TODAY'S BEST NONFICTION

TODAY'S
BEST
NONFICTION

THE READER'S DIGEST ASSOCIATION, INC.
PLEASANTVILLE, NEW YORK

The condensations in this volume have been created by The Reader's Digest
Association, Inc., by special arrangement with the publishers, authors,
or other holders of copyrights. Letters, documents, court testimony, etc. may
have been edited for space.

The original editions of the books in this volume are published and
copyrighted as follows:

Koop: The Memoirs of America's Family Doctor, published at $22.50 by Random
House, Inc.
© 1991 by C. Everett Koop and Allen V. Koop

Circle of Fear, published at $25.95 by Stoddart Publishing Company, Ltd.
© 1991 by Hussein Sumaida and Carole Jerome

Too Tough to Die: Down and Dangerous with the U.S. Marshals, published at $23.00 by
Simon and Schuster
© 1992 by Robert Sabbag

Wall to Wall: From Beijing to Berlin by Rail, published at $19.50 by Doubleday, a
division of Bantam Doubleday Dell Publishing Group, Inc.
© 1991 by Mary Morris

© 1992 by The Reader's Digest Association, Inc.
Copyright © 1992 by The Reader's Digest Association (Canada) Ltd.

FIRST EDITION, Volume 19

All rights reserved. Unauthorized reproduction, in any manner, is prohibited.

ISSN 0893-9373

Printed in the United States of America

Contents

The Memoirs of the
Former Surgeon General
KOOP
BY C. EVERETT KOOP, M.D.

. . . Connecticut Senator Lowell Weicker asked me to meet with Buoniconti and another representative from the U.S. Tobacco Company. I decided to keep cool, hoping that Buoniconti would lose his composure, just as he had shortly before, on *60 Minutes,* when he was being interrogated about the health hazards of his product. Sure enough, in Weicker's office he seemed almost hysterical as he trotted out the old cliché so dear to the tobacco industry: that the scientific studies that demonstrate the hazards of smoking are "anecdotal." Then Buoniconti started a new subject, relating how his wife had quit smoking easily, proving that nicotine couldn't be addictive. I chose that moment to stand up to leave, pointed right at Buoniconti, and said, "That, sir, is anecdotal." Everyone laughed except Buoniconti.

—Koop

Introduction

ON AN ordinary day in August 1980 a call slipped through the screening system in my office at the Children's Hospital of Philadelphia.

"Don't you think it's time the Surgeon General was a surgeon?"

"Who is this?"

"It doesn't matter. Don't you think it's time the Surgeon General was a surgeon?"

I didn't have a ready answer. In fact, like most Americans, I didn't think about the Surgeon General very much, if at all. But my caller urged me to consider the opportunity to serve a new Republican administration. The presidential election was still fifteen weeks away, and I was anything but a politician, but instinctively I decided to keep my options open. I said I might be available. I took the caller's name and number, and tucked it under the corner of my desk blotter. He was Carl Anderson, administrative aide to North Carolina Senator Jesse Helms.

The next day the Heritage Foundation called. "You've turned up in our memory bank as a conservative Republican, one who is pro-life, with a credible experience in academia. How would you like to be Surgeon General?"

I repeated to the second caller, whose name I no longer remember, that yes, I might be available. A new name and number joined its predecessor under the corner of the blotter.

A few days later came the third call. "Dr. Koop, this is John Condon. We met at Billy Graham's when you briefed him on biomedical issues. I am now a headhunter for Reagan-Bush. How would you like to be the Surgeon General?"

"What makes you so sure they'll be elected?"

"Don't worry about that!"

"This is the third call I've had on this subject. Do you guys know what each other is doing? . . . You can say I might be available."

That name and number found its place with the others.

Stretching back in my desk chair, I wondered about the timing of the calls. I was entering the last year of my academic career. I would turn sixty-five the next calendar year, and it was customary at the University of Pennsylvania School of Medicine to retire in June of the year when the magic number sixty-five rolled around.

A member of the medical school faculty since 1942, I had climbed the academic ladder to hold two professorships. In addition, I had been surgeon in chief of the Children's Hospital of Philadelphia since 1948. My retirement had already been planned for April: a farewell party in combination with a scientific program, to which some of my colleagues in pediatric surgery from around the world had been invited. Then I would be old Mr. Chips at the Children's Hospital, with my successor already in my office.

Over the next few weeks the three telephone calls about the Surgeon General position crossed my mind only infrequently. My wife, Betty, mentioned it occasionally, but the prospect never seemed very real to me.

After work on Election Day in November 1980, Betty and I drove down to Deerfield, New Jersey, about an hour away from our suburban Philadelphia home, to watch the election returns with our son Norman and his wife, Anne. As I say, I was not a political animal, but I was fretting about the apparent inability of our country to achieve its potential during the Carter administration. As we watched the Reagan landslide I felt an optimism unlike anything I had previously felt on an election evening.

As we drove home, Betty, with her customary good sense, gave me a bit of advice that changed my life. As usual, she was filling her role as my most valued counselor. Over the years her advice had repeatedly—and wisely—steered our course.

"You do know you're going to be miserable in the job you've chosen for yourself next year after you retire. Have you really thought what it would be like, after being chief for thirty-some years, to be floating around the hospital, operating, teaching, and so on, but with someone else at the helm? You'll be miserable. Why don't you call those people about being Surgeon General."

Driving along in the Pennsylvania darkness, I knew she was right. I didn't have a shred of enthusiasm as I looked at my future. So Wednesday morning, first thing, I found tucked under the leather border of my desk blotter the wrinkled scraps of paper with the three names and phone numbers. Rather miraculously, I found the first two at the other end of the line. John Condon called me back. I said the same thing to each: "When we last spoke, I said in reference to the appointment of Surgeon General that I might be available. I would like to change that now to enthusiastically seeking."

Surgeon General is better known as a title than as a position. The job itself is just a little more than a hundred years old. In 1870 a legislative act placed the Public Health Service, which had been founded in President John Adams' day, under the direction of one medical doctor, called the Supervising Surgeon, a title later changed to Surgeon General. After the creation of the Department of Health, Education, and Welfare, in the early '50s, the Surgeon General's position largely disappeared from sight, except for the landmark 1964 report on the hazards of smoking and the ensuing requirement to print a warning on every cigarette package and advertisement. In fact, by 1980 the Surgeon General's position had become essentially moribund. It had been left vacant under the Nixon presidency, and under Carter it had been combined with the job of assistant secretary of health in the Department of Health and Human Services. The Reagan plan called for reestablishing the position, placing it directly below the authority of the assistant secretary of health. I didn't know for certain what the Reagan people had in mind, but in hindsight it is clear they saw the Surgeon General's job primarily as a means of promoting their social agenda—especially pro-life and family issues.

At the time, though, I naïvely didn't realize that my nomination was a political issue and that my supporters had little idea of my medical background except for my pro-life position. As far as they were concerned, that was my only qualification. And they had based their opinion largely on a program of seminars, films, and books called *Whatever Happened to the Human Race?*, which I had made with theologian Francis Schaeffer to dramatize the issues of abortion, infanticide, and euthanasia. Those programs had become widely known in conservative political circles.

I saw the Surgeon General's job very differently. I saw it as a position of medical leadership, especially in the education of the public about the promotion of health and prevention of disease. And in that misunderstanding lay the origins of my complicated relationship with the people who brought me to Washington.

Once I had decided I wanted the position of Surgeon General, I found myself whipsawed between optimism and pessimism. My name was announced as one of several possible candidates, and I didn't know if and when I would ever hear anything official from the Reagan people. Each day brought more reports, rumors, and suggestions that I was in, only to be followed by similar signs and clues that I was out.

When Richard Schweiker was appointed Secretary of Health and Human Services, the first of three with whom I would work, I saw that as a good sign. I had met Schweiker before, and saw this as a good appointment. On Valentine's Day, Schweiker told me that President Reagan had appointed me deputy assistant secretary of health, with the promise that I would be nominated Surgeon General.

I was excited. And I was not at all concerned about one little technical problem: I was too old. Existing legislation mandated that the Surgeon General could be no more than sixty-four years and twenty-nine days old. I had been alive for about one hundred days longer than that. But, Schweiker assured me, Congress could change the law. After all, the nation had just elected seventy-year-old Ronald Reagan as our oldest President. Certainly no one could imagine that a sixty-four-year-old would be barred from serving as Surgeon General.

So Betty and I tied up our affairs in Philadelphia and prepared to move to Washington. As we drove down on March 8, 1981, I began to realize how little I knew about what I might be getting into. I said to Betty, "If I ever have to say anything I don't believe, or feel shouldn't be said, or if I am forbidden to say what should be said, we'll go home."

Betty and I were among the hundreds of new arrivals to the nation's capital at the dawn of the Reagan era. Our immediate problem was to find a place to live. One of my former surgical trainees, Marty Eichelberger, had assumed a pediatric surgical position at the National Children's Hospital Medical Center, and he and his wife, Nancy, invited Betty and me to live with them until I was confirmed. As things turned out, I imagine they are glad we stayed only a week, declining their further gracious hospitality. They would have had us as houseguests for nine months.

My first day on the job, March 9, 1981, I felt worse than when I was a little boy on the first day at a new school. I had received a letter to report to a room on the seventh floor of the Department of Health and Human Services' Humphrey Building, two blocks down the Mall from the Capitol. The little office was starkly empty except for a desk and a chair. Following instructions, I sat there and waited for someone to show up. And waited. I busied myself by cleaning the telephone. Through my window I could see the Capitol, with the American flag flapping in the breeze. It was a stirring sight, and as I gazed out the window I felt a sense of mission and purpose.

My sense of expectancy and enthusiasm diminished as the hours crept by. In the early afternoon Charlie Miller, retiring deputy assistant secretary of health, took me to meet Ed Brandt, my new boss, who had recently been designated assistant secretary of health. A laconic Oklahoman, Ed simply told me I would have to be sworn in. Tom McFee, deputy assistant secretary of health (personnel) did the honors. I went back to my cheerless office, looked again at the Capitol and the American flag, and wondered if my new role would ever make sense. My sense of isolation began to grow.

If ever I believed in the sovereignty of God, it was during those first lonely minutes in that vacant Washington office. I felt a great sense of God and country, of mission and opportunity. In spite of my misgivings that first day, I believed the only clouds on the horizon were small. Although I had seen a few articles in the press noting the dissatisfaction expressed by some proabortion groups about my appointment, it had not yet dawned on me what vicious opposition I would face from them and other groups.

I faced a long uphill climb against formidable foes. I would need to prove myself each day, each time I met someone. It was going to be just like my first days as a surgeon at the Children's Hospital of Philadelphia, when I had to prove myself to people who said I was not needed, who told me I was unwanted. It was going to be lonely and tough, just like my first days at P.S. 124 back in Brooklyn.

CHAPTER 1
Brooklyn Boy

I AM a Brooklyn boy. I have never understood why people seem to enjoy making fun of Brooklyn—and Brooklyn boys. Most people in Brooklyn don't call the neighboring state "New Joisey," and they don't live somewhere near "Toidy-toid Street." I'm proud to have my roots in Brooklyn, and I have always been fascinated by this unique borough of New York City, on the western tip of Long Island. Although Brooklyn is no longer my home, I return often and visit my old haunts with pleasant nostalgia. I walk by my grandfather's house, making sure it is still covered with that huge wisteria vine. I can smell the fragrance of shady streets I remember from my childhood. I see myself playing stickball on Fourteenth Street. I'm riding my bicycle down Rugby Road in Flatbush. I'm playing baseball with a sandlot team—the Conquerors—at the parade grounds near Prospect Park. I'm a wide-eyed adventurer at Coney Island. Brooklyn still seems much like it did when I moved away in 1941.

I was an only child. An older brother was stillborn; his difficult birth almost killed my mother, who was warned to avoid another pregnancy. But five years later, in 1916, I came along—born at home, like most in my generation. Accounts of my birth always made me wince; it was a textbook case of unsafe obstetrics, climaxed by a risky procedure almost certain to produce a brain-damaged child. My mother was in labor for ninety-two hours, but since my head never engaged, those long days of labor pains were futile. By then it was too late for a cesarean section, so the obstetrician applied forceps to my floating head and somehow extracted me. I often wonder if my traumatic entry into the world had something to do with the path in life I chose.

I was named Charles Everett Koop. My father was John Everett. I hated the name Everett. If people had known about identity crises back then, I should have had one. My father called me Jim. One grandfather called me kid; the other called me boy. When I wasn't with either of them, I was simply the kid or the boy.

Home was a three-story row house on Fourteenth Street in South Brooklyn, between Fourth and Fifth avenues. The house was brick, with a stoop climbing from just inside a wrought-iron gate to a huge door with a fanlight, on the second floor. The first floor was about a foot below street level, and its windows were protected by vertical iron bars, each topped with a sharp finial. When one of my frequent childhood ear infections stretched me out on a couch in the lower room, I dreamed of taking one of those spears and riding off to battle, as knights of old. I was a crusader even then.

Being an only child has both advantages and disadvantages. One advantage was the closeness I enjoyed with my father and mother. My father, J. Everett Koop, was descended from Dutch settlers who, I am told, sailed to New Amsterdam in the seventeenth century. He was a handsome, warm man—I believe without an enemy or even an adversary. He also had tremendous strength of character. Once, when I was home from college for a weekend, my mother approached me in the pantry. "What are we going to do about your father's smoking? He smokes almost three packs a day, coughs all the time, and I'm certain he's shortening his life."

I said, "Forget it, Mom. Pop hasn't got the guts to stop smoking."

That was a stupid, sophomoric thing for me to say, because I was talking about a man who had once pulled out his own decayed teeth with pliers. As I thoughtlessly dismissed Dad's ability to stop smoking, he quietly stepped into the room and overheard what I said. Without a word, he turned, went upstairs, and threw his cigarettes in the toilet, never to smoke again in his life. He proved something health professionals learned only much later: the importance of a self-rewarding goal when you're trying to quit smoking—in Dad's case, his son's approval. With what I now know about nicotine addiction, how I wish I could tell him how proud I should have been of him then.

My father never finished high school, but no one would have guessed it. As assistant vice president of one of America's largest banks, he held his own not only in banking circles but in other fields as well. Once, when I was in the fifth or sixth grade, I asked him what sarcastic meant. He began reciting Shakespeare: Marc Antony's speech at Caesar's funeral. As Dad quoted the line *For Brutus was an honorable man,* he never had to describe sarcasm; he acted it. I was impressed.

At his funeral, his secretary in his early days with the bank described how he had reacted to my unending questions when I was a youngster. Whenever he could not readily answer, he would skip lunch the next day, go to the New York Public Library, and dig out the answer to my question. Suddenly at his funeral it all made very good sense. I well remembered Dad coming home and giving me a complete answer to a question I had already forgotten I had asked the previous day. But even without the library, he was superb.

My mother, Helen Apel, grew up in a large Brooklyn family. She always described her childhood as idyllic but spent her adult life covering up many insecurities and fears. Well read and intelligent, she entered the work force in a secretarial-managerial capacity when many women were excluded. She was a kind and generous woman, who adored me, doted on me, and felt I could do little wrong. We were very close during my growing-up years, and her high expectations of me are in part responsible for much of my striving for achievement.

My mother should have been a nurse or a doctor. She had all the compassion needed, and a good deal of know-how as well. In her earlier years she had administered anesthesia for surgeons who did certain operative procedures in the patient's home. I am amazed at the courage—but bothered by the failures—of surgeons who operated on patients on kitchen tables, with anesthetic assistance from anyone they could talk into the job. Many times I heard Mother's story about trying to give anesthesia to a neighbor's child while the doctor chiseled away his mastoid bone. And of course, she stood anesthetic watch over many a tonsillectomy.

Like many youngsters in those days, it was my privilege to grow up in a three-generation world. I am saddened to read that today only 9 percent of children in the United States live within walking distance of their grandparents. My father's parents, Grandma and Grandpa Koop, lived on the top floor of our house, while my parents and I lived on the lower two floors. When I was thirteen, we moved from Fourteenth Street to a house on Rugby Road in the Flatbush section of Brooklyn, but we maintained the same living arrangements, with my grandparents upstairs.

As a child, I reveled in being surrounded by a large family. Five backyards down Fifteenth Street, I could see the house of my maternal grandfather, Grandpa Apel, a house that he had built for his bride (she died when I was six) and in which he remained until he was in his late seventies. Grandpa Apel never went to school a day in his life—not in the ten years he lived in Germany before sailing to New York, not after he arrived on these shores. Yet he employed his hard-earned, extensive vocabulary in speech that was free of grammatical errors and, like that of many proud new American citizens, free of any trace of a German accent.

Grandpa Apel had transformed his apprenticeship as a tin-smith into the business of heating and ventilating—a precursor of air-conditioning—as well as roofing. As we drove around Brooklyn in his horse and wagon, he would point out to me all the Apel roofs that graced Brooklyn churches.

Until I became a doctor—and my own family's chief physician—my grandparents received more than their share of terrible medical advice. My other grandfather, Grandpa Koop, had developed chronic nosebleeds as a young man. Someplace along the line he was advised by a physician, "John, unless you get a job where you have a tremendous amount of exercise out of doors, you're going to die." My grandfather, thinking he was fighting for his life, decided the life of a letter carrier would provide constant exposure to the elements, as well as nine or ten miles of walking daily. What this had to do with nosebleeds, I am at a loss to say. It may have kept him healthy, but it was not a job to employ his skills. Grandpa Koop had been an engraver on silver and gold. He was happiest with his hands in motion, creating something of intricate beauty.

I have often thought that having two grandfathers who were so facile with their hands shaped my desire to use my own hands as a surgeon. Perhaps I treasured the satisfaction such activities seemed to give them; perhaps it lay in the genes.

BROOKLYN was made to explore. It was fascinating and a little dangerous. On one of my first expeditions, when I was a seven-year-old on my scooter, I was ambushed by two boys much larger than I. In no time at all they had knocked me onto the ground and run off with my scooter. I later learned that the streets of Brooklyn held hazards far more perilous than scooter stealers. Once, during the Prohibition era, I was caught in the cross fire of gang warfare on Fourteenth Street, right in front of my house. I dropped to the ground. One of the gang dropped to the ground, too, but he was dead.

After scooters came roller skates, and with roller skates came my declaration of liberty. Alone or with friends similarly equipped, I roamed the length and breadth of Brooklyn. Roller-skating in Brooklyn was rough business. The asphalt streets were smooth, but unsafe, because the speeding trucks and cars paid little heed to small skaters. The sidewalks loomed like obstacle courses, with pedestrians, vendors, and the large cracks formed by flagstones resting in uneven juxtaposition. I took my share of tumbles, frequently tearing the knees of my knickers and the underlying skin.

Fortunately, there was a place in Brooklyn that offered unending thrills for a little boy, with no actual threat to life or limb: Coney Island. Even sixty years later the mention of the name brings back the marvelous fragrance of five-cent Nathan's hot dogs roasting on griddles, of corn boiling in caldrons, the perfume of cotton candy—the smell of Coney Island was all of those things put together, plus a little dirt and sweat.

I've had a love affair with Coney Island all my life. First I went with Grandpa Koop, who walked me along the boardwalk, with its sleazy, tempting sideshows, then called freak shows. There was the Tattooed Man, the Fat Lady, the Sword Swallower, the Snake Woman, and the Two-headed Calf and other farmyard congenital anomalies. Then there were games of chance that were almost impossible to win. Grandpa Koop would point out a nondescript man in the crowd—the capper. We would follow him for several hours. The capper would be the first to put his dime down to go see the freak show. Grandpa and I would go around to the side door and watch him come out immediately. We would then follow him over to the Kewpie doll boardwalk game, where he'd win a prize easily. We'd follow him to the back door to see him return it. He bought snake oil and boxes of saltwater taffy, only to return it all on the sly. I have frequently said that suspicion is a necessary requirement for a surgeon; I learned it there. And I was intrigued by Coney Island's unusual hospital exhibit: premature infants in incubators. Often I would drag my older cousin Walter there to stare at those babies, neither of us realizing the role premature babies would play in my life.

People should not feel sorry for youngsters born in big cities. I never felt deprived. Indeed, I felt privileged. An empty lot was like a state park. And Prospect Park, especially some of its wooded inner reaches, seemed miles away from the city world, a real wilderness.

When I hiked there on Saturdays with a full knapsack, I could have been hiking on the northern frontier of Canada.

I also expanded my horizons by collecting—anything and everything. The nooks of my room were filled with Indian pottery and arrowheads, cavalry swords from the Civil War, stamps of all sorts, and a collection of teeth. Two molars came from the skull of a South American Indian woman I had found in my high school science lab. When I asked the teacher if I could have one or two of the teeth, he said, "Go ahead. If you can get them out, they're yours." I searched the lab for forceps, pliers, or even wire, but found nothing I could use to extract the teeth. So I seized the Indian's molars between my own and pulled them out. I put the molars on my shelf in a Swedish milk cup dated 1863, between a polo ball and an Italian stiletto.

Teenage summer work in hospitals provided new treasures. One day I came home with a gallon jar of formaldehyde containing an amputated foot. I fully intended to dissect it someday. But I never did, and when I left home to get married, my mother demanded that the foot leave with me. I didn't know what to do with it. I was afraid to toss it into the trash, thinking somebody would find it and cause all kinds of problems. So I took it in its container to an unbuilt part of Flatbush and dropped it over a sewer grate, expecting that the glass would break and allow the foot to fall in. Instead, the glass smashed, and the foot stood resolutely on the grate dripping formaldehyde solution. I drove away. I have no idea what happened, but I have always imagined the police found it and kicked it down the sewer.

My life has always been strewn with stray pieces of anatomy. Years later my children found the left ear of my medical school cadaver, which I'd kept for some silly sentimental reason. I quickly explained it was a trophy from my sword fight with a Spanish pirate on the streets of Marseille. I don't know how much of that they believed, but I know it wasn't for long. A few days later they told me solemnly that Marseille was in France and that the ear had probably come from Cornell Medical School.

Holidays are part of growing up, and for me they bridged the gap between my relatively lonely life as an only child and the often frenzied atmosphere that prevailed in the more boisterous homes of my many cousins. Christmas in Brooklyn, until I was twelve, was a ritual that began on Thanksgiving morning, when my cousin Clinton and I, following a unique Brooklyn tradition, would dress up as ragamuffins and go from door to door asking pitifully, "Got anything for Thanksgiving?" We usually got fruit or candy, but enough people gave us coins, so that we could go Christmas shopping the next day for each of the fourteen cousins expected at Grandpa Apel's Christmas party.

The Koop household—my parents, paternal grandparents, and I— did not acknowledge Christmas with any decorations until the afternoon of Christmas Eve. My mother hung the Christmas wreaths, made of fresh holly, in the four front windows at about 3:00 p.m. on December 24. After a formal dinner we exchanged gifts that evening, because in those days, for letter carriers like Grandpa Koop, Christmas morning was their busiest time. Many people mailed their greeting cards to arrive then.

Later in the day we would leave one grandfather's home for another's to exchange gifts with all of my cousins and their parents. The Apels' house was beautifully decorated, with coal fires in open grates, holly and laurel about the house, and a very festive air indeed. Their Christmas tree reached to the ceiling and was lit with candles, to produce an effect never achieved by electric bulbs.

Brooklyn was important in shaping my young life, but the times spent away from the city on vacation did just as much to prepare me for later life. For a city boy I was unusually privileged to experience the country life and to learn a variety of adult responsibilities early.

In Nova Scotia, we stayed as boarders on a farm in Arcadia village, not far from Yarmouth. It took only a few hours to transform me from a Brooklyn boy into a tiny farmhand. In the Porters' farmhouse there was the smell of baking bread every morning and, after lunch, the aroma of molasses or ginger cookies. Everything we ate was homemade, and the garden produce was either fresh off the farm that day or had been canned the previous season. These Canadian vacations gave me my first excursions alone with my father, when we would paddle a canoe around the northern wilds. These were very special times for me.

On a vacation closer to home but still far from the city, I grew up fast in the summer of 1928, my twelfth year. It was growth in responsibility—responsibility through necessity. My parents had rented a cottage on a peninsula at the end of West Meadow Beach in Stony Brook, on the North Shore of Long Island. At that time Stony

Brook was a sleepy little village; its years as a university community lay decades in the future. Living at the tip of the peninsula, we had a choice of a long walk through sand from the end of the road to our house on the beach or—more convenient—we could take a boat across the creek to the "mainland." Talk about high adventure—it was like living on an island. I was captain of our small rowboat. There were tides to contend with, as well as the rapid Long Island Sound currents that filled and then drained the creek behind our house.

There were fish to be caught, three kinds of clams to be dug, eels to be speared, groceries to be bought, and a car to be driven. None of these could be accomplished without a boat to be rowed, a canoe to be paddled, or an outboard to be started. I learned how to do all this more or less on my own. I suddenly became the man of the house, since my father continued to work in Manhattan, joining Mother and me on weekends and for one week a month from June through September.

The next year, when I was nearly thirteen, we began years of summers a few miles east of Stony Brook, at a beach cottage just thirty yards from Long Island Sound, near Mount Sinai. This was my summer house from ninth grade until my final year in medical school. I continued to prowl the beaches and tidal flats, fascinated by the rich variety of marine life I found nestled in a bewildering variety of environments. For a budding biologist it was a magic laboratory. In nearby Port Jefferson, there was something even more appealing to me: a hospital, even two hospitals. From the time I was sixteen until I was twenty-three my beach prowling and swimming had to wait for the evening hours. Days I worked without pay at Mather Memorial Hospital and St. Charles Hospital for Crippled Children. Because I always wanted to be a doctor.

I CAN'T remember a time when I didn't want to be a doctor. The doctors I knew as a very young child must have helped to plant the desire in me when I was as young as age five or six. One homeopathic physician, Dr. Justice Gage Wright, was a great model. (Homeopathy is an almost abandoned school of medical thought in the United States, in which symptoms are treated by minute quantities of drugs that produce those same symptoms.)

Dr. Wright was a diminutive man—compact, brusque, with an iron-gray mustache and neatly pressed clothing. When he made a house call on me or a member of my family, from the moment he stepped out of his blue Buick, parked at the curb, he was a presence. When he entered the home, my family spoke more softly, as though a normal sound would break the spell. And when he set down his large black bag on a chair in the bedroom, healing had already begun.

Dr. Wright had the biggest doctor's bag I've ever seen—then or since. It contained literally hundreds of corked glass vials three inches high, filled with fluids ranging from clear to amber. To each was affixed an adhesive label inscribed in Latin.

After his examination Dr. Wright always said the same thing: "Get me two tumblers two thirds filled with cold water, two butter chips, and a teaspoon." Soon my family knew to keep these already prepared in the kitchen, and they were produced forthwith. Dr. Wright would drip into each glass three to five drops of two or three ingredients, stir each with the teaspoon, place a butter chip on top of each glass to prevent evaporation, and then lay the spoon across the glasses as they stood on the bedside table side by side, towering symbols of the magic of medicine. The instructions never varied: "Take two teaspoonfuls alternately every two hours." The bowl of the spoon, resting on one butter chip or the other, indicated the next dose. Waiting for the successive hours to roll around was also part of the healing process. The entire family participated.

Office visits ended with the same ritual, except that the drops of magic potion were dribbled into small vials, over tiny sugar pills the size of BB shot. Dr. Wright labeled the corks 1 and 2, and you took those pills alternately, two pills every hour. Even then I wondered and questioned just a little. Such homeopathic wet pills were more concentrated at the bottom of the vial, while those at the top contained hardly any medication at all. It seemed to me that you should get the most medication in the beginning, when you were the sickest, then taper off toward the end.

Dr. Strong was an osteopathic physician to whom our family went for orthopedic problems. Dr. Strong could take an injured arm, hand, or foot in his two most gentle hands, with the largest fingers I think I ever saw, and, without hurting, could make it "all better," as he said. I wanted his gentleness when I became a doctor.

There was another old physician who influenced me, though

largely through the opinion others had of him. He was my grand-father's cousin, Uncle Henry Risch. Uncle Henry had come to this country from Germany a few years before my grandfather Apel, but had never lost his accent. He wore his hair in a wild halo, like Einstein, but his face was much more cherubic.

Every morning, summer and winter, Uncle Henry would jump on his bicycle at his home in Brooklyn Heights and pedal five miles to Coney Island, where he would park his bicycle in the sand, kick off his sandals, and wade into the ocean, still clad in the white linen suit he always favored. Emerging from the water, he'd jump onto his leather saddle and pedal five more miles to my grandmother's home, where he would have homemade coffee cake and coffee for breakfast. In spite of his eccentricities, everybody I knew referred to Uncle Henry as a genius, and people came from far and wide to avail themselves of his care.

Fifteen years after these recollections, when I was a senior in medical school and Uncle Henry had been dead several years, I asked my mother if she knew why he had had such fame as a physician. Her reply was simple: "He cured people of pernicious anemia."

"That's not possible, Mother. The cause and treatment of pernicious anemia are relatively new discoveries. By any chance, do you know what Uncle Henry's treatment might have been?"

"After Uncle Henry had his breakfast at Mama's every morning, he would get on his bicycle and go to the slaughterhouses, where he picked up fresh liver. This he ground and packed into sausages in his own basement and delivered to his patients on his bicycle."

"Mother, they gave the Nobel Prize for that discovery in 1934." Uncle Henry was decades ahead of his time. I knew I wanted some of the genius of Uncle Henry.

Yet none of these men were surgeons, and I *knew* I wanted to be a surgeon. The idea of using my mind, then my hands, to heal someone simply fascinated me. My parents had made me aware of operations, and I knew people who had been deathly ill and then became hale and hearty again after an operation. I think my natural impatience had something to do with my desire to become a surgeon. Surgery requires quick decisions, and it yields quick results.

Even as a young boy, I was certain that I wanted to become a surgeon, so I began my training early. I would spend hours cutting pictures out of magazines with my left hand as well as my right, to train both hands to make delicate, precise, intricate maneuvers. I never became ambidextrous, but I was able to use both hands in surgery better than some. Later I tried to perfect my skills in tying one-handed knots in small corners. I did this by stapling a thread to the bottom of a small wooden matchbox and then tying single knot after single knot with my right hand, snugging them up on the taut thread held in my left.

I decided I could not wait until medical school to see some surgery, so I cajoled my father into asking a bank customer who was a surgeon to let me watch him operate. He accommodated me almost too well. He took me right into the operating room with him while he was doing a submucosal resection of deformed bones in a patient's nose. It was bloody, and I was very close—and very queasy. Somehow I stuck it out.

Soon thereafter, I found easy access to the operating theaters at the Columbia Presbyterian Medical Center. By the time I was fourteen, my size and apparent maturity permitted me to masquerade as a medical student. Paul Strong had shown me how. Paul and his family lived next to us when we summered on Long Island Sound. When I first met him, he was a medical student, and we have been friends ever since.

I would get up early on Saturday mornings, take the subway from Brooklyn to upper Manhattan, and enter the side door of Columbia's Presbyterian Hospital without being questioned; security was unnecessary in those days. As though I had every right to do so, I would take the elevator up to the bacteriology labs, where Paul worked, grab a white coat, and go to the gallery looking over the multiple operating theaters. Few, if any, other observers were in the gallery on Saturday morning, and it was not unusual for a surgeon to look up, see an inquiring face, and reward it with a description of what he was doing. I wasn't only in the gallery—I was in seventh heaven.

After I had seen a fair amount of surgery on those Saturdays, I began to try my hand at it at home. My father and grandfather Koop had built me a lab of sorts in the basement. Here I played with my chemistry set and later did more advanced experiments I had learned from a science teacher at school. Eventually I had white rabbits and too many white rats, all properly housed in cages I had built.

Some of these I anesthetized and operated upon, removing duplicate organs or segments of intestine. My mother was my willing assistant. We would place the animal to be anesthetized in a new, clean garbage pail with an ether-saturated piece of cotton. When the animal was asleep, we would put it on the operating table, and my mother would maintain anesthesia in a style I later learned was pretty proficient. Like those kitchen surgeons of yesteryear, I was remarkably successful. I don't remember losing a single patient.

My first summer job in a hospital, when I was sixteen, put me into the laboratory at Mather Memorial Hospital in Port Jefferson. I started off by slicing pathologic sections on a microtome and then mounting them for the pathologist to read. Before long I was doing urinalyses and the blood counts on the wards.

I seemed to hit it off well with the pathologist at Mather Memorial, and soon he started to bring me the pathology specimens from Pilgrim State Hospital, a six-thousand-bed institution for the mentally ill. I realized he was taking advantage of me, but I kept up with the increased workload. By the end of the summer I had moved up to assisting him in the actual autopsies.

In summers while I was in college, Long Island surgeon Dr. Frank S. Childs invited me to observe him operate, and then he allowed me actually to assist him in surgery. I spent most of my time at the St. Charles Hospital for Crippled Children, where I had to change the dressings of the osteomyelitis patients once a week. This bone infection, which used to be the nemesis of orthopedic endeavors, is now almost unknown because of antibiotics, such as sulfonamides and penicillin. It took me from Monday morning at eight o'clock until Saturday noon to get through all of the patients' dressings once.

One day in the summer before my senior year at college, at age nineteen, I was about to assist Dr. Childs in doing an amputation of a patient's left leg. I took my usual position on the right side of the table when he said to me, "Koopie, you've seen me do enough of these, so that you ought to be able to do one if I help you. Come on over here."

Each day of my youth, whether playing or working, I felt directed toward my eventual career as a surgeon. I thought about it every day in school, except perhaps for those early days, when getting home in one piece was all I could think about.

My grade school, P.S. 124, was on the corner of Fourteenth Street

and Fourth Avenue in South Brooklyn. At the time, the neighborhood was largely Italian and Polish, although a few Irish families still
lived on Park Slope, and, of course, my extended family was there,
scattered on adjacent streets. I left the school at the end of the sixth
grade to go to P.S. 40. Although only a few blocks away, it was in a
rougher neighborhood, and even the tough boys from P.S. 124
looked with some trepidation on going there.

Fortunately, or perhaps unfortunately, there was an escape route.
Brooklyn had four junior high schools—rapid-advancement sections
housed in regular grade schools. Rapid advancement meant that you
took the seventh, eighth, and ninth grades in two years and then
entered the second year of high school. I was chosen to join this
experimental program, and rose to the occasion. I couldn't believe I
was going to a school that had a name instead of a number: Dewey
Junior High School.

But Dewey was eight miles from my new home in Flatbush, forcing
me to take a long trolley ride each day, with a mile to walk at the start
and a half mile at the end. Dewey was in another Italian-Polish neighborhood. The rapid-advancement classes were almost all Jewish. I was
the oddball, no matter how you looked at it. When the school day
ended, my Jewish friends went off in groups to Hebrew school, and I
was left to fend for myself as I walked to the trolley through the tough
neighborhood. Although I never did anything to antagonize the
older boys who hung out on the street corners, I was beaten up just
about every afternoon. I got through that year somehow, but I didn't
know how I would survive the next.

Fortunately, I made an unexpectedly rapid exit from Dewey Junior
High School, thanks to a sadistic art teacher. One afternoon we were
sitting at our desks when Miss Hamilton said, "I have to leave the
room, and I don't want anyone to make a sound."

Of course, as soon as she made her exit, there was a roar as spitballs,
paper airplanes, and other things flew through the air. All of a sudden Miss Hamilton reappeared, to an immediate hush. She asked
anyone who was making noise to stand up. I alone, foolishly honest,
rose, assuming that all my fellow culprits would join me. How Miss
Hamilton could think I was responsible for all the noise she had
heard, I don't know. However, she walked up to me and, without
warning, hauled off and hit my left cheek with the flat of her hand,

hard enough to make me stagger. I went home slowly, but when I got there, the welts were still visible, and my mother saw them.

My father was at a banking convention in Boston, and my mother, timid though she was, took matters into her own hands. The following morning she enrolled me in the Flatbush School, probably the smallest country day school in the nation; it certainly was the smallest one in Brooklyn.

The tiny school consisted of a number of old-fashioned frame houses joined together by walkways and skyways. The layout of many of the houses was just like the one I lived in, so it was like taking algebra in my mother's bedroom or geometry in my grandfather's study. Compared to Dewey, it was wonderful.

Dwight R. Little was the principal, and Mary Ames was the dean. Miss Ames was a very large woman—we were known as "the little school with big aims"—and she was a gem. She appeared gruff and tough, but she had a real concern for children. She knew how to handle their troubles, how to put them at ease. She listened to my story, my mother's account of Dewey, and said, "Everything will be fine here for Everett."

The small Flatbush School helped me lose my timidity and gain self-confidence. The teachers encouraged me to try new things. I loved the athletic opportunities, especially football. Although the school could barely field a football eleven, in my senior year our team remained unbeaten in our division in New York City, thanks to several ringers. I also played baseball and basketball.

Off the playing fields, I joined the debate team, became editor in chief of the school paper, and enjoyed my only effort in politics before I was plunged into national politics as the controversial nominee for Surgeon General in 1981. Student elections at the Flatbush School took place on national Election Day, and we ran campaigns for president with all the hoopla of the Republicans and Democrats. In 1932 I was able to capitalize on the national election as I ran for student president with the slogan:

A double O should have your vote on November 8th—
hOOver
kOOp
rOOsevelt

I won, probably because I also passed out pencil erasers to every kid in school that were printed MAKE NO ERROR—VOTE FOR KOOP.

After my mother died, in 1974, at the age of eighty-six, I found among her treasured papers an autobiographical essay I had written in January 1933, the year I graduated from the Flatbush School. Its final paragraphs distilled the essence of my childhood:

> Now at sixteen I picture myself a great surgeon being consulted by other surgeons no less great. Nothing, it seems, would give me a bigger thrill and would please me more than to operate on a human being from an altruistic viewpoint of relieving his ills, or from the scientific viewpoint of giving to science some information unknown to it.
>
> If my plans take form during the next few years, I will attend Dartmouth College in Hanover, New Hampshire.

CHAPTER 2
The Still North,
The Hill Winds

ON A cloudy September day in 1933, I gazed out the window of the car with intense excitement as my parents and I drove the narrow road winding through the pine-covered New Hampshire hills to the little village of Hanover. In a way I was still somewhat surprised that I was headed for Dartmouth College. My only relative who seemed to know anything about the collegiate world had steered me in the direction of Princeton, in nearby New Jersey. But I had chosen Dartmouth, mainly because Princeton did not have a medical school and Dartmouth did. It was the wrong reason for my choice, but it was the right choice. My four years at Dartmouth were among the best of my life.

At first it seemed all so very new, inviting, and yet intimidating. I had graduated from a school with only fifteen youngsters in the senior class, and now I was at a college of more than 2000 young men, among them 670 freshmen, each eager to show what he could do. I was younger than most—only sixteen when I matriculated. I felt enthusiastic and proud to be part of it all. As we drove up the hill to the campus, the stately beauty of the brick Georgian buildings, the elm-ringed green, and the gleaming white buildings of Dartmouth Row gave me a thrill. They still do.

Right away Dartmouth changed my name. The fellows I met decided that my unusual last name required an appropriate nickname, so I became Chick Koop. Years later, when I began my medical career in Philadelphia, I thought an aspiring young surgeon should not be known as Chick, so I decided to drop my nickname. But the first person I bumped into in Philadelphia happened to be a friend from Dartmouth, who promptly introduced me to everyone as Chick. That's who I've been ever since.

Dartmouth offered an inviting variety of extracurricular activities, but I decided to concentrate on my studies. And football. I have always said that good surgeons are suspicious people. And I have always said that the field of surgery attracts people who are by nature suspicious and compulsive. But I didn't show any of those tendencies my first week at Dartmouth. The first day of football practice I went off with my mother and father for a drive through the White Mountains, about fifty miles north of Hanover. Our outing took much longer than anticipated, and I missed football practice completely. I later learned that because of my high school record, my name had been called out for the position of center on the first team, but since I had missed the first practice, I wasn't able to regain that coveted slot.

But when spring practice rolled around, something happened that changed my life. In the '30s, Ivy League football played a much more important role in national sports than people today might imagine. But Dartmouth had not enjoyed an outstanding season for several years. Therefore, when a new head coach, Earl Blaik, arrived in Hanover from West Point, it made quite a stir in the sports world.

On the third day of spring practice, when Blaik was choosing the first and second squads, I was engaged in running at right angles to a short pass and trying to intercept it. A bunch of other guys were trying out for the same position—the so-called roving center. Before I got up for my next shot at a pass, one of the managers approached me and said, "Coach Blaik wants to see you."

Could this mean that my blunder of missing that first day of fall practice was going to be offset by actually being noticed by the great Earl Blaik? Did he like what he saw? I certainly didn't know, but I jogged over to Blaik and said the customary "Yes, sir!"

"What's your name?"

"Chick Koop."

"I haven't seen anybody run like that since I left the Point."

Later that day, when the first team roster was posted, my name was listed as center. Suddenly my life changed. People who hadn't looked my way as we passed on the stairs of my dormitory now knew my name and seemed anxious to befriend me.

One night, during the second week of spring practice, I walked down Main Street to get my usual toasted cheese sandwich and chocolate milk shake. As I approached Allen's Drug Store, Blaik and three of his assistant coaches were walking toward me. I was with my roommate and several friends, and when Blaik's "Hello, Chick!" was echoed by each of the assistant coaches, I was in seventh heaven. I think my friends would have been willing to carry me home on their shoulders if I had asked them.

A few days later we had a scrimmage, the first team against the second team. On defense I was playing roving center, and the opportunity came to intercept a short pass, just as Blaik had seen me practice. I snagged the pass, found a hole in the line, and must have run about ten yards before I was hit by two very vicious tacklers. I was knocked out cold. I don't really know how long it was, but my friends told me I was on the ground for several minutes. When I tried to walk to the sidelines, I realized that my shoulder was extraordinarily sore. More disturbing, something strange had happened to my vision—I was seeing two of everything, a second image superimposed on the first, somewhat to the right and above it.

Nobody seemed too concerned about my double vision or my intense headache. At first Blaik was solicitous. He advised me to come to practice and walk through the plays, but not to suit up and risk further injury. I did this for the rest of the week, receiving the same fawning treatment when I passed the coaches on Main Street.

When the weekend came and my eyes and headache were getting no better, I decided I would go to the Dartmouth Eye Clinic for a consultation with Professor Bielschowsky, perhaps the most knowledgeable person in the world at that time regarding the function of the extraocular muscles around each eye. He addressed me in moderately accented English after a very complete examination. "What will be your major?" was his first question.

"I'm premed."

"You're premed and you play this foolish game of football? Let me see your hands." I showed them to him, fingers outstretched, palms down and then palms up.

"They're beautiful. They're surgeon's hands. So you not only risk your sight and maybe your life, but your hands and your career. Such foolishness."

He then explained that I had probably had a tiny hemorrhage in or very close to the nucleus of the fourth cranial nerve that supplied one of the extraocular muscles, that it would probably never improve, but that with eyeglasses I could live with it perfectly well. However, if I suffered another head injury, I was risking permanent disaster.

He made sense, and I knew it. But I had to decide if I was mature enough to give up all that big-man-on-campus attention for the much less glamorous life of an anonymous premedical student. I went to see Earl Blaik the next morning in the field house. I told him about my conversation with Bielschowsky and said that after a very painful deliberation I had made the reluctant decision to drop out of football.

Blaik tried to change my mind, arguing that many men had played football and then gone on to be doctors. I don't know how I was strong enough to resist his persuasive tactics, but I was. His next comment destroyed the man in my sight forever. He looked at me and said, "So, in other words, you're a coward."

That night, when I passed the four coaches on Main Street, they looked the other way.

I don't think Dartmouth football suffered much from my absence. Instead, Dartmouth got a very fine center, Carl "Mutt" Ray, who inspired the team for the next three years.

Meanwhile, I was fitted with special eyeglasses, and a new series of problems began. When I woke in the morning and put my glasses on, they seemed to make my vision worse. I could not leave my room until I used my eye muscles to bring the two images together, a difficult exercise that could take as long as thirty minutes. Gradually that half hour of adjustment dwindled, but even now, when I put my glasses on, I see double for a fleeting two or three seconds.

Giving up football was one of the hardest and wisest choices I made at Dartmouth. Not only had I acted wisely to save my surgical ambitions but I also moved into a different social world, choosing a quieter path that would bring me close friendships with other premed students. For my last three years I roomed with Mike Petti, another premed student, from Brockton, Massachusetts. We became good friends with two other premeds: Ed McGrath, from Milton, Massachusetts, and Dan Barker, from Niantic, Connecticut. Two of us came from metropolitan areas, one from a small city, and one from a very small town. Two of us were Protestant and two Roman Catholic. We all shared similar family values, but there was sufficient diversity to permit arguments long into the night.

Most of my time at Dartmouth I studied. My zoology major kept me busy, offering me intellectual stimulation and career preparation, as well as employment. The college lost interest in giving me a scholarship as soon as I left the football team, so I sought out a variety of jobs to help my father finance my education. I washed dishes, sold saddle shoes, ran a laundry service, tutored, and, finally, served as a research assistant in the zoology department. I thrived on work that allowed me to be on the brink of scientific discovery by using not only my mind but also my hands.

One of my professors, Bill Ballard, was experimenting on lens transplants in the eyes of the *Amblystoma notatum,* a strange five-inch-long amphibious vertebrate. After the professor had taken the infinitesimally small lens from one eye of a newborn and inserted it into the other, my job was to see that the little creatures maintained their nutrition. I did this by feeding them chopped newt liver, which I diced up into pieces small enough to pick up on the end of a needle. Another job was to label with india ink all the zoology specimens in the college museum; forty years later I saw my labels still in place.

When the operating season on *Amblystomae* was over, I found other work to do, under Professor Norman Arnold. It was from Norm that I learned embryology, but it was also from Norm that I learned how to teach. In his soft, persuasive, unhurried manner he went to all lengths to explain the complicated field of embryology. Although I could not foresee it at that time, my surgical career would be devoted to correcting the defects that occur in the unfolding of embryology in preborn children.

When I first enrolled at Dartmouth, I planned to take advantage of the special curriculum that allowed certain students to take their first year of medical school as the fourth year of college. But in my junior year I decided against accelerating my education; instead, I would use my senior year to gain greater academic and social maturity before entering medical school. I was also attracted to the opportunities zoology presented in my senior year, when I would be able to have my own little lab, my own equipment, and my own projects. This produced the only wavering of my lifelong desire to be a surgeon. I wondered if perhaps I wouldn't be happy in teaching. It was Norm Arnold who straightened out my thinking on that. As he so aptly pointed out, if I went on to medical school and surgical training, I could always return to the academic world to do what he did, but if I prepared myself to be what he was, I could never do the other.

During those brief weeks of my freshman year when I seemed destined to be a football star, I never would have guessed that in my senior year I would be happy to spend Saturday afternoons looking at a shrimp. My zoology research had taken me into the fascinating life cycle of a tiny crustacean called the fairy shrimp, genus *Eubranchipus.* When full grown, this little pink creature is not quite half an inch long, and under the microscope it looks like a shell being rowed by a well-disciplined crew. The legs shoot out, stroke in unison from forward to back, and propel the fairy shrimp through the water.

In the process of studying *Eubranchipus,* I discovered a new species of shrimp. My mentors told me I could have the little shrimp named for me, and suggested I stay on as a teaching assistant in the department of zoology. I decided that even being immortalized by *Eubranchipus koopii* wasn't sufficiently enticing to postpone medical school another year.

In another lasting contribution to my life, Dartmouth nourished my love of the outdoors. From my first visit to Dartmouth I was enchanted by the beauty of the surrounding countryside. In later life my work would take me all over the globe, to some of the earth's most spectacular scenery, but nothing could replace the special love I developed for the hills and valleys of northern New England.

In the winter I skied. My first skiing experience was in the light of a waning moon on the hills of the Hanover golf course. One of the greatest thrills of my life was to feel myself start down that gentle slope with silence all around me, dark spruce trees stark against the white snow, bitter frost in the air. I became a devotee immediately; every minute that I could spare from my studies went to skiing. My favorite outing was the triple moonrise. I would ski up to the top of Oak Hill, a small mountain about a mile north of Hanover, until the moon came up in the east; then I would schuss down Oak Hill, losing the moon, do cross-country skiing westward, and wait for the moon to rise again over Oak Hill. Then I would descend into the deep valley by the river—a tricky business at night—and wait there until the moon rose once again. I never tired of the thrill of that triple moonrise.

Perhaps because I had learned how to maintain my balance while roller-skating on cracked Brooklyn sidewalks, I became a fairly decent skier and got to the point where I had the temerity to ski the headwall of Tuckerman Ravine, which in those days was a feat usually reserved for experts. Skiing was not only a source of great fun, it was also, at least for me, a risky business.

My enthusiasm for skiing allowed me to get talked into representing my fraternity in the intramural ski-jumping competition. Since I had never jumped on skis, I began to practice. I would get up before my usual hour and attack the smaller practice ski jump at dawn. My routine never varied: I tried the landing hill first to assess its speed and then made three jumps.

On the day of the competition I had a lab and didn't get out until after the sun had gone down behind the tall pines at the top of the jump. As soon as that happened, the slushy takeoff hill froze into ice. Because I was late and a little embarrassed to appear timid, I did not test the landing hill first. That was mistake number one.

Mistake number two was that instead of starting ten or fifteen feet down from the top of the takeoff hill, which was permissible, I went to the top. My third mistake was that instead of standing relatively straight up to slow my takeoff, I crouched. My fourth mistake was to jump when I should have just slipped off the lip.

All of these mistakes combined to make me rocket off the jump much faster than ever before, and I suddenly realized that I was higher than I had ever been—as high as the top branches of the surrounding pine trees. I attempted a kind of somersault to slow my speed and get down as fast as I could. I managed to get halfway around, landed on my back, and slid to the base of the hill, feeling as though I had been hit by a truck.

My friends took me on a toboggan to the college infirmary. No one did much for me, and I lay in bed in quiet panic, because I was partially paralyzed. I could move my arms and legs only with great difficulty. No one discussed my condition with me. I plunged into a deep depression, feeling for sure that surgical aspirations and perhaps even a normal life were no longer in my future. Only much later did I figure out that I had suffered a spinal concussion, from which I began to recover after three or four days. This was the first time I had ever been hospitalized. My case was poorly managed, and that made a lasting impression on me. I resolved that when I finally became a doctor, I would not let my own patients lie in fear caused by an inattentive physician.

A small part of my injury remained hidden at the time, for I had also sustained a very fine fracture in my neck. That would eventually catch up with me in the eighth decade of my life, nearly bringing to a quadriplegic conclusion my tenure as Surgeon General.

Despite my mishaps, skiing was one of the best things about college. But best of all, Dartmouth brought me Betty.

BEFORE the Christmas break in my junior year, I was chatting with Dan Barker and told him I thought it was a shame that he was now in his senior year and had never invited a girl up for Winter Carnival. I knew that Dan had a longtime steady girlfriend at home and that it was a foregone conclusion that he would eventually marry her. But I also knew that in the previous summer he had met another girl, Betty Flanagan, who planned to enter Vassar in September and whose family summered in the Connecticut shore town where he lived.

I said, "Dan, I feel so strongly about this that I would be delighted to invite you and your girl as my guests at our fraternity." I still wonder what was in the depths of my mind as I made this offer.

"That might make a difference. But I don't know which one to ask," he said, looking at two 8 by 10 portraits on either end of his bureau.

"Invite that one," I said, pointing to Betty.

We returned from Christmas break, got through the awful month of January, preparing for final exams in the last week of that month, and then there was nothing ahead but carnival. There was a special something in the air in Hanover as carnival approached. Each fraternity and dormitory prepared a snow-and-ice sculpture, and the Dartmouth Outing Club constructed a huge snow statue in the middle of

Left: the author at eighteen months, with his mother

On a pony, in Brooklyn

Above: Grandma and Grandpa Koop. Right: four generations—young C. Everett with his father and his father's mother and grandmother.

Freshman Koop
the day he left for
college, in 1933

Vassar College student Betty Flanagan

the campus. The social events centered on formal dances with white tie and tails on Friday and Saturday nights and a tea dance after the athletic events on Saturday afternoon. Carnival itself consisted of an outdoor evening on Friday night, a gala affair often featuring an Olympic skating star, stunt skiing, and marvelous fireworks that illuminated the dark pine trees against the sparkling snow. The athletic events included ski races, ice hockey, basketball, and ski jumping.

On Friday afternoon I had just returned to the dorm from a skiing outing and was relaxing in Dan's room when he walked in and introduced me to Betty. I was dressed only in my skiing long johns. It was an unusual beginning to a long relationship.

My date for the weekend was a girl I had known from home, an attractive, popular girl attending Duke, who had little time for me once she saw the other Dartmouth men. After the ski jumping on Saturday afternoon, I returned to the fraternity house and, as was the custom, took off my ski boots so I could be ready to dance, if the occasion arose, in my ski socks. As usual, my date disappeared, but soon the front door opened and in walked Betty.

"Where's Dan?" I asked.

"He's gone to take a nap," said she, "and he thought I should do the same."

"Do you feel like a nap?"

"Not at all."

"Why don't you go freshen up, and I'll take care of you."

Although I might not have admitted it at the time, my romance with Betty Flanagan began that afternoon. Later we often recalled that our conversation had a prophetic quality. Among the many subjects we discussed was the difficulty medical students faced because of the unfair, albeit unspoken, prohibition against marriage.

A week later I sent Betty a valentine, unsigned but obviously from Hanover. At the time I did not know that I had begun a chain of valentines that would extend for more than half a century.

Winter Carnival receded, and springtime of 1936 came to Hanover as spring usually does there—quite explosively after the bleak mud season. I had no plans to have a date for the Green Key Weekend, Dartmouth's spring house party, in early May. So when one of my fraternity brothers was called home to a funeral, I accepted his invitation to drive to New York City with him. I spent Tuesday evening and all day Wednesday with my family and met my friend to return to Hanover early Thursday morning.

It was a gorgeous day, and as we drove slowly north I suddenly said, "We have so much time. Let's stop off in Poughkeepsie, find Vassar College, and visit Dan Barker's girl for a few minutes."

It took some effort to find Betty Flanagan. We were told she was not in her dormitory, but that she would be along if we cared to wait. Eventually Betty arrived from the library. She looked pretty bedraggled in an old polo coat, the lining of which drooped below the hemline on one side. It didn't matter to me.

I don't know why my friend had the good sense to become occupied with some other endeavor, but Betty and I took a stroll around Vassar Lake alone, reminiscing about Winter Carnival, and I realized I was developing an unreasonable attachment to this girl. When we got halfway around the lake, I stopped and said, "This is spring weekend at Dartmouth. Why don't you drive up with us, and Dan and I will squire you around."

I have to admit to some immediate trepidation about having made that remark. First of all, I wasn't clear about the relationship between Dan and Betty, but I assumed it was tenuous. However, I also knew enough about Dan to know that he would not jump at the opportunity of sharing his girl with me for the weekend. Then there was a histology exam I had to take as soon as I returned.

Betty said she couldn't possibly do it, and I coaxed. She softened a little, I pushed harder, and she accepted. But a problem remained. In those days a Vassar girl needed family permission to visit a men's college campus for the weekend. Betty phoned, finding only her grandmother at home. When her grandmother gave her permission, she unknowingly forged a bond between us that we both cherished for the rest of her life.

My friend reappeared, and the three of us were off, up the Hudson Valley to Rutland, Vermont, and across the Green Mountains to Hanover. I put off thinking about my histology exam. I also put off thinking about how I was going to explain all this to Dan, something that was going to be increasingly difficult because the ride up had convinced me that this was the girl for me.

Even all those chemistry courses in my premed curriculum would not allow a thorough analysis of the chemistry that flourished so quickly between Betty and me. She was an attractive girl, exquisitely feminine, but neither frail nor fragile. There was no froth or fluff to Betty. She was solid, genuine.

Betty's father, George Flanagan, the son of an Irish immigrant, had worked in a factory to make enough money to put himself through medical school. As a family practitioner in New Britain, Connecticut, he had earned the title of "beloved physician" because of his compassion and profound sense of obligation to his patients. Betty's mother, Ethel Swartwood, was descended from Dutch settlers who first set foot in New Amsterdam in 1659. With a flair for music and drama, Ethel graduated from Emerson College and then taught English at Syracuse University until she married Dr. George. Among her many contributions to Betty and me was her standard of selfless devotion to her husband's practice of medicine, so that he could do what needed to be done for his patients. She passed this on to Betty, who would nurture it and improve upon it, making possible all I—or, I should say, we—accomplished as a surgeon and as Surgeon General.

Of course, all this lay ahead of me on that long ride from Poughkeepsie to Hanover. What I did know on that ride was that I was in the presence of honesty, loyalty, sensitivity, and understanding. Best of all, Betty had a great sense of humor. I saw a lot in Betty, and I appreciated all I saw.

But I could not have foreseen then what it was that would keep us together and content for over half a century: a true meeting of the minds. As her eyes said as they sparkled that May day, There's more! That has been the priceless ingredient: there has always been more to come.

It was Thursday, and since the great influx of Dartmouth dates for the weekend did not begin until Friday, I was able to find a cheap room for Betty up on the third floor of the old Hanover Inn. It was verboten for the male students to go upstairs to rooms occupied by young ladies, so I left Betty in the lobby, promising that I would be back as soon as I could, after I did some studying for my exam, and that then maybe we could have something to eat. I was nervous about meeting Dan. My attempt at a breezy introduction of the situation to him fell extraordinarily flat. I could tell by the tightening muscles in his jaw that he was angry, and in all fairness to him I have to say that

I was so vague he could not possibly have known what my plans were. I was more than nervous—I was scared.

I was falling in love, and I knew it. I walked back into my room, closed the door, and went through the motions of cramming for the next morning's exam. The pages before me were a blur. I had no interest in the cellular structure of the liver or the microscopic intricacies of striated muscle. After a ridiculous hour I threw in the towel and decided to go back to the inn to take Betty to dinner.

I called Betty's room from the lobby and got no answer. It never occurred to me that she might have gone out. I told the manager that I had called and gotten no answer, and wondered if he could send somebody up to the room to see if she was all right. He looked at me as though I were out of my mind, but nevertheless complied, and returned to tell me that the room was indeed empty.

If love is irrational, disappointment in love is more so. I tore back to the dormitory and found Ed McGrath, Dan's roommate, sitting at his desk, looking very stern. When I inquired where Dan was, Ed said that he had left the room in some anger, muttering, "At least I'll take her to dinner." Then Ed let me know in no uncertain terms that what I had done was something between highly foolish and unkind. He reminded me that in Dartmouth lingo the definition of someone who took a friend's girl was snake. Ed had a high sense of honor. We were, for the first time, on different wavelengths. But wasn't all fair in love and war? I had a definite feeling I now had both on my hands.

I went across the hall, shut myself in my room, and seethed. Again the histology text before me was a blur. When I heard Dan come in and close his door, I took off for the inn. Knowing it was against the rules but unreasonably angry with Betty, I walked up the main stairs in full view of the registration desk, found her room on the third floor, and knocked on the door.

When Betty answered, I said, "Get your clothes packed. I'm driving you to Rutland. You can take a train to Poughkeepsie."

There was never any more sincere consternation than Betty displayed. If I had told her she was responsible for the rumors of the gathering clouds of World War II, she could not have been more startled.

"Why? What did I do?"

"You had dinner with Dan."

"Why shouldn't I? He told me you had sent him to take me to dinner because you had to study."

It was all so very reasonable, so very logical. But I was not. I had foolishly allowed my image of this wonderful girl to crumble over the past hour. But as we talked, we rapidly recaptured the magic spirit of our short time together at the carnival tea dance.

In those few hours a great many things in my life changed. Couples have been through this experience since the beginning of time. They fall in love, go together for a while, get to know each other, build a base on which to form a lifetime commitment. The unusual thing about us was that we compressed all that into the hours between 10:00 p.m. and dawn. Betty has often said, "Chick works with dispatch!"

Dawn made its presence known by the light around the window shade. I couldn't believe the speed with which time had passed or the predicament I was in. Not only was I in a forbidden place, I had been there all night. If I had been caught, I could have been expelled. I said good-bye as though for the last time and started downstairs, looking for an alternate route of escape. There was none. When the registration desk came into view, the clerk was obviously asleep. I sat down on the stairs, took off my shoes, and crept out the front door in stocking feet, unnoticed. Once on the porch of the inn, I put my shoes on and, breathing in the crisp New Hampshire dawn, sprinted back to my room. It was about 6:00. I was able to study until about 8:00. I took the exam, proving that from the start life with Betty would be productive. I got an A.

By the end of Green Key Weekend, Betty and I knew we were headed for life together. After I placed her on the train back to Vassar, I called home. "Mother, guess what! I'm engaged."

There was a long silence. My mother later told Betty, "My legs turned to jelly, but I managed to say, 'That's wonderful, Buddy.' "

I didn't see much of my Dartmouth friends the rest of that weekend, but in time things worked out. Ed came around and grew very fond of Betty. Dan and I remained cool for the rest of the spring term, but eventually he recognized and accepted the situation for what it was. Our friendship resumed.

My senior year at Dartmouth was my best as I reveled in the academic excitement of my major and went to see Betty whenever I could. In the summer she and I were on opposite shores of Long

Island Sound and would use the Port Jefferson–Bridgeport ferry to visit at each other's homes. But during the school year we found that travel between Poughkeepsie and Hanover was difficult. I would hop on the midnight train in White River Junction, Vermont, get off in New York at dawn, take the subway to Brooklyn, borrow the family car, and drive to Vassar.

More than fifty years later, in June 1989, when we had to squeeze into one weekend Betty's fiftieth reunion at Vassar and my receiving an honorary degree at Dartmouth's commencement, we faced a familiar problem: it was *still* hard to get from Poughkeepsie to Hanover.

THERE was something very special about Dartmouth. Many of us felt that at an isolated, all-male college, the depth of friendships was greater than on a coed campus, where social success with women can supersede male companionship. (However, having two Dartmouth granddaughters has let me see the Dartmouth experience in a new light.) Over the years the class of '37 enjoyed what I like to think was a special camaraderie, perhaps because our college years were a brief parenthesis between the worst of the Depression and the war that claimed too many of us.

And there is a special claim that the isolated New Hampshire setting has upon the men—and now women—of Dartmouth:

> *They have the still north in their hearts,*
> *The hill winds in their breath,*
> *And the granite of New Hampshire,*
> *Is made part of them 'til death.*

CHAPTER 3
New York to Philadelphia

As I prepared for my career as a doctor, there was one thing I knew for sure: I would attend medical school at Columbia University's College of Physicians and Surgeons. Paul Strong was the reason. Older than I and a role model of sorts, he was a medical student at Columbia when I was a young teenager. When I went to Columbia for my interview in the fall of my senior year at Dartmouth, I felt very much

at home in the familiar corridors, where Paul had helped me masquerade as a medical student years before. My discussion with the
admissions panel seemed to go well until one of them asked me, "Do
you ever expect to make any major discoveries in medicine?"

It was a stupid question then; it is a stupid question now.

I responded, "Well, sir, from what little experience I have in reading about discoveries in the field of medicine, I rather think that
those who make them are building upon the efforts of many who
preceded them. I would like to be one who makes a major discovery,
but I will be content to contribute to the process."

Good answer then; good answer now.

"We don't think you've got the stuff we are looking for at the
College of Physicians and Surgeons!"

I was devastated. My image of my medical career lay shattered. I was
convinced that whatever happened now, it could be only second best.
Little did I know.

Soon afterwards I went for my interview at the only other school I
had considered—Cornell University Medical College, downtown, on
the other side of Manhattan. As soon as I walked into the main entrance, I sensed a convivial atmosphere. The dean's secretary greeted
me warmly.

When I returned to the dean's office after spending several hours
in interviews in New York Hospital, the dean said graciously, "Mr.
Koop, if you will accept it, Cornell would like to offer you a place in
next year's entering class."

I loved every minute of it. I even loved the course in anatomy,
always advertised as the toughest experience in medical school. Cornell was unusual in that we had only two students per cadaver instead
of the usual four. My cadaver's name was Ira Posey. I knew only that
he had lived in Manhattan and had died of tuberculosis. In death Ira
was one of the most important people in my life, and he contributed
unknowingly to much that I accomplished as a surgeon. His was that
ear I kept in my bureau drawer as a memento of our close association.

I survived anatomy—and the rest of the first year of medical
school—only with the help of my teachers, my friends, and my family.
Yet another skiing accident—this time a broken leg—during my
Christmas vacation incapacitated me for months. The bone had to be
refractured and reset, and I hobbled around in a series of plaster

casts, first with crutches, then with a brace, and, finally, with a cane.

I moved back to my parents' home in Brooklyn while recuperating, and my father drove me to school each day. Our time together in the car became precious to me as I formed a closer bond with him, not only the bond of father and son but that of the closest of friends. His death years later would leave a void that time would never quite fill.

The broken leg taught me a new method of study. Walking around on crutches, dragging a heavy cast, made me extremely tired. I learned to take a couple of short ten-minute naps during the evening, and I also learned to wake up without feeling groggy. I slowly developed a new attitude toward lectures. I concentrated hard on what was being said. If it made sense, I made no notes. If it didn't make sense, I would write it down, check it out at the library, and record it in a black leather notebook. This "cold dope book" became the repository for the information I considered critical to review before exams. The system worked well for me then; it still does now.

During that difficult year Betty came down from Vassar on weekends whenever she could, and we spent much of the summer of 1938 trying to find a way to get married. We had two problems: we had no money, and Betty's father was in ill health, so it seemed unlikely that he could attend a wedding. But we were able to convince our families, as many couples have done, that two could live together on less than two can live apart. In great faith we had wedding announcements engraved, leaving blank the date and place. Less than a week before medical school was to resume classes for my second year, Betty's father was well enough to travel from Connecticut to Vassar College for a wedding on Monday, September 19. It was a small family wedding: four parents, four grandparents, Betty's brother George, and two attendants. Betty and I walked out, married, into an unusually heavy rainstorm. As the wind howled around us I opened an umbrella. It showered confetti all over us, which stuck to our wet clothing like sequins. In the years since, we have celebrated our wedding anniversary with recollections of the infamous hurricane of '38.

Betty's friends had told her that four years at Vassar wouldn't prepare her for much in the world of business, and she discovered that three years did even less. She went to secretarial school, then landed a job in the social-service department at New York Hospital. From then until I graduated, we were employed in the same building and could walk to work together. Though I was always swamped with work, we were home together at night in our tiny apartment, and even in those days she was my sounding board and my confidante.

I HAVE often viewed my life as a tapestry woven of many threads, its ultimate design and purpose determined by the sovereignty of God. So often in my career He had me in the right place at the right time. In the summer before my final year of medical school, my summer plans had just collapsed, and I was walking by the dean's office when his secretary called to me. "Mr. Koop, do you know of any student who would be available to take a wonderful job across the street at Memorial Hospital?"

"It just so happens I do know one, and here he is."

I ran up the street and put on better clothes, and went down to Memorial Hospital (now Sloan-Kettering). There I was interviewed by Hayes Martin, a pleasant, no-nonsense kind of a man, whom I grew to admire tremendously. He told me he was convinced that raw brewer's yeast, which contains large amounts of vitamin B, could help prevent the development of precancerous lesions in the mouth. He wanted somebody to undertake a controlled study to test his theory. I was delighted with the opportunity and readily undertook it. Dr. Martin was right, and we co-authored my first scientific paper.

The outstanding experience of my fourth year of medical school was obstetrics, primarily because I spent two weeks living in Harlem and delivering babies at the Berwind Free Maternity Clinic, on West 116th Street. Four students were assigned there at a time. Of my team, only I had ever seen a delivery. None of us had ever participated in one. My first delivery was born before I arrived. After stepping over a huge dead rat, I found the mother kneeling on a coal pile, the baby and placenta lying between her legs.

I learned fast, delivering fourteen babies in fourteen days, and had practically every complication in the book. It was an eye-opening exposure to the need for adequate medical care in the poverty-stricken neighborhoods of American cities. I tried to do all I could for these neglected patients.

Sometimes while studying late at night, when I didn't think I could cram one more fact into a tiring brain, I would take a walk halfway across the Queensborough Bridge, over the East River, at Fifty-ninth

Street. I'd gaze at the lights of Manhattan from the bridge and realize how much I enjoyed learning to be a doctor and how I looked forward to what I hoped to accomplish. They were tough days, living in New York with no money, but they were days I wouldn't give up for anything. Our children hate to hear us talk about it, but Betty and I did manage to live on five dollars a week for food if we had three weekend meals with my family. We had little time and no money for relaxation or entertainment.

In June 1941 I graduated from Cornell University Medical College. We all stood to sing the Cornell alma mater, "Far Above Cayuga's Waters." I had taken the Hippocratic oath a few minutes before. I was an M.D. My mother and father joined Betty and me for dinner in Chinatown. The bright June days that followed were the last of total freedom that I remember. On the last day of the month I reported for duty as an intern at the Pennsylvania Hospital in Philadelphia, the oldest in the United States.

A pattern for my life was developing, although at the time I did not see it. As with medical school, my quest for an internship brought first bitter disappointment, then something far better.

I had always assumed that after I finished my medical training, I would settle down as a doctor in Brooklyn, practicing in an office in a brownstone. I reasoned that if I were going to practice in Brooklyn, it made very good sense to intern in the New York metropolitan area. There were four or five outstanding two-year rotating internships on the East Coast, two of which were in Brooklyn: the Brooklyn Hospital and the Methodist Episcopal Hospital. The purpose of this rotating internship was to allow the young doctor to sample all the medical specialties before entering general practice or selecting a residency in the field of his choice. Even though marriage and medical school had worked out extraordinarily well for me, I still had to contend with outright prejudice from my profession about mixing marriage and medical training. At both hospitals, interviewers were adamant that you could not be a good intern if you were married.

Discouraged, I turned to a former mentor, researcher Dr. Hayes Martin, who suggested I try the Jersey City Medical Center, a hospital in the news more for its political shenanigans than for its scientific breakthroughs. But when I requested a reference from Dr. C. P. "Dusty" Rhoades, the medical director at Memorial Hospital, he opened my eyes to something I should have seen before. In America, he said, there were two kinds of medicine: there was academic medicine—medicine attached to the teaching program of a university medical school—and there was the rest of medicine. As he put it, academic medicine was in a special league. Once you were out of the league, it was extraordinarily difficult to get back in.

I followed his advice. I set my sights on the top and applied to the best academic-medicine residency programs on the East Coast. When I traveled to Philadelphia for my interview at the University of Pennsylvania, I took the precaution of removing my wedding ring. (The subject of marriage never came up.) I was interviewed by I. S. Ravdin, professor of surgery and director of the Harrison Department of Surgical Research, a man with a reputation as both a brilliant surgeon and a bear who was tough on his residents.

Ravdin was not one to waste time. "Okay, you can get yourself an internship down at the Pennsylvania Hospital. At the end of those two years I'll have you operate in the dog lab for two years. And then you can start the five-year Harrison Fellowship in surgery."

I quickly totaled up nine years of training before I would be a surgeon on my own. Although I realized how much I would learn there, I felt depressed about leaving New York for the steamy summer climate of Philadelphia. Besides, Betty and I had a lease until October on our tiny apartment and couldn't afford rent in two cities, which meant Betty would have to stay in her New York Hospital job. It was our first real separation, and we didn't relish it. I lived at the hospital until autumn, when we moved into our Philadelphia apartment.

Following the established ritual, my first day of duty was July 1, 1941. Every July 1, American medicine changes teams as a new staff of somewhat experienced residents and totally green interns arrives at each hospital. I have always hoped I would never have to be hospitalized in the first week of July.

One day of sweltering in the Philadelphia summer heat and unpacking in my cramped, lonely living quarters made me determined to find a way to get back to New York and Betty. Then I received a call from my roommate, Francis Jacobs, who was in the emergency room. He had an unusual patient, a man of Malaysian origin, complaining of a stuffy nose. Something about the patient's face recalled textbook photos he had seen in med school. Francis confirmed his diagnosis with a microscopic study of the man's nasal discharge. It was leprosy.

My opinion of Philadelphia and of the Pennsylvania Hospital changed in a second. If this hospital could, on the first day of my new internship, provide a patient who walked in off the street with leprosy, it had a lot to teach me. I was right. The year flew by, and it was loaded with marvelous experiences.

Pennsylvania Hospital claimed to be the oldest in the nation; Benjamin Franklin and Benjamin Rush had played a role in its founding. True to its Quaker heritage, the hospital maintained an old tradition of providing a bed, blanket, and bowl of soup for anyone who showed up at its door claiming to be tired, cold, and hungry. Even today, in the Pennsylvania Hospital's modern building, space is set aside in the cafeteria for indigent elderly folks from the immediate neighborhood. I hope no young manager or aggressive board member ever changes that policy.

Each day of my internship at Pennsylvania Hospital and, later, of my residency at the Hospital of the University of Pennsylvania I realized that these two Philadelphia hospitals were among the best providers of medical care in this country. I felt privileged to have joined them.

Very quickly I surprised myself by feeling at home in Philadelphia. It was different from New York. The first time I boarded the Paoli local, the commuter train serving the Main Line suburbs, I was prepared to push, because that's the only way you can get onto the New York subway. As I assumed the posture of a football fullback I was astonished when several gentlemen wearing unpressed seersucker suits and Panama hats motioned me toward the door and said, "After you, sir." The charm of the Philadelphia suburbs worked in combination with the hospital's exciting surgery to keep me a Philadelphian for forty years.

We all had our lives changed by the coming of the Second World War. I completed my training as a civilian physician during the war, and with the shortage of doctors, I was called upon to perform operations usually reserved for surgeons with much more experience. It was nerve racking at times but exhilarating. The few surgeons left behind at the Hospital of the University of Pennsylvania would jokingly say we fought in the Battle of Spruce Street. It wasn't combat, thank God, but even so, lives hung in the balance every day.

My career in Philadelphia was saved because Betty went for a Coke the day after the attack on Pearl Harbor. As she stood in the hospital snack bar she happened to overhear Dr. Ravdin confide in an associate that he planned to fly that night to Pearl Harbor to try a new drug, sulfanilamide, on some of the sailors' wounds. She called me immediately and said, "If Dr. Ravdin goes out there, who knows when he might return. Your future is very much up in the air."

I didn't really know what to do, but I had to do something. Dr. Ravdin's office was full of people, so I went to wait by his car. The December dusk grew colder as I sat on the running board. Suddenly Ravdin appeared. He was a short man—probably no more than five feet five inches tall—and he was wearing, as most men did in those days, a fedora hat. In a very few words he set the stage for the rest of my life. "Don't sign any papers. Before I leave for Pearl Harbor, I will declare you essential to the university for the duration of the war. You will start as a Harrison Fellow on the first of July."

My training, already shortened by war when my two-year internship was cut to one year, had just been further curtailed by the elimination of a two-year stint in the dog lab.

In the next five years I crammed in a decade of surgical experience. With Ravdin away for the duration of the war, the surgical service was in the capable hands of Dr. Jonathan Rhoads. A tall, Lincolnesque man, with a low-pitched voice and a laconic sense of humor, Rhoads was a master surgeon and a master teacher. He was universally admired and respected in the field. I couldn't have had a better mentor.

Jonathan Rhoads was also gentle and generous. He was generous with the number of patients he assigned to me for surgery and with the time he took to teach me. He was generous in inviting Betty and me to his home for a roast-beef dinner in the meatless days of World War II. He was generous with his summer home in New Hampshire, which he let us have after we had gone three years without a vacation. Jonathan became a treasured friend.

As I began my surgical training as a Harrison Fellow, in July 1942, I was elated. I was, at last, an operating surgeon, and I loved every minute of it. A strange surgical case allowed me to assume a position with extraordinary responsibility for a first-year resident. An elderly woman patient was suffering from a serious skin disease known as exfoliative dermatitis; the outer layer of her skin kept sloughing off and falling away. Dr. C. H. Perry Pepper, distinguished professor of medicine, had determined that the dermatitis was being prolonged because of an infection in her gallbladder, but operating to remove the gallbladder would be tricky, in those preantibiotic days, because the open abdomen had to be protected from the infection on the skin. Improvising with sterilized cellophane—from a factory that made Henrietta cigars—and rubber cement, I was able to prepare the patient's abdomen so that Jonathan Rhoads could operate on her safely.

At the time, I had been a surgical resident for only five weeks. Jonathan, detained by another complicated operation, sent word that I should start the gallbladder case. I opened the woman's abdomen, as I had watched Jonathan do a number of times, and it was then my intent to wait until he arrived to remove the gallbladder. But to my great surprise the woman's gallbladder was right on top instead of being in its usual place—buried in the liver. It seemed easy to remove, so I performed the operation just as I had seen Jonathan do it. He arrived as I was putting in the last stitch. He said nothing, but meticulously took out all the stitches I had just placed in the skin, muscle, and peritoneum, in order to inspect my ligation of the cystic artery and duct. Then he replaced the drains exactly where I had them and closed the wound. He never said a word, but I think he was impressed.

Two days later I was in his office when he took a telephone call, turned to me, and said, "Chick, there is a patient who has just come into the emergency room with a bleeding gastric ulcer. Would you operate as soon as possible? Call me only if you need me."

I was astounded. In just five weeks I had graduated to surgery usually reserved for a resident in his third year. That early start, combined with the scarcity of surgeons because of the war and the tremendous number of patients we had for the next four years, gave me an operative experience as a resident that few, if any, had before and none have had since.

If Jonathan Rhoads was my surgical mentor, the senior resident, Harold Zintel, taught me the essence of surgical patient care. Harold shared with me the secret of making rounds: they never end. We would start on the seventh floor at one end of the building and work our way to the first floor at the opposite end of the building, a city block away, checking in on as many as a hundred patients. Then, unless interrupted by scheduled or emergency surgery, we would start all over again. As a result of his guidance, I developed a sense of necessary intimacy with the problems of my patients, and I never lost it.

In later years surgical residents would enjoy adequate salaries and duty schedules allowing them time at home. But when I was a resident at the Hospital of the University of Pennsylvania, I was, well, a resident. I literally lived there, sometimes coming home only once every three days. I was always on call, without a day off in the first two years. It was a busy life and a frugal one. As a Harrison Fellow, I took home $1000 a year for the first three years and $1200 for the last two.

I gave myself to the job completely. My dedication to my surgery was matched only by Betty's dedication to my career. She never complained about the long hours. She knew the life of a doctor—and a doctor's family—was one of sacrifice. It never entered anyone's mind that I should take time off. Who would cover for me?

Besides, I couldn't wait to get to work. My happiest hours were those in the operating room. I felt called to live on the edge of the life-and-death decisions that need to be made there.

The greatest continuing success story of the Ravdin surgical service was the proficiency of its gallbladder surgery. This service had not lost a patient following simple removal of the gallbladder for many years, and the number of such patients successfully treated climbed into the thousands. Each surgeon feared he might be the first one to lose a gallbladder patient.

As it turned out, I was the one who broke the successful series. One evening I walked up to the bedside of a woman whose gallbladder I had removed two days previously. Suddenly she grabbed her throat, tried to say something, and died before my eyes—I believed she'd just had a pulmonary embolism.

I don't know where I got either the courage or the knowledge to do what I did, but in rapid succession I yelled for someone to get the elevator, gave the woman a shot of papaverine directly through the chest wall into her heart, and then ran toward the elevator, dragging the patient's bed behind me. One floor up, I rolled the lifeless patient into an anesthesia room adjacent to an operating room. Without proper sterile clothing, I barged into the operating room—an operation by Dr. Eldridge L. Eliason, chief of surgery, was about to begin— grabbed the astonished surgeon's instrument tray, pulled it back into the anesthesia room, and opened my patient's chest. (This was like rushing into the Oval Office and grabbing a pen out of the President's hand.) I had never before opened a chest, so I didn't do it properly, but I got in there. I located the blocked pulmonary artery, slit it open, and extracted a blood clot over nine inches long, in the shape of a Y. Then I slapped the heart, and it began to beat.

By this time a nurse-anesthetist was giving the patient oxygen, and to my amazement and joy she began to stir. I closed the hole in the pulmonary artery with silk thread and stopped the bleeding. My patient was alive, she was breathing on her own, her heart was beating, and I was trembling.

By this time other surgeons had gathered at the door, simply staring in. Jonathan Rhoads had been called, and he, too, simply stared. I decided to take one more step, which proved to be a fatal gilding of the lily. Since I had opened the patient's chest without sterile precautions, I was concerned about the very high possibility of infection. In the refrigerator in our lab Harold Zintel and I kept Philadelphia's only supply of a new drug—penicillin. This was the new miracle drug, and we overestimated what it could do. I thought that spraying penicillin over the now properly beating heart would prevent any infection. I remember squirting the golden solution over the beating heart with a sense of deep satisfaction that I was adding one more factor of safety for my patient. To my amazement—and horror—the heart stopped immediately. I did not know about the high concentration of potassium in penicillin—enough to stop any heart. By squeezing the heart, I got it beating again, but it was only fibrillating, not forcefully contracting. So my patient, who had already "died" and been brought back to life by somewhat daring surgery, died again.

I wrote Dr. Ravdin, who was stationed in India, to tell him what I had done to save the patient's life—and his gallbladder series—complete with drawings and photos of the embolism. He was very kind and understanding in his reply. Several times in subsequent years I heard him tell about the night his bold resident tried the impossible and succeeded, until he tried to gild the lily.

THE high-quality medical care provided at the Pennsylvania Hospital and the Hospital of the University of Pennsylvania stemmed from the excellent professional cooperation between the physicians and the nursing staff. I learned very early that the best surgery would accomplish little without proper postoperative care. I was able to develop a special rapport with some of the nurses. Betty and I had no money to buy furniture, so I decided to make some in the Pennsylvania Hospital carpentry shop. The yard behind the carpentry shop was separated from the backyard of the nurses' residence by only a low fence. So when the student nurses failed to make their 10:00 p.m. curfew, a common restriction in 1941–1942, they would knock on the carpentry shop door. I would put out the lights, open the door, then lead them through the maze of machinery and lumber, out the back door, and give them a lift over the fence. They were home free.

On the night of their spring dance in 1942, the nurses were unhappy because they would not finish their twelve-hour day until nearly 8:00 p.m., but after the dance had to be back in their residence before the extended, but still unreasonable, deadline of midnight. So with the authority that seemed to have been vested in me by the departure of the senior staff for the war, I dismissed all the nurses on my ward at 6:00 o'clock and told them that I would take care of their duties and give the night report to the next shift.

Not everyone appreciated my alliance with the nurses. The World War I nursing veteran who ran herd on the student nurses complained to the board of managers at their monthly meeting, "There is entirely too much levity in the Pennsylvania Hospital since that Koop boy came down from New York." As far as I could tell, the board did not act on her complaint. But the appreciative nurses put me through a capping ceremony, complete with Florence Nightingale's symbolic lamp, declaring me an honorary nurse.

Even though there was more than enough surgery to keep me busy, I became involved in a medical research project made necessary by the war. The ferocious combat made it clear that the armed services would need blood or blood plasma in quantities that far exceeded the supply. So the National Research Council assigned to various universities the challenge of finding a plasma substitute. The University of Pennsylvania investigated the possibility that a blood plasma substitute could be found in gelatin made by hydrolyzing sun-bleached bones brought from India to the Knox Gelatin Company, just across the river, in Camden, New Jersey. I had the assignment of testing its efficacy, first in dogs, then in patients.

I, too, was a subject of the gelatin experiments. After being bled the equivalent of one and a half donations of blood for transfusion, I replaced the lost blood with gelatin and measured the effects on my cardiac output and vital signs. Despite my lowered hemoglobin levels, I always felt perfectly able to carry on with my work.

We concluded that gelatin was an effective replacement for plasma and that it controlled shock and hemorrhage extraordinarily well. But its viscosity made it congeal at cooler temperatures, so it was judged impractical for combat situations. However, I did get my second earned doctorate, a doctor of medical science—Sc.D. (Med)—then equivalent to a Ph.D. for those in medical pursuits. Years later, while traveling in Egypt as Surgeon General, I discovered an Egyptian physician who was using gelatin as a plasma substitute. She showed me my papers, written decades earlier.

Meanwhile, Betty and I decided that at last we could afford to start a family. Our first son, Allen, arrived in January 1944. He was tiny, had a slow start with jaundice, and kept us up nights—but what a joy! It was the beginning of another set of tensions in my life. I already had all too little time for Betty and now for Allen, too. The effort to balance family and clinical obligations grew with the arrival of Norman in 1946, David in 1947, and Betsy in 1951.

Everyone who lived through the end of the war has a personal memory of that special day in August 1945. I remember the two burned children. They had gone to an automobile graveyard and found that by dropping lighted matches into the empty gas tanks, they were sometimes rewarded with a pop. Unfortunately, they dropped a match into a tank that was partially filled with gasoline. It exploded, covering them with flaming liquid, and they were admitted with almost 100 percent third-degree burns. I nursed those two children by living between their two beds in a small room, leaving only to go to the bathroom. One youngster died in thirty-six hours and the other in forty-eight, and I went home to bed. Betty, with our young son, Allen, who was nineteen months old, was visiting her mother in Connecticut. I had been awake for most of the past forty-eight hours and felt desperate to get some real sleep. As soon as I pulled the shade down, the city erupted with blowing horns, whistles, bells, and shouts in the street. It was V-J Day. The war with Japan was over, and no one, no matter how tired, could sleep. Four of us who were residents went out to a small restaurant not far from the campus. I squandered a week's food money on a black-market steak and then collapsed, asleep at the table.

With the end of the war the end of my residency was in sight. As I contemplated my future I realized that I was at best only halfhearted about my planned return to New York. In many ways I had grown fond of Philadelphia, but I longed for a change of scenery. In late 1945 I made the familiar trip to New Hampshire, with business as well as pleasure on my mind. I talked with the chief of surgery at the Dartmouth Medical School and learned that they would find a place for me. On the train back to Philadelphia, I enjoyed a sense of peaceful anticipation of a move to Dartmouth. Two days later my door burst open at 5:00 a.m. and in strode I. S. Ravdin, resplendent in his army uniform, fresh from the Asian conflict. As usual, he got right to the point.

"Chick, what do you plan to do with your life?"

I had just come back from New Hampshire, where I thought I had arranged my future. So I don't know why I answered as I did. But I said, "Well, Dr. Ravdin, I have grown very fond of the University of Pennsylvania. I'd like to stay here. There is one very weak spot in your program, and that's the tumor clinic. Give that to me, and I'll make it sing for you."

But Ravdin had another idea, one that would change my life. "How would you like to be surgeon in chief of the Children's Hospital instead?" he asked.

CHAPTER 4
Medicine and Faith

THE surgical care of newborns now seems so routine that it is hard to believe it did not exist in 1946, when I started work at the Children's Hospital of Philadelphia. But for the next thirty-five years I was devoted to a new course in the care of infants and disabled children. In a relatively brief time we in this new specialty were able to correct some of the most deadly congenital problems that had taken the lives of countless infants and children over the centuries. When I first encountered these problems, the mortality rate was 95 to 100 percent. In 1981, when I left pediatric surgery, the former mortality rate of 95 percent had become the survival rate for all but one of the five most serious problems in newborns. My belief that all life is precious became the basis of this intense focus on saving the lives of infants.

The offer Dr. Ravdin had made to me involved several stages. First I would spend three months at the Children's Hospital of Philadelphia, then go on to the Boston Children's Hospital to work with William E. Ladd, who was the only person in the United States at that time known as a child surgeon and who also had a teaching service. At the end of that training period I would return to Philadelphia, perform surgery on children exclusively, and become the surgeon in chief of the Children's Hospital, where I was expected to establish the best possible academic service. I was told by Dr. Ravdin to discuss the plan with no one except my wife and parents.

My mind was flooded with doubts. I was about to become a child surgeon—soon I would say pediatric surgeon. But pediatrics had been almost completely omitted from my medical training. I had attended only six lectures on the subject, which covered little more than the feeding of infants. Then when wartime pressures cut my internship from two years to one, pediatrics was one of the rotations left out. At the Hospital of the University of Pennsylvania the children's ward for general surgical patients was tiny—only six beds. During my entire residency I knew of only three operations on newborns, and one of these had been botched.

The chief reason surgeons avoided children was the primitive state of anesthesia. Doctors were afraid to put children to sleep, because they weren't sure they could wake them up. But while most general surgeons avoided children, they saw no reason for anyone to specialize in surgery on children. And for years they actually opposed those of us attempting to get recognition for pediatric surgery as a separate specialty. In the late '40s the large field of general surgery was being splintered into many subspecialties, since wartime had spurred great advances in areas such as plastic surgery, burn management, and orthopedic surgery. General surgeons were forced to yield to specialists, which meant they suffered a loss of patients and income.

So when this twenty-nine-year-old upstart came along, one of only a handful talking about still another new specialty—pediatric surgery—the general surgeons dug in their heels. This alleged insult to general surgery took a long time to heal, and it was years before pediatric surgeons were accepted into the fold.

Of course, I could foresee none of this on my first trolley ride to Children's Hospital. I hopped off the trolley, walked down the sidewalk on Bainbridge Street, and across the Children's Hospital courtyard, which was paved with cobblestones so that the horses drawing ambulances of days gone by could have enough traction. When I opened the oak-framed glass door and stepped into the tiled lobby of the hospital, I was greeted by a young woman, who told me she was the chief medical resident. "Why don't you go back where you came from? You're not needed here, you're not wanted here, and you put four good surgeons out of work."

I was taken aback, and it would take me several years to piece together the entire story that explained why Ravdin had asked me to go to Children's. This, the oldest children's hospital in America, had become dilapidated and languishing, even though it had seen some remarkable research. Its chief pediatrician, Joseph Stokes, was known for a number of accomplishments in pediatrics and for his wartime work with hepatitis in Italy.

The incident that prompted Ravdin to look for a chief surgeon at Children's Hospital had taken place early in 1945. A child with abdominal pain had arrived at the hospital's emergency room. The medical residents diagnosed an intussusception, in which the bowel telescopes into itself, causing intestinal obstruction. Without a simple operation, the child was in danger of peritonitis and death. The resident telephoned the surgeon on call and explained the situation. The surgeon should have operated immediately, but four hours later he had not even arrived at the hospital. They called him again. After eight hours they called him again. This went on for about two days. The patient died before a surgeon ever got there—a terrible case of malpractice and negligence.

After this tragedy the director of nursing gave Dr. Stokes an ultimatum: she would give him one year to establish a service for child surgery, so that this sort of thing would never happen again. She told him if he didn't, she would leave, taking every nurse in the hospital with her. Stokes called the University of Pennsylvania's vice president for medical affairs, who called Ravdin and gave him his mandate.

Apparently, I had not been Ravdin's first choice. He had approached the four general surgeons who were then doing surgery at Children's as a sideline. None of them was willing to take any further training in surgery on children, and none of them was willing to give up surgery on adults. The honor of becoming a pioneer in the new specialty fell to me by default.

THE resident's discouraging welcome was no fluke. It quickly became clear that the pediatricians who worked at the hospital already felt they knew everything about children. With growing trepidation I walked up to the fifth floor to introduce myself to Joseph Stokes, Jr.

Dr. Stokes informed me that any patient that I treated would have to be admitted on his service. He would make the diagnosis. Only when he thought the child was ready to be operated on would he call me, and after the operation had been completed, the patient would go back on his service, where Stokes would manage the child's postoperative care.

My reply surprised him. "That was the procedure until today, Dr. Stokes. The reason I am here is so that will change. I am a surgeon who will soon take the examination of the American Board of Surgery. When I take that examination, I must sign a statement affirming that I will be responsible for my patient insofar as diagnosis, treatment, postoperative care, and follow-up are concerned."

Stokes gruffly said, "I'll see about that!" and telephoned Dr. Ravdin. I could hear only Stokes's side of the conversation, but obviously Ravdin was laying down the rules in no uncertain terms. When Stokes put the telephone down, it was the first victory for pediatric surgery in Philadelphia and maybe in the whole country.

As the years went on, Stokes and I developed a mutual respect for each other, and by the time he retired, we were good friends—to the point that he was even taking the credit for bringing me to the Children's Hospital! But in the beginning we were definitely adversaries.

I found further evidence of my frosty welcome when I saw my "office": a table in the hospital library. I, the future surgeon in chief, would spend many dreary days just sitting there; the staff often would not bother to call me to consult on surgical problems. After the planned three-month trial period Betty and I, our two-year-old son, Allen, and our two-week-old son, Norman, set off for my training session at Boston Children's Hospital.

Although in my later years many people referred to me as the father of pediatric surgery in the United States, that honor belongs to Dr. Robert E. Gross of Boston Children's Hospital. But neither Gross nor I could have succeeded without the earlier vision and spadework of William E. Ladd. Although I learned pediatric surgical technique from Gross, I learned about the art and philosophy of pediatric surgery from Ladd. Following his retirement, Ladd did not give up his contact with children. After eating his lunch at the Harvard Club, he would wander over to the Children's Hospital and walk through the wards where he had been surgeon in chief, hoping to find a resident or an intern with whom he could have a conversation. I always tried to be there when he arrived. We would often just sit and talk, Ladd dangling his long legs over the side of an empty crib. Although I never saw Ladd operate, I learned from him the delicacy of pediatric tissues, especially in newborns, and how easily they are traumatized.

For example, he gave me some pointers about pyloric stenosis, one of the first problems of infancy to be corrected by surgery. This condition, in which the muscular valve at the lower end of the stomach goes into spasm, usually affects babies about six weeks after birth and causes violent vomiting. A practiced finger gently touching a child's abdomen can actually feel this valve, which is the size and shape of a tiny olive. Ladd taught me that infants' abdominal organs were so delicate that even feeling the "olive" with too heavy a hand could injure it. Thereafter, if I was scheduled to operate on a baby with pyloric stenosis, I would post a hands-off order for a day or two before the operation, so the infant could recuperate more quickly. Ladd's lesson was simple, but invaluable.

Although my months in Boston were not easy, my problems couldn't compare to the difficulties Betty endured, mainly because of our housing. Our problem, like that of many young couples, was a lack of money. Betty had her hands full at home, with two small children, and I was still making less than $2000 a year.

The only place we could find in Boston within our budget was a Somerville house that had been abandoned seventeen years earlier. Once an ornate frame house, 15 Adams Street was falling in on itself. We picked our way up the broken steps to the door, brushed aside the cobwebs and filth, and entered the kitchen, the floor still strewn with papers dated 1929. Our newborn son, Norman, was hungry and cold.

The furnace lay on the cellar floor in a pile of rust and iron fragments. Boston is cold in April, and the house was dank and damp. We put Norman in a very small bassinet behind the kitchen coal range that became our sole source of heat until Boston warmed up for the summer.

When Betty's mother first came to visit us, she took a taxi from South Station. There was no number on our house, so the taxi driver went past it two or three times, until my mother-in-law said, "That has to be it."

He replied, "It couldn't be, lady. Nobody would live there."

But live there we did, as Betty struggled with the medieval inconveniences and I attempted to pack in as much knowledge of pediatric surgery as I could. I jumped at every opportunity that came along, no matter how menial. One of the medical interns assigned to the surgical service was called for government work, and I took his place as the lowest of the low on the surgical totem pole. It might have been degrading in a sense, but I learned firsthand everything a doctor or nurse would have to do for a hospitalized infant. Over the years, when I was back at the Children's Hospital of Philadelphia, I was always grateful that I never had to ask anyone to do something for me that I couldn't do myself.

When I returned to the Children's Hospital of Philadelphia, in November 1946, I hoped to find a more receptive atmosphere, but I suppose I should have known better. The hostility still existed, the senior staff was no more eager to have their hidebound, comfortable way of professional life altered by a young kid starting a new specialty, no matter how much it might improve the lot of children.

In offices on the top floor of the hospital, ruling all beneath them, were the members of the senior medical staff, most of whom stood firmly in opposition to me. Among them was a giant of a man in more ways than one: Dr. Milton Rappaport. Unmarried, he had given himself to the hospital and served as confidant to the house staff and as resident philosopher. Rap never forgot anything; he was a walking compendium of medical and scientific knowledge.

But Rap didn't know surgery, and one day we came into sharp dispute on the management of a little boy who had pus in his chest following a bout with pneumonia. I wanted to drain the enclosed cavity surgically. Rap wanted to take out the pus with a needle and inject penicillin into the cavity. I knew that Rap's suggestion had often been unsuccessful in practice and was wrong in theory.

It was decided that the case would be presented at the Friday conference, where perplexing pediatric cases were adjudicated. Philadelphia pediatricians packed the auditorium. There was no better place for a doctor to succeed—and no worse place to fail.

I had been warned by friends that Rap had said if I held out against him, he would ask the board of managers for my dismissal. For two days before the conference, Rap and I, who were no longer speaking to each other, sat on opposite sides of a table in the tiny hospital library mustering our ammunition.

The conference day came. Rap presented the case as a simple one of empyema, a condition in which pus fills the lower half of the cavity in which the lung resides, pushing a partially collapsed lung upward. He had not changed his mind in the least about the cause of or cure for the little boy's woes.

Then it was my turn. I walked up to the X-ray view boxes, where about twelve films of the youngster's chest were on display. The audience leaned forward, eager for gladiatorial combat. I looked at the X rays, recalling an identical case I had seen at the autopsy of an adult several years before. "I think Dr. Rappaport and his colleagues have been extraordinarily fortunate that they have not had a tragic complication from removing the pus in this chest with a needle."

That was certainly unexpected.

"If you look at the edge of the opaque shadow here, which he called empyema, you will note that there is a fine rim of air-bearing lung tissue between the opaque pus and the rib cage. This child does not have empyema. He has an abscess in a congenital cyst of the lung, and the rim of lung tissue, which surrounds the cyst, proves it."

Old Dr. Bromer, the radiologist, squinted at the films. "By George, Rap, Koop is right. I missed it."

Now surprise had turned to consternation. Rap nodded assent, but said nothing. I continued. "The reason I said Dr. Rappaport had been very lucky is that this variety of congenital cyst has the same blood supply as a lobe of the lung, with a large artery coming directly off the aorta. The cyst is lined with vessels of prodigious size. Had his multiple sticks with a needle punctured one of them or, worse yet, torn one of them, you could have had anything from a bad bleed to a fatal hemorrhage. If the infected cyst had been surgically drained, as empyema should be, the drain almost certainly would have eroded a vein, and a fatal hemorrhage would have followed." (That's what had happened in the autopsy I had seen years before.)

"This youngster needs immediate surgery to excise the infected cyst. He should recover without sequelae. If you refer him to my service, I'll talk with the family and operate on Monday."

Something happened that day. No fireworks went off, but I noticed a change in the attitude of the other physicians. Many in the audience would become my referring pediatricians. A victory was won that Friday afternoon—at the conference, in the hospital, in the university, indeed in all of Philadelphia—a victory for pediatric surgery.

THE changes in my professional life, as big as they were, were not as far reaching as the change in my personal beliefs, which happened at the same time. I had always thought of myself as a Christian, and I had been raised in a churchgoing home. My parents had met at church, and I had been a member of the Sunday school from the cradle roll. But I didn't have a clue about who I was spiritually, where I had been, or where I was going. When my family moved to Flatbush and joined the Baptist Church of the Redeemer, I didn't know what a redeemer was, and it never crossed my mind to find out. I must have felt a spiritual yearning, because in 1948, during our summer visit to Maine's Vinalhaven Island, I sat on the rocks amid the splashing surf and read through the New Testament twice. But no new light dawned.

It was Erna Goulding, a nurse at Children's Hospital, who sensed that I was searching for spiritual meaning. One evening, as Betty and I left our apartment to attend a musical program at the First Baptist Church in Center City Philadelphia, Erna suggested we walk a block beyond the Baptist Church and go to the evening service of the Tenth Presbyterian Church. She thought I would appreciate the intellectual approach to Christianity offered by its minister, Donald Grey Barnhouse. But we did not take her suggestion.

The next Sunday, however, I finished grand rounds early, and I found my feet taking me to the Tenth Presbyterian Church, just a few blocks north of the hospital. I entered the back door and slipped up to the balcony. I was just going to observe. I liked what I saw, and I was fascinated by what I heard. I saw the congregation respond willingly and generously to social needs; this was no empty religion. I heard teaching from one of the most learned men I have ever known, and I was interested enough to want to go back the next Sunday morning. And then just a few hours later I returned for the evening service. I did that each Sunday for two years, and except when I was out of town, I never missed a morning or evening service.

After about seven months I realized that I had become a participant and not just an observer; what made sense to that congregation made sense to me as well. And it was new to me. I wasn't just shifting gears from my parents' faith to one of my own.

I was a believer.

Betty became one, too. With the birth of our third son, David, she had her hands full with three small boys, but when I came home from church, she would share enthusiastically all I had learned. We grew as Christians together, and we grew together as Christians. It was one of the most heady times of our lives, with a thousand unanswered questions. Most are answered by now, but it is still heady and still exciting.

It was out of those beginnings that I acknowledged the Lord Jesus Christ in my life and rested in my abiding faith in the sovereignty of God. I came to realize that my life wasn't just a series of dilemmas followed by happy coincidences. I knew there was a plan for my life, and this brought me an assurance I had never known.

No matter what else I did in life, I would be a Christian. I soon discovered that people were not content when I told them that I was a Christian; they wanted to know what kind of Christian, what adjective, what denomination. After I became Surgeon General, the press often referred to me as a fundamentalist Christian. In one sense that is right, because I affirm the fundamental doctrines of Christianity. But fundamentalists are more known for what they are against than what they are for. That label never fit me. I always called myself an evangelical Christian. Evangelist means messenger, bearer of news. An evangelical Christian carries to others the good news of the mercy of Christ.

Faced with the pain and suffering of my patients and their parents, I needed the assurance that there was some greater plan, both for them and for myself. Of course, not all my patients saw eye to eye with me on religion. But just as it has so often been said that there are few atheists in foxholes, I found that there were few atheists among parents of critically ill children. There were times when sharing with them my faith in Christ and the sovereignty of God provided great comfort and strength for all of us.

Each time I operated, after I was gowned and gloved, after the patient was draped, right before I made the first incision, there was always the moment when I established an emotional distance between the patient and me. I don't know how many surgeons have articulated this moment, but for me it made my judgment and perhaps even my technique as free as possible of emotional constraints. Surgeons who have operated upon close members of their families—as I once did—know that the emotional concern is overpowering and in a tight spot can be dangerous, devastating to the patient and to the surgeon.

Furthermore, I realized that for all I might do with my hands and mind, all healing comes from God. Several reporters have portrayed me as a surgeon who prayed with every patient before each operation. It didn't happen that way. Prayer with a patient and the family is of invaluable benefit. I did it whenever I was asked, but it was never routine. Nor did I pray in private before each operation. My faith was bigger than that. I considered myself and my patient to be in God's hands; I trusted that the skills the Lord had given me would be available in time of need.

I had to learn some tough lessons as I attempted to find a working relationship between faith and practice, and early in my newly awakened Christian life I made a mistake in judgment in the tension between family needs and spiritual obligations. Members of the Christian Medical Society from various medical schools expressed a desire to help the men on skid row—the equivalent of today's homeless people. I accepted the supervision of these young men and women, and presumed it would be a chore easy to share with the seventy or so graduate members of the society. That did not prove to be the case, and I found that I was almost always the only available hands-on supervisor.

Every Sunday afternoon for several years, I left home immediately after dinner and went into the city to supervise and teach the students at the Wayside Gospel Mission. That took us well into the evening. My second stint with the students began at the Twelfth Street Gospel

Hall, where we fed 1200 men at 9:00 o'clock and ran a clinic. We never finished before 11:00. My mistake was that I did not spend as much time with my family as I did with the homeless. Sunday afternoons were really the only time I was likely to be home uninterrupted, except by emergencies. I now believe it would have been more important for me to spend half that time with my family. If Betty had not taken great pains to be sure that the children understood that I was doing a service for other people, I think our children could have let my absence lead to resentment, or worse.

As in so much else in my life, my success in the early days of pediatric surgery depended on Betty's support. She continued as my confidante and primary sounding board. But now there was a family to raise: Allen, Norman, David, and a daughter, Betsy. Best of all, our family and our new faith arrived in the same years, so we could raise the kids as Christians. Betty maintained that no matter how busy we were, it was easier to go to church every Sunday than to choose which Sundays to go.

The tension between obligation to family and obligation to profession is constant if you want to be a good doctor and a good father and husband. I took all those roles seriously, but I had the added burden of trying to develop an academic service in a hostile environment. And after the first few years I was absorbed in establishing pediatric surgery as a specialty internationally, not only in the United States. I felt like a juggler with too many balls in the air. And of course, I made lots of mistakes.

Betty and I were spared one common problem. Unlike many couples, we never bickered about money. At first we had almost no money. Eventually we had enough. But it didn't seem to matter one way or another. In almost sixty years together, Betty and I have never had an argument about finances.

The deep satisfaction we feel about our children and the longevity of our marriage are due in large part to Betty's understanding of what I was trying to accomplish and her willingness to take second place to what I saw as my professional obligation. She understood that I would have preferred it to be otherwise, and she knew my striving was not for money or power or position, but to save the lives of my diminutive patients. My wife has always said to me, "Your profession comes first. I understand that. I'd like the time left over." My sorting of priorities was never easy, but two things made it bearable. Betty always said, "If you're happy, I'm happy." And after he was grown, Allen put a blanket of assurance over many years of tensions among obligations by saying—I hope for his siblings as well—"Although Dad was away a lot, Mom never let us feel he was absent from us."

My family understood my work schedule because they realized the importance of my surgery, and they also knew something about it. While other families enjoyed slide shows of the trip to Disneyland, our kids were treated to slides I brought home showing the latest from the operating room: cleft-palate repair, cleft-lip surgery, abdominal operations.

One of the ways I tried to compensate for my professional life away from the family was to try to get home for dinner. Unless an absolute emergency precluded it, I would make it home for the family meal, even if it meant going back to the hospital to operate at 9:00 p.m. instead of 7:00 p.m. The eighteen-mile round-trip between the hospital and our home in suburban Penn Valley was well worth it.

No MATTER how busy life was, I did set aside four or five weeks in the summer for the family to be together, away from Philadelphia and its many demands. Our first family vacations took us to join my parents in a picturesque shack on Vinalhaven Island in Maine. It was a beautiful spot, and the day I discovered that the place was for sale, I decided to buy it. That night, as Betty and my mother were cleaning up after a great lobster feed, my father and I sat on the porch watching the thick fog roll in. At bedtime I carried three-year-old Norman to his bunk and was startled to see a circle of bright red blood on the seat of his pajamas. Few things struck as much terror in me, as a pediatric surgeon, as seeing bright red blood coming from the rectum of a child, because the consequences can be so dire and so rapid in their evolution. I examined Norman immediately, and to my great relief he was bleeding from a mosquito bite that he had scratched. But for the next three days, as the island was fogbound, with no boats coming or going, I wondered what I would have done had the bleeding been serious. Right then I made the decision that we would vacation near medical help that would not be impeded by isolation or fog.

So, no surprise, I returned once again to my favorite place, Hanover, New Hampshire, where in a matter of days I found an abandoned farm on the side of Moose Mountain. The house had lain vacant for several years. The land was beautiful—over two hundred acres of field and forest. But the best thing about our summer cottage was what it lacked. With only two bedrooms—one a bunk room for the kids—it lacked room for any overnight guests, so when the family went there, we were together and alone. Better still, it had no phone, no radio, no television. Each year the month on Moose Mountain bonded us together. Even now Betty and I know of no parents closer than we are to our children. Seven grandchildren have enlarged the family circle, but it remains as close as ever.

From the time Betty was pregnant with Betsy until all the kids had gone to college, the best part of the year was the time from the last Friday in July until Labor Day, when we could enjoy one another and the little house on Moose Mountain. I pitched in with the shopping, and the kids did breakfast. We puttered around the property, swam in a nearby lake, climbed mountains, picked berries, watched the wildlife, read to each other in the evenings, and cemented the love of family that would take us through so much.

These, then, are the three elements of my life: my work in the treatment of critically ill children, my religious faith, and my family. Sometimes, when surgery cannot save a young life, surgeon and family must cope with the death of a child. No one sets out to become an expert in this, but understanding my own family and having a religious faith enabled me to reach out to people in this most heartbreaking of situations.

Often I could manage the disappointment and grief brought by the loss of a baby better when I was alone than when I was with the family. Somewhere along the line some mentor told me that doctors should never cry with parents of pediatric patients. Well, I have to admit, there were times I cried with mine, and I learned that instead of seeing this as a sign of weakness in their physician, parents saw it as a sign of empathy and support.

Then empathy became all too easy—or all too difficult—for me. As a surgeon of the newborn and of children with cancer, I had developed a certain "expertise" in dealing with the parents of dying children. At a conference in 1967 I was asked in the closing five minutes, "What do you tell the parents of a dying child?" Someone with a tape recorder captured my remarks, which soon appeared in several medical journals. In February 1968 *Reader's Digest* printed them as an article, "What I Tell a Dying Child's Parents."

Among the Children's Hospital's many nationally recognized specialists were four doctors who, strangely enough, had children afflicted with the same rare problem for which they had established medical expertise. One day those four doctors and I were talking about this, and I wondered, What is it for which I am well known? I almost shuddered when I realized that my new "specialty" had become dealing with the loss of a child.

I began to have disturbing thoughts that I would lose a child. On Good Friday, 1968, I felt it had happened. Our son Norman was five hours overdue driving from Boston to Philadelphia. When the telephone rang, I was certain it would be the police with grim news. Instead, it was Norman, cheerful as ever, wondering why we were so upset, insisting that he had told us not when he would *arrive* at a friend's home in Philadelphia, but when he would *leave* Boston. A wave of relief swept over me, and I stopped brooding that one of my children would die. They were all safe: Betsy and Norman living at home while they attended high school and college; Allen in graduate school, living a mile away; David a junior at Dartmouth.

However, my feeling of relief was short lived. A few weeks later the most devastating event of our lives occurred. After an uneventful Sunday the phone rang at about 9:00 in the evening. Since we were expecting a call from David, both Betty and I picked up the phone on different extensions. It was the dean of Dartmouth College telling us that David had been killed while rock climbing on Cannon Mountain in New Hampshire.

Roped to his climbing companion, Charlie, David had been hammering a piton into the rock when a large section of the cliff sheared off, carrying him with it. Bound to his tether, he crashed into the face of the cliff like a swinging pendulum. Charlie managed to maneuver David onto a ledge, and climbed down to make a desperate attempt to save his life. David was semiconscious, and bleeding from a severed artery in his knee. Charlie attempted to stop the bleeding with a tourniquet, but it was too late. Within ten minutes David was dead.

Words are inadequate to describe the depth of our shock, hurt, and loss. Losing a child brings a poignant and tender grief unlike any other. We clung together as a family, and the support we received from our many friends and our own faith was enormous. David's death affected each family member deeply and uniquely. Eventually we wrote a book about our experience, hoping that *Sometimes Mountains Move* might be of some comfort and help to others who had lost a child.

I thought that now I might be better able to help parents of dying children, but for quite a while I felt less able, too emotionally involved. And from that time on, I could rarely discuss the death of a child without tears welling up in my eyes.

CHAPTER 5
Surgery and Children

As A physician, I have always been at least a crusader, at best a pioneer. I loved taking on difficult problems, even if there was only a remote chance of success. When parents brought newborns with congenital defects to me, I tackled problems that other physicians dismissed: "We just let those die—we can't fix them." I tried to do everything I could for afflicted youngsters, and because of that aggressiveness, I learned a lot. Many of the operations I performed had never been done before. It was an exuberant feeling but also a little scary.

Above all, in those early years I soon realized that advances in pediatric surgery would have to await advances in pediatric anesthesiology. When I first arrived at Children's, I was horrified by what passed for anesthesia. A nurse-anesthetist would start a tonsillectomy patient under anesthesia with open-drop ether, hook the child to a machine that delivered ether vapor through a curved tube into the side of his or her mouth, then *leave that patient alone* to start another. It was only a little short of miraculous that there were not more misadventures. But at the time, that was standard operating procedure at even the best of children's hospitals.

As I toured hospitals both at home and abroad, I realized that too many children had died on the operating table not because of the surgery, but because of inadequate anesthetic techniques. I needed to find someone who would dedicate himself or herself to pediatric anesthesia the same way I tried to dedicate myself to pediatric surgery.

I found that person in Margo Deming, who had been senior resident in anesthesia when I was a senior resident in surgery at the Hospital of the University of Pennsylvania.

We began to experiment with endotracheal anesthesia in infants. That involved running a small tube from the source of anesthetic through the child's nose and passing it down through the vocal cords and into the windpipe. By squeezing a bag that was interposed between the supply of anesthetic and the baby, we were able to control the amount of anesthetic and oxygen the baby received. The technique not only helped us regulate the amount of anesthesia but also prevented the baby's tongue from falling back into its throat, obstructing the airway.

As far as we knew, no one had ever performed this procedure successfully in tiny infants, so we had to make our own equipment. We took ordinary rubber catheters, cut them to a proper length, and beveled the edges with sandpaper to prevent injury to the lining of the infant's windpipe. We then inserted a wire into the tubing, bent it and the surrounding tube to the proper curve, boiled it all in water, removed the wire, and hoped the rubber curve would retain its memory. Many younger doctors practicing medicine today don't appreciate what a tremendous revolution took place in surgery when plastic tubing came onto the scene.

In the first several years, we used these homemade endotracheal anesthesia techniques on 1200 babies, and we never lost one. We had our share of scares, though, and there were many nights when Margo Deming and I sat up with a small infant whose windpipe had been traumatized, just in case the developing croup might call for a tracheostomy (cutting an emergency hole in the windpipe).

The news of our success spread through the pediatric surgical community by word of mouth, eventually producing a body of literature. Today no one would operate on a child without an endotracheal tube in place.

As we were developing the specialty of pediatric surgery, one cardinal rule emerged: You cannot treat children simply as small adults. They require special procedures. Before pediatric surgeons developed such techniques, the way children suffered under surgery was almost criminal. When I was a resident, a simple inguinal hernia operation on a four-year-old child would start out with an incision three to four inches long, when one and a quarter inches would do. The old procedure produced a large, heavily sutured scar, which made the poor child look like a toy football with thick laces. After the operation the youngster would be mummified in a muslin girdle, which was erroneously believed to provide extra support; confined to a hospital bed for seven to ten days, an eternity to a child; and then sent home with instructions that he could not laugh, sneeze, cough, or lift anything for six more weeks. It was barbaric surgery.

It took pediatric surgery pioneers like Robert Gross and William Ladd to change all that. It was Bob Gross who taught me the hidden, or subcuticular, stitch, which was placed in, but not through, the skin. When you used such stitches, you didn't even need to put a bandage on a child—just cover the wound with a protective liquid plastic, which dried on the skin. Parents would be delighted when their youngster came home from, for example, a hernia operation after only one night in the hospital—later reduced to a matter of hours—with no visible scar or stitches and with no restriction on activity. I never tired of doing those simple inguinal hernias, the most common operation in general pediatric surgery. I performed seventeen thousand of them, and in the latter half of my surgical career I don't think I ever took longer than six minutes.

After hernias my second most common operation was the repair of an undescended testicle, a common congenital problem in young boys. I performed over seven thousand of these orchidopexies. One day, at a pediatric surgical meeting in Chicago, I rose to criticize a new operation, which seemed to me to be inordinately complicated. I was nearly apoplectic when the surgeon presenting the paper said, "And it only takes an hour and a quarter to do." I admit I got a little emotional during my discussion of his paper, and ended by saying, "And besides, the operation I have done several thousand times takes only seventeen minutes." I had never really timed myself, and my surgical colleagues challenged my statement. I returned to Philadelphia and asked the chief of anesthesiology to time me on the next ten orchidopexies I performed. The average was seventeen minutes; some things just work out.

No matter how relatively minor an operation might have seemed to me, however, I always knew that to the parents of my patients it was a monumental episode, and I realized that surgery required more than just good hands. Judgment—when to do which procedure, when to do nothing—is what brings success. I loved the technical challenge of surgery when it could repair what nature had failed to complete, and I enjoyed the challenge of dealing with inflammatory tissue.

Today, in the era of antibiotics, rupturing an appendix while removing it from the abdomen is not the tragic situation it was when I started in surgery. In those days a surgeon who ruptured an appendix could bring on peritonitis, which could ravage, even kill the patient. I delighted in being able to slip a probing finger into the abdomen of a child through a tiny incision, find the appendix, take stock of how inflamed and turgid it was, then blindly deliver it, unruptured.

Another breakthrough came when we put in the first shunt for hydrocephalus—water on the brain—to drain the excessive cerebrospinal fluid and prevent the head from enlarging. When word of this successful surgery spread, children with untreated hydrocephalus came from far and wide. There were days when I would arrive in the hospital courtyard to find a house trailer parked there, driven across the country by a family with a hydrocephalic child. The heads of some of these children were huge—as large as big pumpkins. Some of the children's conditions were so far advanced that they couldn't benefit from surgery, and their frustrated families became the core of one of our early self-help groups. But we were able to relieve the suffering and disfigurement of many.

Among the many people who helped me build the new field of pediatric surgery, I have to give special credit to the nurses, dedicated women whose skills I admired and whose loyalty to our mission I cherished. Nothing in surgery is as satisfying as working with a skilled operating room nurse. You're like dancing partners who know each other's every move; no words need to be spoken in a synchronized duet. Each Christmas I took a page from Flo Ziegfeld's book when I hung a long sign over the door to the operating rooms that said THROUGH THESE PORTALS PASS THE MOST BEAUTIFUL GIRLS IN THE WORLD. The nurses knew I wasn't talking about superficial physical attraction; they knew that I appreciated the beauty of all the things they did to make possible our successes in the operating room.

But I needed more than top-notch operating room nurses. Pediatric surgery also depends upon the quality of postoperative nursing care. In 1956, after many years of searching for funds, I was able to found the nation's first neonatal surgical intensive care unit. At first with only three incubators, eventually with twenty, the neonatal unit worked not only because of the high-tech equipment but also because of the dedication of the nurses. In just a few years I found it necessary to recognize the ICU nurses as I had the OR nurses, so signs then appeared in two places at Christmas.

You might expect an intensive care unit to be a sterile, scientific place, but over the years we saw among all the tubes, monitors, and high-tech gadgets a growing parade of sterilized teddy bears, placed in incubators next to babies half their size. Brightly colored mobiles would suddenly appear above bassinets or incubators. And the nurses would chip in to buy rocking chairs so the mothers could come to the neonatal unit to rock their babies. Most touching, at least once a year a nurse would ask to see me after hours and then timidly but firmly ask me, "Will you help me adopt the baby I'm caring for?" Many of these nurses developed a compelling love for the infants they cared for, and several did adopt youngsters who had been abandoned.

The dedication at the Children's Hospital certainly wasn't limited to the nurses. Charlie Wilson was an operating room orderly when I first arrived at Children's. His grandfather, whom he remembered clearly, had been a slave. Charlie asked little from life and gave much. I was one of the recipients of his concern and care as soon as he saw that we felt the same about protecting children. He brought the patients to the operating room, always comforting the older children as he wheeled them along. He ran the IVs, he kept the instruments repaired, he made certain we never ran out of supplies, and when my back was in a knot from leaning over a small baby for hours on end, he massaged the pain away. Charlie appreciated me before anyone else at the hospital did. I appreciated Charlie, and I loved him.

One morning, after I had removed a huge tumor from a child's abdomen and had only to mop up and close, Charlie whispered in my ear, asking permission to leave early for a doctor's appointment. Twenty minutes later a nurse opened the operating room door and said, "Charlie Wilson has been shot in the street by a policeman."

I left my resident to close. Charlie had been two blocks from the hospital when a child ran out from a house ahead of him, pursued by a policeman holding his pistol and shouting obscenities at the boy. When the cop caught the child, he began to beat him over the head with the pistol. Charlie stepped in and said, "Here, here. You can't do that," and was shot in the chest for his concern. By the time I learned this, Charlie was in the emergency room of the old Graduate Hospital, several blocks away.

Still in my scrub suit, I jumped into my car—parked in the hospital courtyard—and arrived at the Graduate Hospital emergency room five minutes later. Charlie was lying in a bed, completely unresponsive. His usual café au lait skin color now blended with the gray sheets. He had undoubtedly lost a lot of blood, yet I saw only saline solution going into his arm vein. Two doctors lounged down the hall, one reading the newspaper, the other telling jokes to two nurses. I was initially polite, but when I found out that they had not typed his blood and that their plasma supply was not only low but also contaminated, my anger made up for the authority I lacked in that hospital.

I took apart those two disgraces to the medical profession and finished with "If you are very smart in the next few minutes, you might still work here tomorrow. Get me a new IV for plasma. Get this man admitted. Call the chief of the thoracic service and tell him I want him in here now. Alert the operating room for a thoracotomy. Give Charlie a quarter grain of morphine, and move!"

They moved—not as fast as I would have liked, but they were probably out of practice. Meanwhile, I got on the phone to my own hospital and told the chief medical resident, Joseph Rudolph, "Joe, I'm coming through the hospital courtyard in about seven to ten minutes in a black Plymouth. Be at the front door with a boxful of bottles of plasma. I need it for Charlie Wilson, who is bleeding to death in the Graduate Hospital emergency room."

I started the new IV on Charlie, then drove off to the Children's Hospital. Waiting in the courtyard was good old Joe, with a cardboard carton with about fifty bottles of plasma of the small 100-cc size we used for children. He put the box in the front seat of the car, and I roared back to the other hospital.

As soon as I got to Charlie's bedside, I filled the IV reservoir, opened the clamp wide, and watched as the life-giving plasma flowed into Charlie's vein. His blood pressure began to rise, his rapid pulse fell, and soon the bullet was extracted from just above his heart. This frightening episode concluded with Charlie's eventual recovery and the policeman's dismissal from the force.

Not everyone on the staff possessed Charlie's loyalty and honesty. One hot summer in the '50s, the day-by-day management of the Children's Hospital sank so low that essential materials were missing on the wards. On the day I could not find a pair of sterile scissors to take out the sutures in an appendectomy incision, I blew my stack. Without any real authority, I called a meeting of the board of managers of the Children's Hospital. I can't imagine why they responded, but they did. I told them that something had to be done about the supplies problem. The board assigned member John Williams and me to settle the issue. John Williams was a quintessential Philadelphia lawyer, a man so persuasive that his cases seldom came to court. We set up a plan to put those employees on notice that they would no longer get away with stealing.

One afternoon, without fanfare, John and I secured all exits from the hospital complex except the front door and one courtyard gate. When five o'clock came and the employees began to pour out of the building, John and I took our positions on either side of the gate.

The hospital's help filed toward us, each one waddling under the weight of at least one large, heavy shopping bag in each hand. We corralled the first eight or ten employees and announced that we were going to examine their bundles. The others beat a hasty retreat back into the building and returned empty-handed.

Our inspection of the packages turned up whole hams, sides of bacon, turkeys, and assorted kitchen utensils. (I had not been aware of the drain on the commissary.) In other bundles we found packages of sheets and pillowcases, mattress pads, hospital scrub suits, and dozens of surgical scissors. The thievery stopped. Supplies began to build up; indeed, there was a surplus. John Williams and I did two more spot checks. The word was out: you could no longer get away with rifling the Children's Hospital.

With the pilfering issue resolved, I was able to concentrate fully on surgery again. The most common congenital defects I saw that were life threatening but correctable included esophageal atresia (in which the esophagus and stomach are not connected) and diaphragmatic hernias (when the abdominal organs end up in the baby's chest cavity because of a hole in the diaphragm).

In the most common form of esophageal atresia the lower part of the esophagus, which should be connected to the upper part, looks like an elbow on a stovepipe and is attached to the back of the windpipe. This is called esophageal atresia with tracheoesophageal fistula, a congenital defect that must be corrected surgically if the child is to survive.

One night, as I was operating on a premature baby with esophageal atresia, I discovered a strange variation of the defect. X rays had shown no air in the baby's intestine. When most babies with this defect breathe, the air goes down the trachea, through the esophageal fistula, into the stomach. But this baby had an airless abdomen. When I opened the baby up, I saw why: it had no lower esophagus.

Inside this tiny baby, the distance between the upper part of the esophagus and the stomach was about three to four inches—too far to stretch the truncated esophagus down or the stomach up to connect the two. So I opened up the baby's abdomen, removed a section of the right colon, and sewed one end to the short upper esophagus and the other to the stomach. As far as I knew, it was the first time anyone had replaced a missing esophagus with part of the colon. That baby—born premature, with pneumonia in both lungs—did not survive, but the second one on whom I did such an operation did. After earning a Ph.D. in physiology, she went on to graduate from Harvard Medical School.

A revolutionary step that night, forged out of necessity and perfected in the years ahead, a colon interposition eventually became a standard procedure, saving many babies. No wonder I became so concerned as Surgeon General three decades later, when Baby Doe, the ill-starred newborn who would spark a revolution in the treatment of handicapped infants, died of an untreated esophageal atresia with tracheoesophageal fistula just because his misinformed parents and a Bloomington, Indiana, judge forbade the lifesaving operation I had done so often.

I'll never forget my most spectacular diaphragmatic hernia. A garbled telephone call from a nearby hospital described what could only be a dying newborn with a diaphragmatic hernia. Once again I sprinted down to my car in the cobblestoned courtyard, raced eleven blocks to the other hospital, parked my car on the sidewalk, and rushed into the lobby, only to find the elevators were not running. So I ran up to the ninth floor, wrapped the baby in a blanket, ran down the same nine floors, and placed the baby on the floor of my car by the heater. Back at the Children's Hospital, I ran up two flights to the operating room and laid the baby on the operating table. By now the little fellow was dark blue and apparently lifeless. Without taking any sterile precautions, I slashed an incision across the left side of his chest, inserted my fingers, and pulled out the abdominal organs that had made their way up into the chest, thereby relieving the pressure on the lungs and the heart. Then I began to massage his tiny heart with one finger. It began to beat, and—a great sign—the edges of the wound began to bleed. We cleaned the wound as much as we could, and I completed the operation. I made the incision when the infant was only fifty-five minutes old. He remains my youngest patient.

About twenty-five years later my secretary ushered into my office a young man about six feet four inches tall, who stood somewhat embarrassedly before me and said, "My father thought you'd like to meet me. You operated on me when I was fifty-five minutes old." I ran around the desk and hugged him.

Were there surgical failures? Of course there were. There were some children who didn't make it, but fortunately their number diminished over the years. Techniques improved over time, risks were reduced, cosmetic appearances were improved, and rehabilitation became a science of its own.

Yet there are times when I contemplate the failures and have to wonder why. Take the Siamese twins, for example. Ironically, some of my greatest surgical successes became strange failures. My colleagues and I operated on over ten pairs of Siamese twins while I was at Children's Hospital, but three pairs became well known.

First there were the girls joined at the pelvis who came to me in the '50s from a New York suburb. I was elated at last to have the opportunity to separate conjoined twins. Dr. Louise Schnaufer, who would play an important role in two later separations, was my resident. The operation was eminently successful, and for seven years we had two normal, growing, intelligent girls. Eventually the smaller of the twins required open-heart surgery to correct a congenital defect. Her operation went smoothly, but on the fifth postoperative day, as she was sitting up in bed eating breakfast, she inexplicably died. An autopsy provided no reason. At the surviving twin's wedding, only her parents, her husband, my wife, and I knew her medical history.

Then there were Clara and Alta Rodríguez, Siamese twins who were sent to me from the Dominican Republic. The mother had gone into labor in a little village some twenty miles from the town of San José de Ocoa over a road impassable except by jeep. When her labor stalled, she was transported those terrible miles to town, where she delivered by cesarean section Siamese twin girls joined at the pelvis but with complicated internal anatomy—they shared one liver and one colon, and their urinary tracts were intertwined.

The twins were transported to the Children's Hospital in the capital, Santo Domingo, where the father was told it was not possible to separate them. A year later a Philadelphia woman called me and asked what I knew about Siamese twins. She then told me about the Rodríguez girls; her maid was the twins' aunt. I arranged for free surgery, anesthesia, and hospital care for the girls, and the women from the American embassy in Santo Domingo held a cake sale to raise the money for the flight to Philadelphia.

The press took an immediate shine to the cute little girls. The fourteen-month-old twins had two distinct personalities and actually fought with each other, punching and scratching, but without being able to get away from each other. Yet after separation I saw a poignant gesture as one separated twin reached out across an expanse of bedsheet to touch the hand of her sister.

The separation of these twins was perhaps the emotional highlight of my surgical career. After we had arranged the complicated surgery so that each part of it was done by the person on my team most expert at the task, we ended up with two normal girls. Four months later Louise Schnaufer and I took them back to the Dominican Republic, where our arrival was treated as a national event.

Two years later Alta was playing with some beans on the porch of her home in the Dominican Republic. She popped one into her mouth and inhaled, lodging the bean between her vocal cords, and choked to death on the spot. If she had done that even in a hospital, we would have had trouble saving her. Clara grew to become a beautiful and charming young woman.

My most dramatic case of Siamese twins involved newborns who shared one six-chambered heart. It was failing because it could not support the life of the two growing children. In order for one twin to survive, the other would have to be sacrificed. This was an extraordinarily unusual and difficult situation.

The Koops in 1938,
the year they were married

The family in 1963

The family in 1959

Dr. Koop with his sons
Norman and David in 1962,
on top of Maine's Mount
Katahdin

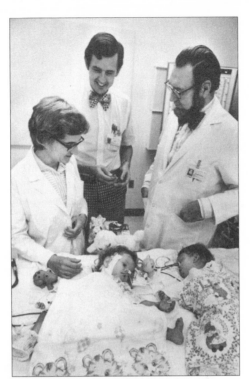

The Rodríguez Siamese twins
and their doctors the day after
their successful operation

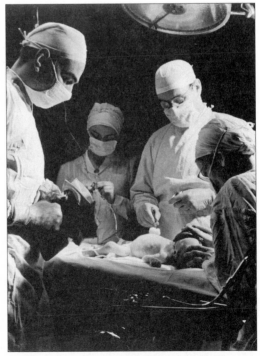

Chief surgeon Koop preparing to operate
at the Children's Hospital of Philadelphia

Religious issues made it even more difficult. Both of the grand-fathers were Hasidic rabbis, and they insisted on a seven-day Talmu-dic argument on the ethical issues involved. I was just as concerned, but I wasn't sure the children would survive the long argument.

Eventually we all came to the same position. One twin, the smaller, was essentially a parasite on the other. It was clear we had no choice about which twin would have to be sacrificed.

The operation was very tense. I had assembled a team of experts to assist me, and then I made the incision in such a way that I could work with an ample chest cavity to contain the six-chambered heart. I would not let anyone else participate in the tying off of the second carotid artery, which spelled death for one twin. For a few moments there was absolute silence in the operating room. It took me a little time to separate the body from that of the survivor. I then tenderly wrapped the body in a sheet and carried it to the door of the operat-ing room, where I was told a rabbi would be waiting to take the body for burial. When I opened the door, I found an old friend, Rabbi Mandelbaum, whose presence somehow made me feel better about the whole affair. I had operated on many of his innumerable children.

No one had ever successfully separated conjoined twins with one heart. Although we all felt a great sadness about the death of one child, we rejoiced that we had succeeded in saving the other. The surviving infant had problems, but her future looked promising. Sadly, she never made it. Forty-seven days after separation she died from hepatitis, probably from a transfusion.

I never forget the failures, but thank God, the successes outnum-bered them by far. Some youngsters stand out among thousands of patients. Jeff was a little boy who came to me because he was a Phillies fan. Jeff was sitting with his mother in the bleachers, watching a ball game while chewing an enormous wad of gum, when a man sitting next to him made some friendly remark about all that chewing gum Jeff was working on. The youngster's mother, defending her son, explained that the boy was only following doctor's orders, chewing gum constantly to get rid of a lump in his parotid gland.

The stranger said, "That is very interesting. Would you mind if I felt the lump in his cheek? I am a radiologist. I know something about lumps in the parotid gland, and I'd sure like to feel it."

After this cursory examination in the ballpark, the doctor turned to

Jeff's mother and said, "On the basis of everything I know, my best advice would be to get your son to see Dr. Koop at the Children's Hospital as soon as you possibly can."

Jeff and his mother were in my office the next morning. The lump in the parotid, one of the salivary glands, had become no smaller on the chewing-gum treatment, and to me it felt like a malignant tumor because it was stony hard. This would be a touchy situation. Surgery on the parotid gland is fraught with the danger of cutting one or more branches of the facial nerve and thereby paralyzing the muscles supplied by that branch.

I operated the next day, and after a seven-hour procedure I had removed the tumor and thought I had preserved every branch of the facial nerve. I was jubilant, but cautious enough to warn Jeff's parents about the possibility of recurrence. That recurrence took place far more quickly than I would ever have anticipated, and two weeks later we were back in the operating room, this time with a different task. Because our first objective was to save Jeff's life, I decided to do a radical removal of the entire parotid gland. This would mean deliberately severing all branches of Jeff's facial nerve except the one that closed the right eye. Jubilation had turned to frustration and depression.

The operation went well, and I did it radically enough to ensure, to the best of my ability, total removal of any malignant cells. Postoperatively, Jeff could close his eye, but he had no other power in his facial muscles. His smile was completely cockeyed. He could no longer whistle, and this seven-year-old boy had been a whistler.

But I had a plan for Jeff, one that could never have been accomplished without two parents, especially a mother, dedicated to achieving the best they could for their son. I told them that I could not guarantee what I was proposing, but it was worth the effort. There are occasions when branches of the fifth cranial nerve, the trigeminal, take over the function of the severed seventh cranial nerve, the facial. So I instructed Jeff's mother to stand behind him as they both looked into a mirror. She was to smile, laugh, bare her teeth, puff out her cheeks—make any facial motion she could think of—and Jeff was to try to imitate her.

To Jeff's father I assigned the task of teaching Jeff how to whistle again. I suggested that they sit opposite each other at a narrow table, and every time the father lit a candle, Jeff would have the pleasure of blowing it out. Initially he couldn't even make the flame waver, but perseverance on the part of all three members of this team eventually paid off.

One day Jeff and his parents stepped into my office. Jeff stepped forward, pursed his lips, and whistled, in its entirety, "Hello, Dolly." I could only weep. I had grown close enough to this family to invite them to our daughter Betsy's wedding. When the orchestra played "Hello, Dolly," Jeff's mother asked me to dance with her to "our song."

Among the patients especially close to my heart was Paul, a little boy with multiple congenital problems. They were so overwhelming in their number and complexity that several surgeons who first saw him decided nothing could be done for him. But doing nothing would lead to newborn Paul's death, a death with the excruciating pain of intestinal obstruction. I knew the problems were amenable to surgical correction, one at a time. Tackling them one at a time took years, and we had to deal with complications along the way. Little Paul thrived through it all and became an admirable and affable young man, even after more than fifty operations. He also became my friend. I admired his family. They coped with great difficulties and managed magnificently. Once, Paul's mother was asked what the worst thing life had brought her was. She answered without hesitation, "Having Paul born with all those defects." Then she was asked what the best thing life had brought her was. Again without hesitation, "Having Paul born with all those defects."

Nothing in humanity is more encouraging than seeing the way parents manage with a child who is less than perfect. The bond between a physically or mentally retarded child and his loving parents is a wonder to behold. Before we had the remarkable self-help movements of today, it was my custom to put parents in touch with other parents who had been through that same circumstance, veterans who could act as mentors and support those who were just starting out. It worked, and it worked beautifully.

Next to surgery, I loved to teach. When I began at the Children's Hospital, the University of Pennsylvania School of Medicine offered no instruction in pediatric surgery. But with the help of my former mentors Ravdin and Rhoads, I worked pediatric surgery into the curriculum.

Of course, the core of any surgical teaching is not in the lecture hall, but in the operating room and at the bedside. A pediatric surgeon needs to learn more than surgical techniques; he or she must also learn how to give parents the emotional support they need. Medical school does a good job of teaching the science of medicine, but there seem to be few teaching the art of medicine.

As a professor at Penn, I tried to impart this blend of art and medicine. After visiting the various wards, I would choose an appropriate patient for final discussion and then withdraw to the nurses' station for a wrap-up with the medical students, residents, and anyone else in attendance. It was on these occasions that I tried to impress on my students that in pediatrics you never have just one patient. You have many: the child, the parents, the grandparents, the siblings, and occasionally the uncles and aunts.

It was my dream to get under the roof of the Children's Hospital of Philadelphia the most comprehensive group of pediatric surgeons anywhere in the world. It took me over thirty years to do it, but by 1979 I had, at last, twenty-seven partners who were bona fide pediatric specialists in the eight subdivisions of surgery.

One important transition made it easier to fulfill that dream. In 1974 the Children's Hospital moved from its ancient and dilapidated buildings in South Philadelphia to a magnificent new building on the campus of the University of Pennsylvania in West Philadelphia.

Moving a hospital is a tricky business. The logistics, especially concerning the transfer of patients, requires months of planning. When the big moving day came, we relied on voluntary ambulance services from the surrounding suburbs and on the cooperation of the Philadelphia Police Department. I watched it all from the roof of the old Children's Hospital, where I was equipped with a walkie-talkie, which kept me in touch with people along the route. Patients were carried out on stretchers or wheeled out in wheelchairs, then lifted into the waiting ambulances.

As the last ambulance pulled out of the cobblestoned courtyard, past the heavy iron gates, I realized I was the only person in the old Children's Hospital except for the security guard. I took a last tour through every room in the old hospital and its adjacent outbuildings. I stood in the tiny area that had been the first surgical neonatal intensive care unit in the country. I stood in the operating room where I had first separated Siamese twins. I stood in my old office, where I had spoken, counseled, laughed, cried, and prayed with so many doctors, nurses, patients, and families over the years. And then I walked out the front door for the last time.

IT WAS difficult to select a resident from those who applied for a position in my training program. Early on, choices were few, but soon pediatric surgery began to attract many very bright young men and women. I didn't care whether an applicant was Phi Beta Kappa, nor whether he or she came from one of the Ivy League medical schools. He or she was certainly not doing it for money, because pediatric surgery is not a lucrative specialty. Ultimately, I chose the people whom I thought it would be fun to teach, who were sensitive and caring people, fond of children.

Regulations prevented my graduating more than one pediatric surgical resident each year. Early on, their term of training was a year, later eighteen months, then two years. Over my lifetime at Children's Hospital, I graduated thirty-five residents and about fourteen foreign fellows. Many went on to become professors of pediatric surgery, directors of divisions of pediatric surgery, and surgeons in chief of children's hospitals.

As I call my patients to memory, I see an almost endless parade going by. I see all the things we did to help them: to repair simple hernias, to make deformed limbs right, to separate webbed fingers, to pin back lop ears, to repair cleft lips and palates, to close spina bifida and treat hydrocephalus, to correct heart defects, to remove tumors, and, above all, to operate on "congenital defects incompatible with life, but amenable to surgical correction."

I have not performed surgery for more than a decade, and still each week brings one or more letters to my home from a grateful patient who may never have known me, because he or she was too young when we first met, or from grateful parents and grandparents. Nothing gives me greater satisfaction. Today, as I travel so much, I don't count a trip complete unless some young adult stops me and says, "You don't remember me, but when I was four days old . . ."

I knew my last operation would be a difficult time for me, so I wanted it to be an operation that would present no unusual problems.

I wanted no fuss made by my colleagues, standing around watching the last procedure of the retiring surgeon in chief. At a few minutes after 1:00 p.m. on March 6, 1981, I made the incision for a right inguinal hernia. Six minutes later, when that was closed, I made the left incision and was finished six minutes after that. My closest associate, Louise Schnaufer, wandered in at the end of the procedure, as she frequently did. No one said anything special, but the realization dawned on me that operative surgery, which had been the most exciting part of my career for nearly thirty-nine years, had now come to an end.

I put the dressing on the infant's two small incisions, waited until it dried, took off my gown and gloves, and walked over to the window separating the operating room from the scrub sinks. I dipped my finger into some soap, then wrote on the window the closing lines from T. S. Eliot's "The Hollow Men":

> *This is the way the world ends,*
> *This is the way the world ends,*
> *This is the way the world ends,*
> *Not with a bang but a whimper.*

The soapy writing stayed on the window until the fall, when one of the janitors washed it away. With it went my last link to the operating rooms of the Children's Hospital. But my bond with all those thousands of little patients will last at least a lifetime.

CHAPTER 6
Confirmation

BECOMING Surgeon General was agonizing, a form of political and personal harassment unlike anything I had experienced in my life. My main supporters, with the significant exception of Secretary Dick Schweiker, seemed to be interested only in how aggressively I would put the pro-life agenda forward. The opposition, therefore, saw my appointment only in terms of the threat the Reagan administration posed to legalized abortion. Those were the outlines of the conflict, and I was caught somewhat haplessly in the middle.

On the morning after Election Day, once I had made up my mind that I really wanted the Surgeon General's job, I decided there was no point in not pursuing it aggressively. I spent a good deal of my time in the next few weeks lining up people who could help me secure the appointment. Some of my connections were tenuous. Nancy Reagan's half brother, Dr. Richard Davis, and I were members of the same department of surgery at the University of Pennsylvania, but he told me he had as many difficulties as anyone else in getting to Reagan, and suggested I work through someone on the transition team. I spoke on the telephone with Dick Schweiker, who then seemed to have the inside track for the job as Secretary of the Department of Health and Human Services (HHS).

The next step was a trip to Washington at the invitation of Senator Orrin Hatch, who had arranged for me to meet a number of Senators. Hatch had just become chair of the Senate Committee on Labor and Human Resources, which dealt with health issues—and my confirmation. I had not met him previously. Strom Thurmond told me, "You look like a doctor. There were nine doctors in my family. I hope to see you around here in the future." And Joe Biden from Delaware, who had lost a wife and child in an accident, credited the Children's Hospital of Philadelphia for helping his surviving children.

My interview with the Reagan transition team, on December 18, seemed to go well, and I was told that after their screening process had been completed, they would submit three names to Schweiker, who would then decide which person the President would appoint.

Then a dark cloud appeared. On the day before Christmas Eve a well-meaning group of Pentecostal Christians purchased time on a Washington television station to show a portion of the movie series *Whatever Happened to the Human Race?*, which I had made years earlier with Francis Schaeffer. Because these movies reflected my opposition to abortion, infanticide, and euthanasia, they stirred up the first antagonism from the public. Planned Parenthood, the National Organization for Women, and the National Abortion Rights Action League began to line up against me, and the first of what would be many negative articles about me appeared in the Washington *Post* and the Washington *Star*.

The days passed slowly, with little purpose, and for the next several weeks I seemed to be sure of less and less. I was told that the field of possible candidates for Surgeon General was growing. But my real problem had become the American Medical Association. I knew the AMA had opposed Dick Schweiker's appointment as Secretary of HHS. Now they were refusing to back my appointment as well; in fact, they fought it.

I decided to tackle this problem personally, so I called the executive vice president of the AMA, Jim Sammons. I asked Sammons why the AMA was opposing my appointment as Surgeon General. Sammons replied that they were not opposing me, but had their own candidate. More than a year later he told me privately that it was my position on abortion that had turned the AMA against me. Most people suspected that all along, but that was the first time it was ever acknowledged.

During the annual Washington pro-life march and rally in January, a selected group visited the White House to press my cause with the President. One of those in the group, Congressman Henry Hyde (Republican-Illinois), reported, "The only thing that I could have done that I did not do was to take a spray paint can and paint Koop's name on the wall of the Oval Office. If I had had one, I would have." Later, as I thanked him for his efforts on my behalf, he said the President had told him that everything he had heard about me from other sources had confirmed that I would be the right person for Surgeon General. I wondered if it was rumor or reality.

Through its lobbyists the AMA continued to fight hard against me. Their choice for the job was former Indiana governor Dr. Otis Bowen. One of my original callers, Carl Anderson, told me that if Bowen were indeed a candidate, I didn't have much of a chance. Bowen was a Republican, a physician, a superb administrator, had been a governor, and would have the support of the two Republican Senators from Indiana. Bowen, as it turned out, was not interested, although later he would serve as Secretary of Health and Human Services, and we would get along famously. As time would tell, I would owe much of my success to Otis Bowen.

The web became even more tangled as the question of my appointment became mired in a variety of schemes to reorganize the Department of Health and Human Services, shuffling around the positions of undersecretary for health, assistant secretary for health, and Surgeon General. Meanwhile, the AMA advanced a new name for Surgeon General and assistant secretary for health: Dr. Edward Brandt of the University of Texas. Finally it was decided to split the only recently joined position of assistant secretary and Surgeon General. Brandt was nominated as assistant secretary, while I would be named Surgeon General. There was one little wrinkle: the Surgeon General would drop down one echelon in the hierarchy and would now report to the assistant secretary. All this mattered little to me at the time, and I understood it even less. I was simply relieved that I would, after all, become the Surgeon General. The story that began with those three long-ago telephone calls seemed to be coming to an end.

Or so I thought. The opposition was gathering its forces, becoming vitriolic. The American Public Health Association, which had supported abortion on demand even before *Roe* v. *Wade*, began a vigorous campaign to block my nomination, trumpeting that I was "almost uniquely unqualified" to be Surgeon General. They claimed, among other things, that I had no experience in public health. A series of articles appeared in the local press portraying me as nothing more than an antiabortion religious zealot. I was disillusioned to see what passed for investigative reporting about the Koop case. It usually amounted to a reporter reading a hostile article about me and then writing a similar article for his or her own paper. Months went by before any reporter asked *me* anything.

The hubbub spread beyond the Washington Beltway. *The New York Times* ran an editorial about me—"Dr. Unqualified"—insisting that my nomination as Surgeon General was "an affront to the public health profession and to the public." In Philadelphia, the *Bulletin*, hitherto a good friend, printed a large cartoon portraying me as a two-headed monster. Across town, the Philadelphia *Inquirer* pleaded with the Senate to reject my nomination. One columnist called me Dr. Kook; many others took it up.

Among the many false labels pinned on me in those early hostile days was that of chauvinist. I have never been sure exactly what that meant. Some people refined the charge by calling me antiwomen. A strange label, I thought, to apply to someone who had trained more female pediatric surgeons than anyone else in America.

One day I decided to have lunch in the Humphrey Building cafeteria. As I walked into the dining room itself, I heard someone say, "Here he comes." By the time I reached my table, the usual hum and clatter had subsided and a hush had fallen over the entire room. As

I walked to my seat I was absolutely astounded to see how many forks were poised in midair between plate and mouth as this unbelievable two-headed monster, the most unqualified Surgeon General appointee in history, prepared to eat his lunch.

My sense of isolation grew even worse. It had been several weeks since the President appointed me deputy assistant secretary, with the promise that I would be nominated Surgeon General. But I still had no job assignment, no obligations to perform. I had lost any sense of purpose, except perhaps my desire to be confirmed. While I was still doing very little, I was introduced to Ted Cron of the Public Health Service Office of Public Affairs, who said he would serve as my speechwriter. I told him I had always written my own speeches and didn't need his services. But Ted insisted—prophetically—that eventually I would be too busy to write my own speeches. He became one of my closest associates, a valued adviser.

In those early weeks Woody Kessel, a pediatrician serving in the Commissioned Corps of the Public Health Service, stopped by my empty office and explained that much of the opposition to me was what he termed theater. When someone like Ted Kennedy blasted off about me in public, he was campaigning for the women's vote in Massachusetts. Woody was invaluable during that first, awful year. And then there was the support of Faye Abdellah—but more about her later.

Gradually the flow of visitors to my office increased, and I welcomed the opportunity to communicate one-on-one with people with whom I hoped eventually to work. So when someone like Bob Graham, the director of one of the agencies of the Public Health Service, or Bill Foegge, the director of the Centers for Disease Control, came by, I had a chance to say, "Let me tell you a little bit about who I am and what my hopes are if I am ever confirmed as Surgeon General."

I shared with these visitors my long-cherished ambition to find ways to avoid overlap and duplication of services for handicapped children, to provide computerized information banks to help physicians and nurses find proper care for defective newborns, and to enable their families to ferret out the resources that communities made available for their upbringing, education, and support.

In retrospect, these became some of my most important weeks in Washington. The delay in my confirmation, as trying as it was, gave me the chance to establish my credibility, and it also helped me slowly and deliberately develop an agenda of the things I wanted to accomplish. Some of the things that I had in mind were issues usually beyond the purview of the Surgeon General. I was able to move in these directions only because of the rapport and confidence I had established with the people I had met then.

For weeks I had been battling titans—the AMA, the press, the proabortion groups—yet my confirmation was almost derailed by devious political shenanigans. When the issue of my being too old surfaced, Senator Jesse Helms decided to deal with it by the customary legislative maneuver of attaching a nongermane amendment to a bill before the Senate. In this case, his amendment, which would change legislation restricting the age of Surgeon General appointees, was attached to a humdrum bill dealing with credit cards. Normally a bill like this, which had already been passed by the House before receiving the Helms amendment, would, after leaving the Senate, be approved by the House or sent to a conference committee. But in this case, Democratic Speaker of the House Thomas "Tip" O'Neill found a way to fight back against Helms, as well as the President and me, by resorting to an old House rule—last used in 1951—to bottle up the issue in the House of Representatives, even though the House has no jurisdiction over presidential appointments. An archaic law discriminating against me because of my age was being used against me by the Speaker of the House, who was four years older than I.

Henry Waxman, Democratic Congressman from Los Angeles, an outspoken advocate of abortion, became my chief antagonist. At the behest of Speaker O'Neill, his Subcommittee on Health and the Environment announced a hearing on the bill. I was asked to testify, but was advised by my supporters that if I did so, the Senate might assume I thought the House had a role in the confirmation process, which it does not, and I might alienate some Senators who were already on my side.

Although it would have been a breach of protocol for me to appear, I had a natural urge to defend myself. Instead, I had to read the transcript of the hearing, in which I was denounced and defamed by representatives from the American Public Health Association, the National Gay Health Coalition, and the United Mine Workers. The subcommittee, it seemed, was not as interested in the age question as it was in harassing the Reagan administration and me on the issue of abortion.

The bizarre parliamentary maneuvering had produced a stalemate. Washington insiders agreed that my cause would prevail on the floor of the House, where the combination of Republicans and pro-life Democrats would yield the necessary majority. But Waxman, it was clear, would not release the bill from committee.

As all this dragged on, Betty and I had to find a place to live. We were going to be in Washington too long to live in a motel but, if confirmation did not come, too briefly to move into a house. So Betty looked around, finally settling on a nice little one-room apartment in Georgetown. We felt we had come full circle—back to a one-room apartment like the one in which we had lived when we were first married. Rents, however, had changed. The Georgetown apartment cost us $1000 a month. I tolerated the steep rental only because I figured that in a month or two I would either be confirmed and in permanent housing, or gone. Nine months later we were still there, waiting, praying, and paying.

But those months in Georgetown were very special for Betty and me. She often said that those were the worst of times, but the best of times in our marriage. It was a time when we needed each other, because we had no one else. We were the only ones who understood the problems we both faced. I had never realized how hard it can be on the family of someone whom the press criticizes day after day, repeating false allegations, defaming character. My worst day in Washington was sometime in late April, when I came home from work and opened the door to our top-floor apartment to see Betty, silhouetted against the partially drawn venetian blinds, with tears rolling down her cheeks as she read the Washington *Post*'s opinion of her husband.

Some people advised me to go visit Henry Waxman, to try to clear things up in a personal visit. I doubted that it would work but was willing to try almost anything. It did not go well. I did not conduct myself as well as I should have. I felt I was in a bitter struggle and no doubt came across brash, antagonistic, prepared to give no quarter.

It was obvious after our brief exchange that there was going to be no change in our relationship. As we walked to the door he pointed to the scarlet thread that went through the buttonhole of my left lapel, signifying that I had been awarded the medal of the French Legion of Honor.

"What's that?" Waxman asked. "Some pro-life ribbon?"

"No. That signifies that I have been awarded the medal of the Legion of Honor by the government of France. And before you ask the next dumb question, recipients are never told why the French government selects them for this honor."

My frustration had given way to rudeness.

I was particularly vexed because I believed that Henry Waxman's support for public-health issues was good for the country, and it was ridiculous for someone who shared my concerns for health to keep his distance over the single issue of abortion. Abortion may be the greatest moral issue facing the nation, but that does not necessarily make it the greatest political issue. The competence of elected officials should never be determined by a single issue.

When I first went to Washington, in March, I never would have thought my summer would be consumed in a parliamentary shenanigan called a discharge petition. This rarely used procedure allows a majority in the House of Representatives to discharge a bill that is being stalled in committee. Republicans in the House started a discharge petition to release from Waxman's committee the legislation changing the age requirement for the Surgeon General. Most Republicans and some pro-life Democrats signed up right away, and we began to approach the magic number of 218 needed to release the bill. But the closer we got to the desired total, the more difficult it became to enlist new supporters. And we began to lose some Democrats who had signed earlier, because signing a discharge petition is very public business. A Congressman had to walk forward to sign the petition, right under the nose of Tip O'Neill. Young Democratic Congressmen did not want to displease their party leader.

But the total crept toward the needed 218. And much to my surprise, in midsummer the first pro-Koop article appeared in the Washington *Post*. Reporter Mary Meehan defended my record, point by point, against the packaged accusations. The article lifted my spirits, and I actually almost enjoyed going to work, at least for the day or two until the next attack, the next political roadblock arose.

As the number of names on the discharge petition grew, shrank, and grew again, suddenly the whole issue was taken behind closed doors. A big deal was being negotiated by Senator Hatch and Congressman Waxman. They were haggling over the various health provisions in the large budget reconciliation compromise between the House and Senate. I never knew what was being traded. I only hoped that no important health legislation would be sacrificed to the sordid political process necessary for my confirmation.

Rumors were born every few minutes, accelerating my rollercoaster ride. Even after the closed-door meetings had adjourned, I had no idea about the crucial wording of the final version of the bill. Two days went by; still no word. I found myself reading volumes into every frown and smile I saw in the corridors. Finally in the parking garage I bumped into a friend from the HHS Office of Legislation, who assured me that the language of the bill had eliminated the age restriction, enabling my formal nomination as Surgeon General.

Getting past the age requirement was not the end of my struggle, however. The actual confirmation hearing still stood ahead of me, and although Republican control of the Senate made ultimate confirmation likely, I was warned to expect trouble along the way.

I kept telling myself I didn't have much to worry about, because that comfortable Republican Senate majority would not deny Reagan his choice for Surgeon General, even if some of them were not all that wild about me. One columnist had written, "With a Republican Senate, if Ronald Reagan wanted Jack the Ripper for Surgeon General, he'd get him confirmed."

But then I would think about how many "sure things" had not panned out already, and I would start to worry. Either way, I wanted to do the "walk around," the customary courtesy calls at the offices of the sixteen Senators on the committee that would deal with my nomination.

My meeting with Connecticut Senator Lowell Weicker, an avowed opponent, started off rather badly, but the atmosphere changed when the conversation turned in a more personal way to the problems of handicapped children, especially those with Down syndrome. Senator Weicker had a child with Down syndrome, of whom he seemed very proud. We shared a common concern for these winsome kids with special needs. We ended on a warm note. But he voted against me. A few years later Weicker would prove a valued ally in the war on AIDS, and we would continue to work together on health issues after he returned to the private sector and until his election as governor of Connecticut, in 1990.

As I made the rounds of other Senators, I was discouraged to learn that each of them had received letters from public-health workers in their state urging my rejection. It was clear evidence of the continuing campaign of the American Public Health Association to cut me off at the hearing.

My chat with Senator Kennedy—up until then my most outspoken opponent in the Senate—proved to be much more cordial than I had expected. He started off by saying to me, "There are a lot of things that you and I can do together in health." We got down to brass tacks quickly and had an especially productive talk about babies who suffer from respiratory distress syndrome, the disease that had killed his nephew, the second little boy born to his brother Jack. I outlined for him the strides we had made at the Children's Hospital of Philadelphia to improve the survival rate of these youngsters and how we had gone on to set up a system of home care for them that provided the same level of care as a hospital but at a tenth of the cost.

What I had feared would be a contentious encounter with Ted Kennedy became instead the beginning of an affable cooperation in a number of vital health endeavors over the next eight years. But during the Senate debate on my confirmation his attack on me was bitter enough to upset Betty to the point that Senator Orrin Hatch was moved to climb to the balcony to offer her a word of much appreciated comfort.

The testimony at my confirmation hearing before the Committee on Labor and Human Resources, on October 1, 1981, brought nothing new. Betty and our daughter, Betsy, sat in the audience, taking it all in. First came the tedious repetition of the summer's charges. Then, at last, I got a chance to defend my record. I told the Senators that the Surgeon General should come to the job with three kinds of prior experience: a professional career in medicine, competence in dealing with the broad health needs of American society, and knowledge of international health issues. So I described my career in terms of these issues, first highlighting my thirty-five years as a pediatric surgeon, which included the establishment of the nation's first newborn surgical intensive care unit and my leadership in the development of the specialty of pediatric surgery.

To reassure them of my requisite background in public health, I reviewed my role in banning the use of X-ray machines for ascertaining the fit of children's shoes, my part in studies at the University of Pennsylvania on hepatitis during the Second World War, and my understanding of the problems of health care for the underserved members of our society, which I had gained first while delivering babies in Harlem and later in the years when the Children's Hospital of Philadelphia was located in a black ghetto.

After reviewing my international health experience in Ghana, Mexico, the Dominican Republic, and with missionary medicine around the world, I concluded by setting out my views of the challenges facing the Surgeon General: the need to revitalize the Commissioned Corps of the Public Health Service, the importance of preserving the integrity of the office of Surgeon General, the special health needs of the handicapped and the aging.

When the hearing ended, I felt relieved and hopeful. But there was yet another delay before the committee vote. So I busied myself with some thorny problems in international health, heading first for Paris, then to Marseille and Madrid, to track down a problem concerning contaminated olive oil. Washington politicking remained as close as the nearest phone. It was during a meeting in Madrid that I was called from the room to be told by a friend that Senator Kennedy had said he would not vote for me, only because I did not need his vote on the committee to win and politics in his home state, Massachusetts, constrained him from backing me. That was a friendly gesture on Kennedy's part and made his sixteen-minute diatribe against me before the whole Senate all the more puzzling. Even so, the committee vote was 11–5 in my favor, removing the next-to-last obstacle. Only the final Senate vote remained. And that kept getting postponed, probably by Democrats still scrambling for ways to defeat me.

As the ordeal dragged on, I went to have a physical done by National Institutes of Health (NIH) physician Tony Fauci, who later became famous as a leader in AIDS research. Although he was thirty years younger, Tony and I had much in common: we were both Brooklyn boys who had graduated from Cornell Medical School, each dedicated to both clinical practice and research. In a private chat before the hearing, Tony turned serious as he talked about my confirmation problems.

"If you don't get confirmed by the Senate, I will have to take a serious look at the rest of my life. If providing excellent patient care and taking care of people to the best of your ability does not qualify you for the job you are seeking, then I ought to leave the government now."

Finally, on November 16, 1981, the big day arrived. Thirty-five weeks after I had arrived in Washington, the Senate got around to voting on my confirmation. I was scheduled to meet with the directors of a Vanderbilt University handicapped program at the same time. While I was in my meeting, someone opened the door to tell me the vote had been 68–24, much more heavily in my favor than we had anticipated. It was hard to believe. I was confirmed. After that long wait, that bitter struggle, I really would be the Surgeon General.

My official swearing-in ceremony and subsequent dinner at Fort McNair for family and friends took place on a snowy evening at the end of January, marking the end of the first chapter of my life in Washington and the start of a new one.

Once I was confirmed, my problems with the press—the cheap potshots, the snide remarks in gossip columns—all fell like leaves off a tree. My life started afresh. With a sense of excitement and humility I realized that each day I was doing something that was counting not just for me, not just for now, but for the entire country and for maybe an endless time ahead. I was grateful to the Lord that the bad days were over and the good days lay ahead.

CHAPTER 7
Wearing the Uniform

ONCE confirmed, I was entitled to wear a uniform with all the regalia befitting my rank as vice admiral. I put it on immediately. The press had some fun with my uniform, calling me sometimes an admiral with no ships, sometimes an admiral in the Ruritanian navy. And there were a couple of times on airplanes when elderly women mistook me for a steward, handed me their luggage, and confidently assumed that I would put it in the overhead compartment. I always complied immediately. But there were reasons for the uniform. Not only did I hope it would give a greater aura of authority to the health messages I wanted the American public to receive but also it was directly related to an important, if relatively unknown, aspect of the Surgeon General's job.

The congressional legislation officially defining the duties of the Surgeon General contains rather broad—even vague—language about the responsibility of warning the American people about risks to their health. It does, however, contain a specific charge about being the commanding officer of the Commissioned Corps of the Public Health Service.

Before I first donned the uniform of the Surgeon General, I, like most Americans, knew very little about the Commissioned Corps, one of the American uniformed services. In fact, I confess I may have shared the prejudice of those in academic medicine who looked down on government doctors. I was wrong. One of the true delights of my service as Surgeon General was my discovery of the excellence, dedication, compassion, and noble service performed by the 6200 women and men of the Commissioned Corps, which made up about 10 percent of the Public Health Service.

However, when I was sworn in as Surgeon General, I found them to be in a sorry state. They knew they were top notch; they knew they were needed. They also knew they were an endangered species. A potent little acronym, RIS, was responsible.

RIS—reduction in strength—is the bureaucratic term for cutting personnel from a uniformed service. One of the first actions of the new Reagan administration was to decide that the merchant marine, which since 1798 had had its health care provided by the Public Health Service, would no longer enjoy that largess at the expense of the government. I was told that someone at the White House had said, "Why don't all of those merchant mariners have Blue Cross–Blue Shield, like the rest of us?"

In any event, the Office of Management and Budget (OMB), with the blessing of the Reagan White House, eliminated that service to the merchant marine. It might have made sense in someone's ledger book, but it had a profound ripple effect, touching the lives and health of thousands. Since the Public Health Service would no longer provide medical care for the merchant marine, the Public Health Service hospitals in major seaports on both coasts and on the Gulf of Mexico were closed down, and the Commissioned Corps's numbers were cut by 2600.

Any reduction in strength weakens a force, but the effect on the Commissioned Corps was magnified because the loss of those hospitals meant a loss in medical training and practice. Commissioned Corps health personnel could no longer be rotated through those hospitals for refreshment training in a wide variety of medical fields. This diminished the corps's ability to discharge its remaining responsibilities to the coast guard, migrant workers, Native Americans and Alaskan natives, federal-prison inmates, and people living in poverty across America.

Luther Terry, the former Surgeon General who in 1964 had released the first report on the health hazards of smoking, wrote to me in February 1982 urging me to do what I could as Surgeon General to preserve the position and integrity of the Public Health Service. Terry and I had been on the same faculty at the University of Pennsylvania before he went to Washington. As the nearly omnipotent OMB accelerated its plan to dismantle the corps, I realized that I had to do all I could to save this little-known jewel in the American crown.

Effective management always requires an appropriate blend of style and substance. Changes in substance might come slowly, but changes in style can become apparent overnight. I decided the corps needed to assert itself and take pride in its mission. As one of the uniformed services of this republic, it ought to wear the uniform with pride. So for the first time in many years, the Surgeon General began to appear in uniform not just for occasional functions where protocol demanded it but whenever he was doing the work of the Surgeon General.

In March 1982 one of my first official acts was to appoint Faye Abdellah my deputy surgeon general. Faye Glenn Abdellah was tall, handsome, and stately, which made her, in uniform, the model of what a commissioned officer should look like. She was the chief nurse of the Public Health Service.

Faye was the first woman to hold the post of deputy surgeon general and became the highest-ranking uniformed woman in the United States. She was a gem in both her offices. Faye had already served the Public Health Service for twenty-five years when I came on board. She was my guide and mentor through many a minefield, providing wise counsel. We had some disagreements, but never an argument. From the day I met her, Faye Abdellah was a true friend and ally to both Betty and me. Faye would be with me, with us, every step of the way for the next eight years.

Wearing the uniform was important both to me and to other officers, and I followed it with more substantive steps. The Indian Health Service needed—and deserved—special attention. My first inspection tour of a small portion of its facilities opened my eyes and bonded my soul to the IHS, especially to the old-timers in the Commissioned Corps who had cut their teeth in public health by serving it. Mine was also the first such visit to IHS outposts by a Surgeon General in anyone's memory. Accompanied by Everett Rhoades, the highly regarded director of the Indian Health Service, I flew to remote facilities in the Southwest. I also visited communities in Alaska.

At every IHS hospital or clinic I went to, I saw excellence. Pharmacies and record rooms were on a par with any in academic medicine. The dedication and integrity of IHS personnel were unsurpassed. At Shiprock, New Mexico, for example, Dr. John Provaznik, a superb surgeon who graduated from Harvard Medical School, was typical of many in the IHS who share a love for the Indians, a dedication to service, and no greed for money. People like this have made the Indian Health Service the professional force it is.

The patients under the care of the Indian Health Service are not an easy population to manage. Native Americans reflect an extraordinary diversity of tribal, cultural, educational, and economic status, and their numbers stretch from the tip of Alaska to Key West, Florida, from southern California to northern Maine. Multiple agencies and congressional committees share the oversight of Native Americans, so to the cultural and geographic problems are added confusing and competing layers of bureaucracy.

On a smaller scale, but a more difficult task, is the Public Health Service's responsibility to supply medical care for the Federal Bureau of Prisons. Both parties benefitted from the arrangement: the bureau of prisons knew by experience that the medical care provided by the Public Health Service was superior to anything else it had ever been able to obtain, while the Public Health Service enjoyed the opportunity to rotate its officers through the bureau of prisons for one more variety of federal health service.

The Commissioned Corps can also meet unexpected health challenges posed to the country, as when boatloads of Cuban refugees, many desperately ill, suddenly landed on Florida beaches in 1981. Castro had opened his hospitals, prisons, and insane asylums, and allowed those inmates to drift to American shores, where their health problems became ours. Almost every disease known to human beings arrived with those Cubans: tuberculosis, leprosy, hepatitis, cancer, and more. The scope of the problem lay beyond the capabilities of the Florida health officials, and federal civil servants responded to requests to assist by saying, "It's not in my job description." But Commissioned Corps health personnel could simply be ordered to report for duty in Florida. They saluted, they went, and they conquered many medical problems. Their work is one of the unheralded healthcare accomplishments of this era.

The other duties of the Commissioned Corps included providing medical care for other uniformed services, the largest of which was the coast guard. I also sought to integrate the corps into the Department of Defense's emergency plans. In an era of tightening budgets and personnel shortages in some military units, I introduced MEDSTARR (Medical Staffing and Training to Augment Reserve Readiness), which allowed understaffed army and air force reserve units to be brought up to full strength by having Public Health Service health personnel fill vacant posts as doctors, dentists, operating room nurses, and so on.

There were some very small, but very special, places where the Commissioned Corps made big contributions to medicine, such as at the nation's only leprosy hospital—the Hansen's Disease Center in Carville, Louisiana, which maintains a public-sector link with the Armed Forces Institute of Pathology. Although leprosy has almost vanished from the United States (there are at present only about five thousand patients), in Asia seventeen thousand new cases arise each week. Carville's experience in protecting leprosy patients from leg amputations has brought new hope to American diabetics. I became convinced that if every American diabetic threatened with a foot or leg amputation could be treated as we treat leprosy patients at Carville, we would be able to reduce diabetic amputations from forty thousand per year to four thousand.

But as successful as we were in these small steps to utilize the talents and skills of the Commissioned Corps, it became obvious to me that a piecemeal approach would not do. In early 1987 I concluded sadly that OMB would not have to kill the Commissioned Corps; it would die by itself. Morale in the corps had continued to languish. Recruitment of minorities and women lagged behind. There was little sense of belonging to a uniformed, disciplined, mobile service: the corps had lost its esprit. I determined that it needed revitalization, and I turned to people with superb management skills, who made it happen—including Secretary of Health and Human Services Otis Bowen, who shared my vision for the corps, and my own chief of staff, Edward R. Martin.

We revitalized the Commissioned Corps, so that it became a dynamic, flexible, mobile, responsive, professional career system for health professionals who wished to dedicate themselves to the problems and programs of our Public Health Service. I look back on that revitalization as one of the most significant accomplishments of my tenure as Surgeon General.

CHAPTER 8

Smoking

As Surgeon General, I took as my mission nothing less than improving the health of the entire nation. I started with smoking.

"A thousand people will stop smoking today. Their funerals will be held sometime during the next three or four days." That is how I would begin my lecture on smoking. It gets people's attention. Why have Americans been so complacent about tobacco, about nicotine addiction? If any other substance, legal or illegal, were killing half a million people a year, the public would be up in arms, demanding action from Congress.

About 45 million Americans still smoke cigarettes, even though health officials have long identified cigarette smoking as the main reason why Americans get sick and die too soon. Cigarette smoking is associated with more death and illness than drugs, alcohol, automobile accidents, and AIDS *combined.*

My first step in the antismoking crusade came with the 1982 *Surgeon General's Report on Smoking and Health,* then the most serious indictment of cigarette smoking the Public Health Service had ever made. During my confirmation struggle I had heard about this upcoming report, but no one had thought to include me in its preparation. It was not until the early weeks of 1982 that I began to realize that I would have to present the report at my first major press conference since assuming office.

As the scheduled date for the press conference, February 22, 1982, drew closer, my tension began to mount. I spent the weekend reviewing the report once more, going over my briefing book, and, I admit, dealing with no small amount of nervousness. The night before the conference I had the same disturbing dream that had visited me regularly for the previous fifty-five years: I am about to go into German class to take an exam. Already on the dean's list, I have not been required to attend classes; I have not studied, either. When I sit down to take the German exam, I discover to my horror that everything on the page is in French.

Shaking off the same old frightening dream, I awoke long before dawn, reviewed my papers, paused for my customary breakfast and Bible reading with Betty, and left for my office, at the Humphrey Building.

Sometimes little things make the biggest impression, and when I walked into the auditorium of the Humphrey Building to meet the press for the first time, I noticed that the thirty or so microphones on the podium left no room for my notes. (It would take me three years to get someone to build a little extension onto the podium.)

After a brief introduction by Assistant Secretary of Health Ed Brandt I explained that the 1982 *Report on Smoking and Health* focused on the clear relationship between smoking and cancer. Thirty percent of all cancer deaths, I said, were attributable to smoking. The 1982 report identified cigarette smoking as a major cause not only of lung cancer but also of cancers of the larynx, oral cavity, and esophagus, and confirmed it as a contributing factor in the development of cancers of the bladder, pancreas, and kidney. New studies also suggested an association between smoking and cancers of the stomach and cervix. The report concluded by pointing to the elevated risk of cancer associated with passive smoking.

Although the report dealt most specifically with smoking and cancer, I also stressed that smoking exacted $13 billion annually in healthcare expenses and over $25 billion in lost production and wages. I said then for the first time what I have repeated so often since: "Cigarette smoking is the chief preventable cause of death in our society."

The press conference received front-page coverage from most major newspapers, and I began to see the valuable ways in which the Surgeon General's position could be used to advance the health of the nation with moral suasion. I also realized that for the first time since my arrival in Washington, I had begun to earn back the credibility I had possessed in my previous surgical career. This marked the turning point in my relationship with the press. They had arrived at my first press conference displaying their preconfirmation hostility, and they left neutral. The next press conference saw them arrive neutral and leave favorably impressed. Eventually the press even became friendly, and in 1986, when I returned to the public eye following neck surgery, some even applauded.

I felt I was off to a great start in the fight against smoking, and I thanked the many people whose work on the 1982 report enabled it to be so well received. I owed an even greater debt of gratitude to the Surgeon General who had started it all, Luther Terry, and to his successors, all of whom had kept up the fight.

Following Dr. Terry's landmark 1964 report, Congress demanded that an annual report on smoking and health be submitted by the Surgeon General. These reports have boasted an unassailable data base, tracking more than 2 million individuals in all fifty states. Each report is prepared by the Office on Smoking and Health, working in close collaboration with a wide range of scientists. And with each Surgeon General's report has come the grim news that more and more deaths are attributable to smoking.

Cancer and heart disease top the list of the health concerns of most Americans. The public recognized smoking's connection with cancer early on, but the connection between smoking and heart disease was not widely known. That changed, I hope, with the 1983 Surgeon General's report, *Health Consequences of Smoking: Cardiovascular Disease,* which stressed the proven link between smoking and heart disease. Many Americans were surprised to realize that smoking caused even more deaths from heart disease than from cancer. Heart disease kills about 565,000 Americans annually, about 170,000 of whom (30 percent) are smokers. The report indicated that the average smoker had a 70 percent greater chance of dying of heart disease than a nonsmoker. Heavy smokers—those who consume two packs or more a day—suffer a 200 percent higher mortality rate.

The 1984 report, *Health Consequences of Smoking: Chronic Obstructive Lung Disease*, presented clear conclusions: cigarette smoking is the major cause of illness and death from chronic obstructive lung disease, including emphysema, in both men and women. At the report's press conference I tried to inject a touch of humor while making a serious point. I asked for a volunteer, someone who was trying to quit smoking, to come forward for a small "reward." Bill Hines, a reporter for the Chicago *Sun-Times*, pushed forward his wife, Judith Randal, a reporter for the *Daily News* in New York. I gave her one of my newly minted blue buttons with the slogan THE SURGEON GENERAL ASKED ME PERSONALLY TO STOP SMOKING. Then I promised her one of my red AND I DID buttons to go along with it if she earned it. A few other reporters came up to me for their own buttons. I was always tickled when I could reward people with the red button of achievement when they stopped smoking. And of course, they felt even better than I did.

There was one skirmish in the smoking wars from which I was relieved to be excluded. It began when Ed Brandt and I, along with other health officials, testified in 1982 before the House of Representatives' subcommittee on health, chaired by Congressman Henry Waxman of California. The issue before the subcommittee was a bill that would change the current Surgeon General's warning on cigarette labels and advertising—"Warning: The Surgeon General Has Determined That Cigarette Smoking Is Dangerous to Your Health"—to a series of rotating warnings against the specific dangers of smoking and the benefits of quitting no matter how long one had smoked. When Brandt and I testified in favor of the bill before a receptive subcommittee, Brandt stated that such legislation was a "high priority" of the administration.

Immediately, and predictably, the tobacco industry dusted off its own research alleging the minimal health consequences of smoking. Under questioning from Waxman, however, R. J. Reynolds Tobacco Company's Edward Horrigan conceded that their industry advertising budget was more than $900 million annually, compared with about $70 million for research.

Just as the administration's commitment to health was winning widespread approval in the press, the powerful Office of Management and Budget caved in to pressure from tobacco-state Congress-men. The next time Brandt and I went to testify on the Hill—this time before the Senate committee sponsoring a bill similar to the one we had supported the week before in the House—Brandt's testimony made it clear that he had been forced to back down. Now, he said, the administration's earlier support of the measure had changed to "no position."

I was as surprised as anyone. When I had arrived in the anteroom of the hearing chamber that morning, I saw Senator Hatch and Brandt looking very grim. Brandt walked over to me and said very quietly that he had been ordered not to support the bill. I replied, "What do you mean? We've already supported it in our testimony before the House." Brandt informed me that OMB had decided to oppose the bill the night before. When it became clear to the commit-tee that Brandt had backed off from supporting the bill, Senator Packwood questioned him aggressively, attempting to find out what had caused this abrupt about-face. Brandt squirmed uncomfortably under the questioning. When specifically asked if he had been in-structed how to testify, he looked straight ahead and remained silent. I was very uncomfortable and relieved that I had not been placed in Brandt's position, because I might have chosen to resign.

I did not assume the position of Surgeon General with the clear intention of being such an active opponent of tobacco, but after I studied the incontrovertible truths about the health hazards of smok-ing, I became at first dumbfounded and then furious at the tobacco industry for attempting to obfuscate and trivialize this extraordinarily important public-health information.

How could the tobacco industry dare to dismiss as unproved the absolutely clear connection between smoking and heart disease; be-tween smoking and death from stroke; between smoking and cancers of the lung, mouth, esophagus, and stomach; and between smoking and a dozen or more serious, debilitating, exhausting, expensive, and humiliating diseases?

How could it do that? The answer was, it just did. The tobacco industry is associated not only with disease and death but also with money. The tobacco lobby is overwhelmingly powerful. It has seem-ingly unlimited funding. Somehow or other it impacts on the lives of almost every member of Congress. The tobacco industry contributes to political action committees, pays Congressmen for lectures, and lobbies Congressmen to support tobacco-related legislation.

One Congressman from a tobacco-producing state, whose name I've somewhat contemptuously repressed, called me at home several nights after the release of the 1983 *Surgeon General's Report on Smoking and Health*. Our conversation ended when he said, "I don't give a good goddamn how many people die of cancer or anything else that you say is associated with tobacco. All I want is jobs and prosperity for constituents in my district. Why don't you lay off all this nonsense about smoking and health?"

Although most people concerned about the health problems associated with tobacco focused—rightly—on smoking, even when there was no smoke, there was fire. My efforts against smokeless tobacco formed a microcosm of the struggle between health and tobacco.

Smokeless tobacco comes in the form of chewing tobacco, dry snuff, and moist snuff, sometimes packaged in paper like tea bags. Just like smoking tobacco, smokeless tobacco is addictive, is protected by a strong lobby, has its own "institute," is advertised to the most vulnerable people, and is heavily promoted to children despite laws forbidding its sale to minors. In some parts of the country it enjoys cultural approval, as many boys are introduced to smokeless tobacco by fathers, grandfathers, and uncles, who are probably unaware of the risk. Its manufacturers have knowingly sunk to the level of introducing an addictive drug to youngsters. At state fairs they have been known to sponsor tobacco-spitting contests by age group, with four-year-olds starting off.

In the fall of 1984 someone from Congressman Jack Kemp's office called asking if I would meet with a Mr. Nick Buoniconti. I knew Buoniconti had been a professional football player, and I guessed that Kemp probably knew him from his own days with the Buffalo Bills. The caller from Kemp's office told me that Buoniconti was representing the tobacco interests but that he was a good guy. Because of Kemp's earlier support for me, I agreed to see the man. Kemp called later, leaving a message that although he did not necessarily share all of Buoniconti's views, nonetheless he was a reasonable gentleman, whom Kemp knew from their common work with parents for drug-free youths. Then I learned that Buoniconti would be accompanied by Lou Bantel, president of the U.S. Tobacco Company.

The next step in the carefully orchestrated pageant was a call from Patty Tyson, special assistant to Secretary of Health Margaret Heckler. (Dick Schweiker had resigned after eighteen months, and Representative Heckler was his replacement.) I was told that Heckler knew I was meeting with Bantel, a large contributor to the Reagan campaign, so would I handle him in my usual charming manner? The message was clear, but I did not know whether it came from Heckler or the White House.

I wanted to get more information on the visitors and their mission. A few phone calls revealed the real agenda: (1) Kemp seemed to want only that I let Buoniconti know that Kemp had called me on his behalf (the issue to be discussed didn't seem to matter); (2) the topic of conversation would most likely be moist snuff (75 percent of the world supply of moist snuff was made by the U.S. Tobacco Company); (3) the company was a defendant in a $19 million suit in Oklahoma brought by parents of Shawn Marsee, a teenage snuff user who had died of cancer of the mouth.

When I first met with Buoniconti and Bantel, the tobacco president took an antique sterling silver snuffbox out of his pocket and tucked some tobacco between his lower gum and cheek, the very spot of the original site of the cancer that had killed Shawn Marsee. I didn't know which bothered me more: his arrogance or his insensitivity. I listened to the same old spiel—that tobacco was being incorrectly blamed for cancer. I told these two men that they were wrong, that my conclusions were guided by good science, and that I strongly objected to their advertising aimed at young people. As I knew it would, the meeting ended in disagreement.

I wanted to fight back against the slippery tactics of the smokeless tobacco industry, but my efforts were being thwarted by Secretary Heckler's obstructive inactivity. We needed to set up a task force to investigate the health hazards of smokeless tobacco. But my repeated requests to Secretary Heckler's staff remained unanswered for more than six weeks. I knew that the tobacco industry could be exerting pressure on Heckler's office. After all, Mike Deaver, once a member of the triumvirate surrounding Reagan, was running the public relations firm that handled the Smokeless Tobacco Institute.

So I took matters into my own hands. I met with people from the Federal Trade Commission, found they were on my side, and told them of my plan to announce the appointment of a task force to investigate the health effects of smokeless tobacco. Joe Cullen of the prevention division of the National Cancer Institute agreed to become chair of the task force, and Jim Wyngaarten, director of NIH, and Vince De Vita, director of the National Cancer Institute, approved NCI's staffing of the project.

Meanwhile, Connecticut Senator Lowell Weicker asked me to meet in his Capitol office with Buoniconti and another representative from the U.S. Tobacco Company, which was based in Weicker's state. I decided to keep as cool as possible, hoping that Buoniconti would lose his composure, just as he had shortly before, on *60 Minutes,* when he was being interrogated about the health hazards of his product. Sure enough, in Weicker's office his voice got higher and louder, and he seemed almost hysterical as he trotted out the old cliché so dear to the tobacco industry: that the scientific studies that demonstrate the hazards of smoking are "anecdotal." The diatribe went on so long that Weicker, who was supposed to be sympathetic to his constituent, made some remarks favorable to the side of health. Then just before our half hour came to an end, Buoniconti started a new subject, relating how his wife had quit smoking easily, proving that nicotine couldn't be addictive. I chose that moment to stand up to leave, pointed right at Buoniconti, and said, "That, sir, is anecdotal." Everyone in the room laughed except Buoniconti. As I shook Weicker's hand his legislative aide smiled at me and said, "You won the first round!"

Even though governmental wheels grind slowly, we finally got our smokeless tobacco committee, congressional hearings, and eventually the Comprehensive Smokeless Tobacco Health Education Act of 1986, which provided for public education concerning the health hazards of smokeless tobacco. The scientific conclusions were clear: a careful examination of the relevant epidemiological, experimental, and clinical data indicated that the oral use of smokeless tobacco represents a significant health risk. It is not a safe substitute for smoking cigarettes. It can cause cancer and a number of noncancerous oral conditions and can lead to nicotine addiction.

The fight continued on other fronts. Shawn Marsee's mother lost her suit against the U.S. Tobacco Company, but eventually we were able to get Surgeon General's warnings on smokeless tobacco, in part because Shawn had repeatedly said to his mother, "It couldn't be dangerous, or there would be a warning on the package."

Over all, I knew the antismoking campaign was making progress, but I also knew we needed a new vision. I was sure the tobacco companies were regathering for a counteroffensive. I wanted to beat them to the punch. The time had come for a bold initiative. I decided to make a public call for "A Smoke-Free Society by the Year 2000"— with the logo SFS-2000. After discussing the idea with Betty, I mentioned it only to my colleagues Assistant Surgeon General Jim Dickson; Ted Cron, my personal assistant; and Matt Meyers, executive officer of the Coalition on Smoking OR Health, an antismoking organization formed by the American Lung Association, the American Cancer Society, and the American Heart Association. I knew if my plan leaked to the administration and thence to the tobacco industry, some way would be found to block the effort. That never happened.

I had been giving speeches since I was twenty-three years old, but never before had I spent so much effort and concern on a single one. I chose the right year to present it: 1984, the twentieth anniversary of the Surgeon General's first report on smoking. I also chose the right month: May, an interlude in the constant barrage of news about the presidential primaries. And I chose the right audience: a combined meeting in Miami of the American Lung Association and the American Thoracic Society.

My speech made clear that this was not just another job for the Surgeon General; this was a job for America. And I said that I was not calling for laws. I was calling upon nonsmokers to stand up for their rights. And I was calling upon smokers to respect those rights. The audience in Miami, who were the first to hear my call for a smoke-free society, were on board right away. Then I carried the call to other groups all across the country.

Next I asked the Coalition on Smoking OR Health to take steps to ensure that the high school graduating class in the year 2000 was a smoke-free class. They got to work right away and in 1988–1989 began implementing a twelve-year curriculum, starting with first graders. By the time these youngsters graduated from high school, in 2000, they would have received antismoking messages throughout each of their school years.

Of all the public appearances I would make, few topped the times

I would speak to youngsters at school. In Honolulu I visited an elementary school where the students had studied the SFS-2000 anti-smoking curriculum. After a few minutes of banter I said, "Who can tell me what's going to happen in the year 2000?"

A hundred hands went up, and I pointed to a little Japanese American lad in the back row, who yelled, "We are all going to die!"

I knew I had to talk fast.

"No, no. You've got that wrong. There are some people who don't make the promise not to smoke that you have just made. *They* might die, but you are going to be alive and well if you keep the pledge to turn your back on cigarettes."

That broke the ice. After a few laughs we were on the same level, and we had a great dialogue, not so much on the dangers of smoking as on the privilege of making choices, which is what the first-year curriculum is all about. I would look at the faces of those kids and pray that they would keep that pledge, that those young lives would not be cut short by smoking, as too many lives in their parents' generation would be.

My personal messages about smoking seemed to be particularly effective, and I found early on that a personal plea from the Surgeon General might be enough to get a smoker to quit. One night, before I gave the banquet speech at the Congressional Country Club, my host introduced me to the two bartenders. At first they were astonished that the Surgeon General was a real person and not just a symbol like, as a cabbie once put it, Betty Crocker. When I learned that each of these fellows smoked more than a pack a day, I begged them to quit for the sake of their health. A few months later I returned to the same club, but with a different speech, and found the same two bartenders. "We ain't smoked since we saw you, Doc!"

After the public began to recognize me, people seldom smoked in my presence. When the nonsmoking tables in a Reno restaurant were all occupied, my hostess said, "I'll just seat you in the smoking section. They'll all put their cigarettes out." Sure enough, they did.

THE next move in the attack on the tobacco interests brought the controversy home. Early on a humid July morning in 1986, as I walked out the door of our duplex home on the grounds of NIH, about ten reporters toting cameras and microphones suddenly sprang from the

Controversy often led to humor during the author's eight years as
Surgeon General. Above: a 1989 political cartoon from the Cincinnati *Enquirer*.

shrubbery and surrounded my car. One reporter stuck a microphone
into my face and yelled, "Is it true that you have been censored by the
White House?" Betty, in the doorway in her bathrobe, was as surprised as I by the ambush. The bungling of Donald Regan, President
Reagan's controversy-prone chief of staff, had brought the intruders
and inadvertently propelled me to a minor triumph.

I had been scheduled for several weeks to testify again on Capitol
Hill, on legislation that would ban all cigarette advertising in magazines and newspapers and on billboards. All congressional testimony
is submitted in advance to OMB several days before.

My White House spies told me that Jim Miller, the director of OMB,
was annoyed by my testimony because of its economic implications.
Miller voiced his displeasure at a White House senior staff meeting,
and Regan said I should not be allowed to testify. The Washington
Post, responding to a tip, called Regan to ask if I had been forbidden
to testify. Regan said, "Yes." I knew none of this at the time. Regan
never called then or later. I would never have withdrawn my testimony under this kind of pressure. But I realized that postponing it
would make things go my way.

It was a pleasure to watch the next events unfold as the heavy-
handed White House tactics boomeranged. Throughout the following days the crusade against tobacco advertising benefitted from fa-

vorable press coverage that we could not have come by for a million dollars. Regan's action made front-page and prime-time coverage out of a story that ordinarily might have been lost. The networks carried interviews with Yul Brynner's daughter (Brynner had recently died of cancer caused by his lifelong chain smoking) and R. J. Reynolds' heir Pat Reynolds, both of whom spoke forcefully against cigarette advertising. Commentators such as *Good Morning America*'s David Hartman summed it all up by concluding that there was a growing ground swell in America to ban cigarette advertising.

When I finally testified, I used the opportunity to say that if the Public Health Service could get equal space in magazines to counter cigarette advertising with the truth about the effects of smoking, the tobacco industry would throw in the towel. I was sure they would prefer not to advertise at all rather than risk having the American people learn the terrible truth about smoking.

By 1986 the antismoking population had become a militant army. They had a goal. They needed a weapon. When I released the 1986 Surgeon General's report on the dangers of passive smoking, the nonsmokers got the weapon they needed. This marked the real turning of the tide.

The *Health Consequences of Passive Smoking* determined without a doubt that passive smoking *causes* disease, including cancer. Stipulating that simply separating smokers and nonsmokers in the same airspace did not solve the problem, the report stressed the especially harmful effects of passive smoking on children.

I felt that future historians would consider this report just as important as the original 1964 report. All across the country smokers were in retreat. Lawmakers and regulators on all levels of government began to protect the lungs of nonsmokers. The General Services Administration restricted smoking in its 6800 federal buildings, affecting 890,000 federal employees. By early 1987 forty states had restricted smoking in public places, thirty-three states had prohibited smoking on public conveyances, and seventeen states had banned smoking in offices and other work sites.

My last Surgeon General's report on smoking, in 1989, confirmed that smoking was still the greatest preventable cause of death in the United States (the annual mortality figures were revised upward, to 390,000) and for the first time stated that smoking can cause strokes, as opposed to just being associated with them. After the report a consensus developed that the mortality figure is closer to 500,000 annually.

The 1989 report was more reflective than earlier reports. It was the silver anniversary report, released twenty-five years after Surgeon General Luther Terry woke up Americans with his 1964 report. Terry, who died in 1985, did not live to read the report that reviewed our progress on the crusade he had started. I count it among my more meaningful accomplishments that I was able to help his family cut through the red tape to enable Terry to be buried at the Arlington National Cemetery with full honors. He certainly affected—and saved—more lives than many of the generals buried there.

We have come a long way since that first report. Cigarette smoking has continued to decline, the percentage of smokers falling from over 50 percent of Americans in 1964 to just over 26 percent in 1989—an amazing accomplishment! And the lives of nonsmokers have improved dramatically. Five years ago most of us still had to spend too much time in smoke-filled rooms. We would not dare ask a smoker to snuff it out. Now when someone lights up around nonsmokers, at the first whiff they turn their heads, glare at the smoker, and make it clear: "Don't poison my air!"

I do not believe the United States will ever again be a growing market for tobacco products. But there are still battles to be fought: cigarette vending machines, cigarette advertising, and the international power of the tobacco companies.

It is illegal to sell both alcohol and cigarettes to minors, because alcohol and nicotine are the two major legal addictive drugs in our society. We would never tolerate selling alcohol in vending machines, but somehow we tolerate cigarette vending machines.

Cigarette advertising is equally pernicious. The tobacco industry spends $4000 per *minute* on promotion, or $2.5 billion a year. Cigarette ads may have been banned from television, but they are sneaking back again through videos. And cigarette advertising still assaults our society in print. You cannot watch a sports event on TV without seeing cigarette ads on billboards, clothing, and equipment.

Although we are beating the American tobacco industry on its own turf, it is scouring the globe for other victims. While smoking in the United States dropped another 5 percent in 1989, American tobacco exports rose 20 percent that same year. In 1989 American companies manufactured 600 billion cigarettes; 100 billion of those cigarettes went overseas.

The tobacco industry has targeted the less developed countries of the world as their most promising markets for the '90s. The transnational tobacco companies travel from country to country with a great deal of cash. These companies build factories and employ many people. They spend large sums on advertising and special events. In some areas they virtually subsidize the media. We see the result in the rising morbidity and mortality rates from Western smoking-related diseases. The recent news that in fifteen Asian countries communicable disease was no longer the number one public-health menace was not really good news. It just meant that in those Asian countries the top three causes of death had become the same three smoking-related causes of death that prevail in the United States: heart disease, cancer, and stroke.

We may have a balance-of-trade problem, but that does not justify exporting disease, disability, and death to developing countries. In my last official act as Surgeon General, I was one of more than thirty witnesses at a congressional public hearing on tobacco and trade. I made my point and concluded by saying:

> "It is the height of hypocrisy for the United States, in our war against drugs, to demand that foreign nations take steps to stop the export of cocaine to our country while at the same time we export nicotine, a drug just as addictive as cocaine, to the rest of the world."

CHAPTER 9
AIDS

WHEN I was designated Surgeon General, in February 1981, I had never heard of AIDS. No one had heard of AIDS, and the handful of scientists who knew about this immunodeficiency disease did not even know what to call it, much less what it really was. AIDS entered the consciousness of the Public Health Service quietly, gradually, and without fanfare. In June 1981 the Centers for Disease Control (CDC), an agency of the United States Public Health Service, published a report concerning five "previously healthy" homosexuals who had been admitted to Los Angeles hospitals with pneumonia caused by a very rare organism, *Pneumocystis carinii.* By the time the report was published, two of the men had died. The other three died shortly thereafter. Soon reports trickled in of cases in other cities as well.

From that small beginning mushroomed the AIDS epidemic of the late '80s. Epidemiologists from the CDC investigated the strange cases and discovered that otherwise healthy, normal people were apparently acquiring some kind of bug—a virus, most likely—that attacked and destroyed their natural immune systems. The bug itself was not killing these people; they were succumbing to other, extremely virulent diseases called opportunistic, because this infectious agent—whatever it was—prevented the body from fighting them off. Since the first cases affected only homosexuals, the Public Health Service dubbed the disease GRID—gay-related immune deficiency. Shortly thereafter, as heterosexuals began to fall victim to it, GRID became the acquired immune deficiency syndrome, or AIDS.

By August 1981 there were 108 cases of AIDS reported, with 43 dead. I knew we were in big trouble. And there was nothing I could do about it. I was told by the assistant secretary for health, my immediate boss, that I would not be assigned to cover AIDS. The department took its cue from him. As Surgeon General, I was not allowed to speak about AIDS publicly until the second Reagan term. Whenever I spoke on a health issue at a press conference or on a network morning TV show, the government public affairs people told the media in advance that I would not answer questions on AIDS. I have never understood why these peculiar restraints were placed on me. And although I have sought to find the explanation, I still don't know the answer.

Perhaps in the first months of the AIDS epidemic, when I was still unconfirmed as Surgeon General, my exclusion went along with HHS Secretary Dick Schweiker's advice that I should keep my head down and my mouth shut until I was confirmed. But even after my confirmation I continued to be excluded from the government's handling of the issue. In 1983, for instance, Assistant Secretary of Health Ed Brandt created an Executive Task Force on AIDS, a high-level group drawn from the Public Health Service to deal with the growing AIDS epidemic. I was not asked to join the task force.

At the time, I never considered myself muzzled about AIDS. I believed initially that my exclusion was simply the result of a division of labor—a very naïve belief, I now realize. It was my job as Surgeon General to communicate with the American people in order to protect their health. It sounds simple. But it did not take long for me to discover how difficult it could be to get the word out, because no matter what the issue, there were always forces trying to keep me from communicating health messages to the American people. I had to wage scores of political battles before I could even begin to do my job.

Within the politics of AIDS lay one enduring central conflict: AIDS pitted the politics of the gay revolution of the '70s against the politics of the Reagan revolution of the '80s. There were reasons why it took a while for public-health authorities to get a handle on AIDS. One was the relatively rare nature of the diseases associated with the AIDS virus: *Pneumocystis carinii* pneumonia, cytomegalovirus and *Candida* infections, Kaposi's sarcoma, cryptococcal meningitis, toxoplasmosis, and so on. In 1981 the United States had relatively few clinicians and researchers who were familiar with these rare diseases that were suddenly cropping up in Los Angeles, San Francisco, and New York. And in any case, we had no cure for them.

Meanwhile, in what was known at the time as the gay revolution, homosexual and bisexual men were coming out of the closet and asserting their civil rights. Unfortunately, most gay activists combined the otherwise separate issues of homosexual health and politics. Their concerns about AIDS were mixed in with other homosexual issues, such as access to jobs and housing, as well as protection against social discrimination. As a result, the first public-health priority—to stop further transmission of the AIDS virus—became mired in the sexual politics of the early '80s. We lost a great deal of precious time because of this, and I suspect we lost some lives as well.

The Reagan revolution brought into positions of power and influence Americans whose political and personal beliefs predisposed them to antipathy toward the homosexual community. In the early years of the AIDS crisis, health officials were shocked by the link between the spread of AIDS and the promiscuity and perversity of many homosexuals' behavior. AIDS patients admitted to an astounding number of sexual encounters with an equally astounding number of different partners in a single day. Such revelations, along with the high incidence of anal intercourse—sodomy—provided valuable information about a possible method of AIDS transmission: semen of one to blood of the other. However, some health officials displayed a profound reluctance to discuss these sensitive issues publicly. So under directions from more than one White House source they simply made vague references to "exchanging bodily fluids," thus considerably slowing down the public's understanding of how AIDS can be transmitted.

In May 1983 Robert Gallo of the National Institutes of Health and Lucy Montagnier of the Pasteur Institute in Paris identified the infectious agent that caused AIDS: a virus dubbed HIV-III, or human immunodeficiency virus. In early 1984 there were over 5000 reported cases of AIDS, with about 2300 deaths. But in a strange way, except for the homosexual community organizations and segments of the public-health community, there seemed to be little outcry for more leadership from the government. In 1985, as the Public Health Service and other branches of the medical community learned more about AIDS, they provided a weapon against the strange disease: a test to identify the presence of antibodies to the HIV virus in the blood supply.

Not many criticisms make my blood boil anymore, but there is one that still does. I still hear people complain that the government dragged its feet and would not release a blood-screening test until 1985. Instead, in spite of the confusion, frustration, anger, and ignorance, the government *did* press forward, and made astounding advances in biomedical science and research. We learned as much about AIDS in six years as we had learned about polio in forty. It is a testament to these unflagging efforts that a reliable blood test was discovered as early as the fall of 1985.

The stakes were very high. The discovery of the blood test saved many lives. Without it, the nation's blood supply would have become increasingly contaminated; people unknowingly infected with the virus by transfusions could have infected their sexual partners; some mothers could have spread it to newborns; infected people could have become blood donors; and so on. We had a close call. Even so, an estimated twelve thousand transfusion recipients were infected with HIV-contaminated blood.

By the mid-'80s we acknowledged that there was much we did not know about AIDS, but we had made extraordinary progress in our understanding of the syndrome. Above all, we learned about how the disease was transmitted. We learned that although the virus had been identified in several body fluids, it seemed to be transmitted only through blood and semen. Researchers were very cautious. For example, Dr. Tony Fauci, later to direct AIDS research at NIH, insisted we check out any study that did not seem to rule out the spread of AIDS by casual contact. But gradually a convincing body of research led us to some important conclusions. The most important thing we knew was the deadliest news: if you had AIDS, your chances of surviving the next two or three years were not very good, and the chances of surviving any longer than that were almost nil.

It was clear that in spite of all kinds of unsubstantiated claims about mosquitoes and toilet seats, there were just four main ways AIDS could be transmitted:

• The first way of transmission was sexual intercourse, mostly, but not exclusively, anal intercourse, which occurred most frequently among homosexuals and bisexual males. This accounted for about two thirds of all cases of AIDS at that time. However, AIDS could also be transmitted through heterosexual intercourse, and even though the statistical incidence of heterosexual transmission was lower, the disease was just as fatal.

• AIDS could also be transmitted into the blood of intravenous drug users who used the needles and syringes of other addicts already infected with the AIDS virus.

• The HIV virus could also be transmitted from an AIDS-infected mother to her infant during pregnancy or at the time of delivery.

• And finally, AIDS could be transmitted through transfused blood or blood products. (The development of the AIDS blood test virtually closed off this avenue of transmission.)

Understanding the means of AIDS transmission was a long way from finding a vaccine, even though research in that area accelerated. Because of the complex nature of the AIDS virus, it became very clear very soon that a vaccine lay years in the future.

A cure seemed equally elusive, as the only drugs that seemed to help, such as AZT (zidovudine, formerly azidothymidine), prolonged a person's life for only a few months or a year, if they worked at all. They did not cure anyone of AIDS, nor did they cure anyone of any condition brought on by AIDS.

Meanwhile, the numbers continued to mount. By July 1985 the CDC had reported 11,737 AIDS cases, with 5812 deaths. Just a week later the toll for each category had risen by about a hundred. That summer the death of Rock Hudson—the first national figure to die of AIDS—raised further the public concern about the disease. For the first time, because of Reagan's friendship with his fellow actor, AIDS seemed to touch the White House, even if indirectly.

It does not take long for public concern and fear to lead to charges of conspiracy. And conspiracy charges about AIDS grew along with the epidemic. One side accused the government of conspiring with the homosexual community to cover up the epidemic. How that would have helped the government or the homosexual community was never clear to me. If ever there was an administration that would not conspire with homosexuals, it was Reagan's. On the other side, homosexuals and their advocates accused the government of a conspiracy to do nothing, to allow the disease to decimate the homosexual community.

I felt caught in the middle but still on the sidelines. Finally, at a July meeting of HHS agency heads, I spoke openly for the first time about the difficulties I was facing concerning the number of requests I had received to say something about AIDS. I had even been forced to decline invitations to provide private briefings for Senators and Congressmen. By this time Ed Brandt had left to go to the University of Maryland as provost on the Baltimore campus and had been succeeded by James O. Mason as acting assistant secretary for health. Since I was no longer the new kid on the block, but actually the oldest kid on the block, Mason made me a member of the AIDS Task Force. He and I also agreed that AIDS demanded a clear spokesperson and that I could make any statement I thought appropriate. At last I could speak up, and my first printed interview on AIDS appeared in the November 1985 issue of *Christianity Today*. I stuck to the issues as I saw them, and I stated for the first time my oft-repeated conclusion that in preventing AIDS, the moralist and the scientist could walk hand in hand.

My intense involvement with AIDS came after President Reagan asked me to write a report to the American people about the disease. For the next two years AIDS took over my life.

I had heard the rumors for a week or so. At the end of January, 1986, at a dinner hosted by then Treasury Secretary Jim Baker and his wife, Susan, two of the White House staffers present slipped up to me and whispered, "You're in the State of the Union message." They said that the President was going to ask me to write a report on AIDS. I thought this unlikely, because about 1500 issues are suggested for the address, and even if the President might finally be ready to talk about AIDS, I knew his advisers were not.

Betty and I watched the 1986 State of the Union speech on television, and it was such an upbeat, frothy address that we knew halfway through that Reagan would never mention AIDS. He didn't, and I said to Betty before we went to bed that night, "I guess I'm off the hook on writing that report."

Then only a few days later, on February 5, President Reagan made an unprecedented visit to the Department of Health and Human Services. The navy band had shown up to herald his arrival. They played a few bars of "Hail to the Chief" when Reagan appeared, and that was it for the music. Dr. Otis Bowen, the new Secretary for Health and Human Services, who had been sworn in about six weeks earlier, spoke first, then introduced the President. Reagan announced that he wanted AIDS to be a top priority in the department and was looking forward to the day when there would be a vaccine. He then declared that he was asking the Surgeon General to prepare a special report on AIDS. That was it. There was never any formal request.

I started the next day. I knew that telling the truth about AIDS would not be well received in some places. One of those places would be the White House. Several months earlier I had told a circle of high-echelon White House advisers that a report on AIDS from the Surgeon General was necessary but that it might bring criticism to the President and his administration. A large portion of the President's constituency was antihomosexual, anti–drug abuse, antipromiscuity, and anti–sex education; these people would not respond well to some of the things that would have to be said in a health report on AIDS.

I said then—and I repeated it frequently—that the Surgeon General was the Surgeon General of homosexuals as well as of heterosexuals, and of the promiscuous as well as of the moral. I am not sure anyone listened. If they had, they would not have been so surprised that my AIDS report was a health report, not the exercise in moral censure they wanted.

I possessed a mandate from the President to write a report on AIDS to the American people. But I knew the normal clearance process sanitized and watered down the message of many a draft document. So I realized that my success in writing an honest AIDS report depended upon my getting the green light from Secretary Bowen to bypass the normal clearance process.

Otis Bowen had already enjoyed careers as a respected family physician and two-term governor of Indiana when he agreed to succeed Margaret Heckler as Secretary of Health and Human Services. Serving as head of our department was not viewed as a plum. When Reagan's first Secretary of Health and Human Services, Dick Schweiker, had taken office, in 1981, Schweiker's father spent a few minutes wandering around the Humphrey Building and looking at the photos of previous Secretaries. Noting that none had served very long, he told Dick that it couldn't be a very good job if people came and went so frequently. But Doc Bowen fooled them all. Although initially regarded as little more than a caretaker, Bowen, a true public servant, would serve with distinction as Secretary of HHS longer than anyone else in the history of the department. He certainly ranks at the top of Reagan's appointees. I found Bowen to be gentle, kind, a superb politician, honest as the day is long, and wise: "If you tell the truth, Chick, you don't have to have a good memory to recall the lies."

Otis Bowen and I shared a common view of medicine, politics, government, and, well, life. He gave me the green light I needed on the AIDS report. I told him that I would seek the best scientific advice and that when the report was ready, I assumed he would join me to present it before the Domestic Policy Council (those Cabinet members dealing with domestic affairs).

Like much of my work in Washington, writing the AIDS report amounted to walking a tightrope. I needed to be in touch with all of the national groups that were concerned about AIDS. I wanted to make sure they knew what I was doing, and I wanted none to say, after the report was published, that they had been blindsided or kept in the dark. But at the same time I had to make sure that the report was independent and objective.

Maintaining control of the report, keeping the circle small, meant that I would have only a very small staff to help me. Dr. Michael Samuels brought with him a broad background in public-health endeavors, and he also brought the part-time help of Jim McTigue, a commissioned officer with whom Mike and I had frequently worked on intergovernmental affairs. We were supported by a small team: Assistant Surgeons General Jim Dickson and Edward Martin; my deputy director of the Office of International Health, Hal Thompson; my personal assistant, Stephanie Stein; and, of course, my deputy, Faye Abdellah.

We learned a lot, and we learned fast. Some groups surprised me, usually pleasantly. For instance, I was delighted by the American Medical Association's aggressive action against AIDS and the willingness of the AMA board of trustees to expend large sums of money on their AIDS Action Plan, which would include plans for education and projections about the spread of the epidemic. The National Coalition of Black Lesbians and Gays, far from adopting the combative posture many expected, was one of the most articulate and caring groups.

A few meetings were critically important. For instance, the National Hemophilia Foundation made a major contribution to our understanding of the disease. (Tragically, 90 percent of severe hemophiliacs became infected with HIV before the blood supply was made safe.) The experience of hemophiliacs nailed down the evidence that AIDS was not spread by nonsexual casual contact. Six hundred families of hemophiliacs were studied. Family members who lived with an HIV-positive male touched each other, used the same utensils, kissed each other, and shared razors without passing the virus. Even the 7 percent who shared toothbrushes (I was surprised by that figure!) did not transmit the virus to their toothbrush partners.

This—and a number of other studies—confirmed that most Americans were not at risk *if* they did not engage in high-risk behavior with sex and drugs. This also meant that persons with AIDS should not suffer discrimination, that the strident calls to quarantine them were misinformed and wrong. Nevertheless, the calls for taking drastic measures against persons with AIDS were mounting each day.

Some California Congressmen had come under the sway of a group who despised homosexuals. They perpetuated a number of myths about AIDS transmission, and one of the Congressmen apparently bought into those myths. He advocated mandatory testing for the entire nation, the quarantine of all those who tested positive, and a law that would make it a felony for people to "exchange body fluids" if they were contaminated with the virus. (How this would be enforced, the lawmaker never made clear.)

One evening he called me at home. "Chick, why won't you get on with mandatory testing of the entire country?"

"I've told you, that's not within the power of the Surgeon General, and I wouldn't do it if I could. But suppose, just for the sake of argument, I could and did. Suppose I called you next week and said I now knew who every seropositive person was in the whole United States. What would you do?"

After a long pause the Congressman, as I recall, replied, "Wipe them off the face of the earth!"

This attitude, I realized as I conducted my interviews on the AIDS report, although not widely voiced, was widely held. I could see where these people were coming from, but I could not agree with them. I strongly disapproved of the forms of behavior responsible for most AIDS transmission. But as a physician, it was my job to save lives and alleviate suffering. It was not my job to make decisions on accepting or treating a patient based upon how he had incurred the disease. Knowing what Christians believe, I felt I was in a unique position to understand their point of view. I also knew that Christians are taught to separate the sin from the sinner and to treat those in need with compassion. Judgment is God's business. As Surgeon General, moved by Christian compassion and the profession of medicine, my course was clear: to do all I could in this report to halt the spread of AIDS by educating the American people accurately and completely.

And education itself, I could see, was going to cause problems. Since AIDS was most often transmitted through sexual contact, my report would have to call for sex education, which in this case was a life-or-death proposition. And I knew that sex education was a buzzword that would drive many conservatives up the wall. But I hoped I could reason with the large conservative pro-life constituency, people who knew me and had supported my confirmation. I hoped that they would be able to see that we would need very explicit sex education, because if kids experimented with sex in the age of AIDS, they could die.

As these problems nagged me, I thought I could save the American people a lot of confusion if I could get around the low-level White House staffers and invite the President to make a statement about the most pressing health threat of his tenure. I saw a great opportunity at the end of July, 1986, when the First Lady and the President would be mounting a new initiative against drugs—the famous Just Say No campaign. I did not think that Just Say No was going to solve our national drug problem, but because the most rapidly expanding group of persons with AIDS was intravenous drug users, I saw a way for the President to address both issues. So one day I called Jack Svahn, domestic policy adviser to the President, and he promised to convey my message to Reagan.

Jack was true to his word and called me at home that evening. He made it clear that the President had grasped the issues completely and appreciated the implications of tying the two together. I was elated.

But nothing happened. The Just Say No program was launched with much fanfare, but not a word about AIDS. One of my White House contacts told me later that Reagan had come to the staff meeting the next morning sold on my idea, but his advisers were simply not interested in the President's doing anything about AIDS.

In August I began to write the first draft of the AIDS report. I wrote. And I rewrote. And I rewrote some more, usually in the evening at the stand-up desk in my basement. The next day Mike Samuels and I would spend two or three hours going over a few pages word by word. Sometimes Betty gave me advice. About the time I had written the fifteenth draft, Jim Dickson suggested that we get additional female perspectives, so I shared the manuscript with his wife, my wife, and Assistant Secretary of Health Bob Windom's wife. They made a few suggestions, which we included.

After the sixteenth draft I asked Tony Fauci, chief AIDS researcher at NIH, to read it, and he made some excellent suggestions. A few days later, on September 19, I completed the seventeenth draft, and Mike Samuels took it to the Government Printing Office. My next step would be to present the report before the Domestic Policy Council.

Knowing the way some on the Domestic Policy Council thought, I could see them nitpicking the report to pieces, but I also knew they did not like to spend money. So I decided to take a psychological gamble. It had been our plan to print this report as a thirty-six-page brochure on cheap paper. We would print 2 million copies—enough, we thought, to cover any requests we might get. (Ultimately, we needed over 20 million to fill the demand.) But I also ordered 1000 copies printed on the best-quality glossy stock, with a cover in the royal blue of the Public Health Service, its seal printed in shining silver, and across the top the title: *The Surgeon General's Report on Acquired Immune Deficiency Syndrome.* I figured that if the Domestic Policy Council was handed a pamphlet shrieking expensive paper and printing, they might be disinclined to make changes because of the cost of reprinting. I think it worked.

As I went to the Domestic Policy Council meeting I was a little nervous, but confident it would go smoothly. I think my first remark took them by surprise. "From what I read in the newspapers, this room has great leaks in it, and I would be very unhappy if this report were to reach the press before it was released by me. Therefore, I am handing out numbered copies, and I hope you will not be insulted if I tell you that I expect to collect each of them at the close of this meeting." A few eyebrows went up.

The report covered signs and symptoms, groups at risk, methods of transmission, and prevention. I reviewed the report page by page but in a rather superficial manner. There was little discussion. The meeting adjourned with the consensus that I would present the report soon at a press conference. I heaved a sigh of relief and drove home more relaxed than I had been in months. I knew some controversy might lie ahead, but I did not know how much.

AT LONG last, on October 22, 1986, I called a press conference to release the AIDS report. The report was brief enough for the reporters to read for themselves. Its main points were clear. I reviewed them, answered questions, said good-bye, and hopped a plane for London, where I had scheduled several speeches, not realizing what a stir I was leaving behind. The press conference television lights had barely been switched off when I was accused of advocating the teaching of sodomy to third graders and passing out condoms to eight-year-olds—words that never crossed my lips. Someone had asked me a question, one of the less important questions of the day, about at what age I thought sex education should begin. I simply said, "Sex education should begin at the earliest age possible." When I was asked to be more specific, I replied, "The third grade." This one comment would unleash a fire storm that would be continually reignited by shrill self-appointed protectors of the public morality, such as Phyllis Schlafly.

Sex education has become such a buzzword and red flag that I often refer instead to human development. But sex education is important to talk about—without buzzwords, red flags, and jargon. Sex education should begin with the child's first question on sex. Until the age of about six, children usually have only two questions: "Where did I come from?" and "Why do I look different from my brother [or sister]?" From the age of six to nine, youngsters generally ask few questions about sex. This lulls their parents into the mistaken belief that their children do not need sex education, and therefore none is given. Parents need to recognize that in our society, children receive constant sex education from siblings, friends, advertisements, and, most of all, television. When children once again begin to ask questions—about age nine—the sophistication of the queries is often embarrassing to parents, who usually give fuzzy or incomplete replies, inadvertently turning their children back to television, movies, and older kids for advanced sex education.

I firmly believe that if parents accepted their responsibilities in sex education, if they worked with their schools, churches, and civic associations, then sex education curricula would teach kind, loving, considerate, and caring relationships in a family context. We might be able to turn out a generation of teenagers less sexually active—and less at risk—than the present one.

I RETURNED from Great Britain to find that the White House was out to do battle with me. Of course, that was not true. The White House is a building. It does not do battle. It does not even make telephone calls. But some people who work there pretend that it does. They telephone the small and the great—"This is the White House calling"—and suddenly knees tremble, machinery stops, and plans are changed. The chief White House resident, the President, does not know how often he is misrepresented by those with White House stationery and telephones.

I don't know who in the White House started the campaign against the AIDS report and me. I know that by using the word condom, I offended Roman Catholics, such as White House aide Carl Anderson, my former political mentor who now worked there. At any rate, my staff informed me that they had been told by the "White House" that printing the AIDS report would have to be "delayed" until "corrections" were made in it. The only correction they sought was to remove the reference to condoms. I refused.

Eventually the presses rolled, the mail trucks ran, and the report went out. The report was sent to anyone who requested it. Congressmen sent it to their constituents, as did many of the groups that had counseled my AIDS staff. At last the American people knew what was myth and what was fact about the AIDS epidemic, and they knew it in plain English. But they wanted to hear more, and I found myself deluged by requests to speak at various meetings and conventions.

At first I did not realize what impact the report would have on the public. Suddenly I found myself praised by my former liberal adversaries and condemned by my former conservative allies. Everybody, or at least those who did not know me, said that I had changed. Conservatives said I had changed, and they were angry. Liberals said I had changed, and they were pleased. But I had not changed at all. All the fuss surprised me. I just did what I had always done as a doctor. My whole career had been dedicated to prolonging lives, especially the lives of people who were weak and powerless, the disfranchised who needed an advocate: newborns who needed surgery, handicapped children, unborn children, people with AIDS.

Suddenly, when I had more to do than ever, I was sidelined by injury. My neck, broken in that spectacular ski-jumping crash at Dartmouth fifty-one years before, had served me pretty well until I awoke in the middle of a November night in Texas unable to move either arm, barely able to wiggle my toes. For a frightening twenty-four hours I thought that I might have become quadriplegic. I had gone to San Antonio to accept the presidency of the Association of Military Surgeons of the United States, and for some reason, while relaxing on a patio for a few minutes, I broke out in a case of hives. Perhaps I had been stung by an insect. Later I figured out that the Benadryl that I took to relieve the hives had put me into a very deep sleep, and my head had rolled off the pillow with my neck bent in such a way that my anterior spinal artery was compressed in my spinal canal, causing the paralysis. It was a frightening experience, and although I regained all of my neurologic function, I willingly underwent spinal surgery to make sure it did not happen again. But it kept me home from work almost every day from early November until early January.

The weeks of postoperative recovery gave me the period of reflection and contemplation I needed. I saw three major challenges ahead of me as far as AIDS was concerned.

First, I needed to capitalize on my new alliance with the moderates and liberals to continue to get the message on AIDS to each American citizen. The report was the first step, to be followed by more speeches than I could count and eventually an AIDS mailer, sent to 107 million American households.

Second, I had to do what I could to align the White House properly in the fight against AIDS. That meant getting around my sniping adversaries to prompt the President to follow his natural instincts of fairness, compassion, and leadership. If I did not succeed, it was not for lack of trying.

Finally, I wanted to mend fences where possible with my critics on the right. I soon realized that it was not worth my time to talk with vitriolic critics, like Schlafly, on the political right, because they had long since stopped listening. But I held out hope that I could reason with the religious right, people with whom I shared the deepest beliefs and values. As I recuperated from my neck surgery I decided to do something that probably no other government official had ever done: spend seven weeks speaking only to religious groups.

When I explained my plan to Jerry Falwell, he immediately invited me to speak in his church, to be televised over a broad network, and at chapel service at his Liberty University, in Lynchburg, Virginia. My speechwriter, Ted Cron, and I spent hours on my address, and then Mike Samuels, Betty, and I went over every word once we arrived in Lynchburg. In morning church service I gave my personal Christian testimony and then spoke briefly about the challenge of AIDS. In the evening I gave my speech, which I repeated again the next day to more than five thousand students at the university. I made similar use of a speaking invitation from the National Association of Religious Broadcasters and gave radio interviews on religious networks. In general, I think my efforts with the religious right were productive. All of us would have preferred not to need to deal with AIDS. But we could agree on the role of Christian compassion in a secular world.

The opposition in the White House would be thornier. I thought the best way to deal with their unrelenting opposition was for all of us to get together and talk through the issues. My convalescence from surgery made that difficult, but one day I was driven to the White House, where I discussed AIDS and sex education with White House aides, including Carl Anderson and Gary Bauer. At this time I think it was sex education that rankled most with Bauer. He was hostile, and Anderson seemed sullen. It was the first of many meetings that left me dismayed.

By then I knew that many people around the country thought the President should be out in front on AIDS, offering the leadership that only he could provide. At least a dozen times I had pleaded with my critics in the White House to set up a meeting between the President and me. And for months I had tried to cover for the embarrassing silence of the Oval Office on the scourge of AIDS. I kept telling myself the President had to speak out soon. As the nation awaited Reagan's penultimate State of the Union address, I was informed that at last he would speak boldly on AIDS. Hopeful and attentive, I tuned in. Reagan covered everything from Afghanistan to defense, but offered not a word about AIDS, as great a threat to the American people as anything on the horizon.

After I returned from a trip to California, I called Gary Bauer to tell him that the West Coast press had intensified its charges that the President was failing the country by his silence on AIDS. Bauer lashed out, saying that Reagan had decided to move further away from me on issues like sex education and condoms. He said the President wanted to say only one thing about AIDS: the nation was facing the problem of AIDS simply because it had abandoned traditional morality, and it would not get out of the situation until we returned to that morality. I said that while I and many Americans might agree with that assessment, the country was not going to accept that as the President's way of addressing a national health threat.

Finally, on April 1, 1987, the President mentioned AIDS for the first time in public, touching on the epidemic briefly and superficially in his speech at the Philadelphia College of Physicians. Striding by a number of reporters shouting questions about AIDS as he went up the ramp to Air Force One, he turned on the top step and said, "Just Say No." That night, NBC anchorman Tom Brokaw reported that the President had not even read *The Surgeon General's Report on Acquired Immune Deficiency Syndrome.*

Congress was way ahead of the White House in meeting the challenge of AIDS, and I suddenly found myself the hero of those Democrats who had most strongly opposed my nomination as Surgeon General. And since the Democrats had regained control of the Senate, my new alliance allowed us to accomplish a lot in a hurry. When Assistant Secretary of Health Bob Windom and I were called to testify before the Senate Committee on Labor and Human Resources, someone tapped me on the shoulder just before the session was called to order. It was Senator Ted Kennedy, who said, "I want to tell you how pleased I am with the leadership role you have taken as Surgeon General in the Public Health Service. We're all very proud of you."

As he smiled and started to walk away, I replied, "Senator, the first thing you said to me when I came to Washington was that you and I could do a lot for health together in this town. Now that you're back in the saddle, let's do it." Senators Lowell Weicker and Howard Metzenbaum, both of whom had voted against my confirmation, were embarrassingly effusive at the hearing about my conduct of the office of Surgeon General—very gratifying words, even if four years later.

I enjoyed a similarly warm reception from the House committee dealing with health, another group that had pilloried me a few years earlier. Chairman Henry Waxman and I had long since smoked the peace pipe—figuratively speaking, of course—because of our joint efforts against smoking. When I was under attack for the report on AIDS, Waxman went on television to say he had been wrong about me: "Dr. Koop is a man of great integrity." I was deeply touched.

But while I had come to like Henry, I did not like what I had to say before his committee. The main subject of one of his committee hearings was condom advertising on television. It was difficult for an old-timer of seventy, about to celebrate his fiftieth wedding anniversary, to talk about condoms. Almost everywhere I spoke, there seemed to be the obligatory condom joke. The most oft told, and a reflection of the times, was about Tommy and his little brother, who were playing outside on the patio. The younger boy ran inside to tell his parent, "Tommy says he found a condom on the patio. What's a patio?" But as people chuckled, I found myself deeply saddened by what had happened to America's sexual morality and by the associated grim epidemic.

I was concerned because the preoccupation with condoms obscured my message. I never mentioned the use of condoms as a preventive measure against AIDS without *first* stressing the much better and much safer alternatives of *abstinence* and *monogamy*. Often I would spend several minutes of a speech extolling abstinence and monogamy, and then at the end I would say that those foolish enough not to practice abstinence or mutually faithful monogamy should, for their protection and their partner's protection, use a latex condom. Usually the press would repeat only the last phrase. That annoyed me.

But in general I must commend the press for the way they conveyed the message on AIDS to the American people. We were making progress. There was still too much ignorance, too much fear, too much prejudice, but the American people were learning about AIDS. I felt I was doing all I could. But for all we had accomplished, one issue loomed large, an issue that would dictate the course of the American response to AIDS and shape official AIDS policy: testing.

At first it made sense to many people. With a killer disease on the loose, just test everybody to see who has it. But a little more thought on the issue revealed the shortcomings of that simplistic solution. First, what would you do with those who tested positive? Of course, I had already heard from those Congressmen and others who wanted to get rid of those with the AIDS virus or put them into concentration camps. And there was that little issue of the Constitution, which did not allow you to round up people because they were ill. AIDS became an issue not only of health but also of civil rights. Widespread AIDS testing could result only in widespread discrimination against people who tested positive. Already the American people, at least those Americans with a sense of justice and compassion, were horrified by the story of Ryan White, the schoolboy who had contracted AIDS from a blood transfusion. Picketed by schoolmates' parents, shunned by his classmates, he had been driven by fear and hatred from his school and town in Indiana.

Although health officials continued to stress the importance of *voluntary* and *confidential* testing for AIDS, we opposed mandatory testing. Millions of Americans concerned about civil rights and basic liberties recoiled from what could happen to people who tested positive for AIDS, even those who had not yet displayed any symptoms. They could lose their jobs, their homes, their insurance, their families. And all these calamities could also befall the small percentage who would register a false positive because of inaccuracies inherent in the test itself. Above all, mandatory AIDS testing would drive underground the very AIDS-infected people who needed help. Driven underground, these people would only continue to spread the disease.

The most important ten days in the politics of AIDS began on May 21, 1987. Two events loomed on the horizon, and the President was going to have to make a clear policy statement on AIDS. He was slated to make a speech at the American Medical Foundation for AIDS Research (AMFAR) gala, featuring Elizabeth Taylor, at which I was to be honored. Ten days later Washington would host the annual International Congress on AIDS, and the administration could not pretend that the congress and the disease did not exist. So when I received a call from Landon Parvin, Nancy Reagan's speechwriter, I figured he might be preparing the President's speech. I took the opportunity to fill his ear for a half hour, giving him some anecdotes for Reagan to use, hoping to make it clear that the President and I were not of different minds on AIDS.

A couple of days later, when I was speaking after dinner in Salt Lake City, I received a summons to a Domestic Policy Council meeting at 2:00 p.m. the next day. On almost no sleep, I zipped to the airport early in the morning, jetted to Dulles, and then ducked out the back of the plane and into a waiting van, which took me to a car that sped into Washington. I reached the southwest gate of the White House at exactly 2:00 p.m., was recognized by the guard, and hurried to the Roosevelt Room. Gary Bauer, who ran the meeting, went over a number of options regarding AIDS, including mandatory testing.

Then I had the chance to make my points. First, I said, we should refer to testing as targeted, not mandatory, to avoid the authoritarian overtones. I went on to discuss the disruptive impact on families and communities of false-positive tests for AIDS. I felt that I was heard, and heeded.

But there was still one big hurdle. At last there would be a full Cabinet meeting devoted primarily to AIDS. As far as I knew, it would determine the Reagan administration's future plans on AIDS. The few of us from the Department of Health and Human Services who were invited sat around before the meeting nervously planning our strategy. Then Secretary Bowen arrived, apparently happy with the advance draft of Reagan's speech for the AMFAR gala. It made us all breathe a little easier. The President was going to follow the path marked by health officers, not by political advisers in the White House. The speech included almost every one of the ideas I had discussed with speechwriter Parvin. But I knew it could all change if the discussion in the Cabinet went the wrong way.

The President came in, took his place at the table, flanked by Cabinet members, told a joke, and proceeded to a discussion of AIDS. It turned out I had the best seat in the house, in the row of chairs one removed from the table but directly opposite the President. By looking between the heads of the two men just in front of me, I had eye-to-eye contact with the President. Unobtrusively I pushed my chair back about six inches, so I was slightly behind the two men seated on either side of me. No one could see my face easily except the President.

The discussions covered the gamut of AIDS questions, ranging from mandatory testing to discrimination to segregation of HIV-positive prisoners to the testing of aliens and those applying for immigration. Whenever the President had a query that I wanted to answer or whenever a Cabinet member made a statement that I wanted to reinforce or rebut, I raised my right index finger beside my nose and almost imperceptibly nodded toward the President. It was like silent bidding at an auction. Reagan acknowledged me on each occasion, saying something like "I'd like to hear from Dr. Koop on that" or "Would you care to comment on that, Dr. Koop?" That system worked eight times; there were no misses. And Reagan ended up espousing the precepts of the Public Health Service on AIDS. The integrity of the AMFAR speech was preserved.

The next evening, at the AMFAR gala, held along the Potomac in a sweltering tent, Reagan's excellent speech—the key sentence was that we would *offer* routine testing—laid to rest the danger of mandatory testing and kept the federal government off the wrong road on AIDS. I was so pleased that I barely noticed the picketers, who were shouting obscenities as they milled around carrying placards: QUARANTINE MANHATTAN ISLAND, BURN KOOP, and other encouraging messages.

For me the rest of 1987, as jottings from my appointment ledger indicate, was an AIDS kaleidoscope: Went on ABC with Tim Johnson to discuss AIDS. . . . Operating surgeons were getting stuck by needles contaminated with the blood of HIV-positive patients. . . . Met with Howard Baker (then White House chief of staff) concerning the composition of the Presidential Commission on AIDS. . . . Had lunch with George Bush to discuss his concerns about AIDS. . . . Went with President Reagan and the new members of the AIDS Commission to NIH, where the President and I, alone in an anteroom for security reasons, discussed AIDS briefly but long enough to have a good conversation. . . . An increase in heterosexual transmission reported in Puerto Rico. . . . Taped a good Public Broadcasting System show on AIDS with Susan Dey of *L.A. Law.* . . . Had supper at the Bush residence and chatted with the Vice President and his wife about the epidemic. . . . In London, Edinburgh, and Glasgow to investigate IV drug abusers' needle exchange programs. . . . In Tokyo discussing "ethics, culture, and morals" in reference to AIDS. . . . Spoke with 365 CEOs from *Fortune* 1000 gathered for a symposium on AIDS at the Work Site. . . . Spoke at the U.N. General Assembly in New York on AIDS and its global challenge. . . . Testified before the House on pediatric AIDS. . . . The Washington *Post* reported that the Conference of Catholic Bishops granted a qualified acceptance of condoms with the publication of *The Many Faces of AIDS.*

THE AIDS report had done its job: it had made accurate information on AIDS available to the American people. But for all its accuracy and simplicity, the report had been distributed very unevenly. So the Public Health Service decided we should send each American household a letter about AIDS. As the number of AIDS cases continued to climb, my repeated calls for action finally got action. I think Congress was embarrassed, so it seized the initiative from the White House, appropriating $20 million for an AIDS mailer. The six-page mailer, *Understanding AIDS: A Message from the Surgeon General,* told the story of

AIDS like it is. It was all set to go by May 1988. It had the largest print order in American history: 107,000,000 copies.

There were the usual critics. One man wanted to prosecute me for mailing obscene material. And there were the usual cartoons and jokes about the explicit text. But AIDS is not a joking matter, and since surveys indicated a clear increase in public knowledge of AIDS following the mailer, I can only conclude that it did what we intended: it saved lives that would otherwise have been lost.

By December 30, 1988, the Centers for Disease Control had received reports of a cumulative total of 82,764 AIDS cases in the United States; 81,418 of these were adults and adolescents, with children under the age of thirteen accounting for the remaining 1346 AIDS cases. During the same period 45,602 adults and adolescents and 742 children had died of AIDS.

The epidemic has continued to grow, claiming more victims each month. AIDS will infect 390,000 to 480,000 Americans by the end of 1993, and 285,000 to 340,000 will have died of it. In the beginning AIDS was a remote threat, and many Americans had little sympathy for the homosexuals and intravenous drug abusers who made up the majority of persons with AIDS, feeling that somehow they deserved their illness. We know better now. AIDS claims all kinds of people. Before long, most Americans will know someone, love someone dying of AIDS. More than ever, we are fighting a disease, not people.

I fear the effect of AIDS upon the healthcare system in our country, especially upon the millions of Americans who exist, often with illness, outside the traditional system of healthcare provision. For the last year of my tenure as Surgeon General, and very forcefully and repeatedly since then, I have called for a thorough overhaul of our dysfunctional healthcare system, how it provides care (or doesn't provide it), how it is insured (or isn't). I am deeply concerned about the lack of national planning to deal with the impact of AIDS on a healthcare system already overburdened and under attack. It could be the straw that breaks the back of America's chaotic healthcare delivery system.

Americans are still afraid of AIDS. They fear this still mysterious disease. They fear its mortality rate, which is virtually 100 percent. They fear the stigma of the disease, of what other people will conclude about their behavior. They fear the consequences of that stigma, which can be loss of a job or housing, expulsion from school, or denial of certain necessary health or social services.

A common response to fear is denial. I am concerned about a growing tendency to deny the AIDS problem. This epidemic is reaching deeper and more broadly into our society every day. And globally, we have seen but the tip of the iceberg. Yet I see a dangerous complacency developing toward a problem many people think is old news. The scope of the problem, which is growing larger all the time, is appreciated less and less.

Soon it will be impossible to deny the statistics: AIDS is becoming one of the top ten leading causes of death in the United States. People may begin to resist paying the cost of caring for AIDS patients, a cost that by the end of the century will run into the billions. This disease, therefore, may force on us one of the most serious tests of social and political will that our society has ever undergone. It may be difficult to come through such a test and still preserve our institutions and our ideals.

CHAPTER 10
Baby Doe and the Rights of Handicapped Children

ON APRIL 9, 1982, the birth of an infant in Bloomington, Indiana, precipitated a controversy that is perhaps less well understood than smoking or AIDS but that touches the lives of millions. At 8:19 p.m. Dr. Walter Owens, an obstetrician, delivered a baby boy. The infant was blue and was further diagnosed as having Down syndrome. It is not certain whether the child suffered the heart defect that occurs in 40 percent of babies with this condition. He also had esophageal atresia with tracheoesophageal fistula.

Baby Doe, as he would forever be known, became a symbol not only of children with birth defects but also of all handicapped infants. From the plight of this single infant sprang a national awareness of the rights of damaged children and a bitter controversy over the government's right to intervene in the private lives of families. And these issues collided in the office of the Surgeon General.

As Surgeon General, I felt compassion for every patient with whom

I dealt, but I could always separate myself emotionally from the issues themselves. The case of Baby Doe was different. Having devoted my career to saving the lives of hundreds of such infants, I could not remain detached.

Baby Doe was a story of failure. The system certainly failed Baby Doe. And the system—the legal system, the medical system, the government—failed to live up to its responsibilities and standards. And yet, after it was all over, I think we accomplished something for America's future Baby Does.

According to press accounts, Dr. Owens told the parents in Bloomington that the child would be severely retarded, was a "blob," and that the chances of his surviving surgery to correct the obstruction of the esophagus were only 50 percent. In sharp opposition, Dr. James Schaeffer, the pediatrician, and Dr. Paul Windsler, the parents' family practitioner, both thought the baby should undergo surgery, and wanted Baby Doe to be referred to the Riley Hospital for Children in Indianapolis for lifesaving treatment. Dr. Owens, the obstetrician, advised the family to refuse consent for surgery, and predicted that the baby would die of pneumonia in a few days. Such a prophecy was not difficult to make. Pneumonia is a very early complication of untreated esophageal atresia. The baby cannot swallow his own secretions from the nose and throat because of the obstruction in the esophagus and therefore inhales or aspirates those alien secretions into his lungs, causing pneumonia.

According to press accounts, our sole source of information, at 9:30 p.m., an hour and a quarter after the birth, the parents of Baby Doe took time to talk it over. By 10:00 p.m., after only a half hour of discussion, they decided, "We don't want the baby treated."

The pediatrician, Dr. Schaeffer, asked, "Do you realize what you are doing?" The family acknowledged that they did.

Dr. Owens said, "You have made a wise and courageous decision."

Dr. Schaeffer then called the Riley Hospital for Children in Indianapolis and made Dr. Owens talk with a pediatric surgeon. The press reported that the surgeon termed Owens' decision not to recommend that Baby Doe be operated on as "infanticide."

On Saturday morning, April 10, Dr. Owens wrote orders for Baby Doe, a task usually expected of the pediatrician or family practitioner. Dr. Owens told the nurses that it was all right to feed the baby, even though feeding him might cause him to choke and die. He ordered the nurses not to administer any intravenous fluids to the baby and to keep him comfortable with sedation. It was clear that all three of these orders could only hasten the infant's death.

Since he could not be fed orally, Baby Doe would need intravenous feedings to stay hydrated and receive the necessary nutrients. Furthermore, Baby Doe was not uncomfortable and required no sedation; indeed, sedation could only diminish the natural reflexes he could muster as a defense against the threat of aspiration.

The hospital administrator pleaded with the family to take the baby home, but they refused. The hospital's attorney asked for a judicial hearing, and Superior Court Judge John Baker complied, with a bedside hearing. In his startling ruling the judge said that as there were two medical opinions, the parents could choose either one. In other words, he would permit the child to die.

Baby Doe was being cared for in the newborn intensive care unit. On Sunday the nurses revolted against carrying out the obstetrician's instructions. As a result, Baby Doe was transferred to a private room, where he was cared for by private-duty nurses, if you can call what he got care.

The agencies that society charges with the responsibility of looking after defenseless children were either unable or unwilling to go to the aid of Baby Doe. The Monroe County Child Protection Committee— set up to prevent child abuse and appointed Baby Doe's guardian ad litem by Judge Baker—found no fault with the judge's decision. On Monday, April 12, using a different approach, three attorneys—Barry Brown, Lawrence Brodeur, and Phillip Hill—sought to declare Baby Doe a neglected child under the Indiana CHINS statute (Child in Need of Services), but an acting judge, Thomas Spencer, ruled that there had been no violation of the statute.

By this time Baby Doe was weak, parched, and spitting blood. At 11:00 p.m. that Monday, attorney Phillip Hill sought a court order so that the child could receive intravenous fluids. This was refused, as was a petition for adoption on April 13. Baby Doe was very much a wanted child. His parents may not have wanted him, but there were several couples who were trying to adopt the dying youngster.

Meanwhile, attorneys Brodeur and Hill appealed Judge Baker's decision to the Indiana Supreme Court. Although the Indiana Supreme Court did not review the substance of his decision, the court ruled that Judge Baker had acted appropriately.

On Thursday, April 15, Lawrence Brodeur flew to Washington to file an appeal with the United States Supreme Court. Back in Bloomington, the staff at the hospital was in an uproar. The chief of staff ordered the pediatrician, Dr. Schaeffer, to start an IV to give Baby Doe the fluids he needed. This resulted in an altercation with the obstetrician, Dr. Owens.

At 10:01 p.m. on April 15, 1982, Baby Doe died.

Even after most of the dust had settled, some of us in government were not in complete agreement as to what had really happened, what it all meant, and what we had to do next. Most Americans felt the same way. From the very beginning the Baby Doe issue had at least two sides to almost every question raised—two sides as to *what* the treatment should be, *who* should make such decisions, *how* decisions should be made, and *which* procedures should be followed when there was no consensus. Except for that first bedside hearing, in Judge Baker's court, the *substance* of the Baby Doe issue had never been thoroughly adjudicated in Indiana, in Washington, in New York—or anywhere.

Above all, it is important to remember that medical opinion at Baby Doe's hospital had been divided. Although the obstetrician's diagnosis of Down syndrome was not contested, his diagnosis of severe retardation and his assessment that Baby Doe had only a 50 percent chance of surviving the operation to repair the atresia of the esophagus raised sharp disagreement. While it is true that surgery to repair esophageal atresia in a newborn can be tricky, it is also true that at the time Baby Doe was born, the success rate for such surgery was high.

There was a touch of irony in the situation. After all, as the Surgeon General called into the Baby Doe crisis, I had been among the first pediatric surgeons to perform corrective surgery for esophageal atresia. My colleagues and I had performed about 475 such procedures in thirty-five years, with an ever improving success rate. As early as the '50s, we were reporting a success rate better than that predicted by Dr. Owens. In my last eight years of active practice I never lost a full-term baby upon whom I operated to correct esophageal atresia; for premature infants the survival rate was 88 percent. So Dr. Owens' advice to the parents of Baby Doe was dead wrong.

Equally open to question was the obstetrician's prediction of Baby Doe's quality of life, whatever that may mean. There is simply no way that a physician can predict with any accuracy just what the quality of life will be for a child born with Down syndrome. The child's retardation can range from mild to severe, and his quality of life is intimately affected by his family, the response of the community, and the kind and degree of medical and health services available to him.

Some people in Bloomington, as well as some of us in Washington, thought that Baby Doe's parents had not been given totally accurate, unbiased information about the condition of their new baby boy. In addition, we cannot discount the role played by the semantic fog. Words can be used to blur as well as to clarify. It is much easier to talk about withholding fluids and nutrition from a handicapped or deformed child than to use the term that describes it more accurately: starvation.

It was not until after Baby Doe had died that the government became officially involved in the controversy. And I became involved only reluctantly. My years in surgery had made me all too familiar with the wrenching discussions associated with the diagnosis and prognosis of infants such as Baby Doe. I was barraged with requests from the press and physicians around the country to do some long-distance hypothesizing about Baby Doe's chances, but I refused. I believed then—and I grew to believe it more intensely later—that those kinds of questions can be answered best by the people who are right there on the scene *if* they think clearly and *if* they act responsibly. Furthermore, we in the government were handicapped all through the Baby Doe crisis by inadequate information. The medical records were sealed by the courts, cutting us off from pertinent information.

When Baby Doe died a week after birth, the death certificate indicated "multiple congenital birth defects." But what did this mean? Were Down syndrome and esophageal atresia, the two defects discussed publicly, the only ones? Or were there others? Did Baby Doe have an uncorrectable heart defect? The mortality rate for such a condition can be very high. In any case, during Baby Doe's brief life the public was denied this vital information. We did not have it then, and we still do not have it now.

The case reflected the double-edged sword of modern medicine—the ability of high-tech medicine to extend human life, for better or for worse. During the last twenty years the dramatic developments in medicine and surgery have made us accustomed to cures. Even though eventually we all must die of something, we have high expectations that medicine can cure most problems, especially problems of children and young adults. People become bewildered, frustrated, even angry when confronted by a condition that cannot be cured, such as Down syndrome.

Baby Doe touched that raw nerve. But American medicine and American ethics cannot use "no cure" as an excuse for "no care." We can offer an incurable patient something just as valuable—we can offer genuine care. Incurable patients still need us as people, even though as physicians we cannot do as much for them as we would like to. That is an important message, and it is a demanding message. It demands that we lay aside our medical texts and instead work through those questions, the answers to which are spun out of the depths of our consciences.

In my pediatric surgical practice I had come upon this kind of situation many times. Those experiences are engraved in my mind forever: a tragically disabled child; parents who were confused, angry, grieving; a divided medical staff. What then?

My considered judgment, worked out over some years, tells me that we ought to do things to give a person all the life to which he or she is entitled, but not to do anything that would lengthen that person's act of dying. And there is a real difference between the two. On the basis of what I could learn about Baby Doe, there seemed to be little doubt that the decision had been made not to give Baby Doe all the life that was his, but actually to accelerate the process of his dying. Once people became concerned about that, the legal system came into the issue.

Those who wished to defend Baby Doe attempted to do so under the laws designed to protect defenseless children. But Baby Doe did not fit neatly into the Indiana state law regarding child abuse and neglect. No one did anything violent to Baby Doe in the usual sense of violent child abuse, although the obstetrician's orders had a violent effect upon the infant's digestive and respiratory systems, so much so that if the same violence had been done to a "normal" baby, there would have been a demand to protect him and perhaps to punish the perpetrators.

Obviously, then, the central issue of the Baby Doe case was the little boy's handicap—Down syndrome. This is what drew the federal government into the case, because it seemed very clear that Baby Doe was a victim of discrimination.

If Baby Doe had been born with only Down syndrome, he would have been nourished and cared for. If he had been born with only esophageal atresia, he would have been operated on and cured. But because he had both Down syndrome and esophageal atresia, he was denied the operation that would have saved his life.

When President Reagan learned about the plight of Baby Doe, he instructed then HHS Secretary Richard Schweiker to make certain that such a thing never happened again. (Typically, his compassion went out to a single individual much more readily than to an issue in general.) What started out as an emotional response from the President turned into a morass of bureaucracy, regulations, and recriminations. HHS churned out one set of regulations and then another, which were successively challenged in the courts.

Eventually the argument centered on a federal regulation, section 504 of the Rehabilitation Act of 1973, which said, "No otherwise qualified handicapped individual shall, solely by reason of his handicap, be excluded from participation in, be denied the benefits of, or be subjected to discrimination under any program or activity receiving federal financial assistance." As a recipient of federal aid, Bloomington Hospital had to follow this federal law.

Baby Doe was not born into a vacuum. For several years ethicists, medicine, the law, and government had been groping toward the resolution of similar issues. Two years earlier, in March 1980, Philip Becker, a thirteen-year-old California boy with Down syndrome, made the headlines because his parents refused consent for the heart surgery he needed to save his life, and the United States Supreme Court refused to hear an appeal on the boy's behalf. The youngster survived only because he was adopted by another couple, who enabled him to have his heart surgery. But concern for what might have happened led to the nation's first conference on infanticide. No official conclusion came out of the conference, but a consensus grew that children born with handicaps must not be neglected.

When the Baby Doe case first hit the newspapers, a number of people claimed the government had no right to interfere in matters of parental responsibility. But of course, the right of government to supersede the rights of parents has been upheld in a number of areas: truancy laws, child abuse laws, immunization laws, and court orders mandating medical treatment for children whose parents attempt to use their religious convictions to deny such treatment.

I have never advocated life at any cost. There are times when the most reasonable action a physician can take is to step back and let nature take its course. But healers should never be killers. And the state has a legitimate role in protecting the life of an infant even if its parents disagree, because they find the situation too difficult to handle.

There is no constitutional definition of how old someone must be in order to receive the protection of the state. There is no minimum age requirement for citizenship. Baby Doe's life began with many tragic complications, but none of those handicaps put him outside the protection of the law. None of them relieved the state of its obligation to protect him. None of them permitted anyone to jeopardize further his health or his life. None of them.

I have always been surprised by the stance of most American liberals in the Baby Doe affair—that the government has no right to intervene in the parents' decision, even if it means death for a viable infant. Usually liberals have rushed to aid the disfranchised members of American society. But in the case of Baby Doe that same liberal faction moved against defenseless handicapped infants. If the country's Baby Does were thirty-five years old, they would have a national advocacy organization and a strong congressional lobby. Unfortunately, they are too small, too weak, and too poor.

Eventually Baby Doe and his successors moved from the realm of physicians and parents into the realm of journalists and politicians, and then into the realm of lawyers and bureaucrats. Three sets of regulations later, three judicial countermanding orders later, several lawsuits later, three Secretaries of Health and Human Services later, two years later . . . Congress, medicine, and the Department of Health and Human Services finally came together on the treatment of handicapped children. But getting there was not half the fun; getting there was bitter.

My position in all this was never very comfortable. First I was on the sidelines; then I was the lightning rod; then I, as a physician within the government, was caught in the middle. The government wanted to protect the lives of handicapped infants. The medical profession opposed government interference. After the complex and often rancorous bureaucratic maneuvering over the way the regulations were framed, finally the law would stand on the side of handicapped children.

The final push to a law, not regulations, stemmed from a ground swell of concern in Congress and in the public. Two episodes fueled the concern. The first, academically laundered but chilling enough, was the publication of an article in the journal *Pediatrics* about what was simply a euthanasia program for babies born with spina bifida. The article reported a program in Oklahoma City that used a mathematical formula to compute the "quality of life" of spina bifida patients to determine which would be allowed to die. Infants whose numbers did not add up right were starved to death.

This was then documented in a Cable News Network three-part television series by Carleton Sherwood, who had already produced a five-part series on Baby Doe. Sherwood's new series depicted the selection of infants at the Children's Hospital of Oklahoma City by the quality-of-life formula. If they did not "pass," they were transferred to an inadequate nursing home in an adjacent building, where their care was euthanasia, but not always by the most direct and painless means. Sherwood's film documented some infants dying of malnutrition, others of infection, some choking to death on feedings poured down their throats.

The Oklahoma tragedy finally got Congress moving, and on February 2, 1984, the U.S. House of Representatives passed legislation extending the definition of child abuse to include the denial of care and treatment to handicapped newborns. The legislation further required that procedures be adopted for reporting and investigating such medical neglect. After losing most of the battles, we had won the war. On October 9, 1984, the Baby Doe amendment became part of Public Law 98-475 when it was signed by President Reagan.

THE case of Baby Doe alerted the entire nation that handicapped newborns have rights. But ensuring that they receive the immediate treatment they require is but the first step in a lifelong commitment to the proper care of handicapped children.

Not all babies are born perfect. Many of the operations I had performed on infants corrected congenital defects that, if left uncorrected, would have cut short the baby's life. There were times, however, when we saved a precious life but ended up with a less-than-perfect child. Some would remain that way, handicapped for life.

Society terms such a result a tragedy, but that may be too harsh a judgment. It is society that transforms disabilities into handicaps, and often the people we too easily label as handicapped become superachievers. As I watched the heroic achievements of so many children with paralyzed lower extremities, I became convinced that Franklin D. Roosevelt probably became a remarkable leader because of his disability rather than in spite of it. Paul Sweeney, my most-operated-on patient—he underwent over fifty surgical procedures—overcame what many of us might call handicaps, and became president of his high school class and a college graduate. But as magnificent as their achievements might be, I realized there was much more we could do for handicapped children and their families to make them more independent.

When I first entered pediatric surgery, children who entered a hospital either were cured or died. Over the years we dramatically reduced the numbers of those who died, but we created a new category of survivor: children who did not go home, children who did not die, but who remained dependent on respirators or ventilators. As Surgeon General, I wanted to continue the efforts I had begun in my last years as a surgeon to move ventilator-dependent children out of hospitals and into their homes. This not only freed them from exposure to hospital infections but also restored them to their family, where they belong. And the financial savings were enormous.

In all my work for the handicapped, I wanted to involve President Reagan, because I truly believed it was an issue close to his heart. But I was continually frustrated by White House staffers, who kept him at arm's length. They seemed to live in a world of happy photo opportunities and did not want to associate the President with anything as "unappealing" as the plight of the handicapped. Once again it was a personal anecdote that finally got Reagan involved. He had heard about Katie Beckett, a youngster whose difficult problems would soon claim national attention.

Katie Beckett was a ventilator-dependent youngster who was being maintained by Medicaid in an institution far from her family's home in Cedar Rapids, Iowa. Her parents talked to Congressman Thomas J. Tauke, who got to Vice President Bush, who told the President, and then things began to move. Reagan sent instructions back down the chain, asking Secretary Schweiker to see that people like Katie Beckett obtained waivers so they could receive Medicaid support for respirator care in their homes. Medicaid had never paid for home care, even though the cost of home care was often a small fraction of that of hospital care. I became chairman of the Katie Beckett Board, which granted similar waivers to youngsters all over the country until Congress eventually made the waiver system into law.

Next I wanted to provide all the help possible to the two groups of people most concerned with handicapped children: parents and pediatricians. In this large, rich, diverse nation there are programs and self-help groups for every conceivable problem, but it is difficult, if not impossible, to keep abreast of what is out there. I cherished the hope that someday I might be able to provide instant, computerized service to physicians concerning the hows, whens, and wheres of repairing congenital defects, especially those that threaten life immediately after birth, and provide families with the support they so desperately need.

I was convinced that the Baby Doe story would have had a different ending if his pediatrician could have produced for the opposing obstetrician all there was to know about surgery and rehabilitation of the newborn's handicap. No physician can be expected to know everything about the latest breakthroughs for all problems presented in his practice. So I began to work with those who could set up a computer network to make the necessary information available. With funds supplied by the Division of Maternal and Child Health of the Public Health Service, we encouraged the University of South Carolina to proceed with the development of computerized access systems for both the profession and parents. By the time I left government, the network had spread to thirty-seven states.

FROM the Baby Doe saga, the first extended issue of my service as Surgeon General, I think we all had the opportunity to learn something. I hope Americans learned about the pernicious practice of infanticide, which had been growing unnoticed in hospital nurseries across the country. I hope Americans learned anew the value of a single human life, no matter how small, no matter how handicapped. I know I learned a lot from Baby Doe. I learned more about how the government works—and doesn't work. I learned even more about the limits of the law when it comes to medicine. And I also learned a lot about how to be Surgeon General. I realized that I was not only Baby Doe's Surgeon General, I was also Surgeon General for his parents and, like it or not, for those physicians in Bloomington.

I did not agree with Baby Doe's attending physicians, but I knew that there were many in the profession who did and that somehow I would have to reconcile with them as well—that is, if I really wanted to prevent the deaths of any more Baby Does. And I did. After a bitter struggle many people worked together to save the lives of other Baby Does and to give their families and their country more of what is needed to care for them.

CHAPTER 11
Abortion

FOR the first fifty years of my life, abortion was a word I rarely heard. And when people talked about abortion, they usually whispered. The American society in which I grew up and the American medical community I joined fifty years ago stood firmly against abortion. The consensus was clear: the fetus was an unborn child; abortion took a human life. Abortion was illegal because abortion was immoral. All that changed with dramatic speed. Future historians may puzzle over the rapidity with which a society system reversed itself on such a basic moral issue. Abortion has become not only a subject of everyday conversation and everyday practice but also the most divisive public issue in American history since slavery.

I have always been predisposed against abortion, but my professional position on the issue matured slowly. It crystallized for me one Saturday in 1976. My residents and I had spent the entire day operating on three newborn babies. Surgery on newborns is time consuming, and although we started at 8:00 a.m., we did not have the third youngster safely in his incubator until early evening. As the three of us sat in the cafeteria, I said to my two colleagues, "You know, we have given over two hundred years of life to three individuals who together barely weighed ten pounds."

One of my residents answered, "And while we were doing that, right next door in the university hospital they were cutting up perfectly formed babies of the same size just because their mothers didn't want them." I knew then that as a surgeon of the newborn, I had to do something about the slaughter of the unborn.

I rose early the next morning and began to write. By Monday evening I had completed *The Right to Live, The Right to Die,* setting down my concerns about abortion, infanticide, and euthanasia. The 120-page paperback, published by Tyndale, sold over one hundred thousand copies in its first year.

I began by tracing briefly my own pilgrimage on the issue. It always seemed clear to me that life begins at conception. After the twenty-three chromosomes of the sperm are united with the twenty-three chromosomes of the egg to become a one-celled living organism, that single cell requires nothing except nutrition to become a baby nine months later. For years I had maintained a firm opposition to abortion but had allowed room for it in certain "hard cases." But then a nurse spoke to me, affirming her belief that the hard cases were just as much in the sovereignty of God as any other event in our lives. Her statement, along with what I had been reading in the Bible about the sanctity of life, brought clarity to the issue. I found I could not justify abortion in any case except to save the life of the mother.

The issue had become clearer, but that did not make it easier. I realized that the decision to have an abortion—or not to have an abortion—could be agonizing and painful, and carry lifelong consequences. The real problem, of course, was that too many women have unwanted pregnancies, and making the decision to abort the child or carry it to term is an inadequate solution to a problem that could have been avoided.

My concerns, though, went beyond the issue of abortion. I became concerned about what abortion would do not only to unborn children but also to American medicine and American society. Abortion would bring along with it deadly consequences that, I felt, even those who favored abortion would not wish to see in our society. My immediate fear was that the 1973 *Roe* v. *Wade* Supreme Court decision, legalizing abortion and thereby denying any rights to the unborn child, would soon be extended to newborn children, especially those with handicaps. I did not think the court would rule directly on this issue. I thought instead that the denial of proper treatment to the handicapped newborn—infanticide—would follow abortion, but it would happen slowly, quietly, in the privacy of the neonatal units of our most respected hospitals. Sure enough, soon after abortion became commonplace, some physicians began to refer to a severely defective newborn—the kind I was able to operate on successfully—as a fetus *ex utero*.

I became convinced that the cheapening of newborn life was a result of the large number of abortions each year. After all, a newborn is more like a fetus in appearance and dependency in the first month after birth than it is like an older baby. Physicians know that the actual moment of birth changes but little in the condition of the baby. If abortion is allowed a few days before birth, how is that different from killing a few days after? Abortion, I saw, was leading to infanticide. And infanticide was euthanasia. What would keep it from extending to older people?

Six months after the 1973 Supreme Court decision that opened the way to abortion on demand, I gave the commencement address at Wheaton College in Illinois, predicting a dangerous domino effect of *Roe* v. *Wade* on life-and-death ethics and medicine in the United States. Many of my listeners, even those who agreed with me, thought I had gone too far out on a limb. I predicted that we would see a rapid increase in demands for mercy killing, demands not only by the patient but also by the family. I predicted a dramatic increase in the number of abortions, as many as 1 million each year. (They exceeded 1.22 million in 1990.) I cautioned that abortion would accelerate our changing sexual morality, with social and health consequences. And I warned that defective newborn infants would be the next to be declared without meaningful life. Within three or four years most of what I had foretold in *The Right to Live, The Right to Die* and in my commencement speech had occurred.

The next step in my involvement with abortion took me back to the past and, at the same time, forward to a new phase of my career. I was at York University in Toronto lecturing to a group of Canadian theologians on abortion, infanticide, and euthanasia. After the question-and-answer session a young man arose and said, "Do you know that

Francis Schaeffer is discussing these same issues at the other end of this campus? Why don't you two get together? He is talking in the abstract, and you have all the examples."

Francis Schaeffer was an old friend from my days as a newborn Christian. Francis and his wife, Edith, later ran a unique Christian ministry to intellectuals. Named L'Abri (the shelter), his home and adjoining campus in the Swiss Alps, above Lake Geneva, had become a refuge for disenchanted intellectuals, searching students, and any others drawn to his philosophical and artistic approach to the role of Christianity in twentieth-century culture. When the Schaeffers first moved to Switzerland, in the '50s, I had done what I could to arrange medical care for their children, especially their young son Frankie, a polio victim. Francis Schaeffer and I had been through a lot together, and he had become a strong friend, although our paths had not crossed for about fifteen years.

I walked across the York University campus to the auditorium where Francis was speaking and caught him just before he was about to begin his final lecture. He spotted me walking down the center aisle and leaned down from the platform so that we could embrace. I repeated what the student had said, and proposed that we get together on my next trip to Switzerland. Little did I realize that I had taken the first steps on the path to Washington, to the job of Surgeon General, and to the continuing controversy over abortion.

A few months later I drove my rented car up the steep, winding mountain road to the tiny village of Huemoz-sur-Ollon. As I walked up to the L'Abri auditorium an elegantly mustached young man standing at the door introduced himself to me as Frankie. I could hardly believe that my patient from long ago, the little boy whose foot had been so seriously hobbled by polio, had become a young man with barely a trace of his earlier disability. He said something rather cryptic. "If you can talk as well as you can write, I think there are some things we can do together."

After I addressed the students Frankie and I walked up the Alpine paths to the next village and then back to Huemoz, stopping briefly for hot chocolate at a roadside stand, discussing all the while the possibilities of doing something significant about the issues of abortion, infanticide, and euthanasia. Late that evening we sat in front of his fireplace and scribbled down the scenario for five motion pictures and the outline for a book, the entire project to be known as *Whatever Happened to the Human Race?* Together, the Schaeffers—father and son—and I determined to awaken the evangelical world, and anyone else who would listen, to the Christian imperative to do something to reverse the perilous realignment of American values on these life-and-death issues.

The entire project, including writing the book, filming the five movies, and holding seminars demanded most of my time for a year and a half. I continued to carry a full load at the hospital when I was there, but I referred the tough cases that required close and long-term follow-up to my colleagues.

We opened the first seminar in Philadelphia, in September 1979, at the Academy of Music, with films, lectures, and discussions spread over three days. In the next four months Schaeffer and I took the seminars to twenty cities in the United States, finishing in Nashville's Grand Ole Opry House, in mid-December, 1979. We also took an international swing, with seminars in Canada, the United Kingdom, Hong Kong, and Japan.

The book sold 50,000 copies, and thousands more people saw the films. About 45,000 people attended our seminars in the United States and abroad. I was reminded of their impact years later as I traveled around the nation and the world as Surgeon General. Many places I went, strangers would come up to me and start one of the three conversations that always delighted me: first, "Thank you for what you are doing for public health"; second, "You operated on me when I was two days old"; and third, "I never understood the sanctity of life until you made it clear in those seminars built around *Whatever Happened to the Human Race?*"

GRADUALLY I had become drawn into the organized pro-life movement. At that time the movement was largely Roman Catholic. Then, with Roman Catholic seed money, a Protestant evangelical pro-life organization was formed, calling itself the Christian Action Council. I was not, as is often reported, one of the founders of the council, but I was in on the organization from its earliest days.

I never unraveled the exact relationships among the various pro-life groups. And although we were allies in the struggle, I was disturbed by the activities of some of the people who shared my views. I found their strident tone and vindictive rhetoric offensive. I was even more disturbed by the lack of integrity and absence of scholarship in some pro-life publications.

Abortion poisoned my confirmation process, even though I had made clear to Secretary Schweiker that I had nothing more to say publicly on the subject. As the struggle over my confirmation revealed, either no one believed me or they wanted to take me to task for my earlier statements. My attempts to clear the air, to put the controversy to rest, accomplished little.

When the confirmation struggle was all over, I kept my promise to Schweiker not to use my post as a pro-life pulpit. But while I made no official pronouncements on abortion, I received over six hundred invitations a year to speak to pro-life and evangelical groups. When some people at Health and Human Services suggested that I automatically decline, I bristled. After all, these people formed a major part of the President's constituency, as well as my own, and I felt obliged to accept some of their invitations, even if I focused my remarks on issues other than the pro-life movement.

Meanwhile, the organized pro-life movement was getting restless. They had assumed that the election of pro-life Ronald Reagan would automatically lead to administration efforts to restrict abortion and to overturn *Roe* v. *Wade*. These people were long on symbolism and posturing but short on political savvy. They and others who had supported Reagan primarily for his social agenda—antiabortion, prayer in schools, and so on—were disappointed when he took no immediate action on these issues. Economic matters, defense, and foreign policy dominated Reagan's first term.

Okay, they thought, he's saving it for his second term. But even then the Oval Office did almost nothing on the abortion issue except make the usual gestures. Once, I was summoned on short notice to the White House to address a group of about thirty pro-life representatives. Since this was during the drawn-out Baby Doe controversy, I welcomed the opportunity to allay the concerns aired by many pro-lifers. Just as I was finishing, Ronald Reagan walked in and made a brief statement about his personal commitment to the protection of unborn children.

I was less than pleased with the conduct of some of the people in the pro-life group; their bizarre behavior was a foretaste of how they would

Above (left to right): Senator Orrin Hatch, Mrs. Koop,
HHS Secretary Richard Schweiker, and the new Surgeon General,
just before his formal swearing-in ceremony

Dr. and Mrs. Koop
in the fall of 1990

With all the grandchildren
in November 1988

inexplicably turn against me three years later. After the President's polite remarks pro-life zealot Nellie Gray berated the President for his inactivity in a manner that was abrasive, brash, and embarrassing to me and some others present. Increasingly I was dismayed by the politically self-defeating character of the pro-life movement.

It was AIDS that once again heated up the abortion controversy around me. It was all based on an awkwardly phrased sentence that the press scooped up and then ran away with. Ironically, I had been trying to clarify the growing national confusion about AIDS. At the end of March, 1987, I had the honor of addressing the National Press Club. Things started out smoothly. The audience seemed very attentive and receptive to my speech, in which I stressed the manner in which AIDS is transmitted and how it is not.

Afterwards I was asked whether a pregnant woman carrying the AIDS virus should have an abortion. I made it very clear that I would never recommend an abortion, because of my personal stand against it, but that a pregnant woman whose unborn child had a 50 percent chance of mortality because of AIDS, as we thought then (now it is as low as 30 percent), was entitled to consultation about abortion if she desired.

I answered the question too quickly. I wanted to make clear that although *Roe* v. *Wade* made abortion a legal option for any pregnant woman, it was an option that I believed, although legal, was wrong.

Betty heard my address on the radio and was very much concerned about the effect of my answer to the question. Sure enough, the next day newspaper headlines blared KOOP SUPPORTS ABORTION.

I became very upset as the news rippled across the country, its effects multiplied, as most press accounts distorted my answer. Predictably, I was taken to task by the far-right pro-lifers. The most blatant attacks came from the stridently conservative Washington *Times*. When I discussed it with Secretary of Health and Human Services Otis Bowen, he counseled, "Chick, look at it this way. Number one, they spelled your name right. Number two, you are getting a lot of publicity. Number three, it may give you the chance to make your position even clearer." I appreciated his attempts to cheer me up, but I realized that I faced a long uphill struggle to undo the damage. I never really did.

As a longtime Republican, I had often heard about knee-jerk liberals. It did not take long in Washington for me to see that conservative knees jerk as readily as liberal ones. The controversy over my remark at the National Press Club not only set some conservatives against me but also brought more liberals to my side. And the very fact that some liberals now cheered me on—correctly for my position on smoking and AIDS, incorrectly for abortion—made the conservative pro-lifers oppose me even more.

I decided to meet privately with some pro-life leaders and pro-life Congressmen. I gently, and sometimes firmly, remonstrated them for thinking that I could so readily abandon my commitment to the unborn, to the newborn, a commitment based upon both years of surgery and years of faith. I think some understood. Many simply chose not to. The public can be fickle.

MY LAST chapter in the abortion saga started when Reagan asked me to write a report on the health effects of abortion on women. Well, he didn't really ask me. He just made an offhand remark in a speech to some pro-life groups that he had asked the Surgeon General to prepare such a report.

It all began with a personnel squabble and a silly idea. The personnel squabble involved a pro-life appointee in HHS who was dismissed because of insubordination. Pro-life issues were not a factor in her dismissal, but the far right was miffed about the affair. It was clear to me that by calling for the abortion report, the President was seeking to mollify them. Reagan had also embraced a silly idea touted by one of the neophyte right-wingers on the White House staff that the evidence of adverse health effects—presumably mental—of abortion on women that the Surgeon General could pull together would be sufficient to overturn *Roe* v. *Wade.*

I did not like the political atmosphere in which this report was conceived. Abortion was more a moral issue than a medical issue. The pro-life movement had always focused—rightly, I thought—on the impact of abortion on the fetus. They lost their bearings when they approached the issue on the grounds of the health effects on the mother.

I also felt from the beginning that this was a no-win situation, that the scientific data that underlay the AIDS report would simply not be available for this one. The AIDS report has remained unassailable and correct in every word, even five years after I released it, because the science on which it was based was unimpeachable. The question of abortion and its health effects on the mother could not draw on the same kind of data and interpretation.

I intended to assume the same control of the report as I had done with AIDS. Assured of Otis Bowen's complete backing, I began to lay plans for the gathering of data. We had to make do with a tiny staff. For the AIDS report we had met with 26 groups, but as we planned the abortion report, 150 groups requested a hearing. It looked as if it would take thirty weeks just for the interviews.

There was much anecdotal information, but anecdotes do not make statistics. Most of the scientific papers had an experimental design that betrayed the author's own bias on abortion. On the first day of my interviews the polarization of positions was clearly evident as I met with a delegation from Planned Parenthood and then with a group from the National Right to Life Committee. A similar climate prevailed throughout the rest of the interviews.

So I met with White House aide Gary Bauer to explain that every bit of literature I had read on abortion reflected the sociological or moral bias of the authors. There was as much evidence of positive effects of abortion on women as negative. I told Bauer that a proper study would cost between $10 million and $100 million. Bauer said he wanted some time to think it over. He eventually got back to me, saying I had to go ahead with the report. A White House staffer told me, "The President never changes his mind."

But my commitment to good science made it clearer with each slanted interview I held, with each biased study I perused, that I could never write the kind of report originally envisioned. By autumn, after I had torn up seven drafts, I came to the conclusion that the only honest way to proceed was simply to write a letter to the President explaining why no current studies could reach a defensible conclusion, one way or the other, on the health effects of abortion on women. (Later, an American Psychological Association committee would confirm my assessment.)

I knew this would disappoint or even anger groups on both sides of the issue who wanted my report to fight their battle. But I had hoped to deal with the issue in as dispassionate an atmosphere as possible. That was not to be. Just as my staff and I were preparing the letter to the President, the Supreme Court announced its Webster decision, which put the right to an abortion more or less in the hands of individual states, thereby bringing the abortion issue to center stage in national and state politics.

Because of the volatile political implications, I did not want the President to be blindsided by the letter, and I also thought it important to inform President-elect Bush, since he would have to deal with the fallout. As Christmas, 1988, approached, I repeatedly attempted to reach John Sununu, Bush's newly selected chief of staff. No one returned my calls.

As Otis Bowen and I approached the White House late that cold, clear January afternoon eleven days before Reagan was to leave office, I had that now all-too-familiar feeling that I was walking a tightrope. Although I thought the matter of sufficient magnitude to warrant a meeting with the President or at least his chief of staff, Otis and I were met only by M. B. Oglesby and Nancy Risque of the White House staff. I handed Oglesby the letter, and then Otis and I explained it. Oglesby said that he would deliver my letter to the President and that he thought the President would be interested in my recommendations. He promised to hold it close. We left feeling elated that it had gone so smoothly.

When I got home, Betty told me that the TV networks, picking up on a distorted wire-service story, had announced that I had issued a report confirming that abortion produced no evidence of negative health effects on women. Of course, my letter to the President had said no such thing. At Betty's urging I spent the rest of the evening on damage control.

I reached Michael Spector at the Washington *Post* and then Marlene Cimons at the Los Angeles *Times;* each later correctly reported the incident. My most helpful call was to Dr. Tim Johnson of ABC, who promised to do what he could to get me on *Good Morning America.* The next morning I could not wait for the first questions from Charles Gibson and Joan Lunden. I welcomed the chance to set the record straight, and I think that in the few minutes of television time available to me I made it clear that I had not wavered at all in my personal pro-life stance, but that as Surgeon General, I had always attempted to separate science from my personal views. In the case of abortion the science was simply not conclusive either way.

No one in the administration responded to my letter to Reagan. The President himself, of course, said nothing. Not surprisingly, the pro-life movement railed against me. I was told that one pro-life leader had complained that I had buried the pro-life movement. If that was true, I thought, they must be in pretty bad shape. I reminded people of what I had said many times: the issue of abortion is not to be decided in terms of its effect upon the mother, but in terms of its effect upon the unborn child. The effect upon the mother is unclear; the effect upon the unborn child is clear—and fatal.

I tried responding to my critics, making it as clear as possible that my position against abortion had not changed at all, but that the issue had to be faced on moral, not medical, grounds. I had personally counseled women who were in deep depression because of the remorse and guilt they felt after an abortion. But I had also encountered women who said that their abortion had saved their marriage or job. The worst thing I could have done for the pro-life movement would have been to write a report that could have been scientifically torn apart.

I admit I have been stung by some of these personal attacks. I have been outraged to see my words distorted, my beliefs doubted, my integrity questioned in public. I believed, however, that no matter how my critics reacted, I had done the right thing.

BY THE time I left the office of Surgeon General, I had become convinced that both sides in the abortion debate had reached a dead end. Webster might move the site of the debate to the states, but it would not alter the issues, nor would it lessen the acrimony. Nor, did I think, would it allow a solution, one way or the other.

I saw two possible resolutions of the abortion issue, each at extreme ends of the spectrum. Far away, but not outside the realm of possibility, lay progress in prenatal care that would allow a fetus to live and develop outside the uterus from the earliest weeks of its life. This would allow abortion without the death of the fetus. It would allow children conceived but unwanted by their natural parents to be brought to term artificially and then raised by adoptive parents desperately seeking children. Although enormous technical and ethical problems loom in this, it would offer a choice that our society might have to face before long. And it would bring into sharp focus the question of whether an abortion means the termination of pregnancy or the destruction of the child-to-be.

At the other end of the realm of possibilities lay the greater likelihood of widespread use of abortifacient drugs, such as RU486. This would have the effect of removing abortion from the public arena, although not from the ethical arena. Abortion would become nothing but an issue between a woman and her pharmacist, beyond the reach of a society concerned about the fate of the fetus. We will need truth in advertising, however, so that the public understands that RU486 is an abortifacient, *not* a contraceptive. At present, we have no idea of the long-term effects of repeated use of this drug.

For the time being it seems that the standoff will continue. The rhetoric comes straight from the days of World War II. Both sides— pro-life, proabortion—are fond of using terms like battleground, combat, and war. They care simply about winning—winning each court case, each legislative battle, each electoral contest. I wonder if each side has not forgotten the human element that prompted the debate: the innocent unborn child, the agonized pregnant woman.

Many of those who have been opposed to abortion have been notoriously unhelpful to unwed pregnant women. Some religious schools and colleges expel a young woman who becomes pregnant, just when she needs all the support she can get to carry her child. Antiabortion people must be more forthcoming with their time and money to assist pregnant women in hardship. Antiabortionists cannot simply rail against abortion; they must press for whatever legal, social, and economic changes are necessary to make childbearing equitable and fair. They should be willing to do anything they can to bring conceived children to birth.

And those who call themselves pro-choice ought to make adoption more of a clear choice. Most children conceived are wanted, if not by their natural parents, then by the thousands of couples yearning to adopt newborn babies. The so-called pro-choice faction needs to do more to make this possible.

I began to search for a compromise. I had not altered my opposition to abortion, my belief that it violates our basic ethical tradition of preserving human life, of defending the weakest members of our society. Ethical compromise was impossible. But I did see the possibility for a practical compromise that would at least lower the number of abortions, the number of unborn children whose death was sanctioned by our laws.

Abortion was not the problem. The problem was unwanted pregnancy. If the number of unwanted pregnancies could be reduced, the number of abortions could be reduced. If unwanted pregnancies could be eliminated, abortions could be eliminated. It was as simple as that. Of course, there were some soldiers in the abortion wars who did not—or would not—see it that way. But there were many others who were weary of confrontation and who might listen to a better way. For example, a growing number in the proabortion group Planned Parenthood began to see that their deep involvement in the abortion controversy had diverted them from their original mission: planning parenthood rather than eliminating it. On the other side, a number of pro-lifers remembered their original concern—the killing of unborn children—and saw the wisdom of at least reducing the number killed.

Twenty years ago, before *Roe* v. *Wade,* a political compromise by the pro-life forces could have averted millions of abortions. In the late '60s and early '70s, as proabortion sentiment was growing in an increasingly unfettered society, there was nonetheless little widespread desire for unlimited abortion. Even abortion advocates knew this. If the pro-life forces had come to a political compromise, firmly denouncing abortion except in the case of a defective baby, rape, or incest, or to save the life of the mother, the proabortion side would have jumped to agree, and the subsequent bitter struggle and the more than 1 million abortions a year since *Roe* v. *Wade* would have been avoided or at least reduced.

There have always been some shades of gray in the debate. Even the most extreme proabortionists would not condone abortion for any reason whatsoever. I would be surprised if proabortion advocates would approve of a woman's choosing an abortion because her child happened to be of the wrong sex. And on the other side, even the Roman Catholic Church allows abortion to save the life of the mother. True, those cases are very rare now, but the Catholic position does provide for abortion in some cases where a judgment is required. I bring this up only to point out that discussion on the practical level is possible.

A large obstacle to practical compromise, to focusing on unwanted pregnancies rather than fighting over abortion, lies in the Roman Catholic stance not only against abortion but also against contraception. As a practical matter, I could never understand the opposition to both at once.

Perhaps the problem could be approached by more clearly defining the role of religious ethics in a pluralist society. This poses a problem for all religious groups in the United States. In some cases, for instance life-and-death issues, we want our religion-based ethical principles to extend throughout society. In other cases, as with holy days and sexual ethics, we limit them to our adherents. So if Catholic opposition to some forms of contraception could be limited to Catholics alone, we could remove a major obstacle to the cooperation needed to reduce the number of abortions in our country. It would allow energy—and government funding—to go into contraceptive research and education, areas in which America lags behind.

In Sweden the teenage pregnancy rate in 1982 was 13.7 per 1000 women, while in New Jersey in 1985 it was 113 per 1000. I do not believe that New Jersey girls are eight times more promiscuous than those in Sweden. Education about contraception can work, but Americans need more education and a national commitment. We also need to focus on contraception research. There may be answers no one has thought of, perhaps ones that are acceptable to Americans of all ethical and religious convictions. It is an area of investigation too much ignored.

I am enough of a realist to know that the abortion controversy in the United States will never offer an easy or popular solution. I wish no abortions were performed. I think most Americans agree with me on that. Even proabortionists will admit that every abortion is a failure—a failure to practice contraception, a failure of our institutions, whether family, economic, or social. Abortions are tragic failures. And for the most part, they are preventable failures. I would like to see both sides of the controversy agree on this. And then they could take steps to avoid the failure that raises the issue of abortion.

The longest journeys start with a single step. In one city, maybe in a dozen, antiabortion groups and abortion-rights activists, while agreeing to disagree on the right to have an abortion, could work together to reduce the number of unwanted pregnancies.

A small step, but also a giant one.

Epilogue

I WAS always proud to wear the uniform of the Surgeon General of the United States. But I also had to look ahead to the day when I would hang it in the closet for good. Because my confirmation as Surgeon General had dragged on for almost a year, my two four-year terms stretched out longer than those of the President who had appointed me. As the election of 1988 drew near, I began to wonder if I would choose to serve with the new administration, either Dukakis or Bush.

George Bush was always complimentary, but never gave me a hint about the future. I had met with him repeatedly on health issues and felt privileged to advise him. My discussions with Bush confirmed what I had always believed from a distance: his preparation for the presidency was better than that of anyone who ever ran for the office.

In late 1988, as I entered what would be the last year of my second term as Surgeon General, I realized that I would never have time to accomplish all I wished to do, especially in the larger area of making major reforms in the healthcare system in the United States. But I realized I could do that just as well out of uniform. The future began to beckon to me as I began to see all I might accomplish as a concerned citizen, one who had fought hard to earn the right to be heard. I more or less decided that I would leave my position before my term officially expired in November 1989.

But no sooner had I made my decision to leave, just after the Bush election, than a new temptation crossed my path. From all across the country came the suggestion that I serve the new administration as Secretary of Health and Human Services.

Of course, I had thought about this job from time to time. No matter where you work, sometimes you think about what it would be like to be the boss. And as Surgeon General, three levels down from Cabinet rank, I had wondered what it would be like to be Secretary of my department. There were many things I thought I could do with the position. But as attractive as the idea was, I recoiled from the apparent necessity to play politics.

A few days after the Bush election I learned that many people were interceding on my behalf, and although I found myself wondering about the outcome, I had a sense of peace about it all. I realized that the heady atmosphere of the Cabinet could be quite enticing, but the more rational side of me said I had better things to do.

In the middle of all the rumors about new Bush Cabinet appointees, Betty and I were invited to a dinner hosted by Secretary of State–designate Jim Baker and his wife, Susan. We had come to know Susan through administration social affairs and Fellowship House, a headquarters for Christian ministries in Washington. She came right up to us and said, "Jimmy gets lots of letters from people to make sure that you are kept on as Surgeon General." I felt I had to say something, so I boldly took Susan aside and told her that although I liked the Surgeon General's job, I had come to the conclusion that I could best help the President if I were the Secretary of Health and Human Services. I simply stated that I had understudied the job for eight years, that I could hit the ground running and accomplish a lot very quickly. Susan Baker's eyes lit up, and she said, "Of course, you'd be just wonderful in that job." I replied that if she felt that way, she should get the word to Jim that I was available. (I thought it would be improper to approach Jim Baker myself. I am a poor politician.)

Once again I was a name on the Washington rumor roller coaster. This time it was not nearly as important to me to be named Secretary of Health and Human Services as it had been to be confirmed as Surgeon General. As I said frequently during those weeks of wondering, if I was not nominated, I would be disappointed for three or four days and then relieved the rest of my life. That is the way it turned out, but not before a few more times around the roller coaster.

Associates called me with "inside information" about the upcoming appointment. I never put complete stock in what they told me, including the statement that the AMA had never lobbied harder for any appointment and that I had unbelievable support in the White House, or that I was still under serious consideration but would have to assure George Bush and his team that I would not be as independent as a Cabinet member as I had been as Surgeon General. I knew I would not want the job with those constraints. I felt I could readily go before Congress and make a plea for increased aid to mothers and children and honestly say, "This is what is needed. I have no idea where the money will come from." But I could never help solve the budget problem by lying, saying something like, "There is no need for further support of mothers and children" or "The states can handle it." Like most Presidents, George Bush required team players. I think my independence had earned me plaudits but was anathema to the Bush administration.

In the midst of all the rumors we were invited to a Christmas brunch at the Bushes', and found that Dr. Louis Sullivan, his wife, Ginger, and two of his children had arrived just before us. I had been in Washington circles long enough to recognize the difference in an approach to someone you are thanking for a job well done as compared to someone with whom you are planning an ongoing relationship. Although George and Barbara were extremely cordial, I whispered in Betty's ear about twenty minutes later, "It's all over. The appointment is made. I've made the diagnosis on the basis of ambience and body language."

The brunch was a pleasant occasion, and I felt very privileged to attend the gathering, obviously arranged primarily for close friends of the Bush family and a few they admired, such as Sandra Day O'Connor and Tony Fauci. George Bush walked Betty and me to the door when we left about an hour and a half later, and said good-bye. It was not good-bye for Sunday afternoon or for Christmas; it was—sprinkled with sincere words of gratitude—GOOD-BYE.

Once Lou Sullivan was named Secretary of Health and Human Services, I felt what I had predicted—a brief disappointment, followed by prolonged relief. That sense of relief was, however, tainted with one regret: I had sincerely desired to have the opportunity to influence the President to appoint a commission to study healthcare delivery in America. I thought I had earned the credibility to bring about a rapprochement in the healthcare and insurance communities so we could at last provide health insurance to the 37 million Americans who live in that fearful world of the uninsured. But I soon realized that I could work even more effectively for my objectives outside the government.

I wanted my resignation to come with as little fuss and with as few questions as possible. So I planned to deliver notice of my decision to resign just before I left for the two-week World Health Assembly in Geneva in May 1989. I hoped the public announcement would not occur until I was winging my way across the Atlantic. Instead, after my letter was delivered to the White House mailroom at 8:00 a.m., the announcement interrupted the morning news programs, and my office and home telephones were swamped with calls. I did an end run around reporters at the airport and settled into my seat on the plane, leaving a lot of stories floating around alleging that I left in a huff.

Weeks earlier I had discussed with Chase Untermeyer of White House personnel how I should go about resigning from the Commissioned Corps. He suggested that I send a letter to the President stating my intent, but inasmuch as the date was not yet settled, to wait until all dates were firm and send a second message. My first letter, in February, had received a lot of publicity, but its full text was never published. So there was some misinterpretation when I sent my second letter, in May. It was, being a follow-up to the first, merely a statement that I would leave office formally on October 1, 1989, but would go on terminal-leave status beginning July 13. Because the letter was short and factual, some reporters interpreted it as being "terse" because I was "miffed." That was not true. George Bush and I remain good friends.

As I contemplated the outlines of my third career I wondered if I should be making so many plans. After all, I was then seventy-two, seven years past the age when so many of my colleagues had retired. Once in a while I wondered what it would be like actually to retire, to do all those leisure-time activities that my life had excluded. But I knew that the contemplative life was not my style, that there was more work to do. Betty often said that I had many talents but that retirement was not one of them. I have always believed that the best way to remain active and alert is to be certain that society expects something of you.

It had dawned on me only slowly that I had moved into a favored place in the public eye. It began when I noticed passersby catching my eye with that look that said, Where do I know you from? Then they would say, "Didn't I see you on TV?" By 1988 it seemed that almost everyone who walked by me in an airport or on the street smiled, nodded a greeting, or said hello. I was most surprised, and pleased, when people would crowd around and start conversations—on the New York subway, on street corners, in airport waiting lounges. I was deeply moved by the personal nature of what they had to say: "You made my mother stop smoking. Thank you." They would ask questions about a son's epilepsy, a nightmare of a problem with medical insurance, or they would ask me to look at a sore elbow. More than any other comment was, "Thank you for a job well done" or "Thank you for what you did for the country."

All this surprised me, because for many years people had told me, only after they got to know me, that I had initially seemed austere, intimidating, even frightening. That always had bothered me, since I never tried to scare anyone. I think I am shy. But suddenly total strangers felt at ease with me, willing to share their personal problems. My son Allen said that the content and style of my health messages to the nation had fostered an image of "approachable authority." Maybe so. But I began to feel like the Surgeon General of all the people. As Betty repeatedly said, I had become family doctor to the nation. As I came to the end of my Surgeon General years I felt that I had gained the public's trust and that I should do something with it.

First, I wanted to make sure I did not use that trust only for private gain. Like many Americans, I was disgusted with the way retired politicians—even Presidents—cashed in on their celebrity status. Offers inviting me to endorse everything from condoms to cereals poured into my office as soon as my intention to resign became known. In one week I turned down more than $8 million. It was a little frightening, since as yet I had no job for the future. And with three children in not-so-profitable careers—history professor, minister, and wife of an officer of a nonprofit organization—there were big education bills ahead for seven grandchildren. But I was not about to sell or rent my integrity and the public trust.

It took me a while to put into words exactly what I intended to do. As so often happens, the right words came to me at a press conference, my final one as Surgeon General. Reporter Jerry Brazda asked how I would like to be remembered. I had never given much thought to a question like that, but the words that came out captured my hopes: "Sometime five years or more from now, I'd like one of you to say, 'You know, after he ceased to be Surgeon General, he continued to be the health conscience of America.' "

I had some idea of what I wanted to do. Like many other people, I knew the entire healthcare system in the United States had become desperately ill. It had grown inefficient, wasteful, and even immoral. I knew there was no easy solution, no quick fix. I knew it would take a judicious and delicate balance of public and private reform. I knew that the American people, the American government, and American medicine could do it. But not without effort, discipline, pain, and leadership. I wanted to do what I could to continue my work in health promotion and disease prevention. I wanted to do what I could to bring to all Americans reasonable health care at reasonable cost. I did not know if I could make a difference, but I knew I had to try.

By the time I left the government, I had gathered around me a little team that would help me. The Children's Hospital National Medical Center appointed me chair of the national Safe Kids campaign, and that gave me a base of operations: an office and a secretary. Longtime colleagues began to work with me to plan a series of prime-time television health specials. My son Allen split his time between teaching history at Dartmouth College and assisting me with my memoirs and speechwriting. And of course, Betty continued in her role of more than a half century as my chief consultant and partner.

No one had attempted what I sought to do. It reminded me of starting out as an untried pediatric surgeon, starting out as an untried Surgeon General. I knew my endeavors to revamp the American healthcare system would bring out opponents, people who were too entrenched and too comfortable in the current system to brook change. Once again, I knew, I would face some opposition, but perhaps not outright hostility. This time there was a big difference. I did not feel alone. I felt I had at my side the millions of Americans who had reached out to support me as I sought to serve them as their Surgeon General. And of course, I rested in the firm faith that my future, like my past, was shaped by the sovereignty of God.

Circle of Fear

Hussein Sumaida
with Carole Jerome

. . . I shook Yusef's hand and walked out into the streets of London. I had done it. I was working for the Mossad. I was an Iraqi working for the Zionist entity itself. Ha! Take that, Dad! And you, Saddam! After all these years— a whole lifetime so far—of them controlling me, now at last *I* was in control.

—*Circle of Fear*

FOREWORD

I KNOW that much of what I relate in this story does not reflect well on me. So be it. I did not write this book to justify my own faults, crimes and misdemeanors. I wrote it to give others a very rare look inside my country, Iraq, and to share with them what I have learned on my odyssey. It's a personal story that holds a global lesson.

Iraq has for decades been a closed book for outsiders. Reporters have been allowed access to political events and figures, but almost never to ordinary people. And people have been afraid to talk openly inside this republic of fear, as one writer phrases it. I call it a small portion of hell. My story takes you into the daily life of my country to evoke the human element that historians and journalists cannot know, and without which nothing can be fully understood.

But because of my unusual background I can also offer an even rarer look inside the machinery of fear—the Mukhabarat, the all-pervasive apparatus of intelligence and secret police. My story is a confirmation of the power and the banality of this secret world of espionage and terror. There are no James Bonds in this real world.

I offer as well a view of Israel that is probably unique, coming as it does from an Iraqi Arab who worked inside the Mossad.

Lastly, I offer this book to my own people as a looking glass. Regardless of what happens to me, I feel it is important to have told the whole story. Only as more and more people gain knowledge can the circles of fear be broken.

Hussein Sumaida

1
VICTIM OF HATE

I CAN run my hand over the scar on my face and feel my father's signature in my flesh. I was barely two years old when, in a fit of temper, he jammed my head in the doorway and closed the lower bolt across my face, just above my right eye. According to my mother, who feared my father greatly, I cried and bled for hours. My mother told me that I was less than two months old when he beat me for the first time.

I know that when I was small, I was an innocent victim of my father's hate. Later, perhaps in order to preserve my sanity, I learned to respond to him with wisecracks, argument and sarcasm. He would fly into a temper, but then at least I could say why he was angry. I also know that if my father had been a normal human being, it is unlikely I would be writing this story today.

For me, for my family, it seemed my father set the deadly pattern of our lives. There was a time when I thought that perhaps I just didn't understand him—though now I find it hard to imagine that understanding would have changed the course of events. Even if you understand pathological violence and fanaticism, surviving it unscathed is unlikely.

Whenever my father got angry, he would hurl the crystal ashtrays and porcelain dishes against the wall, so that there was never a complete set of dishes in our house. I withdrew into books and into my imagination, and I began to nurture a hatred for my father that persists to this day.

His horrible temper flared at trivial things—a meal ten minutes late, or a reply from me that didn't show adequate respect. It was virtually impossible for me to meet his neomilitary standards, because by the time I began to talk, I stuttered, thanks to the constant terror in which I lived. This only made my father more malicious. I was an embarrassment to him, his son who couldn't even speak properly. As I struggled to express myself he would become so enraged that he would pick me up and hurl me onto the floor or into a piece of furniture.

Soon after my sisters and brother were born, they, too, learned to fear him. One sister, Dina, and my brother, Saif, were near to me in age, born in the late '60s. Another little sister, Dalia, was born much later, in 1980. They all were subject to his blows, but I received the brunt of his anger.

My father's favorite weapon was a big blue clog shoe that he wielded like a hammer against our soft skin. We were terrified of it. One day, when I was about seven, Saif and I got up our courage and put it in someone else's garbage. That night, when Father came home, he began hunting for the clog. He bellowed furiously for us to confess. Then he lashed out, hitting all of us in a frenzy of evil frustration.

My mother was, and still is, a quiet, gentle person, who loves her children. How she endured my father, I shall never know. At least he never hit her, because in some strange way he regarded her as his good-luck charm.

My father's full name is Ali Mahmoud Sumaida. He is short, stocky and ugly. He has swarthy skin, a big nose and black hair. My mother, by contrast, is small and frail, with light brown hair and pale skin. Like her name, Suhaila, she is beautiful. They met at university, where he was head of the student underground movement of the Ba'th Party and she was studying social sciences. Everyone who knew them then said she was the most beautiful girl at the University of Baghdad.

My mother, tears filling her eyes, would tell us how unlucky she was to have met my father and to have to live with such a man. If only she had realized in time. Sometimes she would discipline us, too, but somehow my mother retained her peace and kindness. Without her love we children most certainly would have been lost souls. I, in fact, might well have been killed. While my father constantly attacked me, she constantly defended me, drawing a lot of his fire.

Why he hated me more than the others I cannot say. I know that when he ordered me and my siblings to obey a command, they would instantly obey. I would delay, or refuse altogether. If he told us to get out of the room, they would march out immediately. I would stay put, courting disaster. Whether I was insolent because I had learned to hate him, or whether he hated me because I was insolent, I don't know.

Such was life in our family home on Felastin (Palestine) Street. We lived in one of Baghdad's new, posher neighborhoods, in a roomy house with three bedrooms, two salons, a huge kitchen and dining room. It was designed in the style of any modern Western house, with all the appliances. The only Eastern touches were the archways between rooms. The house was looked after by my mother and my maternal grandmother, with the help of a maid and a cook. Like most Iraqi children, we called our grandma Bibi. She was like my mother, small and sweet and gentle. Two nightingales in the nest of a pterodactyl.

If material wealth meant happiness, then I should have been the luckiest kid alive. We had everything that money could buy. The source of all the wealth was my father's politics, and politics were my father's raison d'être.

Apart from using me as a punching bag, my father barely acknowledged my existence. My quarters were a closet he had made into a room for me. He never talked to me, never gave me toys or gifts, even on my birthday. When I was at school, he didn't seem to know or care what grade I was in or what I was learning.

When I was six or seven, my father took a kettle from the stove and poured boiling water on me, shouting abuse. All I recall is the searing pain, not the cause of this atrocity. The burn spread across my thighs and my little private parts, in large painful blisters that made every movement agony. On this and every other such occasion my father refused to allow anyone to call a doctor for me. Instead, my mother would sneak out at five a.m., go and get me an appointment, then come back and take me to the clinic herself.

What I have recounted here is virtually all I remember of my father from my childhood. He flared in my life like an occasional violent thunderstorm. And yet that was enough to make him the driving force of my growing-up years.

Rebellion and revenge dictated almost everything I did in future years. He is like a turbulent shadow, looming over my shoulder. And so he remains in this telling of my tale. But the greater power that he represented became clearer to me over the years. My father was the embodiment of the brutal Ba'thist regime of Saddam Hussein. And I turned hatred of my father into hatred of Iraq's rulers.

Ironically, at school I found I was privileged precisely because of my horrible father. Unlike most Iraqi schoolchildren, I was taken to class in a chauffeur-driven limousine. From my first kindergarten class, at a small private school when I was five, I discovered that the way was cleared for me. Exams, grades, discipline, rows with other kids, were all smoothed over because of my status. I soon learned that my driver was also my personal bodyguard. One of his duties was to supply the teacher with a gift every two or three months. The gifts and the pressure my father's status could exert meant, for example, that I was excused from oral examinations, which with my stutter I surely would have failed.

A child soon learns the uses of privilege. When I was six or seven, I would stuff my pockets with chocolates, which we, unlike most other Iraqis, always had in the house. I'd learned that the other kids would exchange friendship for chocolate. If one of them displeased me or threatened me, I could have him taken care of by my bodyguard.

I was special because my father, Ali Sumaida, was one of the most powerful men in the ruling Ba'thist regime. The privilege came from terror, the tool of raw political power. The special treatment was for my father's benefit, not mine. It denoted his status, not mine. If my father had really cared about me, he would have seen that I was placed in speech-therapy classes, rather than bribing my teachers.

But such actions would have required my father to acknowledge his shameful, stupid son. At all costs a façade of perfection and success had to be preserved. Just like the whole society. Success and promotion were earned by corruption and cheating, and so the country was all just a façade. Behind the façade was rot.

In 1969 my father was made head of the Department of Censorship, but each high-ranking Ba'thist Party member held two key jobs. Father's civil job, as censor, was public knowledge. His party job, as one of the high-ranking officers in Saddam's Bureau of General Relations, was secret.

No book or film was allowed to be distributed or sold without his approval. The Ba'thists were determined to control people by beating their bodies and starving their minds. Ironically, because my father was the watchdog at the closed gates of learning, I was able to pass through those gates with impunity. Our home had a huge library, a warm, snug room lined with all the forbidden books my father had seized and decided unfit for Iraqi consumption. When he wasn't home, I would hole up for hours with one of the illicit books. Most were Arabic editions. There was everything from American novels and biographies to treatises on communism and economics.

My favorite discovery was a book about the life of Eli Cohen, the Israeli spy. After establishing a cover identity in South America as a Syrian émigré, Cohen went to Damascus and worked as an Israeli mole inside the highest echelons of the Syrian political and military system. Cohen's information was a vital factor in Israel's eventual victory in the 1967 Six-Day War. But he never tasted the fruit of his labor. In 1965 he was discovered at his radio set sending messages to Tel Aviv. He was hanged in a public square in Damascus before a cheering crowd.

It was in the pages of Cohen's story that I began to learn what it was like for Israel to live surrounded by hostile Arab nations. (Later, when I was in the West and could separate the propaganda of both sides from the facts, I learned what the Zionists did to earn much of that hostility.) But in school, in Iraq, we didn't learn what the Jews had gone through at the hands of the Nazis. Instead, we learned of the Jewish "conspiracy," and the virtues of Hitler and his Reich. Both were greatly admired by my father and his friend Saddam.

Eli Cohen became my hero. It is hard to convey to non-Arabs just how heinous this was. What unimaginable treason. Devil worship. For my father and millions like him Israel is the archenemy, especially loathed for its usurping of Arab land. And at that level the hatred is valid and comprehensible. But this hatred of Israel is almost pathological, something beyond reason. It marks every moment of our political life and is the foundation of my own story.

As I approached adolescence I figured out that my father's politics were where he lived. If I zeroed in on that, I could make an impact. Hurt him, rile him, anything to strike back. Without giving away the secret of my sources, I began to challenge my father on history and politics.

He always described the Ba'th Party to us as the friend of the people. One night I said, "You and Saddam talk a lot about the rights of the people. Then all you do is kill people or treat them like slaves."

"That's the only way to treat them if they insist on going against us!" he shouted. "They're like stupid donkeys that have to be beaten with a big stick to make them go where they should."

"How do you know they're donkeys if they never get to say what they think?" I replied, knowing it would make him even angrier.

"What would you know about it, you little bastard? The only way to run a country is to have control, and the only way to have control is to make damn sure everybody is afraid to argue. Anybody fights you and zzzztt"—he illustrated by drawing an imaginary knife across my throat—"you're dead."

"Pretty swell revolution you have going. Is this what you all had in mind when you were talking about the rights of the people and overthrowing the corrupt old regimes?"

He moved as though to hit me, and I backed away quickly.

"Get out of here, you little bastard. You're lucky I don't have you killed, too!"

I retired to my closet room.

MY FATHER was born in Tunisia in 1935. His father, part of a large landowning family, had three or four wives and a confusion of children. As a young man, my father began to work in the Tunisian underground movement against Habib Ibn Ali Bourguiba, Tunisia's tyrannical president, who came to power after France granted Tunisia independence. Arrested during a demonstration and sentenced to death, my father somehow managed to escape. He boarded a ferry to Marseilles and eventually made his way to Syria. It was in Syria that my father came into contact with the fateful influence of Michel 'Aflaq, founder of Ba'thism.

The Ba'thist Party was started in Damascus, in 1943, by 'Aflaq and Salah al-Din al-Bitar. In English, Ba'thist translates to Arab Socialist Renaissance Party. The Ba'thist Party has been most important in Iraq and Syria, but it has adherents in all Middle Eastern nations. The party began with reasonably moderate nationalist views, but after Israel defeated the Arabs in 1948, the party grew larger and more radical. Ideologically, Ba'thism is a mix of Arab nationalism, socialism, and Marxist rhetoric. In practice the Ba'thist regimes of both Syria and Iraq are nothing more than ruthless dictatorships.

Ba'thism became just another excuse for a bunch of power-hungry men to take over a country "for the good of the people" and run it for the good of themselves. Arabs were to throw off their chains—and forge new ones.

All fired up with enthusiasm for this new cause, my father joined the Syrian Ba'thist Party. But soon he ran into problems with the Syrian police. In 1957 he moved to Iraq. To enter the country with as many advantages as possible, he pretended to be an Algerian. At the time, Iraq was backing Algeria in its war for independence from France. Since my father's papers were mainly in French, it was fairly easy to alter them to make them look as if he were from Algeria.

My father established himself at the University of Baghdad, where he started to work underground for the Iraqi branch of the Ba'th Party. As far as I know, that was when my father first met Saddam Hussein, another young Ba'thist, who was already known as a thug. Saddam had been expelled from school at one point for beating up a teacher. Brute force was Saddam's only debating tactic.

SADDAM Hussein came from a dirt-poor family whose hometown was Tikrit, in northern Iraq. He was two years younger than my father. The two spent long hours in discussion with their fellow conspirators, in the smoky cafés where men whiled away the time playing backgammon. On occasion such men attended innocent-looking picnics in the parks. There they plotted revolution. The first major act of these Iraqi Ba'thists was an attempted assassination of General 'Abd al-Karim Qassem, in 1959. Qassem had come to power in a coup the previous year, when he and a group of officers overthrew the monarchy of King Faisal II. Qassem was perhaps the first ruler since Nebuchadnezzar who was genuinely popular with his people. Both Saddam and my father were among the group assigned to hit Qassem himself. They failed, and most of the plotters were rounded up. Saddam, slightly wounded in the fiasco, managed to escape to Syria. My father was never even suspected, since he wasn't Iraqi, but an Algerian (who was really a Tunisian).

After the attempted assassination the party put my father in charge of its underground activities at the university while he continued his studies in the history department.

In 1963 the Ba'thists made their first real grab for power in Iraq. My father led the unit assigned to seize radio and television stations. It was a bloody fight, and this time the Ba'th won. Qassem was killed, and his body was displayed horribly on television by the new rulers. They called it a revolution, but it was really a coup d'état. When they succeeded, Saddam Hussein came back from exile to join them. My father was rewarded for his part with honorary Iraqi citizenship and the directorship of Iraqi television.

Saddam was given something more to his particular tastes: he was made chief interrogator at the main prison. Once the palace of King Faisal, it was appropriately called Qasr al Nihayyah—Palace of the End—because King Faisal and his family were slaughtered there. It soon became the end for hundreds of unfortunate Iraqis as well, who fell into Saddam's hands. It was here that Saddam was able to display his full talents as a torturer, using electric wires and prods, nail rippers and other utensils of the torturer's kitchen. Survivors later testified that Saddam personally participated in their agonies.

Saddam did not enjoy his new job for long. In November 1963 they were all overthrown by Ba'thist rivals in the army.

Already the Ba'thist ideology was split into factions within factions. Saddam and my father both went to jail, where they reflected on the reasons for the deterioration of the Ba'th into rival groups and decided it was all the fault of ambitious military officers. Saddam liked to pretend he had genuine military training and rank, but in fact he had none. Deep down he nursed a murderous envy of talented military officers. The decimation of military rivals was to be the hallmark of Saddam's own cannibalistic rule. My father, who was stripped of his citizenship, made a perfect assistant. He was not a part of the military, which automatically made him less of a threat. The two grew closer. Though in jail, Saddam wasn't in as much immediate danger as my father, who was scheduled to be deported. Fortunately for my father he had a friend in the military police who destroyed the file on him. Another friend helped him escape after only three days in jail. Then my father simply took on his Tunisian identity and used his old papers. The Iraqi-Algerian the authorities were looking high and low for was back in business as a Tunisian.

Saddam spent another two years in jail.

My father was despondent. He had lost everything. And now he had a wife, the beautiful Suhaila, whom he had met at university.

On January 20, 1965, she gave birth to me. Since my father didn't want to risk contact with the Tunisians, he had a friend register me at the Tunisian embassy. Years later this action would take on great significance.

In spite of all the setbacks, my father stuck with the Ba'thist Party, and in 1968 it paid off. On July 17 they staged another coup, and this time they held on to the reins of power.

I recall a photograph in our home. It shows all twelve coup leaders standing on the balcony of the palace. My father is one of them. From the time of the coup on, the guest list at our house was a who's who of Iraq's rulers.

Ba'th founder Michel 'Aflaq used to visit with his wife and three sons. 'Aflaq was to Ba'thism what Marx was to Marxism. Ironically, while his theories had spawned the Ba'thist killing machine, 'Aflaq himself was a gentle old soul, who looked like Albert Einstein. He was pleasant, but remote.

Later, a debonair man named Tariq Aziz came by often. Aziz was the only one who showed any human warmth at all, and sometimes he was actually friendly. At one point Aziz had been a journalist, and I always thought of him as one of the few decent human beings in Saddam's circle. It was a mystery why Saddam tolerated someone so intelligent, and it was equally a mystery why someone basically humane could stomach Saddam. But money and power are strong allurements. He became Foreign Minister by dint of being the perfect yes-man.

I also recall Taha Yassin Ramadhan, a rough-hewn character who eventually became the number three man in the country. He could scarcely string together a coherent sentence, but he and my father used to confer long hours over "election" strategy within the party. I already had begun to understand that elections were won with knives and threats. That was the nature of the men and the party that had just taken over my country.

The 1968 coup was led by General Ahmad Hasan al-Bakr, who now became head of the Revolutionary Command Council. Like Saddam, he was from the northern town of Tikrit.

The Tikriti men all called one another cousin and were as close-knit as shrunken wool. The coup that reinstated my father and Saddam was the beginning of the domination of Iraq by these fierce, unpitying tribesmen. At first Saddam depended on subordinates who were from small, insignificant families from all parts of the country, while he brought his Tikriti clansmen up through the ranks as quickly as possible to replace everyone in any position of power.

After the coup Saddam was given the task he enjoyed most: head of internal security. He turned the savage but inefficient system of the prisons into the savage and efficient system of a police state. He set up the innocuous-sounding General Relations Bureau, an apparatus of political surveillance that steadily hunted down and killed everyone who so much as expressed the slightest dislike of the regime. My father was one of its senior officers. Eventually the bureau evolved into the complex system Saddam has today. The Mukhabarat is at its heart.

Mukhabarat is the Arab word for intelligence, but in Iraq it has acquired a definition of its own. A whisper of the word is enough to create an aura of evil power. The Mukhabarat has limitless powers and is answerable to no one but Saddam. It began systematically to place the country under lock and key, controlling everything from commerce to espionage. One word from a Mukhabarat officer could mean someone's death.

Saddam quickly gained full control of the reins of terror. He had discovered the ultimate weapon: fear. Fear now ruled every man, woman and child, every nook and every cranny of Iraq.

2
GROWING UP IRAQI

FATHER did such a good job as censor that he was put in charge of the party's preparatory school as well. It was a factory for turning out ideal Ba'thists. Oddly, he never managed to turn his own children into little Ba'thist sausages. Perhaps we were too insignificant in his eyes, or perhaps he thought we would automatically want to emulate our lord and master. Aside from his natural brutality, I never knew what made him such a devotee of the party line. He seemed to need absolute authority in every walk of life. Most of all, he seemed to need someone to control him as much as he needed to control others. He could only function within a tyrannical state. I don't know why.

Maybe in the act of brainwashing others in his elite school of robots, my father had brainwashed himself, too. He became even more domineering at home. Every word he said was an order. There was never a conversation. We used to count the minutes until he left for the day.

At school, we were subjected to the full blast of Ba'thist propaganda. We learned history as seen through Ba'thist eyes. We learned all about the great King Nebuchadnezzar, ruler of the Babylonians. We were taught his greatest claim to fame: not the seventh wonder of the world, the Hanging Gardens of Babylon; that was insignificant beside his victory over the most evil enemy of them all, the Israelis. It didn't matter that this conquest happened in the sixth century B.C.

In our lessons the Israelis were horrible people who consorted with demons. We were taught always to be on our guard against these evil people who would try to take away our homes and kill our parents. The Israelis were all forms of the devil himself.

Nebuchadnezzar was reputed to have captured the Jews and enslaved them, which made him the brightest star in our Ba'thist history books. After Nebuchadnezzar and on through the triumph of Islam, in the seventh century A.D., we learned more of our glorious past.

It is true that Baghdad and its people were once a shining light, and it is equally true that Westerners are largely ignorant of, or choose to ignore, the accomplishments of Arab culture after the first century. Admittedly, there has always been a Western romance with ancient Egypt and the Fertile Crescent. But it is forgotten that while the ancestors of those living in many of today's industrialized nations were just emerging from the tribal warfare that followed the fall of the Roman Empire, Arab scholars were translating, preserving and adding to the knowledge of ancient Greece, India and other civilizations of antiquity.

Baghdad's golden period came in the eighth and ninth centuries, during the reign of the 'Abbasid caliphates. Haroun al Rashid, the fifth of the 'Abbasids, is associated with *A Thousand and One Nights* and the beginning of the golden period. Later caliphs continued his Bayt-al Hikmah—the House of Wisdom—in Baghdad. Here, Arab-Islamic culture achieved great heights in the fields of mathematics, medicine, philosophy, astronomy, theology, literature and poetry. Ibn Sina, better known in the West as Avicenna, compiled *The Canon of Medicine,* which described every treatment for every known disease. It was the most used medical work between the twelfth and seventeenth centuries. A great hospital was built in Baghdad, where Muslim doctors performed extremely complex operations, including cranial and vascular surgery, as well as operations for cancer. These doctors were the first to use anesthetics. Arabs also gave the West their numerals, the decimal point, and the concept of zero, without which most modern technology would have been impossible.

Educating us in our past glories was fine, but we learned almost nothing about the downside of Iraqi history. The defeats and the cruel tyrants were ignored. I was able to learn about them in my father's library of forbidden fruits.

In 1258 Hulagu, grandson of Genghis Khan, captured Baghdad. Eight hundred thousand citizens perished. In 1401 Timur the Lame, better known as Tamerlane, besieged Baghdad with his huge sling-shots called mangonels. After six weeks of terrified resistance the siege ended. Tamerlane built 120 towers around the wall of Baghdad, using the severed heads of 100,000 victims as bricks.

From 1534, when Suleyman the Magnificent entered Baghdad, till the British took possession, in March 1918, most of Iraq was part of the Ottoman Empire. Following World War I, Britain was to mandate the area. The three provinces—Mosul, Baghdad and Basra—were merged into the political entity that now forms modern Iraq. The new borders brought diverse ethnic and religious groups into one state, but they did not change the essentially tribal nature of the society. In 1920 the emir, Faisal I, led an Arab revolt. He established a government in Damascus and was proclaimed King of Syria. Nationalist agitation spread from Syria, and by mid-1920 the revolt engulfed all of Iraq, except the larger cities, where British garrisons were stationed.

The French, who had been given a mandate over Lebanon and Syria, were determined to enforce it. They ousted Faisal and expelled him from Syria. At the same time, the British wanted out of Mesopotamia. They offered Faisal the throne of Iraq and an Arab government under British mandate. Faisal wanted the throne if it was offered by the people. He also insisted on a treaty of alliance rather than a mandate. His proposals were accepted, and on July 11, 1921, Faisal was declared King of Iraq. The treaty of alliance tied Iraq to Britain, at which point various nationalist groups began to work to end the influence of Britain.

The British soon opted for less influence. Iraq became an independent nation in 1932. King Faisal remained on the throne and was succeeded by his son, Faisal II.

It was this king whose overthrow and murder cleared the way for the eventual rise of the Ba'th and Saddam Hussein.

Above: ancient Iraq's glory days—an artist's fanciful rendering of the Hanging Gardens of Babylon. Right: King Faisal I, who accepted the throne of Mesopotamia from the British in 1921 and formed modern Iraq in 1932.

According to my teachers, our glorious revolution was going to defeat the Jews once and for all, and Iraq would lead the Arab world into a sunlit future of socialism, Ba'th style. That meant eternal vigilance, tracking the devils from within. We children were taught the virtue of informing our teachers if we heard anyone say anything against the government. We were to tell on our friends, our brothers and sisters, and especially on our parents. The least whisper of discontent was to be reported.

In my case, of course, I would have loved to turn in my father, but he was one of the thought police. And all the nail pullers and hot spikes in the dungeons wouldn't have made me do anything against my mother.

As you might guess, this atmosphere caused many to leave. Iraq began to deteriorate from within as more and more of the intelligentsia fled to Europe and North America. Thousands of our best-skilled people left, to be replaced by loyal party cadres whose main qualification for a job was an ability to parrot the current dogma.

My family, though, enjoyed the pampered life of the party elite. Every year we went on trips abroad paid for by the party, which meant paid for by the people whom the party was bleeding dry, and by oil

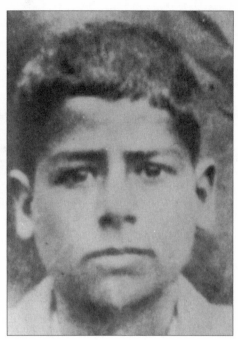

Above: Tikrit, birthplace of Saddam
Hussein and other Ba'thist Party rebels
who would one day seize control of Iraq.
The young Saddam, right, was once
expelled from school for beating up a
teacher. "Brute force," the author says,
"was Saddam's only debating tactic."

revenues. In all, we traveled to more than two dozen countries by the
time I was sixteen, including most of Europe, North Africa and the
Middle East.

After a time I began to realize that my father used different names
and passports. Even in those early years I was starting to see that he
was involved in more than just censorship and party propaganda.

In the summer of 1973 we were in Beirut when news came from
Baghdad that someone had tried to kill Saddam Hussein. Saddam was
still officially the number two man in the country, after Bakr. But
everyone knew Saddam as the Strongman of Iraq. Already he was the
one who counted. Without hesitation my father packed us all up and
whisked us back to Baghdad to be by the side of his leader. He was
betting on the future, and the future was clearly Saddam.

Saddam was unhurt, and we began to spend our leisure time in
Baghdad at the Baghdad Hunt Club, where my playmates were Oday
and Kusai, Saddam's sons. Saddam himself used to sit off to one side
by the pool with his wife, Sadjidah.

I never saw Saddam have anything to do with his sons. He was
remote and austere. But then so was my father in public. Oday and
Kusai and I would play cops and robbers in the playground.

One day they became really interested in me when they saw me in a corner reading a Batman comic. "Can you get us some of those?" they pleaded, much to my surprise. With the money and power they had, I had assumed they could get their hands on more than I could. So I kept them supplied with Batman, Superman and other contraband comics.

As I grew older I liked to go into my father's library and look through the newspapers with holes cut in them, trying to figure out what had been censored. Then when we traveled outside Iraq, I would find out exactly what had been cut from those papers. The censored material was always either critical of Iraq or favorable to Israel or America.

The more I read, the more I began to develop my own ideas about Israelis and Arabs. It seemed to me that the Israelis had a right to exist. So did the Palestinians. And the fanatics on both sides were making sure that neither of them existed in peace.

Our education regarding America was slim. Basically the moral was that the Americans were power-hungry imperialists, who got what they deserved in Vietnam. The only other salient fact was that America was the ally of Israel and was therefore the enemy.

The Soviets were discussed a bit more favorably because Moscow was currently arming Saddam under the Iraqi-Soviet pact of 1972. It was a very loose mutual alliance, the usual treaty providing Soviet military aid and Iraqi cooperation. So later, when the Soviets invaded Afghanistan, a fellow Muslim nation, our government officially condemned the act. But it was empty rhetoric. Iraq did nothing to help the Afghans or hinder the Soviets. Not a word about the conflict was ever reported on the state-run radio and television or in its press. The Afghans were furious, and a deep and lasting grudge was born.

But a clear line was drawn between the Soviets outside Iraq and the Communists inside. While the Kremlin was busy arming Saddam, Saddam was busy wiping out the Iraqi Communist Party in a vicious internal campaign of terror.

My father's work took him to the center of this strange relationship with the Soviet Union. In 1976 he was appointed ambassador to Poland for a four-year term. I was eleven at the time. We moved into an enormous old house in Warsaw, where we lived a life of kings, with three maids and a cook. While the Poles lined up for bread and other food in short supply, we dined on imported delicacies from Denmark and drank expensive French Cognac. Cognac, in fact, was the local black-market currency. It could buy anything.

This was several years before the Solidarity movement of Lech Walesa gained momentum, and Poland was securely in the grip of the Kremlin. My father had to tread carefully. His main task, I learned later, was to find Iraqi Communists and have them kidnapped and shipped home to the waiting hands of the secret police. All my father had to do was put Iraqis in Poland under surveillance and snatch the key figures who might pose a threat to Saddam. That meant, by and large, Communists. Since the Soviet-Iraqi pact, many Iraqis had come to the Soviet bloc for studies, and many of them had become active in the clandestine communist movement aimed at turning Iraq into a Marxist paradise.

I was put in the Iraqi school in Warsaw to finish elementary grades. When I was thirteen, I was sent home to Baghdad for a special exam. For the first time I was at home without my parents. Only my grandmother, Bibi, was there. I felt free for the first time in my life. My reaction was to take up girl chasing with gusto. I became a typical hormonal teenager lusting after girls, whom I treated with superior contempt. I was awful.

WHEN I was growing up, we didn't go to the mosque very often. In Islam the home serves as well as the mosque for the five daily devotions. But every few months we would visit the great shrines of Karbala and Najaf, the two most sacred centers of the Shi'a. Only a minority of Iraqis belong to the Sunni sect of Islam; about two thirds are Shi'a. My mother is Shi'a. My father, Sunni.

The easiest way to explain the Shi'a and Sunni branches of Islam is to compare them with Catholics and Protestants; the God is the same and the basic story is the same, but the rites are treated differently. All sects of Islam trace their beliefs to the Prophet Muhammad. The foundation of the faith is the Koran, the written record of the series of divine revelations Muhammad received from God. All of this was about seven hundred years after Christ, who is regarded by Muslims as the last significant prophet before Muhammad himself. Islam honors all the prophets of the Old Testament and many of the teachings of Christ. It just doesn't regard Jesus as the Son of God.

The Islamic schism occurred with Muhammad's death. Since Muhammad had no male children, there was a dispute over his successor. The ancestors of today's Sunnis decided Muhammad was to be succeeded by a caliph (a leader something like a pope), who would be appointed by the followers of the Prophet. The ancestors of the Shi'a stuck with Ali, the son-in-law of the Prophet, who married Muhammad's daughter, Fatima.

Both Ali and his son and heir, Hussein, were killed in power struggles with the armies of successive caliphs. Ali was assassinated at Kufa, near Najaf. Hussein was enticed into a trap, and he and his small army were massacred by the Caliph Yazid and his men. The tombs of Ali and Hussein are inside the beautiful mosques in Najaf and Karbala.

The Shi'a commemorate the martyrdom of Hussein every year at the time of Ashura, when the men bare their backs and in a frenzy lash themselves with whips. Thirteen hundred years later the Shi'a are still the underdogs of Islam, and they still talk of revenge.

According to my mother, the Shi'a were peaceful, loving, civilized and oppressed. Since she was all of these things, we believed her. For her, Shi'ism was her relationship with God. It was in no way political. She avoided all politics.

I was fourteen when Ayatollah Khomeini overthrew the powerful Shah of Iran in a full-scale popular Islamic revolution. We all whooped for joy. I'll always remember the date Khomeini returned to Iran from exile—February 1, 1979. It changed our world. None of us had much love for the shah. The Persians (Iranians) are traditional enemies of Arab Iraq. Worse, the shah had been an ally of Israel, furnishing it with oil in exchange for military hardware. So even Sunni Arab Iraq was celebrating. But not for long.

Within months Iraq and Iran were back in their old stance of mortal enemies. In Iraq the Strongman finally took over absolutely. Saddam and his fellow Tikritis already ruled the country through the vicious police and security apparatus they had created. They controlled the economy by controlling virtually every product and service, from the oil industry to horse races. Patronage, which had always been a plague, now became the heart of the system that fed the elite and starved the dispossessed.

Ahmad Hasan al-Bakr was only nominally the head of state; Saddam controlled the regime and the country. He had first signaled this with a crackdown on dissidents and by a slaughter of both Communists and Jews. The public execution of seventeen members of a supposed Zionist spy ring in early 1969 was followed by a witch-hunt for Communists, who suffered similar fates after being tortured to reveal their comrades. All of this was a prelude to the main business of eliminating rivals within the party itself.

The first to go was Bakr himself. He was put under enormous pressure from Saddam to resign. His departure allowed Saddam to take over for "the good of the party" on July 17, 1979.

The first thing he did was to purge the party.

I was spending summer vacation with my parents, so we were all in Poland when Saddam took over. One day my father came home in a state of great agitation. We were ordered to pack immediately for home. He told us there was a grave situation in Baghdad. A Telex had come from the ministry, saying a major plot to overthrow the government had been discovered. Father talked wildly of traitors and spies and was in a perfect fury.

"These traitors will be punished," he yelled. "They will regret their mothers ever gave them life. They will die, all of them!"

When we returned to Baghdad, he stormed off to the ministry, leaving us at home to glean what we could from the television news given by the government. What we saw was an elaborately staged purge of Saddam's rivals. This was carried out in a bizarre meeting of about a thousand party members. It was initiated by a "confession" of treason from a Shi'ite member, who then read out a list of his fellow conspirators. As he read the name of one, the camera focused on the man in question, who appeared ready to faint. The confessor then said, "But he refused to join us," and the man went limp with relief. By now all the men in the assembly were either weeping or shouting, "Long live Saddam! Let me die for you!"

This offer to die for the great leader, whoever he is, is a common declaration of loyalty in the Middle Eastern political arena. Tears and other emotional outbursts that would be seen as evidence for need of psychiatric help in the West are part and parcel of men of power in our culture. In this emotionally charged atmosphere other members began rising to accuse others. Executions were demanded.

The traitors were to be executed by their fellow party members. The senior party officials lined up in firing squads at Abu Ghareb prison the next day and shot their colleagues. This was not on television. I knew about it because my father was one of the executioners. It was the kind of work he enjoyed.

The "plot" against Saddam gave him a perfect cover for the elimination of others he believed might be rivals. He was especially interested in the armed forces. Though he had assumed a military title and rank, and commanded the armed forces, Saddam still had a deeply rooted fear and hatred of genuine military officers. In a few years it was a wonder there was anyone left in the military competent enough to clean a rifle, let alone command an army.

Iron rule backed up by firing squads now settled over Iraq.

My family was still part of the pampered elite. In addition to the perks I normally got because of my father's position, I was able to go into business in a small way. Whenever we traveled, I would buy videotapes, small tape recorders, cassettes and, last but not least, pornographic magazines. Beforehand I had sneaked a look at my father's papers to find out his Telex number, as well as that of the Ministry of Foreign Affairs. I would send a Telex to the ministry in my father's name, telling them to have someone at the airport to meet me and shepherd me through customs. Father usually stayed abroad longer. I would then sell my contraband at huge profits to my schoolmates. At the tender age of fifteen I had already developed a taste for secrecy and intrigue. Even in my little black market I kept everything compartmentalized so no one knew who else was buying; sometimes I didn't deal directly, but instead went through a middle man. I wanted to minimize the risk and knew that the best way was to tell everyone a slightly different story, keep them all apart, with no one knowing the whole truth of my operation.

That was how I learned to survive in Saddam's Iraq. Iraqis are a very passionate people—drastically so. If we love someone, we'll give him our heart, our eyes, our lives. But if we hate someone, only God knows what will happen. When Saddam's all-seeing state was imposed over people with such strong emotions, it meant that people didn't even trust their own dreams, let alone other people. Even in sleep we feared we might say something that would displease the beast. I learned early how to live in the shadows.

I also discovered that the revolution next door in Iran wasn't the great liberation of the people we had originally thought. Every day we heard of more killings and people put in jail. Political opposition to the clerical party of Khomeini's mullahs was banned, books were burned, and the universities were turned into centers of Islamic dogma. Women were forced back into the Middle Ages. They were segregated, shrouded in kerchiefs and long robes, forbidden to wear makeup or to be in public with any male who was not a relative. The *pasdars,* or revolutionary guards, roamed the streets of every Iranian town and city, savagely enforcing the new orders. It was a long way from the sunny, tolerant Shi'ism my mother had taught me. Khomeini ruled like other warrior priests of Islam of the past, with blood and brimstone.

Then they took the hostages.

On November 4, 1979, a motley group calling itself the Student Followers of the Imam's Line seized the American embassy in Tehran and proceeded to hold the staff hostage for more than a year. That crisis ended what little power the more moderate Iranian revolutionaries had, and left the radical clergy firmly in charge.

Islam, I was beginning to discover, was not necessarily by nature tolerant. In fact, its original followers had been ordered to conquer the infidels and either convert them or kill them. Khomeini and his men were well within tradition.

And as far as Khomeini was concerned, Saddam was one of the infidels. Before 1979 Khomeini had been preaching Islamic revolution from the safety of the mosque in Najaf—he'd been exiled by the shah years before and taken refuge in Iraq—and when the shah asked Saddam to muzzle him or throw him out, Saddam obliged. Saddam, after all, had no love for Khomeini. The imam was stirring up Iraq's own enormous Shi'a population. The Iranian mullahs preached revolution and broadcast their sermons into Iraqi territory. The cassette recordings of Khomeini's own exhortations, which had been smuggled into Iran with such deadly effect, were now being smuggled into Iraqi mosques and passed around.

The Iranian clergy backed a fanatic group of Shi'a fundamentalists in Iraq called the Da'wah. The Da'wah were busy fomenting Islamic revolution in Saddam's own backyard. Determined to wipe them out, Saddam arrested their leader, Ayatollah Muhammad Bakr Sadr, and his sister. He had them horribly tortured and finally murdered.

Then Saddam went to war against Khomeini himself. Saddam

launched his armies across the Iranian border in September 1980, proclaiming that Allah was on his side and predicting victory in a few days. His stated objective was the reclaiming of a bit of oil-rich border territory Iraq had lost in a long-ago war with the Persians. Instead, the war became a long-drawn-out mortal combat.

At school, we were bombarded with propaganda of how the Americans were getting what they deserved in Iran, but that the Iranians, too, were the enemies of Arab Iraq and the true faith of Sunni Islam.

There was a concentrated effort to turn everyone into America haters. However, in spite of this, everyone continued to love American clothes, hamburgers, blue jeans, music and the rest of the outer shell of American culture. At the same time, deep down, many Arabs had a genuine hatred of American global power. The reason for this can be explained in one word: Israel. America meant Israel. Anyone who fails to understand this will not understand why the situation in the Middle East cannot be solved. Because America is so intimately allied with Israel, and Israel is seen as the root of all evil in the Arab world, then whenever anything bad happens in the Arab world, it is the fault of the Americans. I say this not as a theory, but as a fact. For in our unique system of logic, a theory believed is a fact.

You can have a war between Iran and Iraq, with Iraq using Soviet weapons and with Americans held hostage in Iran, in which both the Iranian and the Iraqi people will tell you unequivocally that the Americans are behind it all. The Americans are the enemy. It doesn't matter that the Iraqis are flying Soviet MiGs; Iranians announce that America is bombing Iran. And Iraqis announce that America is behind Iran's missiles hitting Iraq.

At home, meanwhile, things remained pretty much the same: my father yelling at us, my mother trying to defend us. I was afraid of him, but something always made me defy him. I hated the way he used his power inside our home, like using a cannon against a hummingbird. He always acted as if the slightest disagreement with him were an attempted assassination. I came to realize that my father was psychotic. I also realized that he was precisely the type that functioned well in Saddam's insane regime.

The wonder was that my father took me along when the family moved to Zimbabwe. In 1982 he was appointed first Iraqi ambassador to this former British colony. To do things in style, the Iraqi government had bought a magnificent piece of land with an enormous and luxurious home for the meager sum of $100,000 U.S. Probably the former estate of well-to-do English Rhodesians, long since gone. My mother performed her role as ambassador's wife in a perfunctory but dutiful way. And she was still the one warm refuge of love and affection in my life. I was seventeen and intent on having fun. During the year I was in Zimbabwe, my friends were the sons and daughters of other diplomats who attended the same elite school as I. My pals and I didn't talk about politics; we talked about cars and girls.

In my sixth and last year of high school there I passed my exams, as well as the special test administered by the Iraqi Ministry of Education for university entrance. My first choice was to join the elite air force so that I could eventually take one of the MiGs or Mirages and defect to Israel like Munir Rouffa, an Iraqi pilot who had delivered his state-of-the-art jet fighter to the Israelis in 1966. Saddam's anathema was my hero. Along with Eli Cohen.

My father must have suspected something devious, because he refused to even consider the air force. He wanted me to be a doctor. Not so that I could actually be a doctor. So that he could have his son the doctor. I applied to a college in Los Angeles for electronics and avionics and was accepted. Father said no. Finally my mother was able to make him relent enough to let me go to England, at her expense, to study computer electronics.

So I was off to England and to a whole new world of freedom.

3
INTO THE LIONS' DEN

I WONDER if the British know that Mideastern spies, conspirators and assassins regard their country as the world's biggest playground. And not just London. The provincial towns have been hotbeds of activity, too. I ended up in Manchester, and it was no exception.

I loved England. For the first time in my life I was truly on my own. I was seventeen. It was easy to get to know other students because most of us lived in the comfortable university residences. I had my own room, a big bed-sitter, with a sink and one of those old-fashioned English heaters that have to be fed with coins. Eight of us shared the one bathroom on the floor. Among those on my floor were a Norwegian, an Italian, a Malaysian and a Spaniard.

I could have taken meals at the residence, but I preferred to go out so I could practice my English. I had done well in English at school. Now I wanted to become truly fluent.

Everyone told me, "If you want to learn English really well, get an English girlfriend." I took their advice and began my pursuit enthusiastically. I discovered that many English girls harbored the myth of the romantic desert sheik, and I seemed to be considered more talented in bed than their own chaps. Anyway, I was happy. It wasn't just the sex. It was being able to have a normal friendship with the girls, with or without sex.

Among the other Arab students, especially the Iraqis, I said nothing about my father. The last thing I wanted was for his reputation to follow me here. It was exhilarating. I was free of him. But then I realized I was not free of his shadow, and his imprint was deep in my soul.

Ironically, now that I was free, I wanted to strike out at him more than ever. Politics had always been the surest way to score a direct hit, and now that I was grown, I was in a position finally to take full advantage of that knowledge.

I decided I wanted to join one of the Iraqi groups in England that was working against the regime of Saddam. This meant I had basically two choices: the Communists or the Da'wah. I ruled out the former without even checking them out. Communism hadn't a chance in Iraq, and in any case, what I'd seen of Marxism made me believe it was just another form of tyranny. That left the Da'wah, the Shi'a Islamic movement. I began to feel them out.

At that time I still believed that Shi'ism might really be as my mother described. I thought that perhaps the Iranians had just got it all wrong and used this ancient Arab faith for their own perfidious Persian ends. I held out a last hope that the Shi'a movement would be my answer—until I met the Da'wah face to face.

After classes some Iraqi students would get together and talk of home. A frequent topic was the war between Iran and Iraq. This inevitably brought the conversation around to Shi'ism.

When I mentioned that my mother was Shi'a, the boys in the Da'wah took an interest. Assuming that I would automatically be sympathetic, they'd rant on about how wonderful Khomeini was and how, when he won the war, Iraq would become a new Shi'a Islamic republic just like Iran.

These were Iraqi students talking, but it seemed they wanted Iraq to become a province of Khomeini's Iran. I was both fascinated and appalled. I pretended to agree, not sure of what I was doing or of what I planned to do.

I got to know one of their number, Noman, the head of the Da'wah cells in Manchester. Noman had been trained in Lebanon, where he had relatives. There he and his fellow recruits were taught basic military skills, as well as the specialized skills used by the radical Lebanese Shi'a militia, the Hezbollah, which means Party of God. At the time the world had barely heard of the Hezbollah or its radical core, Islamic Jihad, both of which were supported and in part controlled by Tehran. But in a few years they would grab global headlines as the terrorist kidnappers of Westerners in Lebanon. What they demanded for the release of those hostages was the release of several Iraqi Da'wah guerrillas held in prison in Kuwait after they bombed the American and French embassies there. This was the sort of thing the Da'wah trained for; they learned about explosives.

In 1982, before I went to England, the Da'wah had bombed the Iraqi embassy in Beirut, killing about thirty people. Noman was particularly proud of this exploit, giving the impression he had been part of the overall planning. He talked about how he and his men were waging a jihad, a holy war, against Saddam the infidel. The taking of Western hostages, the Israeli invasion of Lebanon, the bombing of the U.S. Marine barracks and the American embassy in Lebanon, all made headlines in the Western press, but this bit of inter-Arab violence essentially went unreported in the West.

The Da'wah was one of two main religious movements in Iraq. The other drew its members from Sunni Muslims. It was strictly political, without a military wing, since it didn't have a foreign sponsor to pay for arms. It was called the Brotherhood, and at the time it supported Saddam as the least of several possible evils.

The Da'wah was the movement that Saddam was doing everything in his power to wipe from the face of the earth. This militant Shi'a group has both a political and a military arm and is backed mainly by the Iranians. After Saddam killed its leader, Bakr Sadr, it was led by Ayatollah Muhammad Bakr al-Hakim (no relation). Under his leadership the military arm grew more radical and more daring. Bombings became a daily occurrence in the cities of Iraq. The Hakim family controlled other rival Shi'a factions as well. The idea was for the family to control all factions and eventually unite them to take over from Saddam when the moment was ripe.

Saddam wanted to make sure that moment never came. When a Da'wah suicide bomber drove an ambulance loaded with explosives into the headquarters of the air force, the Iraqi regime went to new lengths to identify the perpetrator. To foil pursuit, a Da'wah bomber always commits his final act of glory carrying no identification of any kind. In this case the bomber was blown to bits. Undaunted, Saddam's men gathered up the pieces, sewed them all together and presented this grim reincarnation on television. They offered a reward to anyone who recognized it. When the corpse was identified, they killed the man's entire family.

Unlike party and army people, whom Saddam dispatched by firing squad, Da'wah members merited the special attention of torturers from the Amn, or secret police. Information about Da'wah cells, their members and plots were wrung from those suspected. A favorite method was to tie the captive's hands tightly behind his back and then string him up by his arms with ropes passed under his elbows to a rotating ceiling fan. The agony as the shoulders slowly separated from the body can only be compared with descriptions of the excruciating pain of crucifixion. Few survived it.

Saddam also deported thousands of Shi'ites to Iran, as well as Iraqis of Iranian origin. Among the deportees he included agents of his own to work inside Iran against the ayatollahs. These deportations also provided him with another way to get rid of dangerously talented military officers.

Once Saddam began to move against the Da'wah, a secret department was formed for the job of eliminating any Shi'a who didn't show sufficient support for the regime. Some were sent to walk over Iranian minefields.

By 1984, when I was in England, the Da'wah leadership had been pretty well wiped out inside Iraq. Mehdi al-Hakim, brother of Ayatollah Hakim, was in Tehran. Even the agents that the Da'wah had managed to send in from Iran and Syria were being intercepted, as Iraqi intelligence had penetrated their networks. Hakim was assassinated in early 1988 by the Mukhabarat while he was at a conference in the Sudan.

The Da'wah cells in exile did much the same kind of work that the Iranian revolutionaries did during their years of opposition. They concentrated on recruiting, holding anti-Saddam protest demonstrations in places like Hyde Park and, above all, propagandizing. They had learned from Khomeini to make all the right noises about how they believed in democracy, to woo Western journalists and politicians. What they planned, of course, was a theocratic dictatorship as thorough and brutal as Khomeini's. In fact, they wanted full union with Iran.

This is what I was involved with in far-off Manchester.

Noman was in his mid-twenties, a perfect specimen of a person whose meaningless life finally took on significance when he became a religious zealot. Powerlessness was replaced by feelings of power. Religion provided the answers to all his questions and provided the explanation and the solution for all problems. The cause of all problems, of course, was the infidel Israelis and Americans; the solution was Islam. At a coffee shop one day he decided to try to bring me further into the fold.

"Khomeini is a great man and the savior of our people," he whispered. "Saddam is our enemy, the enemy of Islam and of the people. He's in power only for himself. He tries to fool the people into thinking he's a good Muslim. But he's a fake and a tyrant. We're going to deliver him to Khomeini. Then Iraq will be free."

You got the first half right, I thought silently.

Noman and his friends believed that everything negative that was said about Khomeini was enemy propaganda. Khomeini never killed anyone. People being executed in Iran were being killed by someone who only pretended to be Khomeini. Khomeini was innocent of all the oppression and torture, the horrible, stupid war. At the same time, they would babble about how the war was justified, that to free Iraq, there must be sacrifice for the freedom. What freedom? I thought. Khomeini's? I couldn't believe it. What planet did they live on?

For me the Da'wah were a disappointing bunch of lunatics. Khomeini and his Islamic revolution had built the perfect killing machine, and I had no doubt that these boys would do exactly the same in my country, given the chance. It was conceivable that they would be worse than Saddam, just as Khomeini was worse than the shah.

One night in 1984, around Easter, I made a decision. As I look back I am amazed and a bit appalled at the way I took so many drastic steps, made life-and-death decisions, in a kind of fit. I realize that I was becoming motivated not just by an urge for vengeance on my father but also by my own developing political beliefs. And given what I now knew of the Da'wah and Khomeini's brand of Islam, I could not work for them. That was more important now than my personal vendetta.

On the contrary, I decided I had to do what I could to destroy the Da'wah. I made the decision in spite of the fact that it meant working for the forces that supported Saddam Hussein.

There was another Iraqi student on the campus, named Hassan. From bits of talk I overheard, I knew he had something to do with the Ba'th Party. Hassan, who was a bit older than I, was studying for his Ph.D. in nuclear physics. To study such a subject meant he must have had links with security and been cleared by intelligence. I went to him and told him the truth about my father's identity.

I also told him I had learned a great deal about certain of our Shi'a compatriots in the university. Two days later Hassan brought me to a small lounge at the university to meet two men who had come at his request. I realized I was dealing with Saddam's chosen few. Their aura of power and ruthlessness was unmistakable. The larger of the two was introduced as Auda. Later I realized he was Auda Sultan, one of two Iraqi agents who had been captured in Iran by the shah in 1976 and returned to Iraq as part of a friendship-treaty deal. Auda was a senior agent. He listened intently to my story of Noman and his colleagues, then questioned me about my background. My father's name was enough in itself. My bona fides were above suspicion.

"This will be the first time in eight months we've been able to penetrate the Da'wah," Auda said. "You'll be the mole."

It was only then that I fully realized the ramifications of what I had done. My God! I was working for the secret police. That meant that one way or another I was working for the Mukhabarat itself. In Iraq this is the most powerful arm of the security apparatus.

Auda Sultan was with the Jihaz Amn al-Hezib, the Instrument of Party Security. It was in turn controlled by the Maktab Amanat Sir al-Kutur, which translates badly as the National Bureau and Keeper of

Secrets. Somehow in English it sounds like something out of a children's book. In Arabic it sounded as grim as it really was.

When the security matter in question was outside Iraq, the Mukhabarat took over direction of the Jihaz Amn al-Hezib. And here I was in Manchester, joining forces with these dreaded men.

Auda instructed me to continue pretending that I was in agreement with my Da'wah friends, to learn everything I could and then to report to him. Each Monday and Thursday, if I had anything to report, I was to go to the library at a specific time and to a specific part of the shelves. Auda would be on the other side of the row of shelves, and I would pass my report to him across the books. If I had nothing to report, I simply wasn't to show up. If there was anything urgent, I was to contact a captain in the Iraqi Ministry of Defense, who was studying English at the university.

As I became more accepted by the Da'wah group Noman invited me to attend the sessions they held at the home of a member named Salah. About six or eight of us would gather in the bed-sitting-room upstairs. I used to arrive exactly on time, which meant a while before the others, who were always late. When Salah went downstairs to let the others in, I would go through the papers on his desk, looking for names, bank accounts, anything.

When we were all assembled, Noman would hold forth on Khomeini's latest victory in the war, and the rest would make noises of praise. Sometimes Noman told us about agents going into Syria to train before entering Iraq. And though he never revealed the agents' full names, he revealed their route: it was the same route traveled by the Kurdish resistance and ran through Turkey.

My secret-service colleagues helped my credibility by spreading stories about how I was a dangerous anti-Saddam activist. So by day I went around with the Da'wah putting up stickers that said Saddam was a new Hitler, and by night I went around with Saddam's agents taking them down.

Every few days I passed along my reports in the library, giving Auda names, dates of meetings, and plans of clandestine activities. I gave him Da'wah bank account numbers and revealed the source of their support. Some money was from Syria and some from Algeria.

I never knew what became of Noman and his Da'wah pals. But they were small fry, and I figured Auda and his bosses simply kept them under long surveillance in order to get to the head of the enemy. In any case, none disappeared right away. For a time I rationalized what I was doing by telling myself I knew what fate the Da'wah would have in store for most of Iraq if they got into power.

But no matter how I rationalized, I was not happy with what I was doing. I think what bothered me was the realization that by a horrible twist of fate and politics I was working for the monster Saddam and his killing machine. And my father. One night a strange idea began to form in the clouds of my mind: Mossad.

My old idea of defecting to Israel, of being an Iraqi Eli Cohen, had always been there, hovering at the edge of my thoughts. I tossed and turned and tried to sleep. Mossad. The Israelis.

Maybe I could even the score with my father and his master, Saddam, if I worked for the Mossad. I could offer my services to help them fight Saddam. In the morning I sat down to write a letter to the Mossad. Since I didn't have their address, I simply wrote on the envelope, "Israeli Embassy, London."

I said I was an Iraqi and proposed getting together to fight people we both hated. "If you want to talk," I wrote, "send someone to Manchester, to the Britannia Hotel." I gave a time and date, then added, "Have your man wear a red flower in his lapel."

This was authentically stupid. My only excuse is that I was nineteen years old. Half aware even then of how ridiculous it was, I went to my rendezvous. Of course no one showed up.

Undaunted, I decided to travel to London and go to the Israeli embassy in person. I felt like Daniel headed for the lions' den.

4
WORKING FOR THE ARCHENEMY

THE Israeli embassy in London is a formidable-looking building located in the district of Kensington. When I went there, the street on which it sits was barricaded. The London embassy, like Israel's missions all over the world, was secured because the worst was always expected.

I had barely got to the gate of the Israeli fortress when I was forced through a metal detector and roughly searched.

"Business?" the guard questioned suspiciously.

I fished out my I.D. and thrust it at him. "I must see someone in security and intelligence," I stammered.

The guard narrowed his eyes and motioned to another guard. "This jerk wants to see someone in security and intelligence."

The second guard looked at my I.D. and grinned meanly. "Really," he said sarcastically.

"It's important," I insisted.

The first guard shrugged and phoned. His eyes on my I.D., he spoke to someone in rapid Hebrew, and then put the phone down and returned his eyes to me. "Tomorrow," he instructed, "go to the consulate entrance and ask for Isaac."

The next day, when I was checked at the gate, I was allowed inside after another thorough search and a pass through the metal detector. I was told to follow a winding path past the main embassy building to the consulate, on the other side of the inner garden.

Another guard gruffly directed me upstairs to a small waiting room. A door led to a well-furnished office. It was there that Isaac was waiting for me.

He was a fat man, with spiky gray-black hair. In his gray suit he seemed to me a typical Israeli, businesslike and tough.

"What do you want?" he demanded. "And who sent you?"

"Nobody sent me. I want to work with you," I offered.

"Let me see your passport."

I fished in my pocket and handed it over.

He studied it. "Does your father know you're here?"

So they had checked. I shook my head. "No. He knows nothing. It was my idea."

"Wait here," Isaac instructed.

I waited. Then the door opened, and a tall, distinguished-looking man strode in. He was bald, with dark eyes. He spoke to me in Arabic, and I noted he had a distinct Palestinian accent.

"I apologize for not coming to the appointment you proposed," he said elegantly. "My name is Yusef."

"It was my fault. It was a ridiculous proposal."

"No, no. We just didn't have anyone to send on such short notice. Now then, tell me more about yourself and why you're here."

I told him the whole story. Everything I could think of about my father and his work, and why I wanted to work for them. Yusef made me feel comfortable and confident. But I knew that whatever he did, it was a deliberate strategy. This was a professional.

He gave me papers to fill out, long questionnaires that asked about virtually every detail of my life and my thoughts. I remember many of them: How many cigarettes do you smoke? Do you drink alcohol? Do you take medication? Do you sleep with girls? If so, how many? Who are your friends? What are their jobs? What are their politics? How did you meet them? Do you have any Jewish friends? How much pay do you expect? Have you approached anyone else? It went on and on and took hours to complete. Yusef helped me when I wasn't sure of the question or just how completely to answer. When I finished the questionnaires, he continued to ask me for more information. I told him all about my father and my abused childhood.

"I'm sure you must be hungry," he said after a while.

I nodded, and he picked up the phone and ordered some food. In about fifteen minutes a secretary brought Kentucky Fried Chicken, and we went on with our work. He was helpful, gentlemanly and absolutely impossible to read. I had no idea what he was thinking about my responses. I just answered every question as best I could. I was committed. I was going to do everything they wanted, without reservation.

"Would you like a smoke?" he asked.

"No, thanks. I only smoke one a day. And I had my cigarette for today."

He leaned back, relaxed and lit up. "What will you do," he asked, drawing on the smoke, "if you see me in the street one day?"

"I will say hello, of course," I replied, thinking maybe they wanted to know if I would admit to knowing Israelis.

"No," he said, "you won't. You will walk right on by as if you'd never seen me before in your life. I'm just another stranger on the street. If there's one chance in a million, we take care of that chance. That's why we're still alive. Understand?"

I understood. And I was elated. These were the pros. These were the men who could enable me to fight back, to right some of the wrong, who could help me take revenge on my father and on the regime of Saddam Hussein.

Yusef told me to return the next Sunday.

THE NEXT SUNDAY I WAS TO GO TO the main embassy building, not the consulate. I was thoroughly checked again by guards with a metal detector. Inside I found myself in a large empty lobby with a fireplace and a huge black mirror over the mantel. A guard-receptionist checked my passport, then searched me and everything in my pockets.

He directed me to an office off a hallway to the right. Yusef was there, ready for me.

"Good day," he said, unfolding a map of Baghdad and spreading it out on the table. "I want you to identify some buildings."

"Sure," I replied, looking down at the map.

"Point out the Ministry of Defense for me."

"Here," I said, pointing.

"Now show me the presidential palaces, the Amn, the Rashidiya prisoner-of-war camp and the military airport." They were asking me things that I knew they must know already, but I obliged.

"This is a pretty old map," I said. "If you bring me a more recent map, I can show you better."

"No. We don't need that," Yusef replied.

I told him about the reading I did as a child and how I hero-worshipped Eli Cohen, the Israeli agent who operated on the front lines of the enemy army, bravely finding out everything, down to the last detail of the last soldier's last cigarette. I thought I was going to be a spy like him.

The reality for me was nothing quite as glamorous. I wasn't a trained commando or a specialist in any sensitive area. My special talent was people. Talking to them, getting them to talk to me. The Mossad saw in me an ideal recruiter. If a man is a criminal, then I can act the criminal. If he's religious, I'm more pious than the pope. If he's a gardener, I love flowers. Then I can get into his mind and figure out if this man has a weak spot, a grudge, a reason that would make him spy material.

This talent, I believe, is the natural result of growing up as I did. I became a chameleon because I had to survive in the many environments into which I was dropped.

FOR two years the Iraqi Ministry of Defense ran a special, very private school in England, near the town of Woking, in the hills of Surrey. The entire establishment was rented by the ministry, and every student there was a cadet. A new locale in England was found every few years. About one hundred students were sent at a time. They studied English, history, mathematics, physics and other subjects under the learned eye of top British teachers.

Those who passed their A level examinations were placed in universities throughout England, again at the expense of the Iraqi Defense Ministry. For the most part these students were in high-tech electronics or computer science. Most of the cadets were destined for the elaborate weapon-modifications programs developed by Saddam's minions.

The school was one more illustration of how the Western powers helped for years to build up the military machine they would go to war against in 1991.

This is not to say that every Iraqi student in England was there on His Highness Saddam's service. But it was very difficult for ordinary Iraqi families to send their children abroad to study. A child abroad meant sending money abroad, and this alerted the government to the fact that a son got out. The questions would start. Why did he leave? Did he not pass the government's own security check for a foreign scholarship? Why not?

The security checks on the boys—there were no girls—before they were chosen for the honor of the cadet school in England were incredibly thorough. Political correctness was more important than ability. Still, there were enough bright ones to fill a lot of the places at the elite school. Once they were in Woking, the surveillance continued under the eagle eye of Iraqi supervisors like the Major.

My first assignment for the Mossad was to find out everything I could about the Major and determine if this Iraqi military man could be recruited for the Israelis. Two of my old classmates were at the school, and the idea was for me to arrange a visit and wing it from there. Yusef offered no particular advice, and at this point I was given no special training.

I shook Yusef's hand and walked out into the streets of London. I had done it. I was working for the Mossad. My God, the Mossad! I walked rapidly toward the underground station, a hundred thoughts racing through my mind. I was an Iraqi working for the Zionist entity itself. Ha! Take that, Dad! And you, Saddam! After all these years—a whole lifetime so far—of them controlling me, now at last *I* was in control.

THE GROUNDS AT THE WOKING school were spacious. There was a beautiful garden, and the main building was one of those old two-story red brick English institutions.

My old pals were glad to see me and invited me to stay. Soon we were talking, having a regular class reunion, drinking beer and shooting pool.

"This place isn't bad at all," I said as I checked out the lay of the table for my next shot. "I wonder if there's any way I could be transferred to the Ministry of Defense and join you here?" I lined up the cue and fired.

"You can always talk to the Major," said one of my mates. Bingo.

The Major, a man in his forties, was short in height but long on arrogance. He reeked of the Estikhbarat, the arm of military intelligence for which he worked. He lived off-campus but arrived daily with his wife, whom he left in the car outside the gates as he entered the grounds to check up on things. This daily visit of an hour or two seemed an odd way to keep up surveillance on the school, but the students all figured he had one or two stool pigeons in their midst.

A few days after my arrival I was in the garden with one of my friends when the Major arrived. My friend introduced me to him, and we were left alone to talk.

He knew who my father was. But he was not unfriendly, and we discussed a few innocuous matters, like the high quality of British teachers. My real source of information about the Major was his students, who had made a close study of him. The most useful fact I gathered was that he cheated on his wife. In a small town that sort of thing is impossible to keep secret. It made him vulnerable: the Mossad could use women to get to him.

In any case, school was about to recess for the summer. By now I had figured out that the Israelis really weren't interested in the Major. The assignment had been a practice run. I knew what the Israelis really needed were Iraqi recruits in high positions. And to acquire them, they needed a rover like me. They knew what was going on, but their difficulty was in penetrating Iraqi organizations. They needed to have an agent in place and day-to-day information on the inner workings of various groups.

I returned to London and reported my findings to Yusef. He seemed pleased. The Israelis began to pay me, look after my expenses and anything else I told them I needed. I could buy suits or whatever took my fancy. I remember a gray silk shirt I bought and wore to one of the regular Sunday Mossad meetings.

When I arrived at the Israeli embassy that day and entered the main hall, I saw a face in the black mirror over the fireplace watching me from the other side of the glass. All I could make out was a bald head and dark glasses, but it was a face I would never forget—a huge face, watching from behind a two-way mirror.

This time I was taken to the other side of the embassy, to a lounge with a small kitchen. Inside were four men. Besides Yusef, there was a man they called Mark, who looked like a Wall Street broker and spoke fluent Arabic. Another was a short bald man with thick glasses, who was introduced as Morris. The fourth was an old fellow with hollow cheeks, who had come, they said, from Israel.

We all sat in armchairs around a low, polished wooden table. Morris passed around coffee in chipped mugs from the kitchen.

"Here," said the old fellow from Israel, offering me a cigarette. "Your one cigarette for today."

If he was trying to impress me, he succeeded.

"Tell me again just exactly why you have chosen to work with us," the old man said. He had a deep, raspy voice.

"I want to work against Saddam. That leaves me with three choices: Iran, Syria or Israel."

"Ah," he said with a knowing smile, "Iran. We help them even though they are nothing, they are incompetents. But they're doing us a favor by making war on Saddam. And Syria. Ah, Syria is like a woman wearing a chador. Every time there is a little bit of wind, it lifts up the veil and shows everything. So easy for us. And we"—he grew suddenly serious—"we hit your nuclear reactor, didn't we?"

They certainly had. No one in Iraq would ever forget the day in 1981 when the Israeli jets streaked out of the western skies and obliterated Saddam's beloved Osirak, as it is known in the West. In Iraq it was known as Tammouz, so named by Saddam. Both Osirak and Tammouz are versions of the name of the ancient god of the dead. The name alone gave the lie to Saddam's claim that it was there for peaceful purposes. When I heard the air-raid sirens, I was listening to an Israeli radio station. But by that time the jets had already been and gone, and soon the Israelis were announcing the destruction of Iraq's nuclear threat. Later the Iraqi news broadcasts told us that because of the evil Israelis, we would not be having any of the promised cheap electricity; Osirak was no more. But nobody was fooled. We knew what the reactor was really about: Saddam's nuclear bomb.

"How did people in Baghdad feel about that?" the old Israeli wanted to know.

"They were frightened and astonished that you could come and go like that—could do anything you wanted, it seemed," I told him.

The old Israeli looked pleased, like a satisfied cat.

"And Saddam was livid," I went on. "The head of that defense area was executed, as were all the others responsible for air defense along the route. But I guess you know that."

He smiled a tight little smile. "Morris will be your control officer. If there is anything you need, we will take care of it. Welcome to the Mossad."

MORRIS was an affable type, with dark blue eyes and a bald head. He was clean-shaven and, ironically, looked like a German beer magnate. He could understand Arabic but spoke it poorly, and so we used English. I found myself liking my control officer when we met for our first session. Our meetings now were always outside the embassy, usually in the Churchill Hotel, near Marble Arch, where the noisy coffee shop afforded us public privacy.

The first thing Morris told me to do was to stop working inside the Da'wah for Iraqi intelligence. I was a bit bewildered because it seemed to me the Da'wah and all the other Islamic fundamentalist movements posed an even greater threat to Israel now than its old adversaries, the Palestinians. Give the Palestinians a few square miles and they'd be happy, regardless of PLO rhetoric and fringe fanatics. The Da'wah, Khomeini's faithful followers, would settle for nothing less than annihilation of the Zionist entity.

In fact, it began to look as though the Israelis were making the classic mistake of preparing for the last war instead of the next one. But they were still my best bet for working against Saddam. Maybe they were just testing my obedience and my abilities.

I was to be paid $250 U.S. a month, plus expenses in pounds sterling, and bonuses if I did my work well. But I was to keep at my studies and only do Mossad work on the side. They were insistent on this. In the long run, it was clear, they wanted me to be in a good position for them. Flunking was hardly the way.

Morris then showed me a piece of paper with numbers on it. "This is the telephone number of the embassy," he said, "and this is an extension. If there is anything important, call and ask for this extension and say you want to leave a message. Don't leave your name. If there is nothing, don't call."

Taking the piece of paper, I thanked him and left. I was filled with conflicting thoughts as I considered what I had done: I was now eligible for execution in Baghdad.

AT FIRST Morris put me through my paces in the most basic of all skills for cops, killers and spies: tailing and shaking tails.

He told me to be at the Cumberland Hotel, near Marble Arch, at eleven the next morning. "When you see me, say nothing; act as though you don't know me, and then follow me."

I arrived quite early. I had hardly taken a seat and snapped open a newspaper when a fat, overdressed Arab sat down beside me. He was one of those ostentatiously wealthy types who spend too much money on their clothes and never achieve quite the right effect.

"Hello, my brother," he said in Arabic. "You are Arabic, no? I am Tunisian. And where are you from?"

"Iraq," I said, and returned to my newspaper.

"Ah, Iraq. Yes, fine country. Look, I am ashamed to ask, but, well, I am in such a situation. I'm staying near Oxford," he revealed. "And, well, I don't have the money for the train to go home and . . ."

"I can't help you. I'm just a student, and I don't have much money myself. Sorry about that." How flimsy could an approach be? His suit was worth a small fortune.

He muttered apologies and left.

While I was still wondering what that was all about, Morris came into the lobby, looked around and walked out again. I dutifully trotted out and followed him on the opposite side of the street. He strolled around a couple of blocks, then made a loop over to the Churchill Hotel.

I stuck to him like a hound after a hare. This sort of thing was almost second nature to me. Because of my father's own fears of assassination our whole family was used to looking over its shoulder.

For that matter, so was almost the entire population of Iraq. Prying eyes and ears are simply a daily reality of life in any police state.

I padded into the bar of the Churchill and, ignoring Morris while he sat at a corner table, took a seat of my own across the room. After about five minutes he came over to me.

"Hi," he said casually, sitting opposite me. "Well, that's fine. You're clean." Meaning I hadn't been tailed by the wrong tail. Naturally they had put a tail on me, looking for Iraqi tails.

He ordered a couple of coffees and, when they arrived, began to speak about the Mossad's immediate plans for me.

"We're interested in a Palestinian you told Yusef you knew at Manchester. Name of Abdel."

Abdel, which is not his real name, was taking a postgraduate degree in English at Salford. His thesis was a study of the Shaback, the Israeli equivalent of the FBI. Under the auspices of the British university system, he was looking for the vulnerable points in the Israeli intelligence armor.

Abdel and I had talked on occasion, and from the subjects discussed, I gathered he was with Fatah, the military arm of the PLO. (In 1972 Fatah operatives shocked the world when they murdered eleven Israeli athletes at the Munich Olympics. Since then Fatah has attacked Israeli diplomats, embassies, businessmen, aircraft and ordinary civilians from Bangkok to Madrid.)

"He likes to talk about sex," I told Morris. "What he really seems to like is sex with hookers."

Morris nodded. "Get close to him. Be his best buddy. Find out everything you can about what he's been up to, who he knows."

Getting close to Abdel was easy. All I had to do was express an interest in his favorite hobby. Already I was learning how often the oldest profession was the best weapon in the espionage arsenal. Soon we could be seen most nights roaring around Manchester. Abdel had a lot of money. Whether it was PLO funds or family wealth or whether it came from more insidious sources, I never learned. But Abdel confided in his newfound Iraqi friend about a lot of other things.

One night it would be the Millionaires Club with a couple of tarts, the next dancing till dawn the night before exams. We were carousing around picking up hookers, and we were hung over to boot, but we managed to pass the exams.

In the middle of all these carryings-on, we would talk about Iraqi politics and Fatah exploits. Since I was Iraqi, he could assume I hated Israel and easily believe I was on the side of Fatah. But as far as I was concerned, Fatah were just another bunch of jumped-up pseudomilitary fanatics, who were making life impossible in the whole godforsaken Middle East. I have a lot of sympathy for the Palestinian people, who have been condemned to their own diaspora since the founding of Israel. But I never bought the line that blamed Israel for everything. Maybe I was wrong, but in any case, my war was with Saddam. That meant working with the Mossad against Israel's enemies, whether they were mine or not. There's an old cliché about the Mideast. It goes, "The enemy of my enemy is my friend." A fatuous oversimplification. Instead I prefer, "The friend of my friend isn't necessarily my friend." The key to the Middle East is understanding that you can never really understand it.

I am not writing to defend my actions, but to record them, for better or worse. And at this point what I was doing was informing on the PLO. Abdel gave me some small nuggets of information for my new masters.

One night Abdel and I and our ladies of the night went to an expensive private club. We sat at a secluded table, and while Abdel and I spoke Arabic our English doxies chatted about the Champagne. We got to talking about Fatah operations inside Israel.

"You know how we get the guns through?" Abdel asked. "*Al nuktah al meitah* [the dead spots]," he said smugly.

"Dead spots?" I said, looking interested.

"We prearrange a spot where the weapons are to be buried. Either inside Israel itself or just across the border in Lebanon. Our commandos inside Lebanon handle that part. We have hidden routes to slip across into Israel. Then the actual hit team picks up the stuff for the operation. That way the hit team can cross in clean from the West Bank or even Jordan through the damn checkpoints. And they can rebury the guns and leave the same way. Clean as a whistle."

I looked suitably impressed. Israel had established a sixteen-mile-wide zone north of its border, in occupied Lebanon, to prevent just this sort of thing.

"Where do the weapons come from?" I asked. "It can't be that easy, with the occupation."

"We can easily run them through Lebanon. But the best we buy from Israeli soldiers."

"Israeli soldiers? Sell arms to you guys?" I was stunned.

"Everybody has a price, my friend. Everybody."

When I reported this to Morris, he listened intently and was clearly not happy to hear about Israeli soldiers selling weapons to the enemy. Still, he maintained his poise and pressed for details.

I continued seeing Abdel for a while, gleaning whatever I could about Fatah contacts in England. Morris always told me not to pry too obviously, in order not to raise suspicion. It was more important to keep myself clean for future work. He left it unsaid, but he could only mean work inside Iraq itself.

"Okay," he told me after my third report, "you can drop Abdel now." It was like playing chess on a life-size board. Morris simply moved Abdel off the board. He didn't explain why, and I didn't ask. What they did with the information was their business. Their business, I knew, could be terminal. But that was the game Abdel had agreed to play when he took up with Fatah. The same game I had agreed to play. Abdel, as far as I knew, was allowed to carry on in good health.

"Forget Abdel," Morris continued. "We have something else for you to do. The summer break is coming up. We want you to go to Brussels for the holiday and stay with your father." My father, they knew, was by then Iraqi ambassador to Belgium.

I would rather have jumped into a snake pit for them. "If you say so," I replied without enthusiasm.

"Call me here in London when you get there. We'll have something arranged by then. In the meantime, see what you can find out about security at the Iraqi embassy in Brussels. Don't do anything more than talk to the people you would ordinarily meet there. We'll go into it in more detail later."

I TOOK the boat train to Brussels and was met at the station by my father's driver. My first problem was how to phone Morris.

I told the driver I wanted to call my tutor in England, but didn't want to use the home phone, because that was paid for by the government and this was my private expense. I told him to pull over when I saw a phone booth. He stuck to me like a bear sticks to honey. He leaned against the booth and kept right on talking until London answered. He had probably been ordered not to let me out of his sight or hearing.

I could hardly use my code name to contact Morris as arranged, and I couldn't use his, so I asked for the mythical tutor, using my real name. The secretary didn't twig, and told me there was no such person there, then hung up. Exasperated, I gave up and let the busybody driver take me home.

After a short time we arrived in one of the expensive neighborhoods, where the powerful seem to congregate. People like my father, the ambassador. The house was yet another vast and sumptuous establishment.

My mother threw her arms around me when I walked in. "You've been away too long! Oh, look at you; you're skin and bones." Mothers must be the same all over the world.

My father, though, was his same old self. As usual he was drinking whiskey, which only made matters worse. He barked out an order to get ready for dinner. That was my welcome home from him.

Mama busied herself making a roast chicken dinner, my favorite, and I just stayed in the kitchen with her, talking about my classes and how good the professors were.

It was one of those rare occasions when my brother and sisters and I were all home at the same time. My brother, Saif, was at the International School in Brussels. My older sister, Dina, was studying dentistry in Iraq and was home for the summer. Dalia was only four years old.

Dinner was actually a warm and pleasant affair until I said something unwise about the abysmal failure of Saddam's war with Iran. With a roar Father overturned the entire table and stormed off to his study, shouting all manner of curses at his son.

"Scum. My son is scum! A traitor. I won't have it!"

For one terrifying moment I thought he'd guessed the truth. But it was just his usual ranting. If this is what I was betraying, I thought, so much the better. At the same time, I was aware that I was acting now not only for personal revenge but truly for my own political beliefs.

At least we had pretty well finished eating. While the maid cleaned up, we children tried to console Mama. We brought her hot coffee, and after Father was asleep, late at night, I sat up with her while she read the coffee grounds.

"I don't understand," she said in a small voice, peering into the cup. "I see so many abnormal things—things together that normally are not. I can't read them."

I felt a chill. But I patted her shoulder and said, "But Mama, you live in a completely abnormal family, so it's just a picture of the chaos around here. It's probably the dinner table."

"I suppose you must be right. Why do you have to keep upsetting him? Why can't you try to go along with him?" She began to cry softly. I felt terrible and selfish and remorseful as I tried to comfort her. But I knew I would do the same again.

The next day I was able to get to a phone at a post office without the nosy driver. I dialed the Israeli embassy in London and said I was Franco calling for Morris. Franco was my code name. Sergio Franco.

"Was that you who called last night?" Morris asked angrily.

"I'm sorry. But somebody was standing right beside me, and I had to make something up. All's clear now."

He sounded relieved. "I'll be in on the morning flight. Meet us at the Ramada at noon. The usual precautions."

When I arrived at the Ramada, I heard someone paging Mr. Franco. I went to the desk.

"There's a call for you, sir."

I picked up the phone in one of the booths by the reception desk. "This is Franco."

"Hello. I'm a friend of Morris. Do exactly as I say. Leave the hotel and take the street that is across the road. Walk up and take the first turn right. Follow that street to the end. Turn left and then take the first turn right. Keep walking. I will be there." And he hung up. The Mossad knew by now that as well as having a photographic memory for things I observed, I remembered instructions verbatim.

The sun was shining as I left the hotel and crossed the street. As I walked the prescribed route a car passed me, full of happy sightseers looking out the windows. It was a gray-and-brown Citroën with French plates. When I turned the corner, it passed me again, coming the other way. Then again, as I rounded the next corner.

I willed myself to continue, to ignore it. At the end of the route I found myself on a blocked-off pedestrian street in the old quarter. I was looking around when I saw him. It was the face I had seen watching me in the glass in the hall of the Israeli embassy. The dark glasses, the bald head—he had an indefinable something I could never forget. Just then Morris casually walked up to me with another man.

"Hi," he said. His companion was tall and aristocratic-looking, with light brown hair. "This is Daniel," said Morris by way of introduction. "He will be your contact here in Brussels."

When Daniel spoke, I recognized his voice as the one that had called me to set up the rendezvous. "I'm inviting you to lunch," he said, "before we all get down to business."

During the meal I gave them an account of my expenses, and they paid me with no questions asked, content with a receipt made out on anything handy—a napkin or a match folder.

After lunch Daniel shepherded us up a small side street to a secluded little hotel. The bald man in the dark glasses stayed outside, visible from the front window. The others said nothing about him. I was never to learn who he was.

We checked in at the desk, then trooped upstairs to a room. Since we were a patently suspicious-looking bunch of characters, grown men checking into one tiny room, the hotel was most likely run by one of the thousands of *sayanim*, Jewish sympathizers the Mossad has in every country in the world.

"Everything all right?" asked Morris. We were sitting around the coffee table.

"Fine," I said. "I have some of the information you want." I handed him notes on what I had learned about security at the Iraqi embassy, who the inside guards, chosen by the Mukhabarat, were.

Morris turned on me angrily. "Don't ever do that. Never! Never put anything in writing. Keep it all in here," he hissed, jabbing at my temple with his finger.

I felt my face redden with embarrassment and shock. I had just glimpsed the Mossad side of Morris. My pal was forged of steel.

I was recovering my poise when the door opened and a large bald man came in, carrying a large and obviously heavy suitcase. Not the man I had seen on the street. Another one. My life seemed to be filling up with bald men.

"Ah, hello, Doctor," Morris greeted him. "Just in time." Then Morris turned to me. "The doctor here is going to ask you some more questions. Give him your full cooperation. I'll be going back to London now, and while you're in Brussels you'll work with Daniel here.

You'll have to have a contact point. The phone at your father's house is out of the question. Any ideas?"

"There's a sort of bar-restaurant called the Macao about ten minutes' walk from the house," I said after a moment's thought.

"Perfect. Go there every day at six in the evening and stay for an hour. If there's no call from us, just go home."

Morris and Daniel departed.

"My name is Yusef," the doctor said, shaking my hand. He settled his bulk on the couch and set the large case on the coffee table.

"Well, then," he began cheerfully, "let's see what we have here." He snapped open the case and drew out papers and envelopes, some pencils and felt markers, as well as a cassette tape recorder.

"I think we'll do this first," he announced, handing me a big piece of paper and some colored pencils. "I want you to draw me some pictures. A man, a woman and a child."

The Mossad was certainly full of surprises. But I assumed they knew what they were doing, and I obediently started to draw, wondering what my artwork would reveal about my innermost self.

He took a brief look at my pictures and nodded. Then he read off a list of numbers and asked me to repeat them. With my memory it was easy.

"All right now," he continued, holding up a picture of a ship in full sail. "Something is out of place in this picture. What is it?" There was an anchor in the crow's nest.

He showed me a photograph of a woman sleeping on a couch in a very ordinary living room. She was dressed for daytime, and there was a letter on the floor. "I want you to tell me what happened just before this picture was taken."

This session went on for hours. A Rorschach test. More questions about my childhood. Memories and associations with certain sounds and smells. We spent a lot of time talking about my father, how he had beaten me and generally made life miserable.

"And how do you think people see you?" Yusef asked suddenly.

The question brought me up short. I wasn't sure anymore how I saw myself, let alone how others saw me. "Nothing special," I said. "Likable, I suppose. I mean, I seem to be able to get along with everybody. Except my father of course. I like people up to a point, and on a superficial level I have a lot of friends."

"And how do they see you?"

"As an easygoing rich kid, I guess. Maybe a bit of a playboy. Of course, I don't let anyone know me or get close to me."

"Why?"

"Habit. Maybe because I've spent a lifetime hiding myself from my father." I couldn't help thinking that this aspect of my personality probably made me good material for the spy's lonely trade.

After six hours of questioning, the doctor thanked me and said that was all we had to do, and sent me home.

The next evening I went as arranged to the Macao at six o'clock. It was one of those theme places, all done up to make people think they had walked out of the dreary Brussels weather into . . . well, Macao. It had real palm trees and murals of sunny beaches. I ordered a piña colada and waited. And waited. Nothing.

5

DOING THINGS MY OWN WAY

AFTER three days of piña coladas and endless waiting, Daniel phoned. "Go to the same place we sent you the first time and wait for me—at noon," he said shortly.

I walked to the Ramada. When Daniel arrived, we went to the coffee shop and ordered a simple dinner.

"We want to know everything we can about the Iraqi embassy here," he said to me in low tones. "Names of all the staff, addresses, family situations, how much they're paid, who the Mukhabarat officer is, the other security people, the Telex operators, what kind of Telex they use. Naturally we want to know the codes, as well as who has access to them. We also want to know about your father's office—what it looks like, where it would be best to place a bug." He paused. "Make mental notes of the cars, the licenses and who drives them. We need everything you can find out about how the embassy operates and, above all, any clandestine operations."

In other words, Daniel wanted the embassy in the palm of his hand. The task was actually fairly easy for me. No one at the embassy knew the real state of affairs between my father and me; to them I was simply the son of the ambassador. They assumed that being nice to me would put them in his favor; they were just as terrified of him as I was.

I began dropping into the embassy to chat with and get closer to the guards and secretaries. I should add that they were all men. Women were almost never employed.

As the ambassador's son, I had free access to the building. "I just came to hang around," I'd say casually. Sometimes I'd invite one or two of the men to join me for drinks. The unsuspecting embassy staff told me most of what I needed to know.

I even learned about the coding system—a complex letter code that was changed every so often by a mechanic who would come from Baghdad and alter the decoding machine by the Telex. It was always a four-letter code. For instance, a message like LONDON OPERATION APPROVED might read AMDH BGYR FKPL.

Daniel seemed happy with this information. And I was able to tell him exactly where all the weapons and ammunition were kept.

As for clandestine operations, I learned that the main purpose of virtually all our embassies was to hunt down and destroy enemies of Saddam Hussein. That was the raison d'être of the entire intelligence apparatus and, in fact, of the entire Iraqi government; even the basics of running the country came second. My father, I learned, had ruthlessly performed that task in Poland and now Brussels.

I had always suspected that my father's activities included more than orthodox diplomacy. My conversations with the staff gradually made it clear. One day I noticed two of the security men standing in the embassy's reception hall, enjoying a huge joke. I asked them what was so funny.

"See that big box over there?" said one, pointing to a big crate labeled FURNITURE. It was with parcels for the diplomatic bag.

"What's so funny about that?" I asked, suspecting the horrible truth.

"It's furniture, all right," they said, sniggering. "An armchair, complete with an occupant." At this they doubled up, slapping their thighs.

"Oh," I said knowingly, "one of those. Who's the lucky traveler?" I had heard the stories, but it was still hard to believe.

"One of those Kurdish bastards. He's sound asleep and off to a free vacation in beautiful Baghdad."

I looked at the crate and thought of its poor unlucky occupant, drugged and tied into his very special airline seat. Would he wake up in the baggage compartment and realize his ghastly fate? Would he struggle and scream in vain up there in the sky? Or would he come to only after they had landed and unloaded him into the waiting arms of the Estikhbarat, Iraq's military intelligence?

He was a mere fifteen feet away from me. And there was nothing I could do except tell the Israelis. But I knew they would do nothing to save him. That would be the end of their informant—me—and their information. Fifteen feet away, and already he was in Iraq, another grim statistic. Whoever he was. No wonder the embassy staff was so afraid of my father. He directed agents in these kidnapping operations, hunting down opposition to Saddam even outside Iraq.

The Kurds had been a thorn in the side of rulers of our part of the Arab lands for centuries. They were fiercely independent tribes, whose native territory was a triangle of land at the borders of Iraq, Iran and Turkey that overlapped into all three countries. They had been alternately persecuted and supported by all three, depending on who was trying to cause problems for whom. The Kurds were currently out of favor with Baghdad, and Saddam wanted them hunted down and wiped out.

At first this was done piecemeal, by harassment and arrest inside Iraq and by operations like my father's abroad. But eventually Saddam found this much too slow and inefficient. Saddam wanted a faster, cheaper way to eliminate the Kurds and then any leftover enemies. Like Hitler, he ordered a Final Solution. Orders were given to the Estikhbarat to coordinate the project with army training and testing divisions.

And so they began working in earnest on chemical- and biological-weapons research and development. The Kurds were to be the first to experience the hideous results a few years later.

The unfortunate victim in the armchair would travel first to The Hague and then to Amsterdam, since there was no direct flight from Brussels to Baghdad. In Amsterdam he would be put on board the Iraqi Airways flight to home, torture, and probably death. All along the way, customs inspectors and airport security would wave the crate through because it was protected by its diplomatic status.

This gruesome use of the diplomatic bag was stopped, albeit briefly, in the West. One of these crated-up travelers woke up on the baggage wagon at London's Heathrow Airport. The handlers heard muffled screams coming from their cart and took it back to be opened. There was the usual strain on bilateral relations for a while after that, but then it was business as usual again between Saddam and the British. The Western governments know perfectly well about these horrific goings-on but seem to accept them as just part of the way the world turns.

I FURNISHED Daniel with a few extra tidbits from the annual July 17 party celebrating the 1968 Ba'th revolution. It was the usual formal affair, held at the Meridian Hotel. The guests were a collection of diplomats, journalists, European Economic Community ministers, and members of the Belgian Foreign Ministry. I bribed the embassy photographer to give me copies of the official photos and later, going over them with Daniel, was able to give him a full who's who. In particular, the liberal sprinkling of arms dealers.

One of the most important was a dealer named Gerald Bull. A Canadian with American citizenship, Bull had designed modifications for both artillery and artillery shells that would dramatically increase their range. But he'd had a falling-out with his North American sponsors, including the U.S. Army. When he was charged with breaking trade embargoes by supplying South Africa, they'd hung him out to dry. He was sent to jail for four months.

When he got out of jail, in 1981, Bull was based in Brussels—the arms center of the world. He turned to working for Saddam Hussein, among others.

Saddam's first interest was Bull's modification of the 155-mm howitzer, called the GC-45, a gun with double the normal range. About four hundred of Bull's artillery pieces were supplied to Iraq through South Africa and Austria. That constituted the other main part of my father's work, the work of any Iraqi ambassador in Belgium. Arms. Buying and brokering. And looking after Gerald Bull. By the time my father left Brussels, in 1985, Gerald Bull was the main priority of that post. Gerald Bull's big guns had become the key to Saddam's dream of the conquest of Israel—and perhaps more.

Bull also was working on something that promised even more for Saddam: the supergun. Its barrel was three feet in diameter and one hundred feet long. Bull claimed that it could shoot accurately to a range of a thousand miles. Granted enough money to develop further refinements, he said its shot could go as far as six thousand miles. (Bull had taken old plans from World War II Nazi archives, which showed the design for the V-3, a supergun with the range of a rocket. The Germans had been defeated, and the V-3 prototype destroyed before they could build the real thing. Its main design advance was a sectioned barrel to handle the acceleration of the projectile.)

The Americans had rejected the whole idea years earlier, but now Baghdad footed the bill and began to build the supergun at a plant near Mosul, a city in northern Iraq. Bull kept it secret by ordering different parts from different companies and countries, so nobody had the full picture. Except the Mossad.

The Mossad had had Bull's number for a long time. In March 1990 he was assassinated, allegedly by Mossad agents in Brussels.

How I went about getting the desired information on the Iraqi embassy in Brussels was left up to me. The only proviso Daniel had made was that I not take foolish chances. Therefore the only information I did not supply was the information a search of my father's office might have provided. I had decided that any effort to get into his office would be foolhardy.

Still, Daniel was pleased with what I had produced for him. Pleased beyond measure. There is nothing particularly glamorous, admirable or moral about spying, though at the time I didn't fully realize that. I was still caught up in my need for revenge on my father and Saddam.

In autumn 1984 it was time for me to go back to England for my next year of engineering studies. Soon after my return I met with Morris at a restaurant we both favored in Soho.

As Morris dug into his rich pastry he said, "There's a Syrian in London we want to know about. He's at the Imperial College, in nuclear physics. This one is an important target. It's a kind of make-or-break time for you, too. If you make it, you can rise in our ranks. If not . . . Well, you may just stay where you are."

The Mossad was turning its attention toward Syria. Syria's President Hafiz al-Assad was the only other Ba'thist leader to head an Arab country. He and Saddam Hussein were now locked in a battle to the death for supremacy in the Arab world. They loathed each other.

Syria under Hafiz al-Assad deserved a prominent place in anybody's rogues' gallery. Especially a Syria that had nuclear ambitions.

"Can you get to him?" Morris asked of the Syrian he had mentioned.

"Sure. I have friends at the college. No problem."

I shall call the Syrian Rifaat Khaddam—again, not a real name. He was a nice fellow and a brilliant scholar but a bit naïve. In addition, he was a climber, with big ambitions. That made him vulnerable, and I zeroed in.

It was easy to strike up an acquaintance with Rifaat when I dropped in on friends at the college and joined them for lunch in the dining hall. My friends were in the elite sciences, and they often sat with the fellow Arab doing his Ph.D. in nuclear physics. Rifaat was good-looking, but nonetheless had no luck getting girls.

"I don't seem to have the right moves for the girls here," moaned Rifaat. "They all act as though I'm a dirty old man."

"Never mind," I reassured him. "I can introduce you to girls." In all truth, I hated the idea of introducing him to any of the girls I knew. I didn't want to get any of them even marginally involved in this deadly caper. Fortunately, none of them took to Rifaat, which was all to the good. Trying to find him a girl made me his buddy, though he still hankered after his dreams. And that meant money. At least with money he could buy a woman or two and some decent clothes. He always looked a bit tacky.

So I showed him a good time, all on my now unlimited Mossad expense account. I told him that a friend of my father's was a wealthy businessman, who paid me a lot of money for doing bits of work for his office in England.

While I developed Rifaat's taste for the good life I gradually learned about his work and where he fitted into the plans of his sponsors, the government in Damascus. Like Iraq, Syria paid for scholars overseas and had very definite long-range plans for them.

What Rifaat revealed was dynamite. Or rather atomic. Syria had just begun to build its own nuclear reactor. The hardware was coming from the Soviet Union; some technological help was coming from Germany; and Syrian scientists, like Rifaat, were being trained by the British school system.

It did not take a genius to figure out that Hafiz al-Assad was not

Above: the Ayatollah Khomeini, who ruled Iran throughout the bitter eight-year war with Iraq

Below: on Pilgrimage to the holy city of Mecca in 1988, Saddam Hussein kisses the sacred Black Stone at the Grand Mosque. Critics charge the dictator with making a show of religion to woo the fundamentalist majority.

building a nuclear reactor to lower his people's electricity bills. Like Saddam, he was going into the bomb business.

When I reported this to Morris, he looked stricken. It seemed the Israelis had not known that Syria's nuclear program was actually under way, though in its earliest stages.

After a time Rifaat was thoroughly hooked on the good life, and he openly expressed envy of my relationship with my father's generous friend. He wanted to meet him. So I arranged to meet Morris in the restaurant at the Churchill to tell him this. He was delighted.

"Tell him your father's friend is coming to visit this weekend and you're having dinner with him. Ask Rifaat to come along."

Then to my horror, as we walked out of the restaurant I saw the "penniless" Arab from Tunisia who had accosted me before, in the Cumberland. Was he following me? He was sitting with half a dozen other Arabs. I noticed that Morris averted his face, but he offered no explanation. I decided the Arab might be almost anyone's agent, hanging around hotels, picking up what information he could from fellow Arabs. But who did he work for?

Morris changed our meeting place to another hotel, near Piccadilly. I was constantly on edge now, and over the past weeks I'd begun to lose my hair, until all I had were a few wisps. My hair eventu-

Below: Syria's President Hafiz al-Assad, the only other Ba'thist leader of an Arab country, would lock horns with Saddam for supremacy in the Arab world.

Above: General Ahmad Hasan al-Bakr, pushed aside by protégé Saddam

Above: Iraqi Foreign Minister Tariq Aziz, the "perfect yes-man"

ally grew back, but I was seeing the toll this cloak-and-dagger life was having on me, even though on the surface it seemed so innocuous, so mundane. The mysterious Arab reminded me that I was playing at the ultimate high-stakes table, where a wrong bet could mean a knife in the ribs or a bullet between the eyes.

The meeting between Rifaat and my father's "friend" went like clockwork. Morris called himself Mark for the occasion.

The three of us met for a costly lunch. At a nearby table were others I recognized from the Israeli embassy, seemingly minding their business. Which they were. Our business.

It was fascinating watching Morris in action. He controlled the conversation completely, and deftly maneuvered Rifaat into position. As far as Rifaat knew, "Mark" was a German businessman living in London. His company wanted to expand into Syria but needed some inside information on potential contracts in order to give it a competitive edge. Rifaat didn't really care who Mark was, as long as he was sure of being paid as handsomely as I apparently was. So Morris had a relatively easy job reassuring Rifaat that he would not need to take risks, just pass on information that was easily accessible. That was the bait, of course, and once the hook was firmly in his mouth, he would be asked for a great deal more.

So Rifaat had a new job, as a "consultant" to a German technological firm, selling Syrian nuclear secrets to the Mossad. I saw him a couple of years later looking very well off.

Morris gave me two hundred pounds and a new sound system. That was nice, but material reward was not the reason I was in this game. I still wanted to get my teeth into Saddam. Morris left me to concentrate on my studies for a while. In the winter of 1985 he arranged to meet me again at the Soho restaurant.

"We want you to try to get someone else for us," Morris said this time. "Are you aware of the pilot training program your government runs in the north of England?"

I had to confess I wasn't.

"It's outside Carlisle, just south of the Scottish border. They train military pilots. The head of it is an Iraqi air force major. We want to know everything we can about him."

The following weekend I boarded the train to Carlisle.

Carlisle was cold and dreary. An Austin Mini served as a local taxi, and when I got in, I told the driver to take me to the pilot school. "I don't have the exact directions," I said.

"No need, my lad," he replied cheerfully. "Everybody in town knows where you chaps are."

He took me to a tiny airport on the outskirts of town, and I went into what looked like the main office building—in reality just a shack.

A young Englishman behind a counter greeted me. "What can I do for you?" he asked.

"I'm from the Iraqi embassy," I told him, showing him my diplomatic I.D. "I've come to look up a friend." I gave him a false name.

One of the officers came in as I was speaking, and now greeted me in Arabic. "Never heard of your friend here," he told me affably, "but he might be with one of the other groups. Let's go over to the officers lounge and see if anyone else knows him. Unfortunately, the major is at the embassy in London today."

He steered me across the yard toward the gray bulk of a barracks building. Inside, we joined four other officers in a comfortable lounge. They all greeted me in a friendly enough fashion, including the second-in-command. Of course he had not heard of my friend. But he invited me to join them for tea.

The major's absence was a stroke of luck. It was always easier and

faster to find out about someone from others. Furthermore, the
second-in-command turned out to have a grudge against his superior;
he had ambitions above his rank of captain, which the major was
thwarting. In fact, they all jumped in to complain about the boss with
no prompting at all from me.

"I wish you would report our problem to the embassy," said the
number two man. "It's hopeless here."

"The major is a boozer and a womanizer, and nothing gets done
properly around here," chimed in another. "The boys are doing half
the work they should. This is no way to train an air force."

"I thought the major was a big hero," I offered.

"Was. Now he's a has-been."

"Someone ought to tell them to straighten out the major," the
captain persisted.

"Does it really matter?" I said. "After all, I thought the British
flight instructors handled the work that really matters here."

"Without the Brits we wouldn't have a damn thing going," another
muttered.

Once again I wondered why the British, the Americans and the rest
of the Western powers were so shortsighted. We have a saying in the
Middle East: "Don't despise snakes just because they don't have dragons' horns." It means don't underestimate them, because if you do,
they will grow up to be dragons, complete with horns and breath of
fire. Couldn't the Western nations see they were helping the Iraqi
snake grow up to be a very large dragon, complete with horns and an
air force escort?

It was no wonder many in the Arab world—and for that matter
Western critics—felt that a totally cynical partnership existed between
governments and the arms industry. The arms industry made huge
profits keeping the conflicts raging in the Mideast. The Americans,
Soviets, British, Germans, French, even the Chinese, kept stoking the
fires already burning in the so-called holy lands. The hostilities and
rivalries were our own, homegrown for centuries. The firepower
came from meddling superpowers and arms merchants.

Israel was in there, too. And Israel, just like the rest, played the
game strictly for its own interests. Right now Israel's interest was to
find out everything it could about Iraqi air power. Morris and his
masters wanted a mole in the Iraqi air force at any price. The major

would have been perfect—a war hero, privy to more than the average major, and because of his drinking and taste for hookers he was vulnerable. But the major's men told me he was going on leave almost immediately. Too soon for a safe recruiting operation right now.

I was disappointed. Recruiting the major would have been a clean shot at Saddam's war machine.

When I got back to London and reported to Morris, he was crestfallen but philosophical. "Don't go back. It would look too suspicious. Besides, we have another assignment for you."

We were talking over lunch again.

"Your assignment is a man named Kamal Khatib," Morris continued. "He is a very big fish. Right now he's at Loughborough University, near Nottingham. He's a senior structural engineer on one of Syria's important pet projects—the construction of underground hangars for Assad's fighters and bombers."

I felt a shiver slide up my spine. Anyone involved in such a high-priority, sensitive military project would be no cakewalk. For the first time I felt afraid. The underground bunkers for aircraft had been whispered about in Iraq. Syria's Hafiz al-Assad wasn't the only one building them. Saddam was, too.

The underground hangars were like subterranean aircraft carriers, with several parking levels and hydraulic lifts to raise and lower the jets. The Iraqis were also ironing out the wrinkles on underground runways, which would allow a jet to do the first part of its takeoff without being exposed above ground.

The reason for all this burrowing was simple: every Arab leader had a vivid memory of how the Israelis had destroyed the Egyptian air force while it was still on the ground in 1967.

Of course, any power would seek first to destroy its enemy's air power, as that was the key to controlling a battlefield in modern warfare. So finding out exactly how those hangars were built and what their weak points were was a high priority for the Israelis.

I took the train to Loughborough. At the old train station I found a taxi to take me to the best hotel the place had to offer. I spent a restless, nervous night. In the morning I took a taxi to the university.

I went to the administration building and told the woman at the registrar's office that I was looking for a fellow Arab, a friend of mine named Kamal Khatib. Checking her computer list, she told me he wasn't an undergraduate but I might find him in postgraduate studies. She sent me to another building.

When I asked at the desk, Khatib was indeed listed.

"He may be down in the laboratory," the secretary said brightly.

I quickly located the large lab where they did work on structural stresses and on prestressing concrete.

"Kamal isn't here just now," a genial Englishman said in answer to my inquiry. "Great fellow. Superb engineer. You must be family. Well, you can be proud of his work here."

He chatted on a bit, assuming that someone looking for someone is a friend, not an enemy. He gave me Khatib's address.

I went back to the hotel and phoned Morris.

"Go and see him tonight," he instructed.

Night had fallen by the time I drove up to the small housing development where Khatib lived. I left the taxi some distance from the house and walked up to his gate. It was bitterly cold. Then, not far down the block, I saw two men sitting in a blue Toyota. Its headlights were off, and I couldn't hear the engine running.

I stopped, paralyzed. I wanted to run as fast as I could, but to turn back, I decided, would look even more suspicious than to go in. So, my heart beating about two hundred times a minute, I opened the garden gate, walked up to the door, and pressed the doorbell. The door opened, and there he was. A big man, Khatib managed to look fearsome even in his pajamas and robe.

"Sorry to bother you," I stammered. "Mr. Khatib?"

"Yes?" he snapped.

"My name is Hussein. A mutual friend suggested I come see you."

Standing back, he told me to come in out of the cold and led me up a few stairs to a small vestibule off his living room. I was both relieved at my success so far and more terrified than ever at the thought of being discovered. Already I could see myself in a large armchair. . . .

The mutual friend, of course, was a figment of my imagination. I called him Jabir and had written a letter to Khatib from him, saying he hoped his old friend Khatib would help his young friend Hussein get settled in Loughborough. I was banking on Khatib's having the usual Arab arrogance that would not allow him to admit he didn't know any Jabir.

"I don't know anyone named Jabir," he said, his eyes narrowing as he opened my letter. As he scanned it I could almost hear his mental gears changing. "I don't know anything about this or about you," he said. He folded the letter and kept it in his huge hand.

"I must have come to the wrong place. It must be another Khatib," I said lamely. "I'm sorry to disturb you. I'll be going now. . . ."

I backed out of the room, down the steps and out the front door, trying to move slowly and nonchalantly but wanting to break into a run. Would he signal the men in the car to apprehend me? Or were they Mossad, keeping an eye on my escapade?

Whoever they were, they had gone. I looked up and down the street and saw no one. Nor could I see a taxi. I walked rapidly till I finally saw a pub. I went in to have a drink. Somewhat restored, I made my way to the station and got the last train to London.

Back in my hotel room there at last, I had a hot shower and tried to quell the case of nerves that made my stomach feel like a bag of cats. I slept badly and the next day wandered the streets in a fog of worry, thinking of Khatib and the awful risk I was running. Before, my risk had been kind of theoretical. Now it seemed much too real.

6
"SOMEBODY IS COMING FROM BAGHDAD"

I FELT that the Mossad was constantly testing me while at the same time keeping me in reserve for something bigger. It seemed likely that as the son of a highly placed Iraqi diplomat I was intended to be a mole, one who could be activated whenever I became most valuable to them.

My father was about to be transferred to New York to serve as the Iraqi ambassador to the United Nations. I had already told the Mossad about this, and Morris had made it clear that they did not want me to work for them in America. "We're not allowed to work in the United States," he said. Soon after the Khatib fiasco I met with Morris. "Right now just concentrate on your studies," he said. "Then we want you to go to Brussels again for the summer vacation." He paused, then added, "See if your father can get you a job in the London embassy. Nothing big—filing or something."

I was appalled by the idea. A sudden request to my father from his anti-Ba'thist son to work among Saddam's faithful drones was certain to make him deeply suspicious. In spite of all that Morris, Yusef and the rest of those in the Mossad knew about my relationship with my father, they did not seem to grasp just how out of character such a request would be. Perhaps they thought I had exaggerated.

"My father doesn't trust me. He'd be suspicious if I asked to work in the London embassy—even if I only asked to scrub floors."

Morris didn't look put off at all. "Look, you're to remain in England to finish your degree. We need to have you with a foot in the door of the Iraqi London embassy. Just try. . . ."

I thought the Mossad had been careless in the Khatib affair or, at the very least, that the plan to recruit him had been hastily prepared. This new assignment suggested the Mossad had become even more careless. Clearly, they did not understand the enemy as well as I originally thought they did. This proposal was fraught with risk and almost guaranteed to expose me. But I so wanted to get even with my father and see Saddam toppled that I agreed.

In the midst of this emotional turmoil it was a wonder I found the presence of mind to write my exams. I passed all but one, in electrical circuits and waveforms, which I would have to repeat in September.

THE house in Brussels where my parents lived had a glass-enclosed solarium that overlooked the pool and the garden. It was here that I met with my parents.

My father was angry. "Why the hell do you want to work in the embassy all of a sudden?" he demanded.

"I need more money," I blurted out. "England's expensive."

"I give you more than enough goddamn money!" he exploded.

"It would be good for me. The people at the embassy would appreciate it." I was babbling.

My father just stared at me. Then he turned and walked out, and I knew his leaving meant there was worse to come.

My mother sat still. She looked at me anxiously.

"Will you talk to him for me?" I asked.

I could tell she wasn't any happier than my father about my wanting a job in London. But her reasons were different. Mother disapproved of the way I lived. She assumed I *did* want more money, and she assumed I wanted it to live the life of a playboy.

"Why do you have to live *that* kind of life, anyway?" she said.

Still, she went to my father and spoke to him in my behalf. They had a major argument. A few days later she approached me on the subject. "Why do you want to work in the embassy?" she asked. "Is it really to work, or for something else?"

I knew my father had put her up to questioning me this time, but I let her continue. "You've always fought with your father about the Ba'th, about Saddam, about everything."

She was distraught. Her eyes filled with fear for me. "He's been going through your clothes, your room, your papers."

I felt the blood drain from my face. I had left a book with phone numbers in my dresser. The numbers were in code, but only a simple code.

My poor mother was almost hysterical, even though she knew nothing about my activities. "Please," she begged, "tell me you aren't working for the Iranians!"

I almost laughed in relief. "No, no, Mama. Why would I do such a crazy thing? There, there. Your worry is all over nothing."

My relief was short lived. Her next words turned my blood to ice.

"Your father says somebody is coming from Baghdad. They're coming to see you."

UNABLE to sleep, I sat in the darkness in my room all night. I couldn't even lie down. I was afraid to close my eyes. All I could think was, What is coming from Baghdad? An assassin? The Estikhbarat? A carpenter maybe, to build me a crate.

I had to think. I had to formulate some kind of plan.

By morning I knew I had three choices. I could try to run for it and inevitably be caught. I could contact my Mossad colleagues and ask for help. But I knew that if I was truly exposed, I would be of no further use to them, so their help would be unlikely. Or I could try something as outrageous as it was dangerous. I chose it.

I called the driver and had him take me to the Iraqi embassy. I went straight to the office of the Mukhabarat agent in charge of the embassy, a debonair fellow named Muhammed Salman. "I have something to tell you," I said. "I want you to send it directly to Baghdad without telling my father."

Salman looked at me with mild interest, but as I continued, his expression changed to one of astonishment. And when I confessed, "I've been working with the Mossad," his face went white.

"I was introduced to these two guys by a girlfriend," I went on. "I didn't know they were Israeli, let alone working for the Mossad." This was a lie, but some of what I told him was basically true. "They asked me to find out some things about the embassy. It was small stuff—meaningless, really. They wanted to know about salaries and who the Telex operators were. They paid me well."

Salman remained silent. "I figured out before long who they were," I continued, "but by then I was hooked by the money and the girls. Besides, by then they had me, didn't they?"

It was a stupid story. But I knew my people. I knew that my only chance was to go to them before they got to me. Brazen it out.

Salman pulled himself together enough to ask for details. He hardly knew where to start. "You just tell it," he stammered.

I decided to tell him everything. I gave him names and places. I started with the Fatah drop spots and finished with Khatib and the underground aircraft bunkers. Every word I said could seal my fate. One mistake and I was a dead man.

"I want to get out," I said desperately. It was the simple truth.

It is hard for outsiders to comprehend the enormity of my crime in Saddam's world and the punishment that would await me. An Iraqi working for the Mossad was akin to a Jew working for the Gestapo, perhaps worse.

As I continued my confession I could see that Salman was badly shaken. In this regime heads like his could roll as a result of this sort of catastrophe. He would be seen as having harbored the devil in his post.

"This will all go to Baghdad," he said hoarsely.

The next day was July 17 and time for the annual celebration by the embassy of the glorious Ba'th revolution of 1968. Dressed in their finery, the usual diplomats, journalists and politicians gathered in the Meridian Hotel. I would have preferred to stay in my room, but the ambassador's son had to show up. I found myself a corner by the buffet table. One of the younger fellows from the embassy joined me.

"See that one over there," he said, pointing to a tall blond man by the door. "He just came from Baghdad." Then he leaned closer and whispered dramatically in my ear, "Mukhabarat."

Salman and the man from Baghdad stood talking quietly.

There is a bedouin tribe in Iraq whose members are blond and Aryan-looking. They can pass so well as Westerners that many of their number serve as Mukhabarat agents. They are among the most loyal of Saddam's followers. This man was one of these.

As I looked across the room I knew he had come for me. But the whole picture had changed now. His mission had been thrown off course by my confession. He did not approach me.

The following day Salman informed me that he had received instructions that I was to go to Baghdad, and handed me a ticket made out in a false name. This was not a good sign. It meant that the Mukhabarat did not want a record of my travel to show up on the flight manifests. They could get away with it because at all ticket or passport-control checkpoints my separate diplomatic I.D. was my laissez-passer. With that I.D. I could board any airplane without having to show anyone a ticket. No questions would be asked.

When I told my father I had been summoned to Baghdad, he was angry and perplexed. Usually he was the first to know everything, but clearly he was being kept in the dark. He pressed me for an explanation. "Why do they want you in Baghdad?"

"Something to do with the party," I answered vaguely. "Salman can explain." I had no idea what story Salman would give him. Thanks to my confession, Salman's position was none too good.

On July 19 my father and Salman accompanied me to the airport. My father remained silent for the whole trip. I knew he was scared. I was scared, too. Scared for my life. My father, on the other hand, was afraid of losing his position and prestige. At the airport he made a show of being solicitous. He asked if I had everything I needed and even offered me money. The performance was for Salman.

I boarded the plane, a Sabena Airlines flight to Amsterdam. From there I transferred to the Iraqi Airways plane to Baghdad. Thanks to the procedures I'd followed, no one save my parents and Salman knew I'd left Brussels. I was virtually nonexistent. I might as well have been in one of the diplomatic crates.

ONCE the plane had landed at Saddam Airport, I told myself it was all out of my hands and meekly waited for my escort. Strangely, no one appeared. Still fearful, I glanced about and forced myself forward. My whole plan hinged on my voluntary confession and return.

Then I saw two security types. I walked up to them and asked if they knew the whereabouts of the guys from the Mukhabarat who were supposed to meet me.

They informed me curtly that they were Estikhbarat. "The Mukhabarat is downstairs."

So I set off to find the Mukhabarat agents, but I got lost. Saddam Airport had been built while I was away.

Downstairs I finally found a man with a badge and asked if he had seen the Mukhabarat agents anywhere. I couldn't believe it. Here I was, searching high and low for my jailers.

Suddenly someone behind barked, "Get out of here!" And the man snapped to attention, said, "Yes, sir!" and turned away.

I whirled around, and there behind me was the blond Mukhabarat agent I had seen in Brussels.

"Hello," he said. "Have a nice trip?" Without waiting for an answer to this absurdly out-of-place question, he told me to put away my passport. Then he escorted me through passport control.

"I'm Khaled," he introduced himself as we walked along.

He was about my height—five feet ten—and dressed casually in a striped shirt and trousers. He had an airport security pass clipped on one pocket. We went to the baggage area to claim my luggage.

Then another young man joined us. He looked like an American movie star. He was dressed in a beige suit and had an easy manner.

"Hi," he said. "I'm Jamal. Nice to meet you."

Outside, at the curb, we got into a small Mitsubishi. Jamal drove, and Khaled sat up front with him. I sat in the back. They put their airport badges away, and Khaled took my passport. Officially, I had never left Brussels, and now I had no passport. Nervous as I was, my companions' friendly manner consoled me.

The drive from the airport into the city had a surreal quality. So much was new to me; so much had changed in Baghdad since my departure with my family for Zimbabwe, in 1982. (I had gone straight to England from Zimbabwe in 1983.) A concrete wall stretched along the right side of the airport road. I asked what it was.

"It's a private place for His Excellency Saddam Hussein," Khaled replied. It was, in fact, Saddam's palace, Saddam's bunker and Saddam's lake, I later learned. The whole extraordinary compound had been built as an ultrafortified redoubt to which Saddam could repair either for leisure or for a last-ditch stand in war—nuclear or otherwise. Its walls were three or four meters thick, and much of the palace was underground. The complex, designed to withstand virtually anything, was in the shape of a ship's anchor, making it virtually impossible for any enemy planes to hit it completely in one flyover.

We dropped Khaled off at the Mukhabarat headquarters. People give this compound, with its iron bars and high walls, a wide berth, and if they have to pass by it in their cars, conversation becomes hushed. In the dark it was difficult to see much of this place, just the ghostly shape of a large white building in the rear. Khaled got out and told me he would see me in the morning.

I got into the front seat, and Jamal told me he would drive me to my family's home. What were they going to do with me? Was this some kind of psychological cat-and-mouse game?

On the way Jamal told me he was an officer who taught at the national security college, which was the training ground for the best of the Mukhabarat, the ones who became officers. But right now I didn't want to hear about the Mukhabarat. My fear had begun to recede when I hadn't been taken to Mukhabarat headquarters, and weariness had taken its place. When we drew up to my house, I leaped out and ran up the steps to the door and banged on it loudly, shouting, "Bibi! Bibi!"

Bibi opened the door. Her thin little face lit up when she saw me. "Oh, my! Is it really you? Oh, come in, come in."

"I'll pick you up at nine a.m.," Jamal said, and left.

It was now three a.m. I was home in Baghdad, back in the dragon's lair. Bibi had a hundred questions. Why had I come home? Was there trouble with my studies? My father? But I was too tired to answer. I begged to be excused and went straight to bed.

THE next morning Jamal was just as chatty as he'd been the night before. This time, as we drove along Felastin Street toward the Mukhabarat headquarters, he talked about hookers, drugs and gays. He acted as if we were drinking buddies. I knew he was testing me, watching for my reactions.

At the main gate of the Mukhabarat compound he stopped the car, flashed his I.D., and the gate opened. I looked around, curious in spite of the fear I felt. There was a small stream running through the compound and, on the other side, rows of houses, as in any neighborhood. But the streets were closed. Then I realized that it once *had* been a neighborhood and that it had been taken over lock, stock and barrel by the Mukhabarat.

We drove into the compound, toward the big white building I had glimpsed the previous night. We walked up the long path leading to it, and at the end were made to walk through a metal detector. Then a guard searched us. When that was finished, I looked up and saw Khaled. Jamal left me there with him.

Khaled led me down the main hallway. I could see a large conference room on the right and similar but smaller rooms on the left, each with a couch, chairs and a table. We entered one of the smaller rooms and waited in silence for five minutes, during which I grew more apprehensive.

Suddenly the door opened, and Khaled leaped to attention and saluted. A short, bald, ugly gorillalike man strode in. My heart sank.

"Are you Hussein?" the Gorilla roared.

"Yes, sir."

"Sit there."

He sat behind the table staring at me. "We did not want to end with you like this," he said evenly. "But it has happened."

I was paralyzed. What did he mean?

"But you came to us before we came to you," he continued. "Now you will cooperate with us."

Did he mean it would have been easier to kill me if they had caught me first? Did he mean now that I had confessed, they might consider some other course? That was my desperate hope.

The Gorilla's name was Radhi. Though he was not in uniform, he was clearly high up in the ranks of the Mukhabarat.

He turned to Khaled and said, "You will interrogate him. And you," he added, swiveling his gaze back to me, "will answer him. Then we will see what we will do with you."

He left, and Khaled began to ask me questions, going over the same ground I had covered with Salman, in Brussels. I knew that Salman had recorded everything, so I had to get it all exactly the same. Khaled wanted to know about the Mossad in minute detail: how they handled surveillance, what the officers looked like, what they acted like. He

wanted to know my feelings, observations and judgments. The interrogation went on for eight hours.

I said only one thing that was a mistake. I said I thought Morris was
a very clever man.

"Why? Do you mean you like him?"

I could have bitten off my tongue. One thing an Iraqi must never
do is say anything positive about the Zionist enemy. If the Mukhabarat ever discovered that I had not been trapped, but had willingly
gone to the Israelis, that I actually admired certain of their abilities, I
would most certainly die—and not quickly.

I was protected by the completely unbelievable quality of the act I'd
committed, I thought, as I again tried to push fear from my mind. Any
Iraqi would believe I was seduced by money, women, and life in the
fast lane. No Iraqi would believe I'd actually volunteered my services
to so heinous an enemy.

THE next day Jamal picked me up again and took me to headquarters and the same room. Then he began asking all the same questions
as Khaled had. Perversely I found this reassuring. If they were going
to kill me, surely they wouldn't waste all this time. I had a sneaking
suspicion that because of my experience with the Israelis they wanted
to pick my brain.

At the end of the day Khaled arrived. "We've worn you out with all
this," he said. "Now you're invited out as our guest."

Of all unexpected events, the three of us went out for a night on
the town. They took me to a cabaret club called The 1001 Nights, in
the swank Al Rashid Hotel, a palace of white marble built for an
international fair that never took place, because of the war with Iran.
The floor show featured musicians playing a combination of old Iraqi
tunes, disco for the customers who wanted to dance, then new Iraqi
tunes like "Welcome to the Desert Knight"—all in praise of Saddam.

As the music blared on, Khaled and Jamal tried their drinking-
buddy act on me. They spoke about their days of being trained for the
Mukhabarat overseas, in Rome and Geneva. Just what they were fishing for I don't know. It was a bizarre evening.

I was at home finishing dinner the next evening when Khaled
phoned. "You have something to do," he said. "I'll be right there."

I wondered what treat they had in store for me. We drove to the

Mukhabarat compound, to a large modern building. Inside, all the doors were glass and the floors marble. We went into a room where two men were standing in front of a large painting of sea and mountains. Khaled snapped to attention and saluted the men. One was Radhi the Gorilla. The other was a professorial-looking man of about fifty, wearing glasses.

"You made a mistake," the Professor said abruptly. "Why did you say this Israeli agent, Morris, is clever?"

I went cold all over.

"Are you a traitor?" he asked, then continued without pausing for a response. The questions were all rhetorical. "Yes, you are. Did you work with the enemy? Did you try to destroy the government of His Excellency? Yes, you did. Have people been killed for doing this? Yes, many have already been killed for less than this. Your turn will come."

His voice droned on as he pronounced the sentence. For the first time in my adult life I cried.

I hated crying. But I could not stop myself. They were going to kill me. The seeming friendliness had all been a cruel joke.

"I have never seen a case like this," continued the Professor angrily. "But your father is one of us, so we cannot make the final decision here. We'll refer it to His Excellency, Saddam."

A reprieve! I couldn't believe my ears. Because of my father's status, that final judgment had not been made.

My accusers were clearly furious, though, furious that I had preempted their own attack and had forced them into this position. Because of my "confession and repentance" and my father's position, they were actually granting grace to a Mossad agent.

"We are giving you a chance no one has ever been given before," the Professor said through gritted teeth. "You will return to England. You will be contacted there."

He did not actually say the words double agent, but I realized my big chance could mean nothing else.

"You are in the circle now," said Radhi with cold menace. "And someone who enters never leaves."

AT SEVEN the next morning Khaled took me to the airport. Once again we bypassed passport control. He actually escorted me on board the plane, then left at the last moment.

When I arrived in Brussels, my father was waiting for me. He was standing at the passenger exit, looking both curious and happy. I had never seen him look the way he looked then.

"What happened?" he growled once we were in the car.

I told him I was not allowed to say, on orders of the Amn—the secret police. We lapsed into silence.

At home, my mother was busy packing for the big move to the United Nations in New York. She, too, was curious about my doings, but asked no questions. She was just happy I was back.

Then we were off to the United States for the holidays. My new masters at the Mukhabarat had told me to go with my father when he was transferred and then, when it was time, return to school in England. "We'll contact you there," they had promised.

MANHATTAN overwhelmed me. I wondered how on earth people could live and work in this crowd of skyscrapers. It took me time to appreciate the energy of New York.

We were cocooned, as always, by money and staying in a luxury flat in the Waldorf-Astoria that must have cost $2000 a day.

If I needed anything special done, there was always Yassin. A staff member of the Iraqi mission to the United Nations, he was our fixer. And he could fix anything, from an American passport to a green card, from automatic rifles to cocaine for a party. A green card would cost $7000. I wanted a driver's license without taking the practical exam. That cost me $300.

In all this time, since I left Morris in early July to go to Brussels, I had been completely out of touch with the Mossad. They had known that I was scheduled to go with the family to New York, and so had not expected any contact for a while. Since they did not want me to work in the United States for them, I assumed they were waiting until I returned to England. But they knew nothing, I hoped, of what I now thought of as the five missing days in Baghdad.

It was mid-August when my father was summoned to Baghdad. At the same time I returned to England to repeat my failed exam. Given how cluttered my mind was with my situation, how I managed to pass I don't know, but I did.

First there was the problem of my work inside the Da'wah for Auda Sultan and the Amn al-Hezib, the party security. As I was racking my brains over how to squirm out of that, Auda Sultan contacted me. He had been told by Baghdad that he'd been taken off my case. I would be handed over to a new control later. My new control was called Razzouki. I supposed the Mukhabarat had contacted him.

With that complication out of the way my big problem now was what to do about the Mossad. It was obvious Baghdad expected me to continue working inside the Mossad, as a double agent. But I couldn't work against the Israelis. Besides, if I was caught, they would kill me.

The other obvious possibility was to work as a triple agent for the Mossad. The mere idea was breathtaking: work for the Mossad as an agent in the Mukhabarat, working as a double agent against the Mossad. It would be an almost unrepeatable chance to penetrate the Mukhabarat for the Mossad and feed disinformation to my Iraqi masters about the Mossad.

It was a young man's fantasy—but it was out of the question. The Israelis would never accept me in this delicate role. They would be far safer to cut their losses and silence me.

On the other hand, I could hardly just refuse an order from my new bosses in Baghdad. I had to fix it so that I could *not* stay in England and therefore not work against the Mossad. As usual, I came up with a half-baked plan: I got myself arrested by the British police.

It was fairly simple. I arranged for a friend to steal his girlfriend's Visa card and give it to me. Then I waited a few days until she notified the company and the police. Then I went to an expensive menswear store and tried to make a huge purchase with her card.

The British police who collared me were rough. They took me to a rundown old police station and searched me. After a time I was put in a dungeonlike cell.

A woman came to my cell to interrogate me. She asked about my means of support and the like. I lied and told her my family sent $200 a month—which was far too little to live on. But since I had prepared in advance to leave the country, I had a lot of cash on me, and of course she wondered why. In the end they let me go. I was to return for a hearing September 28. The papers they served me with said that if I was convicted, I would be deported.

The papers were my salvation. They would convince the Mukhabarat that I could not live in England and work inside the Mossad for them. Naturally I never went to the hearing.

7
THE LAW OF THE JUNGLE

WHEN I phoned my father in New York to tell him I had to leave England for good because of a problem with the police, he was furious. By now he knew everything the Mukhabarat knew.

"You goddamn little bastard. You were told to stay in England!" he yelled. Then he smashed the phone down.

When I arrived home, he greeted me with stony silence. The next day he asked my mother to send everyone else out of the house. He demanded to be left alone with his treacherous son.

"So, you are trying to destroy me?" he began. "What the hell do you think you're doing? After they told you to go to England! Who the hell do you think you are? I'll see *you* destroyed before you destroy me, you scum!"

Five days later I received a presidential order saying my studies were to be transferred to Baghdad. It was brought by the Foreign Minister himself, Tariq Aziz, who was visiting the United Nations for a session on the Iran-Iraq War.

It was October 1985, and the war was now five years old. Iraq had been trying to end the conflict ever since Saddam realized more than four years before that it was a lost cause.

I was to return to Iraq on Aziz's private government Boeing 747.

Since it was a diplomatic flight, the only security we had to pass was Iraqi. Everyone on such flights enters and leaves the United States without visas or other American formalities. The plane was parked on a special area of the tarmac. We could simply drive through the gates and up to the aircraft. Several large boxes were loaded into the cargo hold, and I wondered what, or who, might be in them. No American authority ever checked us, our papers, our bags or the boxes. We could have been carrying anything from plastic explosives to dead bodies.

The first-class cabin was ultra first class, with enormous armchairs and the best food and liquor. The center section had been converted into a conference room, while the back portion was set up like any commercial economy section.

I sat up front with some of Tariq Aziz's delegation. They discussed their shopping coups, not the war with Iran, and watched American TV shows picked up on the front screen by satellite.

When we landed in Baghdad, I felt as though I were entering prison on a long sentence.

The senior official from the Makteb al-Khas, the private office of the Foreign Ministry, met me. He was pleasant, and even ordered us some Cokes while we waited for our baggage, but to me he seemed like a jailer.

After I was dropped off at home, I fell wearily into bed, too tired and depressed to talk even to Bibi, who was full of questions about my return. This is my new life, I thought. Inside the circle. Trapped inside the circle.

No one came for me the first few days. I wandered the streets, had coffee in the cafés, looked disinterestedly in stores.

In the streets, shopkeepers were engaged in loud conversation with friends who dropped in. Men lounged on the curbsides under the overhanging roofs, and the aroma of Oriental spices drifted into the air from nearby restaurants. Police and security agents were on every corner. Like most cities, Baghdad teemed with life, but unlike other cities—Paris, for instance—there was no anarchic spontaneity. The police had succeeded in banishing all mystery.

There was, instead, a sense of furtiveness and treachery. Baghdad had changed since my childhood, or perhaps it was just that I was old enough now to recognize what I saw. And what I saw and felt was the law of the jungle. In this regime no one trusted anyone, because no one was trustworthy. Trust had been replaced by fear. Everyone informed on everyone else because if you didn't, someone would inform that you had not informed. Whatever the infraction, real or imagined, whoever committed it, friend or foe, it was reported. Children were taught to turn in their parents for the slightest criticism of the government. Brothers killed brothers. People abused small powers to gain greater ones. Traffic cops extorted money from motorists. The black market flourished.

As each day passed and still no one came to fetch me, I grew jumpy. One day I just took a taxi to the Mukhabarat headquarters and at the gate told the guard I wanted to see Radhi. I thought I'd best go at least as high as the Gorilla. I must have been the only civilian ever to try to get into the dreaded place. The guard was still arguing with me when Khaled, the blond, showed up.

"Hi," he said. "When did you get back?"

They had not informed him of my abrupt departure from the United States—or so he told me. He came to see me regularly for a few days, asking more questions. He asked about everything except the fiasco with the British police over the Visa card. I never knew why he didn't ask about that.

One morning he took me to Baghdad University to register. As it turned out, there was nothing there similar to the courses in electrical engineering I had been taking in Manchester, so another presidential order was issued to enroll me at the University of Technology. This may sound rather grand, but in Iraq a presidential order has to be obtained for almost everything. If you want permission to carry a portable cassette deck, for instance, you need a presidential order. This mountain of paperwork actually comes from the presidential office, and everything is signed by its overseer, Ahmed Hussein.

At the University of Technology I had difficulty with the deputy of the dean, who took an instant dislike to me and tried to create obstacles to my admission. Under instructions from the Mukhabarat the deputy was quickly waved aside by the dean. It was my first small taste of the world that security agents lived in, a world where all doors could be ordered opened. I was not sure I liked it.

But in another area I had some satisfaction. The girls loved me. While the male students eyed me suspiciously, the girls found I was easy to talk to. "You're not primitive, like our own fellows," they said. I was more open, offering genuine conversation and friendship.

There were a lot of girls for me to be friends with at the University of Technology. Perhaps the only accomplishment of Saddam's Ba'th Party was opening the doors of education and the professions to women. Saddam had achieved this by holding a gun to the head of virtually every male in Iraq, a country in which the age-old repression of women was the bedrock of religion, society and politics. It would be hard to find a male of the species more chauvinist than the Arab.

In reality, the change in the status of Iraqi women was only on the surface. Despite all the reforms, little had really changed for women, because the men had remained the same. But at least females had emerged from the worst of the purdah, the traditional seclusion of women, and so it was that I found love in an engineering class.

One day I walked into class and saw her. She was the prettiest girl there. Beautiful, actually, with thick dark wavy hair and wide sensitive eyes. She smiled readily, but quietly, as though to herself. And she was, I soon learned, a Christian. Her name was Ban. She seemed shy, and at first I hesitated to approach her. After years of chasing girls, this was a novel experience for me. One day, as we were leaving class, I summoned my courage and managed to move up beside her.

"What do you think of the course so far?" I asked.

"It's very interesting," she said. "I like the professor."

She walked on, head bent over her books.

"So what made you want to be an engineer?" I asked.

She looked up at me and said evenly, "The same reasons as you, I expect. I want a good job that's a real challenge."

This girl was a real challenge. The old approach would not do. I backed off and said I didn't mean to bother her.

"That's all right," she said. "I didn't mean to be rude."

"Maybe we could talk a bit better over lunch?" I ventured.

"I can't today."

My heart fell. A refusal. "Tomorrow?"

She hesitated, looking me in the eye. "All right."

I was happy out of all proportion to a mere lunch date. At first we saw each other rarely, and always with a group of friends. And slowly I began to wonder if I could be falling in love. For so long, love had not been a part of my life. I just assumed that I was incapable of it. And now this one gentle girl was changing all that.

IT WAS late at night, and the house was still. The ring of the telephone, as harsh as a dentist's drill, jerked me awake.

"I'm a friend," said an unfamiliar voice. "I want to see you."

Terror and panic arose in me. Oh, God, could it be the Mossad?

I hedged. "Give me your number, and I'll call back."

A Westerner would have said, "Who is this?" Not an Iraqi. One simply did not ask such a direct question. If you did, you would only get a question in reply. I saved a step by asking him an indirect question—his phone number.

"No. You name a time and place we can meet," the voice said.

I was afraid to respond and afraid not to.

"Saturday at six. In front of the Mustanseria University."

"I'll be in a blue Toyota, license 155302," he informed me. Then he hung up.

I was terrified. What if it was a setup? What if it was a test by the Mukhabarat to see if I would meet someone from the Mossad?

The more I thought about the strange phone call, the more likely it seemed that this was a setup. First, the approach was not the Mossad style. They would not make a rendezvous in an open space in broad daylight. The man who had phoned had a northern Iraqi accent. This would be rare in foreign agents but common in our own service.

I called the Mukhabarat and told Khaled I had to see him.

When Khaled picked me up, he was nervous and grew more so as I told him my story. "Go to the appointment," he ordered. "We will be in the vicinity."

On Saturday at six sharp the blue Toyota drew up to where I stood in front of the university. License 155302. I still remember that license plate. I also vividly remember the man inside the car: a big man, extraordinarily handsome, with piercing black eyes. As I got into the car those eyes burned into me. I watched his hands as he guided the car through the traffic. He had huge hands, with long strong fingers.

"My name is Abu Firas," he said. "I am with the Special Department. Are you with the Mukhabarat?"

"No. I don't know any Mukhabarat."

"Well, some of my friends want to see you."

"Why me?" I asked plaintively. "I'm just an ordinary guy."

"Don't worry. We're friends of your father."

That was possibly the least reassuring thing he could have said. My father's words suddenly thundered into my thoughts. *I'll see you destroyed before you destroy me!*

We drove aimlessly for about fifteen minutes. It didn't seem to matter anymore if Khaled and his people were on our tail or not. I no longer had any idea which tiger was behind which door.

Abu Firas left me back at the university, telling me someone else would pick me up there the next day at six o'clock.

Khaled told me they had no idea who the mysterious Abu Firas was. "We're checking him out. And the car, too," he said gravely. "You go to the next meeting as arranged, and we'll be ready."

I hardly noticed the man who picked me up the next day—and

drove me straight into the Mukhabarat headquarters. What was going on? This time I was taken into a large conference room.

Abu Firas came in. "You passed the exam," he said, fixing me with those brilliant eyes. "And you called the Mukhabarat to pick me up!" He laughed.

"Now someone important wants to see you," he said.

Probably the Terminator, I thought wearily, tired of this cat-and-mouse, now-we-like-you-now-we're-going-to-kill-you game.

In a second room another man awaited us. He was the only one in military uniform. He had sharp eyes and a thin face, and he looked like a hungry old eagle. He was Fadhil Selfige al-Azzawi, the Mukhabarat second-in-command.

Abu Firas saluted him. I later learned that Abu Firas was a full colonel, the son of a bedouin sheik, and his real name was Farid Shaharabeli. He was head of field operations.

Abu Firas drew out a file from his case and spread out some of the papers before me. "Your case has been settled," he announced.

I looked and saw a document signed by Saddam Hussein himself. "The matter," it read, "is to be left to his father."

There was also a letter in my father's handwriting. Two lines only. It read, "Traitors should always get what they deserve, according to the rules, without regard to family ties."

A death sentence. I *was* going to die. My father's decree did not surprise me. Still, death. . . . I shivered. I was only twenty.

Another letter was produced. "Whose handwriting is this?" I asked shakily.

"His Excellency Saddam Hussein's, may his life be preserved by Allah" was the reply.

I read the words on Saddam's letter. They were incredible. "He is pardoned. But on the conditions of the Mukhabarat."

I could hardly believe it. Saddam Hussein pardoned no one. He had spared my life in return for my father's loyalty. He had stayed Abraham's hand just as he was about to plunge the knife into Isaac's heart. But this Abraham—my own father—would rather, I knew, the deed had been carried out.

"You should thank His Excellency for giving you a chance to live," said Azzawi the Eagle, who then called in a servant to bring soft drinks. He turned to me once again and said, "You are with us now.

Abu Firas will take control of you, direct you, show you true life."
I was unsure what this meant.

"Is there anything you would like to ask for?" he said.

"I'm still having problems with that deputy at the university. He keeps harassing me, lowering my grades, and—"

"See to it!" he ordered Abu Firas.

Suddenly it seemed that they were doing my bidding rather than the other way around. I was astounded.

The deputy must have been astounded as well. He was taken to the Mukhabarat compound for three days and, upon his return, treated me with deference. I found it vaguely disquieting that I could cause someone this kind of trouble. I still failed to realize fully that I was now part of the fearful machine. In fact, I was beginning to feel as though I had escaped unscathed. I lived like any other young student, enjoying nights out with my friends and with Ban. The only ripple on the seemingly normal surface of my life was Abu Firas, who came almost daily to the house to indoctrinate me in the ways of the Mukhabarat.

There was one lesson to be learned above all: the Mukhabarat existed to preserve the life and power of Saddam. The Mossad existed to protect Israel, MI5 and MI6 to protect England, and the CIA made the whole world its business. But the Mukhabarat was there for one reason: Saddam Hussein.

"Saddam is Iraq," Abu Firas instructed me.

Abu Firas told me that first they were going to use my talent for getting to know people. "You will report on them. You are one of us now, and you must feel that completely. You are often undisciplined, and we will correct that. So forgive us if we are critical, but it is for your own good. You must report any time you leave Baghdad. You can call me any time you need advice or help. If you like, we can get some girls and go out."

The sudden friendship, the insistence that I belonged, was mind-boggling. I began to ask myself, Is this the dread Mukhabarat?

But soon I realized that Abu Firas hated my guts, hated me for having been an agent of the archenemy, Israel, and he hated what he was doing. But he had to follow orders from Saddam. I was to be enlisted into the service and shown every respect. His enforced kindness made me realize the full power of the word of Saddam.

I later learned that Saddam had given my father a prize piece of land in reward for his loyalty. It became clear that to protect my father from the scandal, only the very top few officers I dealt with knew about my crime, my involvement with the Mossad. That was when I realized the full extent of my father's power.

I WAS first given a basic introduction to Mukhabarat techniques in the field. Abu Firas and I would sit in the living room. We would drink hot, thick Turkish coffee as we worked, interrupted from time to time by his pager.

On one occasion he brought some maps with him, which he spread out on the coffee table. They were mainly of European cities. "Now then," he said, smoothing out the first one, "a bit about working on unfamiliar turf." It was a map of the city of Zurich. He then outlined a brief course on what to do when arriving in a foreign city, how to study the map in advance and note all the routes to and from the target address, the surroundings, the possible hiding places. It turned out that all this was academic because the agent never did any of this groundwork himself.

In the Mukhabarat a team of officers did all the reconnoitering beforehand, set up all the necessary logistics and the cover. The agent was handed an I.D. kit, complete with passport, credit cards, real money (hundred-dollar American bills were tossed about like small change) and other papers. Usually they would all be genuine, either stolen or those of a corpse.

A car was provided, if needed, complete with changeable license plates. The route and timing were worked out. All the agent had to do was follow instructions and carry out the actual shooting, bombing or robbery. There was no actual elite team of saboteurs or assassins; an agent was picked specially from the general pool of officers and agents for each individual operation.

Abu Firas described a horrible phantom organization called the Kisim Alightialat—the assassination department. It had no fixed staff, no real offices, no senior supervisor. What it had was an open, unlimited bank account. When an operation was initiated, it was financed through this account by whoever was ordered to carry out the operation. The choice of the assassin depended on the nature of the victim and the method to be used. The chosen man was given a bit of special training in explosives, or whatever was required, and sent on his way. There was only one basic requirement: blind loyalty. In some way the agent must have proved to the satisfaction of the authorities that if necessary he would kill his whole family on command and never blink an eye. It seems there are a frightening number of people who, given enough money, are prepared to do such deeds.

With a shock I realized that eventually, if not immediately, I was to be one of the chosen. For what? I felt sick inside.

Then Abu Firas went on to tell me stories about agents who failed or defected. About the officer who was sent to Kuwait to supervise the sabotage of a refinery there. It was to be carried out by an Iraqi-Kuwaiti agent from Basra. Somehow the mission failed, and the Basra agent was executed. The officer managed to escape to Sweden, only to be killed two years later by a Mukhabarat assassin, an Iraqi meat butcher selected for the task.

"This is what happens to traitors," said Abu Firas. It was the closest he ever came to expressing his real feelings about me. The Mukhabarat, it seemed, never tortured its victims. It either killed them or kept them. Torture was handled by the Amn, the secret police. If the fastidious Mukhabarat wanted someone tortured, they sent him to the Amn for the dirty work. Most of the lower orders of the Amn were drawn from the ranks of ex-convicts, rapists and the like. The officers of most of the Mukhabarat departments, however, came from the elite National Security College.

Apart from my case, Abu Firas was a man happy in his work. In addition to casework he taught the recruits at the National Security College. I later took to calling it the goon school. Since they apparently considered that I'd already had enough experience and training, I was not sent to the college.

Every year several thousand apply to the college, and only seventy-six are accepted. The Mukhabarat needs to replenish its ranks every year with about a hundred men—the number it loses on operations, mainly inside Syria and Lebanon. It draws its elite from the top five graduates of the police academy and the top five from the military intelligence school. Some are brought from other places, too—specialists in linguistics, for instance, especially Hebrew.

The Mukhabarat gets a large number of recruits from the goon school. Many of the students are from Tikrit; others are bedouin from northwest Iraq. But some are from the fine arts college, where they have displayed talent in painting or acting. Such skills can be useful to the agent in the field. Often the Mukhabarat will send one of its artists along with a trade delegation when it wants an inside look at a facility not easily penetrated with cameras. For instance, if the Mukhabarat wants to check out a Japanese petrochemical plant, they will manufacture a trade delegation. The artist goes along and later sketches what he has seen. If he needs another look, the Mukhabarat will wangle a second and even a third visit.

On the surface Mukhabarat agents are urbane, well-dressed men of the world. But though the surface has been changed, their minds and souls remain the same: they are fierce sons of the desert, whose obedience to their sheik, Saddam, is absolute. They obey blindly.

I had disdained the Mukhabarat's crude ways of dealing with me at first, but day by day I came to understand that this core of elite officers and their ranks of robots made a formidable and competent organization. They knew exactly what they were doing and how to do it. Sometimes with great subtlety, as with the artist-spies, sometimes with sheer brutality. It worked. It was deadly efficient. My disdain was gradually replaced by the fear and caution I had originally felt.

Finally I cracked under the stress of being Mukhabarat. I was jumpy, unable to eat, unable to sleep and unable to handle my studies. Abu Firas recognized the beginnings of a breakdown and ordered me to rest at home. It was odd, being cared for by the Mukhabarat. I stayed home for five months, with Ban as my only visitor. During that time, I turned twenty-one. It was the worst birthday of my life.

More and more, Ban was becoming the light in the darkness for me. She, though, was unaware of my association with the Mukhabarat. She was from a Christian family, and in Iraq, Christians tend to be very quiet, unassuming people, who stay out of politics. So I was not ready to shatter Ban's peace of mind with revelations about my activities or the reality of my entrapment.

One night when Ban came over, she looked troubled. "What's wrong with you?" she asked. "You seem so nervous."

"It's nothing. Just overwork. Too much studying maybe."

"Are you sure? It's nothing I've said or done, is it? I mean . . ."

"No, no, no. You're the best thing in my life. Don't worry. All I need is some rest and your company."

So she moved closer to me on the couch and leaned against me, and I began to discover that the woman I'd thought shy and withdrawn was very warm and quite daring.

IN THE fall I was ready to go back to university—and once again ran into problems with the administration. They used my failure to appear at a lecture as a pretext to expel me. Another wave of the Mukhabarat wand, and I was in again.

What it all meant, I reflected, was that the whole foundation of society was undermined by corruption. Partisans of the regime got ahead without any real merit. A degree was meaningless because one could not know who'd earned one and who'd extorted one. This rot had spread to almost every facet of life.

In Saddam's Iraq everyone who could be was on the take. That's how the system worked. It wasn't a system really; it was an antisystem.

Take my own case. My official pay was 30 dinars a month, about $100 U.S. at the official rate, $10 U.S. on the black market (the real value). My real pay was in the form of permissions. Since virtually everything is forbidden in Iraq, one needs a special permit to do just about anything. Every time I traveled abroad, I had been bringing computer disks back into the country to sell in my own little black market. A box of floppies that would sell for $8 or $9 in the West I could easily sell for $45 or $50. Especially the 3.5-inch format. Now Abu Firas arranged for me to have a license to do this on a grand scale.

He also set me up in the spare auto-parts business. The Mukhabarat wanted to keep one dealer under surveillance to see whom he was supplying. They suspected that he had partners in the army who gave him army supplies, which he then sold on the public market at high prices. Then he and his partners all split the difference.

The dealer was a young fellow, about my age, so it was easy for me to start up a conversation with him. After the usual talk about girls and movies I broached the subject of our doing a bit of business together. We soon shook hands on a deal.

The Mukhabarat issued an order paper authorizing the government supplies people to give me some of their stock. I drove to the huge government warehouses in the Jurf-Al-Nadaf, a government-controlled market just outside Baghdad. There were long rows of huge sheds full of spare parts for Toyotas, Volkswagens and electrical appliances. It was a bonanza. I would load the stuff into a pickup truck loaned for the purpose, then sell it at my own price to the dealer and pocket the difference, while my colleagues followed the trail of goods.

All this is possible only if commodities are scarce in the first place and if the market is tightly controlled by the security service. That's why I call it an antisystem. And in a horrible way it works. It's a system of terrible beauty. It means that everyone is to some degree beholden to the Mukhabarat that terrorizes them. Everybody is plotting with everybody else, nobody knows who anybody really is, and everybody is kept busy running around in circles inside the circles. No one has time or room left to mount any kind of opposition. You are running around, and everybody is running around you. Saddam is at the center, the still point of the turning wheel.

8
SINKING INTO THE MIRE

IN THE autumn of 1986 my superiors sent me off for Mukhabarat-style military training at a base near Taji, northwest of Baghdad. A spartan place, it had rows of undistinguished brick barracks. The large mess hall featured wooden tables and huge windows.

The most intriguing aspects of Taji, however, were the rows of fake wooden barracks. These empty shells were like sets on a Hollywood back lot. They were decoys, built to deceive enemy bombers. A bit farther out on the grounds I could see equally phony mock-ups of SAM-6 missile launchers, with their three "missiles" aimed at the skies. In 1991, when American planes filled the skies, these primitive-looking stage sets would foil many a smart bomb.

I was taught how to strip and clean an AK-47 rifle and a Browning pistol. Then came target practice on a firing range. I did very well at that.

The rest of my training consisted mainly of being shot at. They would make me stand on the range, holding a waist-high wooden dummy. Then a big Peugeot would come roaring around one of the buildings, its shrieking tires kicking up the dirt as it careered toward me, its occupants firing at the dummy. The idea was to steel the nerves of the trainee. Many agents are great shots but go to pieces the first time they are shot at. The Mukhabarat once again was not as unsophisticated as it first appeared. Spying, I was learning, was usually boring and routine—relieved, as the saying goes, only by moments of sheer terror.

THROUGH my work with the Mukhabarat I learned more information about Saddam's arsenal and his strategies than was healthy for any Iraqi to know. I discovered that if you want to know something, you should ask a secretary, a driver, a translator or someone like Nasar.

Poor Nasar was an old school friend of mine. His uncle Amir was a high-ranking officer responsible for the department handling all arms modifications. Nasar was his bodyguard, so he knew a lot.

Nasar and I became buddies. We liked to go and spend the day at Habanniya, the French-built luxury resort on a lake ninety kilometers west of Baghdad. The resort was just past the huge air base that was home to all Saddam's MiG-25s.

Habanniya was a place for tourists, but because of the war, there was a singular absence of tourists. As a result, in 1986 it was used mainly by the Iraqi upper classes.

Over the weeks Nasar kept me up on the latest in weapons improvements, confident that the weapons meant an eventual victory in the war with Iran. He assured me that Iraq had been working overtime to gain the tactical and technological edge.

French radar systems were modified to capture a larger field. The range was almost doubled, from eighteen kilometers to thirty-four kilometers. Soviet Mi-24 Hind helicopter gunships were modified to carry air-to-air missiles, two at a time. The heavily armored Soviet T-72 tanks were given new computer software programs and night-vision equipment. The big Soviet tanks were dubbed the Lions of Babylon. The Soviet shells were also replaced by new ones that had greater range but less accuracy. Soviet MiG-23 fighter planes were equipped with new suspension points to allow them to carry French-made Magic missiles, which were much smarter than the Soviet ones and had nearly one hundred percent accuracy. The MiGs were also given new French and German communications systems that improved contact with ground control. The small components were copied and produced at a plant in Eskanderia.

French and German technology was used to enhance Brazilian-made weapons systems. As usual, the equipment was taken apart and copied. It was used mainly in armed personnel carriers and other armored vehicles.

If England was a playground for Iraqi agents and terrorists, then France was a supermarket for our armed forces. Anything could be had there, from the famous Exocets to Christian Dior fashions for officers' wives and daughters.

Later I would learn more about the plants in which the ballistic missiles themselves were modified and completed. In a few years the modified SS1 would be a household word around the world: Scud. Meanwhile, I learned that a great many of the engineers in these plants worked under extreme duress. Many were forced into such work against their will. So deep was the distrust and hatred of intellectuals by the party goons that the engineers were routinely beaten by overseers, punished severely for being even fifteen minutes late for work. A sick child at home, a motor accident or a death in the family—no excuse was acceptable.

As I pondered everything Nasar told me, I began to worry. Was he, too, a plant? Was the Mukhabarat checking on whether I would report to them? The more I thought about it, the more likely it seemed. Otherwise, why would he tell me all these military secrets?

I decided to express my concern to Abu Firas. I expected a knowing look and a casual dismissal of the matter.

Abu Firas hit the roof.

Poor Nasar was immediately transferred to the war front. He was fortunate to have Uncle Amir to intervene for him, and he was brought back and put into a safe junior position.

I finally realized that Nasar had been talking to me because he thought that since my father was important, I must be, too, and it would be quite safe to talk to me about anything at all. He got caught between the circles.

It was soon after this that the world learned that Colonel Oliver North and many other misguided fools in the basement of the White House had been selling arms to Iran in hopes of having American hostages held in Lebanon released. North and his partners claimed they had been dealing with moderates in Tehran—moderates like Hashemi Rafsanjani. Of course, Rafsanjani is about as moderate as

Heinrich Himmler, Hitler's Gestapo chief. Few who know the Middle East were very surprised at this further evidence of American naïveté and ignorance in dealing with the region. They were learning, but not fast enough.

Everyone knew that the Americans had been playing a not-so-subtle game in the war all along. They gave limited support to Iraq but did little to stop illicit arms shipments to Iran. The hope was that the two nations would pulverize each other. The Americans weren't the only ones to play this game. France, the U.S.S.R., China and Israel itself were having an arms-bazaar bonanza.

But Iraq had always been led to believe that Washington tilted toward Baghdad as the lesser of two evils. Oliver North's Iranscam made Saddam livid. As appeasement, Washington reflagged Kuwaiti oil tankers, which carried most of Iraq's oil, to put them under American protection from threatened Iranian attack. Saddam was only slightly placated by the American move.

Saddam had been trying to get Iran to agree to a negotiated cease-fire for almost six years of the seven years of combat, ever since it had become clear that the war could not be won. But Iran's mullahs seemed to love the bloodbath.

Saddam came up with a novel Mideastern tactic. At a meeting of the Revolutionary Command Council he set forth the situation: the Iranians' infinite supply of martyrs, their intractability, the option of further bombing of Tehran, the uselessness of that option, the possibility of massive attacks on Iranian ships in the gulf, the dangers then to Kuwaiti shipping, the American policy of sitting on a fence. . . . What was needed was to blast America off that fence.

"You are ordered to destroy an American warship in the gulf," Saddam said, turning to his air force commander, General Hamid Shaaban. "Use the Exocets."

Only in the Middle East would an attack on an American ship be considered a good way to end a war.

The attack was a perfect example of Saddam's cunning. Moreover, there was perfect logic beneath the seeming insanity. America was sitting on the fence because it could afford to; Kuwait and Iran and Iraq were sustaining all the real losses, while America and France and the Soviets and every other nation on earth, it seemed, were supplying arms to both sides. It was just one big weapons testing ground.

Only pressure from America and the Soviets could possibly end the war now. Real pressure. Pressure that would cut the arms arteries of Iran. Bit by bit Iraq was already being curtailed by the Soviets.

The Americans would move to end the war only if they themselves began to sustain unacceptable losses. Like a naval vessel. And, above all, the sailors on board.

On May 17, 1987, one of Saddam's French-built Mirage fighters streaked out of the blue sky over the gulf waters, headed for the U.S.S. *Stark*.

Radar operators on board the *Stark* saw the Mirage, but the commander realized too late that it was homing in with deadly intent. The U.S.S. *Stark* was hit broadside by two Exocets. The *Stark* was able to limp to safe port, but thirty-seven of its men were sent home for burial in flag-draped coffins. Saddam made elaborate apologies, saying it had all been a terrible accident. Exactly how a Mirage could accidentally fire two Exocets at point-blank range was never made clear. The Americans and international agencies were refused permission to interview the pilot. But both parties let the matter drop after Saddam paid the families of the victims a total of $27 million in compensation.

For Saddam it was cheap at twice the price. Washington began to work in earnest for a cease-fire. The war, which would have cost Saddam billions more had it continued, was almost over. The pilot who caused this "accident" was promoted and given charge of the air force college.

THROUGHOUT the war I was spared military duty because I was Mukhabarat. My life went on uneventfully. I continued my studies, and I spent more and more time with Ban. I still said nothing to her about the darker side of my life, not wanting to distress her. She was in no danger as long as I was obedient to Abu Firas.

Later I realized that I had underestimated Ban and that beneath her gentle ways was a resilience and strength far greater than mine. I should have had an inkling of that strength because of the way she handled the difficulties of getting together with me. She had to invent any number of excuses at home, for her parents would have been as happy about her seeing a Muslim as mine would have been about my seeing a Christian. We were an Iraqi Romeo and Juliet, and true to the classic, it was Juliet who was the stronger. But we were happy, and

I grew happier as I discovered that my ability to love had not died as a result of my father's cruelty.

I don't know when it was that I realized I both loved and hated being the property of the Mukhabarat. I hated informing, but finally I had to admit to myself that I loved the special powers. If someone was making life a little inconvenient for me, then abracadabra! They were gone. I was now thinking of the Mukhabarat as *us*, their headquarters as *our* offices.

At the same time, I began to see how easy it was for Saddam to create his goon squads. I hated the man, and yet look how his ways had seduced me! I began to think for the first time of getting out. I knew what I was becoming bit by bit. I was part of the antisystem. I was becoming a goon.

Until now I had just accepted these changes as my fate. But looking at Ban's loving face one evening, I suddenly realized what was happening to me. And I decided to find a way out for us both. I began to watch for an avenue of escape. I knew I must not make a mistake. I would have to play their game better than they could. If I did not, they would eat me alive.

As I found myself mired deeper and deeper in the squalid world of the Mukhabarat, Ban became my lifeline. I knew that with her I had a chance of becoming a decent human being again—if I ever had been. At first I needed her, and then I loved her.

One night, when we were together in my room, I confessed my feelings. I held her close and our kisses grew more urgent. I could feel her passion match my own. She pulled me down on the bed, and we made love like two ravenous lions.

With most Iraqi men that would have been the end of the love story. For me, when Ban and I became lovers, that sealed our bond. Given our new intimacy, I decided it was only right that she know at last just with whom she was involved.

Over dinner one evening at our favorite haunt, the Crystal restaurant, by the Tigris, I told her about the Mossad and my "escape" into the arms of the Mukhabarat. At first she was utterly nonplussed.

"You're an intelligence agent?" she asked unbelievingly.

"I'm afraid so. I try not to get anybody in trouble, but it's almost impossible. Ban, I have to get out of this."

"Can you resign? Will they let you out?"

I realized she hadn't grasped yet what I meant by "out of this."

"No, my love," I said as gently as I could. "They don't let anyone resign. I don't know how yet, but I have to get out of the country. Permanently. And then I'll need you more than ever. . . ."

Her face fell. The full import of what I was saying was beginning to dawn on her. After a time she spoke.

"I don't understand about the Mukhabarat and how it works. But I know you, and I know you share my feelings about life. That's enough for me. My life is with you. Wherever it is."

For the first time in months I felt that I might have a future.

AFTER my confession to Ban I went on as usual. I was buying time and waiting for an opportunity.

As far as my dubious career was concerned, I began to relax a little. Then the Palestinian phoned.

"I have a letter for you from your father," the unfamiliar voice said.

He might as well have said he had a pouch of diamonds for me from the Queen of England. That would have been more likely.

"Can you meet me at the Meridian Hotel?" he asked politely.

I sat on the edge of my bed and tried to make sense of what I knew. First, my caller's accent was Palestinian; that could mean he was Mossad. Second, my father never writes; the Mossad knows this, so maybe the call was a signal from them. But third, the technique was not Mossad. It was too direct, too raw.

I decided it had to be a plant, perhaps by the Mukhabarat.

I met with Abu Firas. He warned me to be extremely careful. "There's something wrong with this guy," he said. Then he handed me a tape recorder. Concealed in my jacket, it was wired to a microphone attached inside my collar. "Leave the machine on the whole time," he instructed. Off I went to meet the Palestinian.

On the house phone at the Meridian I called the room number I'd been given. The Palestinian told me I'd know him by his white hair. Within minutes he appeared. He looked like a businessman, but I still had no way of knowing if he was a Mossad agent brazenly setting up a meeting, or a Mukhabarat agent pretending to be a Mossad agent to find out if I would still play ball with the Israelis. Or he might have been as advertised—a Palestinian.

He greeted me warmly, then steered me out to a secluded table in the breakfast café. He was just beginning to explain his business to me when I saw Abu Firas come in and head our way.

Abu Firas came up and looked at me. "Hi, Hussein."

The Palestinian laughed and said to me, "Did you call him here to catch me? What did you think I was? A spy?"

Very funny, I thought. As it turned out, the Palestinian was genuine. He was in Baghdad as a delegate to a PLO-Iraqi conference. The Mukhabarat had set me up—probably with my father's help. Another test. I was fed up. My nerves were twisted into knots all the time.

Still, I was rewarded in a way for having passed all my tests so well. They let me go to New York for a holiday, accompanied by my father— and my shadows. Even if I had attempted to defect at this point, I would almost certainly have been caught. But I could not run for it just yet. In the first place, there was Ban; I had to get her out of the country. And I wanted to finish my degree and get my diploma, or I would have to start all over again in the West. So I decided to bide my time.

In New York, my father and I barely exchanged three words. I realized he and my mother were at odds, for he was constantly angry and cruel with her. I decided to talk to her.

"He blames me for everything," she said, crying. "I don't even know what it is he's blaming me for."

So I told her that I had got myself into a bit of trouble, but it was going to be okay. Then I told her that my father had ordered in effect that I should be executed for what I'd done.

When she heard that her husband would order the death of her son, she was beside herself. It was the last straw. After a monumental fight with my father she began to pack, with the intention of leaving him forever. Soon after I left New York, she, too, moved back to Baghdad.

By now I was in my third year of university, and in spite of everything, my grades were acceptable. Abu Firas and his men kept me busy watching this student and that professor. The rest of my time was spent managing my various financial scams on the antisystem market, with my computer disks—a fresh load from my vacation—and my auto parts.

I had passed my tests so well that at the end of 1987 the Mukhabarat assigned me to do a security check on a man being considered for employment in a missile factory.

Northwest of Baghdad was a large industrial facility called the Mun-sha'at Nasar, the Victory Factory. The final welding and assembly on most of the large ballistic missiles were done here. The man I was to check out was Ahmed Hassan. In the course of that effort I learned a great deal about this assembly line of death.

The Nasar plant was enormous. Two of its main products were the Al Hussein and the Al Abbas missiles, hybrids made from the design of the Russian SS1—the Scud. Iraqi engineers dismantled, then studied the SS1s in order to reproduce the parts, to which they added their own improvements. All the work in the Nasar factory was directed by a German scientist, who ruled there like a god. No one knew his name except those in the very highest echelons.

The Al Hussein missile was a qualified success. Though it could achieve a range of 600 kilometers, the designers forgot to make the appropriate changes to strengthen the fixed launching pads, and as a result only six missiles could be fired at a time.

The Al Abbas was a dream machine. Its range was up to 800 kilometers, and the fixed pads could accommodate thirty at a time, each one capable of delivering a 250-kilogram payload.

The drawback of both missiles was the lack of a guidance system that could accurately aim them. But to our leaders it was quantity that mattered. Something was bound to hit something important. As always, the target in mind was Israel.

Originally the Nasar plant manufactured containers for everything from household fuel to oil storage tanks. Whenever American or other suppliers of alloys wanted to inspect the Nasar to make sure their materials and technology were in fact being used for peaceful purposes, the stagehands would go into action. The missile-factory set would be struck, and the machines and other paraphernalia from a genuine container factory nearby would be hauled over as replacements. A half-finished container from the original plant was kept on hand for these presentations. It lent an air of authenticity.

The American inspectors—sometimes from a company, sometimes from government—would then be courteously shown through every inch of the factory; they would look closely at it all and nod wisely, sign the required forms and leave.

Abu Firas and my other colleagues loved this and laughed at how completely they had duped the Americans. I was never sure if the Americans needed duping. Money talks, and business is business, especially in the arms business.

The Germans, the Swedes and the Swiss were openly helping Saddam build bunkers and underground hangars for his air force. All of this construction was designed to withstand any attack, including nuclear. One had to assume they knew who the potential enemy was supposed to be.

It was easy for me to strike up an acquaintance with Ahmed Hassan. He lived in our neighborhood, and that gave me the pretext. It is the custom for neighbors to gather together when someone in the neighborhood dies. And thanks to the war with Iran, there was always a house in mourning nearby.

I simply went to Hassan's, knocked on the door and asked him to come with me, because I did not want to go alone to a mourning service. In the Mideast this kind of thing is quite natural and easy between relative strangers. So we set off together for the big tent pitched in the middle of the street for the purpose.

After the funeral Ahmed Hassan and I discovered we had a mutual interest in chess. We began getting together for matches, sometimes at his house, sometimes at mine. Ahmed, it turned out, was a brilliant engineer and, other than that, a very ordinary guy, not interested in politics, drinking, girls or other dangerous distractions. Though I tried halfheartedly to get him to talk about politics or the war, he was only interested in chess and money. He knew how the engineers were treated in these factories by the overseers, but he knew also that the engineers were well paid and often given land and a car. He needed the money. So I gave him a neutral report for working in the Victory Factory.

THE Nasar wasn't the only facility that produced items whose designs were stolen from cannibalized technology. Iraq also had a thriving computer business going, based on the best of IBM and Apple.

There was an enterprising fellow from Basra who had a computer business in southern Iraq, near the Kuwaiti border. Since he mainly supplied the military with weapons-enhancement designs, he had a great business going. His only problem was that since he supplied the military, Apple wouldn't supply him. To solve the problem, he simply acquired the components in Kuwait and the United Arab Emirates, where Apple did a lot of business. Then he shipped the components to phony companies. False end-user certificates—the end user is simply the person, company or country for whom the shipment is ultimately destined—were made out to get around laws that barred export to Iraq and other bellicose countries. Then the parts were put together in his plant. And presto! Iraqintosh Apples.

The main assembly plant was in Baghdad, near Fourteenth Ramadan Street. I was told the computer factory operated sixteen hours a day, two full shifts. These computers helped in programs such as the improvement of the heat-seeking SAM-6 missile. When the Americans developed the phantom heat balloons to fool the missile and draw it away from an aircraft, our researchers went to work and designed special censors to equip the SAMs to distinguish between the balloons and the jets.

When government importers ran into problems in negotiations with IBM for the XT model computer, other ingenious Iraqis dismantled the ones they had, copied the parts and went into business. If they needed actual components, those, too, could be had in Kuwait.

This was Kuwait's main function as far as Baghdad was concerned. It was all pretty much business as usual in the Mideast tradition. No one thought in their wildest nightmares that Saddam would turn those missiles and guns on Kuwait. Except when we lost a soccer game to them. Then the fans would start to grumble that Kuwait used to be a part of Iraq, so we should take it back.

9
OUR MODERN-DAY NEBUCHADNEZZAR

THE war with Iran was still being fought by an exhausted and now resentful army. It was the spring of 1988. The soldiers knew they were dying in a lost cause.

One of the heroes of the war so far was General Abdul Maher Rashid. When the Iranians pushed into the area of the southern swamps, near Basra, Rashid was brought in to save the situation. He did, stopping the Iranians just in time to save Basra. Rashid was a self-confident, swashbuckling type, with natural military skill. His talents would have made him an invaluable asset in any Western army. In Iraq he was doomed, simply because he might one day be a rival to Saddam. Rashid must have known this when he and his brother, a tank-corps commander, began to plot a coup.

They never came close to success. Saddam had ears in their operation, and the tank corps was seized on its way to Baghdad by Saddam's elite Republican Guards. Rashid's brother was killed with great style: Saddam replaced the commander's helicopter pilot with one of his own men and ordered Rashid's brother flown to Baghdad. The new pilot waited until the commander was approaching the helicopter, then turned on the blades, cutting his head off.

General Rashid himself would have suffered a similar fate, but his daughter was married to Saddam's son, Kusai. Rashid was placed under house arrest.

Sadly—for Iraq, for the gulf region, and for the world—Saddam has done such a thorough job of eliminating his opposition that there is scarcely a leader left who could assume power and run the country properly even if the opportunity presented itself.

Saddam deported, tortured and killed opposition among the Shi'a. The gassing of the Kurds, another group who might have risen against him, is also well known. The actions of the Mukhabarat against the Kurds is less well known. The Mukhabarat used to send a female agent to sell a popular homemade yogurt to the Kurds. The yogurt, contaminated with cyanide or rat poison, would kill everyone who ate it. This was also done in Europe, to kill those judged to be a threat to Saddam. It was an alternative to the infamous "diplomatic box."

Members of the Da'wah, Kurds, rebellious party members, and military officers who offered competition to Saddam all had been eliminated. They were delivered in boxes to their front doors after being gassed, shot, bombed or beheaded.

In this atmosphere it is hardly surprising that there is virtually no significant democratic opposition group. There is a collection known as the Liberal Democratic Front, based mainly in England. They have been creatures of the British government since the fall of the Iraqi monarchy. Their leader is the son of Salih Jabur, who was the Prime Minister under King Faisal.

The Liberal Democratic Front busies itself in London with newsletters, pamphlets and meetings, but for the Iraqi people living under Saddam's boot, they are distant and irrelevant.

Perhaps the most telling thing I can say about them is that the Mukhabarat wasn't even interested in killing them.

We all began to wonder if there was going to be anybody left alive to run either the army or the country after Saddam. Ironically, Saddam would turn to Rashid after the humiliating defeat by the Americans, in 1991, to help him try to salvage the ruins. Rashid, still popular with the rank and file and with whatever capable officers were left, would bear watching.

SUDDENLY, after eight years of killing fields, both Iran and Iraq declared victory, signed a cease-fire, and the shooting stopped. It was August 8, 1988.

In Baghdad people celebrated by shouting, dancing and shooting guns into the sky. That night we went out into the streets of Baghdad to join the throngs. It was a rare time of total, open joy in Saddam's Iraq, and it seemed the right time to ask Ban to marry me.

When I made my proposal, we were at a Chinese restaurant. "I know I may bring you only trouble for a while, but one day we'll be free of all this. And I love you. I need you more than life. Please say you'll marry me."

"Of course I'll marry you," she said simply.

Overjoyed, I gave her a beautiful diamond ring I had found for her. She was incredibly happy, smiling through tears, looking at the ring and then at me. I could not believe how lucky I was.

IN OCTOBER, Iraq had a festive spectacle in Babylon to celebrate our modern-day Nebuchadnezzar, Saddam.

Ancient Iraq had two main cultures, one in the north and one in the south. In the north were the people of stone, the Assyrians. They once ruled that plateau with brutal but brilliant efficiency. Though they built their palaces and cities to last, ultimately the Assyrian empire fell to a Chaldean and Medean coalition. The Assyrians left behind only their giant monuments of stone, most of which are near Mosul, northwest of Kirkuk. Some of these huge figures are twenty feet high, and each depicts the body of a mythological bull with outspread wings and the head of a man-god bearing a tall crown. Iraq's second ancient culture, in the south, was that of the Sumerians and Babylonians—the people of the mud. The relics of these desert people did not survive as well as the relics of the Assyrians, because they had no stone. Their monuments were of a different nature, and their ingenuity wrought the seventh wonder of the ancient world—the Hanging Gardens of Babylon. Drawings and writings survive to tell us of the magnificence of this palace of flowers in the desert.

But Iraqi minds were filled more with another of Nebuchadnezzar's accomplishments: the defeat and enslavement of the Jews. We not only studied this in school but we also were reminded of it regularly as adults. Propagandists drew attention to the modern parallel: our glorious Saddam facing the Jewish enemy, ready to conquer Israel.

Saddam decided to build a replica of the ancient palace in Babylon. It was a reconstruction that must have caused howls of anguish from archaeologists around the world. Saddam's idea of restoration was simply to build a new palace over the foundations of the old, burying even deeper the streets and walls of the lost city.

Saddam set about re-creating the Hanging Gardens, too. A public contest was held for the best design for the new gardens and, above all, its irrigation system. To accomplish the final effect he wanted and to irrigate the gardens, Saddam diverted the waters of the Euphrates so that they ran past the doors of the palace he had built on the ruins of the halls of Nebuchadnezzar. It seemed Saddam was a man-god, too.

Nevertheless, like any mortal tyrant, he needed bodyguards. So when he went to Babylon for the great spectacle, I was assigned to go as well. I was one of many to guard the great ruler.

The great spectacle was to be a fashion show. Yes, a fashion show. This was the doing of Saddam's wife (and first cousin), Sajidah, who otherwise stayed out of the limelight—a safe policy in a Mideastern nation. Flashy wives like Sadat's Jihan and the shah's Farah eventually aroused the anger of the reactionary male population—and a lot of the female population, for that matter. So Mrs. Saddam Hussein kept a very low profile, confining her activities to innocuous pursuits like women's fashions. Sajidah had established the House of Fashion to cater to her tastes. Her designers took apart the Diors and Saint Laurents she had sent home from Paris. Just as the missiles and tanks were altered, she had them altered and improved to incorporate the Iraqi features she preferred. Since almost every Iraqi Airways flight carried these Paris designs, people called the flights the Airlift.

Now the House of Fashion was going to give a special presentation of ancient Babylonian costume. Saddam himself would preside. It was a warm night, with a soft wind whispering across the desert. Ban and I arrived in Babylon and followed the crowds to the brand-new ancient amphitheater, because we Mukhabarat guards were supposed to be part of the public and not evident in our official capacity. We did not have time to see the new palace, and I was vaguely disappointed. But we climbed the stairs to a position near the upper-right-hand entrance and took our seats at the back, where I was to be ready to go into action if necessary. There were guards like me everywhere, the elite being in the circle immediately surrounding Saddam. Before us the tiers of seats curved in a graceful circle, descending to the stage. Saddam, Sajidah and their party sat on a dais near the stage.

On all these public occasions Saddam was surrounded by three circles of security. The first was made up of heavily armed men, handpicked from the Presidential Guards, usually relatives of Saddam's. They stayed right by the President's side, and would shoot first and ask questions later. They shot many poor unsuspecting people who'd approached Saddam and, without thinking, reached into their pockets to pull out letters of supplication for help with this problem or that. The second circle was made up of Mukhabarat officers and agents. The officers were in uniform and armed. The agents, of which I was one, were in plain clothes and unarmed. Our job was to handle the public in Saddam's vicinity. Finally, there was an outer, third circle, drawn from the Amn forces of whatever town or city Saddam was visiting. Since their job was to handle overall security and any emergency evacuation, local people who knew the terrain were preferable. The idea was to have security from several different branches in case one branch proved disloyal. Saddam did not want to suffer the same fate as Anwar Sadat of Egypt, who was assassinated on a reviewing stand by his own soldiers.

The amphitheater was lit by torches, which flickered to the strains of ancient Babylonian music. Then war drums announced the beginning of the show. Mercifully, I did not have to watch the parade of ersatz fashions, as I was obliged to keep my back to the stage and keep a watch on the audience. My mind was completely taken up by the task at hand because the punishment for failing to protect Saddam would be unimaginable. Still, I thought the vigilance wasn't really necessary. The devil himself protects Saddam.

On these occasions Saddam presented himself as a kind of godfather, like Marlon Brando, aloof, disdainful, giving lordly blessings with a slight wave of his hand. He was powerful, and a mere blink of his eyes was enough to command his men to obey orders. But he does not have a real natural charisma. His aura, such as it is, grows out of raw power. Rather than inspiring devotion, he instills fear.

Maybe Saddam felt as I did about his wife's pet fashion house, because he left in the middle of the show. I had to go with him, leaving Ban to her own devices. Along with the army of bodyguards, there was, as always, a photographer with Saddam to capture every moment of his public life. Every day, every hour, every minute, every second. Saddam wanted to be sure that any attempt on his life would be recorded. His intimates said he liked to sit later and watch films of failed assassination attempts.

We junior guards were dismissed before we had a chance to follow him to his palace, where he went to commune, I imagine, with Nebuchadnezzar.

10
DELIVERYMAN TO ABU AL-ABBAS

O NE autumn evening in 1988, soon after the spectacle at Babylon, I was visiting the home of one of my computer disk customers. He was an old acquaintance from school, named Ahmed Zaki. I had always envied Ahmed his father. Mr. Zaki was not like any other father I knew, least of all my own. He was warm and friendly and loving with his son. When I visited, we would sometimes play a game called Risk until six in the morning. Then we would arrange for his father to lose so he would have to fix breakfast. Ahmed Zaki's house wasn't at all like our house. His house was alive.

Mr. Zaki had fought on the side of the PLO in the war in Lebanon in 1975 and 1976. Hundreds of Iraqis like him were part of the Arab Liberation Front, a force of volunteer fighters sent by Baghdad to aid the Palestinians. They were trained by the Estikhbarat under Sabir al-Dhoury, who also directed the training of the PLO factions, as well as the Iranian Mudjahedeen, who were staying as guests in Iraq. The Mudjahedeen were one of numerous Iranian groups in exile opposed to Khomeini. This was kept as discreet as possible, since Saddam did not want to be viewed by the world as a terrorist leader, like Qaddafi.

Given Mr. Zaki's background, it wasn't a total surprise when one of the most famous Palestinian terrorists in the world, along with several of his cronies, walked into Mr. Zaki's house one evening. This was Abu al-Abbas, the mastermind behind the 1985 hijacking of the cruise ship *Achille Lauro.*

Abu al-Abbas wasn't the only radical Palestinian who had been welcomed to Baghdad. Long before Abu al-Abbas moved into town, Abu Nidal, responsible for the hideous attacks at the airports of Rome and Vienna, in 1985, also took up residence in Baghdad after his split with Yasir Arafat. Abu Nidal had been sent packing to Damascus when Saddam wanted to be removed from Washington's list of terrorists so that he could receive American aid in 1981. No one was really fooled. The Americans went along with the charade because at that time they were beginning to worry that Iraq might actually lose the war with Iran. There were reports that Abu Nidal moved back to Baghdad later. Saddam's special relationship with these men went back to his violent rupture with Arafat's PLO. In the mid-'70s, Iraq had harbored large numbers of PLO fighters, in sympathy with the persecuted victims of Israeli ambitions. But the PLO had done exactly what it had begun to do in Lebanon: try to form a state within a state. When Saddam learned that the PLO had actually set up its own prisons, its own criminal justice system for its people, northwest of Baghdad, he decided that they had completely worn out their welcome.

An all-out war broke out between the PLO and the Iraqi regime. The Syrians aided and abetted the PLO, allowing fighters based in Syria to stage raids into Iraq. In March 1978 the PLO's Fatah group sabotaged the Iraqi embassy in Brussels. There were attacks on Iraqi Airways offices, as well as car bombs and letter bombs directed at Iraqi targets from Frankfurt to Athens. The Mukhabarat turned on its killing machines in Europe, hitting PLO men from London to Amsterdam. The shooting stopped only when Saddam and Syria's Hafiz al-Assad worked out a very temporary truce.

Both Abu Nidal and Abu al-Abbas led factions of the Palestinians who had broken with Arafat largely over the PLO's too cozy relationship with Syria and over Arafat's moderation. As a result, they were welcomed by Saddam to Iraq.

Abu al-Abbas had been in residence in Baghdad ever since his men hijacked the *Achille Lauro,* in 1985. In that attack Leon Klinghoffer, a crippled Jewish American passenger, was killed. When Abbas and his cohorts were pursued, they were taken in by Saddam. Abu al-Abbas lived in Baghdad like royalty. He had the key to the city. Anything he wanted he could have, from weapons to women. It's odd that cold-blooded killers like this are often so gentlemanly and pleasant at social occasions.

That evening in Mr. Zaki's large salon Abbas and his cronies made themselves comfortable, drinking tea and talking quietly about the arms trade. They discussed where to get automatic rifles. It soon became apparent to me that Mr. Zaki was Abu al-Abbas' number two man, in charge of field training.

In the course of the conversation I piped up and said I knew a fellow who had gone into the arms business. "He brings stuff in from northern Iraq and sells it to anyone who wants it." Everyone's ears pricked up.

"Is he trustworthy?" asked Abu al-Abbas. A great question coming from him, I thought.

"As far as I know," I muttered, and breathed with relief when he changed the subject.

The next day Mr. Zaki phoned me. "We want to talk to you about the matter you mentioned last night."

Reluctantly I went over to see him.

"We trust you," he said. "We want to arrange to buy some small stuff from your guy. Pistols, mainly. Can you set it up?"

I felt like a fly caught in a cobweb. The Mukhabarat spider could be anywhere. What was Abu al-Abbas up to? He had trained in Iraq, and Saddam had supplied weapons. Abbas had everything from defensive grenades to multirocket launchers. Moreover, Abbas could have any pistols he wanted just by knocking on the door at the presidential palace. Why did he seemingly want to go behind Saddam's back? Why go underground? Were they building a secret stockpile? Maybe they planned to do as the PLO had done in Lebanon and eventually become a state within a state (which turned out to be largely true). What should I do? Say no? Report to the Mukhabarat? Were they just playing another cat-and-mouse game with me? I decided I had to play it right back.

"Okay," I agreed. "I can put you in touch with him."

"And you can be the deliveryman. It's better that way."

Better for whom? I wondered, and off I went to the Mukhabarat headquarters to report to Abu Firas.

Abu Firas was inscrutable. He pondered it all for a few moments, then spoke. "We'll supply the weapons. Leave your contact out of it. I'll send a man with you to help deliver them."

Oh great, I thought. So now I was going to sell guns from the Mukhabarat to Abbas, a terrorist. I was going to con some of the most dangerous con artists around. And who was the Mukhabarat conning? I wasn't sure. For all I knew, they were going to rake in a profit, with no one the wiser. Including Saddam. Would anyone like to live that dangerously?

I reported back to Mr. Zaki that I could supply the weapons.

A few days later one of Abu Firas' agents rolled up to my house in a pickup truck. Another pickup followed. We drove to the Zakis' house. Almost immediately a Range Rover came around the corner and stopped beside us. Abu al-Abbas, wearing a light safari suit, stepped out. Taking one of the crates, we all went inside.

Calmly he levered it open, then took out one pistol, then another, giving them each a cursory appraisal. Then he nodded, picked up a brown leather case at his side and opened it for my inspection.

"Do you want to count it?" he asked casually.

"No, thanks," I said, looking at the bundles of money. "That will be fine, I'm sure."

I went into the kitchen and came out with a black garbage bag. I stuffed the money into it, thanked him and went home, later turning over the money to Abu Firas' men. I never saw Abbas again, but friends told me nothing at all happened to him after our little deal.

Saddam had clearly come to some kind of terms with these Palestinians and was as involved in world terrorism as Iran or Syria or Libya. He simply handled it more discreetly.

Only a few years later, when the American bombers flew their devastating sorties over their Iraqi targets, I wondered if they fully realized just what they were unleashing below. Every bomb, I believed, would eventually be avenged in cities around the world if Saddam or his shadowy allies sent out the orders.

My life in the Mukhabarat again settled back to normal, so to speak. One day, during a routine meeting, Abu Firas suddenly acted very friendly. He offered me a way to invest the money I had made from my own little business enterprises—a small fortune of 20,000 dinars, about $70,000 U.S. at the bank rate, $7,000 at the black market rate. He told me he knew an ex-spy from Syria who was now managing the Al Qadisiya Hotel and its nightclub. If I invested money in the hotel— no messy papers to be signed—then Abu Firas would give me 1000 dinars a month on my investment.

It sounded fishy enough already, and then he told me never to go to the hotel or to discuss this little matter with anyone. If this was a test, it was ingenious. Whom would I report to about Abu Firas himself? The Eagle. I went to Azzawi, who was by now head of the Mukhabarat.

The next day Abu Firas came storming over to my house. "You want to get me killed? You want to destroy me? Why the hell did you tell Azzawi about the investment?"

"You were taking money," I replied. "That's the sort of thing I'm supposed to report, isn't it?"

"You don't understand. It's all just a misunderstanding," he said, and gave me back my money.

Now I realized that I was one of them. Deep down I had known it was not a test. I was a Mukhabarat agent informing on another, an Iraqi informing on another Iraqi. No excuses. No rationalizations. And now I knew they would pull me in further and further, so deep that I would forget all my old values. They would brainwash me completely, simply by keeping me doing what I did every day for them.

I realized that I had to stop thinking about escaping and do something about it or I was going to self-destruct. If I stayed much longer, I would inevitably run afoul of my masters. If I made a serious misstep, my original reprieve would be rescinded.

THE only thing that kept me sane and in control was my beloved Ban. Her love for me, and mine for her, carried me through. I decided on a drastic move again. I decided to escape to Beirut.

The Mukhabarat had a program in which it trained a select few men to go to Beirut to aid the anti-Syrian factions fighting in the never ending fratricidal war in Lebanon. I would volunteer. And once in Lebanon, I would make my break.

Since the war with Iran had ended, Iraqis were allowed once again to travel. So my plan was for Ban to go on a vacation somewhere, like Paris, and I would come from Beirut to join her. Then we would disappear into the world. Ban was horrified.

"Lebanon!" she wailed. "How can you even think of it?"

"If I don't take this chance, I might never have another," I argued. "Abu Firas has it in for me after the hotel money business."

Ban began to cry. "I can't bear it. Already there's so much against us. Your parents, my parents, this whole horrible secret police, this whole mess of a country, and now you want to go to Beirut."

"I don't want to go." I tried to soothe her. "But I don't see a better way. And I won't be in Beirut. The operation is based in Junieh."

"Don't go. Lebanon's a shooting gallery."

She was right. And so was I. I had to try it. I wrote to Azzawi and requested assignment to the Lebanese theater of operations.

In the '80s Saddam had changed his tactics with regard to Lebanon. The Arab Liberation Front volunteers were replaced by the more cold-blooded Mukhabarat. Handpicked agents were trained for the assignment. Basically Lebanon was another battleground in his war for Arab supremacy with Syria's Hafiz al-Assad.

Saddam supported the Christian militia, known as the Lebanese Forces, because they were Syria's current enemies in Lebanon.

The reply to the request I made of the Eagle to join in this fray came back almost immediately, in the form of an official approval given by Abu Firas. After the hotel fiasco he was glad to get rid of me.

While I was finishing my courses at the university I went about getting a Tunisian passport. First, I made sure that we, the Mukhabarat, didn't have an agent or informer inside the Tunisian embassy. Otherwise someone would report to my office that I was requesting a Tunisian passport, and the game would be up. A few discreet inquiries among my colleagues revealed that Tunisia was one of the few embassies we hadn't bothered about.

Second, I needed my father's old Tunisian papers so that I could claim a passport as the son of a native Tunisian. I felt nervous as I went through the things he had left in his office at home, as if he would somehow know from across the ocean what I was doing. I found what I wanted and went to class. In the middle of a lecture I slipped out. No one would follow me once they thought I was safely occupied in classes. I went home, though, just in case. Then I crept out the back door, slipped over the neighbor's fence and from there made my way to the car I had borrowed from a friend.

The Tunisians at the embassy were polite and cooperative. But it took weeks of waiting while I grew more and more anxious. Finally they issued me a passport. I was ready. Ban was numb with the strain, but she bravely agreed to play her part.

Then unexpectedly I was called back in to see Abu Firas. With great trepidation I went to headquarters.

"You are being taken off the Lebanon assignment," he said.

I was stunned. "Why?"

"There is too much to do here."

11
THE NUCLEAR GOD

TAMMOUZ/Osirak—god of the dead. Saddam wanted his power. It was as though he wanted to *be* Osirak. And what better way to achieve this than to harness the destructive power of the atom? Saddam had named his nuclear reactor after the god and was on his way to acquiring the bomb.

But the Israelis had shattered those dreams when they bombed the reactor in 1981. Rebuilding was going too slowly to suit Saddam. He had left the reconstruction up to a special scientific department for nuclear power. Now he dissolved that department and put the nuclear program under the control of the Jihaz al-Amn al-Khas, the private security for military and industry.

All pretense that Osirak was a peaceful civil project was dropped. And the Mukhabarat was ordered to run thorough checks on everyone to be employed on the project, especially the engineers.

This was my new assignment. The assignment that would keep me in Iraq. "You are to screen one of the senior engineers," Abu Firas informed me. "And report on even the slightest doubts about him. This is to be a top top secret project now."

Everyone in the West—in the world, in fact—thought that Osirak had been completely destroyed by that Israeli raid in 1981. But Osirak still lived. I was as stunned by this news as any outsider.

"But all the newspapers, the TV, everyone, said that the whole thing had been wiped out."

Abu Firas laughed. "That's the news we put out. Otherwise they might have come back to finish the job. But the core of the reactor is still intact. Now instead of them coming back to finish the reactor, we're going to finish them!"

I was appalled. He meant what he said. The Western powers still found the idea of a first nuclear strike unthinkable, but they failed to realize that Saddam was quite capable of the unthinkable.

I was ordered to get to know an engineer named Muhammad Ali. Because he was in fact a relative of mine, it wasn't that difficult to approach him and encourage a friendship, even though he lived an hour's drive outside Baghdad. Like me, he had studied in England. He'd completed a doctorate in nuclear physics in Newcastle, and we spent afternoons reminiscing about England.

For five or six years he had been head of the furnaces operation at the nuclear plant. After the Israeli raid he was sent to Germany, France, Japan and Kuwait on shopping trips for the parts and materials necessary for reconstruction.

For Muhammad Ali it was simply a job, and he would do it to the best of his ability. Like so many Iraqis, he had completely lost all moral sense in the twisted ethical world of Saddam Hussein. He simply had no concept of what he was doing. Like the Westerners, he didn't think of the unthinkable: a first strike.

Ali was perfect for Saddam. I gave a neutral report on him, saying that he would do exactly as he was told.

When I handed Abu Firas my report, I said, "The Israelis will know what we're up to and just come back, won't they?"

"It won't be so easy this time. We're ready. Those stupid bastards who were sound asleep on the antiaircraft and the SAMs have been taken care of. The new guys will be awake."

"Even so, the Israelis won't give up."

Abu Firas looked at me with a satisfied smirk. "It isn't all there anymore. We've got a lot of enriched uranium stored in the underground channels at the Dokan Dam."

Indoctrination into the party line begins at an early age in Iraq. Above: an Iraqi girl holds up her end of a deadly tradition.

Above: the infamous supergun, developed for Iraq by arms merchant Gerald Bull, boasted a theoretical range of thousands of miles.

I decided to shut up. This was dangerous territory, and I didn't want to know more than was healthy for me. The dam was on the Little Zab River, north of Kirkuk, almost at the Iranian border.

Saddam still intended to be the god of the dead. There were other nuclear projects, at Hammam Ali and Irbil. Just to be sure, Saddam was still manufacturing other forms of death: nerve gas, mustard gas, typhoid. And the most deadly germ of them all, anthrax.

There were chemical facilities around Baghdad, and just about everyone knew about a mysterious Canadian scientist who was one of the key men on the chemical-weapons program. He was a friend of that other Canadian, Gerald Bull.

Bull was still working on the supergun. But the modified howitzers were being adapted to carry what we called binaries. Special chemical warheads, they carried two different chemicals that when exploded together, reacted with each other to create lethal gases. They were being developed by Bull's Canadian friend. At least that was the commonly held belief inside the Mukhabarat.

The ultimate target was, as usual, Israel.

The chemical projects were field-tested on whole villages of Kur-

EXIT خروج

Above: Saddam Hussein's elaborately landscaped summer palace is surrounded by a ten-foot-high security wall. The Iraqi President's Baghdad bunker, left, is designed to withstand virtually any attack, including a nuclear one.

dish men, women and children. The first tests were primitive but effective. They simply flew over in Soviet Ilyushin transport planes and rolled barrels of the stuff out the side. On impact, chemicals in separate compartments combined to form lethal gases.

By March 16, 1988, the Iraqis had refined the process and tried out chemical bombs on the Kurds. The entire village of Halabja was wiped out in seconds. Other villages nearby were treated to a similar fate from the long-range howitzers. This mass killing did not come to the world's attention until after the cease-fire between Iran and Iraq later that same year.

The Kurds were Saddam's whipping boys. He had his military officers use them as practice targets for cluster bombs imported from Chile, then for modified cluster bombs called Siggils, fired by multimissile launchers. The Ababil missile was tried out to see what radius of killing field it would produce. It was a roaring success.

In a more traditional exercise Saddam had his gunships wipe out thirty-six villages in the Imadya sector, in the north, leaving not one survivor. And then special units were sent in to demolish what little was left of the frail little village houses. Eventually they annihilated every village within thirty kilometers of the Iranian and Turkish borders. The war was the excuse for this slaughter. The Kurds were to be wiped out in order to create a no-man's-land along the border. Then, to prevent resettlement, the whole area was mined.

In the summer of 1988 the Kurds were again the guinea pigs for biological weapons. The military scientists tried out their typhoid virus, but for reasons that remain obscure, it was not a success.

Biological-warfare plants were built in Al Kut and Suwera, both to the southeast of Baghdad, along the Tigris. I was never sure what they were busy cooking up in Al Kut, but at Suwera, I knew, they nurtured typhoid. A friend who worked nearby came to visit one day and recounted with glee the latest accident at the Suwera typhoid plant.

"Today they had to run around vaccinating everybody in the area because of some big emergency at the laboratory," he said, laughing. "It was real chaos." And he laughed some more.

In Iraq, people hardly know the difference between life and death anymore, because whether you are dead or alive, it's all the same. Sometimes if you cry long enough, after a while you go right around the circle and start to laugh. In Iraq, if you are going to die, you just take a shortcut and start to laugh right away. You don't bother with crying.

I think this kind of psychology is part of the reason Westerners so often just don't understand what they are dealing with in the Middle East, even on an individual basis. They are completely bewildered, or even antagonized, by the way we react to many situations.

Whether this reaction is the result of living under Saddam's brutal regime or something bred in the bone, Iraqi moral feelings seem stunted. The fact that this death-in-life has wormed its way into our souls may be worse than all the torture and killings.

I WANTED to live. To be really alive. And to do so, I needed two things: freedom and Ban. Again we talked about it, one day when we took a little trip to a lake outside Baghdad.

"As soon as I figure out a way, we get out of here," I said to her as we drove along the highway.

"But how?" she replied, always practical. "They'll find us."

"No. I know how to disappear," I assured her.

Ban gave a little sigh and leaned against my shoulder.

"They've given me a ticket to go to Manila to visit my wonderful father. He's the honorable ambassador there now," I told her.

"Are you going to go?"

"Not if I can help it. But it's one of those tickets with a string attached. If I don't use my exit visa within sixty days, they take my passport and I can't get out of the country for years. So we're going to have to do something pretty soon."

"Did you tell them we were driving here today? You're supposed to, aren't you?" she asked. Her question was prophetic.

As we approached a checkpoint the guards ordered us to stop. I thought as we pulled over that they were probably Mukhabarat; not far away a new palace was being built for Saddam. They hauled me out and pushed me against the car to be searched.

Poor Ban was terrified. I was angry.

Abu Firas again. I hadn't told him about our little jaunt. His long arm was reaching out to remind me just who was boss. They demanded identification papers, then turned even uglier.

"So you two aren't married, eh? What are you going to do? Find a private little spot?" One of them sneered, with a lecherous look at Ban.

"I'm from the Mukhabarat," I finally told them. "If you don't believe me, call headquarters."

This made them break into nasty laughter. They held us there for three hours. Finally they released us.

"You didn't need to do that, especially to Ban," I complained to Abu Firas the next day at headquarters. "You know she hasn't a clue about any of this."

"It's your own fault," he replied. "Next time obey the rules."

If I had ever had any doubts, they were gone now. Ban and I had to get out.

"You are to go to the Philippines," Abu Firas continued. "Then you are to return here to be trained to work with foreigners."

"There's something I want to do first. I want to get married."

Abu Firas looked pleased. A married man was a man with ties that kept him bound to the regime.

"We need your father's approval first," he said cautiously.

"My father says it's okay with him if it's okay with the Mukhabarat and whoever else it's necessary to get permission from."

In the end we needed the permission of all three security services—

the Mukhabarat, the Amn and the Estikhbarat. They all got to work and did a security check on Ban.

She passed, but then Abu Firas said she had to convert to Islam.

I was furious. "No way! I am not going to ask her to change everything she was brought up to believe. I won't ask her."

"We'll see about that," he replied, "but in any case, we have to have her parents' approval."

I sighed. Her parents had been opposed from the beginning to their daughter's going out with a Muslim. They were no different from most other people in my country, where everything was done to keep the various religions separate. But though there was a law that prevented Muslim women from marrying Christian men, Muslim men could marry Christian women if they got all the necessary permits.

So I went hat in hand to Ban's home to plead with her mother. That is the custom when asking for a girl's hand, because a daughter is the mother's charge. In the end she relented, because ultimately her daughter's happiness was more important to her than anything else. Since Ban's mother had agreed, her father did as well, as is also the custom. We decided to go ahead with the legal ceremony. We were not actually considered truly married until we'd had both a legal and a religious service, after which we could live together. Abu Firas was still insisting on her conversion to Islam, but we could at least have the legal procedure done.

Poor Ban. She'd been raised to look forward to a beautiful wedding in white performed in a church, and instead she had a dismal little ceremony in a courthouse.

It was November 11, 1989. I chose the date so that our wedding day was the same as Remembrance [Veterans] Day in the West. That way it seemed even more concrete, something to hang on to in the trials ahead of us. "I promise you," I told her, "when we're out of this country, we'll get married again. We'll have a Christian service in a church, and lots of flowers and a limousine. The works."

"If we get out," she said softly.

I made my first move just before Christmas. Abu Firas' wife was expecting a baby about then, so I counted on that to keep him preoccupied. On the twenty-fourth I bought a ticket for Jordan because I didn't need a visa to go there. It was a trial run to see how I was received at the American embassy. If they would give me asylum, then

I could return to Iraq and finish making financial arrangements and plans for Ban to follow.

At Saddam Airport, I was tense, expecting the long Mukhabarat arm to reach out again. It didn't. With relief I boarded the plane. When we landed in Amman, I was cautious, but my feeling of elation grew. Until I noticed him. He was about fifty and dressed like any businessman. As I walked through the crowds in the terminal toward the currency-exchange booth, he stuck to me.

"Hello," he said jovially, as he took his place in the line behind me. "You're an Iraqi brother, aren't you?"

"Yes," I replied, my heart sinking. "How are you?"

I knew when I was defeated. So I decided to turn their little plan around and stick to him, instead of him sticking to me.

"Say," I suggested, "maybe we could help each other out. I'm here to shop, but I don't know Amman very well, so . . ."

"No problem. I can help."

"And we can share some expenses. Maybe even the hotel."

"Good idea."

And off we went. This kind of casual striking up an acquaintance is very common in the Mideast, so there was nothing unusual on the surface. But we both knew that a game was being played.

We went shopping and even took in a movie together. I came back to Baghdad two days later, with my heart feeling like lead.

Abu Firas had me on the carpet immediately.

"Why did you leave without reporting your plans?"

"I did," I said calmly. "I phoned you from the airport and left a message that I was going for a shopping trip."

He gave me a long, hard look. "Don't play with fire," he hissed in a low voice. "You don't report something like leaving the country half an hour before you do it. Understand?"

I understood perfectly. My time was running out.

I began to make serious preparations for departure, without knowing yet how I was going to do it. I set about getting a passport and exit visa for Ban. With my connections I was able to have the precious documents within twenty-four hours. "As soon as I contact you," I told her, "you will go to London. I'll either send for you or join you as soon as possible." I told her where to stay.

The other major consideration was money. Iraqi dinars were worth zero outside the country. So I set about converting my hundreds of thousands of dinars into tens of thousands of dollars' worth of gold and jewelry: necklaces, diamond rings, emerald and diamond bracelets, pearls and gold coins.

Alone in my room at night, I packed the gold away in small packages. Then I packed them all tightly inside a travel bag. But where on earth could I go? And how? Abu Firas seemed to know wherever I went.

My misery was complete when my father arrived on one of his trips home to the Foreign Ministry. Then I realized that he could help me escape. Of all people, my father was my ticket out—if I could play it just right and maneuver him into position. Ironically, he now wanted me to change money for him on the black market. I got him the very best rate, so in a way he owed me a favor.

We met at his suite at the Rashid Hotel, where he stayed now that his separation from my mother was irrevocable.

"Thanks," he said gruffly as I handed him the money. "You'd better be doing what they damn well tell you the rest of the time," he added.

These references were no longer a mystery to me. While searching for my father's Tunisian papers I had found some others that revealed that he was a senior Mukhabarat officer.

"Yeah, sure." As casually as I could, I said, "But I've been having a few little problems with Abu Firas. Nothing big."

"Like what?" he demanded quickly. I knew he'd bitten.

"Nothing much. A little misunderstanding about money. Some hotel deal they have going. Almost took me for a lot."

"What the hell are you talking about?"

So I told him. And added that since then, Abu Firas had made a point of harassing me, especially about travel abroad. It worked.

"Who the hell does he think he is, messing with my family!" he exploded. "I'll show him a thing or two."

It was that old rule. Inside the family, the lord and master can treat his wife and children as brutally as he wants. But if an outsider gives them trouble, beware. Then it's the honor of the master that's at stake. I knew my man.

We met again the next day in his hotel suite.

He went over to the writing desk by the window and picked up an envelope. "This is a letter of introduction to my friend in the embassy in Yemen, asking him to give you any help you need, any money while you're visiting there."

Yemen? I wondered why he wanted me to go to Yemen, of all places. Then it dawned on me. It killed two birds with one stone. What he wanted to do was to show Abu Firas he was the more powerful. He could send me anywhere he wanted, without any stupid okay from Firas. Yemen was as good as anywhere else. Anywhere but the Philippines. That was the second bird: he averted an unwanted visit from his despised son.

"Here's some money, too, for the trip," he said.

"But what do I tell Abu Firas?" I asked nervously.

"F___ him. I'll show him his place but good."

That was the last time I ever saw my father.

I was to leave on March 17, after my father had departed again for the Philippines. In order to confuse possible pursuers, I changed my reservation on the ninth, a Friday (and the Sabbath), when only the Iraqi Airways offices in the Rashid Hotel were open. I arranged to leave the next day.

Now I set about leaving for good. I gave away virtually everything I owned to a few of my friends. On my last night, Ban and I decided to take a suite in the Rashid, not knowing when we might see each other alone again.

"Do you have to go now?" she complained. "You won't be here for my birthday."

"I know," I replied, stroking her hair. "But you have to understand. This is my last chance. The Mukhabarat are really jumpy these days. They might do anything."

My main concern was Abu Firas. I wasn't sure exactly what the rift between him and my father might cause. The best course for me was straight out of the country. To anywhere else.

We were discussing all this when there was a knock at the door. Ban jumped in fright. My own heart skipped a beat or two. But the best thing was to answer it as if I were innocent.

"Hello," said the old man at the door. I recognized him straightaway. He was one of the escorts for visiting V.I.P.s, from the Ministry of Foreign Affairs. He was short, with wavy white hair. "Oh, I'm sorry. Hello, Hussein. What are you doing here?"

"What are you doing here?" I returned.

"I must have the wrong room. Is this . . . Wait a minute, let me see," he said, looking for something in his pockets. "I've made a mistake," he finished, drawing out a piece of notepaper with writing on it. "I'm supposed to go to room six sixteen, not six ten. Please forgive me."

"Not at all. Why don't you come in?" I said. "Have a drink."

I had said the magic word. He came in and explained that he was expected by the delegation of the Iraqi embassy from Jordan. The ambassador himself was here.

I was extremely pleased by the coincidence. Here was a perfect way to smuggle my gold out of the country. Acting as though he were a trusted confidant, I told him I was taking some gold out of the country and had a pilot friend in Iraqi Airways who would help me for several hundred dollars. He took the bait immediately.

"You can't trust one of their pilots. I can do it for you for less than that," he said. And we made arrangements to meet the next day. Ban listened to this in resigned bewilderment.

"At least I won't have to worry about us having something to live on," I told Ban later.

When it came time for me to leave, she cried, but then made an effort to be brave again. I saw her again only briefly before I left. I went to say good-bye formally at her home. Her mother was there. Ban's father had died at Christmas.

Then I went to my home to do the most difficult thing of all. I told my mother and Bibi I was going away for a long time. They understood they would not see me ever again. They were determined to be brave, not to cry, but the tears welled up in their eyes.

"Don't forget your mother," whispered Mama.

"Never, Mama," I told her. "How could I?"

And I walked away from my father's house forever.

My new contact picked me up at the gate and drove me to the airport. He carried the bag of gold, as we had arranged, and got us through the first security check. After that, he handed the bag to me. They hadn't stopped me at the first post, so I was home free.

As the aircraft lifted off, I took one last look, I hoped, at the country I loved and hated so much. Then it disappeared beneath the gathering clouds.

12
"I'M WITH THE CIA"

THIS was my last chance. I was a spy who had escaped Iraq, trying to come in from the cold. But I was still in the Middle East, a dangerous place, where the long arm of the Mukhabarat could still drag me back to a living hell in Iraq.

Of all the Middle Eastern countries, Yemen was the worst country in the world for a renegade Iraqi in 1990. Saddam Hussein owned Yemen. During the war with Iran he had kept it supplied with oil, and that meant Yemen owed Saddam its life.

When Saddam "won" the war with Iran, he became a hero in Yemen, as well as in a number of other countries. As a result, Yemen was now virtually a fiefdom of Baghdad, and Iraqis were kings of the mountain in San'a, the ancient capital of Yemen. The Iraqi embassy there was, in fact, the seat of government.

I knew I had to walk a narrow line in this ancient town. I could use my Iraqi status to open doors, but I would have to keep as low a profile as possible.

I looked up the hill. The newly built American embassy stands like a fortress overlooking the ancient city. I'd met with the consul earlier in the week and given her a brief written précis of my situation. For the second time since my arrival I climbed toward the iron gates. I was dismayed to see that, as before, there were hundreds of visa-seeking people lined up: men, women and children. The sight of those veiled women, with only their eyes peering out of slits in their long black robes, made me shudder. Where I come from, most of the women do not wear these awful robes. Those eyes with no faces touched some deep nerve of fear in me. Nevertheless, I hurried up a path, crossed the budding new garden and headed for the consular building. Everything in this compound was ultramodern. As with American embassies all over the world, thought had been given to emergency evacuation. The new garden was large enough to land a fleet of helicopters.

The receptionist, a local Yemeni, tried to give me a hard time. "Do you have an appointment card?" He looked at me with narrowed eyes through the bulletproof glass that separated us.

"No, but I was told to come back today—at this time."

He ran his finger down a list he had in front of him. "Do you have any identification?"

"Look . . ." I was getting angry. He suddenly turned around. A short man of about thirty, with thick glasses, had come out of an inner office and now stood behind the receptionist. The man came around out of the cage and held out his hand warmly. "Hi," he drawled in a southern accent. "I'm Steve. I'm with the CIA."

Steve ushered me into a small room furnished with a round table, comfortably padded chairs, and a bar along the wall. The table had a lace cloth and was set for diners. There were no windows. There was, however, a small round bugging device on the ceiling, obvious to anyone who knew what to look for.

Steve ordered us soft drinks and food, and while he asked general questions about my personal background another man appeared with a meal. It was cooked in the Mideastern style. The atmosphere, the meal, everything, seemed so normal—genteel even—considering the subjects we were about to discuss.

I *had* to make this escape good because there was no turning back. I wanted asylum in the United States. I had brought out enough gold to bankroll a new life and was willing to give the Americans whatever information I could.

"Ah!" Steve said, pouncing on my passport. "You have a visa here for the Philippines. Going to pick up drugs for delivery?"

I sat there dumbfounded at this ludicrous question. Then the phone beside Steve rang. He picked up the receiver, listened, then hung up. For a second he glanced at his notes. Then he looked up. "How did you come to work for the Mossad?" he asked.

Apparently whoever was on the other end of the phone was listening to our conversation and knew the ropes better than Steve did.

I told Steve—and our invisible listener—about Mossad operations I had been on in England. I told him how Iraqi agents come and go from the United States and European countries with complete impunity. I revealed how the Iraqi regime kidnaps its opponents in the capitals of the world and ships them home in the so-called diplomatic bag.

I told him what I had learned in the Mukhabarat. I talked about the training schools, the assassination operations, the weapons-modification factories, and horrors such as the accident at the typhoid-virus plant. I was prepared to tell more: for instance, I knew the truth about the missile attack on the U.S.S. *Stark*. But I wanted to keep some cards in my hand. I hinted at the darkest secret of all: Osirak. Everyone believed it was destroyed. It was not.

Ten months later the Americans would hit it again and announce once again that it was dead. But I had reason to doubt even then that Saddam's nuclear ability was completely destroyed. Underwater, in the channels of the Dokan Dam, was enriched uranium. And if they had disguised the Nasar facility by moving another entire factory, they might have moved a lot of Osirak.

"I can tell you about the surveillance of the American embassy in Baghdad," I offered Steve. "Does that interest you?"

His ears pricked up. "Of course. Fire away."

The American embassy sits across the street from the Shahin Hotel. "The Shahin is one big ear for the Mukhabarat," I began. "It's equipped to overhear everything in the embassy.

"Spying is one of the biggest make-work projects in the country," I continued. "It's a major source of employment. As a result, the intelligence services have exhaustive information on everything— even food orders for the American embassy." I smiled a little. "You see, if there's an unusual amount of fancy food ordered by the American embassy, then the spies find out who's coming to dinner. They use that advance knowledge to know when to eavesdrop."

"We run a tight ship," Steve protested.

I shook my head. "In addition to the resident informers on staff, there's one junior staffer in Baghdad who sells American visas. This comes in handy for the Mukhabarat when they choose to send agents, using other means than the diplomatic flights."

Steve looked amazed. Still, he waffled. "I'm not sure we can do anything to help you—at least not immediately."

I felt empty inside and defeated. Didn't he realize how valuable my information might be? Surely the Americans could see that Saddam had new military designs. He had a million-man army with nothing to do. No dictator in the world could let that situation go on for long. He would have to find something to keep them busy before they turned their thoughts to the presidential palace—the way armies do when they have time on their hands.

Saddam might turn his attention to the Kurds again. Or he might turn south to Kuwait. He nursed a long-standing grudge concerning the disposition of Babiyan and Faylakah, the two islands in the gulf held by the Kuwaitis. When the British drew the new borders that carved up the Ottoman Empire, after World War I, they literally cut off Iraq from the sea with one stroke of a pen. The war with Iran had reminded Iraq just how dependent it was on its coastal neighbors. Moreover, Kuwait was making noises about wanting Iraq to repay the billions of dollars Kuwait had supplied for the war against Iran. We Iraqis all knew that Saddam had a very short fuse, and it was burning in the direction of Kuwait.

But Steve and his colleagues at the American embassy in San'a didn't seem to grasp what I was offering them on a silver platter.

I gave Steve all my papers, even my address book with names and phone numbers. "Well," he said, "how do we know you didn't just make this all up, even the phone numbers?"

I stared at him in disbelief. Was that all he had to say?

Once again the phone rang. After nodding several times, Steve corrected his approach. "Well, we'll have to see," he hedged. "We'd like you to go back to Iraq and carry on working there."

I cut him off. "I've had five years of hell there. My last escape attempt failed. This is it. All I want is to start a new life."

"We can't give you a visa, you know—"

"I don't want a visa," I replied. "I need asylum!"

"Is there any other country you could go to? I mean, we might be able to help you later. . . . These things take time."

Since the doors of the United States were clearly not going to open right away, I decided to try my other alternative. "I could go to Canada," I said. "I know someone there."

He nodded. "Right now the main thing is to get you out of here. You've probably been seen coming in here. Yemen won't be safe for you. Why don't you just get yourself to Canada, and we'll get in touch with you there." He put his hand on my shoulder. "And then we'll see what we can do for you."

He was clearly anxious to get me out of the embassy, looking for Iraqi agents over his shoulder. Or rather over my shoulder.

"Sure," I answered. "We'll see."

What I saw was that although Americans and their government are always talking about rescuing people from tyranny, it just doesn't work that way. Geopolitics come first. Just the same, I gave him a phone number where he might contact me in Canada. And he gave me a code and number to reach him in San'a if necessary.

"Well," said Steve as I prepared to leave, "you're *sure* you won't go back to Iraq and work for us there?"

"I can't. Don't you understand? It's all over for me there." I drew my finger across my throat like a knife.

"Hmm. I see," he said, but he didn't. I couldn't understand his attitude. He should have seen me as a spy's bonanza.

I left the American embassy knowing Canada was my best bet. Still, I had to get out of Yemen without arousing the suspicion of any Iraqis who might be tracking me. As a cautionary measure, I went to the Iraqi embassy and called on my father's friend, Ambassador Abdul Hussein.

He greeted me amiably and asked if I needed anything. I assured him I didn't and that everything was fine. Then I detected menace beneath his friendly manner.

"You have been called back to Baghdad immediately," he said. He gave no reason, and I needed none. Abu Firas must have been livid.

I hid my fear that I might have been seen going to the American embassy. I told myself that if I had been, I wouldn't be able to leave this room. I stayed on for a few minutes chatting, then left.

It was clear they had no idea what to do with me. So I bought myself a ticket to Canada. Lufthansa refused to sell me a ticket. Quite properly, they demanded proof of acceptance into the country of destination. At the Yemeni airline counter, however, I just showed my driver's license and said it was my American green card, and they happily sold me a ticket to Toronto.

I went back to my hotel and packed my bag. I could just make a connecting flight to Frankfurt. I went through the airport procedure almost in a trance. The crowds and the noise seemed far away. I felt no elation when the plane lifted off, for I was full of foreboding and worry. After the failure of my meetings with the Americans, I wondered, would anyone help me anywhere?

From Frankfurt I took the first available flight to Bonn. I wanted to get to the Canadian embassy there as soon as possible.

It was raining in Bonn. I took a taxi to one of the small, cheaper hotels in the old part of town. I checked in under a phony name and paid them cash in advance so they would not request my passport to hold overnight as insurance.

My hopes lifted a bit when I entered the Canadian embassy. It was a plain office building on a small side street not far from the Iraqi embassy. I filled out the necessary forms, then handed in my visa application with my I.D. papers to a woman at the counter. As I was explaining to her how desperate I was to go to Canada right away, the consul himself appeared behind the glass. He was an older man with glasses, an old-world gentleman. He came out and ushered me through into his office, explaining that an instant visa was impossible. "You should have your visa in about three weeks."

"Three weeks!"

"Fourteen working days."

All of a sudden I felt terribly alone. Ban seemed a million miles away. And here I was, stuck in Bonn. Well, better Bonn than Baghdad, I said to myself. Shape up. It could be worse.

So I went back to the hotel, retrieved some of the gold jewelry and went in search of a buyer. After asking for estimates in a number of stores, I was directed to a small shop run by a Jewish dealer. When I showed him a hundred-year-old diamond ring, he exclaimed in admiration. I immediately trusted him because he didn't try to pretend it wasn't worth much. He gave me a fair price for several pieces, and so I had some money to live on.

Nearly three weeks later I received a Canadian visa, which is really a temporary visitor's permit. At last. I allowed myself to begin to hope again. But not too much. I knew how closely allied Canada and the U.S. were, and even though Iraq's relations with Kuwait were deteriorating daily, I was afraid Canada would still be reluctant to offend Saddam's government by accepting the son of one of his diplomats as a political refugee seeking asylum.

As THE plane began its descent into Toronto it looked so peaceful below that I felt hopeful. Maybe Ban and I could live here. I decided to get in touch with her and tell her to leave Iraq right away for England. I would send for her as soon as possible.

The officer at passport control looked at my visa, then sent me on to be checked by an immigration officer. She asked the reason for my visit. I could see she was suspicious.

"I'm just here for a trip. My father is a diplomat. I travel a lot."

"How much money do you have to look after yourself?"

"About a hundred and fifty dollars in cash. But the Iraqi embassy will look after me—anything I need," I lied. "I'll register with them here."

Before I made any move at all in this country, I wanted to make contact with the CIA to see if they might handle my case after all. But I could hardly tell her that I was here to see the CIA.

Finally she seemed to believe me. She wrote down the Iraqi embassy as my address in Canada and let me through.

It was a beautiful April day, and my hopes rose again. A trusted friend had given me the number of an Iraqi in Toronto who might give me a room to stay in temporarily. When I called, he welcomed me and gave me directions to his place. It was a beginning.

I waited a week for the CIA to call this contact's number, the one I had given to Steve, in San'a. Finally I decided to call Steve.

"I'm sorry," said the woman who answered the phone at the American embassy in Yemen. "He's been transferred." She passed me on to Steve's replacement. But he knew nothing of my case and said he couldn't do anything.

The next morning I received a call from an American who called himself Jackson.

"Steve passed your name along to me. How are you doing? Sorry to be so long getting in touch. Listen. I should be in Toronto soon. Can we meet at the consulate on Monday at nine a.m.?"

For the first time since leaving Baghdad, I knew I was dealing with a pro. There was something about his voice, his manner, that told me this man knew what he was doing.

"Nine Monday will be great."

"Okay. Tell them you're expected in the office of Mr. Bradley."

The American consulate in Toronto is an elegant building on University Avenue. I used an entrance that avoided the usual lineup of people applying for American visas.

A young man of nineteen or so was at the front desk. I told him I had an appointment. He checked, then slid a book across the desk for me to sign. He called someone on his telephone, then handed me a badge.

An older woman appeared from the elevator. She escorted me to the upper floor, where two men were waiting for me in a comfortable-looking office. One was tall, well dressed, about forty-five. This was Jackson. The other was Bradley.

They began to question me about my story, but not at all about the Mossad. I supposed that meant they must have already checked that out. What they wanted were names of Mukhabarat officers in Iraq, information about people in the nuclear facilities and the chemical- and biological-weapons plants.

"Can you go back to Iraq?" Jackson asked.

"No," I replied, "it's out of the question. Besides, I want to end all that and start a new life, a normal one, in the United States. In return I'll tell you everything I can."

"Well, that kind of decision isn't in our hands, but we'll see what we can do," he promised. "Meanwhile, if you want to go to some other country, we'll vouch for you."

I left disappointed. I had thought it would be so simple. I thought they would jump at the chance of learning more about Saddam and his war machine. I was mystified.

After a week they called to say they couldn't help me. Now I was not only mystified, I was depressed and angry.

I decided to apply for asylum in Canada. On May 23, a few days before my visitor's visa expired, I went to an immigration office and filled out the forms, then submitted them, along with a letter explaining why I feared for my life if I went back to Iraq.

Three weeks later I received an appointment to discuss my case. The woman who dealt with me was kind and anxious to help. She even called the welfare department to see if I was eligible, if need be.

Since I was the son of an Iraqi diplomat, my case was considered delicate. "Others will take it from here," the woman said. "You'll just have to wait for now. Meanwhile, I'm sorry, but we can't allow your wife to join you, not until you have your status here. And you can't hold a job until then, either."

I appreciated her sympathy. But this seemed ridiculous to me. I could draw welfare, but I couldn't work.

I was waiting anxiously for an answer to my request for asylum when Saddam invaded Kuwait. On August 2 Iraqi armor simply rolled into the defenseless little nation and announced that Kuwait was now province 19 of the Republic of Iraq.

13
LINES IN THE SAND

As I sat in Toronto the conquering Iraqi army began to pillage Kuwait. Thousands of foreign workers and tens of thousands of Kuwaitis fled. Among them were Palestinians who had lived there for thirty years, forced to flee, leaving behind their life's savings. This did not stop Saddam from later claiming he had done it all for the sake of the Arab cause, especially that of the Palestinians.

Suddenly the White House was calling Saddam an Arab Hitler who must not be appeased. But as one American journalist put it, Saddam was more of a Frankenstein's monster than a Hitler. Now the media reported how governments and arms dealers from Paris to Tokyo, from Washington to Moscow, from Bonn to Beijing, had had a field day supplying Baghdad—and to a lesser extent Iran—with weapons, technology and advisers.

As usual, no one had thought things through. Now their horrible creation was in their own backyard. As far as the industrialized countries were concerned, the oil nations of the Middle East *are* their backyards. To lose Kuwait was bad enough. But right next door was Saudi Arabia. To lose Saudi Arabia was unthinkable.

President George Bush drew a line in the sand. He sent ships, troops, tanks, pilots, bombers and missiles to Saudi Arabia and the United Arab Emirates to back up the United Nations' demands that Iraq leave Kuwait. If Saddam refused, he would face the awesome arsenal of the United States and Britain, among others.

I knew there would be war. An ultimatum handed to a man like Saddam Hussein guaranteed that he would refuse to back down. Saddam played a clever card when he compared his annexation of Kuwait with the Israeli occupation and settlement of the West Bank, then demanded an international peace conference to deal with all the outstanding Middle East issues, especially those of the Palestinians and the occupied territories. He had a point: the West certainly had a double standard on this issue. Why the Americans had never mustered the political will to buck Israel and do something for the displaced Palestinians, I shall never understand. It was in their own

interest to do so because it would remove the most powerful psychological weapon the hard-line Arabs had: hatred of America as Israel's
ally. Now Saddam wielded that weapon.

When situations like this develop, there is a lot of knowing talk in
the West about how we Arabs need to be allowed a way to save face,
and then we will back down. This is a quaint notion. The truth is,
Saddam couldn't give a damn about saving face or about the Palestinians. What he was doing was playing every card to humiliate the
Americans, with no intention of ever getting out of Kuwait. Even if the
West had agreed to a Mideast peace conference, Saddam would have
strung it out with one new condition after another.

The wonder was that Palestinians from Jordan and the West Bank
suddenly adopted Saddam Hussein as their hero. It was as if they had
instant amnesia about how he had treated the Palestinians over the
years. I would like to have invited all those deluded Palestinians who
were now cheering Saddam as the great Arab hero to visit Baghdad so
they might sample life under the Ba'th Party, the Mukhabarat, the
Amn, the Estikhbarat and all the rest of Saddam's enforcers.

For a while there was hope that the global economic sanctions
against Iraq might bring Saddam to his knees, but that hope assumed
Saddam cared about his people. In government propaganda much
was made of the cruel shortages, but in fact Saddam couldn't have
cared less about what happened to his enslaved public.

The only reason the United Nations could take a stand in the first
place was the collapse of the Soviet empire. For the first time since
World War II local powermongers couldn't play off the White House
and the Kremlin against one another.

When Saddam moved into Kuwait, he seemed to have forgotten
that Moscow was no longer a factor. He also banked too much on the
Vietnam syndrome, believing the Americans would rather sacrifice
Kuwait than get bogged down in another war. Moreover, he didn't
take America's desert expertise into account. The Americans have
deserts. They train on them.

Saddam had completely missed the change of personality America
had undergone during the Reagan years. Americans would fight if
they thought they had to.

Everybody knew it was all about oil, no matter how often President
Bush stressed the oppression of Kuwait and upholding the principles

of the United Nations. Even Bush was candid enough once in a while to say it was a matter of America's strategic interests. And it was. If the United States failed to stand by its Arab allies such as Saudi Arabia and Egypt on this one, those Arab leaders could never again be seen to sit at the American table—if they even lived to tell the tale. As it was, they risked the wrath of considerable numbers of their own populations, who would resent American interference, let alone American troops. There wasn't much love for the fat cat Kuwaiti regime in the rest of the Arab world, but there was a great deal of fear of Saddam.

It became popular to label Saddam a madman. I knew from the inside that he was not a madman in the normal sense of the word. He was a megalomaniac, yes, but a ruthlessly efficient one. One of the best judges of human nature in his own country, he was capable of extremely shrewd psychological maneuvers against an enemy.

Sitting in Toronto, waiting, I hoped that the Americans really did have the backbone to take him on. Nothing else would rid Iraq of Saddam. Unless the Israelis did it unilaterally.

The threat of war should have meant that the CIA would be more interested in me. In early October I left a message for Jackson at the consulate. He called the next day to tell me they were going to work something out and he would be in touch.

I was impatient and frustrated. Ban had made it to England but was alone there, and now, because of the war, her bank account had been frozen, along with all other Iraqi accounts. I had gone through most of the gold, and about all that was left were the pieces of jewelry that I had meant for her. I was on my way out for a walk a couple of days after my conversation with Jackson when a stranger phoned.

"Hussein Sumaida?" he said. "I'm a friend of Abu Firas. He told me to tell you to come back to Baghdad right away."

I froze. There was someone here who knew me, who was looking for me. Someone had given away the phone number. I decided to run. To England. I sold more of the jewelry and bought a ticket to Cairo, via England. Anyone checking the airline would assume, I hoped, that I had gone to Egypt to lose myself in the Muslim masses there.

I LANDED in the hands of the authorities at Heathrow Airport in the early morning.

There were no polite questions here. When I told passport control

I wanted to apply for political refugee status, the reaction was a hostile, "Oh, you do, do you?" And the officer roughly shoved me in the direction of a nearby doorway. I was pushed into a room about two meters square.

Over the next thirteen hours four immigration officers grilled me about my story. The issue that seemed to make them angriest was how I had worked for the Mossad in England without British intelligence being informed of the Mossad operations.

They asked about the chemical- and biological-warfare plants. And about the foreigners that Saddam was now holding as hostages. He had refused to allow many diplomats and foreign workers to leave the country, instead putting them in areas that were strategic military targets to act as human shields. The West was justifiably furious about this. But it had happened after I'd left Iraq, and I knew nothing that would help on this score.

Finally they seemed finished with me. I had been given no food all day, and I was exhausted.

"Don't move," said my last interrogator as he left. A few minutes later a burly officer came in, hauled me to my feet and led me to an underground garage. I was dumped into a white police van and driven to some kind of jail. I was pulled out of the van and hustled into a cold, dark basement cell. A concrete platform with a filthy blue mattress was my bed.

They brought me some food, but I was too wrung out to look at it. I crouched on the floor all night, afraid to have anything to do with the diseased-looking bed. I sat trying not to imagine what would happen if they deported me to Iraq.

In the morning I was taken back to the interrogation room at the airport.

"So what do you think of our government, sonny?" asked one of the officers. "We're a bunch of evil imperialists, I suppose."

"Please, I'm telling the truth. I want to help your side. If you don't believe me, let me talk to your people in intelligence."

"Not bloody likely, sonny. Think we're a lot of fools, do you?"

As far as they were concerned, I was a terrorist.

They left me alone for a time, and I felt like beating my fists on the walls. Then the door opened, and Ban rushed in.

It was like seeing the sunrise. They had called her to come in and had questioned her, too, but apparently with great kindness. She was laughing and crying and hugging me.

Then to our amazement one of the officers came in and informed us that they had decided I could have a hearing in two months. They were giving me a temporary two-month visa.

We took a cab back to the city. Jubilant, happy to be together again at last, alive and well, we hugged and kissed and laughed and cried all the way. We checked into the best hotel I knew, the Regency. To celebrate, we ordered Champagne and shrimp and lobster and all the most delicious things on the room-service menu.

The next day we found a more affordable room at a small hotel and started to prowl about London looking at flats. We finally found one we both loved near Hampstead. I had gone to the bank and arranged for at least enough money to live on week to week, though they would not lift the freeze on the account.

When the authorities called me to come and see them again at the airport, I went right away, thinking they had finally checked out my story and wanted to begin debriefing me to learn what they could about the regime they were on the verge of going to war against.

"We have to send you back to Canada," said the officer.

My heart stopped. I was speechless.

"We can't take on your case, because you already have an immigration case pending in Canada," he said. "It's against the rules. You'll have to go back and continue the process there."

I began to argue, then stopped, realizing it was useless. I felt they were afraid to handle a hot potato like me. They must have imagined the field day the media would have if they were discovered harboring a Mukhabarat agent.

But worse was yet to come. They refused to let Ban go with me.

She brought my suitcase and the gold to the airport. Her eyes were red from crying, and she could hardly speak. I, too, began to cry. Everything was out of reach, no matter where I stretched out my hands.

Ban clung to me and I to her, weeping; then they gently pried us apart. All I could see was Ban's tearful face as they took me away from her, upstairs to the departure lounge and onto the plane.

I arrived back in Toronto on October 19, 1990. The Canadian authorities said Ban could not come until my status was resolved. So I began the long process of immigration hearings for political refugees, alone. In addition, I was interviewed at length by agents of CSIS, the Canadian Security and Intelligence Service. I told them of an informer I knew of in the Canadian embassy in Baghdad, a Christian Syrian girl who routinely gave detailed reports to the Mukhabarat.

The CSIS officers seemed interested in that. I had a lot more information to give them, but they told me they didn't need it. They were a defensive organization, they said, not a foreign intelligence bureau. I was stunned. Canada was going to war against Iraq. Yet the CSIS didn't seem able to take advantage of the intelligence coups I was offering them any more than Steve had in Yemen. I grew more and more despondent.

As fall dragged into winter I waited for the war to start, and pined for Ban.

14
THE BEST REVENGE OF ALL

ON JANUARY 16, 1991, the war began. As American F-15 fighter-bombers streaked across Baghdad's night sky, I sat watching those first astounding live television reports and cheering them on. I wanted the bombs to obliterate Saddam's palaces, the typhoid plants, Osirak, the chemical works, the Mukhabarat headquarters and the arms factories. I wanted all the grotesque creations of the monster destroyed. Most of all, I wanted the bombs to kill him.

I believed the Americans would strike as precisely as they could, but I knew there would be civilian losses. Even so, I believed the total suffering would be less than would be felt if Saddam and his goons continued to rule. Maybe this was easy for me to say, sitting, as I was, safely in Toronto. But I knew that even if I were in Baghdad, I would have been cheering the F-15s from my rooftop.

Like so many others, I realized too late what a total catastrophe the bombing in Baghdad and other badly hit cities and towns was for civilians. I learned in horror of the hunger and privation, then the spread of disease. I had been fool enough to think only the Mukhabarat headquarters and like targets would be hit.

With all communications cut off, I had no idea how my family was.

Someone who had made it out to Austria got word to me that Bibi had died not in the bombing but of illness, a while before. But I don't know for certain if the report is true.

As the war continued, I felt I was on an emotional roller coaster. I reached the depths of despair when bombs hit a civilian shelter and killed hundreds of women and children. I knew the neighborhood, and I was certain this was not a military target. I cursed the intelligence mistake that caused the horror. Then my spirits soared when I heard how many military plants had been hit and how much of Saddam's war machine had been destroyed. Like others, I waited for the ground war.

When the coalition forces rejected a so-called Soviet-Iraqi peace plan and George Bush and his allies sent their armies rolling into Kuwait and Iraq in a massive ground offensive, I knew it was a turning point not only in the war but in America's stand in the Middle East. I felt that for the first time, Washington realized what and with whom it was dealing. The people in the White House and the Pentagon seemed to know as well as we Iraqis that the peace plan was a fraud, just another attempt by Saddam to manipulate the West. Unlike his predecessor, Bush was not drawn into phony talks and deals. Protesters in all parts of the world sent up an angry howl, attacking Bush as a warmonger. But he dealt with Saddam in the only possible way.

In the end the ground war lasted only one hundred hours.

If the Iraqi army had stood and fought, it might have lasted a bit longer. I know that if I had been in uniform, I would have been the first to run toward the advancing enemy soldiers to greet them as long-awaited saviors. And that is precisely what more than 60,000 Iraqi men did. Starved by their own commanders, forced to stay at the front with a gun at their backs, they fell, weeping, at the feet of the allies, half of them not wanting to return to Saddam's Iraq. I know if I'd been one of those soldiers, I would have been terrified, bitter and angry at having to die because of Saddam. I wonder how many died with a curse on their lips—either for Saddam or for America.

That is the nub of the question. Who has won the hearts and minds of the most people?

The rich gulf states and their inhabitants are jubilant at the victory. They praise America to the skies.

The poorer Jordanians, and the mass of Palestinians who live there and in the occupied territories, are bitterly angry at the United States.

U.S. 1st Cavalry Division troops move out into the Saudi Arabian desert,
November 4, 1990. Operations Desert Shield and Desert Storm, the most
massive ground assault since the Normandy invasion, would make short work
of an Iraqi military demoralized by shortages of food, clothing,
weapons, ammunition and leadership.

Many parents in the Middle East are teaching their children that
Saddam is a hero, who stood up to the giant invader. The fact that
Saddam was safe and sound in his bunker and left ordinary soldiers
(mostly conscripts), mothers and children open to the onslaught
won't phase the mythmakers.

Radio Baghdad continued its lurid vilification of the satanic infidel
invader and hailed the lofty and noble courage of the brave Muslim
fighters who repelled the forces of evil in the mighty battle for the
glory of Allah . . . and declared victory.

Above: waving the flag of her liberated homeland, a young Kuwaiti welcomes U.S. Marines, February 27, 1991.

Left: downtown Baghdad in the wake of one of 116,000 allied air sorties flown over Iraq in the forty-day Gulf war

This sort of rhetoric, which in translation sounds utterly asinine, is resonant, powerful and, above all, believable in Arabic. There will be many who know better and have heard from returning soldiers or from the BBC World Service that the war was anything but a victory for Iraq. But just as many will believe it *was* a victory, and be inspired by it.

In spite of all the horror Saddam has wrought on his nation, it is hard for me to picture him departing from his throne. After his military defeat he lost no time in settling the terms of the cease-fire.

This left him free to crush any incipient opposition at home. Saddam hung on to power after causing the deaths of hundreds of thousands of his people in his ludicrous war with Iran. In the Gulf war he lost his hideous arsenal of weapons and most of his army. But these losses would not affect his opinion of himself in the least. He would fight like a tyrannosaur to keep his kingdom.

Perhaps we can hope that the cynical power brokers and arms dealers will rein themselves in and make a genuine effort to prevent the creation of yet another monster. I am encouraged that there is talk of the need to tighten up arms exports and to enforce controls worldwide. But the powers that be must ensure that unconventional avenues of import are tightened as well. I am thinking of how the Iraqi regime has used "diplomatic flights" to fly agents into the West and then out again with everything from weapons to high-tech devices, usually used to enhance the death machine.

At the age of twenty-six, I am jaded enough to believe that the arms merchants and politicians like things the way they are. They build the tyrants, then fuel the wars that have to be fought against them. I will be very surprised if we do not see another war.

And what of Iraq itself? With or without Saddam?

Western news correspondents and analysts speak of possible replacements for Saddam as though they are desirable alternatives: names like Taha Yassin Ramadhan, Saddoun Hamadi and Hussein Kamel are bandied about. These men are not moderates; they are Saddam's henchmen.

A bit of background on these potential successors might be useful. Taha Yassin Ramadhan is a former army sergeant who suddenly became the number three man in the country. His job was to guide the economic development of Iraq. That is, he was comptroller of the antisystem.

Saddoun Hamadi, a Shi'ite, rose from nowhere to ministerial positions, including the Foreign Ministry. Hamadi has been referred to by some Middle Eastern experts on American television networks as a moderate. This term has long since fled the language insofar as Iraq's power elite is concerned. Hamadi is a vicious man, who simply knows how to survive in Saddam's circle of fear.

Hussein Kamel, Saddam's cousin and son-in-law, is equally savage. His chief claim to fame is that he is the husband of Saddam's eldest daughter. The fact that he never finished high school was greatly in his favor as far as Saddam was concerned.

The slippery Tariq Aziz, Foreign Minister, has also been mentioned. He is educated, but like the others, has no popular following. He is a yes-man, who needs a leader to say yes to. And underneath his stylish suits he's just another ruthless Ba'thist.

The ascension of any of these men to Saddam's place will mean a coup every two weeks in Iraq. None of them has a constituency, a power base or the ability to lead. They are followers.

Most of the Iraqi officials who surround Saddam have a poor education. Saddam excuses their lack of schooling by saying, "These men are educated through their struggle to reach the power and heart of the masses." This is typical Ba'thist blather.

Another, sometimes mentioned alternative is the Liberal Democratic Front, headquartered in London and now moved to Saudi Arabia. It has even less of a power base. The Iraqi people have suffered too much while the members of the Liberal Democratic Front have played paper politicians in the West. As I said earlier, even the Mukhabarat was not interested in terminating any of them, regarding them as irrelevant. The Americans and their allies may very well wish to see the Liberal Democratic Front take over, but it would be an almost impossible task. How could they return to Iraq while the police state still functions? How could elections be held in such a rotten system? How could they run a country that is economically bankrupt and morally exhausted?

Another possibility is that Saddam or his henchmen will survive in Baghdad but lose much of the rest of the country. This is a dreadful and most complicated scenario. It *is* possible that the country might endure a civil war and chaos much as Lebanon has endured for more than fifteen years. Because of its ethnic/religious structure, Iraq could revert to its precolonial sections reflecting regional power structures. The British combined the three ethnic/religious divisions to create modern Iraq. Those divisions were Basra, Mosul and Baghdad. Such a scenario could result in the Da'wah's running Basra and southern Iraq; the Kurds' running northern Iraq and Mosul; and Saddam and his Ba'thists would control central Iraq from Baghdad. The splitting of the country would be a disaster insofar as the balance of power in the Middle East is concerned. Southern Iraq—from Najaf to Basra—would become the ally of a now greatly enhanced Iran. Northern Iraq—Mosul—might lean toward Turkey, while Baghdad, where almost a third of all Iraqis live, would be reduced to utter poverty, denied the country's natural resources.

Ironically, this worst-case scenario is a close cousin of what I believe would be the best: a federation of three or more such states. The United States of Iraq. It would be unwieldy and fractious until somehow each learned to live with the other's rights and simply agreed to differ. That, after all, is the core of democracy.

Unfortunately, the group that is best positioned to take over Iraq is the Da'wah. I came to know them in England and found them to be self-righteous zealots who would kill still more Iraqis in the name of Allah and their bitter dogma. The Da'wah did not have much success garnering support under Saddam, partly because he so efficiently eviscerated their organization and partly because Iraqis were less than enthusiastic about anybody resembling Khomeini.

Ironically, the strongest base and network for the Da'wah are the Iraqi POWs who returned from Iran in 1988 full of fervor for the Islamic revolution of their captors. I remembered Noman and the Da'wah gang in Manchester rationalizing Khomeini's barbarities, fired with righteousness. To them democracy means rights and freedom— for everybody who agrees with them. The Da'wah would turn Iraq into another Cambodia. My poor people.

An important factor will be whether or not Washington makes the mistake of deciding to live with the Da'wah. George Bush appears to have learned at last what Saddam is. But it would be too much to hope that American leaders had suddenly, overnight, learned the lessons of all their mistakes in the Middle East. Again I remembered how Noman and other spokesmen for the Da'wah learned to present themselves to the West as harmless democrats. I fear the White House will think that they can do business with the Da'wah.

I know the Da'wah will do business with Washington and then turn and calmly shoot the West in the back. They would do this all over the world if possible. The essence of the Islamic fundamentalist movement is not religion, but rather power through hatred. Hatred of the West in general, America in particular and, beyond all else, Israel.

No peace talks, no settlement for the Palestinians, will change this irrational, visceral enmity felt in the Middle East. Terrorist Abu al-

Abbas and his cohorts will continue to fan those flames whether backed by Saddam, the Da'wah or another, as yet unknown, force emerging from the ashes of Iraq.

The military defeat of Iraq has been followed by some optimistic talk of new hopes for comprehensive peace settlements. But I am not so optimistic. I see only new variations on old, old maneuvers. Canadian Foreign Minister Joe Clark said after a meeting with his Iranian counterpart that what was needed was for the people of the Middle East to trust each other more. The naïveté of such a remark is staggering. Trust? To trust, in my world, is to sentence oneself to death. Perhaps these things are truly beyond the grasp of the West. If that is so, then perhaps the lesson to be learned from my story, from our history, is that the West would be better advised to find another energy source and go home.

There is one other primal element in this mosaic. And it was illustrated graphically by a young Kuwaiti nurse. When the coalition forces arrived in triumph in Kuwait City, they found a people delirious with joy to be delivered from seven months of hell. Somehow the Kuwaitis had managed to make it through, with the help of a small resistance force keeping everyone supplied with food and water. They demonstrated the remarkable human capacity for ingenuity and courage under duress. The Kuwaiti nurse, her face half-covered by a veil, told proudly how she had done her part by administering lethal injections to a dozen wounded Iraqi soldiers.

The calm, cool way she told of her act should reveal to Westerners just what they are dealing with in my part of the world—a deep capacity for murderous hatred.

It is a pathology of our culture. It is not just people like my unbalanced father or megalomaniacs, like Saddam. It is, I believe, bred in the bone. If fear is the engine of Saddam's society, hate is the fuel, and it is a deeper resource even than our oil.

I said earlier that when we Iraqis decide we love someone, we do so with enormous passion. And the same is true of the negative emotions. You rarely hear us say we dislike someone. More often we hate them. There is a large room for hate in each of us. All a leader has to do is fill it.

We are stuck in the emotional ruts of history and cannot escape. I believe these ancient hatreds are almost incomprehensible to North

Americans in particular. The United States and Canada are young nations, without centuries of historical baggage, though the conquest of the native peoples may return to haunt them. In a way, people in these two Western countries have been able to re-create themselves because they have had to make something out of a whole variety of peoples and cultures that came together in this new world. There are problems and passions, and good and evil, but these are not engraved on the souls of North Americans the way my heritage is on mine.

We Iraqis seem condemned to be slaves to these recurring cycles of violence and circles of fear. But I want to believe that we can change this ancient pattern. I want to believe that this war was the beginning of that change.

The rout of Saddam's feared military machine, its exposure as a fraud and a collection of looters are, I hope, the first cracks in the circles of fear. But the Mukhabarat and the rest of the security apparatus are too complex and powerful to simply fall apart. It is not like the Shah of Iran's brutal but incompetent SAVAK, which collapsed when the mullahs gained momentum. Nor is it like Saddam's pathetic million-man army, largely made up of unwilling conscripts who embraced their conquerors.

If anything, my story should show that Iraq's secret services are entrenched. They will remain a force to be reckoned with in some form in any future Iraq. Abu Firas, Radhi the Gorilla, the Eagle, Khaled the blond agent—they will not go gently.

Ba'thism will survive for a time in some form or another. It will survive because such a stain does not come out in one wash. It has not been just a political party, but rather a system of mind control. Children who have been taught to inform on their parents will not embrace the principles of democracy overnight.

My country is a total mess. After so many years of functioning under the antisystem, people's minds and characters have been warped and reshaped until their idea of normal is everyone else's idea of dreadful. It was easy for me to be an agent for the Mossad and then the Mukhabarat because living in Iraq, or anywhere in the Arab Mideast, meant learning from the cradle how to dissemble, cheat, and cut corners. In the culture in which I was raised, it doesn't take a criminal mind to forge passports, work the black market, deal in arms, cheat on exams; it is all just part of the overall character of life.

It is almost impossible to build a democracy out of such raw material. But we must begin somewhere. I don't want to believe we are doomed to tread this horrible path forever. I want to believe that if freed of tyrants, freed of terror, and given knowledge and opportunity, we can all learn that giving life is better than taking it. I like to think we will learn that what we have in common is stronger than our differences. Religions and political systems need to teach us tolerance rather than how to despise and conquer. I want us to return to what is beautiful in Arab culture—the long-lost enlightenment of Haroun al-Rashid's age—but nurtured in modern democracy. I know it sounds hopelessly utopian. But if we give up striving, we are truly doomed.

For my part, I will try to escape my past, with Ban. We will try to find a new identity, a new country, and we will dedicate ourselves to the most irrational affirmation of life there is: having children. More than anything in the world I want a baby with Ban. I want to give life, love a child, cherish it and nurture it so that the beauty I know is possible in the human soul can bloom. I want to give my children fun, knowledge and security. I want to do my part to help make a few more decent human beings on this planet. If my part of the world is to have any hope of peace, we must begin at the cradle. My mother tried, but she was outgunned.

Most of all I want to give love. Then surely love will be returned. That, above all, is what was missing in my own father and in the ideology he has served. I will never fully understand why. But now at least I see that seeking revenge the way I did only keeps the circles and the wheels turning. It is the final irony that the best revenge I can take on my father will be to love my children.

These are strange thoughts from a man who served the Mossad and the Mukhabarat. But love is the only way I know to come in from this terrible cold.

TOO TOUGH TO DIE

Robert Sabbag

. . . The woman did not actually open the door; she simply unlatched it. Oboyski opened it with his foot and a unit of energy equivalent to his 235 pounds multiplied by the speed of light squared. Or something like that. At any rate, his linear momentum carried him over the woman, propelling him directly into the living room of the apartment, where he ended up standing before a coffee table, racking the Remington into the faces of three men seated on the couch.

Oboyski was screaming; O'Flaherty, who came in behind him, was screaming; and everybody behind O'Flaherty was screaming as he or she came through the doorway.

"U.S. marshals. . . ." "Freeze. . . ." "Don't move. . . ." "Put your hands up!"

—Too Tough to Die

Chapter One

ENRY McCarty murdered his first man with a knife. He took the life of a neighbor in New York City in a Saturday-night street fight at the age of sixteen. When he was gunned down by a federal agent at the age of twenty-one, he had shot people to death under four known aliases and put some 2000 miles between his miserable reputation and Manhattan's Lower East Side. When he shotgunned the federal officer who would be his last homicide victim, he had traveled as far as Lincoln County, New Mexico, and the alias he was going by, the name picked up by the local press and moved by wire service to newspapers back home, was Billy the Kid.

Short and slight, with brown hair, blue eyes, almost comical buckteeth, and the overall visual attributes of the stereotypical village idiot, Billy the Kid in the years of his juvenile delinquency was virtually ignored on the Rio Pecos. He was just one more borderline sociopath in a territory where they blossomed like weeds. Virtually unknown outside New Mexico and parts of the Texas Panhandle, he attained notoriety about the time he attained what may quaintly be referred to as his majority. By then, as one of a squalid and rather indolent band of cattle, horse, and mule thieves, he had begun to invite the attention of some of the nation's wealthier ranchers.

Billy the Kid's was to be a uniquely American destiny. More than one cold-blooded murder having accrued to his credit, it would be his depredations against private property, finally, that earned him the kind of attention that doomed him.

In the fall of 1880 he was being pursued with varying degrees of enthusiasm by lawmen of diverse jurisdictions—among others, by cattle detectives in the private employ of the Canadian River Cattlemen's Association and the Panhandle Stock Association of Texas; by territorial authorities in New Mexico's Lincoln and San Miguel counties; and quite probably, though not actively, by the New York City Police Department.

The man who brought him to justice was the only peace officer among them whose authority was recognized across jurisdictional lines. Pat F. Garrett, the newly elected sheriff of Lincoln County, was the man carrying the federal paper on Billy; he was a deputy U.S. marshal.

Garrett entered the field against the rustlers in November, and from that moment on, in more ways than one, Billy the Kid was history.

> There was snow on the ground, it was desperately cold, and Brazil's beard was full of icicles. "Get your guns, boys," said I. "None but the men we want are riding this time of night." We were after the gang, and would sleep on their trail until we took them in, dead or alive.

Garrett, thirty, a cowhand for six years, a buffalo hunter for two, author of the foregoing in April 1882, cut an imposing figure on several fronts; a good rider and roper and an excellent shot, he was over six feet four inches tall. Alabama born, reared in Louisiana, he appeared in the valley of the Rio Pecos at the close of what had become known as the Lincoln County War, the violent economic and political power struggle there in which Billy the Kid, one of numerous cowhands whose guns were for hire, had been an enthusiastic participant. Campaigning on a reform ticket, backed by cattleman John Chisum and by future governor George Curry, Garrett was elected sheriff in November 1880. Perceived as something of a flashy dresser, with a mustache of the long, drooping variety, he was nevertheless a manifestly practical man.

Late in December at Stinking Springs, San Miguel County, his thirteen-man posse secretly surrounded the abandoned stone house in which Billy and four gang members had taken refuge for the night. Garrett, that he might impress upon the outlaws the merits of peaceful surrender, instructed his deputies to kill the first man out the door.

"Our victim was Charlie Bowdre," writes Garrett.

Bowdre went down at dawn, with a feed bag in his hand and seven rifle rounds in his chest. Garrett, almost leisurely then, put a single round—Winchester .44- 40—into one of the mounts that the fugitive had emerged from the building to feed.

"Just as the horse was fairly in the opening, I shot him and he fell dead, partially barricading the outlet."

It is here—with a dead horse in the doorway, a slaughtered man in the snow, and no exit from the cramped quarters but that which led into the gunsights of the posse—that Garrett's narrative achieves the zenith of the ruthlessly matter-of-fact.

"I now," he writes, "opened a conversation with the besieged."

BILLY the Kid was arrested by Garrett on a U.S. warrant for the April 4, 1878, murder on the Mescalero Apache Indian Reservation of Andrew "Buckshot" Roberts. It was a crime Billy the Kid did not commit. His March 1881 trial at Mesilla, New Mexico, was moved, on a technicality, to the territorial side of the district court, where he was acquitted. In the same session he was tried for a homicide he did commit—and for which Garrett, as sheriff, carried a second arrest warrant—the April 1, 1878, ambush of then Lincoln County sheriff William Brady. He was sentenced by District Judge Warren Bristol to be hanged May 13.

Billy the Kid arrived at what was serving as the county lockup in Lincoln with a reputation as an ungracious guest. Judged a serious escape risk, he was outfitted by Garrett in special-order handcuffs— they weighed fifteen pounds—ankle irons, and chains. He was guarded during the entirety of his stay by two experienced lawmen, Deputy Sheriff J. W. Bell, a former Texas Ranger, and Robert Olinger, a bloodthirsty 240-pound redhead who held the commission of a deputy U.S. marshal.

Billy the Kid, as a guest of Lincoln County, did not stick around a week. He left town on horseback, carrying several weapons, among them the handcuffs he wore. The lad—depicted nearly unanimously by his biographers as good humored, with an engaging and guileless grin—left behind the bodies of Garrett's two deputies. Bell, who by all accounts had been especially kind to him, he let bleed to death from the wound of a single large-caliber revolver round. He took Olinger out with a shotgun.

Olinger had been absent when the prisoner, as he was being escorted up an interior stairway, turned on Bell with the cuffs. Where the Kid secured the weapon with which he then shot the deputy is open to debate, but Bell certainly was carrying one, and Garrett's office was replete with them. It was there that he found the side-by-side that he used on Olinger—a 10-gauge Whitney. With Bell down, he waited, taking a position overlooking the street in a second-floor room of the county house. When Olinger returned, he casually stepped to the window and, taking aim from above, opened him up with both barrels.

What Billy did not do is disappear.

"For about two and a half months," Pat Garrett reports, "the Kid led a fugitive life, hovering, spite of danger, around the scenes of his past two years of lawless adventure."

Billy the Kid's possession of limited horizons, his latent instinct for self-destruction, his lack of imagination, and finally (though he was not uneducated) his baseline stupidity are attributes undisguised in the common criminal today.

Among characteristics shared by Garrett and the modern deputy marshal is a talent for ruthlessly exploiting those deficiencies—a brutal aptitude for capitalizing on the predictability of human behavior.

Fatal to the typical fugitive and indispensable to the fugitive hunter is that seductive yet hallucinatory sense of well-being that springs from maintaining a proximity to home. The consensus, not only among historians but among his adversaries themselves, is that Billy the Kid, had he exhibited the foresight or merely the good manners simply to leave the territory, probably never would have been arrested in the first place.

"He had," Garrett concedes, "many friends who were true to him, harbored him, kept him supplied with territorial newspapers, and with valuable information concerning his safety."

Garrett knew more about the fugitive's whereabouts than he admitted at the time or, for that matter, ever was to admit.

"I was constantly, but quietly, at work," is all he would say, "seeking sure information and maturing my plans of action."

What Garrett was doing, the formality of his statement notwithstanding, was getting ready flat out to smoke the son of a bitch. Garrett, in exploiting the manifold deficiencies of a delusional Billy the Kid, did it in classic fashion, and he did it the way federal agents routinely do it today. He used informants.

PAT Garrett, coming off the south plains of Texas, first rode into New Mexico's Pecos valley in 1878. He first made the acquaintance of Billy the Kid in the barrooms around Fort Sumner. (That the two were friends is a literary conceit embraced understandably by modern screenwriters, but unsupported by the facts.) On January 14, 1880, a year before he arrested the Kid, Garrett married the town's Apolinaria Gutierrez. Not only did Garrett have many loyal friends in the area, he had family there as well.

Billy the Kid had been a fixture in Fort Sumner long before his arrest. Having bunked around for about a year, staging cattle raids along the Canadian River from there, he had been captured at Stinking Springs, only thirteen miles northeast. When he continued to haunt the vicinity after his escape, he was underestimating Pat Garrett's determination to a degree that could be expressed in logarithms.

Setting out from Roswell, New Mexico, under cover of darkness, Garrett, with two men—Thomas K. McKinney, one of his territorial deputies, and John W. Poe, a cattle agent employed by the stockmen of the Canadian—started up the Rio Pecos on the night of July 10, 1881. Crossing Salt Creek, the horsemen hit range grass as high as three feet. North of Bosque Grande, where the river widened, the country grew rough, the vegetation increasingly sparse. Picketing their horses by day and sleeping on the trail in their saddle blankets, they covered a total of eighty-one miles.

"We rode mostly in the night, followed no roads," Garrett reports, "and arrived at the mouth of Tayban Arroyo, five miles south of Fort Sumner, one hour after dark on the night of July 13th."

Among Garrett's informants was a rancher named Manuel Brazil, who had been active in the initial arrest. He was to have rendezvoused with Garrett below Fort Sumner, where Taiban Creek emptied into the Pecos River, but failed to appear that night, presumably out of fear of reprisal.

Brazil is the only informant Garrett gives up in print. How many

Garrett utilized is unknown to this day, but almost certainly in complicity were three other Fort Sumner residents: Barney Mason, a local cowboy and a member of the original posse; Sabal Gutierrez, a relative of Garrett's by marriage; and Mason's employer, Pete Maxwell, a local rancher and businessman. Maxwell, the largest individual employer in the area, was owner of many of the cattle and sheep camps at which the outlaw was known to be staying.

On the morning of the fourteenth, Garrett dispatched Poe, who was unknown in town, to make discreet inquiries in and around Fort Sumner. He and McKinney lay low. The three met at moonrise four miles north, at La Punta de la Glorietta. From there they set out for Pete Maxwell's property, arriving shortly before midnight. (The remains of Fort Sumner, including several square miles of land and a collection of buildings built by the U.S. government, had been abandoned by the army. The property had been purchased by Pete Maxwell's family.)

According to Garrett, "We unsaddled . . . and, on foot, entered an orchard, which runs down to a row of old buildings, some of them occupied by Mexicans, not more than sixty yards from Pete Maxwell's house. We approached these houses cautiously, and when within earshot, heard the sound of voices conversing in Spanish. We concealed ourselves quickly and listened. Soon a man arose from the ground."

Later, Garrett says, he would learn that the man, who went unrecognized by him at the time, was Billy the Kid. The man was in shirt sleeves, wearing a broad-brimmed hat, a dark vest, and pants. Garrett says he watched the man get to his feet, go to a fence, jump it, and walk south across the old Fort Sumner parade ground, in the direction of a long row of occupied adobe rooms that had once served as the quartermaster's storehouse.

Garrett circled west, behind a row of what formerly had been officers quarters. One of the larger houses in the line, a long adobe with porches on three sides and separated from the parade ground by a picket fence, was occupied by the Maxwell family.

Garrett left Poe and McKinney sitting on the south porch and entered the rancher's bedroom.

WHEN Billy the Kid returned that night to the room he was sharing with Celsa Gutierrez, Sabal's wife, he removed his gun belt, his boots, and his hat. He lay on the bed, picked up a newspaper, and asked for something to eat. Celsa Gutierrez, offering to prepare the young outlaw some beef if he were willing to fetch it, directed him to a yearling, freshly slaughtered, that hung from a rafter on the north porch of Pete Maxwell's house. Bootless, hatless, leaving behind his double-action Colt, he departed the room carrying a butcher knife.

He died hungry.

Approaching Maxwell's, walking parallel to the fence, he was startled by the presence of Poe and McKinney loitering there in the shadows. Neither knew who he was. Nor could he identify them. Assuming they were Mexicans, as were most of the two hundred to three hundred residents of Fort Sumner, he spoke to the two deputies in Spanish, a language in which Billy the Kid was fluent.

"*Quién es?*" he asked. "*Quién es?*"

Backing through Maxwell's bedroom doorway—away from the strangers, into the dark—he said, "Pete, who are those men outside?"

Garrett's second shot struck a metal washbasin. He put his first into Billy the Kid's heart.

Chapter Two

THE invention of linoleum, credited to an Englishman named Walton, postdates Billy the Kid's nativity by approximately a year. For well over a century the tool designed to shape it has been in reliable service in the city of his birth. The everyday linoleum knife, available at sundry outlets in the city of New York, recommends itself for that purpose to which edged implements today are most commonly turned in the Kid's hometown: armed assault.

Arcing down at the tip like the curling end of a broad mustache, the short, butt-handled tool is a masterpiece of mechanical advantage, its cutting edge on the concave side making it perfect for trimming linoleum and, alternately, for eviscerating the average pedestrian.

It was at this particular intersection of technology and crime, an intersection he would cross in January 1988 in the New York borough of Queens, that a man by the name of Klein, an architect by profession, encountered the phenomenon that is Garnett Leacock.

Leacock, in the course of stealing Mr. Klein's two-door Toyota, had succeeded in securing the ignition key, readily surrendered by its helpless owner, when he decided—why not, for the hell of it?—that he was going to cut off Mr. Klein's testicles. Klein, sixty-four, had already been disabled, his jacket having been pulled down over his shoulders, and he was pleading for his life when Leacock gave him the news.

When Mr. Klein, minus the blood he had lost, was admitted to the hospital that night, the crotch of his trousers had been cut away; his manhood was intact, but his thigh and groin muscles had been badly sliced, and it took five surgeons four and a half hours to stitch together his face.

Leacock disappeared with the car.

AN INDISCRIMINATE predator with a special taste for women—his appetite for rape was gluttonous—Garnett Leacock scoured New York, betraying no discernible rhythm, no semblance of reason, no rhyme. When his path crossed that of a Brooklyn woman by the name of Geraldine Doody, it was as close as Leacock would ever come in his pathological life to poetry.

"At first I thought he was just your usual guy with a long record who'd escaped from jail and could be considered armed and dangerous; but, you know, we get that all the time," she said.

The people who get that all the time, along with Gerri Doody, are the deputy U.S. marshals in the Eastern District of New York.

Gerri Doody caught the Leacock warrant in August 1987. After circulating Leacock's picture to precinct houses in the city, she found victim after victim I.D.ing him to local police. With that kind of intelligence coming in, Leacock, a federal escapee, made the United States Marshals Service's 15 Most Wanted list early the following March. By then his reign of terror had sparked the attention of every deputy in the district, but as case officer, Gerri Doody—the ultimate instrument, as she perceived it, of poetic justice—had come to look at him the way Rome looked upon Carthage.

Garnett Leacock, a native of Trinidad, in the West Indies, a resident of Queens, New York, went to jail for the first time, charged with twenty-eight felonies, in 1967. He was eighteen years old. He had been out approximately a year when he was first rearrested, admitting in 1970 to 110 armed street robberies. His seven months as a federal fugitive, in 1987 and 1988, was, after that, the longest Leacock ever managed to stay out of prison. By then he was pushing forty. The rape that put him in Attica prison in 1973 was that of a Great Neck, Long Island, woman whose family he and two accomplices—one a convicted murderer—had terrorized for hours in one of a series of house-to-house break-ins that night. In the course of the protracted assault they pistol-whipped her husband and threatened her child with death.

Sentenced to twenty-five years, Leacock served thirteen in various upstate prisons, marrying an outreach worker in a local college program during the period of his incarceration. He was paroled in August 1986. His wife, Deborah, thirteen years his junior, who had gone on to become an air force sergeant, was stationed in Rome, New York, living in government quarters. Upon his release, Leacock moved in with her and the young son she and Leacock had conceived during a conjugal prison visit. Ninety days later Leacock was arrested for the rape there of a sixteen-year-old girl.

Because it occurred on an air force base, the rape was a federal crime. Convicted in U.S. district court, Leacock was awaiting sentencing, housed in the Madison County jail, when, with the help of his wife, he escaped. Because she cooperated in his recapture seventeen hours later, no charges were filed against her. Three weeks after that, also with her assistance, Leacock escaped again.

Leacock was sentenced, in absentia, to twenty-seven years in federal prison; his wife, who copped to one of seven felonies in abetting his escape, was sentenced to five years, federal time, in a Kentucky penitentiary. Leacock went to ground in New York.

GERRI Doody, born and raised on Baltic Street in what was then called downtown Brooklyn and is now called Cobble Hill, had come to work for the U.S. marshal for New York's Eastern District in 1971. Probably for the very reason that so many of her friends were police officers—Brooklyn breeds cops the way Beverly Hills breeds blonds—she harbored, at the age of twenty-four, no desire to enter law enforcement. She came to work on the civil desk, employed by the feds as a clerk. Because there were no female deputies in the district at the time, she was called upon now and then—in those circumstances where a woman's presence was essential to the assignment—to accompany deputies working arrest warrants. Also, side by side with sworn personnel, she regularly traveled the country escorting female prisoners. Partaking of the work of the typical federal officer, Gerri Doody discovered that she enjoyed it. With only two years of college, and facing the requirement of a bachelor's degree or sufficient qualifying experience, she would log a total of 2080 field hours before she became eligible for a position. In May 1980, with nine years on the civil desk and after thirteen weeks at the Federal Law Enforcement Training Center, at Glynco, Georgia—where she learned to drive fast, shoot straight, and fight—she was sworn and deputized.

"I was the old broad at Glynco. The kids—I call them kids—were in their early twenties. I was thirty-three."

For the next seven years, as one of some forty criminal investigators answering to Chief Deputy Mike Pizzi, she shouldered the manifold duties of routine district operations in Brooklyn.

Stalwart, ever cheerful, the hazel-eyed blonde was admired not only for her excellent investigative skills but for her altruism and her ability to put others at ease. She was permanently assigned to warrants in the spring of 1987.

In August, Leacock busted out.

THE U.S. Courthouse for New York's Eastern District is located on Cadman Plaza East, in the shadow of the stately Brooklyn Bridge. The office of the U.S. marshal occupies room 172, just beyond and to the left of that international sign of the times, the armed-security setup. On the afternoon of March 8, 1988, Gerri Doody walked to the nurses' station in the building's first-floor lobby to inquire about medication recently prescribed for her father, who was hospitalized with cancer.

The investigation had hit a low. It had been almost seven months now, and the informants were not coming through. They were not putting "heart and soul" into it, in the words of Warrants Supervisor Dave O'Flaherty.

In fact, the Leacock informants posed a special problem. When Leacock fled, he sought familiar territory, as fugitives can be trusted to do—in his case Queens, New York. Leacock subsequently made contact with people he had known since his youth, people who had not seen him in well over thirteen years—the period of his incarceration—and who knew nothing of his case upstate. The majority were law-abiding, hardworking citizens, not the usual street scum to whom criminals like Leacock could be expected to gravitate. They were not susceptible to the wide variety of emoluments and intimidation that one could bring, for example, to the questioning of the typical ex-convict. The effort to win their confidence was a long and tedious one.

There were several informants upon whom the deputies had been putting pressure, knowing that Leacock, of no fixed address, could not survive on the street by himself. Through extensive interviews and the use of telephone traps, they had isolated Leacock's movements to the vicinity of the Albany housing projects, in the Bedford-Stuyvesant section of Brooklyn.

Conducting interviews in the Albany projects, according to Warrants Inspector Victor Oboyski, was not without its share of excitement. "There was shooting and crack dealing going on all the time. A couple of times there were shootings going on while we were there. Right inside the building."

To help snare Garnett Leacock, New York Telephone, which in the typical case might trap a twenty-block area, trapped the entire borough of Brooklyn. A deputy, taking an informant's call, would notify New York Telephone, mobilize a team, and wait for the company to report back with the appropriate location. Given the number of the cooperating party's telephone and the time a call from Leacock had been received, the telephone company, searching its computer, could within five to thirty minutes trace the phone from which the call had been made. Inevitably, however, Leacock's calls were coming from public telephones.

And as Dave O'Flaherty knew, "You can't have ten people respond to a pay phone on Nostrand Avenue."

Instead, with few exceptions, every deputy in the district put in his share of cold nights on surveillance, waiting for Leacock to go into or come out of the projects.

HAVING escaped twice in three weeks from jails upstate, Leacock had brought with him to New York City a certain measure of notoriety. Continually identified in a series of vicious assaults in Queens—a lot of local cases would be closed once Leacock was in custody—he had hit the Most Wanted list for a reason. Deputies in the district all wanted a piece of his arrest, and they were volunteering to work overtime on night surveillance.

"I never took my gun off during the Leacock investigation," Gerri Doody says. "You have to be ready to go out the door. I have my vest, I have my side. You get the call, you just grab everything and run."

But that day in March as she stood there in the nurse's office, ready or not, Gerri Doody admits she had just about had enough.

"The hours, the concentration, you know, you become obsessed with that one person. We'd work early morning. We'd go on surveillance at night, places we thought he might return to, and each day we'd come back without him. We knew he was there in the area and we had all these different leads, but every time we got somewhere, he was somewhere else. We'd sit out till eleven at night, surveilling in different vehicles, just sitting in the car, staring, looking and praying and hoping. I'd gotten calls, I'd be home in bed. We'd get false alarms. I don't know if it'll ever happen again, but I just couldn't think of a thing except him."

She was also paying necessary attention to her other warrants—and to those of her fellow deputies (they made their arrests as a group)—and thus going out, with regularity, on routine six a.m. hits.

She was working days, nights, and weekends. What personal time she was able to steal she was determined to devote to her father; she was unfailing in her visits to the hospital, as she would continue to be until eventually he died there of cancer.

It was hard to see how things could get worse.

WHEN Gerri Doody finally heard that Garnett Leacock had been arrested, she heard it from a police officer in Queens. She had been circulating copies of Leacock's photo when the officer gave her the news. "Yeah, we locked that guy up," he said.

Garnett Leacock, after losing a very brief car chase to them, had gone on to lose a follow-up fistfight to two New York City cops. No sooner had he staggered the first cop with a sucker punch to the nose than the second kicked Leacock so hard in the chest that he knocked the fugitive out cold. After taking him to the hospital, the cops took Leacock to jail and booked him under the alias Jerome Jackson: black male, five seven, with brown eyes, black hair, and a one-inch scar on his right cheek. They charged him with assault, resisting arrest, and possession of stolen property; locked him up; and misclassified his fingerprints.

Her fugitive, the officer told Gerri Doody, had been in police custody for three days. Three weeks ago.

"He was allowed to post bond. We released him."

BECAUSE she was talking to the nurse at the time, Gerri Doody, that March afternoon, did not take the call that came in from the informant she had spent so many months rigorously cultivating. All she remembers is walking back to the squad room and Dave O'Flaherty's bearing down on her. "Grab your gear," the supervisor shouted.

Oboyski sped past with a shotgun. Everyone was racing for the door.

Some later claimed that as O'Flaherty hung up the telephone that day he actually yelled the words "saddle up." Whatever he first said was unimportant, they agreed, because the next thing he said was, "Leacock." In the projects. Right then. In a sixth-floor apartment. O'Flaherty had the number.

Six deputies on the move—all visibly armed, clutching bulletproof vests and raid jackets, one of them carrying a 12-gauge riot gun out onto the streets of Brooklyn—engineered a familiar broken-field run under the eyes of several court-security officers and through the pedestrian traffic in the lobby of the Federal Building.

A three-mile drive to the Albany projects—it was lights and sirens until the entry teams were two blocks away. In front of the projects, hanging out when the three two-man teams pulled up, were maybe a dozen teenagers. All of them scattered instantly when Oboyski hit the grass. On the run, with the shotgun out, the 235-pound Oboyski entered the building by running straight across the lawn and vaulting a four-foot fence. O'Flaherty's instructions, transmitted over the radio as the deputies approached the projects, were to seal the staircases immediately.

"Keep him from the lobby."

With no fire escapes, and with the apartment six floors up, it was Leacock's only way out.

If, in fact, Leacock was still in there.

Gerri Doody and Deputy Marvin Mack, moving fast, took one stairway; Deputies Tony Crook and Billy Thrower, the other. O'Flaherty and Oboyski (the senior men) took the elevator.

"Me being the supervisor," O'Flaherty explains, "I take the elevator. [And] I want my guy who goes in the door first with the shot-gun to be fresh. First guy going in the door, I want him to be ready." On the elevator, O'Flaherty acknowledges, "My weapon's out be-cause if the elevator door opens and Leacock's standing there, I want him to meet . . . my friend."

Everyone arrived at the apartment door wired, pumped up, shak-ing under a rush of adrenaline, sweating under the weight of a second-chance vest and the nylon of a raid jacket.

Everyone had his weapon out. Everyone was breathing hard. And everyone was hugging the wall.

Another day at the office.

Dave O'Flaherty gave them plenty of time to calm down. "Relax," he told them. "We're here. He can't go out the window. If he jumps, he deserves to get away."

In a rapidly conducted tactical meeting held there at the threshold of the apartment, the deputies decided against immediately breaking down the door. Instead they would first try to open it, and they would do so with Marvin Mack.

Deputy U.S. Marshal Marvin Mack, fifty-two, was no stranger to the Albany projects. He had grown up in Bedford-Stuyvesant. Today, and too often, unfortunately—because it was so often on business—he found himself back in the neighborhood. If Mack was breathing as heavily as everyone else, it was probably for a different reason. At five eight, weighing 260 pounds, Mack had just run up six flights of stairs, and to him it had felt like twelve. Not that Mack was unaware of the danger he and the others faced.

Garnett Leacock was, according to the informant, in possession of a gun. He was, far more importantly, facing the rest of his life in prison. He was a man with absolutely nothing to lose. It was very possible that there would be some shooting on the other side of the door.

On the landing that day, outside the apartment, everybody was frightened, and everybody had been there before. But not one of them knew the meaning of sheer, flat-out terror the way Marvin Mack had once experienced it.

It was October 1973. He had been two years on the job, dispatched on special assignment to the U.S. district court in Baltimore. Mack was standing adjacent to the defense table in a hearing room—with the defendant standing before a judge—when his supervisor turned to him and said, "Marvin, if he's remanded, I want you to take him."

It was then, as he confronted the prospect of actually throwing handcuffs on the felon in question, that Marvin Mack experienced the Fear. "I stood there thinking," Mack recalls. "I wondered if my legs would move. I was proud to be where I was—for my family, for my race. I'd come a long way. But I was worried that if the time came, my legs wouldn't move. What a country. I was Marvin Mack, a kid from Bed-Stuy, and I was going to put the Vice President of the United States in jail."

Marvin Mack, DUSM—who had been there the day Spiro Agnew resigned the vice-presidency, pleading nolo contendere to a single charge of income-tax evasion—now back in Bed-Stuy, holstered his Smith & Wesson. He turned his navy-blue raid jacket inside out, obscuring the embroidered patch and the large yellow lettering that identified him as a deputy marshal, and zipped it up to conceal his body armor (100% KEVLAR ARAMID—better living through chemistry from the wonderful people at Du Pont). He knocked on the apartment door and announced that he was from the New York City Housing Authority, an agency whose personnel were always conducting inspections.

Standing to the right of the door, his back to the wall, was O'Flaherty. Oboyski stood to the left. In the several minutes they had waited there listening, they had heard inside the apartment both men and women talking. If no one had answered the door, the deputies, with a nod from O'Flaherty, were prepared to take the door out fast—"I guarantee that door would have been down in a matter of a minute . . . the Halligan, the ram, or the sledge"—knocking it broadside into the apartment, carrying the entire doorframe in with it.

The woman who answered Marvin Mack's knock did not open the door to him. She asked whom he wanted to talk to. Mack gave the name of a woman, the apartment's tenant of record.

Oboyski would be the first man through. As soon as the door was off the latch, Oboyski, with the field pump, was going. Having loaded the five-shot in the car coming over, he had refrained from chambering a cartridge.

"When I get inside, I'm gonna slide one in," he said. "I want them to know I'm rackin' a round."

The sound is an inimitable one, and natively unmistakable. A round in the chamber—a noise so ominous it is audible to the deaf.

A second woman opened the door.

Gerri Doody, commenting on the roles played by the various participants in the events that immediately followed, volunteered what many considered to be an understatement of oceanic proportions.

"Dave and Victor, they're not the kinds of personalities to stand around in the background. They're pretty rambunctious, yeah."

Yeah.

Victor Oboyski is six feet three; Dave O'Flaherty, six feet even, and together—unarmed—they weigh 460 pounds. If you have federal paper outstanding against you, the only thing worse than coming up against one of them is coming up against the two of them together. It is like looking over a cliff. Add to that the likelihood that one of them is staring at you over the bead of a cut-down, 12-gauge smoothbore charged with 00 buck, and it gives an entirely new meaning to the concept of misfortune.

Of the junior members of the entry crew that day, the heir apparent to the legacy of the two senior men was the youngster, Tony Crook. While Crook, twenty-seven, will never be as frightening to look at as either of his immediate superiors, he poses as clear and present a danger to American felonry; his enthusiasm for police work is on the order of magnitude of Byron's passion for poetry.

Billy Thrower, thirty-six, had almost four years on the job at the time. A Brooklyn native, as were most of the deputies in the district, Thrower had come over from the Immigration and Naturalization Service, but it is unlikely that anything at INS had prepared him for the kinds of partygoers that he was crashing through doors with these days.

This assorted half dozen—call them the authority behind the warrant—having delivered themselves to the door of an apartment in the Albany housing projects in Brooklyn on the afternoon of March 8, 1988, stood on a sixth-floor landing, waiting with guns in their hands, not altogether impatiently, to serve a piece of paper representing the American taxpayer.

The woman did not actually open the door; she simply unlatched it. Oboyski opened it with his foot and a unit of energy equivalent to some function of his 235 pounds multiplied by the speed of light squared. Or something like that. At any rate, his linear momentum carried him over the woman, propelling him directly into the living room of the apartment, about six feet distant from the door, where he ended up standing before a coffee table, racking the Remington into the faces of three men seated on the couch.

". . . and just very simply told them, in the nicest terms possible, that if they moved, they might upset me."

Actually, Oboyski was screaming; O'Flaherty, who came in behind him and immediately over him, was screaming; and everybody behind O'Flaherty was screaming as he or she came through the doorway, *"Police. . . ." "U.S. marshals. . . ." "Freeze. . . ." "Don't move. . . ." "Put your f---ing hands up!"*

Gerri Doody came through behind O'Flaherty, immediately freezing the woman who had unlatched the door. Clutching a child and screaming herself, the woman was one of two standing there when the feds came crashing through—a total of twelve people, then, all of them terrified, at least six of them armed and on an emotional trigger, wreaking pandemonium in the room.

As Vic Oboyski, jacking a cartridge into the chamber, loomed there bellowing, his voice amplified by adrenaline as he shouted instructions—many of which were repetitive, all of which began with what sounded like the word don't and came down to the proposition that as an acceptable form of behavior, not even breathing was encouraged—O'Flaherty jumped over the coffee table with a pistol in his hand and started throwing people onto the floor. Crook and Marvin Mack moved in behind him, and while he and they held their weapons to the heads of the three men there, Oboyski and Billy Thrower moved quickly to the back of the apartment, where they swept the bedrooms. They found a young woman with an infant in one and two unattended infants in another, gathered them all together, told the woman to stay put, and wasted no time returning to the chaos in front.

The woman who had opened the door was by now struggling to leave the apartment, screaming so hysterically, "Don't hurt my child!" that Gerri Doody had holstered her revolver to try to keep her under control and at the same time protect the baby. Other apartments on the floor had started emptying into the hallway; the residents, at the sound of the young woman's screams, were crowding around the doorway, firing questions and screaming themselves.

"You really can't hang out in the projects too long. Once you get your man, you get out. We were no more than five minutes in the apartment."

Dave O'Flaherty, who earlier had said the investigation had been so intense for so many months that he "could pick this guy out without a picture," was not encouraged by what he had on the floor. As, left to right, he studied the suspects who were pinned face down in front of him, he thought, The first two, they're definitely not him. The third man did not make O'Flaherty much happier. The only way this character was going to be Leacock was with some hair on his face and a lot more weight on his bones. It was a cinch that there was paper on the man somewhere—for whatever it was worth—because whoever he was, O'Flaherty concluded, the guy clearly had been living like a real street skell.

Cops have a lexicon unique to their work. The expression skell, probably derived from the word skeleton, is applied by police to criminals of sickly, somewhat scurvy appearance—the drug addicted, the diseased—and is employed frequently by Brooklyn deputies.

When Vic Oboyski returned to the living room, O'Flaherty was taking names. And it was Oboyski, the entry team's public relations director, on behalf of everyone assembled, who congratulated the man under the barrel of O'Flaherty's automatic—the third man from the left—when the latter identified himself as Jerome Jackson. Smiling quite jovially—"Jerome, we been looking for you"—he conversed with him until Gerri Doody took over.

O'Flaherty cuffed his hands, Oboyski his ankles, and together they hoisted him off the floor—less like a dragon slain, more like a road kill—and presented him to his case officer the way one might surrender a trophy. "Gerri," they said, handing him up in as courtly a fashion as possible.

The chivalry may have eluded Leacock; the poetic justice did not.

It was Gerri Doody who explained very clearly to the rapist that he was being arrested by a woman—not another of whose company he was going to enjoy for a while, she wanted him to understand. Gerri Doody, armed and dangerous, spoke for so many of his victims when she looked Leacock in the eye and told him, "Take a good look. It's going to be your last."

They carried him out face down, parallel to the floor.

But Gerri Doody was wrong in the assumption that she was the last woman that Garnett Leacock would get a good look at.

At a federal hearing scheduled to have him classified a dangerous special offender, Leacock, soon after his capture, enjoyed the company of various women in a Syracuse, New York, courtroom, at least one of whom testified against him. He was to do so again when the state of New York held a similar hearing. Judged a predicate felon in the latter proceeding, Leacock received a guarantee from the Empire State that as long as he lived, he would not see a prison from the outside. To say that he will not see the light of day for a while is something of an exaggeration—he currently sees it, according to Assistant U.S. Attorney Craig Benedict, for fifty minutes every twenty-four hours in a four-by-six exercise pen located in the maximum-security facility at Marion, Illinois. When he sees it, he is alone. Under twenty-four-hour lockdown, like everyone at Marion—the federal system's only level 6 penitentiary, it replaced Alcatraz—Leacock spends the remaining twenty-three hours and ten minutes of the day indoors in isolation, in a cell three stories belowground. And after Leacock serves his twenty-seven-year federal stretch, the state of New York will take him into custody and lock him away for the rest of his life.

Chapter Three

"**E**VEN police officers. . . . In my earlier days on the job, I'd go into the precincts and say, 'I'm with the U.S. marshals'; they'd say, 'Where's your horse?' I'd hold up the star, and they'd say, 'What? Are you with Texaco?' "

Gerri Doody is not employed by Texaco, the international petroleum giant whose corporate trademark is the same five-pointed star behind the authority of which Pat Garrett, Virgil Earp, Bill Hickok, and others either advanced or managed to delay the closing of the American West. One of 2700 sworn deputies who, among other things, execute fugitive arrest warrants in the nation's ninety-five federal judicial districts, she works for the President of the United States. Under the supervision of the U.S. Marshals Service, she and her fellow deputies in 1988—the year they captured Garnett Leacock—

hunted down and arrested 14,000 fugitives from justice, more than all other federal law-enforcement agencies combined.

Today's deputies are heirs to a legacy that enjoyed its most dramatic expression on the American frontier, a heritage that came to romantic flower over a century ago, when the deputy U.S. marshal was the law west of Fort Smith. It is a tradition that in the fall of 1880 was anything but new. When Pat Garrett set out from Lincoln County to bring in Billy the Kid, the inheritance he acceded to was just short of a hundred years old.

The U.S. Marshals Service, postdating by fewer than six months the inauguration of George Washington, is the oldest federal law-enforcement agency in the country. Established by the Federal Judiciary Act of September 24, 1789, the offices of U.S. marshal and deputy marshal were instituted by the First Congress as a part of the same legislation that empowered the federal judicial system. Marshals and their deputies, mandated to administer to the newborn nation's federal courts, were assigned to serve all legal process—writs, warrants, summonses, subpoenas—make arrests, handle prisoners, disburse fees and expenses, and in general ensure the orderly conduct of the administration of federal justice. Commissioned to carry out within their districts the orders not only of the courts but of Congress and the President as well (they took the national census every ten years until 1880), they projected federal authority across the far reaches of the young republic, providing local representation of an emerging national will.

Marshals, as they continue to be, were appointed by the President— the original thirteen were appointed by George Washington—subject to confirmation by the Senate. Until 1853 they reported directly to the Secretary of State, after which their supervision came to rest with the office of the Attorney General. Paid on a fee basis until 1896, when Congress established a salary for both marshals and their deputies, they escaped national organization until 1961, when a chief marshal, James P. McShane, was appointed. In 1969 a Washington-based agency—the United States Marshals Service—was superimposed over the districts.

Under its first three directors the Service began rapidly to professionalize recruitment and training. By 1988 its fourth director, Stanley Morris, had engineered legislation that ensured that his successors would be appointed not by the Attorney General—as Morris and his predecessors had been—but by the President himself.

The deputy marshal today is the embodiment of both personal and institutional survival in modern America. His story is the story of the survival of the institution itself, its passage from vitality to morbidity to ultimate almost miraculous recovery.

FOR more than a century after ratification of the Constitution, marshals and their deputies remained the only federal officers with power of arrest; and because they represented that essential barrier between civil and military control of the union it was their destiny thus to become the general practitioners of American law enforcement. Their broad federal mandate put them, at every critical juncture, into the history of the republic.

The story of the "men and women [who] fought and died in support of the ideal of self-government," according to Marshals Service historian Frederick S. Calhoun in his official history of the agency, *The Lawmen: United States Marshals and their Deputies, 1789 to 1989*, is "the story of the clumsy, inefficient, and peculiar method by which we Americans choose to govern ourselves. The history of the U.S. marshals and their deputies is a history of Constitutional implementation, of how the Constitution worked—or failed to work—over the past two centuries."

In the decades between ratification and the War Between the States, that history insistently expressed itself as a struggle to strike some balance between federal and regional interests.

In 1794, five years after the founding of the Service and three years after the republic's first Secretary of the Treasury, Alexander Hamilton, endeared himself to the people of the new nation with an excise tax on domestic spirits, the grain farmers of frontier Pennsylvania honored Hamilton's boss with the first armed insurrection against the U.S. government. U.S. Marshal David Lenox, riding out of federal district court in Philadelphia to serve summonses on seventy-five distillers who refused to pay the tax, took the initial gunfire in what was to become known as the Whiskey Rebellion. Some five months later, setting out from the nation's capital with a 13,000-man militia raised by four states on the orders of the President and marching under the command of Revolutionary War general Light-Horse

Harry Lee, Lenox was one of three civilians required by the Commander in Chief to take the field against the rebels. Lenox was there to make the arrests, establishing by his presence the law-enforcement authority of the constitutional government.

At those points in American history where parochial and federal interests inevitably came to collide, the office of the marshal, as the personification of federal power, was very often the target of most immediate opposition. Upon no circumstance prior to the outbreak of civil war was the collision between those interests to be more dramatic than it was on the issue of slavery.

One of the few early political victories over slavery enjoyed by the North in the years preceding secession was an 1819 measure enacted by Congress equating the importation of slaves from Africa (formally prohibited in 1808) with piracy, a crime that was punishable by hanging. Over the same period, concessions to the South were more numerous and, in at least one instance, more inflammatory. Among the measures passed collectively as the Compromise of 1850 was the infamous Fugitive Slave Act.

Numbered among the casualties in the political war engendered by these two statutes were the marshals mandated to enforce them. Natives, traditionally, of the districts in which they served, marshals inevitably found themselves caught between their sympathies and their duty. Sworn to uphold the 1819 law, southern marshals boarded vessels intercepted offshore by the navy, confiscating the "cargo" and bringing merchant captains to justice, only to confront recalcitrant jurors, reluctant witnesses, and the scorn of their neighbors. Sworn to enforce the Fugitive Slave Act, northern marshals, who were dragged into court periodically by state and local officials in challenge to federal authority, met with vilification, riots, and bloodshed. The death by gunshot in 1854 of Deputy U.S. Marshal James Batchelder, at the hands of an angry mob of Massachusetts abolitionists attempting to liberate the captured fugitive slave Anthony Burns, best illustrates what federal lawmen in the free states confronted in the ten years of accelerating conflict that foreshadowed the capture of Fort Sumter.

With the inevitable collapse of the union, marshals throughout the South resigned their commissions to join the Confederacy.

It was during the Civil War that greenbacks were introduced, and by that time as much as a third of the legal tender in circulation in the United States (until the twentieth century, American money existed in a variety of forms) was counterfeit. The Treasury Department on occasion hired detectives to investigate the traffic—Allan Pinkerton, the original private eye, had gained fame cracking a counterfeiting ring as an undercover cop in Chicago—but such special agents were rare, and until 1865 the suppression of counterfeiting was assigned to the U.S. marshals.

In the twelve years that passed between Robert E. Lee's surrender at Appomattox and Rutherford B. Hayes' election to the American presidency, U.S. marshals, entering the most dangerous period in their history, would take casualties as the vanguard in a losing war to ensure the rights of the nation's newly enfranchised southern Republicans, citizens who were being systematically victimized by their former owners throughout the South. (It was a war that deputies would come back to win, but not until a hundred years later.)

Reconstruction of the South saw the states of the former Confederacy occupied by the Union Army and forced to modify substantially their political and social institutions. Washington's determination to prohibit the South from denying the rights of citizenship to former slaves gave rise to such night-riding social clubs as the Ku Klux Klan and to legislation designed to suppress such organizations.

By 1877 deputy marshals backed by the army had arrested more than 7000 people for violations of the civil rights laws, the most radical of which were the Klan Acts of 1870 and 1871. The marshals paid for their success; attempting to serve process, they faced arrest by state authorities. But that of course was the least of it. Scalawags in the eyes of the South, many of them simply were murdered.

The federal government's power to defend citizens from one another, a power that theretofore had fallen to the respective states, was eventually denied by the Supreme Court, which in 1876 ruled that the more forceful provisions of the Klan Acts were unconstitutional. In his bartering for the presidential election of 1876—in which he had lost the popular vote to Samuel Tilden—Hayes, in exchange for southern electoral votes, promised to pull the federal troops out of the South.

By 1877 Reconstruction was over. But the killing of deputy marshals in the South had just begun. The region's determination to resist the authority of the U.S. government was most violently expressed in its citizens' outright refusal to pay the reinstituted federal excise tax on whiskey.

The moonshine wars, in which more deputies would lose their lives than in any theater of operations outside the boundaries of Indian Territory, were a legacy of the larger conflict in which North and South had so recently engaged. The excise, a tax repealed by Congress in 1809, was revisited upon the nation in 1861. It was legislated to underwrite the Union Army. At an original seventy cents per gallon the tax inspired the Whiskey Ring scandal that typified the corruption in which the administration of Ulysses S. Grant was so thoroughly soaked. With the tax's rise to ninety cents per gallon, the customary bribery of revenue agents gave way to the more profitable practice of clandestine manufacture.

The authority of revenue agents extended no further than to the seizure of illegal stills and whiskey. Power of arrest lay with the U.S. marshals and their deputies, some of whom reported entire counties in rebellion. The murder of a federal officer was not a federal offense, and local authorities, in their opposition to a government from which they had fought to secede, were more readily inclined to prosecute deputies for destruction of private property—the stills in question— than to prosecute the moonshiners who routinely gunned the deputies down.

Not until 1889 did the Supreme Court provide the federal government with the means to protect its officers from the authority of the states. That year Deputy U.S. Marshal David Neagle, assigned to protect the life of Supreme Court Justice Stephen Field, shot and killed in the discharge of that duty a man named David Terry. Charged with murder in California, Neagle, appealing to the ninth circuit court, was ordered released on a writ of habeas corpus. The Supreme Court decision upholding the order did little to discourage state authorities from arresting federal marshals, but it created a clear precedent for releasing them.

IN THE returning Confederate soldier, in the bitterness of his defeat, flashed a spark of lawlessness sufficient to ignite a prairie fire that would burn for a quarter century across the American West. And across the scorched earth of that untamed frontier the deputy marshal would ride into folklore.

Nowhere did the bitterness that fueled the combustion exist in greater abundance than in the ravaged landscape of postwar Missouri. The state had been occupied by Union forces as early as 1862. Resistance was sustained throughout the war by well-trained guerrilla armies riding under such famous commands as those of William Quantrill and Bloody Bill Anderson. Denied amnesty after the war, unlike their brothers in arms across the South, the Kansas and Missouri raiders entered civilian life as outlaws.

Emblematic of the lost Confederate cause, these outlaws and their grievances found support in the hearts of the local population. The brutal experience of the Missouri farmer under Union occupation was amplified in its aftermath by an unsympathetic government's failure to address his desperate struggle for economic recovery. A victim rather than a beneficiary of postwar federal policy, he bore little if any respect for the nation's institutions.

Least of all for its banks.

It was on the tinder of this resentment that the fire of lawlessness would feed. And never would there be more successful keepers of the flame than a pair of young Missouri irregulars named Frank and Jesse James.

The James gang virtually *invented* bank robbery. At that moment on Saint Valentine's Day, 1866, when William Bird, clerk of the Clay County Savings Association, in Liberty, Missouri, was told over the barrel of a gun, "I'd like all the money in the bank," he entered the annals of American criminal history—so unimaginable was it that an American bank be knocked over during business hours.

The take was estimated at $60,000.

Imitated but never equaled by desperadoes for over a century, their like never to be seen again—they *owned* the railroads *and* the stage lines—Frank and Jesse James, by measure of sheer innovation alone, would stand forever unchallenged as the first family of American crime. Not the least of their accomplishments was that they managed to remain at large for more than fifteen years.

On April 3, 1882, Jesse James was murdered—shot in the back of the head by fellow outlaw Bob Ford, who had made a deal to save himself with the governor of Missouri. Frank James thereupon surrendered to Governor Thomas Crittenden. Tried for murder and, with dispatch, acquitted by the people of rural Missouri, Frank would live to the age of seventy-two, dying on the eve of the First World War.

In the shadow of these two men, across the Great Plains rode outlaws such as the Daltons and their cousins, the Younger brothers, who had gained fame riding against the banks as members of the James gang. The three Youngers were taken alive in the great Northfield, Minnesota, raid, in 1876. (A penitent Cole Younger, after serving twenty-five years, would take to the American lecture circuit.) Emmett was the only one of three audacious Dalton brothers to survive the failed 1892 simultaneous raids on two banks in Coffeyville, Kansas. He would serve fifteen years in prison. Others came and went, but it was the death of one outlaw, more than that of any other, by which the end of the era was measured.

Uninvited to take part in the catastrophic Coffeyville raid was a Dalton understudy named Bill Doolin. His death, in Oklahoma Territory, in August 1896, was a significant moment in the triumph of law and order on the American frontier. And it was just as significant a moment in the history of the U.S. marshals.

Between the end of the Civil War and the turn of the century, more deputy marshals were killed in the line of duty than at any other time in their history. A dozen died fighting the Klan. Two dozen died in the moonshine wars. But of all those slain in the 200 years since their office was established, no fewer than a quarter lost their lives on the 74,000 square miles of real property that is occupied almost entirely by present-day Oklahoma: between 1872 and 1896, 103 deputy marshals were killed in what at that time was known as Indian Territory.

"A rendezvous of the vile and wicked from everywhere"—in the words of a Fort Smith, Arkansas, newspaper—Indian Territory, unorganized until the Oklahoma land rush of 1889, was officially established by the Intercourse Act of 1834. Until congressional passage of the act, which was designed to protect Indians from depredation by whites, the territory had existed as a vaguely defined wilderness of undesirable land upon which the Five Civilized Tribes, as they were called, had been resettled by the government after being forced to vacate the East, the region to which they were indigenous.

Indian Territory was the sorrowful product of the nation's Indian removal policy, journey's end on the Cherokee Trail of Tears.

In 1870 the only authorized permanent residents of Indian Territory were 50,000 Native Americans, principally Cherokee, Choctaw, Chickasaw, Creek, and Seminole, whose ancestral lands had been stolen from them by settlers of European descent. But by that time history had begun to repeat itself. In the wake of the Civil War, Indian Territory had become swollen with squatters, the worst of the nation's whites, drawn there by commerce and the utter absence of local law enforcement.

Tribal law, the local law of the land, did not cover the behavior of white men.

Jurisdiction over Indian Territory emanated from the U.S. Court for the Western District of Arkansas, located in the town of Fort Smith, which was situated on the Arkansas River, no more than a hundred yards from the territory's eastern rim. The court had become so corrupt by 1875 that the district judge, his clerk, the U.S. Attorney, the U.S. marshal, and most of his deputies had all been forced to resign. Into the vacuum of authority created by their departure would step, that year, a thirty-six-year-old two-term former U.S. Congressman from St. Joseph, Missouri, to make more than twenty years of judicial history.

Isaac Charles Parker, appointed U.S. district judge for the Western District of Arkansas by Ulysses S. Grant, arrived in Fort Smith on May 2, 1875. Within nine weeks of his arrival he had sentenced six men to hang. Simultaneously. The gallows built upon his orders were designed to execute twelve at a time. Parker—among other things, a great ally of the Native American—in his twenty-one-year tenure would sentence hundreds of criminals to prison, 160 to die. After appeals and commutations, a total of 79 would be executed.

The condemned did not make their way to Isaac Parker's court voluntarily. Keeping the "Hanging Judge" busy, a force of 200 deputy marshals, over a period of twenty years, scoured Indian Territory on horseback, riding out of Fort Smith on the most celebrated manhunt in history. The motives of some deputies were questionable. Some had questionable pasts. All had only one thing in common. Their skills were those of the gunfighter.

Of the deputies who "rode for Parker" the most famous was a native Georgian whose reputation as a frontier lawman was well established by 1886, when he was recruited out of Texas. Quiet, resolute, avuncular, he would ride into modern history as the prototypical western marshal. Take away the ivory-handled six-shooters, the lever-action Winchester .44-40, and the fabled number eight shotgun; talk him out of the badge and the knee-high boots; stand him up for a photograph in a three-piece suit and Heck Thomas still looked saddle weary.

He once rode into Fort Smith out of Indian Territory with thirty-two prisoners in custody.

Heck Thomas, in August 1896, was riding for E. D. Nix, U.S. marshal for Oklahoma—the territory carved out of Indian land and opened to white settlement in 1889—when he finally caught up with Bill Doolin. The outlaw had been brought in once already, captured by famed deputy marshal Bill Tilghman after being tracked to Eureka Springs, Arkansas, but had managed to escape the territorial jail in Guthrie six months later. Thomas tracked Doolin to his father-in-law's farmhouse in Lawson, where the outlaw was holed up with his wife and young child. On the night of August 24, as Doolin and his family, under cover of darkness, were setting off from the house, Thomas and his posse got the drop on him. After a brief exchange of gunfire—in which Doolin managed to discharge first his Winchester, then his six-shooter—Thomas, as he explains it, "got the shotgun to work and the fight was over."

The death of Bill Doolin, leader of the last of the great outlaw gangs to ride out of the Midwest, did not put an end to crime on the frontier. It did, however, provide evidence that law enforcement in the territories had finally become organized. The manhunt itself signaled a change in the tide of local civilian support—running in favor not of the outlaws, but of the lawmen who pursued them.

With the closing of the West and the onset of the new century, the deputy U.S. marshal would enter upon a twenty-five-year decline and a plunge into obscurity that would last another twenty-five.

With the organization of the western territories came local rule on the frontier, and with the emergence of local, county, and state police forces there, the deputy marshal eventually fell victim to operational atrophy. After that, it seemed he was doomed—when he received attention at all—to receive only negative attention.

In the spring and summer of 1894, led by its founder Eugene V. Debs, the year-old American Railway Union, fresh on the heels of its first victory in a strike against the Northern Pacific, struck the Pullman Palace Car Company just south of Chicago. Protesting massive wage cuts, 18,000 workers walked off the job, bringing rail operations across the Midwest to an abrupt halt. The federal government sided immediately with management. Citing interference with the movement of the U.S. mail, Grover Cleveland's Attorney General obtained an injunction against the union and authorized the deputizing of 5000 men, most of them thugs in the employ of the railroads, to break the strike. Eventually followed in by over 2000 soldiers, the deputies served as the shock troops in what proved to be a stunning setback for organized labor. For the better part of the next forty years the deputy U.S. marshal would provide the federal muscle in the government's war with the American labor movement.

During the First World War deputy marshals arrested, delivered, and registered enemy aliens, who were then interned by the army; deputies also provided perimeter security against saboteurs on the nation's docks and around its industrial plants. During Prohibition they provided arrest power for Treasury agents and also conducted the property seizures. It was deputy marshals, one of them a woman, Norma Haugan, on warrants issued in the Northern District of Illinois, who in 1931 arrested Al Capone.

The deterioration of the office was accelerated in the new century by a rapid expansion of the federal bureaucracy. New law-enforcement agencies were chartered, and not only were they specialized but, more important than that, they were centralized—headquartered in Washington with ready access to the decision makers who controlled their destiny. Their growth was assured.

The decline of the deputy marshal would be cast into sharp relief in the 1930s when, capitalizing on manhunts for such celebrated gangsters as John Dillinger and Pretty Boy Floyd, a publicity-savvy bureaucrat named J. Edgar Hoover transformed a minor agency in the Justice Department into what was soon to be the most famous law-enforcement organization in the world. With the rise of the FBI the office of the deputy marshal would substantially depreciate.

Once the long arm of the law, the deputy was by now reduced to bailiff and professional process server. A glorified jailer. With no central headquarters to lobby the federal bureaucracy on his behalf, he was a civil servant without a career path. Held to no professional standards, he was a lawman at the occupational pinnacle of whose job sat local ward heelers and party hirelings. For a quarter century the office of marshal would serve as a refuge for aging political hacks, sustained solely on the fruits of congressional patronage.

EVENTUAL revitalization of the office had its roots in the American civil rights movement. When communities in the South, in the wake of the 1954 Supreme Court ruling *Brown* v. *Board of Education of Topeka, Kansas,* defied federal court orders to desegregate their schools and public facilities, the Justice Department turned to the U.S. marshals to enforce the courts' decisions.

It was deputy marshals who in 1960 escorted black first graders to school in desegregated New Orleans, who in 1965 walked from Selma to Montgomery with Martin Luther King, Jr. But it was on the night of September 30, 1962, in Oxford, Mississippi, in pressing the most incendiary confrontation of the era, that the deputy marshal walked out of the obscurity cast by the shadow of history to recapture the errant glory that was destined to be his again.

By the end of September, 1962, several attempts to secure the registration of James Meredith as the first black student at the University of Mississippi—his admission having been ordered by the Fifth U.S. Circuit Court of Appeals—had been thwarted by state officials under Governor Ross Barnett. Attorney General Robert Kennedy, to guarantee Meredith's enrollment, detached to the Ole Miss campus on the afternoon of Sunday, the thirtieth, 123 deputy marshals. Their force was augmented by specially deputized Border Patrol and Bureau of Prisons officers, for a total of 536 men.

By five p.m. they had attracted a crowd. By nightfall the crowd had grown violent. In the vanguard of the riot that ensued was a small corps of university students. The mob that eventually formed, however, was dominated by outsiders; over the course of the confrontation their number would reach 3000. Backed by the white columns of the Lyceum, the antebellum building that housed the office of the university registrar, helmeted deputies, who had been ordered to hold their fire, soon started hitting the ground under an onslaught of rocks, bricks, and vials of acid. Using tear gas, the deputies held their positions.

Gunshots eventually erupted, and the deputies were forced to take cover. They took sniper fire throughout the night. By two a.m., when the army arrived and cleared the campus of rioters, there were, among the officers who had taken part, 180 casualties, 27 of them wounded by shotgun or rifle fire. Five were cited for bravery. There were two fatalities that night—one a young Mississippi spectator, the other a French journalist.

Marshals arrested 200 rioters, fewer than 50 of them university students.

At eight a.m. Meredith, a transfer student, registered for classes. He would remain on campus for almost a year. Until he graduated, on August 18, 1963, he was guarded by deputy marshals twenty-four hours a day.

The fight for civil rights did not end with James Meredith, but after Oxford, the days of state-defended segregation in the United States were clearly numbered. That night in Mississippi was a turning point, not only in the social history of the nation but in the history of its oldest law-enforcement agency. Deputy marshals, by demonstrating their professionalism, had earned new stature in the eyes of the public and in the ranks of the federal bureaucracy. What followed was a period of expansion and rebuilding that would bring them, belatedly but dramatically, into the twentieth century.

In 1969 the United States Marshals Service was established. By 1974 it had achieved bureau status within the Department of Justice. Headquarters enjoyed control over the Service's budget, over the hiring and training of deputy marshals, and over the nature of the Service's various missions. The ninety-five U.S. marshals themselves, the political appointees, were tolerated.

By the time of the marshals' bicentennial, in 1989, the Marshals Service had secured a broad operational mandate that was reflective of its deputies' unique status in the federal bureaucracy. Because they are both officers of the federal courts (the judicial branch) and law-enforcement agents of the Attorney General (the executive branch), theirs is a widely diversified mission.

THE Marshals Service, as it has been for 200 years, is responsible for the security of all federal judicial proceedings. That responsibility includes the personal protection of judges, magistrates, jurors, witnesses, prosecutors, and officers of the court, both in and out of the courtroom. The Service responds to all reported threats against members of the judiciary. Responsibility for the physical security of the more than 500 judicial facilities in the ninety-five districts was consolidated within the Marshals Service in 1983.

The Marshals Service receives, processes, and takes custody of all federal prisoners brought before the court for arraignment. (In 1990 it processed approximately 87,000 of them.) It contracts with state and local jails for housing unsentenced prisoners when federal facilities are not available. On March 30, 1991, in one place or another, the Service was holding a record 15,000 prisoners for trial or sentencing.

The Marshals Service is also responsible for transporting all federal prisoners, producing them for legal hearings and meetings with counsel as well as for trial. It moves sentenced prisoners to penitentiaries and transfers them between penitentiaries. Short-distance prisoner moves are handled by district personnel in surface vehicles; long-distance moves are accomplished by the Service's National Prisoner Transportation System (NPTS). Budgeted at up to $18 million annually, NPTS operates a scheduled airline, Con-Air, a sixteen-plane fleet that includes two Boeing 727s. With stops at some thirty cities and six military installations around the country, it flies five to six days a week at an industry-enviable capacity of seventy percent. Headquartered at Will Rogers Airport, in Oklahoma City, it moves state and local as well as federal prisoners and charges state and local authorities for the service. Cheaper and infinitely safer than commercial transportation, Con-Air has enabled local authorities, reluctant to seek extradition of felons because of high transportation and personnel costs, to do so at a fraction of the expense traditionally incurred.

As administrator of the National Asset Seizure and Forfeiture Program (NASAF), the Marshals Service is custodian of over $1.4 billion in cash and property seized in criminal cases brought by the various agencies of the Justice Department. It is the responsibility of the Marshals Service under NASAF to secure, inventory, appraise, store, maintain, and ultimately dispose of the assets seized.

The Marshals Service is still responsible for the expeditious service of all federal process; it executes some 354,000 court orders, not including warrants, every year. Because its deputies have arrest powers on the nation's public highways, which are not granted to the Department of Defense, the Marshals Service provides security assistance to the Strategic Air Command during the intermittent movement of

Minuteman and cruise missiles between military installations. The Marshals Service also oversees the security of all international spy swaps; it accepts custody of fugitives surrendered to the United States by foreign governments pursuant to extradition or expulsion; it is one of the principal U.S. agency participants in Interpol.

To respond to emergencies—civil disturbances, terrorist incidents, hostage takings—and to provide security during high-threat trials and prisoner moves, the Marshals Service maintains a paramilitary force, the Special Operations Group. (It was they who put the handcuffs on General Manuel Noriega in Panama in January 1990.)

A modern law-enforcement bureaucracy, sustaining and expanding a jealously guarded federal mandate, the Marshals Service owes much of its new purpose to its Office of Congressional and Public Affairs. As engineer of the Service's publicity, the office has successfully promoted the agency, constructing an image for the deputy marshal modeled on the prototype of his frontier predecessor. Notwithstanding the agency's professional handling of the programs outlined above, however, mass production of that image would have been impossible prior to 1979, the year of the fugitive program.

That year, in a Department of Justice policy move, responsibility for the majority of federal fugitives fell to the Marshals Service. Under a memorandum of understanding between the Service and the FBI, the Marshals Service assumed authority over certain categories of federal fugitives, including those who had violated the conditions of their parole or probation or had jumped bond after being convicted. The backlog of fugitives at the time had grown to unprecedented levels, primarily because the FBI was giving them no priority. (In investigative agencies, no institutional credit is given for fugitive arrests; agents are rewarded for opening new cases and making *initial* arrests.)

With the fugitive program came jurisdiction over those who had escaped from federal prison. And with that authority the Marshals Service made its first move in the campaign that would eventually carry it to the forefront of American law enforcement.

CHRISTOPHER Boyce, it is arguable, when he broke out of maximum security at Lompoc, California, did more for the U.S. Marshals Service than he had ever done for the KGB. The young California native, celebrated in the book and subsequent film *The Falcon and the Snowman,* who was convicted in 1977 of selling American satellite secrets to the Soviets, escaped prison in January 1980. He remained at large for over a year and a half. It was deputy marshals, invigorating their reputation as the law west of Fort Smith, who brought him back alive. The Service capitalized on the attendant publicity with such shameless sophistication that its budget and manpower were summarily increased. With the trackdown and capture of Boyce, the deputy marshal as manhunter was clearly on his way back.

Just as celebrated was the apprehension in 1982 of rogue CIA operative Edwin P. Wilson. Indicted in April 1980, Wilson had been wanted on several charges, including illegal weapons trafficking—he had supplied Libyan colonel Muammar al-Qaddafi with explosives and had trained an army of international terrorists in their use. Assistant U.S. Attorney for the District of Columbia Larry Barcella, who had made the case against Wilson and was seeking to extricate the former agent from his sanctuary in Libya, turned to the FBI, under whose jurisdiction Wilson fell. The Bureau, finding the political risks of involvement too great, and citing as futile any effort to bring Wilson to justice, wanted nothing to do with the case. The young prosecutor, finding a court of last appeal in the Marshals Service, approached Howard Safir, its associate director for operations. The inevitable arrest of the cunning Wilson was both a coup for the Marshals Service and a significant embarrassment to the Bureau.

Under Safir's direction, deputy marshals attracted international attention again when, in 1985, they tracked down the Nazi "Angel of Death," Dr. Josef Mengele—last seen at Auschwitz forty years earlier—corroborating his death in South America and ultimately exhuming his body in a Brazilian cemetery.

But these and other successful high-profile fugitive efforts were merely the more dramatic plot points in the larger story. Capitalizing on the restoration of its historic authority, the Service inaugurated various Special Enforcement Operations run out of headquarters, the most successful conducted under the acronym FIST, for Fugitive Investigative Strike Team. Designed to grab headlines and boost arrest figures, and conducted in cooperation with state and local agencies, the nine major FIST operations engineered between 1980 and 1987 resulted in almost 15,000 felony arrests. While grounded in traditional police investigative techniques, the operations often attracted attention for the innovative nature of those arrests—for the scams occasionally employed by deputies to snare fugitives en masse, several dozen at a time, without violence.

THE U.S. Marshals Service, with a work force that hovers in the vicinity of 3300, is about a tenth the size of the New York City Police Department. Of the 3300 personnel, about 2700 are sworn operational people; 150 of those are women; nine to ten percent are black, and five percent are Hispanic.

A deputy's livelihood, like that of any cop, incorporates survival in its most elementary manifestation. His is an endeavor where mortality is a preoccupation. The typical deputy marshal devotes a large part of his average workday to averting violent death on the job. Even at its most routine, the job is decidedly dangerous. Prisoner transportation, "almost half of what we do," puts a deputy in continual contact with some of the nation's more desperate people.

"They are ingenious," as one deputy explains it. "They have twenty-four hours a day to think of how to beat you."

Survival is the story of the deputy marshal in another, ironic way.

A large part of the Service's resources are dedicated to the survival of members of the criminal class. Public relations successes aside, the future of the Marshals Service, in the absence of anything else, is secured by the one activity it does not go out of its way to advertise, an activity by which the course of law enforcement in this country has been changed forever. The U.S. Marshals Service is proprietor of the Federal Witness Security Program (WITSEC). It is with the Service's assignment to witness protection, in 1971, that the modern era of the deputy marshal truly begins.

Chapter Four

DONALD "Bud" McPherson, like many of his contemporaries in the Marshals Service, had come on the job with a background that one could honestly describe as checkered. A "pre-Miranda cop" in Brooklyn, New York, McPherson had quit the force at thirty, resigning with an associate's degree in police science and fewer than ten years on the roster. In 1963 he joined the New York City Fire Department. Then, in 1966, leaving the city, his first marriage, and that job behind, McPherson moved to southern California. There he went to work as a Burns Detective Agency supervisor and, after that, as a fire fighter for Warner Brothers Studios, eventually being laid off. He tended bar for a while. He then bought a truck. In time he landed a contract to haul furniture for a van line. In the fall of 1970 he was sitting in his rig in a rainstorm, unable to load because of the weather, when he ran across a newspaper item announcing a test for sky marshals.

And far be it from Bud McPherson to ignore any opportunity to broaden his occupational horizons.

Air piracy, as a criminal occupational specialty, came into its own in the early years of the Nixon presidency. Responding to its sudden worldwide popularity, the White House issued orders that armed undercover agents be placed aboard U.S. carriers as expeditiously as possible. Bud McPherson went to work as a sky marshal under the authority of the U.S. Customs Service, but characteristically, not for long. In August of 1971, hitching his perpetually double-parked career wagon to a familiar five-pointed star, he applied to fill one of two openings for deputies in the office of the U.S. marshal in Los Angeles.

In 1990 he was still there.

How McPherson, in the winter of 1973, came to be standing in a blinding snowstorm in Rapid City, South Dakota, dressed in yellow golf pants is a story which as accurately as any illustrates the day-to-day vicissitudes of the career into which he had stumbled.

McPherson had not been on the job a full five months when he applied for duty with the Service's paramilitary wing, the Special Operations Group (SOG), a year-old unit of volunteers organized to respond within hours to civil disturbances and national emergencies. The group at the time conducted its tactical training at the U.S. Border Patrol Academy in Los Fresnos, Texas. Soon after he trained there in 1972, McPherson found himself on SOG duty in Washington, D.C., where that November's Trail of Broken Treaties protest march by American Indians had escalated to a five-day occupation of the Bureau of Indian Affairs (BIA). McPherson, a combat veteran, who as a teenager had served with the 187th Airborne in Korea, took to the prospect of rappelling out of a helicopter onto the roof of

Washington's BIA building with a certain measure of equanimity. (Ultimately the plan was abandoned in favor of negotiations.) He did not, however, see in Special Operations his future as a deputy marshal.

Three months after he returned to Los Angeles from the nation's capital, on a sunny February morning, McPherson received orders to report to even sunnier San Diego on a routine court-security assignment. Those who know McPherson well will tell you that what he grabbed first were his golf clubs. No sooner had he packed a suitcase, however, than a second call came in, instructing him to fly to Denver, where he would be joined by other deputies assigned to Special Operations. In Denver, McPherson was briefed.

He was dispatched immediately to South Dakota, there to touch down in the aforementioned Rapid City snowstorm. He hit the tarmac running, like a paratrooper for the PGA—dressed rather optimistically, he discovered, for what would prove to be the opening round in the ten-week occupation of Wounded Knee.

Within hours he was wearing a royal-blue jumpsuit—with SOG patch and silver star—an orange neckerchief, and combat boots, about to participate, however reluctantly, in the continuing history of his government's oppression of those people native to North America, a continent that, somewhere in the dark backward and abysm of time, had given majestic rise to the gold-latticed coal-and-uranium-rich real estate that would come to be known as the Black Hills.

After helping deny access to the BIA building on the Pine Ridge Reservation to members of the Oglala Sioux Civil Rights Organization (OSCRO)—a five-day assignment—McPherson returned to Los Angeles. Again, as it happened, rather optimistically. He had been home no more than two weeks when several hundred Indians, under the leadership of OSCRO and the American Indian Movement, occupied the Pine Ridge village of Wounded Knee, site of the December 29, 1890, massacre in which more than 200 defenseless Sioux—men, women, and children—had been slaughtered by President Benjamin Harrison's decorated 7th Cavalry. Within twenty-four hours of the occupation, the community was surrounded by federal officers—FBI agents, BIA police, and deputy U.S. marshals, McPherson among them—equipped in short order with armored personnel carriers, semiautomatic rifles, and enough ammunition to make the original massacre measure up like a motor-vehicle fatality.

The siege lasted seventy-one days.

"This is not Korea, this is Wounded Knee," McPherson would later explain of a snapshot taken of him at the time, in which he is pictured armed with a modern assault rifle, aboard an armed personnel carrier. "We were shooting at each other every day."

Royal blue inevitably gave way to camouflage.

Exclusive of secession, the siege of Wounded Knee stands as the longest civil uprising in American history.

According to John Haynes, a Special Operations deputy who would go on to become the unit's commander, "We figured we could have ended it within six hours anytime we wanted to. But nobody wanted another Wounded Knee massacre, like the original thing that happened. Nobody wanted that. Nobody."

Storming the hamlet was estimated by the military to be possible at a cost of fifty percent casualties to the assault force. As negotiations with the Indians over their grievances were pursued, the siege dragged on into the spring.

"We were settin' in the same positions that the Seventh Cavalry had set in. And you would visualize, here we are, the cavalry, settin' up there, lookin' down, just like they were back then. We set in and deployed in some of the very same positions. And to sit up there at night and listen to them beatin' their tom-toms and dancin' . . . We all grew up watchin' cowboys-and-Indians movies and stuff. It was a hell of an experience."

The siege, when it was over, was marked by the deaths of two Indian fighters and the permanent paralysis of a visiting U.S. marshal whose spine was severed by a rifle round.

BUD McPherson's evolution as a witness-security specialist began in 1972. He had attended court-security school within a year of his basic training, and it was from graduates of this school that the Service took its witness-security specialists in the early days of the program. (Advanced training in WITSEC itself had yet to be formalized, and until such time as it was, WITSEC remained a subspecialty of court-security work.) As a court-security specialist, McPherson had handled, among other cases, the trial of Daniel Ellsberg, the erstwhile defense analyst who had leaked the Pentagon Papers to *The New York Times.*

It would be upon his return from Wounded Knee, in 1973, with a year of court security behind him, that McPherson was assigned as a district specialist to WITSEC. And if he was looking for a clue to his future, he did not have to look very far.

THE call came in from Washington. McPherson's orders were simple. He was to meet an American Airlines flight at Los Angeles International Airport.

The orders ended there.

"Your man will be on it. You'll recognize him."

End of conversation.

Security on the witness was that tight.

"In the early days of the program everything was a secret. Not only did they operate on a need-to-know basis, but they wouldn't even tell you when you needed to know."

McPherson, with two cars stationed outside the American Airlines terminal, put a low-profile, three-man detail on the arrivals gate and waited, ready for anything, open to whatever wild card headquarters had decided to deal. Studying passengers as they deplaned the transcontinental flight, McPherson made out his man immediately. Blond, bespectacled, all-American, a young man of medium stature, the fellow was unimposing in the extreme, yet at the same time unlikely to benefit from any serious attempt at disguise. Not even a marginal attempt had been made. He was dressed the way McPherson had always seen him dressed—a little bit less than elegant, a little bit more than uptight. A lot, indeed, like a lawyer.

"He comes over to me and says, 'You must be Bud.' *He* knew who he was meeting. I guess he had a need to know and I didn't."

Washington had not been fooling. McPherson's man was recognizable. Unmistakable, in fact. He was using the name John West, but his real name was John Wesley Dean, and he would spend the rest of his time helping to orchestrate the inevitable fall of the political administration of the thirty-seventh President of the United States.

In the summer of 1973 virtually all participants in the witness-security program were members of organized crime. John Dean, the White House counsel, far from being typical of the witnesses McPherson was assigned to protect (a majority of the American public probably held racketeers in higher esteem), was not even *in* the program. Dean officially was just one more federal witness—a cooperating one, to be sure—but he was so high profile a witness that security on him was essential. Not only was Dean vulnerable to death threats, but simple injury to him, however slight or accidental, held a promise of political embarrassment the enormity of which the Justice Department could ill afford. What Dean shared with McPherson's other witnesses—really only a couple of things—were things as prevalent in Washington as they were on the New Jersey waterfront. A couple of things like (a) a felony indictment and (b) a desire to trade.

"I'd been around a lot of guys who got religion because it was in their best interests. But I liked Dean. I believed him."

McPherson would grow friendly also with Watergate superstar G. Gordon Liddy, whom he was charged to deliver—not as a witness but as a defendant—to the 1974 conspiracy trial that stemmed from the burglary of the Beverly Hills office of Daniel Ellsberg's psychiatrist.

"Behind his back, we referred to Liddy as Unit Twenty-six. We figured he was playing with half a deck. His best buddy in [the Federal Correctional Institution at] Terminal Island was [New York mobster] Bill Bonanno. They jogged together."

In witness security, a line of work in which forced camaraderie was an essential condition, McPherson would eventually develop a soft spot in his heart for an array of racketeers, crooked politicians, and twisted individuals in general, especially for their innocent families. But the collapse of the Nixon administration, which had overseen so dramatic a shift in the destiny of the deputy marshal, posed a singular irony for the specialist working witness security. It was under Richard Nixon's Attorney General John Mitchell that the Service as such had been created. And it was under his authority, by way of the Organized Crime Control Act of 1970, that WITSEC was codified and entrusted to the Service as an essential component of its mission. McPherson's assignment to protect John Dean coincided with Dean's testimony in the Watergate-related trial of John Mitchell and Maurice Stans, and Dean was up against the politics not only of a critically convulsed Justice Department, but of an institution both older and closer to home.

As McPherson explains it, "The U.S. marshal here [in Los Angeles] is appointed by Nixon. There's a Republican administration going down. No one wants to protect John Dean."

McPherson's association with Dean predated the discovery of the

White House audiotapes that were to corroborate Dean's testimony. And McPherson had been a cop for too long, he had been around too many witnesses, to take anything Dean said on faith.

"In the beginning I didn't know, and I tried not to make a distinction. I got to like John, and I got to appreciate the situation he was in. He was tough. Most people hated him—he's a snitch, he's talking about the President, trying to save himself—he was [perceived as] a lowlife. [But] John was basically a decent human being when you got to know him. And as I got to know him I was pulling for him. Still, I didn't know for sure."

McPherson was with Dean the day that Dean and the rest of the world learned of the existence of the tapes, and McPherson says that Dean's euphoria that day was an expression impossible to fake.

"In the beginning I was pulling for him. But that day, when he found out about the tapes, I would have bet my life on him."

McPherson was not alone in growing to like the soft-spoken man who routinely over the telephone identified himself as John West. McPherson's wife, Claudette, following the Watergate hearings on television, like many incredulous Americans had become somewhat captivated by Dean.

"I watched, I think, every minute of Watergate," Claudette McPherson recalls. "John Dean totally fascinated me. I wanted to know, Is this guy Dean for real? What kind of a person is he?"

"She never knew, until later, that she was getting calls from him every day," McPherson says.

Dean came under McPherson's protection upon completion of his testimony before the Senate committee investigating the Watergate break-in; he had been called as a prosecution witness in the Mitchell-Stans trial in New York. Like many of McPherson's witnesses in the days before electronic satellite paging (during office hours deputies, very likely to be in court, were more often than not unavailable), Dean, when he needed him, telephoned McPherson at home.

Claudette McPherson, who ran a printshop during the day, took most of Dean's calls in the evening. "I'm following Watergate, and this guy kept calling at different times. 'Damn it, Buddy, it's that John West again.' I'd be watching the [taped] hearings on television [at night] and this man would be interrupting."

When her husband was not at home, Claudette McPherson would take messages. And he was not at home a lot. Her husband was not at home, for instance, when John Dean was called as a rebuttal witness in the Mitchell-Stans trial in New York.

Claudette's epiphany came one late afternoon as she was catching the news at work—"The first time I saw Bud on television."

There on the screen, as the two men were leaving court together, Claudette saw McPherson and Dean.

"I was at work and I saw him on TV. I got so mad at him. He called me that night, and I said, 'I saw you on television, and I know what you're doing, and now I want to know everything.' "

McPherson's blown cover was inevitable, he admits.

"When you're on the network news with John Dean every night, it doesn't take a genius to figure out what you're doing."

There were few safe houses at the time, and while prisoners could sometimes be held in secure county jails and government offices— the former were difficult to trust, the latter required heavily armed deputies—nonprisoners, like Dean, had to be handled outside the system.

Travel vouchers from headquarters came cheap—official government transportation requests were issued to the typical WITSEC deputy as freely as ammunition.

" 'Here's a book of GTRs. Go somewhere. Keep him alive.' "

And by the way, keep him happy.

Dean, going over his testimony at the Nashville, Tennessee, home of government prosecutor James Neal, wanted to visit Opryland USA—take in the Grand Ole Opry and the Country Music Hall of Fame, maybe hit a couple of rides at the amusement park.

"I finally said okay," McPherson remembers. "I assigned six or seven guys to the detail. I told Dean to dress down."

The snapshots would tell the story. They would show Dean— seated with his wife, Maureen, and McPherson—a hat jerked down over his eyes, superimposed stiffly upon the backdrop of a crowded Opryland USA.

"He got nervous," McPherson says, "when he saw a lot of guys staring. He said, 'Maybe we better leave.' "

McPherson, who was more than happy to oblige, did not share his suspicions with Dean.

"They were looking at Mo. I don't mean to sound . . . you know. But she was really built."

Maybe they were looking. Maybe not. Maybe McPherson should have known better than to take the guy out of a suit. But rarely again would it be as much fun to speculate. Later in his career, entrusted with the care and feeding of Jimmy "the Weasel" Fratianno, McPherson, acceding to a similar request, would face far less entertaining imperatives when he took the cigar-smoking hit man ice-skating.

Chapter Five

BUD McPherson, now WITSEC chief for Region XII, which encompasses the states of Washington, Oregon, California, Hawaii, Alaska, and parts of Nevada, works out of an office in the Federal Building in Los Angeles. His responsibility is twofold. Not only does he direct the security of all federally protected witnesses over the course of their testimony in his region, he oversees an enormous share of the relocation program that WITSEC in practice represents.

One September day, which was a typical day at the office with a single exception—that he was actually *in* his office—he gave an explanation for his imminent departure therefrom that spoke to the ongoing needs of racketeer redocumentation.

"I gotta go get some birth certificates in Nevada," he muttered into the telephone.

Soft-spoken, articulate, management material to the max, McPherson, a twenty-year resident of southern California, has been hanging out with hoods for so long that there is little hope now that the Brooklyn will ever leave his voice. His speech, by no means inelegant, carries with it a vaguely perceptible upper-register rasp. Over the phone he sounds like a very upscale underboss.

Taking pains ever to dress as though he were on emergency call to photographers for *Gentlemen's Quarterly,* as do most of the people who work "metro"—district jargon for WITSEC—McPherson invariably sports a matching tie and handkerchief, and until recently could be seen driving around greater Los Angeles in a late-model BMW confiscated by the Service under its National Asset Seizure and Forfeiture Program. He is six one and weighs 195; he has a full head of light brown hair steadily going to gray, and blue eyes you will never see. He is a man with a flair for the dramatic. As something of a personal trademark he always—day and night, outdoors and indoors—wears shades.

"And I'll be wearing sunglasses," he told a stranger over the telephone that day as the two made arrangements to meet.

Among the many telephone messages that awaited him when he returned from the meeting that day were two from a celebrated television producer who had been courting him as a source of material for the better part of a year and whose efforts had doubled in the face of McPherson's mandatory retirement, which was now fewer than two years away.

But McPherson had more pressing problems. One of them concerned an Asian witness he had relocated years before. The witness's daughter had just been accepted on a full scholarship by a medical school in Chicago. She had lived in the United States almost all of her life, but was not a U.S. citizen. As the expatriate of a friendly nation, she was ineligible for asylum, and the Immigration and Naturalization Service would not grant her immigrant status. McPherson was trying to get her a green card.

In addition to everything else that day, McPherson, with the help of a SOG detail, was overseeing the security of a high-threat trial being conducted across the street. In the lockdown of the U.S. courthouse, a focal point of media attention, he had René Verdugo and two other high-profile prisoners—one had been convicted, the jury was still out on the others—implicated in the 1985 kidnapping, torture, and murder outside Guadalajara, Mexico, of U.S. Drug Enforcement Administration agent Enrique Camarena. These three, collectively, could be put away for several hundred years (Verdugo, alone, would eventually draw 240). They had access to an effectively unlimited source of cash, and it did not take much of an education to judge that the risk of their escape—or their murder by confederates in the drug business, should they choose to cooperate with the government—was a serious one. Witnesses by no stretch of the imagination, they were nevertheless, as defendants, the responsibility of WITSEC, which handled all of the Service's sensitive, high-threat, high-profile moves and most of its international action—spy swaps being an example.

On top of all that, McPherson had his routine duties.

Bud McPherson's routine duties as a witness-security inspector can best be appreciated in light of a legal opinion once eloquently rendered by Louisiana Mob boss Carlos Marcello. When the late "Mafia kingfish" was finally indicted for labor racketeering, a piece of artwork he treasured was confiscated. It had hung from the wall of his New Orleans office, mounted there much like a sampler, catching the eye of many a dignified visitor like the proud needlework of a properly educated young lady. Imprinted thereon was an adage, an observation that might easily serve as the unofficial motto for WITSEC. It was the adage by which the old racketeer lived.

It read THREE DO NOT MAKE A CONSPIRACY IF TWO OF THEM ARE DEAD.

Call him the Oliver Wendell Holmes of wiseguys.

Honor among thieves as a keystone in the edifice of crime has always been of questionable strength. The willingness to betray one's brothers-in-arms did not begin with the witness-security program. What WITSEC did was simply to elevate the song of the stool pigeon to a legitimate American art form.

There was a time when doing time was an acceptable part of the cost of doing business. And as often as not it was an essential part. Rare was the made guy in the Italian rackets who had not proved he could take a fall. An indoctrinated member of La Cosa Nostra, a right guy, a wiseguy, was by definition a stand-up guy. He could be trusted to do what was correct.

The moral compunction attributed to the old Mafia bosses on the matter of narcotics is nothing more than a literary convention—what the old men of respect knew was that the heavy penalties for drug trafficking increased the possibility of the rank and file's cooperation with prosecutors. Heroin, as it happened, was to be the least of the bosses' problems. The sentences that came down under the nation's modern racketeering statutes were enough to push family enforcement operations to the limit.

With the coming of the witness-security program, the code of silence was all but dead.

Until Congress passed Title V of the Organized Crime Control Act of 1970, protection of an individual government witness was the responsibility of the investigative agency making the case in which that witness was testifying. With establishment of the witness-security program the following year, that responsibility—on the Attorney General's authority—was entrusted to the Marshals Service.

The truth is, nobody else wanted it. Underfunded and understaffed to begin with, the program instantly became the Department of Justice equivalent of bureaucratic Siberia. If you were in trouble at Justice, according to McPherson, you could count on becoming WITSEC director.

In the beginning it was thought that between thirty and fifty people a year would require the services of the relocation program, which was funded at under $1 million. It was not long, however, before the program was taking on 400 and 500 principals annually. By the end of September, 1990, some 5600 witnesses and 7000 dependents had been protected, relocated, and provided new identities, and the budget for the program had reached $43 million. While the program enjoyed immediate, quantifiable success from a prosecutorial standpoint (the government claims a conviction rate of better than eighty-six percent in cases where protected witnesses are used, and a recidivism rate among program participants that fluctuates between seventeen and twenty-three percent, which is less than half the national average), the program at the outset was in many other ways a disaster.

Because the program, by design, was so heavily layered in security, it generated publicity only in its negative manifestations. Disgruntled witnesses went running to reporters with disturbing regularity, while the details of the program's triumphs, out of necessity, remained a secret. Not the least of the program's unqualified successes was the fact that of those witnesses who followed its guidelines, none had ever been killed. (Thirty of those who have left protection have been murdered.) The program's perfect record at providing protective services had much to do with the ingenuity of its early deputies, but not in the way one might assume.

McPherson is very candid about it. "We never got caught in those days. We didn't know what we were doing. How could the wiseguys know?"

In the days before the 1978 memorandum of understanding, a document requiring the signature of every witness entering the program, deputy marshals took the heat for a lot of case agents and U.S. Attorneys who were inclined to make outrageous promises upon which the Marshals Service could never deliver. When the witness did not get the new Cadillac he was promised—or that mansion in the

Cayman Islands, the Park Avenue plastic surgery, and the 3000 Balinese dancing girls he dreamed of—battle lines were rapidly drawn. It was the witness, the case agent (usually FBI), and the U.S. Attorney on one side and the WITSEC deputy on the other.

"The case agent's the guy's rabbi," McPherson is quick to point out. "He's the one the witness goes running to. The case agent and the U.S. Attorney. He's testifying for them. And they're getting something in return. We're not. We're providing a service to these other agencies. They're not restricted, like we are."

Not, at any rate, until the memorandum of understanding, which stipulated that the only promises that were in any way binding on the government were those that were made by the Marshals Service itself.

In 1977, McPherson acknowledges, he relocated a horse. He will not identify the U.S. Attorney who originally made the promise, nor will he identify the U.S. marshal who so readily agreed, in writing, to honor it, except to point out that both were politically appointed and that the two "were close." And of course he will not identify the witness—a female witness, he says. Her Thoroughbred required a legal name change. A tattoo change as well.

"The woman," he explains, "we sent first." He is parsimonious with the details, adding only that, "The woman was easy."

McPHERSON says, "I'd never ask a person to come into the witness program if he had any other option. I tell people before they come in, 'It's the toughest thing you'll ever do.' "

The witness-security program is a relocation program. The lifetime protection of the Marshals Service presumes redocumentation and relocation—a permanent identity change for every member of the family and permanent extirpation of that family from the community in which it is rooted. Communication with relatives and friends, when it is permitted, is handled through secure mail-forwarding channels administered through the Marshals Service. There is no going home ever again. No weddings, no baptisms, no high school graduations. One minute you are in New York taking commissions on your six-figure extortion contracts, drawing on your investments in bookmaking, loan-sharking, and narcotics, and the next minute you are selling secondhand Oldsmobiles for short money to a community of Mormons somewhere in Utah.

Nobody said it was going to be easy.

Take all the problems any family ever had. Add to them an emasculated father—a man from whom the making of all major decisions has been taken away and who is everything he hated most in the world from the moment he learned to shake hands, namely a stool pigeon, a fact that his wife is only too ready to throw in his face, along with the saucepans when they happen to go flying. A wife with no girlfriends to talk to, who misses talking to her family. And children who, when they finally make friends, have to lie to them on a regular basis. And there you have a day in the life of the typical WITSEC family.

One mistake by anyone and it is a new name all over again, and maybe this time you are promoting Chryslers to Lutherans outside Des Moines.

The relocated family's lifeline is the WITSEC inspector, a combination of social worker, religious worker, doctor, banker, and bodyguard. A deputy must have a year in grade as a journeyman before applying for advanced training in witness security, a curriculum that includes courses in counseling and psychology and methods of documentation as well as a refinement of such basic deputy skills as defensive driving and protection of high-profile dignitaries.

With the reorganization of WITSEC in the late 1970s emphasis was placed on identifying the better, more upwardly mobile deputies in the agency and channeling them into the program. Selection carried a higher rank and grade. It was as a means of encouraging application to WITSEC that the rank of inspector was created.

Transfers within WITSEC are not encouraged. Essential to the success of the program is that the inspector be an insider, that he make a long-term commitment to the relocated family. Continuity is the glue that holds the arrangement together. And a knowledge of the witness's case is very often as crucial to the arrangement as the establishment of a personal rapport. Inexperience of course creates the ultimate nightmare—the witness walking all over the deputy.

"These guys," McPherson advises, "are protecting the best con men in the world."

McPherson hypothesizes a WITSEC inspector working in the American heartland. His boss is in Washington, D.C. The deputy sees him only at conferences. He gets "chummy with a witness out in the boondocks."

McPherson paints the following picture: "Then comes a time you tell the witness he's got to go to work, he's terminated from funding. Now, all these witnesses, no matter what you tell them in the beginning, they want a pension for the rest of their lives. Smart witnesses, when it comes time to work, say, 'You got to relocate me.' Why? 'Well, this inspector, I think he's dirty. He went out to dinner with us. I bought dinner for him.' The deputy gets in trouble. He either gets fired or shifted out of WITSEC. And this witness, he's got a certain amount of credibility, he's got to be relocated. Now he starts all over again."

And does not have to go to work right away.

For the naïve deputy it is very easy to get sucked in, very often while trying to do the right thing.

McPherson has lost a lot of good people.

"A conservative guess? Twenty to twenty-five inspectors, over the history of the program, compromised by the witness. That's only since '78. Before that, there were no rules."

One of McPherson's deputies went into business with a witness. Many deputies get fired; some go to jail.

"WITSEC is very dangerous that way."

An individual's acceptance into the witness-security program is the decision of the Office of Enforcement Operations in the criminal division of the Department of Justice. Application for protection is made by the various U.S. Attorneys' offices and organized-crime strike forces throughout the country.

The suitability of an applicant, according to the Marshals Service, is determined on the basis of the following information: the possibility of securing similar testimony from other sources; the relative importance of the testimony; the risk the witness might pose to a relocation community, as determined through psychological evaluation; and an assessment as to whether acceptance will substantially infringe on the relationship between a child who would be relocated and a parent who would not. In cases where only one parent enters the program with a child, the Service arranges and monitors secure visitation between the child and the nonprogram parent. It also oversees visits between relocated witnesses and nonprogram children pursuant to court orders allowing them.

In 1987 the Marshals Service opened the Witness Security Safesite and Orientation Center in metropolitan Washington, D.C., through which all witnesses now enter the program. The center, which can accommodate six families and four prisoner-witnesses, includes temporary living quarters, interview and polygraph rooms, and medical and dental examination facilities. Here witnesses, before being relocated, complete a comprehensive admission-and-evaluation program and receive psychological counseling to prepare them for the move.

Participation in the program is voluntary, and a witness, by formally releasing the Service of its protective responsibility, may terminate his participation at any time.

Upon acceptance of a witness into the program, redocumentation begins with a court-approved name change, the new name being chosen by the witness himself. With the change in effect, most agencies will supply backstop identity papers, the basic portfolio including birth certificate, Social Security card, driver's license or state I.D. card, and school and medical records. The Service will issue only those documents to which a witness is actually entitled. A diploma will not be issued, for example, to a witness who has not graduated from high school. Every witness must pass a driver's test before being licensed. Foreign nationals are not given proof of citizenship; they receive immigration papers instead.

"You get a new family, you're going to deal with them on a daily basis, a Monday-through-Friday basis, for maybe a month," says WITSEC Inspector Bill Wagner. "You're going to spend a lot of time with them when the process first begins. Schools, furniture, medical records—to obtain the records is a piece of cake, but to do with them what we do with them and then finally get them into the family's hands is a lengthy process. There are a lot of things in the program that take a lot of time, and that's probably the major complaint. You need the cooperation of literally eighteen agencies. And not everyone cooperates with the federal government, believe it or not."

Many federal agencies cooperate only reluctantly, and marginally at that—the Immigration and Naturalization Service being a good example—while a lot of state and municipal agencies will not cooperate at all.

Modern WITSEC guidelines require that all new paper be legal. The guidelines are about ten years old. Bud McPherson was redocumenting people when there was no redocumentation program, making it up as he went along, manufacturing birth certificates in an instant printshop to get relocated children into the little league.

McPherson still gets calls from some of those he handled as far back as 1971. Many will deal only with him.

"I can't tell you how many graduations I get invited to. How many weddings. To the kids I'm Uncle Bud."

FEW things are more difficult than finding employment for the program's participants, the vast majority of whom are career criminals. To say that they have limited job skills is something of an understatement. The Marshals Service administers a battery of vocational inventories to incoming witnesses, who receive a stipend from the Service until such time as they are self-sufficient; the amount of the allowance, based on the size and geographical location of the family, is determined by the Bureau of Labor Statistics. During that time the Service also covers the cost of any necessary medical treatment.

Essential to a witness's successfully going legit is what the Service picturesquely refers to as "a readjustment of expectations"—its way of saying that selling cocaine pays better than pulling the night shift at the International House of Pancakes. The Service will not support a witness indefinitely, and the disgruntled witnesses whom the public generally hears from are typically those who have simply been cut loose from funding.

Regulations require that the Service notify prospective employers of a witness's participation in the program and of a criminal record, if any. Where documentation is required and either is unavailable or represents a security risk, the Service, rather than provide records, will "make representations."

One of the more legitimate complaints about the program comes not from the witnesses themselves, but from the long-suffering American taxpayer. Into the communities of law-abiding citizens, career criminals are routinely injected, with completely sanitized backgrounds. Gone only are the days of the more severe violations of the public trust, when case agents intervened with local law enforcement on behalf of the protected witness. When a protected witness is arrested today, WITSEC instructs local authorities to treat him as they would any other suspect, with one exception: WITSEC asks that he not be put where his enemies can get to him. Which rules out putting him in with the general population of a lot of American prisons.

"If that means putting him in the hole [solitary confinement], so be it. But we'll give him up in a heartbeat. And we tell him that [before he comes in]."

Often local authorities are asked to allow the witness to serve any time he draws in the lockdown of a secure federal facility.

Located around the country in the seven busiest metropolitan areas are the respective WITSEC safe sites used to house protected witnesses when they are returned to the danger area for court appearances. Layered in physical and electronic security, the safe sites, according to McPherson, are relatively new. Ingenuity, he confides, is as essential as ever.

"I used to rent trucks—mail trucks, bread trucks, a lot of trucks. Once I rolled a guy out of court in a wheelchair. You take a couple of guys, not drawing attention—no red lights, brakes aren't squealing. You just sneak in, sneak out. You can have a guy on the roof with a shotgun, just don't have him carrying an American flag and a searchlight. You do it low key, they don't know where you are. But there are times when they know you're coming and times when there are only one or two ways to get in."

And that, in witness security, is when the fun begins. They call it going high profile. Drawing unashamedly on the power of advertising, it is the quintessential show of force.

"If I'm going to take a guy on a dangerous move, I've got guys on the roof, I've got a couple of inspectors and four SOG deputies with automatic weapons. SOG can wear their black ninja outfits—if we have a shoot-out in the street, I'd like the locals to see some uniforms. We move a lot of hot people. We use private planes, air force planes, a lot of automatic weapons. It's fun and it's twelve-hour shifts. Everybody in WITSEC wants to be at 37,000 feet with an Uzi. You don't have to worry about the kid with an earache, all the kids the mother can't handle because she's having trouble with the father, the witness who's having psychological problems. You give a deputy a break, you let him go to 37,000 and get away for a few weeks."

BUD McPherson's agency career vivifies the bridge between the old and the new Marshals Service. His success as a deputy and as an individual parallels the success of the agency itself. But for several years after he pinned on the badge, McPherson's commitment to the job was marginal at best. Viewing the Service in terms of a career, McPherson had always been one move away from making another move.

And then McPherson got word that things were about to change.

The word came down from headquarters in 1978. On a trip to the training academy at Glynco that summer Bud McPherson saw the word made flesh.

His name was Howard Safir.

Howard Safir was a thirty-six-year-old Drug Enforcement Administration supervisor when, in 1978, his boss, DEA administrator Peter Bensinger, put him on loan to the Marshals Service to rescue the witness-security program. Tall, lean, square-jawed—nephew of a New York City police detective who in 1952 had arrested bank robber Willie Sutton—Safir grew up in The Bronx. He entered federal law enforcement in 1965 as a special agent for U.S. Customs, and went immediately from there to the Federal Bureau of Narcotics, the precursor of the DEA. Having worked undercover in New York, Miami, and San Francisco, Safir then worked several temporary overseas details, assigned to heroin interdiction in Southeast Asia, France, and Turkey. Street-cop tough, no stranger to a gunfight (his first shootout came six months into the job, and came to an end when he put a bullet into his suspect's chest), Safir nevertheless swelled to full lawenforcement blossom as a bureaucrat.

"If anybody is responsible for the changes in the modern Service," according to Bud McPherson, "it's Howard. Little by little, things got better, more professional. Money here, a piece of equipment there. We started holding our heads up, started thinking about the future instead of just apologizing for the past."

WITSEC is a case in point. Marshals in the districts had no affection for the WITSEC program at all. Run directly out of headquarters, it bypassed them completely. All it did was cost them deputies, whom they assigned as contact men only because they were forced to and only, McPherson suggests, "on a slow afternoon."

"There was no funding, no staff, no equipment. No *regulations*. It was the cause of the bad press, much of which was justified. Then Howard came along and we had regulations. We had a memorandum of understanding."

McPherson, seeing in Safir the breath of air that would carry WIT-

SEC out of the doldrums to which it had been condemned, was not above running an occasional con on the new WITSEC chief in the interest of accelerating the pace of change.

"I set Howard up a couple of times. We're at Fort Hamilton, in Brooklyn, with Fratianno. He's going to testify [in New York]. I can throw a snowball from Fort Hamilton to [boss] Joe Colombo's house, to [Genovese boss] Funzi Tieri's house. We're in an abandoned WAC [Women's Army Corps] barracks. And at the downstairs door, absolutely no security. We didn't have any. So I got some wire coat hangers, and I hung some beer cans above the door. And that kind of nonsense—little trip things in the hallway . . .

"We were in the confines of a military base, so we had a *modicum* of security. I knew the wiseguys. They are *not* going to come onto a military installation. I knew Howard was coming, so I overplayed it to show him what we needed. Howard comes in and sees my elaborate beer cans strung up, sees the army blankets tacked over the window. We start talking, and he says, 'Don't you have any [anti-intrusion] equipment?' I said, 'We don't *have* electronic devices. We've been promised them for years, but no one ever gets them.'

"Howard says, 'You'll have them.' A couple of months later we had them all [infrared seekers, motion detectors, video surveillance]. Now we can wire windows. We have control units, perimeter security—the stuff we should have had all along. We got it. We got it fast."

The first major turn in WITSEC's path to elitism was Safir's institution of the "metro corridor," an organizational move the result of which was the creation of twelve WITSEC regions and a chain of command that circumvented completely the politically appointed marshals. Today WITSEC is so layered in security that its individual operations are virtually impenetrable to anyone without a need to know, including WITSEC deputies not assigned to the operation in question.

Detailed to the Marshals Service for a year, Howard Safir, at the end of it, was asked to stay. Promoted from WITSEC chief, eventually to become associate director for operations, he would go on to help revolutionize the organization.

THE transition between the old and the new Marshals Service is measured by many events—the desegregation of the University of Mississippi in 1962; the arrivals, respectively, of William Hall, in 1976, and Stanley Morris, in 1983, as directors; the appearance of Howard Safir, in 1978. But however one measures it, the transition coincides with an observable shift, at the federal level, in the typical cop's notion of organized crime.

It is said that during the administration of Ronald Reagan the only thing in America that went down in price was cocaine. With the rise in the Reagan years of the Colombian cartels, organized crime in the United States came inevitably to mean dope. When federal lawmen today talk about organized crime, they are talking about the traffic in contraband drugs, and when they do so, they manifest what translates as an outright nostalgia for the Mob.

Nowhere is this phenomenon more evident than in the witness-security program.

In the words of Bud McPherson: "Give me wiseguys any day. Who made us experts on Colombians, on terrorists? Give me a good old wiseguy any day. I got their book of rules."

With Caribbean nations providing the manpower, the face of organized crime has changed. New World American gangsters, for example, do not limit their revenge to stool pigeons; they slaughter entire families—the wives and children not only of their enemies but of their competitors as well. Nor do they subscribe to a code of conduct that prohibits their killing the police.

With a lock on the nation's headlines, the trade in Southeast Asian heroin and Latin American coke has drawn attention away from the old Sicilian families who, according to Bud McPherson, are as active as they ever were. They may not be playing leading roles in the nation's nightly news, but they still provide the overwhelming majority of the WITSEC honor roll.

It was the Mob that gave WITSEC life, the Mob that brought it to the attention of the American public at large, and it is the Mob that still gives the program its unquestionable star quality.

The veritable Gloria Swanson of the witness-security program is a guy named Jimmy Fratianno.

ALADENA Fratianno, a made guy in the Italian rackets, was born in 1913 in a small town near Naples, Italy. He arrived in Cleveland, Ohio, at the age of four, the son of a landscape contractor. Before he was out of his teens, he embarked upon one of the few careers that offers no dignified retirement, and at about the same time he started calling himself Jimmy because Aladena sounded too much like a "broad's name."

A precocious gambler, Jimmy the Weasel, as he would come to be known, began by making book at local tracks. He progressed rapidly from gambling to sticking up gambling joints, and by 1935 he was cracking heads for the Teamsters. He was twenty-three years old when he went to prison for the first time—for roughing up a bookie who was too slow to pay off.

In 1946, one year into his parole, Fratianno moved to Los Angeles where at the age of thirty-three, under the sponsorship of celebrated syndicate tough guy Johnny Roselli, in a winery on South Figueroa Street, he got made—initiated into La Cosa Nostra—in a ceremony reminiscent of his First Communion.

"For a while there," he told Roselli, "I felt like I was in church."

The rest is underworld history. Fratianno, who has confessed to committing several murders as a soldier in Jack Dragna's Los Angeles crime family, entered the witness-security program in 1977, and his testimony has been nothing if not comprehensive—a treachery-ridden who's who of postwar racketeering.

In 1981 Fratianno collaborated on a book about his life. Six years later he collaborated on another. A darling of the media for over a decade, he single-handedly made WITSEC famous and, in the course of doing so, raised the visibility of Bud McPherson, whose destiny it had been to escort Fratianno into the program.

One of Fratianno's more recent attempts to make Bud McPherson's life miserable was his well-publicized claim that the Marshals Service had terminated him, leaving the public to assume that after years of dedicated service to the government he had been cut loose to fend off the enemies who had contracts out on his life. What the Marshals Service actually had done, years later than Fratianno had any right to expect, was cut him loose from funding. Jimmy Fratianno, more than ten years in the program, had managed to avoid getting a job. He invented the most popular ploy to that end—once settled in a particular community and on the verge of ultimate employment, Fratianno would spot a suspicious vehicle or a suspiciously familiar face and so convincingly identify a threat that WITSEC would have to relocate him.

Fratianno has been redocumented so many times in so many parts of the country that rare is the field inspector who has not, however fleetingly, met him at least once.

"Not the most pleasant guy in the world to be with," asserts the Service's director of training, Duke Smith, who worked WITSEC early in his career.

Smith's is an opinion held by many who have rotated through the program. Active WITSEC deputies, on the other hand, appear reluctant as a matter of policy to speak ill of any individual witness.

"Fratianno is used to having things his own way," according to Mike O'Neil, a WITSEC coordinator in New York. Which is probably true of most mobsters, especially those who have been around for a while—many of whom, admittedly, can be very entertaining. "After they get immunity, they tell you Sinatra stories, they tell you Kennedy stories, they tell you everything."

Bud McPherson, for his part, has never had a serious problem measuring up to the various requirements of keeping the temperamental hit man happy. During one stay in Los Angeles, McPherson, for Fratianno's recreation, supervised several afternoon visits to an underutilized ice rink; deputies, strapping on skates, flanked the murderer as, circling the arena, he relived the more innocent moments of an ill-remembered childhood.

Security, to the veteran McPherson, was not a significant worry.

"Wiseguys don't carry guns. They got to go home, get a gun; they got to get backup. The same with funerals. There's plenty of time to get out before anybody can dime you."

Fratianno, in his constant relocating, likes to serve as his own travel agent, and one of his more recent requests for transfer was to Saint Croix in the Virgin Islands.

"I took him there," McPherson admits. "We stayed twelve or fourteen days. There were chickens crossing the highway. It cost fourteen dollars for breakfast. And there was only one TV network. He couldn't watch the Cleveland game. It pissed him off. We left."

As any deputy marshal will tell you, the ruthless-murderer-as-lovable-curmudgeon is nothing more than a myth, and in Fratianno's case it is a fable nourished by the mobster himself. Fratianno's romance with the press is resuscitated every time he opens his mouth. And in the endurance of Fratianno's notoriety there is a questionable reciprocity: thanks to Fratianno, there are few racketeers in the country who do not recognize Bud McPherson on sight.

When McPherson moved to Los Angeles, he built a house east of the city, in part because he wanted to partake of the privileges of the Via Verde Country Club. Studying the membership list when he joined, however, he saw the name of Louis Dragna, the nephew of Jack Dragna, who with Fratianno had been acting co-boss of the Los Angeles family just before Fratianno turned government witness.

As McPherson explains it, "I told my boss, 'I'm never gonna play golf with the guy.' He said it was okay to join."

One Saturday, to play as his guests, McPherson invited two strike-force attorneys and "another law-enforcement guy."

"We're in a foursome right behind Lou."

McPherson and his guests played golf all day and retired to the clubhouse for a drink. McPherson excused himself to use the men's room. Inside he happened to run into one of Louis Dragna's golfing companions.

"He says, 'Hey, Bud, who are those guys you're playing with?' I told him who they were. He says, 'Bud, play behind us every week like this. Louis thought there was a wire in the golf cart. He was a nervous wreck. He couldn't make a putt. Heh, heh. We took all his money.' "

To HEAR Bud McPherson tell Mob stories is to hark back to one's school days, specifically those days on which one walked wretchedly into one's American history class, having failed to complete the previous night's reading assignment. McPherson drops contract murderers' names as though they were part of the country's cultural vocabulary, recounting events of routine bloodletting on the cheerfully innocent assumption that they carry the mythic freight of Civil War engagements.

When McPherson tells stories about protected witness Joe Bish, "the greatest cook in the world," then starts talking about Luparelli, "the button man [who drove the car] on the Gallo hit," you are expected to know that Joe Bish and Luparelli are the same guy, that a button man is a Mob soldier, that a hit is a syndicate contract murder, and that Luparelli—after spotting "Crazy Joe" Gallo— "dropped a dime," that is, made the phone call that resulted in

Gallo's being gunned down in lower Manhattan's Little Italy, in 1972, in Umberto's Clam House, on Mulberry Street. Knowing these things when you talk to these guys is like knowing that Stonewall Jackson in 1863 lost his life at the battle of Chancellorsville.

"You can dislike a witness and not have him know; you can dislike him and not be able to hide it—it's so obvious it shows. Then there are what my wife calls your friendly murderers; you may not like them, but coming from Brooklyn, as I do, you have an ability to understand them."

Coming from Brooklyn, as Bud McPherson does, means coming from Borough Park, a neighborhood dominated heavily by Italians when McPherson was a kid.

"I grew up with all the wiseguys. Joey Gallo and I went to school together."

In the fall of 1978, preparing to testify in the racketeering trial that followed an investigation into the construction of the Westchester Premier Theatre, Jimmy Fratianno, under McPherson's protection, was being held at Fort Hamilton, in Brooklyn. Home to the nation's five wealthiest and most powerful Cosa Nostra families—there were 2500 made guys in New York—the city was a criminal Disneyland; and one afternoon, with nothing better to do, McPherson, with several deputies, took Fratianno on a driving tour of Brooklyn, pointing out to him all the bosses' houses.

"For Jimmy it was like going to Washington, the seat of government. He was like a kid. He couldn't control his excitement."

Bud McPherson brings far more to bear upon his knowledge of the Mob than his merely having grown up in its shadow. He is not shy about asking questions, and for twenty years he has been asking questions of the racketeers under his protection. After all, he assumes, if you want to know how to protect a witness from a professional hit man, who better to ask than the hit man himself.

And over the years, at the Marshal Service's training academy, he has shared his knowledge by delivering a series of lectures he created as a part of the required curriculum of the Service's witness-security school. The title of the course is eloquent testimony to the academic credentials McPherson has brought to the federal government's endless war on organized crime. Informally known as Bud's course, it bears the official scholastic title Wiseguys 101.

Chapter Six

OPEN to rapid evacuation by both interstate and intracoastal, the city of Brunswick, Georgia, is situated seventy-five miles south of Savannah, in the state's maritime Glynn County. Hence the name Glynco, applied to the former naval air station there, where in 1975, in fulfillment of a congressional mandate, the Federal Law Enforcement Training Center was established as a bureau of the Treasury Department. FLETC, as the training center is bureaucratically known—serving some 16,000 students annually on the outskirts of a city that is home to fewer than 18,000 civilians—is a consolidated facility providing basic and advanced training for the personnel of sixty-three participating federal organizations, from the National Park Service to the Border Patrol. The sprawling installation incorporates over a hundred buildings on 1500 acres of land and approximates nothing so convincingly as a theme park for cops.

Not only does it house the largest indoor firing range in the country, it features four outdoor ranges as well, not including that range devoted exclusively to shotgun training. The northern third of the facility is given over almost entirely to a driver specialties complex— three defensive-driving courses, two highway-response courses, and a pair of water-fed skid pans. Isolated, off in the northeast corner, is an expanse of conspicuously unimproved real estate dedicated to what is identified on the visitor's map as "Explosives Demonstration." Adjacent to the outdoor firing ranges on the southwest edge of the complex is the international border practical-exercise area. Abandoned in various locations about the property are airplanes, boats, and assorted motor vehicles for hands-on training in search and seizure.

Indoors at Glynco the troubleshooter of the new century may attend classes conducted by the computer- and economic-crime division, enroll in advanced law-enforcement photography school, or receive advanced training in technical investigative equipment— acoustics and microphones; the installation, operation, and maintenance of electronic surveillance; audio enhancement; and radio-frequency tracking. Glynco offers advanced programs in marine law enforcement, in archaeological-resources protection, and in a language called law-enforcement Spanish.

Much of the training here is audible for miles.

Defensive driving at Glynco does not mean what it meant when you first heard the expression in your senior-high driver education class. The water-fed asphalt pads are for practicing controlled skids, performing 180-degree J-turns and bootleg turns. Defensive driving is evasive driving—jumping curbs, executing controlled crashes through roadblocks.

The sedans parked on the firing range serve the requirements of barricade shooting: roll out, take cover, and fire over the fenders—*do not shoot the photographer.* There are more pop-up and swinging targets indoors and outdoors at Glynco than in a thousand penny arcades: the tough guys with five-o'clock shadows flashing press cards or pump-action shotguns, the blonde cradling the baby, the brunette clutching the large-caliber pistol, cartoons flying at you from everywhere—*fire but don't f___ up.* A freeze-frame four-color nightmare. And before you graduate, the Marshals Service sends you through an indoor version of it in the dark: loud music, flashing strobes, and amplified human screams—you and a partner and, only in the U.S. Marshals Service, live ammunition. "The maze is where we really stress 'em out; if they're going to lose it, they lose it there. We've seen them come out weeping."

And then, too, there are those combat silhouettes of the three-dimensional variety, the ones that walk and talk and improvisationally scream obscenities in your face. These are the training center's role players, the actors and actresses—civilians—who portray the criminals and the innocent bystanders whom the students confront on the streets and behind the closed doors of the practical-exercise area. A three-block complex of former enlisted quarters exhibits the look of the typical postwar suburban subdivision. Here, in some thirty-five abandoned bungalows—the interiors of a couple of which have been rearranged to resemble commercial establishments, barrooms, for example—potential deputies are tested on what they have learned about working fugitive warrants and what they have learned about walking away from such confrontations alive.

On a typical day at Glynco, traveling the streets you will see aspiring Broadway performers growling and spitting and verbally abusing future officers of the law (when they are not trying merely to gun them down) as the former are questioned, arrested, jailed, or ignored by the young students in question. You will find the actors riding in the backs of limousines, impersonating visiting dignitaries or Mafia big shots, as those same fledgling civil servants usher them cautiously around town—potential deputies walking the fenders as the vehicles cruise to a stop on Second Street, just outside building 20, the training offices of the Marshals Service.

DUKE Smith, director of training, U.S. Marshals Service, is not of the British peerage. He is not the Duke *of* Smith—not as far as anyone at Glynco is aware. But then, neither can anyone there, if pressed, tell you what his given name actually is. Officially he is G. Wayne Smith, born in July 1948. But Duke is what his wife, Suzy, has always called him, and the two have been going steady since Smith was thirteen years old.

An erstwhile amateur opera singer, a former college athlete—he majored in music at Western Carolina University, which he entered on a football scholarship—the bespectacled Smith, if not of the royal family, is the man, it is generally agreed, whom the Marshals Service would send first if any of them needed arresting.

Six feet three and weighing in at 230 pounds, Duke Smith came into the Marshals Service in 1974, in Greensboro, North Carolina. The principal prerequisite of employment at the time was that a deputy own a full-sized car.

"When you signed on in the old days," says International Branch chief Larry Homenick, "before they gave you a gun, they gave you a set of handcuffs and leg irons. That was your equipment."

The mission of the Service as the local marshal saw it—as U.S. marshals everywhere saw it—was the delivery of prisoners for trial. In default of that, a deputy's duties were limited to the service of process. In Greensboro, however, neither activity filled up a deputy's day.

"Deputies," according to Duke Smith, "were goin' fishin' most of the time."

For Smith, who had gone to work as a cop before completing college (he returned eventually, to graduate with a degree in criminal justice), it was an inauspicious beginning—the more so given the reality that he had gone to work first in Miami.

"When you're a cop in Miami, that's war every night. There's something happening all the time. You'd just walk into stuff. Once a week I'd come in, my uniform'd be ripped off—I mean, you're out there fightin' all the time. When you're twenty-one years old, and the sap is still rising, it's a great place to be."

The same could not be said of the U.S. marshal's office in Greensboro. Smith walked into his chief's office one day and saw warrants all over the desk.

"What are you doing with these warrants?" he asked.

"We have 'em in NCIC—when they catch 'em, they'll call us," the chief replied.

NCIC, the National Crime Information Center, is run by the FBI. Its computer contains the name and fingerprint classification of every wanted person in the country. The information is contributed by, and accessible to, every cop in the United States.

"Who are 'they'?" Smith wanted to know.

"Anyone who picks 'em up."

"Do *we* work warrants?"

"Well, every once in a while the judge'll ask us to go out and pick up a guy who failed to show up for court."

Every once in a while. "On downtime," it was later explained to Smith by one of his fellow deputies.

Downtime in Greensboro, to Smith's way of thinking, was a metaphysical concept. "You get a summons, a complaint, to serve, you'd drive thirty miles down the road, serve it, then take the rest of the afternoon and fish."

Smith wondered why he should not ask permission to work some of the warrants stacked on the chief's desk.

"You're gonna be mighty unpopular if you do," he was told.

Smith was ready to call it quits.

"I'd been a pretty successful, an aggressive, policeman. I went home and told my wife, 'I don't know if this job is for me.' "

He finally summoned the courage to press the warrants issue with the marshal. Two days later the chief, who saw warrants as the equivalent of make-work, approached Smith's desk with three fugitive warrants in his hand.

"You want to work warrants? Have at it."

"And he gave me three cases so cold— I mean, people hadn't

looked at them for years. These people had been gone, like, since Methuselah was around."

One of the three had failed to appear for trial nine years before.

"The advantage," Smith knew, and the only advantage, "was that these three guys had forgotten that anybody was lookin' for 'em."

Smith's alienation of his chief deputy was complete when he cleared the warrants in three days.

"That really pissed him off."

As soon as the opportunity presented itself, Smith escaped Greensboro by way of the witness-security program. It is still the agency fast track. He attended witness-security school in 1978, a member of the first class of specialists, all of whom were graduated with the newly created rank of inspector. He worked WITSEC for only two years—in a service that was growing rapidly, Smith immediately drew the attention of headquarters. In nine years he jumped ten grades; his ascent through the bureaucracy was unprecedented.

When the Marshals Service inherited the fugitive program, in 1979, Smith was selected by Howard Safir to initiate the study that would gain the Service status as a participating member of EPIC.

The El Paso Intelligence Center was founded in 1974, a joint venture of the U.S. Border Patrol and the Drug Enforcement Administration. Established as a central repository of criminal intelligence on the international traffic in narcotics, it was focused initially on the transportation of marijuana and heroin across the nation's border with Mexico. By the time Duke Smith arrived, EPIC had grown to include four other participating agencies—the Customs Service; the Bureau of Alcohol, Tobacco and Firearms (ATF); the coast guard; and the Federal Aviation Administration. Since that time four more agencies have entered into memoranda of understanding (the FBI, the Internal Revenue Service, the State Department, and the Secret Service), and the center's charter has expanded to encompass tactical intelligence on aliens and firearms, as well as on dope.

Smith's reception at EPIC was memorable for its lack of enthusiasm. Interagency cooperation in government is a consensual hallucination. In 1979 the situation, as Smith confronted it, was made worse by the perception of the Marshals Service—by then no longer justified—as a kind of terminally stumbling stepsister in the federal law-enforcement family. Its participating status at EPIC, which Smith helped to engineer, contributed significantly to the agency parity that the Service enjoys today.

Smith's sales pitch was very simple: "We don't want your dope; we don't want your investigations; we want the bodies. We want the guys. What have you got?"

In the United States, *initial* arrests account for all the institutional credit in law enforcement. Agents of the other investigative agencies receive no credit for *fugitive* arrests. Smith saw to it that the Marshals Service specialization in fugitives—the mission to which its investigative mandate was restricted—would come to be seen not as a threat, but as an asset by every federal officer with warrants to work.

In October 1979, with the federal fugitive program, the Marshals Service inherited some 8500 FBI fugitives. When Smith arrived at EPIC, he discovered seventy-seven percent of them documented there. "In over three quarters of our cases, we had automatic leads. It had been an untapped resource for years."

In 1980, when the Marshals Service started dragging in fugitives, it was not uncommon for the federally departed to greet deputies with a statement like, "I've been here for ten years. What took you so long?"

Smith remained EPIC program coordinator until 1983, when he was assigned to Glynco as the Service's director of training.

"THEIR training's more for real," a federal agent who has taught at Glynco will tell you about the Marshals Service. He is talking about their survival training.

In the words of Duke Smith: "Our human resource is the most valuable resource we have, something we take very seriously. We stress officer survival. We make it clear early on, 'You don't do us any good if you're dead.' We put a lot of emphasis on survival skills."

Survival skills in the U.S. Marshals Service include mental and physical conditioning and rigorous tactical training. But because, more often than not, life-and-death transactions are conducted in an exchange of the all-too-familiar currency of gunfire, greater emphasis is placed on a proficiency with firearms than on anything else.

Deputy United States marshals do not respond to traffic accidents. They do not rescue cats from trees. They do not take reports of burglaries or escort elderly citizens across their districts' busy streets.

Top left: Isaac Charles Parker, "the Hanging Judge." Top right: one of Parker's deputy marshals, Heck Thomas, once rode out of Indian Territory into Fort Smith with thirty-two prisoners in custody. Right: the men who tamed Dodge City—toughest cattle town in the West—included Wyatt Earp (seated, second from left) and Bat Masterson (standing, right).

Above: Pat Garrett, the deputy U.S. marshal who killed Billy the Kid in 1881

Above: Henry "Billy the Kid" McCarty, "just one more borderline sociopath in a territory where they blossomed like weeds"

Left: young Jesse James in uniform as a Missouri rebel. "In the returning Confederate soldier flashed a spark of lawlessness sufficient to ignite a prairie fire that would burn across the American West."

Left: Chicago mobster Al Capone, hiding handcuffs with his hat, in the custody of deputy U.S. marshals

Below: showdown at the University of Mississippi, September 26, 1962, as Chief U.S. Marshal James McShane (center) confronts Lieutenant Governor Paul Johnson (left) in an effort to compel the enrollment of transfer student James Meredith (right)

Left: Deputy U.S. Marshal Donald "Bud" McPherson (left) in 1973, protecting Maureen and John Dean (in hat) on a visit to Opryland USA, in Nashville, Tennessee

Left: Christopher "the Falcon" Boyce, convicted spy, in custody of U.S. marshals a year and a half after his 1980 escape from prison. His capture invigorated the U.S. marshals' image.

Right: Brooklyn chief deputy Mike Pizzi (right), with a bust of Alphonse "Allie Boy" Persico. The sculpture was used by marshals in their manhunt for the fugitive crime kingpin in 1987.

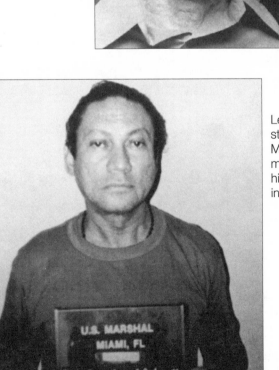

Left: former Panamanian strongman General Manuel Noriega. U.S. marshals put the cuffs on him in Panama in 1990.

Left: Stanley Morris, Marshals Service director from 1983 to 1989. "When the FBI made an arrest, they got the credit. But when we did, the story credited 'federal agents.'"

Right: at the Federal Law Enforcement Training Center, in Glynco, Georgia, trainees learn to drive fast, shoot straight, and fight. "There are more pop-up and swinging targets at Glynco than in a thousand penny arcades." Below: practical training pays off for Deputy Marshal Gerri Doody (left) when it comes to work warrants in New York City.

Murder, rape, armed robbery, and other violent felonies, it is not their duty to investigate. They are not in the business of gathering evidence. Their interface with crime is with the criminal himself: the indicted, the convicted, the incarcerated, the escaped. They come in after the fact. And virtually everything they do on an operational level requires possession of a gun.

Deputy John Butler, EPIC program coordinator, in acknowledging a rather unique contribution to the Service's recruitment effort, effectively articulates both the realities and the official limits of the typical deputy marshal's job. The occasional recruit, Butler says, when asked why he is drawn to the Marshals Service, will cite as one of his professional ambitions—often because he thinks it is expected of him—the rehabilitation of chronic felons.

"I tell him," Butler says, " 'You're in the wrong business. Our job is to put scumbags in jail. Ninety percent of these people need to be rehabilitated by Doctor Smith and Doctor Wesson.' "

While the number of those incarcerated for victimless crimes is admittedly growing—the population's determination to dope itself will one day, out of necessity, be handled outside the criminal justice system—and while miscarriage of American justice is not so rare as one would like to believe, the truth is that a plurality of those doing time in the nation's prisons today clearly belong there. And for the rest of their natural lives.

Many are the career felons who, in a strictly clinical sense, are uncivilized. They have demonstrated over the course of their lives a chronic inability to coexist peacefully in a society elevated above the primitive. Theirs is a degree of personal development that, in at least one significant way, bears resemblance to the infantile: they are characteristically unable to recognize a connection between action and consequence. For them, the only thing that distinguishes right from wrong is who happens to be doing it.

It is for people such as these that prisons were created. The etiology of their criminality (some are born to it, many more are bred to it by the environment in which they are reared) is worthy of study. But it does not alter the reality of their existence. In abundance. These are people who have absolutely nothing in common with you. And they form the core of the nation's prison population. Charlie Manson is in there with people who understand him. To assume anything else of those who dwell today in the American penal colony, as fashionable as it may be to do so, is delusional.

And cops deal with these people all day. Every day. It is these people whom cops are dealing with when they are not dealing with you.

Deputy John Haynes, a Special Operations Group commander, admits that routinely coming into contact with such people is not something one takes in stride. It affects the average cop, and it affects him every time it happens.

"Yeah, I think it does. I've never gotten used to it, and there are thousands of penitentiaries I've been in and out of. It bothers me every time I go in a penitentiary."

And his discomfort has nothing to do with fear, Haynes says. Though when he talks about it, his voice carries the weight of an elemental, almost spiritual, dread.

"To me, when I walk in there, it's like walking into hell, what hell must be like. I'm not talking about the living conditions. I'm talking about the . . . sin, the hatred, the perversion. You know, I believe in God. And to believe in God you got to believe in hell. And when I walk in one of them places, I think that's as close as getting to hell as you can come, because you can just feel the energies in that place. And I just cannot wait to get out of there, you know, when I put a prisoner in there."

What the typical deputy marshal faces on the street in the form of parole violators, probation violators, and escapees, is one part desperation immersed in a solution of depreciated expectations.

"They know they're going to die anytime themselves," Haynes says, "from overdoses, from the police, from other criminals. They don't expect to live a long, productive life. So if you get in their way, that's your problem. 'It's me or you, and it might just as well be you. Why let you live?' "

Survival in the U.S. Marshals Service is contemplated in the black light of the foregoing realities. And these days, survival, when deputies talk about it "for real," is inevitably discussed in the dark context of what has come to be known as the Roanoke event.

THE city of Roanoke, situated in the Blue Ridge Mountains, is home to the office of the U.S. marshal for the Western District of Virginia. By the late winter of 1988 the U.S. Marshals Service was conducting some 140,000 prisoner movements annually, and the district that includes Roanoke, covering two thirds of the geographic area of Virginia, was conducting its healthy share of them.

One of the prisoners in federal custody in Roanoke that year was a career bank robber named John Anthony Taylor. On March 9 Taylor, forty-two, who was being held at a county jail pending trial, was scheduled to keep a physician's appointment at the nearby Roanoke Valley Medical Clinic.

Taylor's appointment, a follow-up visit, had been made two weeks before. Its date and time, as a matter of policy, had been kept secret from the prisoner. He remained officially uninformed of its specifics until deputy marshals arrived at the jailhouse to escort him to the clinic.

Taylor, a suspect in several East Coast bank robberies, had been complaining for weeks about chest pains. Though his heart problems were probably genuine, he did have a history of faking ailments. A convict with a record of armed robbery and escape that dated back twenty-five years, he was known on one occasion to have eaten a light bulb, on another to have swallowed a razor blade, in efforts to get out of prison.

Taylor was reported to be unusually chipper that afternoon when deputies Mike Thompson and Sherry Harrison picked him up at the county jail. During the checkup the doctor remarked that Taylor appeared to be in good spirits. Taylor's blood pressure measured much higher, however, than it had on his previous visit.

Mike Thompson, forty-one, married, and the father of five, was a fourteen-year Marshals Service veteran. A native of Alexandria, Virginia, he was assigned to Roanoke in 1979. Sherry Harrison, twenty-four, raised in Stanley, North Carolina, had joined the Marshals Service after working three years for the Gaston County, North Carolina, sheriff. She was assigned to Roanoke in 1986, the year she came out of Glynco.

At 2:05 p.m., Taylor's examination complete, the two deputies walked the prisoner, in leg irons and handcuffs, out the door of the Roanoke Valley Medical Clinic. As they prepared to put Taylor into their government sedan Sherry Harrison was approached by a heavy-set man who had stepped quite suddenly from behind a utility van parked nearby. He had long hair and a beard and wore a Harley-

Davidson T-shirt. His name was Barry W. Dotson. He was thirty-three years old, a self-employed carpenter from Fredericksburg, Virginia. Walking up to Harrison, he raised a revolver and held it to her face.

"Don't do anything," he said. "We're just as nervous as you are."

The word "we" took on meaning as an armed twenty-two-year-old woman came up behind Mike Thompson. Her name was Tina Marie Julian. She was also a resident of Fredericksburg. Later identified by a witness as "the woman in pink," she snatched the car keys from Thompson's hand.

Barry W. Dotson had a minor criminal record. He had served two years at a state prison farm for a couple of small-time burglaries he had committed in his late teens and early twenties. "A follower, not a leader," in the words of a friend since childhood, "he never," according to another, "hurt anyone in his life." He was a stranger to John Anthony Taylor.

Tina Marie Julian—characterized by friends as "a bubbly person," by federal investigators as "a bubblehead"—had no criminal record. She had met Taylor the year before, when he was flashing money around the Fredericksburg bar in which she worked as a cocktail waitress. Taylor had moved in with her shortly thereafter.

It was she who had recruited Dotson—with a promise of money, according to federal investigators. Having arrived in the city in a pickup truck earlier that day, they checked into the Econo-Lodge motel on Roanoke's Franklin Road. From there, carrying bolt cutters, duct tape, and their weapons, they drove to their rendezvous with Taylor, parking the truck within walking distance of the medical center. In constant touch with him by telephone and mail during the period of his incarceration, Julian, authorities say, had, at Taylor's urging, somehow obtained from the clinic the date and time of Taylor's appointment.

Taylor, when the ambush went down, gave no indication that he was surprised. "Give me your gun, give me your gun," he shouted at Thompson as he and Julian together proceeded to shake the deputy down for his revolver.

It is the practice of the well-trained deputy marshal never to let a prisoner see his weapon, never to let him see the holster, even when it is empty. Neither Taylor nor Julian knew what kind of sidearm

Thompson carried, nor did they know on which side he happened to carry it.

Marshals Service regulations governing sidearms are not so rigid as they are specific. The weapon issued by the Service is a six-shot revolver, caliber .357 Magnum, and because it is meant to be carried concealed, it is issued with a three-and-a-half-inch barrel. There are those deputies who, for various reasons, prefer an autoloading pistol over a revolver, and once he qualifies on it, a deputy may carry the semiautomatic pistol of his choice.

The Marshals Service does not encourage the use of shoulder holsters. Cross-draw holsters of any kind are a hazard on a firing line, so deputies are not given an opportunity to train with them. Though Glynco holds to the proposition that "you play like you train," it bows to 200 years of rugged individualism and enforces no standards where holsters are concerned.

Because most people are right-handed, odds favor your finding a deputy's gun holstered to his belt, inside or outside the waistband, just above his right hip. And that is where John Anthony Taylor expected to find Mike Thompson's gun.

Orthodox in one way—he carried a revolver—Thompson was unorthodox in another. He carried it in a shoulder holster.

Screaming at Mike Thompson while Dotson's trigger finger quivered within inches of Sherry Harrison's face, the handcuffed Taylor, standing on Thompson's right, pulled Thompson's shirt out of his waistband, looking for the deputy's gun.

"Where is it?" he shouted.

It was Tina Julian, standing behind Thompson, who discovered the weapon in the shoulder holster under Thompson's left arm and reached for it.

Marshals Service historian Frederick S. Calhoun characterizes what Mike Thompson did next as better shooting "than Earp or Hickok ever did."

"He didn't think, he didn't reason," Duke Smith maintains. "His motor skills took over. He reacted to a situation. It's a motor response. You're conditioned [by training] to do that."

What Mike Thompson did was what he had done so many times facing combat silhouettes at Glynco.

Reflexively he drew his gun.

He shook Julian off and favored Dotson with what the Service teaches as the law-enforcement-standard "double tap." He put one round in Dotson's chest and one in his head, killing him before Dotson could pull the trigger on Harrison. Either shot would have been fatal—Dotson was as good as dead before he hit the ground. Mike Thompson did not see him go down; spinning, he fired twice at Tina Julian, whom he had fully expected to have killed him by then (shooting him in the back, but giving Harrison time to draw). Thompson hit Julian once in the chest. She collapsed to the pavement, and there she immediately died, Thompson's car keys clutched in one hand, a can of chemical Mace in the other, a .25-caliber semiautomatic pistol tucked in the waistband of her blue jeans.

Seeing Julian go down, Thompson threw Taylor to the ground, holding him there with his foot while Sherry Harrison, with her side-arm drawn, kicked the revolver from Dotson's hand. The two deputies then scoured the parking lot for additional people with guns.

Taylor was sobbing when the police arrived.

The choreography of the encounter, studied carefully and recapitulated time and again, serves as a training model in the officer-survival course at the academy.

"It went down absolutely by the numbers," according to Frank Skroski, Smith's deputy director for training. "Absolutely textbook," he said, adding that Thompson, from start to finish, was in complete control of the situation.

It was Thompson's officer-survival training, in 1984, coupled with his advanced deputy training, in 1986, that prepared him for the event, according to Skroski. When he arrived at Glynco in 1986, Thompson was a no-better-than-average shooter. Out of a possible 300, he was scoring 240s and 250s. When he left a month later, he was well on his way to being an expert, consistently scoring 290s. Not only had he sharpened his skills, but he had sharpened his confidence as well.

"So much of defensive shooting is in the mind," says Deputy Joe Trindal, firearms instructor at Glynco. Shooting is sight alignment and trigger control, but more than that, he says, "it is mind control."

From his street-survival seminars Thompson knew there would be an instant at which Dotson would become distracted. It was at that instant, the instant Dotson's glance shifted, that Thompson drew and fired. The time it took him to clear his holster and release two rounds was probably no more than three seconds.

Thompson's performance, remarkable in light of what he managed to do, was as remarkable, according to Skroski, for what he did *not* do. He did not waste a third shot on Dotson (he did not even watch him fall), nor, having missed Julian with his first shot, did he fire at her again once he saw her go down after the second. Spinning away from Julian, he had two rounds left in the cylinder of his revolver to protect himself from any additional shooters he might encounter.

"You never assume the ones in front of you are the only ones involved," Frank Skroski says. "We teach that if there are two, you think three; if there are three, you think four. You never underestimate your adversaries. You always look for the next perpetrator."

The encounter, start to finish, went down in a matter of seconds. The typical gunfight—which typically takes place in the United States and which typically turns out to be lethal—transpires, it has been calculated, in about seven seconds and within a range of fewer than ten feet. An average of four rounds is exchanged.

Both Thompson and Harrison appeared shaken after the shooting, and neither, until later, was able to talk about it to the press.

Thompson did, however, call Duke Smith at Glynco.

He said, "Training saved my life."

WHEN Duke Smith arrived at Glynco in 1983, out of a basic-training class of twenty-four students, the academy was losing an average of ten percent; within five years, with class size increased to forty-eight students, those washing out and dropping out were doing so at a rate reduced to one or two percent.

"Training hasn't changed that dramatically," Smith asserts. "The screening process has. We're getting a different caliber of cat."

The price the Service pays, says Smith, for its better-educated higher-caliber recruit is a relatively small one.

"They have no military or police experience, and bring with them no innate sense of chain of command."

Brooklyn's Victor Oboyski, who earned both his bachelor's and master's degrees at night school while working as a deputy in New York City, observes that many of the new recruits have never been away from home.

"Their maturity level is pushed back; many, as a result of college, are still dependent upon their parents. A lot of guys, their mothers are still making their beds. When I came in, there were nothing but [armed forces] veterans, a lot of guys out of service. You come in with a military background, you don't question as much as these kids do. You understand chain of command. For many now, it's their first job. Most of the time you're working long hours. You work twelve to fourteen hours a day, a kid says, 'What? I got concert tickets!' After three or four years they get with it."

As a witness-security specialist, Bud McPherson, very early in his career, had grown accustomed to spending the better part of his working day in the self-conscious company of FBI agents, U.S. Attorneys, accountants, and law school grads, all of whom looked as if they had been born in suits. And it was part of a personal policy of McPherson's always to outdress them. McPherson does not remember when he started dressing like a Wall Street millionaire, but neither does he remember a time when he dressed as though he were anything else; it is not unreasonable to assume that, coming from New York, where one of the few crimes of consequence is being out of style, McPherson, like many of his contemporaries, took to it the minute he started paying for his own clothes. Certainly of no little significance, however, is the neighborhood from which he hailed. McPherson had been surrounded by wiseguys from the moment he was able to walk. The neighborhood was acrawl with made members of the Mob—characters who never passed the barbershop without stopping in for a trim, a generation of tough guys who paid more for their shoes than their wives did.

"I didn't know I wasn't Italian until I went to school." Bud McPherson, his hands in his pockets, was pacing back and forth, laying claim to the academic territory that stretched between a blackboard and a dozen WITSEC students in a small classroom at Glynco. He had flown in from Los Angeles the day before, arriving by way of Savannah, but apart from the off-season suntan he sported, there was nothing West Coast about him. The conservative charcoal threads set off a red-and-blue paisley necktie. The collar bar was gold. The eyewear was military standard, full tint, G-15. He looked like a radar officer in the air wing of the Gambino family.

The one-day course McPherson had come to teach represented the academy's entire curriculum in the field of social studies: Wiseguys 101, a basic history of La Cosa Nostra in the United States.

McPherson's tale would open in turn-of-the-century Sicily, progress through the 1920s by way of New York and Chicago, and then move on to postwar Las Vegas before entering the modern era and the realm of McPherson's personal experience with the Mob.

"I went to P.S. 179 in Brooklyn. Two of my classmates," he would declaim, "were 'Crazy Joe' Gallo and Pete 'the Greek.' . . . In the New York City Police Department, I worked in the Sixty-second Precinct, Bath Beach—that's close to Coney Island. It was Funzi Tieri's neighborhood, boss of the Genovese family. Joe Colombo lived there. . . ."

His voice rising and falling, conjuring star-studded "sit-downs" and perpetual "beefs" among executives of "the liquor business," McPherson now and then would step to the blackboard to inscribe there the names of his story's principal characters. And returning periodically, with a sweep of his hand he would run chalk through the name of each player as he went into corporate transition. Colosimo: rubbed out (Johnny Torrio and Al Capone move up in Chicago). . . . Frankie Yale, in Brooklyn: whacked. . . .

Big Jim Colosimo's was the prototype of the gangland funeral— the long cavalcade of limousines; the huge horseshoe-shaped floral pieces spelling out SO LONG, PAL; underworld dignitaries from everywhere paying their flamboyant respects; pallbearers packing heat; everybody crying dramatically. Even Johnny Torrio was crying—the man who had had Big Jim bumped off. It was an ostentatious show of regret that set the standard against which all future burials were to be measured.

"They gave him a terrific send-off."

The Roaring Twenties were rich with stereotypes that make themselves felt today.

When Legs Diamond, working for the illustrious Arnold Rothstein, pulled his enormously ill-advised free-lance job and hijacked a liquor shipment, in 1924, that belonged to Irish bootlegger Big Bill Dwyer, it was Dwyer's partner, a young Italian tough guy by the name of Francesco Castiglia, who went to Rothstein to say, "Hey, Legs didn't do the right thing. We're going to have to go and collect."

In capitalizing on Prohibition, Rothstein, the underworld gambler who had fixed the 1919 World Series, had always been more banker than bootlegger; he was eager to distance himself from the escalating violence. He said, "Do what you have to do."

Following Legs Diamond's removal (Legs survived the attempt on his life, but he got the message), Rothstein assumed the sponsorship of three young New York hoods. One of them was Meyer Lansky, a Russian Jewish immigrant to New York's Lower East Side. It was he who would eventually teach members of organized crime to dress like bankers and businessmen. Another of Rothstein's protégés was the young Salvatore Luciana—"Lucky" Luciano—who, in victimizing his classmates when he was eleven years old on the Lower East Side, launched the protection racket in the United States. He would graduate to narcotics after the Harrison Act. The third was Francesco Castiglia.

Born in Sicily, in 1891, Castiglia, the oldest of three children, arrived in New York at the age of four. His family settled in East Harlem. After elementary school he became the leader of the 104th Street Gang. At twenty-one he was arrested twice, but served no prison time. At the age of twenty-four he went away for a year on a gun charge. Castiglia owed much of his eventual success to a thoroughgoing lack of prejudice; he would form business alliances with anyone, regardless of national origin. At a time when it was unthinkable for Sicilians to marry outside their ethnic circle, Castiglia went so far as to marry outside the faith. He wed a Jewish girl named Loretta and remained married to her for fifty years. His street name made him a natural to serve as liaison to the Irish politicians who controlled Tammany Hall.

McPherson moved to the blackboard. He said, "His street name was Frank Costello."

And when McPherson said it, his voice fell apart. Yes, that crepitant wiseguy whisper, that classic, stereotypical rasp associated in Mob mythology with the early elderly dons, is the legacy of Frank Costello—legendary boss and immediate progenitor of what was to become the Genovese crime family in New York. Costello was to the mobsters who followed him what Chuck Yeager was to postwar fighter pilots.

He was . . . *the voice* of La Cosa Nostra.

As Bud McPherson explained it that day, immigrants in the early years of the century took their medical problems not to the doctor but customarily to the neighborhood midwife or sometimes to the local barber. Tonsillectomies and the removal of inflamed adenoids, routinely performed on children, were primitive surgical procedures conducted with even more primitive instruments—often they were no more sophisticated than the cleanest of the kitchen scissors. And botched operations were common in the neighborhood.

"They wanted their tonsils out, they went down the block. And a lot of them went around for the rest of their lives . . . *talkin' like this.*"

Frank Costello was the archetype.

Wiseguys today who affect the growl in the absence of any pharyngeal damage do so in tribute to him.

As BUD McPherson's recitation was coming to a close, Mike Pizzi's nonstop flight from New York was touching down in Savannah. Pizzi's arrival at Glynco was anticipated there with an enthusiasm no less palpable than it was infectious. His lecture on district operations, delivered to every basic-training class just prior to commencement, was legendary in the Marshals Service.

Respected throughout the Service, even by those who did not know him personally, the Brooklyn chief, a character in every sense of the word, occupied a very small circle in the nationwide chain of command: he was one of the few men under oath for whom affection appeared to be universal.

The mere mention of his name was good for a smile.

"A wild man, a professional Brooklynite," was not an unofficial assessment of him. It was the evaluation of him tendered on the record by the Service's Office of Congressional and Public Affairs.

A tough guy in the eyes of his fellow deputies, Pizzi was that rare member of the Service who had lost none of his street-cop edge in mastering the skills of the effective manager. At the root of his success was an enthusiasm for his work and for everyday life that was almost childlike.

A year before, Pizzi had brought down upon the Marshals Service a shower of political sunshine by having orchestrated, where the FBI had failed, the tracking down and ultimate arrest of Alphonse "Allie Boy" Persico, former underboss of the Colombo organized-crime family in New York. A fugitive on the Bureau's most-wanted list since June 1980, Persico had been at large for over seven years. A task force was formed under Pizzi in May 1987. By November, Persico was in jail.

"Allie Boy was a very likable guy. We didn't go knockin' on his family's door on holidays."

Pizzi's understanding of the protocol, like McPherson's, was acquired at an early age. His grandmother's house in Bensonhurst, the house in which he grew up, looked out on the local wiseguy clubhouse, and Pizzi's nocturnal comings and goings as a teenager were met by his grandmother, who harbored no romantic notions about the Mob, with the following: *"La notte è per il lupo."*

The night, she told him, is for the wolf.

One of Pizzi's childhood friends, one of many who eventually would fall in with the Mob, had as great an influence on Pizzi as did his grandmother's advice about predatory creatures of the night. Pizzi was at marine boot camp at Parris Island when he received "from two sources" photographs of his good pal Freddy—the late Freddy, as it happened. The nineteen-year-old—"very handsome, very tough"— had been strangled and shot, and his body eventually crushed under the wheels of a car.

"It really wakes you up."

Another friend, "another legendary tough guy," named Tony, was knocked off soon thereafter. "My career as a wiseguy," Pizzi would say, "was never to materialize."

Pizzi entered the Marshals Service in 1965 and, like McPherson, brought a young Brooklyn girl along for the ride.

The two men, while at Glynco, were staying at the same hotel. That night, in the hotel bar, they traded stories, a couple of hometown boys going on about the girls they had married, swapping memories of their early days on the streets of the old neighborhood, catching up on the news, updating each other on the latest being carried on the gangland grapevine. . . . "You know who else is dead?" To the residents of Brunswick, Georgia, who staffed the city's largest hotel, these two colorful characters, so clearly from out of town, sounded for all the world like the very troublemakers about whom they were talking. But if Pizzi and McPherson sounded like a couple of wiseguys, it was only to the unpracticed ear. What was audible in their conversation was a singular music: it was not the Frank Costello crisscrossing their speech; it was the treelined avenues of Brooklyn.

Chapter Seven

R ALPH Burnside, thirty-six, was a week and a half into a three-week assignment, 1200 miles from home. He was one of several out-of-town deputies detailed to the 1988 sedition and conspiracy trial of fourteen members of The Order, the enforcement arm of the Aryan Brotherhood, which was being conducted in Fort Smith, Arkansas.

It was just after five p.m., and the defendants were about to be moved, escorted down the rear steps of the Federal Building and loaded into a secure van. The prisoners were to be transported back to the county jail now that court had adjourned for the day. There were points of cover in the compound, but Burnside did not enjoy one of them; holding a position securing the street, he was standing out in the open.

There were six deputies posted on the ground, three vehicles in addition to the van—a lead car and two backup sedans. There were four SOG deputies on the stairway, another six or eight, dressed in tactical gear, holding covert positions on the roof. Armed with a WITSEC shotgun—a cutdown Remington 870—Burnside, wearing a knee-length leather trench coat over a three-piece summer-weight suit, had been standing for fifteen minutes, holding his post, when the sky opened. He could see the squall line as it came rolling in from the direction of the old gallows two blocks north—Isaac Parker's gallows, on the timbers of which seventy-nine men had met their destiny in the twenty-one years that the "hanging judge" had held jurisdiction over Indian Territory—a landmark in old Fort Smith.

Burnside had never seen anything like it anywhere in the country— thunderclouds off the Great Plains, rain hitting the hardpan, prairie rain—and it was on top of him before the prisoners came out of the building. He had known there would be moments like this. And Burnside knew what was required of him.

Burnside did not leave his post. Resolute, redoubtable, rain cascading off the heavy lenses of his eyeglasses, he stood at port arms— "stood there like a fool"—watching the barrel of his shotgun fill with water. The suit was a blue cotton poplin, forty-six regular, maybe $250 retail—DRY CLEAN ONLY it said. Burnside knew it was gone. It was five minutes before the prisoners were brought down, another ten before all were loaded. By then Burnside's pockets were filled with water. The suit was a total loss.

As one of the prisoners was hustled through the downpour he shouted through sheets of rain, "Burnside, what are you, crazy?"

Burnside gave an answer that was more than ample to explain things to every other deputy on the detail.

"No," Burnside replied. "I'm Brooklyn."

OVERWORKED and understaffed and perpetually out of style, the Eastern District of New York is notorious within the Marshals Service. Its deputies handle more trouble before lunch every day than the average district sees in a month. The spiritual heart of the only American city that can claim over 2000 homicides a year—two dozen on a summer weekend, twenty in a single day—Brooklyn is occluded by neighborhoods where the sound of gunfire is almost orchestral.

Magnificent, ineffable, eternal, a source of centuries of civic pride, the borough, awash today in the workaday bloodshed endemic to some of the world's darker pockets of political insurrection, currently enjoys a reputation as the nation's answer to frontier Tombstone, "the town too tough to die."

One good look at the action here—on the streets of Bedford-Stuyvesant, Brownsville, or East New York—would bring the Earps to their knees. Working three years as a deputy in the bad neighborhoods of Brooklyn, New York, is like working maybe fifteen years almost anywhere else in the country.

"We had the Ohio Seven come in here," Victor Oboyski reflects, "the United Freedom Front. They thought they were going to come in and be tough guys. Maybe in Akron, Ohio, yeah, they caused some trouble. But in New York, forget about it. We took them all down, I mean down on the ground. We knocked them down, cuffed them, and dragged them out of the courtroom. And we all went back to work laughing. This is no big deal for us. This is going on all the time. Want to get tough? We'll get tough. We handle tough guys all the time. This is one tough borough. New York's one tough city. Our guys have a battle just commuting to work. If you're going to come to Brooklyn, and you think you're going to be a tough guy, you better bring lunch."

November 10 FELL ON A THURSDAY in 1988, so Friday came a day early to Parker's.

At the waterfront saloon in Brooklyn Heights terrorized weekly by Mike Pizzi and his crew, deputies had gathered to celebrate a birthday. It was seven p.m., the U.S. Marine Corps was 213 years old, and at the instigation of his chief, who was hosting the event, Ralph Burnside was drawing attention.

Standing at the bar, he and Pizzi were comparing tattoos.

And Burnside had his boss beat pants down.

Burnside, a martial-arts instructor before he joined the Service, was a contemplative man given to a deep appreciation of Oriental thought. His reverence for the ways of the East extended to the elaborate ornamentation of his lower torso—on the upper hip flexor on either side of his pelvic girdle was a full-color fine-line tattoo, each measuring four by ten inches and representing six hours of intricate work with a hand-held seven-point pencil.

Like that of many highly trained martial artists, Burnside's body art was an expression of spiritual values—loyalty, strength, and grace—in his case symbolized by a dragon on the right side, a tiger on the left. It was not something he was inclined to exhibit. Had anyone but the chief asked him to do so, his answer would have been no.

Burnside's opinion of Pizzi was not one of those things he disguised.

"He's one of the few people in the Service I would go to the gates of hell with."

The best that Pizzi, for his part, could do was a Kewpie doll surrounded by three hearts, etched into the flesh of his right shoulder, and a U.S. Marine Corps bulldog (inspiration for all the undressing) imprinted on the tricep below it. A pretty lame statement by artistic standards, the layout spoke eloquently to Pizzi's operational style.

"Keep things simple. The more elaborate the plan, the more difficult it is to execute."

MIKE Pizzi is five feet ten, weighs 160 pounds, and his graying hair is as slick as a wet deck on a destroyer. He buys his clothes from Sears, Roebuck & Co., leans toward landscapes when he paints—"my middle name is Angelo"—and he has the best posture in the U.S. Marshals Service. He speaks fluent conversational Italian with the same forty-weight Brooklyn accent in which his punctilious English is immersed.

Pizzi entered the Marshals Service in June 1965 after four years in the U.S. Marine Corps and two years spent driving a truck. He was twenty-three years old at the time. Taking a $3000 pay cut, he was sworn in, given a badge and a gun, and put to work in the Southern District of New York. Pizzi's formal deputy training amounted to two weeks of instruction in prisoner handling and in the use of firearms at the federal penitentiary in Atlanta, Georgia. Pizzi worked three years as a deputy in Manhattan before being transferred to Brooklyn.

"We had no radio equipment, no backup, no vests—we used wits, stealth, and cunning. We had no computers, no access to intelligence; all we had was what we could develop in the street. We worked day and night; we worked fugitives on our own initiative, usually before nine or after five."

Pizzi was assigned to Air Piracy in 1970, and within a year he was the deputy in charge, directing the screening of all departures out of New York, assigning deputies to selected flights. As a supervisor, he also was overseeing twelve WITSEC details and had two men working warrants. Four years later, with the end of the air piracy program and the formalization of WITSEC as a program conducted out of Washington, he was promoted to operations supervisor. He was made acting chief in 1975 and became chief deputy in 1977.

From the start of Pizzi's tenure as chief, all the lies they told about Brooklyn were true.

"We never asked for help or pity, never asked for anybody to give us a break. We never asked judges to reconsider orders. We took everything they threw at us and we did it. What we established in the eyes of the Service was that we were the toughest, strongest people they had on the job, and in Brooklyn only the strong survive."

Not many districts, Gerri Doody observes, would have handed the Leacock warrant to a woman. When she brought him in, she says, "Mike was ecstatic. It was just pandemonium [in the office]. Anywhere else, they'd remember it for years. [But] it's hard to make an impression in Brooklyn." Usually, she points out, "when you have a top fifteen, headquarters sends in a task force. Not in Brooklyn. In Brooklyn *you* are the task force."

Ask Mike Pizzi where he comes by his management and leadership skills and he will give you the three-word answer that embodies every-thing about America he sees as noble.

"The Marine Corps."

In Pizzi's paneled office, on the first floor of Brooklyn's U.S. district court, flanking his government-issue desk are two standing flags: one the Stars and Stripes, the other the Marine Corps banner. On the wall behind the desk hangs a photograph of Lieutenant Colonel Oliver North, autographed, and inscribed "Semper Fi." Interspersed among the special-achievement awards and other honors bestowed on Pizzi by the Marshals Service, and occupying frames adorning the walls of the office, hang, among other things, a photograph of the flag raising on Iwo Jima's Mount Suribachi, snapshots of Pizzi as a teen-ager on military duty overseas, and a large photograph of the legend-ary leatherneck general Lewis "Chesty" Puller.

And on November 10 Pizzi wore a Marine Corps necktie.

"The Marine Corps birthday," in Brooklyn, according to Vic Oboyski, "is bigger than Christmas."

DETAILING the capture of Garnett Leacock, Gerri Doody remarks, "We were ready. The chief trained us. We still have training on Thurs-days. But back when we had more time, we had practical exercises. He'd blow a whistle and we'd have to run, have all our gear ready, like in the army."

Mike Pizzi is an inveterate teacher, which makes him such a natural for the district operations seminar at Glynco.

The Glynco lecture typifies Pizzi's style.

"I heard a rumor," he will tell the students, "that the last time I came to this class, I took the manual and threw it in the garbage pail. I didn't do that. I wouldn't do it. It's too big to fit in the garbage pail. It's now in three volumes. The manual is a guide, okay? There's numerous ways of doing something right. . . . Please don't say [when you get to your district], 'That's not the way it's done at the academy.' When you leave the academy, it's over."

In fact, the Brooklyn chief has abiding respect for what transpires at Glynco, and what he offers students is really only an amplification on various techniques.

During his two-hour lecture he engages the students in street sce-narios he considers typical. In the scenarios Pizzi plays the part of the suspect and chooses a student on each occasion to play the arresting officer. For the first scenario Pizzi always selects the best shooter in the class, arms him with an unloaded revolver, unloads his own, and in the course of the scenario—in which he gives the deputy the advantage; that is, the deputy has the drop on the suspect—quickly succeeds in shooting the deputy's character to death.

"You have to play by the rules," he explains, "and this bastard don't have to play by no rules at all. You're talking, your lips are moving. You can't pull the trigger. You're a decent human being, and you don't have it in you to do what this bastard can do. There are a lot of things a bad guy can do that you can't do [by law]. We do not want to lose any of you. I would rather [see] half the goddamn prisoners in the institutions today [go free] than lose one of you."

The advantage a deputy gives away in any potential confrontation is essentially twofold. A criminal need not observe departmental guidelines governing the use of deadly force; he need not wait to be threatened with a gun before pulling the trigger. Nor does a suspect have to consider bystanders and passersby, innocent civilians who happen to be in the line of fire or in the path of ricocheting lead.

What Mike Pizzi's scenarios reinforce is the inadvisability of working alone.

"The toughest thing in the world is to take a guy alone. Some of us are here only because the guy chose not to do us in."

Having said that, Pizzi will choose a second student from the class, and in a scenario similar to the first he, in character, will deliver an injury to the arresting officer as devastating in its own way as was the earlier lethal gunshot. While the student, having put the freeze on suspect Pizzi, recites instructions over the barrel of a gun—"Hands where I can see them. . . . Do this. . . . Do that."—Pizzi simply walks out the door of the classroom, closing the door behind him.

"Could happen," warns Pizzi, reentering the room to the uproar of laughter. "What's going to stop me. Guy walks away. Now you got a foot chase. You can't shoot the dude."

Vic Oboyski, elaborating on the point that the scenario makes, acknowledges that "you get a lot of that in New York. Guy goes, 'F___ you. I'm not putting my hands up.' What are you going to do, shoot him? 'I'm going. Bye.' And he walks away. You're standing there with your gun and your badge in your hand. What are you going to do with the guy? You have a lot of guys, you point a gun at them, they could care less, because they've had guns pointed at them their whole life. You're going to have to do something. You're going to have to put your gun away, put your badge away. You're going to have to roll your sleeves up and get down with this guy. Because in this city they don't really care."

"Sometimes too much equipment can confuse you," Pizzi tells the students. "You got a radio, you got a gun, and you got a badge, and you got a slapper. And you only got two hands. You think you could put those handcuffs on me? I'm going to tell you now, you ain't going to put them on. What are you going to do with the piece? You got a disadvantage, and I'll tell you why. You got to fight me one-handed. You think you could fight me with one hand? Can you shoot me? No, I'm unarmed. I turn my back, you can't shoot me in the back. There's a lot of things you can't do. Now you got handcuffs in *this* hand. *Now you can't even push me off.*"

Vic Oboyski tells of one New York City arrest he made in which he had pulled a car to the side of the street, jumped out of his own car, identified himself, and ordered the driver to step out. The driver hit the accelerator and tried to run Oboyski and his partner down.

"I shot the guy in the face, in the *head,* and he got out of the car *mad* at me. What am I going to do, shoot him again? He's unarmed. I shot him in the *head* and the only thing I did was piss him off. The guy wanted to tumble."

Pizzi tells of a Special Operations Group training exercise in which his boss, U.S. Marshal Charles Healey, participated. "Healey was a former homicide cop, very tough guy," Pizzi tells the class. "Worked TPF in New York—the Tactical Patrol Force. Worked riots; knows his way around the street. They're doing a felony car stop and they asked him to be a role player, and he decides he's going to play the role of the brother of the guy who's handcuffed on the ground. He walks over. He says, 'Hey, what happened? This is my brother.' The marshal [playing the arresting officer] says, 'Stand back, man. He's under arrest—felony.' [Healey] says, 'What do you mean, arrest, felony? He's my brother. He works in a grocery store.' 'Stand back.' 'What are you telling me, stand back?' Now, they go through this for about five minutes. He got the guy so excited, the marshal *shot* him. Here's an unarmed guy arguing in the street, and this guy *shot* him.

And *then* tried to justify to the rest of them why he shot this guy. 'He didn't listen!' You can't shoot somebody for not *listening.*"

The confusion Charlie Healey employed on the untrained marshal, the same confusion Pizzi utilizes in the street scenarios, serves the experienced felon well. The volatility of an arrest and the exploitability of confusion are why deputies do not work single-handed.

"We never work alone," Southern District warrants supervisor Frank Devlin insists. "We do not conduct interviews alone and we never arrest with two people. We always go out with at least three or four. We do our homework. We try to pick the location, the time. We want to *control* the situation."

As SOG commander John Haynes explains tactical response: "A show of force is a tactic itself."

Vic Oboyski, after fifteen years on the job, attended enforcement school at Glynco, a course in advanced training for journeyman deputies. Veteran instructor Bob Natzke one day was conducting a practical exercise.

"He goes like this," Oboyski recalls. "He says, 'Hit the door. And hit it the way you would do it on a regular hit.' I said, 'You really want us to do that?' 'Yeah.' 'Okay.' . . . *Boom! Boom! Boom!* 'Open the f___ing door!' Natzke busted out laughing. He says, 'No, no, no. You know what I mean.' I said, 'That's what I do.' I know the bad guy's in there? . . . 'Open the door or we'll kick it in, you son of a bitch!' That's the psychological factor. I want the bad guy to think that the biggest monster he can imagine is coming through that door. That's what I want him to think. You know [and here Oboyski assumes a falsetto], 'Excuse me, federal agents.' I don't want him to think, you know, like, some five-foot-one IRS agent's coming in. I want him to think that King Kong is coming through that door and is going to eat his gun and eat him and his kids and just leave an empty apartment."

In gauging Mike Pizzi's popularity throughout the U.S. Marshals Service, one cannot overlook the singular impact upon his superiors and fellow deputies of Pizzi's proven ability to annoy the FBI.

"I'd like to say we're all in this battle to fight crime and/or evil and the Red peril together," Duke Smith concedes. "But you know that's not the real world."

To understand FBI agents, think of them not as policemen, but as lawyers and certified public accountants with gun permits. Trained to conduct fraud investigations, unsurpassed in their ability to follow paper trails, they are acknowledged experts at gathering evidence in a variety of white-collar crimes. In the early years of the cold war they managed to distinguish themselves in the field of counterespionage. But much of the work for which the Bureau has always sought statutory authority is what might be considered traditional police work, and for that its employees are poorly trained. In truth, the only time FBI agents have ever made history as street cops is from ambush.

In its pursuit of bank robbers during the Great Depression, the FBI's principal success was in the field of public relations. The agency's gunning down of John Dillinger in July of 1934 helped establish a preeminence in the media that the Bureau has never relinquished. The Bureau's ascendancy in Washington can be attributed to J. Edgar Hoover's understanding of both the sophisticated and elemental uses of power—he held his job for forty-eight years—and to his preternatural gift for the manipulation of publicity.

As Marshals Service director Stanley Morris points out, "When the FBI made an arrest, they got the credit, of course; but when we did, the story credited 'federal agents.' "

Effective application of the principles of self-promotion was not developed by the Marshals Service until a little more than a decade ago. And its public relations triumphs, as they mounted, cast its sister agency in an unflattering shadow.

International Branch chief Larry Homenick, touting the speed and efficiency with which the Marshals Service hauls in fugitives, points to a paralysis in the FBI, a symptomatic impairment of initiative induced by a complex chain of command. Special agents, in order to operate at all, first have to navigate their own bureaucracy, he says. While a deputy marshal on his own might close a case in a matter of days, his mechanism for doing so, Homenick suggests, is incompatible with procedure as observed by agents of the Bureau. "We're hungry. In the Marshals Service you got to do it on your own. On a fugitive case, we send two guys. They spend millions. They'd spend a week giving it a code name," he says.

The Bureau, notorious for its disdainful treatment of state and local police, is no less self-aggrandizing in its official dealings with the investigators of other federal agencies.

"The cooperation is all one way," one of those investigators reveals. "They show up with a notepad at your office. They share no information. They don't aid law enforcement; they hinder law enforcement."

WHEN J. Edgar Hoover in the late 1960s turned down President Lyndon Johnson's offer of a share of the federal dope mandate, he was acting counter to established tradition, but he was not acting out of character. Nothing, Hoover knew, was a greater threat to the rank and file than narcotics.

"He didn't want his apple-cheeked agents in their Brooks Brothers suits getting dirty," explains a deputy marshal.

However, with the entrenchment of dope on the criminal scene and its feeding on the lion's share of the nation's law-enforcement budget—and with drug enforcement sucking up all the nation's headlines—the FBI has finally cut itself in.

"And they're not prepared," the deputy points out. "They can make mass conspiracy cases, but they can't do it like the DEA does. The DEA gets down in the street and rolls around in the gutter with these guys. That's the only way you're gonna fight narcotics. You're not gonna fight narcotics with wiretaps and putting a guy under surveillance for five years like the Bureau does. You have to get out there in the street."

And, he adds, not irrelevantly, the DEA delivers the drugs.

"The Bureau comes up with these multi-multi-conspiracy indictments, and they come up with one kilo of heroin. You have all these guys on trial. Where's the drugs? There's no drugs."

Nor, in 1979, were there any fugitives. When President Jimmy Carter, that year, assigned responsibility for their capture to the Marshals Service, it was in part because the FBI for half a century had neglected to deliver on the mandate. Once the Marshals Service started generating headlines for succeeding where the FBI had failed, it was only a matter of time before the Bureau filed an official grievance.

The complaints, quite audible by the end of 1987, were to escalate rather rapidly to a full-scale Justice Department turf war. The actual outbreak of hostilities in the official territorial battle between the nation's largest law-enforcement agency and its oldest—eventually resolved with compromises on both sides—came one morning that

November when newspapers arrived at the FBI field office in New York with Mike Pizzi's picture all over them.

The FBI had not been ecstatic over Christopher Boyce. Edwin P. Wilson very clearly had been a humiliation. And now, finally, there was this.

As Duke Smith, in characteristically deadpan fashion, points out, "Persico didn't please them."

Chapter Eight

VICTOR Oboyski's approach to police work is probably best illustrated by a story Southern District chief Flip Lorenzoni tells about their days together as deputies in Manhattan. Lorenzoni and Oboyski were transporting two federal prisoners from New York to Pennsylvania. One, convicted of armed bank robbery, was to be driven to the maximum-security penitentiary at Lewisburg; the other, convicted of bribery, was to be dropped at the minimum-security Allenwood facility.

The two felons hooked to each other in the rear of the sedan—in leg irons, waist chains, and handcuffs—were also locked for much of the journey in aimless conversation. But it was not until the car arrived at Allenwood that the bank robber was suddenly put wise to the fact that his fellow prisoner was a justice of the New York State Supreme Court.

Stepping out at Allenwood, the irrepressible Oboyski, opening the rear door of the sedan, slapped the palm of his hand twice on the roof of the car, and ceremoniously barked, "All rise!"

As Lorenzoni saw it, the move was classic Oboyski. "He loves his work," Lorenzoni insists. "He's *always* in a good mood."

"As a cop," Oboyski will readily tell you, "you take yourself too seriously and you got a problem."

VICTOR Oboyski, a native of Ozone Park, Queens, entered the Marshals Service under the Veterans Readjustment Act, in 1971, after one year of college and three years' experience as a military policeman with the U.S. Army in Germany. A deputy by day, Oboyski attended school at night, receiving his bachelor's and master's degrees—in police science and public administration, respectively—at New York's John Jay College. While his physical attributes bespeak the stereotypical, old-school deputy marshal, the fair-haired, 235-pound Oboyski is modern law enforcement personified, clearly a Renaissance door kicker.

After a stint working Air Piracy out of Brooklyn, Oboyski was assigned to New York's Southern District. He put in ten years there before recrossing the East River to answer to Pizzi. At district awards ceremonies in 1988, when he received his twenty-year pin (the Marshals Service credited Oboyski with three years for his military experience), his fellow deputies fondly presented him with an occupational aid—an army-surplus M72 rocket launcher, a 66-mm light antitank weapon—in observance of his advancing years and his abiding affection for forced entry.

"NO MATTER *what* he does," says his former partner, Frank Devlin, "Vic makes people laugh."

Exiting that day at Allenwood, the first person to laugh was the judge.

The bank robber, however, did not find it funny.

"That dude a *judge?*" the bank robber asked.

Oboyski said that he was.

Indignant, the holdup man said, "Next I'll be ridin' with Richard Nixon."

"Well, him," Oboyski said, "I think you'll recognize."

"Man, you people be lockin' up *everybody.*"

Oboyski could not argue with that.

Little did Oboyski realize at the time that one of the people he would be locking up in the course of his career was the most-wanted organized-crime figure in America.

A WARRANT for the arrest of Alphonse Carmine Persico, underboss of the Colombo crime family in New York, who had been convicted on three counts of extortion, was issued on June 23, 1980, three days after his failure to appear for a presentencing hearing in Brooklyn's U.S. district court. "Allie Boy," whose criminal record dated back to 1949—assault, fraud, firearms violations, possession of stolen property, loan-sharking—and who had previously served seventeen years of a twenty-year sentence on a second-degree murder conviction, was facing, on each of the three counts, twenty years in prison and a fine of $10,000 when he defaulted on his $250,000 bond and vanished.

For the more than seven years that he was at large, Persico was the technical responsibility of New York's Eastern District, where the arrest warrant had been issued, and in that time more than one task force answering to headquarters had been unsuccessful in locating him. Persico was not the typical fugitive. He had access to the protection and to the unlimited resources of the Colombo family, only a few of whose members had knowledge of his whereabouts; he could be assumed to have the help of organized-crime figures in whatever region he had relocated; and he did not follow any obvious wiseguy pattern: he did not run off to Florida, for example, only to show up at Hialeah at the hundred-dollar window, flashing money. Persico went underground and stayed there.

Over the years, thousands of investigative leads were developed, but nothing of substance materialized. In May 1987 a new task force was formed out of New York. Mike Pizzi, who had grown up in Bensonhurst in the shadow of the Colombo family clubhouse at Seventy-sixth Street and Thirteenth Avenue, assigned the case to himself.

"The case was ours because it was failure to appear postconviction," Pizzi explains. "The FBI would have retained it had it been preconviction."

The FBI, putting Persico on its 10 Most Wanted list, claimed jurisdiction on the grounds that the warrant grew out of an organized-crime case.

"When he failed to appear that day," says Pizzi, "I sent [Inspector] Bob Leschorn out to look for him. From that point, it was Leschorn's case."

For three years Bob Leschorn worked the case, reporting to Pizzi. With the establishment of the 15 Most Wanted list in 1983 and Persico's appearance thereon, and with weekly progress reports thus required by Washington, Leschorn found himself answerable not only to Pizzi but to headquarters as well, to the chief of the Enforcement Division directly. An untenable command structure, from Mike Pizzi's point of view, it was made impossible by Leschorn's promotion and transfer to headquarters in 1984. At that point Pizzi prevailed upon Washington to let Leschorn take the case with him. For the next three years the investigation was run by Washington. In early 1987, with little to show for its efforts, headquarters invited Pizzi back in.

"I said, 'I'll take it, but under one condition. No interference. And I'm telling you now, I'm going to run it my way. And I'm going to assign it to me.' "

Pizzi, over the next several months, was answerable, by agreement, to only one man in Washington—Chad Allan, the new deputy chief of the Enforcement Division. Allan gave Pizzi room to operate.

"Whatever I asked for, I got. People, funding, no interference—we asked, we got it. And he never asked me for anything."

Washington did ask for *one* thing.

"When they gave me the case back, they also asked me to sit down with the FBI. One more time. So we sat around a table and we divided tasks. Same results. We gave them everything, they gave us nothing."

The information upon which Pizzi proceeded was that developed over the years by Leschorn.

"It started out as an enormous task."

Going over all the case files, Pizzi's investigative team discovered its greatest problem to be not a lack of leads, but an overabundance of them. There was information putting Persico in Europe, in Florida, and in Mexico; he was reported sighted in Japan and Brazil on the same day. The truth was that no reliable witness had seen him since the day before he was to have appeared for presentencing in 1980.

"There was not one positive sighting on the guy from anybody."

Speculation that Persico was dead, however, was nothing more than that and ultimately could not be accepted. Of the thousands of leads Pizzi inherited, the more encouraging led to Connecticut.

"Connecticut came from intelligence sources on the street—stoolies, tips—from locking up organized-crime guys, and from talking to NYPD. The rumble was that he was in Connecticut."

The Colombo family's connection to Connecticut was impossible to dismiss in light of a discovery that many of its members, when arrested, had been in possession of Connecticut driver's licenses. That Allie Boy might actually be there was reinforced by intelligence gathered by District of Connecticut deputies Art Roderick and Don Donovan. In their search for another high-profile Mob fugitive, Salvatore Caruana, they had begun to uncover what appeared to be a kind of underground railroad for racketeers centered around Hartford.

"The rumble was that the Patriarca crew, who Caruana's hooked up with, was hiding these guys," Victor Oboyski recalls. "They had a system just like the government has safe houses. They would do the same thing. You go up there, you sign in. . . ." New England Mob operations were overseen by the Patriarca crime family in Providence, Rhode Island, and if Persico was in Connecticut, he was no doubt there with their knowledge.

"There were too many times that we heard Connecticut for it not to be pursued," Mike Pizzi explains. "We decided to resolve the Connecticut issue once and for all. We went into Connecticut and said we're not *leaving* Connecticut until we can say he's *not* there."

Before dispatching deputies to Hartford, however, Pizzi developed a rigorous investigative protocol.

"We conducted no interviews, *not one,* in the Persico case," he says.

With the exception of that—in fact, one interview was conducted, but not until the weekend of Persico's arrest—the investigation represented classic police work, a marriage of old-fashioned shoe leather and contemporary electronic software.

Pizzi proceeded upon the assumption that Persico, if he was in Connecticut, had obtained a driver's license there; Pizzi was looking for a man who had received his first license at the age of fifty or thereabouts, and who had done so after 1980. He was also looking for a man who had no credit history up to that point. And no telephone listed in his name before then.

Assuming Persico would choose a date of birth that was easy to remember, Pizzi took Persico's birthdate, December 6, 1929, opened it up one day in either direction, did the same with the month and year, and targeted his search on people whose birthdays fell within those parameters. Allowing for two inches on either side of Persico's height, he sought a man between five ten and six two.

"We were looking for somebody with no background."

Somebody whose first name began with the letter A.

Pizzi, no stranger to the fugitive's life history, knew that the word Al was tattooed on Persico's fist. The tattoo would limit the mobster's choices when it came to assuming an alias.

"I thought that somebody with Al tattooed on his hand would at least have his first name begin with the letter A. I didn't want to limit it to the name Al, because I thought it would narrow down our investigation. So we expanded the investigation to cover having the first name begin with the letter A."

Pizzi also searched for people whose last names, like the ethnocentric Persico's, ended in a vowel.

"Old habits die hard. Usually somebody would use a name he was comfortable with. Or at least somewhat comfortable with. So we thought he would use the letter A for his first name, and at a minimum his last name would end in a vowel."

Establishing these parameters and taking bits of information gathered from sources over the years, Pizzi assembled a task force. As field supervisor, he assigned Victor Oboyski.

IT WAS on the Department of Motor Vehicles (DMV) computer in Hartford that Oboyski and the task force began their investigation, and as the information came back, Mike Pizzi was immediately confounded.

"Who in the world would have thought that thousands and thousands of people would have gotten their licenses after they were fifty years old."

Persico, if he was in Connecticut, was not the only one, Pizzi discovered, to have moved there postretirement. Of those drivers licensed in the state who had received their permits after 1980, more than 7000 fell within a ten-year age span of the fugitive.

Motor vehicle records represented only a fraction of the data base.

"Studying all the intelligence over the years," Vic Oboyski says, "we believed he had had a heart attack. We believed he'd been in a boating accident, that he'd been in a car accident, that he had been burned. We knew that he was an alcoholic. And that he drank Scotch—Cutty Sark, we believed. All this information had been gathered through street people. And a lot of things on his profile were true."

In fact, only that Persico had been burned was untrue. (That and the fact that the quart of Scotch he drank every day was Cutty Sark. It happened to be Dewar's.) While the DMV records were being collected, Mike Pizzi put deputies to work simultaneously assembling others.

"We got guys checking ambulance runs. We also had guys checking with the coast guard. And we're looking for a common denominator.

The computer wasn't doing the work for us. It was legwork. It was guys actually going through all of the accident reports, all of the ambulance runs, guys going through all the coast guard accident reports—*boxes* and *boxes* of files."

Connecticut deputy Art Roderick estimates that the task force sifted through 175,000 records.

Pizzi instructed his deputies to proceed upon the assumption that nobody could be trusted.

"You don't want anybody to know who you're zeroing in on. You want one record, you ask for ten. You find what you're looking for, you go right past the name. Discipline, that was the key. Whenever we got a lead or a fact, we had to sit on it. We had to stop, refrain from asking the question which could take us over the top, or at least save us lots of time. If we asked the wrong person, he was gone."

Not only would it turn out that Persico had been receiving assistance from a crime family other than his own, it would later be discovered that a former official of the Connecticut DMV had been a part of the conspiracy. The underground railroad that Pizzi's investigation ultimately exposed, the network that the official was alleged to be a part of, had been operated by the Patriarca Mob for close to a decade and had been used to shield high-ranking members of at least three organized-crime families.

It was Mike Pizzi's belief that in the past the investigation had suffered because too many leads had been abandoned, often in favor of others that appeared to be more promising.

"Every time they got a lead, they ran out on it. But that was not the way we were going to run this case. We were going to do this slow and methodical and leave nothing behind us. When we said 'clear,' it was clear. If we had jumped on a lead, we would have left the state of Connecticut more than once. But we moved like a plodding Roman army. We weren't going anyplace until everything behind us was destroyed and devastated."

The task force, assuming that Persico had had a heart attack, obtained records of over 10,000 ambulance runs alone. Sifting through these and through vehicle and boating accident reports, they also compiled lists of dry cleaners, barbers, opticians, and subscribers to New York newspapers.

"Later we learned that we were right on target," Pizzi notes. "He had suffered a heart attack and was taken to one of the area hospitals. Once we had gotten to the hospitals, we were going to look for someone who didn't have hospitalization [insurance]. I mean this thing was going to go on ad infinitum."

PIZZI's list of 7000 licensed drivers included 700 whose first names began with the letter A and whose last names ended in a vowel. Credit checks on each of them reduced the list to 150 people.

Twenty-six of them actually shared Persico's exact date of birth.

One of them was named Anthony Perri.

Anthony Perri had been issued a permit to operate a motor vehicle in August 1982. His application for the permit showed that he had been born in Middletown, Connecticut, and that he had attended Hartford High School. Payment to the DMV for the permit had been made in cash.

"We started checking."

The task force, disguising its target, sent a deputy into the high school with four names in addition to Perri's. While one deputy handled that, the others continued feeding data into the computers.

Hartford High School showed no record of Perri's attendance. The state Bureau of Vital Statistics had no record of his birth in Middletown or, for that matter, anywhere in Connecticut.

Pizzi was not about to abandon any other investigative leads, but the street cop in him was nobody's fool.

"It was our first live son-of-a-bitchin' clue."

It was now September, and with the hit on Perri, the Persico task force set up a command post in a Hartford hotel. Of the six deputies under Oboyski, three had fewer than two years on the job; one, Janet Doyle, out of eastern Pennsylvania, was right out of the academy. The task force had been formed over a period of months, reaching full strength, Oboyski explains, just in time for the move to Hartford.

"We got the whole complement of people at the exact time that we hit on Perri. We had brought them in to do record searches. Now I had them doing investigating."

Each deputy took a room at the hotel. They rented cars, ran in their own telephone lines, put their own locks on the doors, set up a typewriter and a fax machine, and went to work.

To his application for a road test Anthony Perri had affixed a signature. Upon cursory examination, the signature displayed similarities to that of Alphonse Persico. Had the document offered up nothing more, Pizzi would have been encouraged. But on the application Perri had also deposited a latent fingerprint. That was another matter altogether. Yet as Mike Pizzi would later explain, "You can't just go with some dust on a piece of paper that's seven years old and expect to get a print. It has to be done with special chemicals. People who are experts can do it. So we took it to a friend in the NYPD and let him put some chemicals on it, without telling him who it was for or what it was about. He did it for us."

Pizzi responds to the obvious rhetorical question in the affirmative. "Yes," he soberly agrees, "ordinarily you would go to the FBI."

Pizzi matched Perri's print to that of Persico's left index finger.

"There had never been a confirmed sighting of him," Vic Oboyski points out. "Up to that point everybody was telling us he was dead. They were laughing at us."

Pizzi called Chad Allan in Washington. "Chad," Pizzi said, "he's alive."

Perri had taken his road test in a car registered to a man named Albert Longo. The task force pulled the records. Longo's signature also bore similarities to that of Alphonse Persico. A background investigation of Longo produced a profile similar to Perri's.

"Longo was a backup," Oboyski explains. "Longo was also Persico." (In fact, Perri was the backup. Longo was the name under which Persico was living.)

Running title searches of all cars registered to Perri and Longo, deputies discovered that all had passed through wiseguy hands before and after Persico owned them.

"Some wiseguy's girlfriend would ultimately end up with the car. Artie Roderick would recognize the names. Artie was our biggest asset. He knew all the local wiseguys in Middletown, Connecticut."

Deputies charted all the addresses used by Perri and Longo both to obtain driver's licenses and to register their cars. Using yellow pins to signify Longo, green pins to signify Perri, they transferred the charts to a map. The pins formed a distinct cluster in the Hartford-Bloomfield area. The address most recently used was in suburban Bloomfield. It had been used by Persico as Albert Longo. In 1985.

After that the task force lost him.

MEETINGS WERE held every night.

"We'd discuss everything in committee," Oboyski says. "Each team would explain to the other what it had done that day. I took notes. I would take input from everybody. We would reach a consensus on our next move. The chief and Dave [O'Flaherty] were getting subpoenas and everything else we needed and faxing them to Connecticut. We had no direct contact with headquarters."

Not only was the task force insulated by the district against interference from Washington, it was also sheltered by its own precautionary measures from the scrutiny of greater Hartford.

"We ate breakfast, lunch, and dinner together," Oboyski says. "We would drink together in the evening. We did not mention his name in the state of Connecticut until we got him. We never mentioned the word Persico. We were all talking code; he was 'our guy' or 'that other guy.' We were all talking like gangsters."

Deputies would later discover that one of the hotel bartenders had once moved Persico's furniture. Quite innocently, as it turned out. But it was one of those coincidences that would infuse memories of the investigation with a gratifying measure of intrigue.

Oboyski, driving to Connecticut every Monday, was driving home every Saturday afternoon. As Thanksgiving approached, he and the task force began to grow desperate.

"We were under the impression that we were going to be severely cut after Thanksgiving, and we said, 'We have to get this guy before then.' Also, we were worried about the agreement with the Bureau. There were negotiations going on at the time."

Oboyski's fears proved to be well founded. Under the agreement reached the following year with the FBI, the Marshals Service would be forced to yield the investigative prerogative in cases of organized crime. Under the new agreement Persico would have been off limits.

On Monday, November 2, Oboyski arrived in Hartford only to tell his troops, "We gotta dig in. We're only one or two pieces of information away from this guy."

"Yeah, Vic, like his address."

On Saturday, November 7, 1987, the task force conducted its first interview.

"Up until that point," Oboyski maintains, "we had not shown Allie Boy's photo anywhere. Or the photos of the bust."

THE BUST TO WHICH OBOYSKI refers is the plaster bust for which the investigation would ultimately become famous—a forensic sculpture that had been commissioned by Pizzi, a rendering of what Persico might look like seven years after his disappearance. A stunningly accurate likeness of what proved to be a rapidly aging Persico, the work of art, in the wake of the investigation, received an enviable share of press attention.

However, when he is asked to estimate the bust's ultimate impact on the investigation, Victor Oboyski, upon due reflection, readily concedes the inevitable. "The bust was meaningless," he replied.

BY RUNNING a background check on the Bloomfield house, Persico's last known address, Oboyski established that its owner over the period Persico was in residence (the house had since been sold) was by occupation a salesman. The man sold pinball machines and was currently in Las Vegas. Call Victor Oboyski prejudiced: he wrote off the former owner of the house as a source of information.

On Saturday, November 7, Oboyski took a chance on a neighborhood dentist.

"We didn't tell the dentist who we were looking for. We walked in. We said, 'We're federal agents. We're interested in the people who live across the street.' "

Oboyski, of course, was not interested at all in the people who lived across the street. Once he received an answer, he asked, "Who lived there before that?"

The dentist, unable to provide information on previous occupants of the house, directed Oboyski to neighbors who, he said, could. After running a quick check on them, Oboyski approached the neighbors in question.

"I'm there with the little redhead, Janet."

Oboyski and "the little redhead," Deputy U.S. Marshal Janet Doyle, made it only as far as the neighbors' front door.

"I interviewed the husband. He doesn't know much. He starts telling me, 'Well, I really don't know. Let me ask my wife.' He wouldn't let me talk to his wife. He relayed the questions. He leaves; he comes back. This goes on three or four times. I said, 'Well, thank you very much.' I wanted to get into the house, but I could see that the old man was very hesitant. And I don't blame him. So I leave."

Oboyski left somewhat confused. The information he left with, while rather limited, was at the same time distressingly specific. The man who two years before had occupied the house in question had lived there with a woman, Oboyski had been told. A daughter would come and visit. Alphonse Persico had a daughter, but his wife's whereabouts had always been known. Oboyski was not encouraged by what he had learned, but Vic Oboyski was not done yet, either.

He and Janet Doyle went for a cup of coffee.

"I've found," Oboyski says, "in investigations, when I meet you for the first time, you're a little hesitant. We're establishing a relationship, back and forth. You're feeling me out. A half hour later if I come and see you and say, 'Oh, by the way . . .' we've already established something. You've seen me once. I'm not a stranger. You trust me now. A half hour later, believe it or not, you'll give me more information. . . . It works."

It was not the luck of the draw that put Janet Doyle at the scene of the interview in the company of the strapping Oboyski.

"I'm a threatening guy. That's why, right away, I want to sit down. I'm a big guy; I look intimidating. So in order to get somebody to talk to me, I have to sit down, lean back, and joke and laugh and get over the intimidation end of it and get them talking to me. It's good to have a female deputy if you're interviewing a female. I'll ask the question, and the female will answer the female—won't even answer me. I'll ask the questions, and she'll look right at the female marshal and answer her, like I'm not there. There's that bonding or whatever you want to call it that takes place between the two of them."

The two deputies finished their coffee. Now it was time to go back.

"Sir, look, I'm very sorry to have to bother you again, but it's *very* important that I talk to your wife. All I want to do is show her some photos. Would that be all right?"

He said his wife would come to the door.

"I open the album up," Oboyski says.

The wife identified Alphonse Persico. "That," she said, "looks similar to him."

She was pointing to one of the early photos. Oboyski, assuming that in 1985 Persico would have had some more age on him, had expected her to identify, if anything, the photo of the bust.

"Where do you think he was from?"

"I believe he came from New York."

And then she gave Oboyski the information that completely ruined his weekend.

"He was with a British gal." An attractive blond woman with a British accent.

That really threw Oboyski. Persico's wife, Oboyski was well aware, was a blonde. But now he had a blonde whose English was inflected. He asked how old the man's daughter was. A young girl, he was told. And that threw him even more. Persico's daughter was in her mid-thirties.

"Did she live with them?"

"No, she would just come and visit."

And that was it.

"I was kind of down, I'll tell you right now. I wasn't sure it was him. But even if it was, I didn't have a hell of a lot more to go on."

Oboyski had *nothing* to go on. Deputies, having scoured the local post office files, had already come up empty. Neither Longo nor Perri had received mail at the house, let alone left a forwarding address.

"I sent everyone out again."

Oboyski instructed his fellow deputies to search the post office records for the names of any and all people who had received mail at the address during the time Persico lived there.

And then it happened.

"We came up with two names."

Both of the names belonged to women. One of them had given as a change of address a box number at the same post office, then canceled it. The address she had given when she subscribed to the post office box was fictitious.

On Monday, November 9, the task force started looking for the women.

"Teddy [Brooklyn deputy Ted Gloo] comes up with a phone number. In Hartford. Roderick comes up with the DMV information on both women. Sure enough, they're a mother and daughter."

The records search showed that the addresses given by the daughter for her driver's license, her automobile registration, and her telephone were all the same. The mother herself—tall, trim, forty-two years old—had not been so straightforward.

"The mother has everything scattered—the car, one place; the driver's license, another; the phone, still another. What do we go for? The phone. It has to be the most current."

The telephone was billed to a ground-floor garden apartment in a red brick building at Five Highland Street, West Hartford.

"I gave Artie and his partner the album and sent them out. Joey and his partner [Brooklyn deputy Joey Orlando and District of Idaho deputy David Meyer] had to go get a tire changed. Teddy Gloo had to head back to Brooklyn. So I was left there with Janet. We were by the phone. I was in touch with Mike."

Mike Pizzi had made the decision to keep headquarters twenty-four hours behind. He had asked Chad Allan merely to be within reach within a reasonable amount of time. But on Friday, the sixth, after the task force had made the decision to show the photo spread for the first time, Pizzi called Allan in Washington and said, "I want to know where you're going to be twenty-four hours a day, starting now."

"Before everyone went out," Oboyski recalls, "Artie turned to me and said, 'I got a good feeling about this.' I said, 'So do I. I like this.' "

Art Roderick, at Five Highland Street, interviewed the building's superintendent. Roderick asked her who lived in the apartment.

"Well, there was a woman living there," she said, "but she's gone."

The woman, the superintendent acknowledged, spoke with a British accent.

Roderick asked, "Who's living there now?"

"Just the guy's living there now."

"Who?"

"Al."

Roderick showed her the photo spread.

"That's Al," she said.

Roderick called Oboyski at the command post. "I think we got him," he said.

"What have you got?"

"The name Al. The blonde."

"Sit tight."

Oboyski called Pizzi in New York.

"Chief, I think we got him."

"What are you going to do?"

"We're going to go out and arrest him."

"What about surveillance?"

"Screw surveillance. I'm tired of surveillance. I'm tired of mincing around. We're going to go out and collar this guy."

"Call me immediately."

Oboyski's plan was to try a scam telephone call to make sure the man identified as Al was at home.

"I'm not going to knock the door down," he would later explain, "because if he's not there, then we blew it. That's why I didn't want Artie to make a move. Slow. We had been so slow and methodical up to that point, we had to hold back."

Mike Pizzi says he knew better than to try to make tactical decisions from New York. It was Oboyski's call from that point forward.

"Years and years and years of searching for this guy," Oboyski says, "and now, here we go."

But Oboyski did not want to make his move without his other team.

"Now I sit there, and I'm waiting for the other two guys to show up. I'm trying to get them on the air. I can't get them on the air. I call up the Texaco station they're at. They're not there. I'm pacing back and forth in the room now. I got Persico sitting in the apartment. I want the other team. I don't want to go there without the other team."

When Orlando and Meyer showed up, Oboyski split up the teams. He put Orlando with Janet Doyle, took David Meyer in his car, and told Roderick over the radio to meet him behind the apartment complex. He did not want to risk being seen rolling up in front of the building. He had Orlando park on the street and sit there with his arm around Doyle; acting as an innocent couple, the two deputies watched the apartment window. He had Roderick take him to the superintendent.

"Look again," he said, and opened up the photo spread.

"That's Al," she said again.

He asked her if she thought he would be home. She said that he should be.

"The super had no idea who he was," Oboyski says. "All she knew was she had a whole bunch of deputy marshals there who were coming out of their skin. We were trying to act as calm as possible. But this is November ninth. This thing's going to end Thanksgiving. We were coming to the end of the road, as far as I was concerned."

Oboyski discovered that workmen had been in the apartment the previous week to repair the bathroom ceiling. He instructed the superintendent to call the apartment and get the man she knew as Al on the phone and ask him if it was okay if the workmen returned to do some touch-up. He sent Roderick and Meyer downstairs to stand outside the apartment door with their radios turned low.

The superintendent made the call.

Alphonse Persico answered the phone.

"When I heard that Brooklyn accent," Victor Oboyski says in his own, "I knew it was him."

"Yeah, no problem" came the reply to the superintendent's request. "It's okay. Don't worry about it."

"Right away I get Artie. I give him the word. Joey, outside, picks it up on the radio. They get out of the car. We're all going in together. And we want to get in quick."

At five p.m., with a passkey provided by the superintendent, the task force, guns drawn, entered the Highland Street apartment.

"I put the key in the door, turn it. *Boom.* I give it a knock; the door swings open. He's standing in the kitchen."

Alphonse Persico, underweight and old beyond his years, a victim of heart disease and cirrhosis of the liver, wearing a T-shirt and house slippers, his trousers unbuttoned, $1000 in his pocket, was standing over the stove with a wooden spoon in his hand, stirring a marinara sauce he had prepared that day and was about to serve himself for dinner. The table was set for one.

"Hey, Al. How ya doin'?"

"Who are you?"

"We're with the U.S. marshals, Al. You're under arrest."

"Okay, anything you say. Just tell me what you want me to do. No problem," he said.

Oboyski told him to put down the spoon.

Persico put down the spoon. They cuffed the mobster, frisked him, walked him, and sat him down in a chair.

"Joey, read him his rights."

Persico was alone in the apartment. One team had quickly swept through, careful not to disturb any fingerprint evidence that might be used in a prosecution for harboring; the racketeer, on the run for over seven years, had not managed to remain free on his own. In the pocket of a jacket hanging near the door deputies found an additional $6000.

"The woman was gone," Oboyski explains. "He beat her up. There was broken furniture in the apartment. She was gone. He was living alone."

Using a handkerchief, Oboyski picked up the telephone. He dialed New York and said, "Give me the chief."

When the phone in Mike Pizzi's office rang, Pizzi was standing about four feet away. Dave O'Flaherty had been trying to get him a helicopter. Pizzi had tried but had been unable to sit. He was having trouble controlling himself. O'Flaherty handed Pizzi the receiver. Pizzi took it and immediately spoke.

"Tell me something good."

And Oboyski spoke the words his chief had been waiting over seven years to hear.

"We just put the irons on him," Oboyski reported. "Alphonse Carmine Persico is in custody."

Oboyski, in Connecticut, could hear the pandemonium in the office as the news was passed around.

Pizzi says, "I wanted to take my gun out and fire a shot into the ceiling."

Chapter Nine

"ARE you sure?" Chad Allan said.

"Do you have a bottle of whiskey?"

"Yeah."

"Well, start drinking it, 'cause he's in," Michael Pizzi said.

He was Alphonse Persico, and he was seated, cuffed, in the back of Victor Oboyski's rental car, on his way to the lockup in Hartford.

Oboyski was engaging the killer in casual conversation.

"Allie, did you ever think we'd get you?"

"I figured you'd get me someday," Persico replied politely. "I figured somebody would have to drop a dime."

Oboyski, somewhat frightfully, spun around in the front passenger seat and fixed the gangster with a glare.

"If you knew what we went through to get you, you wouldn't believe it!" Oboyski said. "I wish somebody *had* dropped a dime, because I'm sick of Connecticut. Probably the only good food in the whole state is in your kitchen right now."

"The sauce is still there," Persico told him. "You want to go back, you can help yourself."

Persico had calmed down quickly in the aftermath of his arrest. His body language almost immediately had begun to feature a special vocabulary. Deputies knew it well. Having spent seventeen years on the inside, Persico had become, in Mike Pizzi's estimation, firmly and quite understandably institutionalized.

"These are not people who give you trouble. These are not people who smart-talk you. This was a fairly likable guy. He was *always* a gentleman. Very polite. The Persicos, from our perspective, were always likable people, always joking, always pleasant. I don't know how they would be from the other side—you're a storekeeper and you're being made to pay them off—but always in a pleasant frame of mind, always pleasant speaking."

On the afternoon of Persico's arrest the Service's enforcement chief, Louis McKinney, telephoned his counterpart in the FBI.

"We're taking Persico off the Fifteen Most Wanted list," he said.

"That's good," came the agent's reply, "because he's dead, and it doesn't pay to have him on there so long."

"No, no, no," McKinney responded. "We're taking him off because he's in custody."

"There was no way to deal with them on this case," Mike Pizzi would later report. "All the crazy stories you heard throughout the years, about how they could be so damn uncooperative. It was true in this case. It was disgusting. They never shared anything with us."

FOR Mike Pizzi, the obligatory FBI beef is just one more entry in the daily log. Pizzi, as a district chief, has more important things to worry about. In the districts, according to Duke Smith, priorities tend to set themselves. Assignments frequently unfold there like triage in the emergency room at New York's Bellevue Hospital, and even on a slow day the chief deputy may as well be wearing a lab coat.

Says Smith, "You might get a phone call that says, 'Hey, we got a collateral lead for you. We've got a top-fifteen guy, we think, in a hotel down the street.' And you've got five trials you're trying to work, and you've got to haul five prisoners to the West Coast, and two of your guys are off on special assignment working witness security, and three guys are ducking out the door during lunchtime trying to catch a fugitive, and you say, 'Wait. Time out. We've got to go over here and do this.' Or you'll have to go up and arrest a boat. You'll get a court order— A 3000-megaton ship with Norwegian registration is leaving the harbor. It just left, and you got a seizure order. You jump down and get the coast guard. They have you fly out in a helicopter. You land on the deck—maybe you take a boat—and say, 'Captain, the ship's mine. Take her back.' . . . You never know what you're going to have to do."

The argument can be made that when it works at all, government is inefficient. And if you do not think that is true of the criminal justice system in particular, you need only go so far as to debrief the chronic felon. He will tell you unequivocally that the arithmetic is very much on his side.

"We got about six hundred warrants on file" in the Southern District of New York alone, Warrants Supervisor Frank Devlin volunteers. "Six hundred bad guys out there, wanted by us. We get forty in a month, new ones, on top of that. And we make about forty arrests a month. We're never going to catch up."

It is with such staggering numbers as these that the Marshals Service's FIST operations were specifically designed to deal.

FIST. Ask Duke Smith. "In government, you can't have anything successful unless you have an acronym."

FIST (Fugitive Investigative Strike Team) is designed to strike a blow against those fugitives from justice whose resident population in the United States of America on any given day is just about half that of the state of Montana. Of prime importance in the neology of FIST was that the operations sell on page one. And so the Marshals Service to that end etched its FIST operations with a cachet that made them irresistible to newsmen. Mike Pizzi and deputies like him, with the resources of Washington behind them, took a traditionally ugly and very dangerous business and opened it up like a three-ring circus; they took a time-honored theme, the classic criminal manhunt, and played it like rock and roll.

"All of us who work fugitive cases know how dangerous it is to have to go into somebody's house, especially by force," Pizzi says. "It's a very very difficult thing. You never know what you're going to experience. Sometimes people react in such a way that you have to use more force than you want to. And it's sometimes heart wrenching because there are kids in the house. Nobody wants to see Daddy or Mommy leaving in handcuffs. You try to avoid that when you can, if at all possible."

"Going in with guns out, throwing handcuffs on the father, dragging him out—that's going to terrorize a child. You can't do that," agrees Frank Devlin. "When we know there are kids around, we don't take guns out."

"Going into somebody's home," Pizzi says, "is probably the least desirable way to make an arrest—less even than a felony car stop, which is a very dangerous thing to do. You want as many of the odds in your favor as possible. And there comes the concept of a sting operation. It's a relatively safe, inexpensive way to arrest people."

The Atlantic City bus tour engineered by Mike Pizzi in the summer of 1985, which netted more felons than had ever been taken down in any single operation of its kind, was typical of the sting operations routinely conducted by the Marshals Service. It came at the culmination of a FIST operation run out of the Eastern District of New York. The mini-FIST, as such regional operations had come to be called, had been instigated by Pizzi himself, and over the course of that spring had resulted in the arrest of over 300 fugitives through conventional investigative means—working informants, following leads, breaking down doors—good old-fashioned police work.

In the sting itself, which was conducted in cooperation with the NYPD's Brooklyn warrants squad and in which state and local fugitives were also targeted, Pizzi would oversee the arrest of twenty-one fugitives—sixteen men, five women—in a single day, in a space of four hours, in fact. The combined task force would arrest only felons—people wanted for assault, armed robbery, armed burglary, felony narcotics violations, and other serious offenses; it would do so at a quarter of the cost of the typical arrest; and it would do so without recourse to the use of a lot of muscle.

The heavy lifting came in the creation of the scam. A thousand fugitives were notified by mail that they had won a free trip to the Sands Hotel and Casino in Atlantic City, New Jersey, along with $100 in bonus money, $50 of it in cash. The bright green one-page circular designed, printed, and mailed by the task force contained a telephone number at which the winners were to respond to a Miss Bridewell, employed by a fictitious tour company, who would schedule appointments for them to claim their prizes.

"We anticipated that out of the thousand we would get about two percent. If our estimates were correct, based on our past experiences, we would manage to arrest about twenty people," Pizzi explains.

Miss Bridewell—named, in Pizzi's characteristically mischievous fashion, for the sixteenth-century City of London house of correction, and portrayed by secretary Frances Nespoli—scheduled appointments for the morning of July 20. Bus departures were to begin at eight a.m. from Hansen Place in downtown Brooklyn.

Each winner was assigned a lucky number. It was derived from the number of the actual file folder in which the fugitive's warrant was kept. A registration table was set up on Hansen Place, at which Gerri Doody, wearing a hidden transmitter, would greet the individual respondents and read the lucky numbers aloud. Task force members aboard the tour bus parked half a block away, receiving the transmission, would pull the corresponding folders. Then, training binoculars on the respondents through the blacked-out glass of the rear window, they would I.D. each against the mug shot of the fugitive sought. Impostors—relatives, for example—were turned away, either at the point of arrival itself, or if closer observation was required, as they were walked from there to the door of the bus.

"There were six or seven people on the bus anticipating the fugitives getting on. One deputy acted as the driver. The final escort, standing outside the doorway [of the bus] was a New York City cop."

Walking fugitives between the registration table and the bus was Dave O'Flaherty. Pizzi, Vic Oboyski, and Deputy Bob Meltzer posed as a Con Edison crew working on a manhole nearby. There was one NYPD cop standing in a flower shop across the street; one, posing as a tourist, standing at the entrance to the Long Island Rail Road station, not far away; two more, dressed as telephone repairmen, working on a booth at the far corner of the block. In addition to all the pedestrian heat, there were two chase cars on the scene. In all, there were probably forty cops assigned to the operation.

The location had been selected for a reason.

"It's a very popular area, and it's kind of a busy area. And when you are in a busy area, there are lots of invisible people. The setup was perfect. Hansen Place in Brooklyn, under the big clock."

The big clock Pizzi refers to is the clock on Brooklyn's landmark Williamsburgh Savings Bank Building. A further advantage of the location, he notes, was its access to a variety of public transportation.

Of those clever fugitives who cased the setup before approaching the registration table only to flee because they grew suspicious, three were apprehended by one or another of the teams working surveillance. The bright green fliers the fugitives carried worked to give them away.

For added authenticity, each fugitive was invited to bring a companion along on the tour—a wife, husband, girlfriend, or boyfriend, as the case might be. That companion, for obvious reasons, had to be admitted to the bus with the fugitive.

"We would have them sit down, keep them under observation until we rendered the fugitive safe, and then we'd escort them off the bus and out of the area."

As the fugitive was admitted to the bus, he or she was greeted with a handshake by its driver, Deputy Tony McHale. McHale's grip was unusually firm. Members of the task force, weapons drawn, immediately immobilized the fugitive—grabbed him, cuffed him, searched him, and sat him down—and the felon was under arrest before he knew what hit him.

The bus, making periodic trips to a prison van parked about ten blocks away, dropped fugitives off in groups of five or six, returning each time to Hansen Place to welcome a new handful of suckers. One late arrival, eager to catch the bus as it was pulling away for the last time, came running alongside, waving his flier, pleading to be let aboard. McHale, at the wheel, pulled the bus to a stop, opened the door, reached out a helping hand, and hauled the man inside. When six unpleasant passengers instantly put guns in his face, the prize-winner wet his pants.

Five months later, in Washington, D.C., a similar operation was run out of headquarters. Three thousand fugitives were notified by mail that they had won free tickets to a Washington Redskins–Cincinnati Bengals football game as well as the chance at a grand prize, an all-expenses-paid trip to the upcoming Super Bowl in New Orleans. Winners were invited to collect their tickets at a free brunch to be held at the city's convention center on the morning of December 15. In the midst of the festivities a total of 166 officers drawn from the

Marshals Service and the city's metropolitan police department arrested 96 fugitives en masse. In terms of sheer numbers the sting was unsurpassed.

AMONG the differences between the Brooklyn sting and that conducted by headquarters was the participation in the latter of the Service's Special Operations Group.

"We handle our own muscle," Mike Pizzi says of the Eastern District. "We handle our own details, our own problems."

According to Ralph Burnside, the scarcity of SOG details in Brooklyn is attributable to a fundamental inconsistency in the operational styles of the Brooklyn chief and the Service's paramilitary wing. SOG, in the words of its commander, John Haynes, takes its strength from "regimentation and discipline, willing obedience to command," while Pizzi, according to Burnside, "encourages individualism. There is no mold to fit, in Brooklyn. You are encouraged to be your own best self."

Pizzi, who underwent SOG training in 1972, says that "a lot of good guys didn't make it," and admits that he "got a bad taste for it" back then. (Pizzi was asked to leave on the day before graduation.)

Organized under then director Wayne B. Colburn in 1971, the Special Operations Group today conducts its four-week training on the 15,000 acres of Camp Beauregard, a National Guard installation situated on the Red River outside Pineville, Louisiana. There a permanent staff of thirteen answers to SOG commander John Haynes, who reports through a chief in Washington to the associate director for operations. Of the thirteen staff members, three are civilians, their duties solely clerical. The other ten are deputy marshals, and when they are not acting as instructors, they serve as the group's first-response team, the only deputies in the Marshals Service who work SOG missions exclusively.

"When there are no classes, they're making arrests," Haynes says.

John Haynes, recruited by the Marshals Service in 1971 after eleven and a half years in the Marine Corps, first went on the job in his native Oklahoma. A graduate of the SOG class of 1972, he was made an instructor shortly thereafter. He has been with SOG ever since. His brown hair and mustache going to gray, the trim Haynes, pushing fifty, takes justifiable pride in his ability to keep up with his recruits.

He became the unit's commander in 1986, at the age of forty-three, and hopes, he says, to be the first deputy U.S. marshal to retire out of Special Operations.

In addition to training its own deputies, the Special Operations Group regularly offers training to the police organizations of foreign governments. Under Marshals Service contract with the State Department, SOG has provided advanced instruction in counterinsurgency, hostage negotiations, fugitive tracking, interrogation, and judicial security to police from Mexico, Colombia, Bolivia, Ecuador, Honduras, Costa Rica, Czechoslovakia, Poland, Hungary, Italy, Greece, Turkey, and the Philippines. The program conducted at Camp Beauregard is one of several sponsored by State's Anti-Terrorism Assistance Division.

A tool available to each of the several Marshals Service divisions, the Special Operations Group takes its manpower from some 125 SOG-qualified personnel dispersed throughout the rank and file, working deputies called as needed from districts around the country.

SOG offers no special pay or rewards and is strictly volunteer. That forty percent of those who occupy positions of leadership in the Service—inspectors, supervisors, chiefs, etc.—have passed through Special Operations speaks both to the cachet of having belonged and to the raw ambition inherent in those who apply. Training, Haynes argues, is accessible to every deputy in the Service.

"The door," he says, "is open to everyone. We're not elitist. The standards are not that tough. They're fair. We don't ever want to be thought of as something everybody can't belong to."

The door may be open to everyone, but it swings both ways, and fast. Out of an average-sized class of about fifty, half can be expected to wash out.

"We don't give a written test. They're tested every day, every hour, mentally and physically. I want to see you do what you got to do."

What you have got to do first, to be accepted for instruction, is shoot seventy percent with a pistol. That is *before* you apply. After that, you must survive a month of rigorous paramilitary field training, conducted in a disciplinary atmosphere similar to that of Marine Corps boot camp—drill and command, marching to chow, regular inspections, punitive push-ups, routine verbal assault—full Parris Island. The training itself is in traditional SWAT, special weapons and tactics; deputies undergo exercises in tactical property entry, wilderness survival, and hand-to-hand combat. They are trained in rappelling—required to free-rappel from the skids of helicopters coming in at ninety feet; they are put through combat trials and officer-survival drills; and outside WITSEC, they are the only Marshals Service personnel to qualify on automatic weapons.

"Pistol for us is a secondary weapon," says Haynes. "We go operational, a deputy's going to have a shotgun or a rifle or a machine gun in his hands—Colt SMG, an MP5. WITSEC uses the Uzi. SOG uses counter-sniper weapons that the Marshals Service [otherwise] doesn't use—a .308 or .30-06 scoped rifle. Right now we use the [.223-caliber Ruger] Mini-14 as our long gun.

"We tell them right from the get-go, this is not a military unit. We are first and foremost civilian police officers. [But] tactics is tactics, and it comes from the military."

Special Operations training, though it once did, no longer incorporates paratroop jump school.

"The basic philosophy is to locate, isolate, contain, and control. The LICC principle. Making an entry is the last thing you want to do. Make 'em come out—that's their turf in there. If you locate 'em, isolate 'em, contain 'em, and control 'em, you only got three things they can do. Surrender, fight, or flee. That's the only three options any human being's got in any situation. But once we contain you, you can't get away; once you see you're outnumbered, you don't want to fight. That only leaves you the option of surrendering. And that's the theory we work under in the Marshals Service."

It is the theory, in fact, under which successful SWAT teams everywhere operate. Haynes calls it "team-concept firepower," and it is the civilian variation on the theme of military fire control. But where the latter is orchestrated to inflict casualties, the former is arrayed to discourage them. A show of force, as Haynes points out, is a tactic itself, and the measure of any SWAT team's success is its ability to neutralize confrontation. More often than not, such response teams bring suspects in alive. By the very nature of their training, successful police paramilitary units will characteristically complete their missions without ever firing a shot.

SOG today participates regularly in a variety of district operations, backing up local deputies in sensitive prosecutions, high-threat prisoner moves, fugitive operations, and large-scale property seizures;

and with the current plethora of major dope trials it has become something of a handmaiden to WITSEC.

Haynes says he seeks diversity in his deputies and grants that he has been fortunate in being able to draw from a large pool of talent and experience. And he says he is getting a new breed of deputy.

"A lot of them are single. They've gone to college, remained single, and are just coming into the job."

There are character traits that Haynes identifies as typical of the SOG recruit. "You just about have to put a bit in their mouth. You won't see any of these guys backin' up. They're all hard chargers. They're all strong-willed people." And it is instructive to look at those qualities against the backdrop of police work in general. For there is a very good argument to be made for the fact that they are merely an exaggeration of the attributes of the average American cop.

THE well-adjusted human from infancy is programmed to recoil from danger—to avoid it, and, failing that, to flee. Policemen are programmed by training to run in its direction. Theirs is a career, characteristically, that thrives on confrontation and their willingness to initiate it. According to Victor Oboyski, it has always been that way.

"A cop [is a guy] banging his nightstick. 'Gimme the corner. Gimme the corner!' You have to assert your authority. 'It's *my* corner now.' "

Cops are physical people. The image of the typical officer is that of a man with a gun in his hand. The impression is a false one; most cops spend their entire careers without ever drawing their weapons. In truth, what street cops, both men and women, spend most of their time doing is fighting. Putting their hands on people. Wrestling, mixing it up, getting in people's faces, throwing their weight around.

"In our profession, you're meeting the worst people, the dregs of society—and you're meeting *good* people at their worst."

People do not call the police when things are going well at home.

Police work is all about muscle. Apparent fearlessness in a cop—a display of fearlessness, genuine or not—is an instrument of survival.

"Just like an animal can sense fear, you get these street people," says Vic Oboyski, "guys that've been arrested ten, twenty times, you know. They can sense fear. They can look in your eye, or they can actually *feel* it, like an animal can. They can *tell* you're afraid. Once they know you're afraid, that's it. You're on the defensive."

As a veteran, Vic Oboyski has learned how to turn the authority on quick. With reference to Mike Pizzi's semiannual shenanigans in the classroom down at Glynco, Oboyski is quick to point out, "If I had Mike pulling that s___ with me, I'd crack him. I'd knock him down. *Bing*. 'Now what are you gonna do?' If I'm arresting a guy, and the guy starts acting a little funny, he's on the ground. If he acts cool and everything, fine, you know, I'll treat him like a gentleman. But I ain't gonna play with him. Everyone wonders why cops throw guys against the wall. That's the initial I'm-not-gonna-play-with-you routine. You got to take the high ground. You got to be aggressive right away."

A cop making an arrest wants a suspect in handcuffs before the suspect has time to think. One reason is the gun. The gun belongs to the cop only as long as he or she is at a distance from the offender. Once a cop closes in, the gun belongs to whoever gets his hands on it. When an arrest attempt results in a fight, the cop more often than not is fighting for his life. And that is why such struggles are characteristically so ugly to watch.

Coming on strong, for a cop, is a weapon like any other. Coming on strong at the wrong time, Victor Oboyski acknowledges, can escalate what would otherwise be a relatively peaceful confrontation. Being an effective cop is all about knowing when to turn it on and when *not* to. There are times when, handled properly, everything goes down smoothly, and others when, as one big-city cop puts it, you "have to take control of it and start screaming."

Times, unfortunately, tend to favor the latter.

"They don't fear cops now," Oboyski says, cruising the mean streets of Brooklyn. "A cop now is just an obstacle. People here don't fear jail. You and I do. They don't."

Retired customs investigator Bill Hughes waxes almost nostalgic when speaking about the bad guys in whose faces he flashed his badge.

"The game was a lot different then. When the jig was up, when you put that government tin on them, they knew you meant business," he says. "The old-timers thought the feds were bulletproof."

Bad guys today, he acknowledges, are far less likely to go quietly and far more likely to go the limit.

"Now they kill the feds."

In 1987 the U.S. Marshals Service's FIST operations—those that SOG was backing up—went the way of the seventy-eight long-playing-record album. That was the year FIST became WANT—Warrant Apprehension Narcotics Team. With the advent of WANT (conducted in collaboration with the DEA and local authorities and under which the Service for the first time pursued prearraignment fugitives), the agency's famous fugitive sweeps suddenly took on a new rhythm, a switch in emphasis as audible as that heralded by the release some thirty years earlier of Bill Haley's "Rock Around the Clock."

For deputy U.S. marshals, the arrest of bank robbers, rapists, and racketeers had officially entered the realm of the classics.

Number one with a bullet was dope.

And while the agency, through its fugitive and National Asset Seizure and Forfeiture mandates, arrayed its forces on the domestic front—WANT was nothing more than the public relations arm of the incursion—there were selected deputies who carried the battle deep into enemy territory.

Same war, different theater.

Chapter Ten

"HE THOUGHT we were going to kill him. They put him through the fence. We grabbed him. He was still blindfolded, handcuffed behind his back. Down he goes, down on the deck. And you can smell the adrenaline—'Please don't kill me, I'll tell you anything you want to know, don't kill me, I got a family'—and at that moment I felt great. I felt that at that moment that son of a bitch paid. At least, through his mind the thought crossed, 'They're going to blow me away'; and he knew that it was payback. At least for that little bit of time I felt like a million dollars. . . . That minute, maybe three, that he was down there, that made it all worthwhile for me."

The arrest of René Martín Verdugo, on January 24, 1986, was the first of what would become known in the months that followed as Tony's black bag jobs.

"What it is," says Deputy U.S. Marshal Tony Perez, "is you convince the people on the other side to do the right thing. And they do it. Most of the time. But if you tell them to cross *t*'s and dot *i*'s—if you gotta do it diplomatically and through diplomatic channels—it doesn't get done. And I'm not saying what I did was right. I'm saying what I did was effective, and it was not illegal. I got a clean heart."

Arrests such as Verdugo's, essayed at the outer limits of the agency's statutory authority, are the utmost manifestation of the deputy U.S. marshal as the long arm of the law. An expression of the Service's federal fugitive mandate only in its most ruthless interpretation, such operations entered the realm of inevitability only when law enforcement became personal.

On Thursday, February 7, 1985, U.S. DEA agent Enrique "Kiki" Camarena, thirty-seven, was abducted by five men outside his agency's offices at the U.S. consulate in Guadalajara, Mexico. A month later, on March 6, Camarena's mutilated body and that of Alfredo Zavala, a local pilot Camarena had occasionally employed, were discovered seventy miles away, buried behind a ranch in the neighboring state of Michoacán. There was speculation that Zavala had been buried alive; Camarena had been beaten to death. Both men had been tortured before being murdered, Camarena for perhaps thirty hours.

The search for Camarena and the investigation of his death revealed a sustained, systematic conspiracy between some of Mexico's most successful traffickers in cocaine and marijuana—Félix Gallardo, Rafael Caro Quintero, and Ernesto Fonseca Carrillo—and the officials and former officials of several of its government agencies. Eventually nineteen foreign nationals, all but one of them Mexican, would be indicted in the United States, among them the former head of Mexico's federal police and the former Mexican Interpol director. Also indicted was Dr. Humberto Alvarez Machain, a Guadalajara gynecologist alleged to have kept Camarena alive that he might sustain the amount of torture necessary to extract information from him.

The success of U.S. agents in bringing the indictments was bitter fruit, nurtured by a passion on the part of Camarena's fellow officers to make his murderers pay. To this day it is questionable whether all will ever be made to do so. DEA agents, in exacting but a taste of revenge, relied heavily on back-channel maneuvering. They did it without the help of President Ronald Reagan, and they did it in spite of his Secretary of State. And when they had gone as far as they themselves could go, they turned to the only man they knew who could take it one step further. They turned to Tony Perez.

I been chased by cops all my life. If I was out on the street today, and Tony Perez was after me, I'd surrender.

—Jimmy Fratianno

What Jimmy Fratianno saw in Tony Perez, he probably saw in his eyes. Dark, flickering, firm of purpose—the kind of eyes some women associate with the bedroom, they are the kind of eyes some men associate with the ring. They look like they give off heat. And Tony Perez looks like a guy who sleeps with them open.

If your house were on fire, you could call Tony Perez, and if he said he would be there to handle it, you could roll over and go back to sleep.

Soft-spoken, well spoken, sometimes shy, with dark, curly hair and a mustache to match, Perez is strung together like a prizefighter, something like a fast light heavyweight. Straightforward, stand-up, forever young, Perez is the kind of guy who gives cops a good name, and he is the heart and soul of the U.S. Marshals Service.

"Good man, good kid, and he was from the first day," according to Bud McPherson. "He was fresh out of the marines, and he had a degree of maturity that was far beyond his young age at the time."

José Antonio Pérez escaped from Fidel Castro's Cuba on May 1, 1965. He arrived in the United States of America in a fourteen-foot rowboat with an uncle, after eight nights and seven days at sea. He was not yet fifteen years old, and like many Americans who earn their citizenship the hard way, he was quick to identify not only its rights and privileges but its duties.

There was more than one star in his future.

Before he was sworn as a deputy marshal, Perez, honoring those duties one late afternoon near An Hoa, South Vietnam, drew attention to himself as a U.S. Marine Corps platoon sergeant, "holding some folks back while the better part of our platoon got the hell out and got some reinforcements." Of the "folks" in question, a force of enemy riflemen who had overrun his unit, Perez concedes, "There were a lot." Perez held his position "for two or three hours—me and a guy named Petersen, a black guy with red hair, green eyes. I had the machine gun; he was my assistant gunner."

The two escaped under cover of darkness, each pausing only to pick up the Bronze Star for heroism.

With a Bronze Star, a Navy Achievement Medal, and a Purple Heart, Perez, returning from Southeast Asia, entered the Marshals Service in 1972 and was assigned to its Los Angeles office. In 1973 Perez "got going on warrants," and it was not long before he developed a reputation as a body snatcher.

Tony Perez, as chief of major-case investigations, oversees the Marshals Service 15 Most Wanted program, under the purview of which fall fugitive cases selected not only for their complexity but for their high visibility as well. The 15 Most Wanted list functions primarily to support a public relations effort, and its blueprint was stolen by the Marshals Service *in toto* from the FBI.

To make the Marshals Service's 15 Most Wanted list a fugitive must be a class-one violator. Misdemeanor warrants carry no weight. National media exposure is not essential, but its power cannot be ignored. Violence, of course, invites star quality, yet there are avenues to criminal celebrity that stop short of a tendency to cut throats. One of them is big-time drugs. But however you make the list, the paperwork your case generates will cross the desk of Tony Perez.

CONFIDENTIAL informants are as indispensable to deputies like Tony Perez as they were to Pat Garrett over a century ago.

"There's no case where everyone is stand-up and solid," says Perez. "There's always someone that you can break down. I can tell you who is a lazy deputy marshal and who is a smart, hardworking deputy marshal by [the measure of his] informants."

And a cop never gives up his informants.

In 1984, working a FIST operation in Los Angeles, Perez and his partner, LAPD officer Manny Mata, chiefly by developing informants, arrested thirteen homicide suspects in under six weeks, an extraordinary achievement by any measure. The informants, like the suspects, were Cuban.

"Mariel boatlift people—these were criminals themselves. There's nothing we can do to these people. We can't *threaten* them; they've been in worse jails. They've eaten that rice and beans for years. The way we deal with them is with the truth. . . . We spent time with them, talking their talk, walking their walk, convincing them this is the only way to go. Manny and I slept in a station wagon for days on end because we told one guy, 'You are very important to us. Without you we can't break this case, and that's a fact.' He was very scared to give us any information because he was going to get bumped off if word ever got out—and only *he* knew this guy's movements. We promised him we would 'cool off' the information to the point that the guy would never know it had come from him. Three days sleeping in the station wagon to cover the guy, but I kept my word. It's respect. Word gets out: You can deal with Tony; Tony's stand-up. You can deal with Manny; Manny's stand-up."

But there is more to capturing fugitives than the cultivation of confidential informants.

"It's like hunting an animal," Vic Oboyski believes. "What you do is you lay traps. You try and push him out of where you think he is and lay traps to where you think he's going to go."

"You know in your heart when you've done it all," Perez says.

TONY Perez is one of those deputies who is reluctant to hang his citations, and it is the speculation of some of his colleagues that there are very few offices in Washington with the wall space to display them, anyway. With questions on the part of his superiors as to whether he was management material, Perez, following his assignment to headquarters in 1984, went about earning Marshals Service promotions with a diminishing ceiling in the bureaucracy. To put him back out in the districts, his bosses would have had to make him a chief, and because they were reluctant to do so and because he was so downright talented they essentially invented a job, major-case investigations, into which to promote him in 1988.

Back in January of 1986 Perez was an inspector, a regional manager in enforcement operations at headquarters, and René Martín Verdugo was just one of the several thousand fugitives on whom the Marshals Service was holding paper. Outstanding against Verdugo was a routine felony dope warrant issued in San Diego by the U.S. Court for the Southern District of California. Insulated by money, enjoying the unofficial protection of the government of his native Mexico, Verdugo was virtually untouchable, immune to capture by the United States, into which he now was moving marijuana by the ton as a lieutenant of drug trafficker Caro Quintero.

When an FBI forensics team in 1985 recovered from the scene of Kiki Camarena's interrogation and murder a hair sample belonging to Verdugo, indictments in the Camarena case were still a good three years away. A grand jury had yet to be empaneled when, shortly after the evidence was recovered, Tony Perez, in the Mexican resort town of San Felipe, brought to Verdugo's attention the matter of his outstanding San Diego warrant.

Perez had received a call from the DEA on December 17.

"I had the pleasure of meeting Mrs. Camarena. She was there in the task force room when I went to DEA headquarters. DEA had called me and said, 'Hey, Tony, come over. Let's talk.' I met the woman there. I met the guys who were running the show."

Their opening line was innocuous enough: "We want to see if you can do something for us."

"I'm thinking, Why doesn't DEA do this? Why don't they avenge their own thing?"

The Drug Enforcement Administration, in the wake of Camarena's abduction, was having serious problems operating in Mexico. They had already coughed up a lot of international trouble and as much stateside bureaucratic trouble as they could handle.

"We're just not going to be effective," Perez was told by the agents in the room that day.

Perez looked at Mika Camarena, he says, and "I knew it was for real."

As Perez saw it, it went way beyond dope.

"Just a guy sending dope over here, it's like . . . At some point, although you see the tragedies and all, at some point it's like it's become a business. But *this* . . . I could touch people. . . . I can touch Mrs. Camarena, whose husband was tortured and killed for trying to do the right thing in a place I knew very well."

Perez, whose stepmother and stepbrother are Mexican, identifies Cuba and Mexico as "very tight, very close culturally."

Perez says, "I promised nothing."

His first move was the obvious one.

"I went to Mr. Safir."

The DEA's request of Perez, when all the delicate language was peeled away, was essentially for the kidnapping of Verdugo. Even if handled lawfully—and for that adverb it would be a stretch—it would be one of those operations that, if it received any attention at all, would redound to the discredit of everyone. The request, however heartfelt, however appealing to the instinct of the cop in everyone, was a request in which any bureaucrat, in any response short of summary denial, would see nothing but wholesale disaster. It was a request that arrived at Marshals Service headquarters with little more than love on its side.

And Howard Safir immediately said yes.

WHEN Howard Safir favors the world with a smile, he does so with such apparent difficulty that to see it happen is almost heartbreaking. On the operational side of the Marshals Service, good humor does not bleed from the top. Painfully uncomfortable in the presence of others, at the same time driven by ambition, the associate director makes it effectively impossible for others to relax in his company.

To think of Tony Perez as enormously fond of Safir would probably be a mistake. Perez does not dislike him, but his respect for the man, like everyone's, is tempered by such apprehension as to make camaraderie unimaginable. In the rank and file Safir inspires a mix of sincere admiration and flat-out fear.

"Up here [at headquarters] credibility is everything. Mr. Safir will back you all the way; he'll let you follow incredible hunches. If you get results. But the man takes no prisoners if you f___ up."

"The Service," according to one chief whose experience predates Safir's arrival, "needed a tough and tense boss. Howard's the ultimate survivor. He's going to be hard to beat. The man never gets tired. [And] he has the intelligence and the demeanor to go along with his working habits. He's a good boss and a good leader."

If, as novelist Joseph Conrad suggests in the imperishable pages of Lord Jim, "You shall judge a man by his foes as well as by his friends," let it be said of Howard Safir that numbered among his enemies are Edwin P. Wilson, Christopher Boyce, Josef Mengele, Alphonse Persico, and thousands of garden-variety scumbags on the order of Garnett Leacock.

And, yes, René Verdugo.

ON JANUARY 13, 1986, four weeks after meeting Kiki Camarena's widow at DEA headquarters in Washington, Tony Perez and three other deputy marshals traveled to Calexico, California, to talk to the DEA's resident agent in charge, and from there crossed to the Sonora, Mexico, side of the border, into neighboring Mexicali, where René Verdugo lived.

"I went down to Mexico. *We* actually went in and did the work, as far as looking [for Verdugo]. We went in, spotted the guy. We knew his comings and goings. It would have been easy for us to grab the son of a bitch, put him in the car, bring him across the border, and lie."

Instead, Perez enlisted the aid of members of Sonora's judicial police.

"We got six officers there to help us out."

Which was really the germ of the operation.

"It's really human relations. We talk to people; we convince them to do the right thing. No heavy compromises, no heavy demands on these folks, just one-on-one. I go to a police organization in another country, go to someone in command. I tell them this is what I need. I'd like to have this man back. The moment we start pointing fingers at Mexico, Colombia—start saying, 'You're all corrupt. Your cops are corrupt. You're all into this and that'—the moment we start doing that, we're finished.

"We got six officers there to help us out, and they took a good ten days of watching him and waiting; and finally he went to San Felipe, to a party. Laughing and joking, he left the party to get some more beer, and he was under surveillance, of course. We said, 'Do it now.' And we grabbed him—*they* did—out of a party. They grabbed him, took him to the car, and they went over."

Over the border.

"It was his daughter's party, or someone very close to him in the family—maybe a birthday party. He owned the house in San Felipe. He had houses everywhere. He was a very well-to-do man. San Felipe was, like, his beach house.

"Once they were close enough—just two Mexican males, plain-clothes, with a rental car from here (I gave them the car to do the thing) . . . said they were judicial police—a fact; they *were*, at the time. 'We'd like to see you, like to talk to you a little bit.' . . . Down on the station wagon floor, and off they went. . . . Instead of taking him to their station, they made the choice of bringing him to the border, to the Americans. They did the right thing."

It was no typical evening drive along the Baja peninsula. Verdugo's wife and his Mexican lawyer were on the telephone within minutes of his abduction. Perez is understandably vague on some of the details of the caper, but it is apparent that there was a certain urgency in the timing of the actual snatch.

"We grabbed him there. His friends saw it. He broke away from a group. It had to be done there. We suspect one of those people called, and roadblocks were set up. There were police barricades already set up. . . . It was, like, a sixty-mile drive, and it wasn't no freeway, either. You had to do certain things to get away from these folks."

Perez and the three other deputies—Mike Carnivale, Ernie Tautimes, and David Mendoza, the core of what some in the Service call Tony's Tigers—had been joined in Mexico by then International Branch chief Don Ferrarone. In Calexico, Perez had rented three vehicles for the caper: a sedan, a station wagon, and a van. On the run for the border Verdugo went into the station wagon with the six Mexican police officers. Running up front, at the wheel of the van, was Perez, with Tautimes and Ferrarone. Mendoza and Carnivale brought up the rear.

"We had to get off the main road in a couple of instances, actually go *off* the road and get into the desert and drive around [the roadblocks] that way. I let [the Mexicans] take the lead after a while because these guys knew where they were going. Now I was in the middle, and the tail car—the chase car—continued to be Mike and David. We were running without lights and were going eighty miles an hour *off* the road, across the desert; and it worked. These people knew exactly what they were doing."

It took about an hour to make the run.

"I remember it was dark. . . . It was not dark when we picked him up. There was a moon. It was pretty good. It was like a movie in slow motion, the way everything happened."

Perez says he experienced no sense of danger as such, save that inspired by the speed at which he and the others were traveling. Apprehension at what might befall him at the hands of Mexican authorities—what had befallen Camarena—was not uppermost in his mind, he says.

"Once you're in a situation like this, you just roll with the punches. It crossed our minds collectively, and we talked about it, but when we shook hands over here with DEA at headquarters, the deal was done. We never dwelled on that kind of stuff."

They made the border at twenty past six. The niceties of customs and immigration were bypassed. Five miles west of Calexico, Perez, at an unmanned crossing, climbed the fence to receive Verdugo.

"They put him through the fence—the Mexicans pushed him through. We grabbed him; we put him on the ground. We laid him down, and there were no sounds whatsoever, because I made it clear, I didn't want anyone speaking English, Spanish, Chinese . . . nothing. 'Don't say a word throughout this whole thing, because people are going to get killed behind this arrest if he recognizes that Mexicans were involved.' "

One of the more problematic considerations governing Mexican participation evokes understatement on the part of Perez.

"Their sense of how this stuff ought to work is a little bit different than ours as Americans."

A little bit, indeed. Perez was forced to speak to the issue.

" 'This is your country. These are your people. Your system is what it is. But we're working together now, and I can't have one bruise on this guy. No bruises, no cuts. Treat him as if he were the president of the country, with all the honors. No slapping, no hurting no one. That's one of the things, that's part of the contract here. Whatever you do, don't give me a bruised spot.' And he didn't have a bruise on him. We undressed him; we took photos.

"Things started getting worse and worse for them. Because as word got out that [Verdugo] had been abducted, and it was believed to have been by police, [his friends] started making inquiries. This man was a man of means. So a lot of pressure was put on the officials there, and they started closing in on these people. And that's when the guy I coordinated with, he said, 'Tony, you got to get us out.' They're in the witness-security program, thirty-two of them. Their families had to come out, too. . . . They firebombed their houses, took their businesses over. . . ."

IF YOU want to know how the politics of dope poisons national priorities in America, ask your local fisherman, nostalgic for the days when the U.S. Coast Guard had a search-and-rescue budget, when uniformed sailors and chopper pilots fighting force-ten gales risked their lives to pull the drowning out of twenty-five-foot seas.

It is those same brave officers who are paid now to notch the prows of their cutters with quaint pictures of marijuana leaves, to steam the ocean in search of dope.

It is also that branch of the U.S. armed forces whose personnel can be seen today being dragged off to federal prison half a dozen at a time for drug trafficking.

Of those diseases associated with dope, none is as infectious, none is as thoroughly contaminating as the money. The billions in revenue that dope generates today has suborned more people in the criminal justice system than was imaginable a decade ago. The indictment of police officers in south Florida on narcotics and murder charges is now not even enough to lead the local news broadcasts there. Neither is it uncommon in federal drug prosecutions to see lawyers indicted with their clients, nor are members of the bench immune. No man's price is so high that the dope market cannot support it.

If there is one endeavor that currently generates more questionable cash than drugs, it is the White House war on drugs. Dope is a growth industry not only for those who traffic in it; dope is a growth industry for cops.

As any law-enforcement bureaucrat will tell you, "That's where the money is."

The Marshals Service, by the very nature and the statutory limits of its mission, plays an entirely *re*active role in federal law enforcement. It does not bring people *into* the criminal justice system. Choking the nation's courts and prisons are people ushered thereto by its investigative agencies and federal prosecutors. But though drawn there by forces beyond its control, the Marshals Service nevertheless thrives, prospers just as vigorously as do all the nation's cops, at that bureaucratic trough polluted by the politics of dope.

CIVIL forfeiture proceedings can be traced through common-law England to the ancient Romans and Greeks. The United States has had provisions for property seizure since the founding of the republic, since establishment of the Customs Service, which was authorized from the outset to confiscate the ships of smugglers apprehended evading import duties. The U.S. Supreme Court, after the Civil War, upheld the wartime forfeitures of southern-owned property located in the North and reaffirmed the principle during the years of the Volstead Act (1919–1933).

There are currently more than a hundred civil forfeiture statutes in the U.S. Code; they are designed to enforce an array of federal laws ranging from agriculture violations to copyright infringement. But not until the advent of the Racketeer Influenced and Corrupt Organizations Act (RICO), in 1970, and expansion of the controlled-substances laws (the Comprehensive Crime Control Act of 1984 and the Anti-Drug Abuse Acts of 1986 and 1988) did these statutes threaten to distort the focus of criminal prosecution in America.

Today about a quarter of all federal cases involve offenses that subject defendants to the nation's forfeiture statutes. Not only has civil procedure begun to overshadow criminal prosecution in America, in many cases it has come to replace it. Under its ever expanding drug and racketeering statutes the federal government is now seizing the real estate and other private property of its citizens, not simply in the absence of an owner's conviction but in the absence of bringing criminal charges.

When seizing real estate—for instance, your home—the government is required only to allege in court that probable cause exists to believe that a crime was committed there, that the property, for example, was used in the possession of drugs or to aid in the distribution of them, or that it was purchased with the proceeds derived therefrom. The Drug Enforcement Administration can seize cash and other property, such as cars, boats, and airplanes, with no court proceedings at all. It is the owner's responsibility to bring the proceedings in court and there to prove his innocence. At his own expense—and presumably with borrowed money, since all his assets have been confiscated. That such seizure might violate the Fourth Amendment to the Constitution is irrelevant; the law does not impose the penalty on the owner but, by way of a legal fiction, states that the property itself is guilty and that the property has no constitutional rights.

It is the fear of many Americans, many federal officials among them, that the lure of seized assets is distorting the priorities of the nation's law-enforcement agencies. Increasingly, the statutes are being applied to seize very valuable property for very minor offenses. Increasingly, case agents and their supervisors, in deciding what to investigate, are asking themselves, "What can we seize?" Their seduction by the revenue available—asset forfeiture funds come back to the agencies in the form of national drug-war budgeting—not to mention the high visibility that major seizures promise, is clearly skewing the choices authorities make as to what cases to become involved in. The tendency exists to concentrate on relatively safe operations, to pursue the wealthiest criminals, not the most dangerous.

Adding a profit incentive to law enforcement, which up to now has been commonly associated with the corruption of Third World police forces, draws official attention away, it is argued, from securing the safety of the public. Arrests for homicide, rape, robbery, and assault yield dividends that are not negotiable.

THE Marshals Service administers two key features of the Justice Department's asset seizure initiative: the National Asset Seizure and Forfeiture Program (NASAF), which manages and disposes of assets, and the Assets Forfeiture Fund, which distributes the proceeds.

The Service is currently managing over $1.4 billion worth of property, half of it real estate. The assets must be secured, inventoried, appraised, stored, and otherwise generally maintained. Much of the work, including the profitable operation of businesses that have been seized, is accomplished through hundreds of property managers and commercial vendors under contract with the Service.

The Marshals Service hires countless appraisers and auctioneers. It uses brokers, sales agents, and other liquidation services, disposing of property by way of public sale or other commercially feasible means; transfer to federal, state, or local law-enforcement agencies (cars, boats, airplanes, and other crime-fighting equipment); and salvage, scrap, and destruction.

All forfeited currency and all the money received from the sale of forfeited assets is deposited in the Assets Forfeiture Fund, the primary function of which is to underwrite the expense of carrying out additional seizures. Injected into the fund in fiscal year 1990—in which the Service processed and maintained paper records on 34,000 asset cases—was $460 million. Nearly $56 million of that was used to pay for the program: asset management costs, case-related expenses, and payment of third-party claims. Another $115 million was earmarked for new prison construction. More than $175 million went to state and local law-enforcement agencies.

Assets seized over the years have included cars, trucks, other motor vehicles, boats, ships, and aircraft; residential and commercial real properties such as horse farms, recording studios, golf courses, banks, office buildings, ranches, restaurants, and retail stores; cash, jewelry, coins, precious metals, art objects, antiques; laboratory equipment, chemicals, foodstuffs, and weapons.

There was a brass-and-aluminum foundry in Wisconsin (operated for a year by the Marshals Service before being sold for $1.9 million); a nursery and flower shop in Massachusetts; a quarter-horse racing stable near Floresville, Texas; a championship Thoroughbred show horse with stud fees worth $2.5 million; an island off the coast of Florida; 21,000 baseball cards in a collection auctioned in Newport; a handmade 1981 Italian Stutz Diplomatica automobile; a herd of cattle in Muskogee, Oklahoma; a topless bar in Syracuse, New York; and $2 million worth of rare U.S. gold coins.

In New York, application of the forfeiture statutes has proved to be an effective law-enforcement tool for shutting down, at least temporarily, certain lucrative drug operations. In raids on numerous crack-and-heroin enterprises there, deputies, to the delight of local residents, have seized apartment buildings by the dozens.

In the Eastern District, Mike Pizzi's crew has developed what amounts to an entire subspecialty in seized real estate.

"TAKE the door! Take the door!"

Dave O'Flaherty had hollered so many commands through the dilapidated wall of the apartment—he could actually see through it in places—that the occupants beyond it now had no idea what to do. And before the bad guys had time to think, before they got creative and came up with something on their own, O'Flaherty wanted in.

Oboyski hit the door.

Operating openly as a crack factory and a twenty-four-hour drug supermarket, Crack Castle, as it had come to be known, comprised a pair of adjoining, three-story residential buildings, 395 and 397 Westervelt Avenue, in the New Brighton section of Staten Island, New York. To walk-in and drive-up customers, the group occupying the apartment houses had been moving up to 2500 vials of ten-dollar crack a day. Intimidated neighbors had been complaining for years, and in the four months before the hit, the two locations had been host to thirty-four drug arrests by city police.

The buildings, located within walking distance of a public

elementary school, had fallen into disrepair. As Dave O'Flaherty would later concede, the front door came down easy.

And since just before the moment they hit it, O'Flaherty had been hollering. There was more than one reason to do so. O'Flaherty says that screaming "lets out [your] anxiety," as much as scares the opposition. But more than that, it "lets them know who you are."

Put a tape recorder on a typical hit and you will hear the word police! yelled out more times than you are able to count. The last thing a cop wants is to be mistaken for a stickup man.

The first floor had been empty. The stairway had been shaky; it was hanging off the wall. And now O'Flaherty, on the second floor, over the barrel of a shotgun, had totally confused the occupants of the apartment he was about to enter, screaming contradictory commands. He had given maybe a dozen or so, shouting through the holes in the masonry, when Oboyski hit the door.

The apartment door was nothing special. It had not been reinforced, no security gates—nothing like that. A standard steel fire door, New York City, up to code. But for some reason it resisted the sledge. It was going to go eventually, maybe in several seconds, but that was not quick enough for O'Flaherty.

"Take the wall!" he said.

It was one of those shining moments in the course of human events where a man is invited to accede to a dignity reserved for him by destiny. Victor Oboyski—exploding plaster, lathing, and structural carpentry, crashing in much as King Kong would—actually entered the apartment through the wall. On any other planet in the universe he would have been allowed to eat the people inside.

Deputies followed him in.

Fifteen people were arrested that day—nine women, six men—and a total of three buildings were seized.

When Pizzi's crew hit the sidewalk, they witnessed a piece of street theater that was like nothing they had seen in their lives. Yet over the months that followed, it would be played out again and again for them, set against the ravaged backdrop of an ever changing urban landscape. And soon it would cease to bewilder them.

The citizens of Staten Island, New York, stood applauding the federal government; they stood there, in force, cheering deputy marshals with repeated cries of "God bless America."

Chapter Eleven

"**O**KLAHOMA is still woolly. . . . Some youngster would try to put me out because of my reputation. I would be bait for grown-up kids who had fed on dime novels. I would have to kill or be killed. No sense to that. I have taken my guns off, and I don't ever want to put them on again."

Bat Masterson, a former lawman of wide and well-earned reputation, was a national celebrity when, in 1905, he declined Theodore Roosevelt's offer to appoint him U.S. marshal for the Oklahoma Territory. Having given up for good the gunfighter's life, earning his living as a newspaper columnist for the *Morning Telegraph* in New York (he would moonlight as a part-time deputy marshal in the Southern District for four years), the man who had tamed Dodge, the toughest cattle town in the West, told the twenty-sixth President, "I am not the man for the job."

Oklahoma may have been woolly in 1905—a fifty-two-year-old gambling man whose eyesight and reflexes were finally beginning to fail him, Masterson would be in a position to know—but by then the territory and what remained of the frontier could only loosely be considered wild.

The conquest of the Great Plains and subsequent taming of the American West are traced officially through U.S. history to a single date: to February 15, 1876, the day the first patent was issued for the manufacture of barbed wire. But across the frontier of the American imagination, along the trail of the national character, the closing of the wilderness is tracked to another no less momentous occurrence and a patent issued three years earlier—to the development of the first .45-caliber Colt cartridge revolvers, marketed alternately and written into folklore as both the Peacemaker and, rechambered for .44-40, the Frontier Six-shooter, the weapon that mythopoetically *won* the West.

Every soldier, every lawman, and every significant scumbag on the American frontier did at least part of his killing with one of these gate-loaded revolvers, the official cavalry pistol of the U.S. Army. From Ben Thompson to Belle Starr, from John Wesley Hardin to

Tom Horn—they all went about littering the landscape with the help of the late Sam Colt's case-hardened "equalizer."

Wild Bill Hickok, who is famous for having carried a variety of guns, was carrying any number of them—but holding in his hand only aces and eights—when Jack McCall blew the back of his head all over the floor of a Deadwood saloon, in 1876, with a Peacemaker. Jesse James was similarly dispatched six years later by the outlaw Bob Ford.

As an expression of the problem in the West and not its solution, the Peacemaker was showcased quite dramatically—there were several of them on hand—in what may be the most celebrated half minute in American frontier history. That episode, destined to illuminate the annals of the nation's folklore indelibly, was a small-time street fight devoid of all honor, conducted in a dust-blown silver boomtown in the high desert of southeastern Arizona. It is an incident also indelibly linked to the U.S. Marshals Service.

It was in his official capacity as a deputy U.S. marshal that Virgil Earp, accompanied by his brothers Morgan and Wyatt, enjoyed his first encounter with Frank McLaury on the morning of July 25, 1880, at McLaury's cattle ranch on the Babocomari Creek outside Tombstone, Arizona. The confrontation followed a misappropriation of government property earlier that month: six U.S. Cavalry mules that had found their way into the cowboy's possession.

The showdown came fifteen months later on Tombstone's Fremont Street, in a vacant lot between the home of lumber dealer W. A. Harwood and a rooming house owned by photogapher Camillus Fly and his wife, near the rear alleyway exit from the O.K. Corral.

On that cold fall afternoon of October 26, 1881, on the high plateau, in a town that boasted "a dead man for breakfast every morning," when the Earps and a homicidal dentist, the tubercular "Doc" Holliday, dispatched three unfortunate cowboys—Frank and Tom McLaury and the young Billy Clanton—to Tombstone's Boot Hill, the frontier lawman, however ignominiously, secured a legitimate lock on American gunfighting legend.

It is out of the mythology of such events that the deputy marshal rides today. From the overworked saddle tramp wearing out federal horseflesh to an underpaid pair of them putting too many miles on the clock of a low-octane Ford, the deputy marshal exits his second century much as he did his first: setting forth to bring government, however unwelcome, to the vast reaches of the nation. And surprisingly little has changed.

Out of a field office in Moscow, Idaho, a deputy marshal named Denny Scieszinski today patrols terrain stretching from Hells Canyon east to the Bitterroot Mountains, from the Salmon River all the way north to the border of British Columbia, 41,000 square miles of some of the most beautiful and rugged country in North America. And he covers the territory alone. In a four-wheel drive, carrying a radio and a gun—"I have more than one of those"—he serves process and tracks down fugitives, riding the range much as Pat Garrett did in 1881, bringing law and order to a landscape that has changed not at all in 200 years and, if God and Denny Scieszinski have their way, never will.

Garrett survives in Scieszinski, just as he survives in every deputy from Gerri Doody to Tony Perez. He survives in deputies like Bill Woolsey, who tracks fugitives today on the squad that some fifteen years ago Perez put together in the Central District of California.

Born in 1951, raised in Arcadia, California, Woolsey, enforcement supervisor in the Los Angeles office, will tell you that police work runs in the family. You can trace it back four generations, he will tell you, to his maternal grandmother's mother's father, an Alabama-born peace officer who served as a sheriff, a deputy marshal, a Texas Ranger, and a collector of customs, a frontier lawman who retired to ranching until, at the age of fifty-seven, he himself died by the gun, at close range, from ambush, shot in the back of the head.

"Yes," Deputy U.S. Marshal Bill Woolsey will tell you, "Pat Garrett was my great-great-grandfather."

Epilogue

GERRI Doody continues to work warrants in the Eastern District of New York. In the year 2000, having put in twenty years hazardous, she will be eligible for retirement.

Dave O'Flaherty in June 1991 replaced Mike Pizzi as the Eastern District's chief deputy.

Victor Oboyski, currently acting warrants supervisor in the Eastern District, was elected in 1990 to a three-year term as president of the Federal Law Enforcement Officer's Association.

Marvin Mack and **Billy Thrower** continue to serve as deputies in Brooklyn.

Tony Crook left the Marshals Service in 1991 to join the Bureau of Alcohol, Tobacco and Firearms.

Garnett Leacock has yet to leave the federal penitentiary in Marion, Illinois.

Bud McPherson retired from the Marshals Service in the fall of 1990. He is president of Donald McPherson and Associates, a security and investigative network in Los Angeles.

Jimmy Fratianno continues to serve as the Gloria Swanson of the witness-security program.

Howard Safir, failing to be named Marshals Service director with the 1989 change in presidential administrations, departed the Marshals Service in 1990.

John Haynes continues as Special Operations Group commander.

Duke Smith in October 1990 was named the Marshals Service's number one cop—he is its associate director for operations.

Frank Skroski replaced Smith as the Service's director of training.

Mike Thompson, honored for his heroism on that March afternoon in Roanoke, Virginia, received the highest award the Marshals Service bestows—the Robert Forsyth Valor Award, named for the deputy marshal who in 1794 became the first to die in the line of duty. In July 1991 he was invited to share his expertise with the Service's incoming deputies and was promoted to the position of instructor at the training academy at Glynco, Georgia.

Sherry Harrison, who shared the Forsyth Award with Mike Thompson, left the Marshals Service in April 1989 to return to work in local law enforcement.

John Butler in January 1991 was promoted from the El Paso Intelligence Center to chief of the Air Operations Division of the Marshals Service, headquartered in Oklahoma City.

Ralph Burnside continues as a deputy in the Eastern District of New York.

Mike Pizzi in the fall of 1990 was invited to cross the Brooklyn Bridge when he was appointed chief deputy for the Southern District of New York.

Bob Leschorn in 1991 was transferred to the Service's Office of Congressional and Public Affairs. The first sworn officer ever to be assigned there, he is charged with coordinating operational activities with that office and with enhancing Marshals Service visibility within the various news and entertainment media.

Art Roderick, assigned to headquarters, was promoted in July 1991 to branch chief of Domestic Investigations.

Chad Allan is currently deputy chief of training for the Marshals Service.

Alphonse "Allie Boy" Persico, on December 18, 1987, in Brooklyn's U.S. district court, was sentenced to twenty-five years in prison on his federal loan-sharking conviction. On Tuesday, September 12, 1989, the sixty-one-year-old Persico died of cancer of the larynx at the medical center for federal prisoners in Springfield, Missouri.

Flip Lorenzoni, replaced by Mike Pizzi as district chief for the Southern District of New York, in 1990 was dispatched to Philadelphia, appointed by the Attorney General to serve as interim U.S. marshal for the Eastern District of Pennsylvania.

Frank Devlin was promoted in July 1991 as U.S. Marshals Service representative to Interpol headquarters, in Lyons, France.

Tony Perez, as field supervisor of Marshals Service personnel in Panama in late 1989 and early 1990, oversaw, among other things, the surrender to the United States of Panamanian general Manuel Noriega. In December 1990 he was named chief of the Enforcement Division of the Marshals Service.

Larry Homenick currently serves as EPIC program coordinator.

Stanley Morris was nominated by President George Bush to be deputy director (supply reduction) of the Office of National Drug Control Policy. His appointment confirmed by the Senate, Morris was assigned to the position in October 1989.

Billy the Kid was buried in the military cemetery at Fort Sumner, New Mexico, on July 15, 1881.

WALL to

WALL Mary Morris

Something there is that doesn't love a wall,
That wants it down.

—Robert Frost

. . . Stretching some four thousand miles across China's northeastern frontier, the Great Wall was built to keep the barbarians away. Evil forces were said to dwell in the north, where the desert—the void, the unknown—lay. Today the Great Wall remains the quintessential symbol of China and, in a sense, of the Chinese.

. . . If the Great Wall of China was intended to keep people out, the Berlin Wall was built to keep them in. On August 13, 1961, the people of Berlin woke to find their lives shattered. In the night, as they slept, a twenty-six-mile barrier of barbed wire had been stretched. The Iron Curtain, once imaginary, was made flesh.

—*Wall to Wall*

SINCE I journeyed to China, the Soviet Union, and Germany in 1986, much has changed. When I traveled, democracy and free enterprise were being spoken of openly in China, glasnost and perestroika were just beginning to grow current in the U.S.S.R., and the Berlin Wall was quite intact. Since then, there have been the crackdown on the democracy movement and the abuses of human rights in China, the remarkable altering of the Soviet state, the opening of the Berlin Wall. As some walls have come down, others, perhaps more solid than before, have gone up. While this work is a travel memoir, it is also a travel history. But I am not a historian, nor a political theorist. What I have written about in these pages is what I witnessed in 1986, a time when these countries were on the brink of promise and change. The world I saw then is not the same world now, but the hints, the suggestions of what was to come, were already in the air.

The Great Wall

FROM the outside, on a tree-lined residential street of Beijing, the Mongolian embassy didn't appear as if it would present any problems. It stood serene, with its brown stucco façade—the color of the desert I longed to cross—a low wall of scrub pines, a pink gravel driveway, and an open gate, reminiscent of an Italian villa. The moon-faced girl with the sleek black hair and a reddish complexion greeted me at the gate with a faint look of recognition. This was my third visit.

The first time I had come to this gate was just as she was locking it, three weeks before. I'd grasped the bars, like a monkey, pleading silently with her. The embassy was open for visas only a few hours a week. In order to cross Mongolia on the Trans-Siberian Express, as I intended to do, one needed a Mongolian transit visa, and the only place in the world to procure one was at the gate where I stood. The first time, I had been told to return in two days' time. I had returned obediently on schedule and was informed that I had to leave my passport for twenty-four hours, which was impossible at the time, because the following morning I was to depart at dawn for Chengdu.

I then spent several weeks traveling through a steamy Szechwan province, flying to Tibet, where I had experienced the wonders of the Jonking Temple. I had sailed through the Yangtze Gorges, dined on delicacies and touched silks in Shanghai, all the time thinking that the one thing I truly wanted might elude me—the stamp on my passport that would enable me to enter the land of my Russian ancestors by rail.

This time the moonfaced girl ushered me through the gate into a small guardhouse, where I handed her my passport. She opened it, looking at my picture, then at me. "Come back tomorrow," she said.

"Tomorrow," I repeated. "Tomorrow is Saturday," I said, knowing that the gate would be locked.

"Tomorrow," she said. I stared into her placid face, at her rustic beauty. She was a descendant of the roving Tatar tribes, the fiercest conquerors history has known. United under Genghis Khan in the thirteenth century, the Mongols spread their terrible conquest from eastern China to Poland. Indeed, in my own family of former Jewish peasants, males are sometimes born with the "mark of the Tatar"—a blue spot at the base of the spine from an elongated coccyx, a genetic trait that made Genghis Khan sit far forward in the saddle. My own brother was born with the blue spot, which faded shortly after birth— the vestige of rape and inbreeding during the Tatar reign.

Now this Mongolian woman who was in a sense both enemy and ancestor stood with my passport, my fate in her hands.

I folded my hands before my face in a Buddhist supplication, a prayer. "Tomorrow," I said. "I'll be back tomorrow." I walked away from her backward, then headed down the quiet Beijing street.

EVER SINCE MY GRANDMOTHER TOLD me about being buried alive, I have wanted to travel to the place where the little graves were. To find, if not the town, at least the part of the world my ancestors came from, the place of my grandmother's stories.

My maternal grandmother, Lena Malkov Zimbroff, came to America from Russia, from a small village in the Ukraine, when she was twelve years old. My mother's mother was a teller of tales, a dreamer, with translucent blue eyes that made me think of globes and oceans and distant lands. She told me of the small graves dug in the backyard of their home, some thirty miles north of Kiev, in the district of Chernigov, on the outskirts of the town of Nezhin.

When the cossacks rode into town—those fierce, marauding men who were in part remnants of the Tatars—mothers trembled, clasping their children in their arms. My grandmother told me of a young cousin skewered on a saber, of another swept away in a torrent of hoofbeats. To protect her children, my great-grandmother buried them in the ground, with reeds sticking out of their mouths.

With a misty look in her eyes my grandmother told me that she had to lie down on her back in a tight, moist hole of earth. It was dank and slimy, and the dampness penetrated her clothing, entering her flesh. My great-grandmother stuck the reed into her daughter's mouth and frantically hurled dirt over her face, for she had eight children to bury in this way. When she was done, she smoothed the grave, while Lena clamped her eyes shut and waited, wondering what would happen if her mother was captured, if she never came back. When Lena told me this, my mouth tasted of soil. I found it difficult to breathe.

Even though she lived in downtown Chicago, my grandmother's house was the first foreign country I ever traveled to. The whispers in thick, impenetrable tongues, the smells of baking breads and savory fruit stews, the fairy tales—they all came from another land. In a wistful, mysterious voice my grandmother told me Russian folktales—of Baba Yaga, the cannibal witch, or Jack Frost, whose embrace was death, or the girl turned into a firebird, her feathers spreading beauty across the land. Marushka, she called me, after the firebird girl.

And in that same voice, conspiratorial almost, she told me of a village, a girlhood, a flight to America—stories more compelling to me than the made-up kind. At times the stories took a dark turn. She told me of the cousin jailed for political reasons, and of her own daily trips to the jail, traipsing through the mud with baskets of food. She told me of the cossack man who was kind and gave children bits of bread. Then one day he carried off a girl from the village, and no one ever saw her again.

My grandmother made things up. I don't know if half of what she told me is true: if I really had a cousin who was lawyer to the czar, another who married Trotsky's daughter, and another who discovered a way to keep the Leaning Tower of Pisa from falling down. It is possible all the stories were pure invention, but none stayed with me more than the image of my grandmother buried with a reed in her mouth, the clatter of hoofbeats overhead.

In contrast to the Mongolian embassy, the Chinese International Travel Services office felt like a commodities exchange. The hot, airless room was stuffed with people, most of them shouting. Europeans in jeans, with dirty rucksacks, Eastern Europeans in dark polyester suits and ties, Central Asians in their caftans and skullcaps were all jockeying for position, shouting, waving vouchers, trying to grab the attention of the Chinese bureaucrats, who shouted back at them, snatched vouchers, disappeared, came back, saying over and over, *"Mali. Mali."* We don't know. We don't know.

My heart sank. It did not seem possible that the ticket I had prepaid in New York, which had to be picked up in Beijing, would find its way to this office and into my hands, enabling me to board the train early next week. Already this had been a journey of obstacles, and now it seemed as if this one more thing would stand in my way.

I found what appeared to be a line, cozied up to the person ahead of me, and stuck there until, after a long wait, a neurasthenic young Chinese man stared at my voucher, then at me, as if I were somehow to blame for his trouble. He motioned for me to wait as he wandered off. Then he came back and motioned for me to sit down.

I sat on the floor beside two men. They wore burlap caftans, small skullcaps, and sandals. Their features were more reminiscent of people from Arabia than from China, and I recognized them to be Chinese Muslims from Central Asia. These were the descendants of the Arabs and Persians who traveled the ancient Silk Route as merchants or mercenaries.

Not wanting to stare, I took out a small notepad and a fountain pen and began to write. As soon as I moved the pen across the page, I felt them staring at me. I paused, looked at the one next to me, then handed him the pen. First he tried to write with his left hand, as I had done, and his friend began to laugh. Then he tried to write with his right hand, and his friend laughed some more. They laughed and laughed, then gave the pen back to me.

Next the man beside me made a sweeping motion with his hand that encompassed all of Asia, afterward giving me a questioning shrug. I thought for a moment; then I picked up the pen. I drew a rectangle, four wheels, and a track. The man stared at my train; then he smiled a toothless grin. Both men shook my hand, introducing themselves. "Moscow, Mecca," the man beside me said. I pointed to myself. "Moscow," I said.

IN DREAM journeys I had imagined crossing the Hindu Kush, retracing Marco Polo's steps. I had stared at maps of the South Seas, of Madagascar, and made and remade my journeys as many times as I'd made my bed. But the trip I always wanted to take was the one to the place where the little graves were.

In 1986 I was invited to China with my companion of several years to tour the country under the auspices of the Chinese Friendly Contact Association. I had first debated seeing China in this official fashion, but then it occurred to me that I could use that as a jumping-off point to take the trip I had always wanted to take.

I pleaded with my companion to accompany me. In the years we had been together we'd hardly had a vacation. But there were concerns on his side. A conference in Sri Lanka he wanted to attend, a demanding ex-wife, difficult teenage sons. Night after night we discussed it, and finally I made up my mind. I would leave him in Shanghai, traveling on to Beijing and then across Asia. I would visit the area of the Ukraine where my family originated, then fly home from Moscow. I would do the journey on my own.

For months I planned the trip. I had everything arranged, as was necessary when traveling to the U.S.S.R. in 1986. But on April 28, ten days before I was supposed to depart from New York, something on the morning news made me pause. Technicians at the Forsmark nuclear power plant, sixty miles north of Stockholm, had reported an abnormally high level of radiation. Frantic engineers ran every check they could on their own reactor, fearing a problem there, but could find none. Meanwhile, in other parts of Sweden, Denmark, and Finland, similar readings were being taken. From some mysterious source, radiation was spilling across Scandinavia. As the northern countries turned their suspicions to their powerful and stony neighbor to the east, the Soviet Union met their demands with silence and denials.

All day I followed the news. Then at nine p.m. Moscow time a Soviet newscaster read a four-sentence statement as follows:

> "An accident has taken place at the Chernobyl power station, and one of the reactors was damaged. Measures are being taken to eliminate the consequences of the accident. Those affected by it are being given assistance. A government commission has been set up."

On the news a red, pulsating circle reached out from Chernobyl, its circumference pounding at the edges of Chernigov and Nezhin, in the Ukraine, and Gomel, in Byelorussia, where my great-grandfather was born—the region north of Kiev that was my intended destination. As the worst nonmilitary nuclear disaster in history unfolded, I had ten days to decide. No one knew yet the extent of the injuries, deaths, evacuations, long- and short-term effects. Its realities were cloaked in secrecy.

The advice of friends divided sharply along gender lines. All my women friends of childbearing age who knew I was approaching forty and wanted to have a child told me to stay home. All my male friends, except for the family doctor and my Russian shoemaker, told me to go ahead. "It'll be interesting," they said.

I spoke with a journalist who had written on nuclear fallout. He said it was still too early to predict the extent of the radiation and that the half-life of that kind of radiation was very short. Possibly, by the time I was to travel there, it would just be like getting a few extra chest X rays. He suggested I buy a Geiger counter—or a dosimeter, for measuring how many rads I was getting. He said I could get one in those electronics stores around Penn Station. He also advised me to avoid eating while in the Soviet Union.

I was laughed out of every electronics store in New York, but I packed an extra duffel bag full of Eastern Mountain trailpack dinners (beef Stroganoff, sweet-and-sour chicken, sloppy joes), a heating coil, iodine pills, cans of sardines, beef jerky, candy bars, fruit juice in cans, canned tuna, crackers—determined to go despite the dangers. On schedule, in early May, we departed New York.

THE Chinese International Travel Services office wasn't emptying, but people were coming and going. European tourists exited smiling, tickets in hand. Students in denim jackets, who looked sweaty and spent, were now laughing, smiling, tickets about to arrive. My Chinese Muslims heard their names called and scurried to the counter, leaving me. My journey seemed ill fated, star-crossed.

Suddenly the neurasthenic Chinese man who had taken my voucher appeared and beckoned me to follow him through a maze of back corridors and darkened stairways. I puffed up six flights, careful to count in case this was not my last time here. We came to a dingy office, unlit, with a dark linoleum floor. A woman sat at a desk reading what appeared to be a novel. A man in a corner was dreamily practicing his t'ai chi. The bureaucrat who led me thrust my paper in their face. They looked at my voucher as if being shown a street address in a city they'd never seen. *"Mali. Mali,"* they said. We don't know. But the man practicing his t'ai chi stopped, looked again at my voucher. "Monday," he said. "Ticket here Monday."

It was Friday, and Monday was two days before I was to leave. The weekend without ticket or visa stretched before me like a vast, barren plain. Making my way downstairs, it occurred to me now that I was not going anywhere. That I could sit on the floor of the Chinese International Travel Services office and watch others come and go, but somehow I would never go anywhere again.

DEJECTED, I wandered down Jianguomenwai Avenue—the official façade of Beijing—past the Beijing Hotel, then cut over to Wangfujing Street, the main shopping street. Wangfujing, meaning the Well of the Princes' Residences—this street of storefronts selling cheap underwear, pirated cassettes, mascara and lipstick, polyester shirts—was once a thoroughfare of palaces. Little alleyways jut off the main artery, with names like Pig Market and Lantern Market Street that are remnants of the imperial past, reflecting trades that no longer exist.

Once you have left behind the buildings of state, the wide imperial highways, and the commercial arcades, Beijing might as well be a village still living in the ancient, agrarian past. Leaving Wangfujing, I entered the maze of side streets, courtyards, and alleyways that make up the heart of Beijing. Here women in skirts with anklets or knee-high stockings squatted by the side of the road. The children had bows in their pigtails, many with gauze over their faces to protect them from the dust that blows across the Gobi Desert. Old men, with long white facial hairs, sat in front of houses in navy-blue suits, canes in hand, toothless, nodding.

The smell on these side streets was of aging meat, urine, dust. The heat was strong. The streets seemed lined with rusting bicycles. The houses consisted of boards hammered together. Thick, elephantine plants engulfed the entranceways, where young girls with dark, inscrutable eyes swept. I peered into living rooms, bedrooms, as I passed, seeing concrete floors, barren rooms, unmade beds beside tables piled with bowls of rice, an ancient woman swatting flies.

I thought of my companion, whom I had left behind in Shanghai. He would return to New York, then depart for Sri Lanka. I would travel across Asia alone. I could see his face as we parted, assuring me that he would be at the other end. But now, peering into the lives of the Chinese, I wondered what they would think if they could suddenly peer into mine. A man too busy and perhaps untrue. A woman in need. The prospects for a family small, vague. I had traveled the world on my own for years—the Middle East, Europe, Latin America. But now suddenly, here in China, a fatigue came over me, and I felt as if I could not go on for another minute alone.

I came to a Chinese apothecary, the kind I'd seen in the provinces. On one side, behind a white marble table, stood pharmacists in white coats, looking quite earnest. Behind them were neat rows of white bottles of medicine. On the other side of the apothecary an old man sat behind a glass cabinet filled with oddly shaped tubers, antlers and horns, desiccated insects, twigs, and leaves—the ancient cures of Chinese medicine. People went in, some to the modern, Western-medicine side, others to the old man for his ancient cures. I smiled at the pharmacists in the white coats, but went to the old man.

Before some of his cures were little cards written in a shaky English scrawl. I found potted deer antlers, a do-it-yourself acupuncture kit, strong-and-healthy tablets, recovery-of-youth tablets, moisten-one's-throat tablets, antiobesity pills, general-weakness herbs.

The herbalist smiled at me. With his hands he showed me how some cures you grind, some you boil and drink. I indicated I was traveling by making several circling motions around an invisible globe, and then I dropped my shoulders in a tired slouch. He nodded and laughed, pointing to the strong-and-healthy tablets. I purchased a small quantity. They looked like rabbit pellets. I would carry them with me for five thousand miles, never taking a one.

As I left the pharmacy an old woman walked out of one of the houses, heading toward me. She hobbled with a cane; her tiny feet, no more than three inches long, rose like hillocks. I recalled descriptions I had read of the pain when the bones break, of little girls screaming as their mothers bind them even more tightly. I felt my own feet beneath me, and found myself walking even more briskly through the streets of Beijing.

THOUGH I had been avoiding this for weeks, I knew it was time to go to the U.S. embassy and find out what the present traveler's alerts were on Kiev and the outlying regions. Perhaps I also had an ulterior purpose. After days alone in Beijing I was gripped by a desire to speak my own language, to carry on a conversation, regardless of how mundane.

I reached the entrance to the embassy, and a blond, crew-cut marine asked for my passport. "I don't have my passport," I said. "It's at the Mongolian embassy, getting a visa."

"I'm sorry," the marine said, "but we need proof of citizenship to allow you into the embassy."

"Do you think I'm Chinese?" I asked.

The marine laughed. "I'm sorry," he said, "but I need a passport. Those are my orders, ma'am."

"Then can you get me an information officer? I need to talk to someone about Kiev."

He looked amused, then picked up the phone. A sandy-haired man arrived, in khaki pants, shirttail out, sweating profusely in the heat of the day. He looked at me and sighed, then looked at the marine. "She can come with me." He led me into a small antechamber, where we sat on red vinyl couches. "How can I help you?" he said.

"I have an itinerary that takes me to Kiev and Chernigov, which is thirty miles from Chernobyl. Do you have any current information about the situation in that part of the Ukraine?"

He ran his fingers through his damp hair. "We have a traveler's advisory on Kiev. I personally would advise you not to go there. I definitely would not go to any outlying areas, and I am certain the Soviets won't let you."

I had already worked out a plan for this situation. I would go to Kiev, then rent a car to take me north. Even if I could not get as far as Nezhin or Gomel, at least I would see the area. "But I can go to Kiev."

"You can go at your own risk."

"But what is the danger? Do you know the risk?"

"The Soviets have been very circumspect. We don't have all the facts. Do you know anything?" he asked me hopefully.

"You're the information officer," I said.

"Oh, we know what we read in the newspapers, but we don't have an exact report."

"But I can go if I want."

"I don't think you can go outside of Kiev, but you can go to Kiev if you want." Now he was beginning to lose interest in me, finding me rather crazy, I think.

"Can you give me a fact sheet?"

"Well, I just don't have anything very informative." He stared at me for a moment, then snapped his fingers, as if a light bulb had just gone off in his head. "I'll loan you my copy of *Time* magazine," he said.

"Oh, that would be great" was my bemused reply.

"Here, I'll photocopy it for you. You decide."

I followed him to the copier, where we both looked ill in the green glow from the machine. Then he thrust the pages into my hands and wished me a safe journey. As I left, I saw him shaking his head.

Stopping for a Coke at the soda machine, I sat on the steps of my embassy and read what I had not known before departing. All pregnant women and schoolchildren had been evacuated from Kiev. People had been told not to drink water, to avoid milk products and leafy vegetables, to wash often and keep their windows shut. The area north of Kiev had been evacuated. No one could travel there. According to *Time* magazine, the reactor was still on fire.

WHY I wanted to continue on this journey remained a mystery to me. Even as I sat on the steps of the embassy absorbing the facts as they were known, my purpose seemed vague and unsure. My parents had pleaded with me not to go. "You aren't going, are you?" my mother asked in that same way she always phrased her statements, ending them with a question that inspired doubt. My father took the more tempered, businessman's approach. "Do you think it is advisable? Have you given any thought to staying home?"

But I am a person who has always searched for home. The German poet Goethe once said that writers are people who have the disease of homesickness, that being a writer is being on a constant search for the place where you belong. I have always longed for the place that was mine on the planet. Perhaps this made me restless, made me wander the earth, never putting down roots.

Once, when I was living in the American West, I met a man who came from a valley called Puerto de Luna—Gateway to the Moon. He had lived in that valley all his life, and his ancestors before him. He took me on a tour—the sinkholes, the decaying adobe churches, the path Coronado took as he searched for the fabled cities of gold. He showed me the house in which he, and his father before him, had grown up. This geography was in his blood. Everything he knew or loved or remembered was here.

But my family are Jews, Russian Jews at that, and we have been called the wanderers of the earth, though our wandering was forced upon us not by nature, but by necessity. My own family, which lived for troubled centuries on the steppes and farming land of the Ukraine, has been scattered like seeds, and only by chance has landed where it has. I have heard of a psychological disability whose symptom is restlessness. The inability to stay put. The need to move on. It is the condition of a person who must flee, who cannot stay, yet who is always looking for somewhere to rest. I seem to be so afflicted, though perhaps it is the affliction of my race.

The truth is that where I belong comes to me in my dreams, but I know I cannot go there. For years the image has always been the same. Tracks through the snow, leading down familiar streets lined with snowmen, sleds, children at play. These tracks take me back to Illinois, to Hazel Avenue, above the shores of Lake Michigan, and my childhood home.

The house is gone, long ago sold to a man who married a woman half his age. An American flag flies on the lawn; white wrought-iron furniture, antebellum style, sits on the front porch. I know this because when I am in Illinois, I visit my neighbor, and from her house I spy upon my former life. I try to envision someone else sleeping in the room where my father tucked me in. Where I read my first books, whispered my first secrets to girlfriends on the phone. Now a stranger lives inside that life, while I wander, searching perhaps still for the tracks that will lead me home.

CHEN Bao, a Chinese writer who was an acquaintance of a friend from New York, lived on the outskirts of Beijing, and I made my way there in the evening. I walked through a narrow passageway that separated his rather large four-story house from another. Yelping dogs nipped at my heels. I rang, and Chen Bao met me. He was a stout, broadfaced man, with thinning hair, and he greeted me with a wide smile. "It is good to see you," he said, as if he had known me for a long time. "You see, ten years ago I couldn't say hello to you on the street. Now I can have you in my home."

He led me four flights up a red linoleum stairwell. The doors were open to other apartments as we passed. An old woman cooked at a gas stove. An old man stared at me with frightened eyes that kept blinking as we passed. "We are very lucky, my family. We all live here together. My family and my wife's family. We have different floors, but we are all together. It is a very good arrangement."

We entered a living room that had been set up for tea, complete with small cakes and sweets. I gazed around me at the plastic plants, which were everywhere—bonsai, wisteria, evergreen, pineapple. The room was decorated with Chinese lanterns, and scrolls on the walls.

Chen Bao poured the tea. "Oh, yes, we are very lucky. A decade ago I could never have had you in my home. Why, it wasn't even my home during that time. Ten families were living here. You would not have believed the filth, the vermin."

"Where were you?" I asked hesitantly. "Where were you then?" It appeared he wanted to talk about that decade of collective madness called the Cultural Revolution. It was the time when China wanted to purge itself of anything tinged with Western privilege or thought. Scholars, scientists, doctors, officials, writers, artists—anyone in an elite profession was subject to reeducation by means of humiliation, torture, exile into the countryside. Tens of thousands were bludgeoned to death for playing the piano, keeping pets, reading novels.

Anything viewed as personal, individual, self-centered was condemned as Western decadence. A generation of the country's most gifted thinkers and creative people was destroyed. By the end of it, in 1976, at least a million were dead.

"Where was I? In the country, planting seeds. Actually, I fared better than most. I was gone for seven years. Lost seven years. But I have done all right. I work for a newspaper. I write my own books. I have been able to get some of it back. Not like my father. He did not do so well. He was a teacher of philosophy. His mind is not the same. They made him kneel for days on broken glass. They did other things to him, things he won't talk about. I know they shaved his head and made him walk the gantlet while they beat him with bats. But there are worse things you can do to someone. He was a man of principles. He believed what he taught."

"Is he alive?"

"Oh, yes, he is alive. You saw him as we came up the stairs. But as you could see, he is not the same. But you know, they persecuted everyone—stamp collectors, people who raised goldfish, who kept bonsai." He waved his arm at his plastic plants.

"But that is over now," Chen Bao said. "What happened is over. It will not happen again." He sipped his tea, the complacent look gone and a more troubled one in its place.

Then he poured more tea as we grew silent, gazing into our cups. We were like two people who have been thrust into a premature and uncomfortable intimacy, and suddenly we were aware of the embarrassing place to which it had led us. "That is over now," Chen Bao said, his face growing jovial again, passing me a cake. "Tell me about New York. Tell me what is going on in the rest of the world."

UPON returning to my room, I decided to phone New York. I wanted to talk with my companion, who had by now arrived from Japan. I asked the operator if I could place a call. She said she would call me back. I waited and waited, listening to a cassette of conversational Chinese, practicing the sound over and over.

I cannot say that it was the happiest time of my life. I had been in an angry state, given to outbursts, rages, sudden tears. I was not getting younger, and I had been with this man for over three years. What I thought I wanted with him—marriage, a child, a place of our own—had somehow eluded me. I had shut out others for his sake, and now it all seemed to be a mistake.

As I fell asleep that night, waiting for the call that never came, I dreamed I was traveling by train through a foreign country that had fields of wheat. Each row is a different color—red, blue, gray, and green, repeated in the same pattern over and over again. My companion is with me, and at last we come to an enormous walled city. We enter and find ourselves in a central plaza lined with giant doors painted the same colors as the rows of wheat. No one is there except the two of us. He says he will go and find a hotel, and he leaves me standing alone.

I stand before these giant doors, looming hundreds of feet high. I cannot reach the knocker, cannot reach the handles. I am left standing there for a long time. In the dream my companion never returns.

STRETCHING some four thousand miles across China's northeastern frontier, the Great Wall of China was built to keep the barbarians away. Evil forces were said to dwell in the north, where the desert— the void, the unknown—lay. To protect themselves from threats, both real and imagined, the Chinese have traditionally turned their backs on the north. Yet the wall, intended to contain those threats, did little to hold back the Mongol invasion of the thirteenth century. Today the Great Wall remains the quintessential symbol of China and, in a sense, of the Chinese.

A few weeks previously I'd spent my thirty-ninth birthday climbing the wall. With my companion I'd walked its reconstructed ramparts, gazed across the North China plain. Now, under the assumption that I was leaving early the following week, I decided to return to pay my respects. Prior to getting the bus that would take me, I made my requisite visit to the Mongolian embassy.

At the embassy, I stood, as anticipated, before a locked gate. I was kept from despair by the fact that a fellow traveler, a man in raggedy jeans and a dirty khaki jacket, a well-used rucksack dangling from his hand, stood shouting, "Hello, is anybody here?" in French. But the gate remained ominously closed. Still, the presence of another human being made me think that they had told at least one other traveler to come back.

The Frenchman saw me and said, *"Vous allez Trans-Siberia?"*

"Yes," I replied.

"June fourth?" he asked in almost accent-free English.

I smiled. "So we'll be on the same train."

He shook his head. "I've had such a hard time getting this visa," he muttered.

His name was Pierre. He was French, but lived in Amsterdam, where he played the saxophone. He'd been traveling in China for two months. "But now," he said, "I'm afraid to go home."

"Why?"

"Chernobyl," he replied.

I was about to ask him more when the moonfaced girl came, jangling a large key, with which she unlocked the gate. She motioned, and we followed her into the dark, austere entranceway of the embassy. Here, without ceremony, she handed him his passport and me mine. We both opened them at once and saw the red-and-blue stamp that would make our passage possible. "So," Pierre said, picking up his knapsack, buoyant now, "I'll see you on the train."

"Yes," I replied, thinking that in fact I would.

"We'll have plenty of time to talk then." He whistled as he walked away, making several Chinese stop and stare.

I BOARDED the bus to the Great Wall, glad to be going somewhere, if not yet on the train. I was trying not to think of what would happen on Monday if the travel services did not produce my ticket. Instead I let the excitement of this small adventure carry me.

The bus took us to the outskirts of Beijing, through the throngs of bicyclers (five million of them), to where the houses and apartment buildings dwindled to hamlets, finally into the countryside of rice paddies and small farms. A breeze blew, and I was content to stare outside, watching the rural landscape pass like some misty painting on a Chinese scroll.

Within a little more than an hour the Great Wall was in sight. I disembarked and joined the throng of tourists, for it was a Saturday and the crowds on the wall felt more like the attendees at some major sporting event. All afternoon I climbed the wall or sat on its parapets, watching the Chinese scurry up and down this symbol of their nation, as much representative of who they are as, say, the Statue of Liberty is of America or the Eiffel Tower is of France.

I thought of how this wall cut across the North China plain, along the rim of Inner Mongolia, until it reached the Yellow River, how for another thousand miles it snaked along the edge of the Gobi, turned toward the distant autonomous region of Xinjiang, then came to an end along the ancient Silk Route. The age and scope of this wall are beyond comprehension. Even the man credited with its construction— Qin, first Emperor of China—was merely connecting a series of already existing walls.

Qin, the emperor from whom China draws its name (Ch'in), intended for his dynasty to endure for ten thousand generations instead of fourteen years, from 221 to 207 B.C. However, in those years Qin, a great warrior, managed to unify China. He was the ruler to whom Mao Tse-tung compared himself when he wanted to justify his tactics to unify the nation. Qin was proverbial in his cruelty. During his reign he burned books and had scholars buried alive. Mutilations, brandings, and other forms of ingenious cruelty were commonplace.

Qin thought nothing of sending hundreds of thousands of laborers to their death as they connected walls to form the Great Wall. The wall stands twenty-five feet high, and twenty-five feet thick at its base. Five horsemen can ride abreast along its ramparts. It is the largest structure ever built by man—the only man-made structure that can be seen by astronauts in space. Built and rebuilt over generations, the wall as we know it now was mainly reconstructed by the Mings, who ousted the Mongols.

To understand this wall, one must first understand something about the Chinese. They have the oldest recorded continuous civilization (dating back four thousand years). Although spoken Chinese varies so much from province to province that a person from Canton literally cannot understand a person from Shanghai, its written language has been uniformly the same for more than two thousand years.

The Chinese have always wanted to protect themselves from the north, and from the nomadic tribes they feared. Yet I could not help thinking as I wandered its ramparts that the wall represented something less substantial—a deep psychological fear, the need of a people to protect themselves not only physically but emotionally as well. A recent study showed that while the Chinese have the lowest crime rate on earth, they are more afraid than Americans to venture out alone in the dark. Even in their personalities they tend to keep their feelings hidden, if they are aware of them at all. Yet fear of the unknown has historically been a national trait, reflected in modern times in the politics of terror.

I had been having my own childlike fears of late, and so I felt a certain affinity with the Chinese and their need of this wall. Sleep had not been coming easily, and when it did, I struggled with troubled dreams. I would wake shaking in the night, knowing there was no one I could call. I felt like a prisoner, condemned by language and race, within a strange kind of solitude I had never known before.

I felt invisible in this scrambling crowd as they rushed up and down the ramparts, and suddenly I found it more lonely to be in the crowd than to be really alone. I ascended to the northwestern part of the wall, until I reached the end of the reconstructed part. There I looked out and saw miles more of wall, crumbling, with blue flowers growing out of its cracks. At the base, stones tumbled into the North China plain. A few boys had crossed onto the broken part of the wall, and I decided to do the same. I climbed easily over the small barricade and put my foot on shaky stone, rough hewn.

I walked for a little way, then found a place between two rocks, where I sat down. The breeze was strong and warm, and I turned my face to the north, to the flat, verdant plain that seemed to fade into a burnt sienna at the horizon, where the edge of the Gobi lay. I stared across Asia, until I thought I could feel what it would be like to see Genghis Khan's men bearing down from the north, like my own worst fears, or to see a train leading me away across this same great plain.

It was late afternoon when I hopped a tour bus heading back to Beijing via the Ming tombs. I had already visited the tombs, and was not anxious to return, but the bus was making a forty-five-minute stop. I decided instead to revisit the gardens and the cardboard hill of photographic fantasies, where just weeks earlier my companion and I had been photographed in a cardboard airplane, vintage World War II. Now I tried on all the disguises—a princess, a warrior, a concubine. I stuck my head into the hole that put me astride horses crossing Arabia, in the bow of Viking ships. But in the end, with a strange compulsion to repeat myself, I opted for the airplane again. I climbed in, and as the photographer held up his fingers, trying to get me to smile, I soared for an instant solo, breathless and alone.

Forbidden City

SOMETHING was wrong with my body, I thought, returning to the hotel. Fatigue seemed to flow through my blood. A weakness had entered my bones. I felt as if I were wrapped in gauze, as if I were floating down a river. Perhaps it was the heat of summer in Beijing, or perhaps something really was wrong. I brushed this thought aside. Probably I am suddenly growing old. I have reached that point where the bones ache, the spirit languishes.

I put on the tape of conversational Chinese and let my body ease onto the bed. An overhead fan whirred, and I closed my eyes, with no intention of sleeping. But I slept, then awakened, startled to find myself in darkness, famished and ready to go out.

I went to a restaurant not far from my hotel. Many of the restaurants I had frequented in Beijing were accustomed to foreigners, and in some cases their menus were translated. But the restaurant I walked into was not this type.

It had concrete floors, about a dozen round tables with dirty tablecloths. The kitchen, which was part of this main room, had huge boiling vats containing rice and soups. The air was hot and steamy. The chef was a tall, skinny Chinese man who was missing his front teeth. When he laughed, he smiled a somewhat maniacal smile.

As I walked in, I stepped on rice and bones tossed onto the floor by previous clientele. Finding nothing smaller, I took a large round table next to a Chinese family. There sat a husband and wife, who stared into their bowls as they shoveled in their food, a small boy just past toddling age, two ancient grandparents, and a few other people, whom I assumed to be members of the extended family. Their table was literally piled with food, dishes on top of dishes, and one of the men kept shouting to the cook to make more. When he did this, the chef laughed a maniacal laugh.

I sat down and was handed a menu by a woman in a dirty apron. I opened the menu to find it was entirely in Chinese. I pondered my dilemma. The proprietress returned, pencil and paper in hand, prepared to take my order. Not knowing what else to do, I pointed at the table of the family beside me. "I'll take that," I said, "and that." I pointed at a few things until the woman seemed satisfied. Once she was gone, I turned my attention back to the Chinese family. The father was helping his little boy eat his rice with chopsticks. Patiently the father showed him how to hold the chopsticks, how to pick up rice, which kept falling into the boy's lap. One of the men across the table kept shouting, laughing. Then the whole table burst out laughing.

Food was put before me, but I could not find the strength to eat. Instead I watched as the father repeated his chopsticks lesson, and now the relatives laughed less as the boy began to learn. Feeling like an orphan waif, I wanted this family to invite me to join them, but when they did not, I raised my chopsticks and slowly began to eat. The chicken dish I thought I'd ordered turned out to be pork, something I rarely eat. It also seemed that I had ordered sea cucumbers, those slimy creatures—half animal, half plant—that the Chinese love. I picked at my food.

A beggar woman came into the restaurant. The proprietors ignored her as she went from table to table, plucking whatever she could off pushed-away plates and from the floor. She paused at the family beside me, and the father shoved a plate her way. She scooped what was on it into a burlap sack.

She came to me. She began taking food from one of my plates, stuffing it into her toothless mouth. Her face was wrinkled and looked as if it were covered with ash. She kept her eyes on me as she took the food, the way a cat might do.

Then she pointed to my plates. With a wave of her hand, she asked if I intended to eat. I thought of China, with a billion mouths to feed, and signaled for her to help herself. She dumped it all into the dark, fetid bag; then she ambled away, her sack over her shoulder.

I HAVE done what I can to trace my ancestry. There are ships' logs, immigration records. These are the facts, from what I can discern: My great-grandfather came from Gomel, a town in Byelorussia. Later he married and moved to the Ukraine, into the Jewish Pale—the area within which the Jews were required to live—to the district of Chernigov, somewhere outside the town of Nezhin.

The history of the Ukrainian Jew is miserable and long. In the pogroms of the nineteenth century, millions fled, emigrating to Europe, Palestine, the United States. In World War II a million and a half were slaughtered. But before these events decimated the Ukrainian Jewish community, Jews had been in Russia for centuries, living apart in small communities and working as merchants, tradespeople, or farming the land as peasants.

Nezhin, where my grandmother Lena was born, was one of the centers of the tobacco trade. I believe it was during the Chmielnicki massacres of 1648, in which over a hundred thousand Jews were slaughtered, that my ancestors fled to Gomel, where my great-grandfather was born. Later he would return to Nezhin, where he would raise his family. But in 1881—and 1882, the year my grandmother was born—pogroms broke out again. Twelve years later, with persecution continuing and the promise of America before them, my family left.

My great-grandfather brought Lena first, by ship to Canada, planning to send for his wife and the other children once they were settled. They traveled in steerage for thirty days. Lena was sick for the entire crossing. She thought she would never see land again. But at last the boat docked in Halifax. My great-grandfather made his way to Chicago, because he had cousins there. It would be a few years before the rest of the family could follow, arriving through Ellis Island.

In Chicago, a small but emerging city on a seemingly endless prairie, the winters were difficult, and my great-grandfather tended to pray rather than work. With his wife and eight children he lived in two rooms in a cold-water flat.

My great-grandfather was named Isaac. I have seen him in pictures. A man with a long, dark beard, a sturdy body, and, I am told, piercing blue eyes. For a living he peddled a cart of notions—shoelaces, pins, needles, buttons. He was, my mother told me, a handsome, austere, distant man.

Because Isaac made little money, his children went out to work in the sweatshops and factories and lumber mills. From the time she arrived in America, my grandmother sewed pillows in a sweatshop, as did the other girls.

IT WAS Sunday, and Wong had reluctantly agreed to meet me for an hour or so at the Summer Palace. Wong, a thin, frail-looking man with fine, intelligent features, worked for the government and had arranged the official part of our trip. We had met several times briefly, but had struck up a friendship. He had an affinity for contemporary American authors and said he would like to spend more time with me. However, actually getting together proved difficult. There were many demands on him, he had too much work, and in the end I sensed a hesitancy on his part.

Still, we met at the entrance to the Summer Palace, the bucolic setting that had been the summer home of the Emperors of China. It was here that the last emperor was sent when he was banished from the only home he had ever known, the Forbidden City, in 1924. But the Summer Palace was as open, fertile, and warm as the Forbidden City was enclosed, sterile, and cold. I was happy to wander its grounds for the afternoon.

Wong and I strolled the paths along the edges of the lake, where little boats sailed. We walked across narrow, arching bridges and paused to peer at family scenes—photo opportunities where young girls posed in crinoline dresses, boys assumed karate postures in kung fu jackets, grandmothers wrapped arms around resisting grandchildren. Here Wong, who had been talking almost nonstop about Norman Mailer, Henry Miller, and other writers prominent in literature courses at Beijing University, drew a deep breath. He sank into a bench as our gazes both drifted to the family scene.

"I have a little boy," he said at last. We had not spoken in any personal way before, so I took this as an indication that he wanted to open up.

"How old is he?" I asked.

"He's three. Do you want to see his picture?" He reached into his wallet and pulled out a picture of a bubbly, smiling boy dressed in a short blue suit. "He lives in Shanghai. With my wife and my parents."

This confused me. "You are apart?"

"Oh, not in that way. It is because of our work units. She is a doctor, and her work unit is in Shanghai. Mine is here in Beijing."

"You can't go and work in Shanghai? Or she can't come here?"

"Oh, no, it's not like that at all. You can't just move around. You need a work-unit transfer."

"But separating families?" I tried to fathom what it would be like— to have a child, but not be able to live with it—but I could not.

"I feel lucky," he said. "Some couples are apart for many years. I think we will be together soon, but then there are other problems."

"What other problems?" I asked.

"You see, if my wife and I were both in Beijing, with no grandparents to care for my son, he'd have to go to boarding kindergarten."

"What's that?" I asked, thinking I already knew.

"It's a boarding arrangement when the parents are separated or have long work schedules and cannot provide adequate home care."

"How old are the children when they board?"

"Oh"—Wong thought for a moment—"well, when they are three or so. They might start very young. So this is better. He has my parents; my wife is there. . . . I think about this all the time," he said. "I'm never sure what to do. But I see them forty days a year, and my son has his grandparents and his mother. The father is dispensable, no? . . ." His voice trailed off. "Still, I worry. Last week he fell down. He had to have stitches in his head. I couldn't tell how serious it was from here. I was worried. I couldn't sleep. My wife said it was just a few stitches, but still it is my son, my only child."

He stood up, and we began to walk around the lake again. "You Americans have such a different family life, don't you?"

"Yes, it is different." I could not bring myself to say more to Wong, whose mood had grown somber. "Are you pleased you have a son?"

He laughed. "I am pleased I have a child. We are not peasants, you know. We do not drown our daughters," he said, referring to the alleged practice in remote parts of China of drowning female infants, due primarily to the fact that female children, when they marry, leave home for good, whereas male children remain and work. "We are happy to have a son. We would be happy with a daughter."

"Would you ever consider having another child?"

Wong, a man of perhaps not more than thirty, looked at me, shocked. "Oh, never. It would be impossible."

"Impossible?"

Again he laughed. "Well, not impossible, but in terms of the state it is not possible. The second child would receive no public funds, no schooling, no health care. We could not do it." He smiled. "I have my son, and I am happy with this. What more do I need?"

I HAD been feeling a pain in my neck, a stiffness in my back, the result, I assumed, of too much time on the road. I also felt weak, the general malaise that I had tried to explain to the Chinese apothecary.

I had been told that there was an acupuncturist in my hotel, so I decided to go before going out for the evening.

I walked into a smoke-filled room. A soap opera was on the TV, and two men and two women, all in white coats, sat watching. One of the men was smoking a Camel. In the soap opera, a woman, shouting in Chinese, clutched a child, pulling it away from a man. The child was screaming. It appeared as if the man had struck the child.

The man smoking the Camel motioned to a table made up like a bed and told me to lie down. The sheet was stained. A man in the next bed groaned as needles went into his feet. The acupuncturist sticks needles into my neck, my heels, my shoulders. I am gripped with a sudden fear of needles. The woman in the soap opera screams. Her child cries. Tears come to my eyes, but I cannot wipe them away.

THAT evening I met an acquaintance from New York, a professor of world politics who was teaching at Beijing University. The professor himself was Asian. I told him of my meeting with Chen Bao earlier in the week and my afternoon with Wong. He spoke to me very frankly and softly about China. "I came here with a very positive outlook," he said. "I was very very pro-China, but it just doesn't work. The system is a failure. It contains the worst of capitalism and the worst of communism. The worst of capitalism because it is so class-conscious. Rank is all that matters here—the cadre system, the work unit, and so on. And the worst of communism because the Chinese want to exert complete control. The politics in everyday life is terrible here." He glanced around to see if anyone was listening before he continued to speak. "A student cannot come to my office without permission from his chairman. The chairman must know what the student wishes to discuss, when, where, why." He ran a hand wearily through his dark hair. "It just isn't working. And"— he leaned ominously toward me—"I think it will get worse. I think we haven't seen the half of it yet."

"But what about all the economic reforms?" I asked. "The attempt at a market economy. And what about what Chen Bao told me—how things are much freer?"

"Only to a point," he said. "And then you'll see. It will all change. It won't go any farther than that. It is a precarious balance here."

LATE FOR A PERFORMANCE OF THE Chinese acrobats, I left my friend, feeling a bit depressed by what he'd said. Then I hailed a cab. The driver was fairly young, with slicked-back hair. I had been practicing my Chinese with tapes, so I decided to try a conversation. "How are you?" I asked him.

To my surprise, he replied, "I am fine. And you?"

"Good," I said.

"Where are you from?"

"New York," I told him. "America."

He laughed and smiled. "You speak Chinese," he said.

"I am studying," I told him.

"Oh, that is good. That is very good."

The lights of Beijing went by, and I felt light-headed for the first time since I had been alone in China. It was as if I had suddenly deciphered the enemy's code, broken some terrible silence. Still, I was at a loss. I wanted to talk with this man more, to learn what his life was like, but I had exhausted my meager vocabulary. He dropped me off in front of the theater. "Enjoy our acrobats," he said. He waved as he drove away.

Just as I found my seat the lights dimmed, and there in the darkened, almost empty theater I watched the acrobats. Women folded their bodies together like Siamese twins, legs and arms interlacing like vines. A man shaped his body so that it fit through loops so tiny that only my arm would have fit through. Another man stacked glasses filled with colored liquid, one after another, on top of his nose. The movements were what I had come to anticipate of the Chinese—controlled, exquisite, and in a certain sense pointless, yet perfectly learned.

Then came the one who amazed me most, the woman who balanced seven porcelain bowls, which she moved from head to feet, to her back and her shoulders while performing acrobatics on the head of her partner. I was transfixed by her steady, reptilian movements. I thought of China and the delicate balance my friend had spoken of. How precarious it suddenly seemed. The woman moved assuredly, bowl to head, to feet, to nose—but one false move and it would all topple. I thought of my own precariousness, how fragile life seemed. Love itself was a kind of delicate act that could not be done alone; it was nothing without the bowls.

THOUGH THE FACES OF THE TRAVELERS were different, the Chinese International Travel Services office seemed the same as it had a few days before—a sign I did not find encouraging. The Chinese bureaucrats were still shaking their heads, shouting, *"Mali. Mali,"* and exasperated tourists were waiting, pleading, slamming fists into counters. But I did as I had done before. I stood in line, voucher once again in hand. When I reached the front, perhaps an hour later, the same nervous bureaucrat I'd seen the week before shook his head. He passed my voucher from person to person, but still no one seemed to know where my ticket was. Now I knew that I would never see Russia. I would never get on the train.

I left in utter despair, about to burst into tears, when a Chinese student accosted me. He had crooked, overlapping teeth and thick glasses. "Do you like Chinese food?" he asked. "Are you married? There are fifty states in the United States, including Alaska and Hawaii, and only twenty-nine provinces in China," repeating as a litany the lines all Chinese students who want to practice their English say.

It occurred to me that perhaps he could help, and so as a last-ditch effort, I explained my problem to him. He listened intently, nodding, then grabbed me by the arm and dragged me inside. He led me to the front of the line, shouting in Chinese the way the bureaucrats had. A man looked up, stared at me, shouted something back, then pointed to the door that I now knew led to a maze of corridors and stairs.

I followed the student as he raced up six flights into the office I had been in the other day. The man was still practicing his t'ai chi, the woman still reading a novel, as if this were some time warp from the previous week. The student shouted at them. The woman shouted back. The shouting became more polite. The man who was doing t'ai chi nodded, listened, then went off.

He was gone for a long time. The Chinese student kept telling me to be patient. "No way out," he said. "No way out." I began to pace. "You must be patient. You've got an altitude [sic] problem," he told me. I tried to make conversation. "I want to go to America and study," he said. "I want to eat pizza and watch American TV."

"There are other things to do in America," I said.

"Like what? Tell me and I'll do them."

"You can drive around the countryside. You can go to the beach. There are many museums." He hung on my every word. "You can

visit the Washington Monument, the Statue of Liberty." I was beginning to grow homesick, when suddenly the clerk returned, a green-
and-pink ticket flapping in his hand. "Here," he said. "Your ticket."

I stared, reading, "Peking-Moskau via Erhlien." I thanked him. I
thanked the woman reading the novel. I found myself walking out of
the room kowtowing.

Outside, I thanked the student profusely. "Oh, no thanks," he said
over and over, beaming through his crooked teeth. "My pleasure. No
thanks."

Then, on a whim, I offered to take him to lunch. "Maybe we can
find a pizza," I blurted, but then saw that I had made a mistake. "Oh,
no. No need." His pride was injured. He walked away from me backward. "I go back to work. You are welcome."

"You can practice your English," I called to him, but he was gone.

IN THE thirteenth century, having easily traversed the Great Wall
and conquered the North China plain, the invaders from the north
decided to build a great city. On the site of the old Ch'in city of
Chung-tu, the great Mongol leader Kublai Khan spread out the parameters of his palace, which would be its centerpiece. The Mongols
would call it Da Du, and the Chinese Ta-tu—Great Capital.

It was here that Kublai Khan built the great palace that Marco Polo
describes in his writings. Marco Polo tells of thick walls stretching a
mile on each side, whitewashed and fortified. Of a game park between the outer and inner walls, where white harts and musk deer
roamed; ponds where the animals drank; paths where the khan might
walk. He speaks of walls bedecked with pictures of dragons and birds
and horsemen, of a dining room that could seat six thousand, of a
roof ablaze in scarlet, gold, blue, and green, varnished like crystal.

Then in the fifteenth century the Mings threw off the Mongols and
transferred their capital from Nanking to Ta-tu, which soon was
called Peiping—Northern Peace. On the site of what had once been
the palace of Kublai Khan, the Ming ruler Yung-lo set his own palace.
From that day until the early part of this century, imperial China was
ruled from within the walls of the Ming Palace, which most people
refer to as the Forbidden City.

The palace was built according to the laws of geomancy, with every
major structure representing a part of the body, enabling the power

of the emperor to radiate out in four directions, as if he were himself the sun. Yet within the city's four concentric walls the rulers of China reigned in virtual isolation. Almost no one saw them except for their eunuchs, their concubines, and their immediate family. And then at the end of the civil war between Mao Tse-tung and Chiang Kai-shek, after Mao proclaimed victory, on October 1, 1949, the gates of the Forbidden City were thrown open for all to see.

I WALKED through the Meridian Gate into the entrance to the Purple Forbidden City—once considered to be the heart of the capital, the empire, indeed the world—where, according to ancient Chinese texts, "earth and sky meet, the four seasons merge, wind and rain are gathered, and yin and yang are in harmony."

I walked the Imperial Way, across the Canal of the River of Golden Water, toward the Hall of Supreme Harmony, across the marbled terrace, and down the steps toward the Hall of Complete Harmony and the Hall of Preserving Harmony. As I recalled the cruel and unharmonious history of this country, the names seemed like wishful thinking. But to the Chinese, this was the center of their universe, the place where balance was supposedly kept. Along this axis, from the emperor's throne, his divinity and benevolence were extended to all the reaches of the realm.

Chinese tourists gazed impassively at the throne of their emperor. Some held their children up to see. So rooted is it in their culture that this city is closed for only the emperor that they moved through it as if they expected to be ousted at any moment.

I found myself stunned before the expanse of walls, courtyards, terraces reaching more than half a mile, whose marble was carried from the Burmese border on the backs of elephants. The main buildings existed on the central axis, with the lesser buildings laid out asymmetrically around them. At the far end were the Palace of Heavenly Purity, where the emperor once lived, and the Palace of Earthly Tranquillity, where his empress had her chambers.

I walked among the pagodalike structures, with their red tile roofs with the steep pitch, jutting edges, and upturned corners. Gazed into the faces of carved stone owls and dragons representing the imperial virtues. I continued through the open promenades into a maze of alleys, sequestered walks, struck by how impersonal it all seemed.

There was no sense of the people who had ruled here. No trace of an emperor. Yet here the Son of Heaven dwelt, never leaving the walls of the Purple Forbidden City. He existed without a single view of the city of Peking or of the people he ruled.

As I made my way from palace to palace, down steps leading to fountains where concubines had played the lute, into apartments where eunuchs had served their aging consorts, into throne rooms where emperors had bestowed grace or handed out punishment, I thought less of the art objects before me—the gilded furnishings, the jade figurines—than of the intrigues, the passions, the cruelties and loves.

I moved somewhat uneasily through the sacrosanct walls, as if I could overhear a plot being hatched. I recalled the story of the hapless concubine who had pleaded for her emperor in the midst of a coup, only to find her own self hurled into the depths of a putrid well. Now all this history—from Kublai Khan to the present—was stored in this rather sterile museum that the Purple City had become. As I crossed bridges, moving from palace to palace, the words of Coleridge came back to me, a poem I had not read since college:

> *In Xanadu did Kubla Khan*
> *A stately pleasure-dome decree:*
> *Where Alph, the sacred river, ran*
> *Through caverns measureless to man*
>   *Down to a sunless sea. . . .*
> *A savage place! as holy and enchanted*
> *As e'er beneath a waning moon was haunted*
> *By woman wailing for her demon-lover!*

SITTING on the steps between the Palace of Heavenly Purity and the Palace of Earthly Tranquillity, I stared at the ring on my finger. Ten days before, I had stood with my companion at another sacrosanct place, the Jokhang Temple, in Tibet, the seat of Tibetan Buddhism. Monks in red robes, heads shaved, lay prostrate on the ground, praying. The temple was lit with candles sitting in red glass, casting a reddish light, and the smell of incense was intoxicating and sweet.

Outside the temple a flock of Tibetan women had gathered, draped in turquoise jewelry and brightly woven cloth. They pushed beads, amulets, earrings, baubles, necklaces, and rings in my face, laughing as I began to bargain with them. One woman caught my attention. She had jet-black hair pulled back, revealing her clear, glowing, burnished skin. She had playful dark eyes and seemed to be about my age.

I examined an amulet, with a dancing woman inside, and a strand of coral beads. She indicated with her fingers thirty yuan. I shook my head, held up all my fingers twice. "Twenty," I said. We made a deal. We did this several times, until I had made my purchases for the day.

My companion, who had gone off to buy small Buddhas, returned, and we thanked the woman, waving good-bye. I had not walked far when she came back to me. She opened my hand and put a blue turquoise ring in it. I shook my head. She thrust the ring onto my ring finger, smiling at me and my companion. "No," I said, shaking my finger. I felt his hand touching my shoulder. She pointed to the ring, then to the two of us. I tried once more to refuse what I now understood to be a gift. She put her fingers to her lips to shush me.

Now I sat alone on the steps of the sterile Imperial Palace, thinking how different this felt from where I'd been ten days before. No one had come to bargain with me playfully. No one had put a caring hand on my shoulder. For a moment I thought I could pick up the strains of a lute, but it was just the wind whipping around the palaces. I thought of the wailing woman crying for her demon-lover. If I listened, I could hear her cry.

A PEKING duck dinner in an old Chinese restaurant was advertised for tourists in my hotel, and wishing to celebrate my imminent departure for Russia, I signed up to go. I had one traveling dress and one pair of heels with me for such occasions, and I dug these out of my duffel. The dress was wrinkled, but would do. I showered, combed my hair, put on a little makeup, and then slipped into the dress.

It was a snug-fitting dress that zipped up the back, and while I did not feel I had gained weight, it seemed a little tighter than usual. I was thinking about this as I began to zip it up. Distracted perhaps for a moment, I let the zipper snag midway up. I tried to force it, but it was stuck. I tried to take it off my shoulders and shimmy out, but I was immobilized there, like a madwoman in a straitjacket as I turned this way and that, determined to be free.

I thought I would remain caught there forever. Whom could I call for help? Would the woman at the front desk understand my plea? Whom would she send to rescue me? The thought made me more determined. Like the Chinese acrobat who worked his way through the loops, I willed my body small and managed to crawl out of the dress and into another outfit. I caught the bus to the restaurant just as it was pulling away.

THE entrance to the restaurant was a courtyard with a small fish-pond, and we tourists made our way inside. Our hostess, dressed in a traditional Chinese gown, seated us at a large circular table, and we introduced ourselves. An English human rights activist sat to my left and a bodybuilder from Chicago to my right. Across from me was a man from New Zealand who loved Reagan and wanted to discuss him with me during the meal.

The bodybuilder wore a Zen symbol around his neck. He was huge, and his shoulder mashed against mine. "I'm from Chicago," I told him. "I grew up there."

He had been traveling in Asia for over a year. "I can't wait to get back and eat Gino's pizza and coconut cream pie and Cap'n Crunch with bananas," he blurted.

A waitress brought in our first course. Sesame chicken feet (only the skins) and marinated sea slugs. I tried to pass, but the offerings were automatically placed on my plate.

The English human rights advocate turned to me and began speaking, for reasons I do not understand, about the Tibetan habit of chopping up their dead and feeding them to the vultures. As the duck was brought in, the Englishman said, "You know, it became such a tourist attraction that they had to stop it. The monks got so angry that they were chasing the tourists around with people's guts."

"I'm sick of Asia," the man from New Zealand said. "Give me America any day. America with Ronald Reagan, that is." He looked at me for some agreement, but I was moving the sesame chicken feet around on my plate.

IN THE evening, when I returned to the hotel, Wong was waiting in the lobby, a guitar resting between his knees. He had come to say good-bye. I had a gift for him, a wool blanket I had purchased at the friendship store—where Chinese cannot shop—knowing that blankets were very dear in China and winters could be cold. "Oh, no," Wong said. "I cannot accept this."

"But you must."

"Oh, I cannot. I cannot. I have neglected and abandoned you. I have not spent much time with you. I was preoccupied with many things. No, I cannot accept."

"But you must. Send it to your wife. For your little boy."

He seemed more tolerant of this idea but remained mired in guilt. "Next time I will show you more of my country."

"That would be lovely," I said, thrusting the blanket into his hands.

"I thank you for my wife and family. I thank you for my son."

"It has been my pleasure."

"I consider you my friend. I will do anything I can to help you."

"I consider you my friend as well."

Finally he took the blanket. Then he opened his guitar case. "I wanted to sing you a song. For your departure," he said. He sat down, and with a thick Chinese accent and a rather tinny sound to his guitar Wong sang for me—many verses—and I applauded tearfully when he was done.

THE next day, my last day in China, I rented a bicycle in a small shop off Jianguomenwai Avenue. Unable to communicate a single word, I pantomimed again with my hands. I held out money. The man took it, and I was off.

First I rode through residential streets to test my skill. I rode past people's houses, their gardens, their laundry. People shouted as I went the wrong way down a one-way street. I rode on, like a deaf-mute, until I crashed into a man with a bike loaded down with live ducks. He cursed me under his breath, the ducks squawking.

Now I crossed over to Jianguomenwai Avenue, joining the crowd riding in the direction of Tiananmen Square. I joined the steady stream of men and women, in their navy-blue suits, their Mao jackets. I rode until I came to the square. There I rode out of the mass and paused beneath the huge poster of Mao, founder of Chinese communism, hero of their revolution, author of their darkest hour.

I watched as toddlers ran, their faces covered in gauze. Couples held hands. Old people, perched on canes, sat in the shade. It all seemed so peaceful, as if nothing could go wrong here. It was hard to remember that this was the same people who in the 1950s set out to destroy its birds, which were eating too much grain. For twenty-four hours the Chinese beat tin cans and blew whistles so that the startled flocks would find no place to rest, and millions dropped from the sky, dead of heart failure.

When I had first read about this, it seemed to sum up China perfectly. But now I was not sure. I had seen the streets of China pulsing with life. And I had sipped tea, listening quietly to the tales of the Cultural Revolution. I could not help but feel ignorant; as I stood in Tiananmen Square on June 3, 1986, China's fate seemed as inscrutable as the faces riding before me.

Suddenly the wind picked up. The sky darkened. As I gazed to the north I saw coming toward me a thick yellow cloud, like pudding. People began scurrying, seeking a wall, a corner to protect them. Bikers hurled their bicycles down. They covered their faces. Some pulled their coats and sweaters over their heads.

It was the yellow loess dust from the Gobi, a storm of dust that worsens each year as the desert grows closer and the evil of the north approaches. Before I knew what to do, it was striking my eyes, my face, my throat. Blinded, I groped for cover, but I was caught in the middle of the great Tiananmen Square. I staggered toward a wall and beneath a tree found some shelter from the wind. I pulled my sweater over my head and waited, still as a statue.

Then the dust was gone, as quickly as it had come. I got back on my bicycle and rode once again with the throng that, it seemed, had never stopped moving.

Across the Gobi

FOR me, trains are the stuff of stories, inside and out. From windows I have seen lovers embrace, workers pause from their travail. Women gaze longingly at the passing train; men stare, with thwarted dreams in their eyes. Escapist children try to leap aboard. Narratives, like frames of film, pass by.

On the inside, I have had encounters as well. I've met people who have become briefly, for the length of the ride, lover or friend. A strange and sudden intimacy seems possible here. I've been invited off trains into homes, into beds, into lives—each time, I am sure, because people know a train traveler will never leave the train.

My life, even as a little girl, was intimately tied to trains. When I was five, my parents concocted a train journey to Idaho, a family vacation at Sun Valley. My father was not with us on that ride. He would be joining us later, flying in after a meeting, coming for a short spell, his vacation time always being trimmed, like lean meat.

So it was my mother, brother, and myself in our tiny compartment, my mother a frazzled woman—lonely, I think—but dedicated, as mothers were then, to us. She didn't get angry about the toothpaste flushed down the toilet, the small suitcase that kept falling on her head. She wore lipstick and a blue dress and high heels to dine in the dining car. My mother's agenda was London, Paris, Rome, maybe Hong Kong, but we were en route to Boise, Idaho.

So I escaped and sat, hour after hour, beneath a glass dome, staring at the light over the cornfields. I sat—a dreamy, somewhat forlorn child of five—watching the stars coming on like city lights, until my mother retrieved me back into our cramped compartment. Here I kept my eyes open, peering into the night at the dark expanse of prairie, as the world I knew receded and we moved into the West.

In the morning, before daybreak, I made my way—still in my nightclothes—back to the dome car to await the rising sun. Slowly it came, and there before me suddenly stood the white peaks of mountains. I had never seen a mountain before, and these shimmered, their glacial caps sheathed in sunlight, against the endless blue sky and the flat green midwestern plain from which they rose. There on the Union Pacific Railroad the mountains came upon me as my first truly complete surprise—the way the remarkable events of life have come upon me since. Even my mother, as she came wearily to try to coax me back to our compartment, paused for a moment in awe.

In the high-ceilinged, dark-wood waiting room for the Trans-Siberian Express, Chinese Muslims, the women with veils over their heads, sat on sacks of bulgur and rice. European students studied their travel guides or slept on their duffel bags. Eastern European diplomats, in dark navy suits and shirts with frayed collars, milled close to the doors. Announcements in Chinese blared through the static of speakers overhead. Anxious travelers—bound for Ulan Bator, Moscow, Warsaw, Berlin, and some even for Mecca—checked their watches or bade their good-byes.

I went through my papers. Everything seemed in order as I leaned into my duffel, once again overcome with fatigue, as if I had sunk there, never to rise again. But suddenly the gate was opened, and the travelers surged, like an obedient flock, for the train.

I moved slowly from the rear, dragging my duffel behind, until I passed through the doors onto the platform. There it stood—an army-green train with perhaps a dozen or so cars, circa 1950, PEKING-MOSKAU on its side, Chinese porters in red caps standing ready at each car. I stood amazed and thrilled.

I made my way to carriage number 3, where a very tall, very un-Chinese-looking porter—who would take care of our car for the entire ride and who spoke enough English and French to make brief conversation possible—took my duffel out of my hand. He led me into the first compartment and wished me a pleasant journey.

I stared at the lace curtains, the small lamp, the writing table with lace tablecloth, the chair, the small sofa that would convert into a bed. I opened the door to the semiprivate bath, which consisted of a hose shower and a sink. On the advice of a friend I had purchased a deluxe ticket, as opposed to first class. First class consisted of a hard bed and four people in the compartment. Deluxe was a soft bed and two people in the compartment. For six days, at a cost of two hundred dollars, I knew I had made the right choice.

I sat down at the small table by the window. Travelers scurried outside. Porters helped them with their bags. My porter brought me a pot of tea and said that the samovar was always hot.

I breathed a sigh and settled in. I was opening my journal when Cecilia arrived. She sported a full pack and a loud Liverpool accent. "So here we are. We're roomies. Isn't this great!" She was large, a dishwater blonde with square features and a boisterous voice. In a matter of moments I learned that Cecilia was English, living in Singapore with her second husband and her two children, having marital problems, and also, she hinted, an affair. "Going to London," she said. "I needed a break." I predicted rather accurately that Cecilia would not stop talking for the entire six days and that if I wanted to think or rest, I'd have to work my way around her, which did not seem very easy in an eight- by six-foot room.

I got up to stretch, and Cecilia took the window seat facing the direction in which the train was traveling. There she planted herself for the rest of the trip, with her tea, her rock and roll tapes, and the snacks she'd eat all day long, never seeming to have a meal.

I left the compartment and stared out a window. Soon there came a whistle, a brief announcement in Russian and Chinese. The wife of a Yugoslav diplomat, who had the compartment next to ours, stared out the window as well. When she heard the announcement, she turned to me and said in English, "Now we are leaving." She gave me the only smile I would see on her face the entire trip. Suddenly the whistle came again, and in a matter of moments I felt the tug of wheels, the power of engines as the journey began.

I found a jump seat at the window. I pulled it down and watched as the streets of Beijing drifted away; the stream of bicycles receded, then disappeared. Rice paddies came into view. Oxen pulled plows across yellow-earth fields. I was oblivious to the other travelers, all with noses pressed to the glass, until someone shouted, "The wall, the wall." There it was, snaking across the mountains, crumbling here and there, careening down a ridge, only to rise again; the Great Wall of China wended its way like a mythological beast, fortified and useless. Then slowly it diminished, until it was only a thin line, like a crack in the earth. And then it was gone.

I GUARD my grandmother Lena's naturalization papers in a vault back home. But I made a copy, which I carry with me on this trip and hold in my hand as we leave the wall behind. In the same vault I keep her wedding ring, which I am intended someday to wear. It sits wrapped in tissue, with its beveled edge, its interweaving pattern that could be leaves or pebbles on a beach; I often stare at it, trying to decide. Sometimes I want to wear it when I leave the vault, but always I put it back in its tissue, locking it away, believing that the right time will come.

I cannot look at the ring or at the papers that I keep there without thinking of a picture I have of my grandmother, an aging bride at twenty-two. In the picture she is unsmiling, something rare for her, and there is already a middle-aged thickening around her waist.

I do not believe she wanted to marry. She wanted to be a dancer, she told me once, twirling around the room. Never mind that Jewish

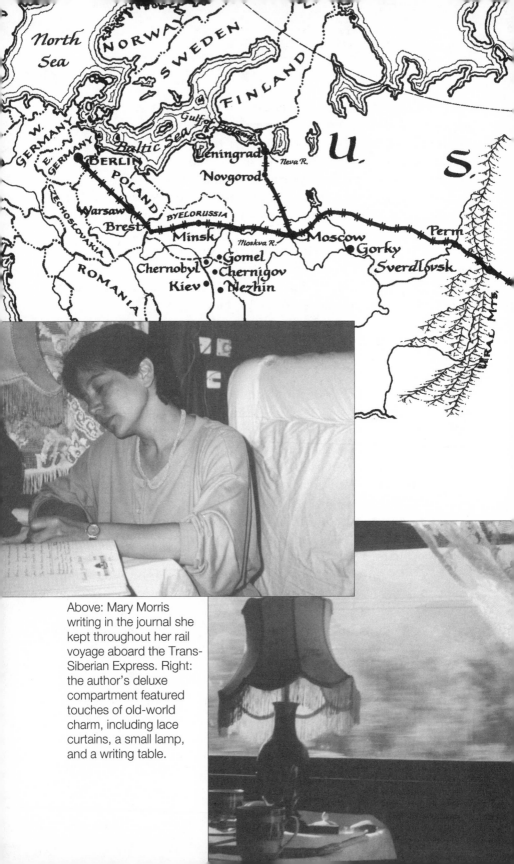

Above: Mary Morris writing in the journal she kept throughout her rail voyage aboard the Trans-Siberian Express. Right: the author's deluxe compartment featured touches of old-world charm, including lace curtains, a small lamp, and a writing table.

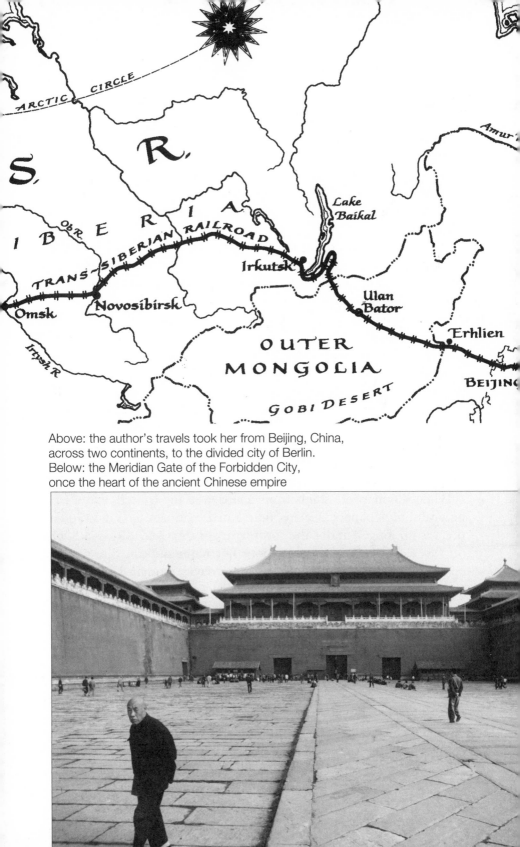

Above: the author's travels took her from Beijing, China,
across two continents, to the divided city of Berlin.
Below: the Meridian Gate of the Forbidden City,
once the heart of the ancient Chinese empire

girls could not be dancers then, or that her petite, buxom frame was not what one traditionally associates with Russian ballerinas. My grandmother wanted to dance her way around the world.

Instead she married a redheaded man with a fiery temper and a sad, complex history. His name was Zimberoff, though the *e* was dropped when a sign painter couldn't fit all the letters over my grandfather's saloon door. Her marriage was an arranged one, though over the years affection would grow between them. They produced three redheaded, fiery children, my mother being one. My grandmother was widowed suddenly at forty-five and lived more years than that before she died, but she never married again. She didn't seem to mind her solitude, even when blindness made her doubly alone.

People said Lena had psychic powers. She was said to predict births, calamities, deaths. The day of my grandfather's death, a picture he had hung dropped off the wall. It was a picture the family hated— Little Bo Peep playing a banjo. My grandparents had fought over it. At lunch my grandmother looked at the wall. "The picture," she said, "the picture," moments before it fell. When her husband died that evening, my grandmother said she knew.

I believe she knew what was happening to me without my telling her. I felt she knew everything there was to know about me. Even though she is long dead, I feel this is still true.

When she married, she became a citizen of the United States. Her naturalization papers declare that Morris Zimberoff (my grandfather) is no longer under the sovereignty of the Czar of Russia. Only on the back of the document does her name appear. She was his chattel, my mother explained. In those days a woman belonged legally to her husband and all legal matters were in his name.

There are family members who can tell me more of the things I long to know, but many won't answer my letters or return my calls. We have been split apart by personal rifts, contested wills, assorted griefs. People who grew up in the same house will not say hello in synagogue.

I think of the dinners at my grandmother's house when forty or fifty people would eat steaming bowls of soup, roast chickens, specially baked breads. Now the only keeper of these recipes is my grandmother's failing alcoholic maid. I always think I will call to get these recipes. That I will learn to bake those sweet meats, those sugary rolls. I imagine for myself a household full of guests, relations reconciled.

When holidays come around I go to films, buy tickets for shows. Sometimes I go to synagogue for memorial services, wondering for whom it is I mourn.

THE dining car looked more like a Chinese laundry than a restaurant—noisy, frenzied, boiling hot. Warm Chinese beer was being handed out, and I grabbed one from a passing tray, as everyone else seemed to do. The car was packed, and I saw no seats, but then Pierre, the French saxophone player I'd met at the Mongolian embassy, waved from across the room, pointing to half a seat. "So," he said, putting an arm around my shoulder, "you made it." He was sitting at a boisterous table of European travelers—Swiss, French, German, and Dutch—speaking assorted languages. When I joined them, they switched to English, but I told them French or German was all right.

A small fan blew overhead, but the heat continued to rise. Everyone was sweating. Plates of delicious fried meats, sautéed vegetables, rice were being passed. "Open a window!" Pierre shouted in French. The soaking waitress ignored our pleas. Someone opened a window, and the cook went wild, screaming in Chinese, slamming it shut. "Dust!" he yelled. "Dust!" We drank our warm beer and ate hot food as we baked in the sun.

The heat did not let up, and felt close to a hundred and twenty at times. None of the Chinese porters would permit windows to be open. "The desert," our porter explained to me. But back in our car, protests were mounting. At last he let us open the windows in our individual compartments if we kept the doors shut. Cecilia had gone to the dining room to sit, and left me alone at the open window, dust blowing in my face.

The landscape had altered. From the farmlands and rice paddies we moved into a mountainous, more arid terrain as we crossed Inner Mongolia. Though we had yet to reach the desert, a scrub grassland reached to the horizon. I sat as the day shifted to evening and the heat subsided.

AT EIGHT forty that evening we reached Erhlien, the border town between Inner and Outer Mongolia. It was the gateway to Russia, Outer Mongolia being a Soviet protectorate. The station was old-fashioned, like something out of the American West—a small wood-slat structure. Chinese border guards came onto the train. After checking our passports and visas, they told us we could leave the train.

I stood on the platform, breathing the cool evening air. It was unclear how long our stop was, but to my surprise and almost fear, suddenly they took the train away. Then I recalled the words of a friend who'd taken this trip before. At the borders, he'd told me, they have to change the wheels because the track has a different gauge. Each country also has its own dining car, and now for Outer Mongolia the new car had to be attached.

I was happy to leave the train and walk in the cool night air. It was a lovely night now, and a full moon shone overhead. I went into the station, where a small postal service was open. I bought stamps and began to write postcards from the border of Inner and Outer Mongolia, seemingly the most remote place on earth, though in fact it was fairly accessible. I sat on a wooden bench writing, while border guards patrolled around me and bullfighting music played incongruously on the overhead speakers.

On the platform an hour or so later I ran into the Chinese Muslims I'd sat next to on the floor of the Chinese International Travel Services office. We greeted one another like long-lost friends. One made a sweeping motion, as if to wipe sweat off his brow, indicating how hot they had been. Then they pointed to the yellow moon over Mongolia, clasped their hands as if in blessing, and smiled.

AT ABOUT midnight the train returned with new wheels and a Mongolian dining car, and we crossed into the Mongolian People's Republic. After perhaps half a mile the train stopped, and Mongolian passport officials boarded. They had wide bronze faces, reminiscent of the indigenous peoples of America. Some theories of human migration say that these ancient Central Asian peoples crossed the Bering Strait and were the first inhabitants of the Western Hemisphere, from whom all the Native Americans descended. But now it was clear that they were part of the police state. Bunks, overhead racks, and suitcases were thoroughly searched for contraband. Then at one a.m. they left, and we entered Mongolia.

I found I could not sleep, so I wandered to the new dining car, which, with arching windows, scalloped seats, and red curtains, looked more like a mosque. Pierre was sitting with two Dutch girls. The Mongolian dining crew—a man and his wife—were already setting up for breakfast. They worked noiselessly in the background.

Pierre ordered a bottle of Mongolian vodka and poured drinks all around. The man, who wore a small, brightly colored skullcap, and the woman, with a scarf around her head, brought glasses out and joined us. They raised their glasses, and we raised ours. Then we sat in the darkened car, watching the beginnings of a moonlit Gobi rush by, drinking Mongolian vodka into the night.

MONGOLIA, the homeland of Genghis Khan and his grandson, the great ruler Kublai Khan, is a land of towering snowcapped peaks, and forests, rivers, and lakes. But it is hemmed in by a wall of mountains in the east, west, and north that prevents precipitation, and the Gobi Desert, to the south, is the result. Suitable for neither a pastoral nor an agricultural economy, it is almost lifeless. Its heat is unbearable in the summer. Piercing winds and snow make it miserable in winter. Only a few humans, and sturdy animals, can survive this inhospitable land.

In the morning, just after five, I woke in a cold and dusty compartment. Bending back the shade, I peered at half a million miles of golden sand. Camels and yurts—those large round nomad tents the same color as the desert in which the wandering traces of the warrior race still dwell—appeared. They were infrequent, but they were there, camels blending into the sand, the round yurts in which Mongolians had been living for millennia.

It was not long before sand filled the air of the train, covering our pillows, our belongings. A fine golden dust seemed to settle on everything. The porter would not permit any windows to be opened as the heat of the day grew, and we baked, like prisoners of a sauna. Cecilia could not bear it, and she staggered to the dining car, where she would remain for the morning. I munched on a breakfast of melba toast, sardines, V8 juice, transfixed by the emptiness beyond, longing to get off the train. I imagined a horse awaiting me. I fantasized my yurt, a caravan, me munching on yak meat. I had a desire to flee across the great Gobi flat. I pondered the life I'd left behind—no job, one cat, good friends, devoted family, a questionable companion, who, it seemed, was always on my mind. It would all be there, I reasoned, when I returned.

IN THE THIRTEENTH CENTURY Genghis Khan, whose original name was Temuchin, which means ironworker, unified groups of nomadic tribes that roamed the Gobi Desert and began one of history's most remarkable military conquests. His father, the chief of a small tribe, was poisoned by an enemy, and at the age of thirteen Temuchin became the leader. Temuchin and his family lived a harsh, miserable life as herders of a few head of livestock, digging roots for food.

But soon Temuchin began to attract followers. He built an army—a superb fighting force—using rigorous training and discipline. He ensured that his troops were well equipped, and he appointed officers on the basis of achievement, not connections. In this way he made his officers loyal to him. Temuchin used his army to extend his power, and by 1206 he was ruler of all Mongolia. That year an assembly of Mongolian chieftains proclaimed him Genghis Khan, which means limitless strength.

In 1211, with a hundred thousand fearless horsemen, Genghis Khan penetrated the Great Wall of China and conquered a million people. He then swept through Central Asia into Persia, through the mountains of the Caucasus, and into the Russian steppes. Mongol cruelty on these campaigns was legendary. Once they executed defiant Russian boyar captives by placing a platform on top of them, and then proceeded to have a banquet on it, crushing them to death.

Neither Russia nor China would ever be the same again. Genghis Khan established, and his grandson Kublai Khan consolidated, the greatest empire the world has ever known. It stretched from Korea to western Russia, from Burma to Iraq, from the Arctic Circle to Canton. In their conquests the Mongol armies—the Golden Horde—razed once beautiful cities, burned churches, destroyed libraries. They killed and enslaved mercilessly. They abducted women and smashed sick children into trees. Yet their empire brought Europe and Asia into contact for the first time, helping to unify the vast country that was then the unknown territories of Russia.

With the death of Kublai Khan, in 1294, came struggles for succession. The empire dwindled back into tribal conflict, wandering bands. However, invasions of the Tatars, successors to the Mongolians, continued to ravage Russia into the sixteenth century.

Then in 1691 the Manchus conquered Mongolia, reducing the Mongols to serfdom and poverty until 1911, when Mongolia declared itself an independent state. But Mongolia's independence would be short lived. Neither China nor Russia would ever forget the havoc Mongolian rule wreaked on their countries. Mongolia would become a political pawn in the hands of its neighbors until finally it became a Soviet protectorate. Now it is a country of collective farmers and herders, not a place travelers think of with interest. But for a time the Mongols ruled the world.

AT MIDDAY we pulled into Ulan Bator. Located some nine hundred miles from Beijing and a staggering thirty-seven hundred miles from Moscow, the capital of Mongolia looks like a Muslim city, bespeckled with mosques and houses, with scalloped windows and domed roofs. Yet plunked down amidst these, like the legs of storybook giants, were Soviet-style apartment complexes and government buildings.

On the platform, to my surprise, Soviet police—blond, enormous, wearing knee-high leather boots and tight-fitting green uniforms— patrolled, while russet-skinned, broadfaced Mongolian women dusted the tracks with colorful green or purple feather dusters. I wanted to take a picture of the women, but when I raised my camera, a Soviet guard put a finger across his face. *"Nyet,"* he said. I put my camera down. I crossed the platform to a small park, and was about to sit for a moment in the shade when another guard emerged, with the same practiced finger across his face. Slowly I backed away, toward the train.

Some passengers were leaving the train at Ulan Bator, where they'd stay about a week, until the next train arrived. I watched as they lugged their duffels, happy to be getting off. I wanted to be among those who were leaving. At that moment I decided I had planned this trip all wrong. As a traveler who always followed her impulses, I had gone wherever the bus would carry me, but this trip had clipped my wings. Soviet travel must be preplanned, prepaid. You can't just get off the train on a whim and show up the next week.

My mood was gloomy as I returned to our compartment and found Cecilia and her newfound friend Janet munching on biscuits and tea. Janet was also English, and thinking about moving to South Africa, a place Cecilia had lived. "You know," Cecilia said, "the Africans are like little children. Of course they should rule—everyone knows that. But they need to learn how. You have to teach them everything."

"Oh," I said. "I imagine, like most people, they learn quickly."

"We had a woman working for us once, and every day we had to show her again and again how to put the dishwasher on."

"I never get those things right either," I said.

"Now, I'm against apartheid, just like everyone is," Cecilia said, "but in South Africa they are little children." She leaned toward Janet. "You know, I've never told anyone about this before, but . . . ."

I grabbed a book and my journal and headed for the dining car, the only place on the train to escape to. It was fairly empty, it being after lunch, and I took a seat by the window, feeling suddenly old, stodgy, trapped in an itinerary. But then as we started to roll, I pressed my face to the glass, thinking of what might await me, and how, if nothing else, there was the motion of this train to carry me along.

Pierre came into the dining car and joined me for a late lunch, which the chef reluctantly prepared. We ordered kefir—fermented milk—sourdough bread, Mongolian borscht, a cabbage stew with some kind of broth, and to my surprise, it was all delicious.

"So," Pierre said, finishing his soup, "tell me, what's your story?"

I told him I was traveling on a magazine assignment—which was partially true—to find my childhood home, which was thirty miles from Chernobyl, and that all in all it seemed like an ill-fated trip.

At the word Chernobyl he shook his head. Then he paused. "That's not the real story."

I laughed, knowing he was right. "Well, tell me yours first, and then maybe I'll know what to say."

"All right. I have three daughters. Twins by one woman and another by a second woman." He was smiling. Obviously he had delivered this information before. "And the girls are all the same age."

My eyes widened. "Do they know about each other?"

"Oh, we're all great friends. The kids all play together. I baby-sit for them all the time, except since I've been away."

"For two months," I reminded him.

"I needed a break," he said. "Now you tell me. What is it? Are you running away? Is it a secret you carry? Unrequited love?"

"All the above," I said. "You choose."

"Is there somebody in your life?"

I thought about where he would be right now. Perhaps on the

tennis court or with friends eating Chinese food. This was the longest we had ever been out of touch. I have no memory of not speaking with him for more than two days. "Yes," I said softly, "there is."

"So what's wrong?" he asked.

"Nothing's wrong," I said. "I wish he were here, that's all." A wave of homesickness came over me. Perhaps a letter would be waiting in Moscow. Perhaps I would have some word.

Pierre pursed his lips. "So why isn't he?"

"He had other things to do," I said.

Gathering up my books, I told him I was going back to my compartment. I needed to rest. When I returned, Cecilia and Janet got ready to leave. It was a rhythm we established. Except for sleeping, we were hardly in the compartment at the same time if we could help it. I settled down, my door open, with a book I had been meaning to read. An anthology of Soviet writers. I had not been reading for long when the wife of the Yugoslav diplomat came into my room. "We are approaching the Soviet Union," she told me. "I'd tear the cover off that book if I were you."

I turned the book over; Aleksandr Solzhenitsyn stared me in the face. I opened the book and skimmed the contents. Pasternak, Solzhenitsyn, and others—exiles, dissidents, or dead in Stalin's labor camps. I looked back to say something to the diplomat's wife, but she was gone. I couldn't bear to tear the cover off the book. Instead I hid it on a shelf above the bathroom, hoping they wouldn't look there.

Digging into my pack, I pulled out my copy of *Anna Karenina* and a Rachmaninoff tape, which I put in my cassette player. These, I assumed, would offend no one.

AT ELEVEN p.m., with little fanfare, we reached the Soviet border. Suddenly I heard the sound of clomping boots on top of the train. Loud stomping noises. Voices shouted in Russian. Doors and compartments were opened, then slammed shut. Without being told to, the Eastern Europeans had already left their compartments and were standing with rehearsed indifference in the corridors of the train.

I climbed to the shelf above the bathroom and ripped the cover from the book of Soviet writers. Then I dropped two packages of Marlboros, which I'd brought for such an occasion, onto my bunk.

Guards came into the compartment. Half were Mongolian. The

others were large blond Russians. I had planned to hand them the cigarettes, but they motioned for us to leave. From the corridor I listened to the sound of beds being lifted, suitcases pulled down. The wife of the Yugoslav diplomat looked at me askance.

Suddenly they left, as quickly as they had come. We were told we could exit the train where a small money exchange was open and purchase rubles, which we would need from now on in the Soviet dining car. I was about to leave, when one of the blond Russian guards returned. He shut the door behind him. I had no idea what he wanted. He leaned forward, and I thought he was going to kiss me. Instead he pointed to the cigarettes, which I gave him. Then he pointed to my Walkman, which I did not want to give him.

Instead I slipped it onto his head and turned on Rachmaninoff's First Piano Concerto, with Van Cliburn playing. He closed his eyes and swayed back and forth, swooning in another world. Then he hesitated, returning the Walkman to me. I took the tape out and slipped it into his hands. "Rachmaninoff," I said. "Thank you," he whispered, and the next thing I knew, he was gone.

At the money exchange, I ran into Pierre. "Meet me in the dining car for a drink," he said, his breath forming a cloud in the cold Siberian night air. It was one a.m. when they brought the train back with its new wheels and dining car, and he waved to me as he leaped on, his car separated from mine by the dining car.

As the train crossed into Siberia, I tried to make my way to the dining car. But the door was locked. I pounded and pounded, for I was accustomed to being able to pass through whenever I wanted. Moments later the door was flung open.

A huge, walleyed old Russian peasant in a soiled apron sat in complete darkness, peeling potatoes. "*Nyet,*" he said, slamming the door in my face. It was late, and who was I to argue? I left the lonely potato peeler, with his wandering eye, to his darkness.

I went back to my bunk, cold as could be. I could see my breath inside. Cecilia snored beneath the layers she had put on, and I dug into my duffel for a flannel shirt and an extra sweater, which I would wear all night for several nights to come. But I did not care. I lay awake all night, thinking of what surprises lay ahead as the train carried me into the ancestral homeland, the first of my kin to return.

Mother Russia

I N EARLY times the men of Novgorod marched into the remote lands beyond the Ural Mountains again and again, never to return. The legend grew that only Alexander the Great had ever succeeded in crossing the Iron Rock, as the Urals were called. It was said that he forded an icy sea until he came to a land with inhabitants who ate carrion, corpses, and all kinds of filth. The people of Novgorod called this race the Yugrians, which means the impure, for they were warlike, heathen and vile. When one of their tribe died, it was said, there was no burial. There was a feast instead.

So Alexander prayed to God to free the world from such monsters. God heard his prayer and bade a great rock to close before these impure tribes. He left one single copper gate in the great rock, and this gate he locked and bolted, to be opened only on Judgment Day. Behind this gate lay a land of ice and snow, a rugged terrain of primordial forests and pathless bogs, the place of abandonment and exile that we have come to know as Siberia. The name is perhaps derived from the Mongol word *sibir*—the sleeping land. Bounded on the north by the Arctic, the east by the Pacific, the south by Mongolia and China, Siberia is all the land east of the Urals—the Asian dominions of the Russian Empire.

For centuries the world beyond the iron gate of the Urals was shrouded in mystery and superstition, until in the early sixteenth century an ambitious and clever man named Anika Stroganov, along with his sons, began sending out expeditions across the mountains to bring back the fur of an animal called a sable, distant cousin to the mink. Besides fur, Anika discovered salt, precious to Moscow, and a land fertile for growing corn. He told Czar Ivan he believed precious minerals would be found in the mountains. He spoke to him of gold.

The czar granted Anika and his sons a twenty-year lease over five and a half million acres. With a faulty map and a lease to land the czar did not own, the Stroganovs set out to explore the Siberian terrain. They found a land of salmon- and pike-swollen rivers, of luxurious furs—beaver, ermine, black fox, and sable—of forests so dense and sinister, even the bravest could become disoriented there.

In order to consolidate their territory, the Stroganovs put together a reserve of men who had had their falling-out with the laws of Moscow. They were robbers, escaped peasants, and condemned murderers. They called themselves cossacks, forming a kind of Robin Hood band, and became the conquerors of Siberia. With flintlocks and harquebuses they launched successful attacks against the native peoples, who were armed with only bows, arrows, and swords. Under them, Russia came to control its Asian frontiers.

Under Peter the Great, exploration was carried further. Peter sent Vitus Bering off to explore the easternmost recesses of the land. Peter opened semiprecious-stone mines in the Urals. For the Russians, who had witnessed two centuries of darkness when the Mongols swept without obstacle across the land, the conquest of Siberia became essential to national security as well as to economic policy.

Stretching from the Caspian Sea to the river Amur, Siberia's five million square miles presents the largest expanse of pastureland in the world. Its steppes, or grasslands, seem to go on forever. Combined with the taiga and the other, less dense forests, it is six times larger than the whole of Europe, not including Russia.

The climate, however, is renowned for its grimness. The peculiar climate of Siberia comes from the structure of its surface, unprotected from the keen cold air that descends from the polar tundra. Separated from Central Asia by a barrier of snow-clad mountains— the Hindu Kush and the Himalayas—and essentially landlocked, Siberia is shut off from mild winds from the south. Its ground has been found to be frozen as deep as sixteen hundred feet, and even in summer it never warms. This unyielding land proved to be rich in minerals and ores, and for centuries men would be sent to Siberia for the most minor of crimes to work as slave labor in its mines or, later, to build the railroad upon which I was traveling. But it is the climate that has given Siberia its true reputation—as the place of desolation, of exile, of gulags. The place where you send people to punish them.

I woke to an icy compartment, frost covering the window. I lay beneath all the layers of clothing I had—flannel shirts, warm socks, two pairs of pants—freezing under the thin blankets as the train whipped across the frigid Siberian plain.

Peering through the open shade, I saw frozen ground, ice-trimmed lakes. Stocky railway workers in small villages—mainly women with picks or shovels in hand, red scarves around their heads—waved. Siberia was settled quickly to protect the eastern frontier. Its boomtowns attest to this fact. Wood-slat structures, the kind you might find in the gold rush ghost towns of the California hills, lined the track. Occasionally we came to a town of gingerbread houses, their scalloped trim painted in bright yellow or green, but most of the houses were drab, and when we left them behind to plunge once again into the dense poplar forests and fields of wildflowers, I was relieved.

The fatigue I'd experienced at various stages of this journey returned, and I lay in bed for a long time, finding neither the strength nor the will to rise. Diagnosing it as travel fatigue, I decided a shower would make me feel better, but still I could not bring myself to get up. At last, forcing myself from beneath the blankets, I peeled the layers off and went into our small bathroom. I made myself bathe beneath the hand-held hose, in water that was only slightly warmer than the air. The dust of the Gobi swirled down the floor drain. Drying quickly, I put my clothes back on and returned under the covers.

Back in bed, I watched the Siberian landscape pass by. I contemplated the vastness of this land. My vision obscured by the thick forest in which I found myself, I could only imagine the thousands of miles of tundra or the sweeping steppes to the south. Even in spring it seemed to be a miserable stretch of wintry tracks, broken only by abundant rivers and a few glacial lakes.

I do not know how long I lay there that morning, reading, sleeping, thinking about the land. Cecilia hadn't budged either. It was beginning to occur to me that she had died in her sleep when I heard her stir. Then I made my way toward the dining car.

DIMITRI had been a waiter on the Russian dining car of the Trans-Siberian Express for fifteen years. He wore a black bow tie, a white shirt, and had a trimmed black mustache and a portly belly. A kind of lethargy seemed to have settled over the train, and the dining car was empty. With a great flourish, Dimitri invited me to sit down.

The cook, who wore a gigantic plastic bag that stood straight up on her head—she would wear it for the entire trip—and the dining car manager (her husband, it turned out) didn't want me there. Breakfast was over. Lunch hadn't begun. A sharp exchange took place between them. Igor, the old potato peeler who'd stopped my passage the night before, stared dumbly among them. At last I spoke, and they turned to me in silence and awe. I was Russian, I told them in halting college Russian—one hundred percent. "My name is Marushka," I said, telling them my grandmother's pet name for me.

Dimitri was overjoyed. "A Russian! Yes, you have Russian eyes," he told me. "A Russian face." He shaped his hands into a flower. The cook and her husband agreed. And later, when the cook and her husband had their backs turned, Dimitri indicated by making sweeping cups with his hands that I had Russian breasts as well.

He handed me a menu that included chicken Kiev, beef Stroganoff, blintzes. "Oh, I'll have blintzes," I told him, already tasting those rolled pancakes stuffed with jam and smothered in sour cream.

Dimitri held his hands together and tilted his head. *"Nyet.* I'm sorry, we don't have them."

"Oh." It was almost noon, and I was getting hungry. "Then I'll try the mushrooms and Stroganoff."

He tilted his head the other way, twisting his hands as if to plead with me. "I'm sorry."

I put the menu down, smiling. "What would you recommend?"

"Oh, the cabbage is very good. And there is beef borscht, but perhaps you'll want that for supper." He made his recommendations, as he would each day, and I would no longer embarrass him by ordering what was listed—but unavailable—on the menu. I ordered a breakfast of fried eggs, kefir, sweet cabbage, and bread with cheese and butter. The cook rose with great ceremony to fry my eggs.

Dimitri asked politely after my husband as he served me, and I told him I was traveling alone. He looked saddened; then he smiled. He had a son he adored, but his wife, he told me, was so-so. "Sometimes it is better"—he gave me a reassuring pat—"traveling on your own."

As I ate, I stared out the window. We had reached the fringes of Lake Baikal, the great lake near Irkutsk. People in boots fished along the pebbly shore or huddled before driftwood fires outside the fishermen's shacks. I rubbed the frost off my windowpane so I could see.

As we made our way around the lake, women in babushkas, stoking the fires in front of log cabins and clapboard houses or pausing from their housework, waved as they shivered in doorways. I thought I could see my grandmother from the train. She waves a feather duster, seeming to scold the wind. Her long skirt rises, as if she can fly. The babushka flaps around her head. I sip my tea and feel a presence float through the dining car. It is a freezing morning as I think of my grandmother, a little girl in the Ukraine.

I come from the Midwest, from the most suburban place on earth. I grew up with all the modern conveniences, the same set of friends. Streets were paved, the trees lush and green. Danger never crossed my mind. But my grandmother came from this strange place of mud-lined streets, cossacks, and pogroms. Her early years were years of hiding and flight.

I never really became friends with her until the winter I was eighteen and had embarked upon my first journey without parental supervision—to Florida for spring break. I tried to forget that my grandmother was there for the winter. Miami Beach proved boring. The boys were dumb, the weather lousy. I called my grandmother one day, and she offered to show me around.

She took me to a place where flamingos stood on one leg, where alligators could eat out of your hand. She took me to Wolfie's, where we ate Dagwood sandwiches and strawberry egg creams. I gave up my hotel room and moved onto her floor. And it was there that I began to understand how she had lived a life different from mine. How her mother had put her in a grave in the ground. How she had grown up with the fear of kidnapping and rape. And how, when she was twelve, she said good-bye to everything she knew.

She lived only a few more years after that visit, but every time I saw her, she told me more. What she could not remember, I'm sure she made up, just to keep me at her side.

When she was ninety-two, she complained of pain, and I took her to the hospital. For weeks she lingered, and I went back to New York. Then one day my mother phoned and said I should come. For five days I sat beside my grandmother as she lay in a coma. Finally I told my mother I had to go. There was school. I had things to do. On the way to the airport, on an impulse, I told my father I wanted to see her one more time, and he detoured for the hospital.

She sat up in bed, her long silver tresses bound with yellow bows the nurse had tied for her. I clasped her hand. The skin was soft, like doeskin. The flesh felt as if it could slip off into my hand. It will be fine, I told her. I'm going back to school. I'll get my Ph.D. I'll marry a nice man. Smiling, she clasped my hand, blessing me.

She died as my plane rose. When I got to New York, I called home. Then I turned around and flew back. The nurse had told my mother she'd seen this happen before. That a person in a coma will wake up to say good-bye.

ON MAY 14, 1891, Czar Alexander III wrote to his son Nicholas—the future and final Czar of Russia—who was traveling back from the Far East:

> Your Imperial Highness!
> Having given the order to build a continuous line of railway across Siberia, which is to unite the rich Siberian provinces with the railway system of the Interior, I entrust to you to declare My will. At the same time, I desire you to place the first stone at Vladivostok for the construction, which is to be carried out at the cost of the State and under the direction of the Government. Your participation in the achievement of this work will be a testimony to My ardent desire to facilitate communications between Siberia and other countries of the Empire, and to manifest My extreme anxiety to secure the peaceful prosperity of this Country.
>   I remain your sincerely loving,
>   Alexander

THE question everyone was asking, however, was not why Alexander wanted the railroad built, but rather why he had waited so long. Russia badly needed an ice-free port on its eastern frontier, and it needed a stronger foothold in Asia to keep that port open. The best way to consolidate its political hold in Asia was to unite the country. Alexander was beginning to realize that communication was the means to unite Russia, and back then that meant building a railway.

Though Vladivostok at the time was a miserable port, icebound 110 days a year, it was Russia's best exit to the East. And so it was here that on May 31, 1891, the future czar Nicholas II dug the first turf and ceremoniously filled a wheelbarrow to signal the groundbreaking for the Trans-Siberian Railroad.

Prior to the existence of the railroad, travel was primitive. The only route across Siberia was the Trakt, basically a trail of mud, dust, or snow trudged by exiles and convicts. To this day there is no transcontinental Soviet highway. Frequent changes of horse and driver made travel terribly slow, not to mention the hazards of frost and snow. At last, when eastward expansion became inevitable, the czar proclaimed that a railway from the Urals to Vladivostok would be built.

The Trans-Siberian Railroad was not only intended to link Russia to Siberia. It would also link Europe to eastern Asia. It would open a new path to world trade, the modern equivalent of the old Silk Route. It would enable Russia to take part in the struggle for the Pacific and would open the markets of China and Japan. In a word, the building of the railway was a way of making Russia a true power in the world.

The construction was to begin in five different locations, building only one track. The workers were a mix of Turks, Persians, Italians, Chinese, Koreans, and Russians, and some twelve thousand of the twenty-nine thousand laborers at the height of the building were convicts, offered reduced sentences for working on the railroad. Stonemen, riveters, and bridge builders were hired in winter, when the rest of the crew departed.

Conditions were grim, to say the least. Bridge builders often lost their grip and were hurled onto the icy surface of the river below or drowned in the freezing waters. In summer, workers toiled amidst swamps of fever-spreading mosquitoes. Horses were wiped out by Siberian anthrax. Rivers rose to unbelievable heights, sometimes sending mountains of water crashing between the passes. Bubonic plague, cholera, bandits, and Manchurian tigers attacked the workers.

But in 1897 the first official train thundered down the track to Vladivostok at a speed of nearly ten miles per hour. In 1903, at a cost of some 250 million in U.S. dollars, the Trans-Siberian line—5778 miles, making it the longest continuous track in the world—was completed, and in 1916 the entire railroad, with all its additional routings, including the China route, was finished.

IRKUTSK, a onetime cossack fortress and gold-mining boomtown, was our first Siberian stop. Once again some travelers departed for good, and I was left with the feeling that I was missing something.

I wandered to a flower stand, where a woman with translucent blue eyes and stark white hair was selling bouquets. "How is busi-

ness?" I asked, and she laughed. "Good when the train comes in." I
bought a small bouquet and told her she was very beautiful. She
laughed again and said, "No, no, not beautiful at all." I told her again
she was beautiful and said I wanted to take her picture. She laughed
again, refusing with modesty. But when I raised my camera, she began
to pose, turning playfully this way and that, like a model.

Suddenly a man ran up. He wore a dark jacket and trousers, a gray
vest, and he had those gray middle-aged features I saw on so many
Soviet men. "No pictures," he shouted. The flower lady, ashamed,
hid her face as the man chased me back toward the train.

On the platform, I again tried to take a picture, this time of the
train itself, but a soldier stopped me. The military attaché from the
U.S. embassy, who was on our train, explained. The Russian train
system is electric and vulnerable to sabotage. "They think pictures are
a security risk." He laughed. "That's how backward they are."

No ONE on the train knew what time it was. Some people said the
train traveled on Moscow time but operated on local time, if you can
figure that out. But half the people were on Beijing time, and one
diplomat said he was on Tokyo time. And the dining car was on
continuous service, so nobody really cared.

The car was packed now as I sat with the two Dutch girls and a
woman from France. A middle-aged Swedish man joined us, and he
asked about Chernobyl. Hardly anyone had dared bring it up on the
train, as if there were some taboo, but he asked if we had any news.

"We've heard that thousands have died," one of the Dutch girls said.

"I don't think that's true," I said, "but many will."

"Those poor people." The Swedish man shook his head forlornly.
"I am afraid to go home. I have heard that our crops are ruined."

When they left, I noticed that Dimitri's mood had turned very
glum, and I wondered if he had understood our conversation. I
would spend the rest of the train ride watching Dimitri's moods go up
and down, but this time he seemed particularly saddened. Dimitri
wore his feelings on his sleeve, the way my mother said I did.

I went back to my compartment and returned with the flowers I'd
purchased in Irkutsk. These I gave to Dimitri, who accepted them
with such an effusion of thanks that it sent the cook almost tumbling
out of her plastic hat.

RUSSIAN CARS FROM THE FAR REACHES of Siberia, from the place where the train begins, in Vladivostok, had been added in Irkutsk. For the first time, Russian passengers were on board. They never came to the dining car, but remained enclosed in their compartments.

One of the drawbacks of the Trans-Siberian Express is that there is no lounge car where one can just sit and relax. With no possibility for exercise except on our short stops, being constantly in the dining car was making me feel bloated and stuffed. I began to walk up and down the corridors of the train.

ON ONE of my pacings I met Sonya, a schoolteacher from Vladivostok of Tatar descent. As I stood, nose pressed to the glass in the Russian car, the door to her compartment opened, and she handed me some sweets. Her daughter, named Tina, had giant red bows in her hair, and a perfectly ironed dress. She looked as if she had just walked out of the house ready for school.

Sonya invited me in, and I sat on the bed while Tina showed me her toys—a stuffed animal, a book. Sonya told me she taught second-grade reading. Her husband was an engineer. She opened a box of smoked salmon. She told me how her husband had carved a hole in the ice and sat there for hours waiting for the fish.

Though I protested, Sonya insisted on giving me two fish. I held them in my hand. They were desiccated, flat, their eyes little dried-up beads. Feeling honored but slightly embarrassed, I wandered between cars carrying these fish, wrapped in last week's *Pravda*. Thinking Dimitri might know what to do, I made my way to the dining car.

He was ecstatic with my find. "This is excellent fish," he said, "the finest." The cook came out of her kitchen to examine them. Even her husband came over, pinched them, and nodded in assent. "We must celebrate," Dimitri said, and the cook and her husband agreed.

The car was virtually empty as Dimitri pulled out his personal stash of vodka, which was completely illegal, and poured balalaika cocktails (vodka straight up). He brought out a jar of caviar and a hunk of Russian rye. He showed me how to cut slices of the fish, which was tough and salty, but both Dimitri and Cook said it was great.

We were laughing, Dimitri telling me stories about his life on the train, as Pierre came in, whistling the way he had when he left the Mongolian embassy. The manager of the dining car, resuming his somber expression, told him to stop. Pierre sat down with us, picked up a slice of fish, and continued to whistle. Dimitri got up quickly, cupping his hands in supplication, asking Pierre to stop.

"You know, the Russian conductor told me to stop whistling. Now this guy's telling me to stop whistling. What's wrong with whistling?" he shouted in French.

Now I told him to stop, but he kept on defiantly. The manager of the dining car disappeared and returned with Victor, the short, compact Russian conductor. Pierre whistled in his face. "Get out," Victor said, "or I'll throw you out."

I got up and walked out. In my compartment, I found Cecilia and Janet having tea and some kind of sandwich. "And so," I heard Janet say, "I told him it was her or me, and he, of course . . ." I dug into my pack for some chocolate and headed toward the Russian cars.

Left: the author with acquaintance Pierre, a French saxophone player from Amsterdam, in the corridor of the Trans-Siberian

I found Tina and Sonya stretched on their bunks, half asleep. I apologized, but they invited me in. I handed them the chocolate, thinking it was a paltry offering in return for the gift of remarkable fish in whose pursuit her husband had almost frozen. But they were as grateful as if I had handed them a winning lottery ticket.

Leaving Tina munching on a chocolate bar, I made my way back toward my car. It was dark now, and the cold had settled back in. Pierre was standing between cars, and I realized he was waiting for me. "You're crazy," I told him, thinking about the dining car scene.

"I don't like authority," he told me. "It makes me nervous."

"Well, you think you're going to change the world by whistling," I said, wondering if this weren't as good a place as any to begin.

"I might," he said. "I just might."

I stood beside him, the night air in our faces, watching a now dimly

Left: a herdsmen's wagon train on the grasslands of Inner Mongolia, in China

Right: Sonya, a teacher from Vladivostok, and her daughter, Tina.
Left: a Siberian frontier town reminiscent of the old American West, as viewed from the train.

lit Siberia zip by. He put his arm around my shoulder and pulled me
to him. I tried to squirm away, but he held me, his arm firmly around
my shoulder. I wanted to get away, but I also wanted to stand there. I
didn't want anything more to happen. I just wanted to let myself rest
against his arm. He seemed to be looking for the same thing, for
neither of us moved from the spot. We stood like that for a long time,
his arm like a barricade holding back the world.

At last I excused myself and slipped away, leaving Pierre standing
alone between cars. The compartment was empty now, and dark.
The vodka had gone to my head; I pulled up the shade and collapsed onto my bunk. Floodlights shone in. The train's whistle
screamed through my sleep.

Suddenly I am dreaming my dream of winter, of snowy roads and
twisting ravines, of Indian paths I followed as a child, the place I go
back to. As we rush through the pine forests of Siberia, frost on the
panes, the ground snowy in mid-June, it is as if all my dreams become this one dream, and it is my dream of return, of reconciliation, of home.

FARMLANDS raced by. Mile after mile of wheat, blowing in the wind.
I sat, face pressed to the glass. It was the first real farmland we'd seen
since we'd left Beijing, and yet the sight was bittersweet. I could not
look at these acres of grain and not think of Stalin's collectivization
plan, carried out mostly in the Ukraine but also here. In a massive and
brutal effort he appropriated the land and created the low-producing
state-sponsored farms. In protest, kulaks—the well-to-do farmers who
profited from the labor of peasants—cut the throats of their livestock.
Sixteen million horses were killed, cattle reduced by forty-five percent. A hundred million goats and sheep, two thirds of the entire
stock of the nation, were slaughtered. But the kulaks were rounded
up and marched into the depths of Siberia. Two million of them were
executed. Grain shortages began. The Russians have been hungry
ever since.

I was relieved by a knock at my door. Tina stood there, big red bows
in place. "My mother would like you to have breakfast with us." I
packed up juice, crackers, sardines, and fruit and followed her.

Sonya had taken the train many times before, and she came well
prepared. Along with her fish, she had brought homemade breads,

cheese, tea, a heating pot, and yogurt. She had made a small spread for us, to which I added my contributions. She was thrilled with the sardines. She picked one up by the tail, sniffing it, examining it with her round Tatar features. Like a pelican, she dropped it down her throat and swallowed it. She clapped her hands, and then she fed her daughter in the same way. "These are wonderful," Sonya said. I told her I'd brought two dozen cans and was beginning to tire of sardines. In the course of the train ride I would give her half my supply.

Sonya's family came from Kazan, the birthplace of Lenin, a fact of which she was very proud. This was her annual trip home. They were going for the summer, although it always made her sad, because the summer in Vladivostok wasn't bad. They would stay with her family until August. Her husband would join her in July, when he had his holiday. "I am a teacher, you know. I get a longer holiday."

"I am a teacher too," I told her, which was from time to time the case. I had made a decision not to tell many people I was a writer, something I'd been warned not to do. "I teach at a university."

"Oh." She looked a bit ashamed. "You must be smart."

"You must be patient," I said. We both laughed.

Tina clung to her mother, beaming at me. She was radiant, like an advertisement for a healthy child, and I envied Sonya, traveling with her daughter by her side.

"So what do you think of all the changes in Russia?" I asked her. "What do you think of Gorbachev?"

"Oh." She smiled, clapping her hands together. "Gorbachev is wonderful. He is very good. A fine leader, a hero."

"But is he helping the Russian people? Is life better for you?"

"You'll see. He will do great things. Many changes will come. Already he has made many changes," she said, beaming. "Jobs are easier. There is more food. We have more freedom."

"How do you have more freedom?"

"The newspapers are freer to print what they think. People are freer to travel abroad."

"And Gorbachev, is he a good man?"

"Oh, he is a very good man. He has recognized the mistakes of Stalin and is trying to correct them. He is a man dedicated to change. He will make my country great again."

Suddenly, despite agreeing with much of what she said, I had the sense that Sonya, the teacher, had been well taught. I could not help but feel that what she was saying to me—the generalizations, the platitudes—she had learned by rote. There was something missing.

I was happy when Tina changed the subject. She handed me some hard candy and said I must come to Vladivostok to visit them. I told her I would like that very much. "And bring your little girl," Tina said, grinning at me. My harsh thoughts melted now. I'd made no mention of a little girl, but I promised Tina I would.

DULLNESS had settled over the train. The cold, and almost five days of perpetual motion, had sapped our strength. The dining car was empty more and more, in part because there was very little food, and the kitchen staff had begun a card game out of tedium. The rules seemed vague. At first I thought it had to do with suits; then it seemed it was about sequence. The cook tried to explain, but it made no sense to me. Nobody seemed to care. They dealt me in.

Dimitri sat next to me, directing my hand. The cook smiled. Igor, the potato peeler, his walleye wandering every which way, held his hand, never making a move. I kept thinking that now the cook would take off her hat, but it remained upright, eight inches high, like a cream puff on her head. She began talking about her life. "Fifteen years on the train, fifteen married years," she grunted, nodding at her husband, who was concentrating on his cards. "Try making love in one of those compartments," she said with a laugh. "Try making love with him . . ." She didn't complete her thought, but her husband was rotund—huge, in fact—and I could see her problem.

"We have children, two grown children. But since they were seven years old, we hardly see them. My mother takes care of them. We are home for a few days; then we turn around."

"It's a good living," her husband said. The cook sneered, shuffling her cards around.

Dimitri, I could tell, was growing depressed. "I've been at this for fifteen years too. I started when I was twenty. My boy is ten. I see him for a few days, then turn around. I always bring him something—a trinket, some small thing." He handed me a small carved wooden boat from Vladivostok. "I'll give this to him when I see him tomorrow." His eyes seemed to brighten at this thought.

"Do you ever get off the train? Do you ever get to visit?" I thought of how much I had wanted to get off and stay at various points.

Dimitri shrugged. "In fifteen years I've never visited a single stop. I've never gotten off." He put a card down for me. Igor suddenly rose, tossing in his hand. His hulking form banged the table. "There," Dimitri said, "you won."

I WENT back and lay down on my bunk, exhausted from doing nothing. I was growing more and more tired, it seemed, by the day. The motion of the train rocked inside me. Overhead, Chinese music played. I took out a tape of balalaika music and put it in my Walkman, dreaming of troikas, vodka, snowball fights. I imagine a bonfire; someone lifts me into his arms, sweeping me away.

Later I woke to late afternoon sun pouring in. Suddenly it was a beautiful spring day outside, sixty-five degrees. We made an unscheduled stop in the middle of a small woods to check the brake pressure. It was unclear how long we'd be delayed.

Off to the side of the track, in a dense grove of blue-green pines, a pond shimmered in the light. Bluebells and buttercups danced along its banks. Ducks skirted its surface. I stood between cars, scanning the platform. Like an animal set free, I jumped down and raced into the Siberian woods. I stood for a moment at the edge of the pond, giant spruces around me, breathing in deeply the pure air.

Then suddenly I bent down, plunging my fists into the dark, cool, Russian soil. This was Mother Russia, I thought. To the Slavs, all the destinies of living things were linked—people, plants, animals. They reveled in the cycles of nature—birth, death, rebirth. Their Easter gift was the egg, the giver of life. The earth, the notion of eternal motherhood, was the Russian ideal.

Now I had touched Russian soil. I thought of my own mother and grandmother. How far away I was from someone who would hold me. I let my body sink to the earth. If my journey stopped here, it would have been accomplished.

The porters started shouting, for others had also run away. But I lay on the sodden green earth, thrilled to be touching my homeland for the first time. All I wanted to do was breathe the air, feel the ground. I never wanted to go anywhere else again.

The train whistle sounded. I was aware of scrambling, shouting. I heard Pierre. "What are you doing? You're crazy. Get on board." My

tall Chinese porter was signaling the chief engineer, motioning for
him to wait. I rose and ran in the direction of the train. The porter
caught me by the arm and hoisted me on board.

ON A brilliant spring morning we crossed the Urals, penetrating
the Iron Rock, through the copper gate that was intended to be
bolted shut until Judgment Day. After five days and a distance of some
four thousand miles, we left behind the frozen, sleeping land and
crossed the spiritual border between Asia and Europe. I gazed at the
mountains and thought how this could be Switzerland or the Rockies.

The industrial north rose outside, a gray, smoky blotch on the
landscape. Huge chimneys of refineries spewed smoke. Miles of housing complexes, all the same, monotonously flowed by. I stared out the
window thinking of what lay ahead. Several more weeks of solitary
travel, uncertainty about Chernobyl and my visit to the Ukraine,
doubts about returning home. I thought of my companion, who was
by now in New York, and suddenly I was seized with the urge to call
him. We had not spoken in a few weeks, and now, as the possibility was
soon to be before me, my urgency seemed difficult to bear. I was like
some schoolgirl in class, longing to see her boyfriend, anxious for the
bell to ring. But thousands of miles, cultures, and other things stood
between us. A world of differences. An emotional wall.

I thought of how we had met. En route to a faculty meeting, I'd
asked an older man tying up his bicycle where the meeting was. He'd
shown me inside. Then I sat down beside a friend. "You see that man,
the one you came in with?" my friend said. "That's the man who
changed my life, who changed the way I see the world."

Later that afternoon as I stood on the platform, going to New York,
he was there as well. We rode the train into the city. We rode the
subway. "Are you following me home?" I asked. His wife, from whom
he was estranged, and sons lived around the corner from me. The
first time we had dinner together, he made me laugh. He told me
stories that had me doubled up with laughter.

It was a difficult time for me when I met him. My work wasn't going
well. There was no one in my life. Nothing seemed to be right. When
I told him that I felt alone, he listened to me as intently as anyone ever
had. And when I told him I was going to apply to law school, he shook
his head. "I think," he said, "your destiny lies elsewhere."

It was not long after we met that I accompanied my mother to Paris, where a Gypsy in a ragged fur coat pulled me into an alleyway. Turning my palm over in her filthy hands, she said, "You are falling in love with a married man. He is older than you. He will leave his wife. You will be happy for the rest of your life."

EVERYONE was packing, preparing to depart. Pierre had tossed a few things into his rucksack. He was filthy, looking as if he hadn't bathed in weeks. But then it occurred to me that we all looked filthy. Touching my own hair, I recalled that I hadn't washed it in a week.

I went to Sonya and Tina's compartment with half a dozen cans of sardines as a going-away present. They were thrilled to have them. Sonya gave me her address in Vladivostok and told me that when I next took the train, I must come and stay with them and go ice fishing with her husband, which I assured her I would do.

I packed up my few things and then went to the dining car, which was closed for service—but the card game was going on. The four of them dealt me in. And suddenly I seemed to know how to play. I was making good plays, raising bets. I knew when to ask for a card and when to back down. Even Igor looked at me, amazed.

Then Cook put down her cards and with great ceremony, as if she were about to abdicate a throne, removed her white plastic hat. "Moscow," Dimitri said, as if this were the signal. Outside were suburbs, housing complexes, children playing in the street. Dogs, women with groceries in their arms. Everyday life. Then suburbia receded, and tenements—monolithic brick buildings, block after block in the Stalinist neoclassical style—rose, gray against a gray sky.

Cook took a beautiful enameled comb from her pocket and began to comb her rather dry, brittle hair. The handle of the comb was etched in luminous colors. Flowers in interweaving patterns. I touched it admiringly.

Now there was a scramble to leave. Everything had to be done quickly. Dimitri kissed me on both cheeks, tears in his eyes, and said, "You must ride my train again." As I made my way to the door, waving good-bye, Cook intercepted me. Her face looking very severe, she pressed the comb into my hand. I tried to hand it back to her, but she wrapped my fingers around it firmly. "For Marushka," she said.

Moscow

ACCORDING to legend, when the cathedral known today as St. Basil's was completed, Ivan the Terrible had the architects blinded so that they could never repeat their marvels anywhere else in the world. Though the legend is without basis in historical fact, this conglomerate of churches, consisting of eight cupolas and eleven multicolored domes, is one of the world's greatest architectural splendors, the crowning glory of Red Square, of Russia itself.

Two hours after my train arrived, I walked across the street from my hotel to Red Square. It was late afternoon, and the square was almost empty. A few soldiers patrolled as I ambled for the first time in six days on somewhat shaky legs, like a newborn colt.

Despite what many Americans think, the "red" of Red Square does not refer to the political persuasion of the Kremlin, nor to the color the flagstones take on at dusk, but rather to the Old Slavonic word for red, which was synonymous with beauty. Before the Revolution, Red Square was a bustling marketplace, where bears on leashes performed and Gypsies whirled. Here you could buy fish or cabbage, silks and religious icons. Stands overflowed with plums, cherries, red currants, and apricots. Furs Russians needed for their winter hats and coats were sold in abundance—sables and foxes, beaver and silver mink.

But now at dusk I traversed the near empty, austere seat of the Soviet regime. Even the endless queue before Lenin's tomb along the Kremlin Wall was gone. But at the end of the square, rising in its whimsical, magnificent way, was St. Basil's. Its curlicue onion domes, in brilliant shades of blue, red, green, and yellow, captured the light of the setting sun and seemed more fantastic than real.

In 1552 Ivan, who was not yet called the Terrible, ordered his architects to build a great church. It was to be named the Cathedral of the Intercession, in celebration of the feast day when Ivan's troops conquered Kazan, one of the last Mongol fortresses. He ordered the church to be built in the shape of the eight-pointed star of the Virgin, surrounded by a cluster of chapels of different heights and colors. The architects managed to incorporate the features of Russian wooden churches into masonry, creating one of the most unique pieces of architecture in the world. Whether its architects were blinded or not, no church like it has ever been built, before or since.

The Cathedral of the Intercession popularly came to be called St. Basil's, after a holy fool whose bones lie consecrated in the cemetery. Basil the Blessed was said to be one of the holy fools who dared to stand up to the czar—renowned for his cruelty—and criticize him. But instead of executing him, Ivan listened. It was not uncommon in the Middle Ages for a ruler to listen to an inspired individual who bore the stigma of madness.

It is here in Red Square that Byzantium meets bureaucracy and the two sides of Russia stand face to face. Somewhere between the onion domes of St. Basil's and the towering brick walls and crenellated medieval towers of the Kremlin, the real Russia lies. During the Mongol invasions Russia had sought help from Europe, only to be met with indifference. Once it had thrown off the Mongol yoke, Russia continued to look with fear toward Asia and distrust toward Europe, a pattern that persists and has marked Russia's centuries of isolation.

After standing awestruck before St. Basil's, I strolled back toward my hotel, deep in thought. This was a history I thought I understood. Yet now that I had arrived, I found myself faced with what I had been avoiding thinking about for a few weeks—my intention to journey south, to Kiev and the outlying districts of the Ukraine. Russia's isolation seemed all the more poignant when I thought of how it was so slow to inform Europe about Chernobyl.

It had been almost two weeks since the information officer at the U.S. embassy in Beijing had given me that copy of *Time* magazine. Although it was still some weeks away, the thought of my actual departure for the Ukraine loomed, and I found myself frightened by what remained unknown. Radiation has no smell or taste, no palpable traces. Eventually I would have to find someone who could inform me of what the present situation was.

Reflecting on my next move, I became aware of shouting, of loud noises around me. I turned and saw that the large gates of the Kremlin had opened and a cavalcade of official-looking motorcars with police escort was careering straight at me. A man along the side of the road motioned for me to jump in his direction, and I shot toward him just as the cars passed where I had been standing. It occurred to me that they would have run me over if I had not jumped out of the way.

Outside of border guards, this was my first encounter with the state, and the feeling was not a pleasant one. I walked with my head up, looking both ways, more cautious now as I crossed Red Square.

WHEN I returned to my hotel room—a small, dark room with a tiny, hard narrow bed—the phone was ringing. This seemed odd, but when I picked up the phone, I heard someone say my name. Then I recalled that a friend of my mother's had a nephew who worked in Moscow at the U.S. embassy. Ted Cavendar welcomed me and said, "There's a dinner and screening of *Out of Africa* at the ambassador's tonight. Can we pick you up in an hour?" I said I'd be downstairs.

The shower was a hose I held over my head, and the tub was the size of a large sink. I had to squat in order to bathe, but the water was hot, and it was the first time I'd washed completely in days. I dried myself with towels the size of washcloths, then took out my traveling dress and carefully pulled up the zipper. Only hours after I'd left the Trans-Siberian Railroad behind, I walked out into the June night air of Moscow in high heels and a dress.

SPASO House is located on a residential street in Moscow that could be a side street of Washington, D.C. Ushered into the giant marble hall of the ambassador's residence, greeted by a well-dressed crowd and waiters in tuxedos passing trays of caviar, smoked salmon, and deviled eggs, I felt not unlike Cinderella, my life momentarily transformed.

The guests included the elite of Moscow—"the real bigwigs," Ted whispered as he grabbed two vodkas off a passing tray and handed me one. Diplomats and correspondents, photographers, artists, and business people all flitted from person to person, moving like flocks of birds each time some new dignitary entered the room.

Ted introduced me as an American writer "of some note." But my real claim to fame seemed to be that I had just gotten off the Trans-Siberian Express. One extremely tall man, who looked like Abraham Lincoln, got down on his knees and kissed my hand as Ted told him that I had just arrived via Beijing. Others looked at me as if I had returned from the moon. "Mongolia," one elderly statesman muttered. "You've just crossed Mongolia."

Ted left me in the hands of the scientific attaché to the U.S. embassy. "What are you doing here?"

"Here?" I said, pointing to the room around me.

"No, in the Soviet Union. What brings you here?"

"I am planning to travel to the villages my family came from."

"Oh? Where's that?"

"Around Gomel, Nezhin, and Chernigov."

"Oh, really? That's interesting," he said, clearing his throat. "I don't think anybody's going there these days."

"Well, I thought if I got to Kiev, I could perhaps get a driver to take me north."

He shook his head, indicating he would not do that. "I don't think you can. I think the roads are blocked."

"Well then, I'd settle for Kiev and the outskirts. Do you think it's all right to go to Kiev?" I did not mention to him that my itinerary had me scheduled to be in Kiev for a week.

"Sure, you can go for a day or two." He spoke cheerfully now, as if this seemed like a fine thing to do. "Are you planning on having children?" He grinned as Ted caught my arm, dragging me away.

Someone announced that *Out of Africa* was about to begin, I paused at the hors d'oeuvre table for Russian rye and caviar. Someone leaned against my arm. "I understand," a man with a thick Russian accent said to me, "that you are thinking about going to Kiev." I kept leaning into the table, not looking at his face, but I saw the blue sleeve of his jacket as he reached for something. "Don't go," he said. "It isn't safe." Then he walked away.

All through the movie I thought about what the man at the hors d'oeuvre table had said. I squirmed in my chair, trying to find him in the darkened room. When the movie ended, the doors to the main hall opened, and a buffet a city block long was revealed. Giant serving casseroles of beef Stroganoff, chicken Kiev, blinis with caviar and sour cream, mushrooms in cream sauce simmered over blue flames. I gathered food as if this were my last meal, which for a time it actually would be. Off in a corner, plate in hand, I stood alone, devouring.

Ted caught me and dragged me over to an American correspondent for ABC. "Did you cover Chernobyl?" I asked him as I tried to balance my plate and a glass of champagne.

He had a nice youthful grin, a blond mustache. "Sure, I covered it." He paused, smiling at me. "From Moscow."

"You didn't go to Kiev?"

"Are you kidding? My cameraman said he'd quit before he'd go near the place."

"And the network didn't insist?"

"You know, I've been in lots of war zones—Nicaragua, Lebanon— but I don't know a correspondent who'll go near the Ukraine."

I was growing despondent. "I planned this journey," I told him, "around going to the villages my family came from. Near Kiev. I could just take a day's drive."

"I wouldn't touch it. We don't know half the story. The Soviets haven't been exactly forthcoming." He turned to walk away. "I know someone who can help you. Talk to Nicholas Daniloff. He's the correspondent with *U.S. News and World Report.* He knows everything, and he's a good guy."

Once again I stood alone, and was beginning to feel overwhelmed by the vodka, the food, the sudden array of people and problems thrust upon me. I was about to leave, when through the crowd I spotted the blue suit of the man who had walked away before the film began. I moved near him and did what I would find myself doing a great deal in the Soviet Union. I whispered. "May I speak with you?"

He had a handsome face and sharp blue eyes. He took me by the elbow and led me into a corner. "I was told you are trying to get to a town north of Kiev." He dropped his voice, and I had to lean very close to him to listen. "When the reactor was on fire, the people from the town came out to watch it burn. No one did a thing. There was no evacuation plan. When the people were told the water was bad, they boiled it. The government told us nothing."

"Who told you about me?"

He ignored my question. "They let the children stand and watch the fire. They let people go about their business. Those children and people will probably all die. You can say something about all of this. The other journalists can't write the truth, because they'll lose their contacts or they'll be asked to leave, but you don't have to come back again." He turned to go, then spoke again. "But be careful. What you write and who you write about can be identified. There are people who will dig salt for the rest of their lives because of what some journalist has said."

Joseph Brodsky, the Soviet émigré poet who now lives in the United States, once wrote that the Russians have more difficulty accepting the breaking of ties than anyone else. The Russians, he says, are a very grounded people. For them a house, a village, a country are all forever. Their sense of permanence is deeper; their feelings of loss also run deeper.

I have contemplated how it was just by chance that my family was thrust upon the midwestern soil. Wrenched from their native land, the Jewish Pale of the Ukraine, my family would count itself among the lucky, the ones who got away. They could have gone anywhere, because after leaving Russia, nowhere would really be home.

In an odd, hardly dramatic way, I felt I understood. I myself was thrust out into the world, unprepared, at the age of eighteen, when my parents drove me from the safety of the Midwest to a college in Boston. I had the sense that my own parents were kidnapping me, forcing me away. Though at times I tried, I was never to return. Once a year or so, when I am gloomy, my parents say, Why don't you come home? At times the possibility draws me, but I try to envision lunches at the Country Kitchen with high school friends. Gossip about who will divorce, who will remarry. Sundays spent with my family, watching a football game. It is a reality that is incomprehensible to me.

I am caught in this web between a desire for permanence and a deep sense of loss. It is as if my dark Russian soul has been exiled, banished to another place. I thought that by traveling to the country my grandmother called home, I would somehow find an answer. I would recognize what I had been looking for all along.

For years I have thought of buying a house on the east coast. Sometimes a real estate agent takes me on a tour. Always there is something wrong. The rooms are too spacious or too small. The house needs too much work. There's noise from the street. The agents keep calling, but after a while they stop. Eventually they catch on.

I used to think that none of the houses were right. But the truth is, all the houses were probably fine. I just didn't want to live anywhere. I had already had a home in Illinois.

I didn't want to live with someone else's memories. I didn't want to live in rooms imbued with others' hopes and dreams. I wanted whatever foolish loves and pointless disappointments there might be to be mine.

THE LINE AROUND THE CRENELLATED red brick wall of the Kremlin to see the embalmed father of the Russian Revolution snaked five city blocks. Foreigners, I was told, were quickly ushered to the front, but so far no one had recognized me as a foreigner, for which I was both grateful—for I was passing as Russian—and regretful, as the heat of the day and my own fatigue were mounting. The estimated wait was three hours, but I had been standing still for forty-five minutes.

The Kremlin is the heart of Russia, troubled and tormented perhaps, but a heart nonetheless, and from here the lifeblood of Russia pulses. At the beginning of the thirteenth century, when the Mongols swept through Asia, they established a stronghold on the Eurasian plain where the great culture of Kiev thrived, and they managed to turn the brilliant and rich civilization into a wasteland. All who could, fled north, into the forests. When the Tatar reign ended, a sizable population settled in the land between the Volga and the Oka rivers, united by a *kreml*—small fortress—on a hillock on the banks of the Moskva River called Moscow. The word kremlin derives from the Russian word *kreml.* A view of the Kremlin from the banks of the Moskva River makes it easy to understand why this hill, protected by the river, played such a strategic role in the middle of these vast plains. It was here that the reconquest began and Moscow grew supreme.

With the fall of Kiev and the move in 1326 of the head of the Russian Orthodox Church from his seat, in Vladimir, to Moscow, Moscow became "the holy city," the third Rome, and grew rapidly. By the fifteenth century the frontier settlement had reached a population of a hundred thousand. It grew in concentric circles, walled city within walled city, with many fabulous churches and wooden structures (most of which would be burned to the ground during Moscow's many conflagrations, including the spectacular burning that forced Napoleon to retreat).

The walls of the Kremlin, which have loomed for centuries impregnable, wrapped in mystery and intrigue, were built by Italian architects in the fifteenth century. Within these walls judgments were handed down, tortures performed. Czars were born, rose and fell. Revolts were quashed, liaisons conducted in its secret passageways.

The brick walls of the Kremlin, twelve to eighteen feet thick, are lined with passages and storage spaces, twenty towers, and five crimson-colored doors. The great walls, combined with the ideal location, made the city virtually impenetrable. The Kremlin, with its series of forts, armories, cathedrals, palaces, and convents, was at its height during the sixteenth and seventeenth centuries. The splendor of this small city was legendary. Cupolas rose in brilliant gold. Gold, silver, and colored tiles gleamed from the walls.

Within its walls dwelt the czar and his entourage. Here was also the Terem, or female quarters, that gilded cage where the czarina and her ladies languished in tedious seclusion, passing their days at religious ceremonies and embroidery, preening, decking themselves in ermine and silver fox, in rooms replete with Persian rugs, jewels, ivory combs, mirrors, but with no one from the outside world to admire them. They never went beyond those walls, oblivious even to the marketplace of Red Square, just a few feet away and ablaze with life.

Few penetrated the Kremlin's walls. Few ever gained admittance to the upper echelons of its power. In modern times not much has changed. The seat of government is now the presidium, but essentially much of what happens behind the Kremlin walls, though they were opened to the public in 1958, remains cloaked in secrecy. Glasnost has begun to cast some light into this darkness, but until now the isolation has been complete.

BEHIND me in the line to Lenin's tomb an aging couple, arms intertwined, stood motionless as statues. I assumed from their dress and their patience that they had traveled across half their country for a glimpse at their revolution's hero. The woman in front of me clutched at her two children as if she were dragging them to safety. Dressed in a suit of gray gabardine, sweat dripping down her face, she turned to me. "It's very hot," she said. The children—a boy and a girl about a year apart—gazed at her with such adoration, I could only assume they were desperate to persuade her to take them to the zoo or the circus.

"Yes," I said, not wanting to think about it, "it is very hot."

"Oh, you are not from here. Where are you from?"

"America," I said. "New York."

"Oh, New York. New York."

The old couple appeared visibly moved. "New York," I heard one of them whisper.

"And you?" I asked the woman.

She smiled halfheartedly, then looked over her shoulder. "Kiev," she whispered. Then she began speaking quickly—long Slavic sentences whose sense I lost almost before they began. She kept taking her children's hands, holding them up in the air. Tears came to her eyes. Slowly I began to make sense out of what she was telling me. Chernobyl. They had been evacuated. But she was frightened for her children. She was afraid because they had drunk the water, breathed the air.

I explained to her as best I could that I was supposed to go to Kiev in a few weeks' time. "Nyet." She waved a finger in my face. "Don't go," she said. "It's not safe. No one is there." Then she turned her back on me, and would not look at me again. I stood there another hour, until I thought I would faint. The line had barely moved, and I pondered whether I really wanted to see Lenin, thinking how in truth the dead do not interest me. I have never been the kind of person to visit mausoleums, tombs.

I left the line and headed over to the state emporium, GUM department store, thinking I would buy something to eat. But the lines to buy food were long, and I had no strength for another line. I slumped along the rim of the fountain that forms the centerpiece of the shopping center. Toddlers played at my feet, dipping hands into the water. Lovers and hopefuls tossed coins. A rosy-faced child splashed water on me with glee, while his ashamed parents scolded and uttered endless apologies.

The faces of the two children in front of me in the line would haunt me. Years later I'd watch a newscast of the victims of Chernobyl, children who had acquired leukemia. I would stare at pictures of hospital beds, rows of them, filled with dying children, and search for the faces of the children whose anxious mother had clutched them as if they were bundles she might lose.

Wondering now if I would indeed go on to Kiev, I wandered Gorky Street in search of food. At last, in the very late afternoon, I made my way back to my hotel to see if I could get a late lunch. There was an hour's wait. I sat until I at last pleaded with the maître d', explaining that I was starving. He begrudgingly sat me at a table with a few Russians and an American film distributor from Arkansas.

"Boy," the distributor said, "I just love doing business with the

Soviets. Nicest people to do business with. Honest, easy to get along with." He didn't speak a word of Russian, though he'd been coming to the U.S.S.R. for some time. "They all speak English," he said.

He had a nice fatherly way about him. A roundish red face, a puffy body, the kind of person you think you can entrust your life's story to. I told him a relatively small amount of mine. He didn't pry, but listened to whatever I said about my journey. "Boy, a woman traveling in this country alone." He smacked his lips. "Don't see that every day." Our orders of borscht and beef Stroganoff were slow in coming. But the vodka was not. He told me about his daughters, back in Little Rock with his loving wife, Lorraine. Then he asked me hesitantly about my personal life. "There's someone back home," I said. "I think we'll get married soon."

That evening I took a stroll through Red Square, pausing before the moon rising above St. Basil's. The air was cool and fresh, and I felt my body starting to relax. Then I went back to my room, opened the window wide, and collapsed on the bed. I drifted into that kind of deep sleep that only comes when your fatigue is great and your conscience, for a moment at least, is at peace.

I was in the deepest sleep of all when in the middle of the night the phone rang, the man from Arkansas on the other end. "I'm sorry," he said. "Did I wake you? You seemed kind of tense when I saw you this afternoon. I thought maybe you could use a backrub."

I thought of how much I would love a backrub. "I don't think so."

"I don't mean anything strange by it."

"No, thank you," I said, slamming the receiver down.

It would be hours before I could get back to sleep. I found myself sitting up, thinking about the person I didn't want to think about, the one I'd left behind. I didn't want to think about him, because I harbored the hope that my life with him might turn around. I hadn't really faced the reality of our future together. That he was too old and had been married too many times, traveled too much, and probably was seeing other women was lost on me. I was blindly in love with the person I believed understood me better than anyone had.

Even looking back now, it is not a love I can completely understand, but it seemed as if he saw through barriers, as if he knew how to reach inside. Never mind that after the first three months together I already felt he was slipping away. There were always reasons, excuses, and now, I assume, lies why he could not be there.

I struggled for his time. For a family trip to Florida, I'd beg for a week. He'd say four days. We'd settle on five, but then his ex-wife would call and one of the boys was being thrown out of school. The vacation we'd negotiated for so long dwindled down to three days.

Why was I so needy? I asked myself. Why couldn't I accept things as they were? You are the sea in which I swim, he'd say whenever I complained that I felt alone. If only you could relax, not be so dependent. Let go. If only I could be more confident, trusting, and self-assured. I was trapped, and I knew it. Only his voice would soothe me.

AT LEO Tolstoy's house they ask the visitors to put paper slippers over their shoes. Ahead of me a tour group of widows shuffled, their feet sounding like sandpaper on the bleached wood floors of what was more like a country house than an urban dwelling. I stayed behind in the dining room, letting the widows shuffle on, examining the everyday life Tolstoy lived in Moscow, a city he detested.

It was in October of 1882, at his wife Sofya's insistence, that the Tolstoy family moved to this house. Tolstoy himself had no desire to leave his beloved Yasnaya Polyana—Clear Glade—the estate 130 miles south of Moscow where he was born, in 1828. It was from Yasnaya Polyana that Tolstoy drew his strength. He loved the peaceful country life. He walked among the birches and lilacs, paused beside his ponds, visited the 350 peasant families that lived on his land. He wrote *War and Peace* and *Anna Karenina* there. Yet Sofya, concerned for the education of her children and longing to be near her friends and family, urged him, against his will, to buy this house in Moscow.

As I roamed from room to room, pausing to examine a book left open, a pair of spectacles on a desk, I thought of how unhappy Tolstoy was here, how prophetic those words that open *Anna Karenina* became: "All happy families are alike, but an unhappy family is unhappy after its own fashion." Tolstoy abhorred Moscow city life, seeing here only a seething mass—the impoverished, the miserable. "Stench, stones, luxury, poverty, debauchery" was how he phrased it.

I shuffled upstairs, up a small, narrow stairwell. Pausing before the children's rooms, with toys neatly lining the shelves, I thought of what life was like for the Tolstoy family. Tolstoy's mother died when he was eighteen months old, his father when he was seven. He was raised by devoted servants and, when he was sixteen, sent away to board. For years he lived a life of gambling, debauchery, and indolence, dreaming of a great and pure love.

When he was thirty-four and she was eighteen, Leo Tolstoy wedded Sofya Behrs. The first years of their marriage were a flowering of love and work, and Tolstoy produced his masterpieces then. But he was a seeker, this orphan, who had looked for meaning in life first through freedom, then through love and marriage, through literature, and finally through God.

In these benevolent rooms, where children grew, and in the park outside, where they played, Sofya and Tolstoy drifted apart. She had borne him thirteen children, eight of whom survived. She had copied his work night after night, recopying *War and Peace* some seven times. And yet on August 26, 1882, Sofya wrote in her journal:

Left: renowned Russian novelist Leo Tolstoy and his wife, Sofya, in the garden of their country home in 1910. Below: Tolstoy's work area as it appears today at the house in Moscow.

It was twenty years ago when I was young and happy that I started writing the story of my love for [Leo] in this book. Twenty years later here I am sitting up all night on my own, reading and mourning its loss. For the first time in my life, [he] had run off to sleep alone in the study. Lord help me, I long to take my own life, my thoughts are so confused.

I stopped at the study, recalling Sofya's words. That night he would return to her, but he left her in small ways again and again over the next thirty years, until at the age of eighty-two he wrote a note saying definitively that he was leaving her, going on a pilgrimage from which he would not return. Sofya, reading his note, threw herself into a pond and would have died had one of her daughters not saved her. Tolstoy only got so far as Astapovo station, where he lapsed into a coma, from which he never recovered.

I MOVED through rooms that showed no sign of acrimony and grief, rooms that seemed to depict only the simple joys of domestic harmony. I thought of my grandmother's house. With its foreign accents, smells, furnishings, it bore no resemblance to the antiseptic world of my own suburban life. Indeed, as I moved through the house of Leo Tolstoy, it was as if this were the house I had journeyed through all my life, as if I could close my eyes and smell my grandmother's sweet breads, her kasha, her savory fruit stews.

I thought of how much sadness dwelt within these walls. My own family was beset by strife, though I never quite saw it as a child. My father was a perfectionist; my mother was a housewife who should have been a fashion designer. He wanted a spotless house, meals served on time. She wanted to be living in London, or at least downtown Chicago. My father tried to teach my brother and me the proper way to do things, but nothing, it seemed, was ever done right. Battles sent us fleeing into our rooms. Doors were slammed. My brother fled to his television; I went to my books. My father was buried behind newspapers; my mother took refuge in sewing. Here we fortified ourselves. We hid within the safety of our walls.

My world was a made-up one. I invented roles for myself, parts I played. Usually they evolved out of the pioneer past of my little Illinois suburb. A mother on the prairie, a wife leading a wagon train, a sister tending to an injured brother. In my dreams, along the banks of Lake Michigan, in the ravines behind the house, I was in charge. When I came home, I gave in to the demands upon me. I practiced piano. I studied hard. Meanwhile, I was seething inside. I built strong walls around my world. No one came in. Nobody knew.

Then one day I exploded, and what I'd built around me came tumbling down. I shouted words my family never knew I knew. I stomped out, barefoot, in the rain. I slept at one friend's house, then in my boyfriend's arms. I shouted again, but no one heard. How I could never be myself. How there was a part of me I always had to hide. I set out on journeys, wandering the world. I would find that part of me, uncover what I'd lost, like buried treasure. And then I'd be able to tell my family, and they would understand.

SUDDENLY I felt stifled within the confines of the Tolstoy house. I made my way down the back stairs, where I deposited my paper slippers and walked into the summer day. A large enclosed park, with rising linden trees—majestic, cool—loomed to my right. Here Tolstoy walked and pondered, searching for meaning in his life, for belief.

A wave of despair overcame me as I walked among the lindens in Tolstoy's garden. Even the great ended up in disappointment. Earthly pleasures never satisfied Tolstoy's longing. Literature never satisfied his imaginings. The love and compassion he sought would never be found for him. Tolstoy, the man who preached peace, would spend his final hours in rage and isolation, dying alone in a train station.

I stretched out on a bench and contemplated my own life, the man I loved, who himself was a great student and lover of Tolstoy. Perhaps, I thought, history will prove things different. Perhaps, in my own case, it would all work out. I closed my eyes, content for the moment, with the breeze overhead, Tolstoy's lindens waving above me. I folded my arms across my face and slept.

A sharp banging awakened me. A guard with a billy club pounded on the bench. Cruelly I was ordered out of the garden, where I had found a moment's peace. But in truth I was shocked at myself. I am not given to falling asleep on park benches. Now it seemed apparent that something was wrong. A parasite I'd picked up in China, a brain tumor, radiation sickness. I found I could almost not stand. Like an old woman, her life behind her, I made my way to the gate.

I DESCENDED INTO THE BOWELS OF Moscow on a steep escalator, deep into the underground—that remarkable feat of engineering which has become as popular as a tourist attraction as it is a mode of transportation. Begun under Stalin, the first fourteen stations, using more marble than all the palaces built by the Romanovs, are veritable works of art, with their colonnades, sculptures, paintings, and mosaics glorifying the major events of Russian history.

Now the Muscovites milled about, leafing through *Pravda,* chatting in a friendly way. Some looked anxiously at their watches. The train came, and people rushed inside. I sat on a comfortable plastic seat in the well-lit, graffiti-less subway car, contemplating my illness and what I should do. Checking into a Soviet hospital seemed out of the question. I would wait until I got home.

We had reached what I thought was my stop, and I got out. I ascended on another great escalator and found myself in a tree-lined neighborhood that bore no resemblance to the heart of the inner city, where my hotel was.

I walked and walked, but the streets remained residential. I stopped a man and asked if he knew the way to my hotel. He frowned. Then I asked him where the Kremlin was. "Kremlin!" he exclaimed. He pointed in the direction I was going, shaking his head.

I walked for perhaps an hour, then collapsed onto a bench. It was beginning to occur to me that I had taken the underground the wrong way and that I was perhaps miles from my hotel. Opening my map, I assessed the damage. By the time I made my way to another station, I could be at the hotel. I walked on.

It was midafternoon now, and I was famished. I found a bakery, but it had a very long line. I longed for a restaurant, a café, a bar. I wanted to sit at a table with a sandwich and a beer and watch people wander by. But there were no signs, no places to pause, rest, have a bite.

All the stores had three lines into the street—the one where you made your selections, the one where you paid, the one where you picked up your purchases. The average Soviet housewife spends two hours a day in lines. I had neither the patience nor the strength. I pushed on until I came to a kolkhoz—a market where individuals sell their own crops. Here the lines were shorter, though the cost high. I bought some apples, a warm bun, a bottle of soda. Pausing in a small park, I sat down to eat. I ate as if I'd never eaten before in my life.

As I left the park an old woman with gold and silver teeth, a red babushka around her head, grabbed me by the arm. She was asking directions, pointing in different ways. I told her, I am not from here. At first she laughed at her own foolishness. Then she grew serious. Where? she asked, breathless. Where? America, I said. Suddenly she began to cry, leaning toward me, whispering rapidly into my ear.

I realized that she thought I spoke Russian fluently, not the few words I could say to negotiate my way down the street. She gave me a message to take to someone she loves. Someone who had gone away. A son, I imagined from the intensity of her sobs. Or a daughter who had promised to send for her. She took my hand, pressing it to her heart. Thank you, thank you, she said. She kissed my hand innumerable times, blessing me through her gold and silver teeth. And then suddenly she was gone. But what is the message I am supposed to carry? I asked myself over and over again. Whom is it for?

AT EIGHT thirty that night I staggered into my hotel, exhausted, famished. I showered, put on my dress, and headed down for dinner. I tried all the restaurants in my hotel—there were five of them—and the wait was two hours, minimum. There were restaurants outside as well, so I walked to a few of these. In front of each was a long line.

I returned to my room and tried to place a call to my companion, in New York. The operator said the call would take ten hours, so I wrote him a letter instead. I wrote until about eleven thirty. Then I made myself a package of beef Stroganoff, which I cooked with a heating coil. I drank a shot of vodka and went to bed.

In the morning I decided to ask Intourist, the government agency in charge of tourism, if I could change my vouchers for Kiev. Travel in the Soviet Union is all prepaid, prearranged. In order to make any changes, one must deal with Intourist. I had not yet made up my mind that I would not go to Kiev, but I wanted to know if it would be possible to alter my plans.

At Intourist branches in each hotel, nine or ten women—whose job it is to procure theater tickets, train tickets, excursions, and guides—all sit in a row. I approached the woman in charge of travel vouchers. I asked if she spoke English. She nodded without speaking. "I would like to know if it is possible for me not to go to Kiev," I said politely.

She was blond, perhaps my age, with severe features, a gray shirt.

She gave me a cold stare. "Oh"—she spoke indifferently, flipping through my vouchers—"you must go to Kiev. It is open for tourists."

"My embassy has a traveler's advisory against going into that area."

"Yes. I would not go." She spoke breathlessly, like Garbo. "Russians will not go, but you"—now she smiled—"you must go."

THROUGH a contact I managed to get the number of the man who had warned me, at the ambassador's a few nights before, not to go to Kiev. I will call him Ivan, although I am told I do not have to protect him, because they have done everything that can be done to him. Ivan has been forcibly separated from his wife, who is American. He has lost his profession. He has been declared a parasite. He cannot get a visa.

I am told other things. My phone is probably tapped. My room is wired. The maids work for the KGB. They will copy my address book if I leave it in my room. I am told that ten million people work for the KGB in some capacity and that you cannot know whom to trust.

I phoned Ivan from my hotel room. He said he wanted me to meet some people, but he could not arrange it right away. He wouldn't say anything more on the phone. "I know your itinerary. I will arrange something before you leave. You are not going to Kiev, are you?"

I went down to Intourist again. A new woman sat at the voucher desk. She was older. Perhaps she will be more sympathetic, I thought. I handed her my voucher. "I am scheduled to go to Kiev, but I don't want to go."

She looked at my voucher, then glared at me. "Then you must leave the Soviet Union," she told me. "It is the only way."

THERE is a picture on my desk at home that I treasure. It is a picture of my family shortly after they had all arrived in the United States. They sit before a backdrop that in their lifetime they will never know—a farmhouse, a trellis, cherry blossoms, a picket fence. In the middle sits my great-grandfather Isaac, with his long, dark beard, his blue eyes—my inheritance, I am told—and a stern, opaque face. My great-grandmother stands with her hand obediently on his shoulder. Around them are their children—the ones she buried alive. Dave and Harry, with their long blond curls; Bunnie and Herman, older and not very attractive; Hannah; then my grandmother Lena, a beauty about to turn ripe; Eva; and Morris, the oldest. For me they have stopped at this moment before the fake backdrop, not long after they got off the boat.

In a drawer in my desk I keep all my other photographs—the ones I intend to put in albums someday. Sometimes I even buy albums—smooth, tanned-leather books that I keep in a pile, empty, expectant for what I fear will never come. The ordering of my life. A chronology made clear. Though it is some plan I seek, it is what I seem to scrupulously avoid.

The truth is, I like the way, in this drawer, time blurs over the years. I can reach in and retrieve myself at sixteen or thirty-three. I can find my grandmother, a young woman with small children, or older, eyes glassed over with glaucoma, squinting for the camera. Moments are frozen here. My Russian family for me is forever in front of that picket fence. The picture makes me feel secure, as if we will all—everyone we have ever loved—live on in one dazzling moment. What I want is this blur, these moments standing still, frozen like the winters of my youth.

The author's great-grandfather Isaac with his wife and eight children. Lena, the author's grandmother, is in the back row, second from left. Chicago, circa 1900.

NICHOLAS DANILOFF LIVED IN A tree-lined residential district on the outskirts of Moscow. When I reached him by phone and told him what I was trying to do, he suggested I come over. Daniloff was a pale, thin man with glasses, a studious type. He did not make small talk as he handed me an enormous map. "Here is the area where you want to go," he told me, pointing in a circle around Chernigov, and for the first time I saw a detailed map of the Ukraine, with all the little villages and towns.

Daniloff had been writing a book about a Russian relative of his, and he understood the difficulties of doing research in the Soviet Union. "You need a special visa, and with Chernobyl, you won't get it now. You need to learn more Russian. You need contacts here. You can't just go do whatever you want in this country." He made it quite clear that getting to the Chernigov area on this trip would be impossible.

"And I would not go to Kiev now. There is nothing you can do. No one will take you out of the city, and it probably is not safe."

"I thought if I could just see the outskirts, a few towns . . ."

He shook his head. "It is highly unlikely that you will be able to. You could go to Kiev and sit and try it, but in my opinion Kiev is not safe now."

"I've been trying to change my itinerary, but it doesn't seem to be working."

"Keep trying," he said. He spoke in a dry, straightforward manner, and I believed him more than I had believed any of the others. Then he showed me around. I saw his research room, filled with newspapers and clippings, all neatly filed. He said he kept everything because he never knew when he would need it.

After about an hour I thanked him and left.

Three months later Nicholas Daniloff would be arrested by the KGB for spying.

IN MY hotel room, I waited for the phone to ring. I wanted to meet with Ivan. I also had been promised a meeting with the Russian poet Andrey Voznesensky. It was hot, and there was no air-conditioning, so I lay naked on the skinny bed in tangled sheets, a hot, dusty breeze blowing in. My breasts felt distended, my belly large. This seemed like a foreign body to me, not the one I'd known.

A new level of loneliness set in. I wrote an impassioned letter to my companion, in New York. I don't want to travel alone again, I told him. On a sheet of notepaper I made a list of the guests I would invite to our wedding. Then I tore the letter up and tossed it into the trash.

The phone rang, and it was Ivan. He told me that he was trying to set up some appointments, but nothing could be arranged now. If I returned to Moscow after my visit to Leningrad—instead of going to Kiev—he would have an appointment for me then. I told him that I had tried, but couldn't change my vouchers. "Keep trying," he said.

"You're the second person to say that," I told him as we hung up.

Hunger grabbed me, and I headed out the door. I had discovered the cafeteria at the Intourist Hotel by now, and there I filled a plate with stuffed cabbage, stewing meat, potatoes. I could not imagine how I would ever eat so much food, but effortlessly I did.

In the morning I was determined to change my vouchers, and headed straight for the Intourist desk. There was a new woman, and I asked her what language she spoke. French, she told me. So in French I explained my problem. "Oh, you can change," she told me, "but it will cost you twice what you have already paid."

The women, I knew, switched posts frequently, so I went to the cafeteria for breakfast and took a walk around Red Square. I contemplated for the last time a visit to Lenin's tomb, but the line seemed longer than before, and instead I wandered back to my hotel. Since I was departing tomorrow for Leningrad, this would be my last try.

A new woman had appeared at the Intourist desk. She had soft, gentle features and warm brown eyes. As always, I asked her if English was her language, and she replied, "No, Spanish." This pleased me, since Spanish was my best foreign language and I knew Latin culture well. I thought to myself, standing there, What do Latin women care more about than anything in the world?

I said, "I am going to have a baby, and I am supposed to go to Kiev. I would like to change my vouchers."

She nodded, making it clear she understood. "Of course. No, you should not go." I leaned toward her across the counter. She glanced at my body, a questioning look in her eyes.

"Only a few weeks," I replied.

"I will be happy to change your vouchers. There will be no charge."

"I would appreciate that," I said as she flipped through my vouchers.

"Would you like to return to Moscow, then?"

"Yes, that would be fine."

And then I knew what perhaps I'd known all along. That I had been intending to travel to the place where the world's worst nonmilitary nuclear disaster had occurred and that I was, by a quick calculation, six weeks pregnant.

"What is your name?" I asked.

"Natalia," she told me.

"Thank you, Natalia," I said.

I walked outside. It was a warm afternoon, but there was a breeze in the air, and I began a slow walk around Red Square, trying to absorb the facts of my life as they now stood. I was not going into the Ukraine, which was the purpose of my journey, and I was going to have a child, which was taking me by surprise. I felt thwarted, and yet at the same time I experienced a sense of completion. Still, I could not bear just to get on a plane as scheduled and fly home. If I could not go to the Ukraine, I wanted to continue on and return to the West by rail.

Natalia was still at her post when I returned. "Excuse me," I said, handing her all of my vouchers, my plane tickets—everything. "I am supposed to leave Russia in about two weeks by plane from Moscow. I'd like to cancel my flight and take the train to Berlin."

Natalia looked at me askance. "You will need transit visas. You'll need to change this airplane ticket. I'll have to check with the railroad. I don't know. . . . Where will you stay in Berlin?"

I shrugged. "Somewhere. It doesn't matter. Is it possible?"

"It will be difficult," Natalia said slowly, a smile crossing her face, "but it can be done."

LATER that evening as I packed for Leningrad, the pieces were clear, and suddenly I understood. I wasn't even sure how I had missed it for so long, but when one is traveling, time is sometimes forgotten. Now as I thought back, reading through my journal, I knew that it was true. In fact, I had dreamed my daughter before I had her. I had dreamed her on the Yangtze River boat ride, where the dead bodies of pigs and cattle and humans drifted by. On the river the Chinese say is the river of life and death, I imagined my daughter, and there I conceived her.

On that journey through China with my companion, I had met a young girl, with copper-colored hair, who liked to paint with watercolors to pass the time. Her name was Axelle, and she was eleven years old. Her family, who lived in Fiji, traveled all over the world. I admired this family of intrepid travelers—each child wearing his own backpack—and I knew then that I wanted to have a child to journey with, to see the world. In the afternoon, as our boat sailed down the muddy green river, Axelle came to my room and we sat on the floor and painted the sailboats and the sunsets we saw. We exchanged our paintings and promised to write.

That night in Moscow I read in my journal:

> May 23, 1986. Arrived Wuhan, 6 p.m. Spent day painting and reading with Axelle. I long for a little girl—have a deep desire for a child, boy or girl, but a girl would be best. A child who will want to see the world.

For years I had wanted to try to have a child, but my medical history made the prospect dubious. Ten years before, in Mexico City, an abscess on an ovary ruptured. A surgeon's knife saved me, but a child was an unlikely goal. But in Tibet, perhaps in a moment of folly or great love, I'd told my companion I wanted to try.

Later, one night in Wuhan, we left the boat and entered the steamy furnace city of the Yangtze. The heat was visible, in undulating waves. I walked with Axelle and her family, my companion at my side. As we walked those sweat-drenched, stinking streets, a coursing pain shot through my side. Yet it was not unpleasant. Rather, on the banks of the river of life and death, it had been like a fire burning inside.

THE Intourist official was waiting for me in the lobby of the hotel to take me to the station for the train to Leningrad. He was a large gray man, with a dour face. He directed me to his car. A few moments later we were at the station, and he was walking ahead toward the platform while I dragged my bag behind him. I kept thinking he would turn to see if I needed a hand, but he didn't. He passed car after car, moving farther and farther along the train, which seemed quite full.

At last he turned around, took my bag into a compartment, and flung it onto a seat. I followed and saw that I was sitting in the last seat in a completely empty car. He pointed, instructing me to sit. He did not seem like the kind of man to argue with, so I obeyed, feeling somewhat diminished. Then he left.

I sat for a long time, and no one came. It occurred to me that perhaps foreigners were kept separate from Russians on this train, which was not the overnight tourist train to Leningrad. I got up and looked into the compartment behind mine. It was full of Russians, laughing, passing bread and cheese among themselves. I had just decided to take my bag and go into the next compartment when people began to file into the car.

This railroad, ordered to be built by Nicholas I, has a mythical past. It is said that the railroad has a curve near Leningrad because when the czar indicated its route, he drew a line with a ruler between Moscow and Leningrad (then St. Petersburg) and the pencil slipped around his finger near the top. No one dared ask whether he meant the curve to be there. They just built it that way.

This was also the train where Anna Karenina met Vronsky that snowy night when her fate was sealed. Not unlike Anna, with emotions shuttling between private passion and societal propriety, I contemplated my fate. As a young girl growing up on the banks of Lake Michigan, I had made a pact with myself. If I ever got pregnant, which was a very dim possibility in my girlhood, I would fling myself off the bluff where I walked my dogs. This way I would not be a burden to myself or my family. I would hide my shame. But now, years later, I envisioned for myself a different scenario. I was no girl of sixteen. I had a companion with whom I had spent the last three years. I was almost forty, with a career. I could take care of myself, and I had someone to share my life with.

A PRETTY woman in a cotton shirtwaist came into our car. She was followed, like a duck, by a procession of small children and then an old woman. Oddly, they all took seats in different places.

The train started up and soon left the station behind. As we snaked through the outskirts of Moscow, I peered forlornly at building after building of government housing. Then the government housing was gone, and we were in the suburbs. I stared out the window, the sun in my face, and watched then as the landscape alternated between farmlands and more industrial sites, as it would for much of the journey.

I was content to be moving ahead. And now I devised a plan for myself. I would call my companion from Leningrad and tell him the news. We would plan our future. On a sheet of paper I remade the list of the guests who'd come to our wedding.

The pretty woman in the cotton shirtwaist asked me a question I didn't understand. My response made her look at me quizzically, then ask where I was from. America, I told her. *Amerikanska?* she replied. From New York, I said. Suddenly she took me by the arm and paraded me up and down so that everyone knew that an American was in their car. People got up and looked at me as if I were a rare specimen in a zoo. Others gave me small tokens. An old man handed me a pin of Lenin. I had brought pencils with the Statue of Liberty perched where the eraser should be for such an occasion, and I began handing them to the children, who took them with gleeful shrieks.

After a while my novelty wore off, and most of my fellow travelers went to sleep. I made my way into the dining car. It was almost full. The old man who'd given me the Lenin pin was squeezed into a seat with some women and a young girl, and he beckoned for me. American, he shouted, so everyone turned. Here, sit with me. He pointed to a nonexistent space.

Somehow everyone made room. We introduced ourselves, and the old man told the waiter—a handsome young blond Russian with a dark mustache and lovely dark eyes—to bring me tea and whatever else I wanted. The next thing I knew, a plate of steaming kasha with melting butter sat before me, and no one seemed to care that he had served me before the others or that he would never hand me a bill.

When they had all finished their meals, everyone got up at once, it seemed, waving good-bye, and I was left almost alone in the dining car. I was glad for the respite, thinking I'd have a little time to myself, when suddenly the waiter sat down.

"My name is Sasha," he said. I told him my name. "I want to visit America," he told me. "I've heard wonderful things. I like it here. It is my country. I have a good job. I meet interesting people, but"—he looked over his shoulder to see if anyone was listening—"sometimes it is not enough. There are things . . ." An official-looking person was counting receipts in the back, and Sasha seemed uncomfortable.

"How long have you worked for the railroad?"

He held up three fingers. "I am an engineer, but for now I must do this." He shrugged, clearly not happy with his lot. "But eventually I will be an engineer. This is just my training period."

"What do you want to do when your training period is over?"

"Build bridges," he said proudly, "or perhaps hydraulic dams."

I had my phrase book with me, and we flipped through it when we could not find a word. He pointed to the word synagogue, again looking behind him. I looked at him strangely. "Are you Jewish?" he asked. "Many Americans who come to Russia are Jewish."

I nodded.

"My mother," he said, "she is Jewish. So I am Jewish." He took off his railroad pin and handed it to me. "Saturday morning, be in front of your hotel. I will take you to synagogue." And I said I would.

Leningrad

IT HAS been called the Venice of the North, the Second Paris, Babylon of the Snows. To Peter the Great, it was his window on the West. It was of Leningrad that Russian poet Aleksandr Pushkin wrote in "The Bronze Horseman," "I love you, Peter's creation; I love your severe, graceful appearance . . . the transparent twilights and moonless gleam of your still night."

Like a once great but troubled starlet, Leningrad has led a tormented past. For its beauty it has paid a high price. Tens of thousands died building this city under Peter's relentless command. A million and a half died trying to defend it during the nine hundred days of its siege in World War II. To Stalin, it was the city he feared might rise up against him. Some feel that when he knew the Nazis were planning an assault on Leningrad, he turned his back. Leningrad suffered almost beyond belief in World War II. The packing crates of the Hermitage museum were used as coffins; children's sleds transported the sick, the dead. When the blockade was lifted and the starvation of half its population was over, the renovation began. Its power depleted, Leningrad became a living museum.

But for me its potency remained. As the taxi hurtled along Nevsky Prospect en route to my hotel, I was immediately captured, taken in. Perhaps it was the shock of arriving at eleven o'clock at night and finding broad daylight, for it was White Nights—that time of year in the north when the sun never dips very far below the horizon. Perhaps it was the whirl of colors—the buildings of green and blue, pink and creamy white that darted by. Or the austerity of its imperial structures, bathed in northern light and reflected in the waters of the canals. Cold, expansive, indifferent. Leningrad, St. Petersburg, Petrograd, Sankt Piterburkh, or just Peter—as its denizens like to call it—casts a spell that won't let go.

THE lobby of my hotel was filled with the most beautiful women I have ever seen. Women dressed in silk of shiny mint and pale gray, electric blue and soft violet. Women in shoulder pads and spike heels, with tresses of spun flax or the darkest Mediterranean shade. These were the women of Leningrad who emerged from their stale desk jobs or secretary pools every Friday night to service the Finnish men with coarse ways and wads of money who arrived like clockwork for the weekends. My hotel lobby seemed to be the ideal spot for this salient example of free enterprise.

I checked into the hotel, my room a quaint study of lace curtains and dark wood, a four-poster canopy bed tucked into an alcove. But I felt restless, so I walked outside. I wanted to have a drink and be among people. There was a bar next door, so I went in.

The bar was also filled with these same women, who sat like mannequins, lips perfectly glossed, eyelashes thick as horsehair. They reminded me of actresses wearily awaiting their audition. Their dead eyes gazed at me as I entered their midst dressed in jeans, a bulky shirt. I thought about turning back, but it became a matter of pride.

The reality of my pregnancy had not yet truly sunk in, so I ordered vodka. After a few moments a Finnish man sat down at my table and spoke to me in Russian. "I'm American," I said, wondering what had prompted him to select me out of all the possibilities in the room.

"Oh, I thought you looked different, but I could use a little company that's different. These women, they're all lonely. You know what they want more than anything else? They want to talk."

"I can identify with that," I said.

"What're you doing in this place?"

"I wanted a drink," I said. "I wanted to get out."

"It can be taken wrong," he muttered. He was stout, with thinning yellow hair. He wore a wedding ring.

"Are you here on business?"

He laughed. "Well, my wife thinks I am. A couple times a year I get over here, but"—his hand swept the vapid faces of the women—"it's getting a little tedious. But my wife, well, you know how it is."

Actually, I didn't know, and wanted to ask him more, but he took another line of discussion. "Let me tell you something." He spoke in a fatherly way. "You've got to be careful here. In this city people will buy anything—your shirts, your jewelry—but mainly they want dollars, so be careful with your money. But you can trade anything you've got." He slapped me on the leg. "Anything." I was enjoying his company and was sorry when he got up to leave, though clearly he did not just want to talk.

When he was gone, I looked around and saw that except for the bartender, the room was filled with women. I was hungry to talk to a woman. I looked for sympathetic eyes and found only blank stares and suspicious looks. They must have been having a slow night, or business was generally bad. I sat nursing my vodka, staring into its cold glass.

AT TWO a.m. I emerged from the bar into broad daylight. Unable to sleep, and with a long, sunny night ahead, I decided to go for a walk. I wandered to the small square near my hotel, across from the Russian Museum, and found myself before the statue of Pushkin. This was his city, and he was their poet—the father of Russian literature. Descended from an Abyssinian prince, Pushkin was, and remains, Russia's most beloved writer. A free spirit, he lived intensely, gambled compulsively, and died in a duel with a man with whom his wife was probably in love, leaving generations of Russians to mourn.

As I sat beneath his statue the sun shone, still bright, and the wisteria was in bloom. The air, fresh off the Gulf of Finland, was redolent with the smell of jasmine. Sweetness was everywhere. The park was not empty, nor were the streets as the citizens of Leningrad ambled, as they would for two more weeks of White Nights, aimless and confused as a disoriented migrating herd.

With no map, I set off, thinking I'd make a loop, then return along the wide boulevard of Nevsky Prospect in the direction of the river. But it was not long before I left the main street and was wandering down a side street lined with canals, across a footbridge crowned with gold-winged griffins. The buildings of imperial Russia loomed before me, painted in their shades of blue like robins' eggs, the pink of Norwegian salmon, the soft yellow of cut wheat, the white of fresh cream, all reflected in the brownish green waters of the canals.

I cut through other side streets, crossed other bridges, until I stood on the cobbles of Palace Square, before the astonishing Winter Palace. With hundreds of rooms, its blue-and-white façade shimmered like ice. Here thousands of peaceful demonstrators—men, women, children—were met with the gunfire of the imperial guards, touching off the Revolution of 1905. I stared into its vastness and imagined the slaughter that had occurred, the dark side of all this beauty.

Continuing on, I reached the Neva, where I paused before its wide, turbulent, exquisitely blue surface and the stately, palatial buildings that lined its banks. Frozen solid for six months of the year, the Neva now flowed into the Gulf of Finland with a force that astounded. Small fishing boats floated by. Two lovers in light jackets sat on an old boat ramp, kissing with abandon. Gulls hovered overhead.

Pushkin immortalized the city in his poem "The Bronze Horseman," written in 1833. Now I found myself standing before the statue from which the great Russian epic draws its name, with Peter astride his rearing horse, symbol of Russia itself, trampling a serpent representing the forces that tried to oppose his reforms. I felt the rising hoofs of Peter's horse could easily trample me.

Then I turned back into the maze of winding side streets. I made my way along the murky canals, down the narrow alleyways. I told myself I should go back to the hotel and sleep, but I was being sucked in, amazed at how easily I'd fallen into step with this city and its inhabitants. I was like one obsessed, overcome, a fly in the radiant web.

I wandered the streets as one does through a museum, silently, with reverence. Or as you might after committing a crime, with stealth, yet feeling contemplative, planning your next move. I could imagine, as Pushkin had, the statue of Peter coming to life and stalking men along the ancient cobbles of this city. It seemed I had walked into a Russian fairy tale and I could play any part—criminal, prostitute, destitute mother, coy mistress, woman alone—but not in some cardboard tourist attraction, as I'd done at the Ming tombs. This was all too real.

I found myself back at my hotel at about six a.m., the sun still in the place where it was when I left, but I was now exhausted, spent. I crept into my room, bones aching, and pulled down the shade. Then I made my way into the small sleeping alcove. I lay down on the narrow bed and pulled the canopy curtains around it.

I lay in the small alcove, on that narrow bed, enclosed in lace, and I felt the small body contained within my own. We lay there together, one inside the other, inside the bed, inside the alcove, the room, like those Russian dolls I carried with me as gifts, each one smaller and smaller, tucked inside the other.

PETER the Great stood at the delta where the Neva meets the Baltic, his soldiers behind him, miserable in the inhospitable swampland, and declared that here he would build a great city by the sea. Here where the Neva divided into four branches, creating a marshy archipelago of islands, Peter would realize his dream of a city like Amsterdam, with pristine winding canals and tree-lined streets.

On May 16, 1703, on land that he had only recently seized from Sweden, he cut into the ground and laid the first stone of what would become the fortress of Saints Peter and Paul.

Peter the Great was a giant, standing six feet seven, renowned for his appetites for drink, lovemaking, smoking, and bawdy humor, and for his dark side—his sudden rages, his cruel vengeance. In the very fortress where he laid his stone, he would have his own son beaten to death for treason. Even as he heaved his country out of the Middle Ages, he would torture the *streltsy*—his own palace guards, who rose up against him—by having them flayed, then roasted over slow flames.

From boyhood Peter lived with a hatred of the Kremlin. Its dark, secret corridors and its musty rooms only served to remind him of the horror he had witnessed in the first *streltsy* revolt, when he had seen people he loved—mentors, relatives—stalked and cut to pieces as he trembled in his mother's arms. For the rest of his life the Kremlin was a prison to him. He dreamed of light, fresh air, open space, the sea.

As a man of gargantuan energies, Peter wanted Russia to be more like the West. He wanted Russia to turn away from its Byzantine and, he felt, barbaric Eastern ways. He cut the beards off his boyars, at times wielding the razor himself, and thrust women from the seclusion of the Terem, unveiled, into the world.

Peter didn't care about any resistance he met. He believed there was nothing he could not do. Indeed, he is said to have mastered fourteen skills, including gunnery and shipbuilding (which he learned in a Dutch shipyard, where he went incognito). He was an expert at papermaking, etching, leatherwork. He cobbled his own shoes, made his own furniture. Once, as a present, he gave his beloved wife, Catherine, an ivory chandelier that he had crafted himself.

A man of vision, he created for Russia a modern army and—his true dream—a navy. At the delta of the Neva, Peter knew he would put his ships. Ironically, from this same harbor in World War II the navy would fail the very city Peter had created it to protect.

Some say it was the curse of the bones upon which the city is built. For Peter spared no one. He rounded up tens of thousands of Swedish prisoners of war, peasants, workers, and criminals from all over Russia and forced them into swamps of freezing mud. Working barechested in the middle of winter, tens of thousands died. More were rounded up, until, in seven years, Peter had his city. Then he needed people to live in it. So he simply invited his aristocracy to summer with him in his new city, which required that they build houses at their own expense. No one could refuse the czar.

Until Peter, Russia had never acted as a single entity. The forced labor and coercion exercised by Peter to get his project accomplished united Russia for the first time. No one knows how many died in this effort. A hundred thousand. A million. They came to dredge the swamps, hold back the sea, build the city of Peter the Great's dream, cursing him as they died. They died of malaria, influenza, and colds. They died in the floods that came as the Gulf of Finland swelled.

The city rests upon its dead, and one can only wonder that so much beauty came from so much death. The people of Leningrad do not forget this. Some told me they felt the dead stirring in the ground. Others believed that the nine-hundred-day siege by the Nazis was the payment due to those who died building the city. To this day it is standard practice for the brides of Leningrad to take their bouquets after their wedding service and place them on the mass grave at Piskarevsky Cemetery, where hundreds of thousands who died during the siege are buried. That cemetery is bedecked in bridal bouquets. In the words of the Leningrad poet Olga Berggolts, "Let no one forget; let nothing be forgotten."

THE Peter and Paul fortress stands along the banks of the Neva, its ramparts and bulwarks formidable, its golden spire piercing the sky like a lance. Here under its cathedral dome the later czars and czarinas of Russia lie buried in cold white sarcophagi adorned with simple gold crosses. Only at the tomb of Peter were a few flowers laid.

Descending into the dungeons, now a prime tourist attraction, I gazed into musty cells that had once held the likes of Dostoyevsky. Peter's own son Alexis was tortured to death in these dingy rooms. The dank coolness of the dungeons and the pressing need of tourists to gaze into their misery rankled my nerves, and I ascended, crossing over swiftly to the park and the promenade of arching oaks.

It was here that St. Petersburg was born. In 1703, in a small three-room wooden cabin, which has been preserved, Peter lived during the building of his city. He was too busy to have a house built for him, and throughout his life his personal needs and tastes would be simple. But from here he could watch the city rise out of the swamp, and this was all he required.

I paused on a bench beneath the trees, in the cool shade of the small promenade, and contemplated what it was to watch your dream unfold. Or the opposite, to watch it collapse. I pondered the things I had wanted in this world. What had I accomplished? Where had I failed? The roster came out about even, I decided. But I knew that there was something I had to do now. I could delay it no longer.

RETURNING to the hotel, I placed a call with the concierge, asking if I could please reach the States. I gave her his number. She said they'd call me when they had my party on the line. I went into my room and collapsed on the bed. I have no idea how long I had been lying there when the phone rang.

When I picked it up, he was on the line. "How are you?" he said.

"I'm fine," I said, "but I miss you."

His voice was soft, gentle, on the other end. "I miss you too."

We made small talk for a few moments. He told me about his work, the children. One of the boys was in trouble again. His ex-wife wanted the boy to live with him. He sounded weary, speaking of all the difficulties. It occurred to me that this might not be the moment to tell him what I needed to say, but he would be departing for Sri Lanka soon. It would be many weeks before we'd speak again.

"I don't mean to add to your complexities," I told him, "but I'm going to have a child."

Transatlantic silence was deafening. Water seemed to fill the line; minutes ticked away. "Did you hear me? I'm going to have a child."

"Well, a child is a wonderful thing. . . ." His voice was full of pauses, something rare for him. "Of course," he added despondently, "I'm not sure I've had great luck with mine."

"Well, maybe you're being given another chance."

He said nothing; then I heard a soft "Perhaps."

"I want to have this child," I said, emphatically now, as if I had made up my mind. "And . . . and I think we should make it legal."

Again there was silence, oceans of water flowing between us. "Legal?" he said. "In what sense?"

I paused, taking a deep breath. "We've been together a long time now. I think we should get married."

"Well . . . let's wait and see," he said. "Why don't we discuss it when you get home."

When you spend years of your life with someone, you get to know his turns of phrase, his little habits. I'd heard him say "wait and see" to others. To ex-wives he was trying to placate, to children making too many demands. To all those he intended ultimately to disappoint or ignore.

We hung up, agreeing to discuss it later in the summer, though I knew what the outcome would be. Lying down on the bed in the alcove, I thought of my grandmother. It was a Saturday morning, and I was fifteen years old. We sat in her darkened living room, a plate of prune strudel before us, and my grandmother asked me about boys. Was there a special one I was seeing? Did I like them at all?

Then she gave me her only piece of sex education. She told me that if a man touches a woman's body before marriage, she disintegrates.

"Disintegrates?" I asked, incredulous.

She nodded, held up her fingers, as if they contained an exploding spore, and then let them go. "Puff," she said. "Nothing at all."

FROM 1764 the czars of Petersburg collected works of art and put them in the buildings beside the Winter Palace. These buildings have come to be known as the Hermitage. After the Revolution the palace, with its fifteen hundred rooms, became the perfect spot for displaying the treasures of European painting. Here the old masters—Leonardo, Titian, Rubens, Rembrandt—are on display. For two hours I followed my guide—a necessity, it seemed—until I was overwhelmed and could go on no more, my head reeling not only from the magnificence of the art but also from trying to imagine the balls held in these malachite, agate, marble, and gold-gilt ballrooms, the dinners eaten in the grand dining room.

I needed to walk. I headed along Nevsky Prospect, then found a farmers' market, where I purchased apples and a sweet roll. Then I made my way to the Dostoyevsky house and museum.

Dostoyevsky lived in a small apartment, and the contrast to the impressive Tolstoy house in Moscow surprised me. The ordered simplicity of his life was evident in the toys his children played with, the dark, austere furnishings. Under glass there were letters and manuscripts written in his own hand, along with the careful budgets his wife kept that enabled the family to stay afloat. I was touched by the normalcy surrounding a mind so possessed, and felt relief to be away from the enormous successes of Peter to these more conceivable accomplishments—at least to me—of a great writer who lived as an ordinary man.

As I made my way slowly back to the hotel I found myself in stride with "Father Time." He had a long white beard that fell halfway to his

Below: the onion domes of St. Basil's Cathedral, in Moscow. Right: visitors lined up along the towering brick walls of the Kremlin to view Lenin's tomb.

chest. He wore a green army suit, vintage World War I, bedecked with every conceivable medal, and walked with a carved wood walking stick.

He took me by the arm. "You are French?" he asked.

"American."

"I am a Bolshevik. One of the original fighters for the Revolution."

I looked at him, amazed. "How old are you?"

"I am almost a hundred years old."

"You are a hero," I said, touching the medals on his chest.

He smiled, a twinkle in his eye. "We are all heroes. Every Russian is a hero." We were crossing Nevsky Prospect now, walking toward Pushkin Park. Some people smiled at the old man. Others, tourists, looked at him as if they were seeing a ghost.

"You know, when I was a boy, I saw them once, the czar and the czarina. They were in a carriage, going right down this road." He stopped to point. "They were so beautiful, and they looked so happy." Then his eyes turned dark. "And we were all so hungry. Still," he said with a sigh, "it was so sad."

We had reached Pushkin Park, and the old man now eased himself

Below: the author met "Father Time" on the streets of Leningrad. Bedecked with medals, he claimed to be one of the Bolsheviks—the original fighters for the Revolution—and nearly a hundred years old.

down onto a bench. Someone stopped and asked if they could take his picture. He stood up solemnly and stared into the camera. Then, weary, he sat back down again. "I have lived through everything," he said. "We are all heroes. Remember I said so."

On Saturday morning, when Sasha, the waiter from the train, did not arrive, I made my way alone to Lermontovsky Prospect, to one of the oldest synagogues in Russia. It was a brown stone structure— crumbling, it seemed—and though there were some young couples with children, most of the Jews waiting for the service to begin were older, stooped. These were faces that had lived through the siege of Leningrad, with Hitler's troops threatening at the door. They had also lived through the Stalinist purges and the ongoing persecution of the Soviet Jew. There was something dead in many of their eyes, something gone. I had read much on the suffering of the Soviet Jew, but seeing it here, in the flesh, stunned me.

Yet as I walked in, faces lit up. Hands reached out; strangers greeted me. They seemed to know right away that I was a visitor, someone they had never seen before.

I went upstairs to the balcony, where the women prayed. All the women had colorful babushkas in bright floral silks with spangles. Some cried as they prayed. A woman beside me recited the *Kaddish*, the prayer for the dead, over and over again, beating her breast, crying. With them, I stood and recited the *Kaddish*, tears welling in my eyes, as if I were praying for all the living, and the dead.

After perhaps half an hour a young woman turned to me. "You're American, right?" She was a foreign-exchange student living in Leningrad for the summer. As we left the synagogue Sally introduced me to two medical students, Michael and Josh, who were also visiting. I was speaking with Michael when a frail blond man approached us.

"I would like to take you to hear some music," he said quietly. "It is not near, but you will meet some interesting Jews. Refuseniks, like me."

I had not yet met any Jews who had dissented against the Soviet system and in exchange lost whatever small privileges they might have had. We agreed to go. David introduced himself and gave us instructions. "Do not walk in a group or speak English loudly," he said. "Don't look as if you don't know where you are going."

The four of us jumped on a trolley, and it sped down the middle of the street. We paid our fares while David stood a few feet behind us. His eyes kept shifting over the crowd. I had ballet tickets for that night, and I found myself concerned about when we might be back. I mentioned this to Sally, and she turned to David. "How far are we going?" she asked. And when he did not reply, she said, "Is it very far?"

Suddenly we realized our mistake. David looked at us strangely, as if he had never seen us before. He turned his back to us. At the next stop he jumped off the trolley and never looked back.

THE vice consul of the U.S. embassy, Scott Rothman, who was a friend of a friend, had invited me to go with him to the ballet and to dinner. Scott picked me up, a Finnish girl with him in the convertible, and we sped to the Kirov Theater.

This great ballet company had once been the pride of Russia, but when Lenin moved the capital back to Moscow, in 1918, the Kirov became little more than a training camp for the Bolshoi. Still, it had produced some of Russia's finest dancers.

The ballet that night was *Giselle*, a story about betrayal. Giselle, a peasant girl, falls in love with a disguised prince, who cannot marry her, because he is engaged to someone else. Upon learning this, Giselle dies, presumably of a broken heart, and joins a group of betrayed spirits, the Wilis—women jilted en route to the altar who have died. The Wilis condemn the prince to death, but Giselle's assistance and the crack of dawn break their spell. I watched this ballet in which women are viewed as wraiths, invisible and lithe, and at the same time vengeful, full of spite. Its meaning was not lost on me.

The restaurant, situated on the beach, right on the Gulf of Finland, was huge, and packed. From our table I could see the blue shores of the gulf. The sun was still high in the sky. A waiter in a tuxedo brought three silver platters, piping hot, of what Scott said was a real Russian specialty—mushrooms in sour cream sauce.

Suddenly I was famished, and the mushrooms looked delicious. As I picked up my fork to eat, Scott said, "Well, I hope no one is pregnant at this table."

I lowered my fork. "Why?"

"Because of the milk products. You know, the cows ate the grass after Chernobyl, and it goes right into their milk."

Imperceptibly I pushed my plate away. The Finnish girl was already eating, but Scott, with diplomatic panache, raised his hand. "Waiter," he said. "Menu, please."

It was two in the morning as we drove back along the canals and the banks of the Neva. We drove in silence. When we reached my hotel, Scott said, "If there's anything you need . . . If I can help you with anything . . ."

I thanked him for offering and said good night.

Once in my room, I placed a call to my parents. It took three hours, but at last I heard my mother's voice, tired, on the other end.

I blurted it all out tearfully. "I'm not going to Kiev," I told her. "I'm not going into the Ukraine." I heard her breathe a sigh of relief. "I would have gone," I said, "but I'm going to have a child."

"Good," she said, her voice seeming to wake up. And then, "A child. Well, I think that's good."

"You do? I'm not sure it's good," I muttered.

"When's the wedding?" she asked, her voice hopeful.

"There's not going to be a wedding." I told her about the phone call. "I'll probably have an abortion when I get home. I don't know. I can't go through with this. I can't do this on my own. Don't tell my father," I told her. "No matter what, don't tell him." Again the vision of the bluff down which I'd fling myself came to me.

"You sound confused," she said.

"I'm fine. I just needed to talk," I told her. "But promise me you won't tell anyone."

She promised.

AT THE synagogue the day before, I had briefly made contact with a dissident named Vladimir Meyerhoff, who asked me to meet him in a park the following day. While I did not anticipate that he would appear at this meeting, I went, and to my surprise, he was there. Vladimir was dark, intense. When he saw me, he rose, extending his hands. "You came," he said. "Please"—he spoke quickly—"my house is only a few blocks from here. You must come. I'll fix you tea. We can talk more easily there."

His house was on the canal Dostoyevsky used to roam. En route, we paused before a narrow three-story building. "This is where Raskolnikov killed the pawnbroker and her niece," he told me, as if Dostoyevsky's novel *Crime and Punishment* were historical fact. We went a few blocks more, then began our climb up a dreary staircase in the building where Vladimir lived.

His apartment reminded me of the rooms where my grandparents used to live. Grim Oriental tapestries, gloomy landscape paintings on the walls, dark wooden furniture. Darkness seemed to surround Vladimir. He told me his wife and children were in Estonia for the summer. He went into the kitchen and made tea. Then for two hours I sat listening as he told me the story of his life.

Sixteen years ago, he said, the Soviets convicted some Jews of a plot to hijack an airplane and fly to the West. Someone named Vladimir as a co-conspirator. Immediately he lost his job as a computer technician, and had been working ever since as a house electrician. Ten years ago he applied for a visa to emigrate to Israel. Nine years ago his parents left. He had not seen them since.

"Every year I reapply," Vladimir said, "and every year it's a different story. When I applied for a visa on the basis of reunification of families, they said my parents were no longer close family members, because I had not seen them in nine years. When I pointed out that I had not seen them in nine years because I had been denied a visa every year, they shrugged. They try to break you down, wear you out."

That spring, Vladimir said, a documentary had been made about enemies of the state. It was called *Mercenaries and Traitors*. It showed a map of Leningrad, and then the picture zoomed in on a street and finally on Vladimir's house. The movie said an enemy of the state lived in that house. Since then, his son had been persecuted at school and his daughter had been refused entry into the same private school as the son, which by Russian law she had the right to go to. "You know," he said, "I have 'Jew' stamped on my passport. Just like the Nazis. It's not different. That's how we are treated."

As I was leaving, Vladimir said to me, "In Russia when refuseniks toast, we don't say cheers. We say visa." Freedom suddenly felt as precious as it ever had. Vladimir raised his teacup, and I raised mine. "Visa," we said, clicking teacups. Then I said good-bye.

WHEN I returned to my hotel, I found a message from Michael and Josh, the medical students I'd met at the synagogue. It said there was a party that evening at the place where they were staying and I should come. I took a cab in the early evening to the outskirts of Leningrad, to a kind of dormitory complex that was part of the university. These students were on an exchange with Soviet medical students and doctors, working on issues of world peace. They were all members of International Physicians for the Prevention of Nuclear War, the organization that had won the 1985 Nobel Peace Prize.

I walked into a small, smoke-filled room, where medical students in various states of inebriation were talking about medicine and the future of the world. Three Soviet doctors were present. One was a woman with short black hair, simple, dark features. I sat down next to her. Her name was Tanya. She was doing a residency in surgery in Moscow, and her English was excellent.

Tanya told me that she lived with her mother in a flat with four other families. "It is not so bad," she said. "Some people have ten families in their flat." She smiled softly, and I liked her immediately.

Tanya said the smoke and the noise were bothering her and suggested we go outside and take a walk. We took the elevator down and began to walk along a fairly active thoroughfare. "So you're a doctor," I muttered as we got outside. "I could use a doctor."

"Yes." She smiled, looking at me. "I believe you could."

"What do you mean?"

"You are going to have a child, aren't you?"

"Yes, but how did you know?"

"You have a glow. I knew the minute you walked in the room."

"I don't know what I'm going to do. The circumstances," I said, "aren't great."

"The father, you know him?"

"Very well. I thought we'd marry."

"Oh." She shook her head. "That *is* sad."

We followed the thoroughfare to a park and kept walking.

"I was supposed to go to Kiev, then into the Ukraine," I told her.

"Oh, you made the right decision not to go. It isn't safe. Not for you, not for your child."

"Yes." I nodded, not quite comprehending the sense of *my* child, since I was now deciding not to have this child.

"Look," she said, "I'm going to Moscow tomorrow. I'll be there when you get back. Let's see one another. Maybe I can help you. Make things a little easier."

I took her phone number. "Tell the doctors I was tired and went home, would you?" I asked her. "Tell them I'll call them tomorrow."

I hailed a cab, waving good-bye to Tanya. In half an hour I was back at the hotel, where I lay down on the bed, not falling asleep. I'm not sure how long it was before the phone rang. I heard my father's voice on the other end. He was eighty-six years old, but he sounded like a young man. "This is your father," he said.

"I know."

"How are you?"

"Great," I said, tears coming to my eyes.

"Well, I spoke with your mother," he said, making it sound as if they were suddenly separated and living in different cities.

"She promised . . ." I blurted, realizing how foolish it had been to exact such a promise from her.

"Never mind. You know, you aren't getting any younger. I mean, you're going to be forty years old."

"Yes, I know."

"Well," he said, "men come and go." He was right about that. "But you know, a child is forever."

"You can live with this?" I asked timidly, never having imagined a conversation like this with my father.

"I can live with a lot worse," he said.

My LAST night in Leningrad, I met Michael and Josh and their American guide, who Michael assured me was CIA, for a walk along the canals. I promised I'd show them the house where Raskolnikov killed the pawnbroker, but as we moved along the canal all the houses looked the same. It could have happened here, I said, or here. Realizing I had failed in my mission, I offered to introduce them to Vladimir, whose apartment didn't seem far away.

It was eleven thirty when we called, but Vladimir told me he doesn't sleep on White Nights, and he invited us up. This time he took out a bottle of wine and poured drinks all around. Then he began to tell his story again, the same story he told me the day before. The charges, the documentary, the persecution of his children. Everything. "Visa," we said as we toasted. "Visa." We raised our glasses dozens of times.

When we left, it was two in the morning and broad daylight. The medical students walked me back toward my hotel, but then I invited them to the bar where I'd gone my first night in Leningrad. The

Finnish men had gone back to Finland, and now the bar was filled with tired prostitutes, makeup faded or running down their eyes.

This was no longer the pick of the crop. The impeccably dressed women who could model anywhere in the world were asleep, having completed their weekend's work. What was left were the derelicts, discarded and sad. I walked in with three men, and the women perked up like deer at the scent of the hunter and stared at me with envy and disgust.

We had not been sitting down long when a young woman came over. She introduced herself as Veronica and pulled up a chair, next to Michael. She ran her hand over Michael's knee, and he pushed her away. "I want a man," she said. "You have three, and I have none. Can't I have one?" Veronica pleaded with me. "Just one." She put her head down on the table and sobbed, "Just give me one."

THE next morning as I was leaving, a man helped me get my suitcase into the elevator. I thanked him in Russian. Then he asked me in broken English if he could buy my underwear. "My girlfriend likes American underwear." I told him I was wearing my underwear and what I was not wearing, I needed. He thanked me anyway, somewhat sadly, then helped me again with my suitcase as we reached the ground floor.

Moscow

ON THE plane back to Moscow, when fellow passengers realized that I was an American, they gave me small souvenirs: the generic pins of Lenin, bits of hard candy. To the children beside me I gave my remaining pencils with the Statue of Liberty perched defiantly on the tip, and they squealed with delight. Still, I felt dejected, as if the fact that I had decided not to go into the Ukraine were an act of personal cowardice. For the first time in my life I found myself backtracking, taking a route I'd already taken. But more than that, something was gone, never to return.

The Ukraine was sprinkled with lethal dust. Many would die. Children, years from now, would languish in hospital beds, their bone marrow destroyed. My defeat did not seem personal—more global, in a sense. I thought of my own child and wondered what kind of world she would be born into. A world divided, or one at peace? A world on the brink of destruction, or on its way to new solutions?

Not long after I was back in Moscow, Ivan called. He wanted to take me to a gallery run by a friend of his named Lev. Lev exhibited from his home the work of his friends, mostly dissidents and Jews.

Lev was a large, rather heavy man, with obvious health problems. He chain-smoked the entire time I was there. The apartment was small and cluttered, but it had a big living room, and on its walls were photographs and paintings, none with very political themes—portraits of women, men. And a few social-realist themes, such as an impoverished-looking old man on a bench carving wood.

Both Lev and Ivan had spent a good deal of time in Soviet prisons, Lev because he was Jewish and ran a private art gallery, where he exhibited "anti-Soviet" art, and Ivan because he was Jewish, had married an American, refused factory work, and wanted to be a photographer. He had in fact defied authorities consistently for years. Both men had been declared parasites of the state.

"The worst sentence," Lev told me, "is two weeks. If you are there longer, they give you something to do. But for two weeks, you do nothing. You sleep in a room six yards by three yards, with twenty-five men. You have no blanket, no mattress, no pillow. You cannot wash. You go to the bathroom three times a day with a guard who points a gun at you while you are on the toilet. Imagine fifteen days spent this way."

"It seems terrible," I said feebly.

Lev's wife, a large woman who breathed heavily, brought us some cakes. "You see my wife," he said. "Her heart is ruined. She cannot breathe. They have broken her with worry."

I told them I was going to be seeing Andrey Voznesensky in two days and that I was going to ask him about a woman poet, Irina Ratushinskaya, who was in prison. They looked at each other. "You know," Ivan said, "he could probably get her out if he wanted. He doesn't risk anything. Or he risks just enough. He knows how to play the game perfectly." It was clear they thought little of him.

Later as we were leaving, Lev said, "You might be in for some fun. The KGB has been following me. Perhaps they will follow us now." We walked along, but no car followed us. I must admit to a slight feeling of disappointment.

As we were about to go our separate ways, I said to Ivan, "And if you get your visa, what if you go to the States and your marriage falls apart and you have no work and you have nothing?"

Ivan smiled. He had beautiful blue eyes, and they were sparkling. "The only thing I want," he said, "is to never see their faces again."

"I'd sleep in the street," Lev said, "just for one thing."

"Just for freedom," Ivan said, completing the thought.

"You know," Lev said, with a sweep of his hand, "sometimes I go out in the morning and I see the trolleys and think to myself, Why don't they just stop? Why doesn't all of this just stop?"

THAT evening Tanya called, and we went to eat in a small restaurant, where the service was slow. We sat and talked. She told me about her mother, a medical doctor who, because she was older—in her fifties—and because Moscow had too many doctors, worked as a pharmacist. "Isn't that difficult for her?" I asked.

"Oh, no. She's happy they let her stay in Moscow. They could have sent her to practice medicine in the provinces. This way she can stay here. Of course, it has been difficult since my father left."

"Oh, he left?"

"Well, actually he barely stayed. I'm not even sure if they were married. For many years now it has been just my mother and me. We get along all right. It is best to get along with someone if you sleep in the same room."

"You share a room with your mother?"

"We used to share a bed," Tanya said with a laugh, "until recently. I told her I was thirty and it was time I had my own bed."

"I could never sleep in a bed with my mother," I said.

"Oh, we all do what we have to. In some ways," she said, "our lives are easier than yours. Our jobs are guaranteed. Our housing, our medical care, our old-age benefits. We are taken care of."

It was true. I'd seen no homeless, no slums, no extremes of wealth and poverty. But it all seemed so dreary. No one seemed to care much.

"But we are"—I hesitated to say it—"we are freer."

She reflected on this. "Yes," she said. "Yes, you are. We are mirror images of one another, aren't we?" meaning our two countries.

After dinner we strolled through Red Square. Tanya told me a little more about her life. Marriage and children didn't really matter to her.

She viewed them as fetters, things to tie her down. "Of course," she said, afraid to hurt my feelings, "I think for some people it is fine."

"Oh, I don't think marriage is coming my way," I said.

"You really don't think he will marry you?" She seemed saddened at this.

"No," I said, "I don't think he will."

We walked back to my hotel. In a short time we had grown very fond of each other. I felt as if Tanya had become a friend, almost as if she had been sent to help me. "Is there anything I can do for you? Is there anything you would like for your journey?"

I thought about this for a moment. Then, overwhelmed by a desire for fresh fruit, I blurted out, "Oranges. I would love some oranges."

Tanya looked at me in dismay. "I will try. . . ."

"Don't bother. It was just a thought." Now I was embarrassed by my wish. As I thought about it I realized I hadn't seen oranges anywhere in the Soviet Union.

"It will be difficult," Tanya repeated as we said good night, "but I will see what I can do."

A CONTACT had arranged a meeting with Andrey Voznesensky, the superstar Russian poet, at his dacha in a place where writers live, outside of Moscow, called Peredelkino. The contact was going to drive me, but I got stuck in the elevator for half an hour, and by the time I got downstairs, he was gone. The only way to get there now was by taxi, which was going to be costly.

Outside the hotel where the taxis were assembled, I asked who would take me to Peredelkino. They all shook their heads, turned away. No one wanted to go.

"I am going to visit Mr. Andrey Voznesensky," I said. The drivers perked up. They negotiated among themselves. Finally a young man with a mustache, named Alan, stepped forward and said he would take me, but it would cost fifteen rubles an hour, or about twenty-five dollars. I estimated I would have to hire him for at least four hours, but I still wanted to go. At about eight p.m. we set out.

Alan and I sped in his small Volkswagen taxi toward the outskirts of Moscow. I had only sketchy directions, and I communicated them as best I could. We drove and drove. Alan kept stopping people, asking directions. At last we reached Peredelkino, only to learn that Mr.

Voznesensky's house was on the other side of some railroad tracks that could not be crossed. We drove back twenty miles.

An hour and a half after we left, I reached Mr. Voznesensky's dacha. Voznesensky, a rather pallid-looking man, came out and kissed me flat on the mouth. "So," he said, "you have made it. It is wonderful that you have come. Tell me, how are my friends at P.E.N.?"—the International Association of Poets, Playwrights, Editors, Essayists, and Novelists. And in a moment we were catching up on New York gossip.

The dacha was a charming little summer cottage he and his wife, Zoja, shared with someone upstairs. The table in the country kitchen was spread with strawberries, chocolate, and wine. "These are not Chernobyl strawberries," he assured me. "We pick them ourselves." He poured me a glass of wine. "Cheers," he said.

We talked about the upcoming Writers' Union Congress. "A revolution is happening here," he said. "Enormous changes. Like with the film industry. It will happen to the writers as well."

"What kind of changes?" I asked. Although I had a sense of what they'd be, I wanted him to say it.

"Less censorship, free expression, what you call your First Amendment rights."

"Really? You really think changes will occur?"

"You will see. Nothing will be like it was."

Then he led me into his studio. "Here," he said. "There are things I want you to see." The studio was a mess. Papers, books, pictures were everywhere, spilling onto the floor. He dug around until he pulled out a sketch of a monument. He held it up to me with great pride. "This, you must see this. I designed it and had it built. It is a monument to Russian poets. But when you see it, you will understand how it won't be as it was before. That time is past."

It was almost midnight, and all I could think about was how much the taxi was costing me. Just as I was leaving, Zoja rushed out, bringing me a beautiful Russian scarf—a green-and-pink floral pattern with a black fringe—and she wrapped it around me. "To remember us by," she said. Touched by her generosity, I kissed her on both cheeks.

Then Andrey walked me to the cab. When we reached the taxi, we paused. "Andrey," I said, "there is someone I am concerned about. A poet. She has been in prison for a long time. Her health is very poor." He looked surprised, as if he'd never heard of such a thing. I told him her name. Again he seemed surprised.

"I have never heard of her, but why don't you write down her name for me. I'll see what I can do." I wrote down her name. "I'll see if anything can be done." He slipped the piece of paper into his pocket. "But you know"—he cocked his head—"this is Russia."

Six months later I met Irina Ratushinskaya at a reception in New York. I wondered if Voznesensky had somehow made this possible.

Andrey kissed me good-bye. It was now almost dark, and an incredible orange moon, full and shimmering, rose over Moscow. Few cars were out, and we drove quickly but in silence. When we reached my hotel, I asked Alan how much I owed him. He shook his head. It had been taken care of, he said. Voznesensky had paid him. I was amazed by this generosity. I gave him ten more rubles and said good night. "Good luck," he said to me in Russian, "and thank you."

ON SUNDAY, my last day in Moscow, I decided to go to Novodevichy Convent to attend Mass. I walked through a garden to the stone building. Old women, lacework around their heads, crossed themselves before the religious statues in the park. Men in dark suits and ties walked solemnly into the church.

Russian orthodoxy had reigned supreme until the time of Peter the Great, and then with dwindling power until the Revolution, in which it was for all practical purposes institutionally eliminated, but here it flourished. It was Prince Vladimir of Kiev who in 987 brought orthodoxy to Russia. Vladimir had examined all the great religions of the world, sending emissaries out to bring back word, in order to determine what Russia's religion should be. He rejected Islam, because the Russians could not live without drink, and he rejected Judaism, because he could not accept the condemnation to wander. He rejected European Christianity, because he saw "no glory there." But when his emissaries returned with word of Byzantium and its churches with thousands of shining lights, the richness of its ornaments and vestments, its mosaics and jewels, he determined that Eastern Orthodoxy should be the religion of Russia, because God dwells in beauty.

For the next thousand years the church played a major role in Russian political, spiritual, and cultural life. Then, in the Revolution, this profoundly religious people suddenly found themselves with a new god thrust upon them, in the guise of communism. By 1939 only a hundred churches were operating in the U.S.S.R. When I visited, seventy-five hundred, a fraction of what once existed, were open across the entire land. Still, though revolutionary zeal endeavored to replace spiritual belief, it had never quite succeeded.

People flocked into Novodevichy, filling the aisles. Covering my head with the scarf Zoja had given me, I entered the dark, cavelike church, whose air was thick with incense. The cathedral was emblazoned by the light of thousands of candles, small beacons glowing in the darkness. Flowers filled the nave. People milled about; children ran to and fro. Some knelt and crossed themselves. Others moved forward to take the Eucharist. There was a remarkable sense of disorder. The service reminded me of a Jewish service where people come and go, talk, and no one seems to mind.

Neighbor leaned over to gossip with neighbor. A fleeing child was returned to its bewildered parent. It all seemed vibrant, full of life. I stayed for a long time. Then I lit a candle for my unborn child. Scarf over my head, I warmed my hands at the flame.

THE next day, an hour before my train was to leave, Tanya stood in the lobby of my hotel, a bag of oranges in her hand. They were small and brown and hard, but they were oranges, and only then, seeing her holding them, did it occur to me what trouble she had gone through to procure them—the search, the hours spent in line. "Here," she said, holding them up. "It was the best I could do."

I would never see Tanya again. The letters I wrote never received replies. But these oranges sustained me. All the way to Berlin I sucked their bitter fruit, grateful for this gift.

BY NIGHT the train made its way west, across Byelorussia—White Russia—a land of timber: oak, silver birch, and pine. And of farmlands now covered with the fine dust of radioactive fallout, which four years later would make the death rate of children in Minsk from leukemia leap from one a year to one a week. I missed its tragedy as the train sneaked, like a thief in the night, across this tainted land.

To my relief, I had a two-person compartment to myself. All night long we chugged across White Russia. I am not certain when I slept, but the next thing I knew, it was morning and the border was in sight.

When we reached Brest and the border between the Soviet Union and Poland, two women customs officials entered my compartment.

The women had been moving quickly through the train. They were of a stocky, solid breed, the stereotypical Soviet female bureaucrat. When they reached my compartment, they asked me to take down my bags, then emptied everything I had—pills, cosmetics, every article of clothing, every souvenir, fifty canisters of film, my address book, my journal, and some other writings. They laid to one side my journal, film, and writings as they slowly picked through my personal effects.

One of the women spoke English, and she began translating an endless barrage of repetitive questions from the other woman— older, larger, more severe. Why are you traveling alone? Why isn't your husband with you? What is this writing? How do you know this poet? Does this roll of film show people's faces?

I came to the land of the firebird, I told them, to find my family's trace, to see the villages my grandmother told me about, the ones that made up my dream. I came alone because my husband could not join me. He is in Berlin on important business. He is waiting for me there.

The older, more austere woman was not satisfied with my responses. She barked an order at her subordinate. "You must come with us," the one who spoke English said gently. "Please bring your work."

I watched as the older woman flipped through my journal, which contained everything that had happened on this trip. Tears came to my eyes. I was frightened, as frightened as I'd ever been on the road. "I am going to have a baby," I told the woman who spoke English. "I am very tired. I am feeling sick." She said something to the older woman, who did not seem to care.

"Please," said the kinder woman. "Come with us."

I had written many things in my journal, and I had no idea whom I might have implicated. I could live without my film, I told myself. But I could not let them confiscate my journal.

I made a snap decision. As I trailed behind them I slipped my journal under the blanket on the upper berth in my compartment. In half an hour the train would leave. The station was some distance from the train, and there would not be time to send me back for the journal, so they would have to either detain me or delay the train, neither of which I thought they would do.

The cold station house was filled with Russian soldiers and a few

Eastern European tourists, all of whom looked at me askance. The soldiers seemed amused. The chief of customs, another woman, asked me to spread my work out on the table. I was feeling faint as I put down my pack and displayed my film and some short stories. "Where is your writing?" the older woman asked, annoyed.

"Oh," I said dumbly. "I thought you wanted my work. That was just my personal diary. This is my work."

"Your diary? We asked you to bring your diary."

"I misunderstood. Shall I go back to the train and get it?"

Simultaneously we glanced at the clock on the wall. It was a quarter to eleven, and the train was to depart at eleven. If they detained me further, I'd miss my train. The head of customs took the film out again, all fifty rolls. What is on this roll? Where did you take this? I had no idea, but I answered the questions. Beijing, Shanghai, statues in Leningrad, architecture in Moscow. No people, no faces. No one.

At last, weary of me, they sent me to a window, where a guard held my passport. He handed it to me, the visa removed, with no stamp in it. It was as if I had never been there at all.

I had to run to reach the train in time. I was in tears, and I felt hideously alone. I sucked on one of Tanya's oranges for strength. It was not long before the train pulled out. As we crossed the river into Poland, I breathed a sigh of relief.

Divided City

A CROSS Poland I stared at fields of wheat, miles and miles of grain, meadows of tall grass. Soon the light shifted, and the fields turned from a shimmering gold to late afternoon shades of pink and blue. I recalled the dream I had had in China of being in a train, passing fields of colored wheat. Now all the emotions I had felt on this journey—from passion to sadness, from despair to hope—rushed past me in a rainbow of colors.

My grandmother had been buried alive as a child, and I understood now, carrying my own child within me, why this image had stayed with me all this time, why it had sent me on this trip. I thought of how we all bury the child within us or have it buried for us—through impoverishment and violence, through domestic strife and abuse, through prejudice and fear. In my own way I had buried a child of my own. Not the one I was going to have, but the one I had been. Now I felt her within me, beginning to dig her way out.

As a child, I could never do anything right. I could never set the table, make a bed, turn in a report card that was just right. Try harder, my father always said. Reach for the stars. I reached until I thought my arms would break, until I could reach no more. I reached for love, for immortality, success. I wandered for years unsure and alone, with dreams of home. I found lonely nights in a too small apartment, sipping vodka, distractions that left me empty, the arms of men who didn't love me, the shunning of those who would.

And yet I am not a child of exile or war-torn grief. My parents were parents who loved me. They were good to us in the best way they knew how. Still, there are many ways, I thought, to hurt a child.

Watching the wheat fly by as the train hurtled to the West, I felt somehow protected, yet I realized that many others had crossed this terrain thinking they were safe. My parents' lives were lived far away from the battlefields of Europe. Yet in 1947, when I was born, they named me Mary so no one, my mother told me years later, would know that I was a Jew. Outside my window the scene was peaceful, yet between 1939 and 1945 six million Poles died on this plain I was crossing; half of them were Jews. Even now recent history hovered over these fields, tainted by the Chernobyl cloud.

In Warsaw, on the station platform, I bought sweet bread and munched on it, my supply of sardines at last depleted. For once when the train made a stop, I did not want to stay. My thoughts were of home. In a matter of hours I would cross into the West. This eight-week journey would come to an end.

At nine thirty that night, under a sea of floodlights, we entered a kind of large concrete warehouse with huge platforms, room for many trains. We had reached the German border. For a long time the train just sat. A few guards marched by, but no one came to inspect our passports. I had my transit visa in hand and did not expect any difficulties at this crossing, but still I felt within me a growing sense of unease. Germany was a country I had avoided for many years, and I wondered now why I had chosen to come this way.

Two guards arrived, blond and tall, and inspected my transit visa.

They were formal and efficient, and within moments they were gone, but my heart was pounding. The train began to move again. I heard the endless clack of the wheels, whose rhythmic sound I'd listened to for weeks now, but suddenly the sound took on another meaning.

In an hour we'd be in Berlin. I lay back on my bunk and thought about the parents of friends who had taken similar train rides going in the opposite direction. These were, you might say, the lucky ones, the ones who got out in the early days of Hitler's Reich.

When they were small children, their parents took them to the train station, in Berlin. Their parents told them that they were going to a summer camp in Britain, which was true, and that they would be home soon, which was not. The father of a friend of mine was put on a train when he was twelve and never again saw anyone he'd known before. The great-aunt of another friend recalls seeing her mother on the platform waving good-bye, sobbing. But her mother clung to her youngest, a four-year-old girl, declaring that she could not let all of her children go. Later they would die in Auschwitz.

Now on the train, riding into Berlin, about to be a mother myself, I tried to imagine. What would I do? Would I let go? Or would I hold on? Would I put my daughter on a train bound for England, knowing I would never see her again, or would I keep her with me and hope against all probability? I tried to imagine my orphaned child growing up, thanking me for the gift of life I had given her. Or silently cursing me for sending her off, leaving her alone in the world. I knew which decision was the right one, but there, for the first time, as the train hurtled toward Berlin, my unborn child became real to me, and I wept because I did not know for certain what I would do.

AT THE end of World War I, Germany was a hungry, defeated, and bankrupt nation. Plagued by unemployment, runaway inflation, and general despair, the German people were searching for someone who would make Germany strong again. At about this time an extreme right-wing nationalist party began to rise to power. This group, who called themselves the German Workers' Party, wanted to punish the "criminals" who had agreed to the Versailles Treaty, which had taken away much of defeated Germany's territories, forced the nation to disarm and pay huge reparations. The leader of this group, which later changed its name to the National Socialist German

Workers'—or Nazi—Party, was a young Austrian named Adolf Hitler.

The son of a cruel, authoritarian father, Hitler was brought up to believe that order, obtained by any means, was the highest value. Paranoid and unstable, a vibrant speaker with piercing blue eyes, Hitler had a remarkable ability to rally people to the cause, and the cause that made people cheer him was the return to Germany's past glory. He said he would build an empire that would last a thousand years, in words oddly reminiscent of a similar unstable historical figure, the first ruler of China and builder of the Great Wall, Qin.

In the Jew, Hitler found his true enemy. He managed to blame most of Germany's ills on the Jews and to equate its return to greatness with their annihilation. After Hitler became chancellor, in 1933, he began to systematically deprive the Jews of their rights, starting with their exclusion from the civil service. In 1935 the Nuremberg Laws made Jews no longer citizens, but subjects, and declared that all intimate relations between a Jew and an Aryan, including marriage and friendship, were forms of "racial pollution." In the next several years thirteen additional decrees, taking away rights such as attending university and owning property, supplemented the Nuremberg Laws, until the Jew would be outlawed entirely.

In the early years of the Reich, emigration was difficult, though not impossible. Jews were prevented from taking money out of the country or selling property at a reasonable rate. Those who left sometimes found they had no opportunities elsewhere in Europe, so they returned to the country of their birth, thinking that the situation, while grim, would not worsen. This hope was dispelled during the organized assaults of November 9, 1938, referred to as *Kristallnacht*—Night of Broken Glass—when seventy-five hundred Jewish shop-windows were shattered, all the synagogues went up in flames, and twenty thousand Jewish men were sent to concentration camps.

On January 30, 1939, Hitler declared that the result of the war would be "the annihilation of the Jewish race in Europe." On September 1 he invaded Poland. The deportations, the construction of concentration camps, and, ultimately, the Final Solution began.

The statistics of Hitler's insane atrocities against the Jews are appalling. Poland lost 3,000,000 of its 3,300,000 Jews, the U.S.S.R. lost 1,100,000 of its 3,000,000, and Germany lost 141,000 of its 566,000 (half of Germany's Jews went into exile at the beginning of the war).

Berlin, which had 172,672 Jews in 1925, declared itself officially *Judenrein*—cleansed of Jews—on June 16, 1943. The numbers are staggering, the human suffering and loss beyond comprehension. This collective assault has come to be known as the Holocaust, from the Greek words *holos,* for whole, and *kaustos,* for burned, meaning the complete destruction by fire.

The complex psychological roots for Hitler's hatred of the Jews, the collusion of the German people, and the roots of anti-Semitism in Europe have all been well documented elsewhere, but now I found myself entering Germany with great uncertainty, in a state of disbelief.

IN THE darkness, the lights of the city appeared. Brilliant white floodlights shone on the stately classical buildings of East Berlin— those that had been left standing after the war. Beyond these, the city seemed cloaked in darkness. A sprinkling of lights here and there, but mainly these floodlights on the buildings of state.

And then I saw the Wall, illumined by these same lights. It wended its serpentine form through the city, eerie monster that it was, stretching twenty-six miles—pristine, silent, sinister in its whiteness. It was a scar across torn flesh. It split this city in two.

And then, so quickly it startled me, we were on the other side. A shout, a sigh, seemed to go up from the train. And now the Wall turned into a playful beast bedecked in brilliant colors, defiant and irreverent, a blaze of graffiti in contrast to the starkness of the East. I felt as if I had been holding my breath for weeks, and now suddenly I could breathe again. Before me was West Berlin—neon lit, noisy, decadent, materialistic, and beckoning.

Soon we pulled into the station in West Berlin, and everyone began to disperse. But I stayed where I was, gazing from the window of the train. For this was the place where child had been wrenched from mother, where sobbing parents had tried to explain their tears as they said good-bye. It was also in well-lit stations such as this that cattle cars had stood, their windowless darkness about to hold the Jews of Berlin, or of Warsaw, or of dozens of other European centers.

The Office for Jewish Emigration, administered by Adolf Eichmann, was the agency in charge of deportation and extermination. The German Reichsbahn, or state railroad, secured special trains— *Sonderzüge*—for the Jews, who had been promised that they were going to live in another place, where there would only be their own kind. They paid their own passage. (One-way group fare was provided. Children traveled half price; infants under four traveled free.) But for the most part, the Jews were transported as cargo in freight cars.

It was on the platforms from which tourists were now running off to find taxis to take them to the bright lights of West Berlin that the deportees were processed and stuffed into the airless cars in which they rode standing for hours, sometimes days, without food or water, without sanitary facilities. Many—the old and infirm—died during the journey. Some were crushed to death.

Families had clasped one another, praying they would not be separated. Exhausted, they clutched small children in their weary arms, for if the child slipped from their hands, he would be trampled under the feet of their fellow passengers. Families were forced into trains that would take the route I had just taken, or routes south, to Auschwitz, to Dachau. In this train station where my journey had ended, other people's nightmares had begun.

I GOT my bags down and dragged them through the deserted depot. Competition for cabs on the street was stiff, but after about half an hour I found one. I had no idea where to go, so I said, "International Hotel," assuming there must be one and that it would have good rooms and a hot shower, and the cab sped through the streets of Berlin. I found myself bedazzled. Shops, discos, stores, restaurants— all the accoutrements of commercial capitalism missing in the East— were alive here, and the change startled me.

Checking into the hotel, which was in fact the nicest I'd been in for a long time, I went to the roof garden for a drink. It would be soft drinks from now on. The view of the city was dramatic, for the East was truly monochromatic, stark, pale, and the West aglow.

Beside me sat an American and an elegantly dressed German businessman, both speaking English. The American was spouting off, his conversation shifting from the price of the dollar to television advertising. So at last it seemed I was back in the West.

IF THE Great Wall of China was intended to keep people out, the Berlin Wall was built to keep them in. On August 13, 1961, the people of Berlin woke to find their movements truncated, their lives shattered. In the night as they'd slept, unbeknownst to them or to their allies, a twenty-six-mile barrier of barbed wire had been stretched.

This operation, ordered by Khrushchev and carried out by Erich Honecker, former leader of East Germany, was performed with as much secrecy as all the great surprises of history. Nowhere was it written what had been planned. Almost nowhere had it been talked about. "How the hell could they build that without our knowing about it in advance?" an angry President Kennedy asked when he received word, some seventeen hours after the Wall had gone up, while he was sailing in Hyannis. But the fact was, they had.

On August 13 the barbed wire was laid. The Iron Curtain, once imaginary, was made flesh. Bridges across the Spree were blown up; Friedrichstrasse Station was closed; Brandenburg Gate was sealed. Families and friends who had easily moved in and out of one another's lives were irrevocably separated. And gradually construction began of a twenty-six-mile cinder-block wall that would zigzag through the city, more ominous and escape resistant than many could imagine. There would be ingenious attempts—tunnels, balloons, border crossings by East Germans dressed as Soviet soldiers—but these were treacherous. When they succeeded, the West was exuberant. When they failed, the results were tragic and all too palpable.

The cold war had taken a new, icy turn. Its symbol became Berlin. When Kennedy came to Berlin, in 1963, he spoke the memorable words to three fifths of West Berlin's population: "Two thousand years ago the proudest boast was *Civis Romanus sum.* Today in the world of freedom, the proudest boast is *Ich bin ein Berliner.*" He challenged those who did not know the difference between communism and freedom. "Let them come to Berlin," he said.

AFTER a buffet breakfast of fruit salad and scrambled eggs, of which I had many helpings, I made my way to Checkpoint Charlie, the American entry point into East Berlin. It was there that American and Soviet tanks had faced one another in a standoff on October 27, 1961, from which the Soviet tanks would eventually back down, before the world learned to live with the Wall.

At the Museum of the Wall, I stood in tears before pictures of brides waving across barbed wire at their grandparents, of riddled bodies, faces of the brokenhearted. I read unbearable accounts of families divided, of children taken from their escaping parents, never to be seen again. While the parents languished in East German prisons, the children were put up for adoption. To this day some parents and children are still searching for one another.

In a somewhat shaken state I made my way back into the East one last time. Displaying my passport to the U.S. customs official, I received a visa, a stamp, and wandered through the maze of tunnels, where the East German border guard examined my passport and waved me in without a word.

It was as if I had stepped into a period piece, a Hollywood version of life in the 1950s. Fashion, cars, hairstyles had stepped back a quarter of a century. I made my way to Unter den Linden, the broad main street of East Berlin, lined with the government buildings of the Reichstag as well as record and book shops. Music poured from old Victrolas. Beethoven, Haydn. There were no modern record shops, no video stores. The bookstores seemed antiquarian, dated.

I walked slowly along Unter den Linden, once Berlin's greatest avenue. To Frederick the Great, it was the centerpiece of his royal capital, and for the wealthy and aristocratic, it was the most prestigious address in the city. Still, it was along here on May 10, 1933, that thousands of students marched in a torchlight procession, carrying books by Thomas Mann, Albert Einstein, H. G. Wells, and Jack London, to be burned as anti-German literature.

I walked slowly, in the heat of the day, until I came to the Pariser Platz. Here I stood, with the grand Reichstag to my right and the closed Brandenburg Gate before me. The gate, once the supreme symbol of the city, was now stuck in the no-man's-land between the end of Unter den Linden and the Wall.

I moved to the grass, where I stood beneath the shade of a tree. Here a young man, perhaps of college age, approached. He spoke in German. "Right here, where you are standing"—he pointed to a grassy spot beside me just off the sidewalk—"that is where his bunker was. That is where he killed himself. Right there, but you see, there is no marker. Nothing. But this is where it happened."

"Who?" I asked dumbly, surprised by his outburst.

"Hitler," he said. "The man who ruined my country."

"Right here?" I pointed to the ground, where there was not a trace of what had happened. "There should be something. A plaque."

"Perhaps we want to forget."

"Maybe that's not such a good thing," I said, the words of Santa-yana looming within me, but their translation eluding me: "Those who do not remember the past are condemned to relive it."

"You are from . . ."

"America," I said. "New York."

"You are"—he hesitated, pushing his sandy hair, straight and silky, off his face—"a Jew."

I nodded without speaking. Then I said, "Yes, I'm a Jew."

"Yes," he said. "I can understand. My country, my people, we have a terrible thing to overcome. But we are not the same people who did this, you understand. Hitler was, well, a monster, you see, and now"—he pointed at the Wall—"this is what we must live with. This is what we must understand. How this could have happened. But then you are a Jew. I do not know how you must feel to be here. The world should be a better place." He grew excited, sad, then weary all at once, and I couldn't help but feel how somehow he typified this new generation of Germans, burdened with guilt, political strain, the pres-sures of living in a divided country, a divided city.

"You live in the East?" I asked.

"No. My grandmother lives here. She is sick. I am given day passes once every few weeks. But I don't like to come here. I hate going through the checkpoints. It is like coming to a zoo. Often I come to this place and try to piece it all together."

"You are a student?" I asked.

He laughed. "Yes, a student of life. No, I am a laborer. I work with my hands," and he held them up for me to see. He seemed so very weary, too old for his years.

I looked once more toward the Wall. "Maybe they'll tear it down."

He looked for a moment with me, his eyes suddenly filled with brightness. "*Ja*," he said, "maybe they will. . . ."

I WANDERED along Unter den Linden and bought an ice-cream cone, which I sat on a bench eating, thinking about the young German and his hope for a better world. We have lost our innocence. Someone should give it back.

The Russian poet Osip Mandelstam must have thought this when he wrote, in "The Last Supper":

Heaven fell in love with the wall.
It filled it with cracks. It fills them with light.
It fell into the wall. It shines out there . . .
And that's my night sky, before me,
and I'm the child standing under it.

I longed myself to be that child, gazing with wonder up at the night sky, innocent again, and I thought that perhaps, with a child of my own, this might be possible.

I made my way back through the matrix of concrete and chicken-wire tunnels, through assorted checkpoints with armed guards and patrol dogs, all of which made me feel I was in some peculiar initiation rite. It was easy to get in. Getting out was another matter.

Now I flashed my visa and passport to the American official, who stamped it, with a tired smile, and sent me into the light. I emerged fatigued, somewhat abashed, into the side of freedom and democracy and crass capitalism, and inequality and poverty and so on, having left behind a dour, somber other reality. I pondered where I had been and what awaited me.

Meandering along the side of the Wall, I passed an image. The shadow of a man escaping over the Wall and tumbling into a giant can of Coca-Cola. What is better? I asked myself. What is worse? It should all blend together. Somehow this should all come down.

I paused at the memorial for a boy, age eighteen, shot in the back. He had bled to death in the no-man's-land between East and West. His name was written, his dates, a cross. THERE WILL BE NO WALLS IN HEAVEN graffiti scrawled beside his memorial read. Here I lingered. My fingers touched the Wall's cold façade, because any boy now was someone's child to me.

About the Authors

When he left the office of Surgeon General, in 1989, **DR. C. EVERETT KOOP** said that he wanted to remain the "health conscience of America." With the help of his wife, Betty, he has been keeping that promise. Through speaking engagements and public appearances Dr. Koop continues to deliver the no-nonsense health advice Americans have learned to expect from him. In 1991 he hosted a series of prime-time television health specials for NBC, covering such topics as medical insurance, the doctor-patient relationship, and the future of health 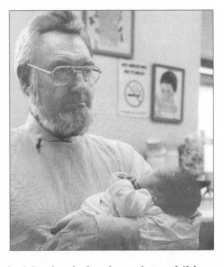 care. Dr. and Mrs. Koop live in Bethesda, Maryland; they have three children and seven grandchildren.

Twenty-seven-year-old **HUSSEIN SUMAIDA** is currently living undercover in Canada and, as of this writing, is seeking political asylum there. He lives in daily fear that his former spymasters at the Iraqi secret service will find him or that Canada will seek to return him to his native country. "I'll be killed immediately if I'm sent back," he says. He hopes that someday he can lead a normal life with his wife, Ban. **CAROLE JEROME** is a Canadian television-news journalist and a free-lance writer specializing in the Middle East. Her previous book, *The Man in the Mirror,* is a behind-the-scenes account of the Iranian revolution.

ROBERT SABBAG worked as a general-assignment reporter for the Washington *Daily News* and the Boston *Record-American* before becoming a full-time writer. His previous book, the best seller *Snowblind: A Brief Career in the Cocaine Trade* (1977), details the true-life adventures of a drug smuggler. Sabbag spent five years researching *Too Tough to Die,* including a stint at the Federal Law Enforcement Training Center, in Glynn County, Georgia. A graduate of Georgetown University, he divides his time between a New York City apartment and a house he built himself on Cape Cod, in Massachusetts.

MARY MORRIS was born and raised in Chicago and attended Tufts College and Columbia University. She is the author of five previous books, including two novels and the critically acclaimed *Nothing to Declare: Memoirs of a Woman Traveling Alone,* a chronicle of her journey through Mexico and Central America. Currently teaching creative writing at Princeton University, Morris is at work on a book about her travels in the American Southwest with daughter Kate Lena. Mary Morris lives in Brooklyn, New York, with her husband, Larry O'Connor, and her daughter.

CREDITS

Reader's Digest Fund for the Blind is publisher of the Large-Type Edition of *Reader's Digest.* For subscription information about this magazine, please contact Reader's Digest Fund for the Blind, Inc., Dept. 250, Pleasantville, N.Y. 10570.